Communication
Research Methods

GERIANNE MERRIGAN
San Francisco State University

CAROLE LOGAN HUSTON
University of San Diego

With Foreword by
Brian A. Spitzberg

THOMSON
— ★ — ™
WADSWORTH

Australia • Canada • Mexico • Singapore • Spain
United Kingdom • United States

THOMSON

WADSWORTH

Publisher: Holly J. Allen
Editor: Annie Mitchell
Assistant Editor: Breanna Gilbert
Editorial Assistant: Trina Enriquez
Technology Project Manager: Jeanette Wiseman
Marketing Manager: Kimberly Russell
Marketing Assistant: Alanna Kelly
Advertising Project Manager: Shemika Britt
Signing Representative: Tracy Rashbrook
Project Manager, Editorial Production: Mary Noel
Print/Media Buyer: Doreen Suruki

Permissions Editor: Sommy Ko
Production Service: Linda Jupiter, Jupiter Productions
Copy Editor: Ken DellaPenta
Proofreader: Elinor Lindheimer
Indexer: Medea Bogdonavich
Cover Designer: Gary Palmatier
Cover Images: All PhotoDisc/Getty Images, except: (on left) PhotoDisc/
    Getty Images/Mel Curtis; (fifth from left) Image Bank/Buzz Bailey
Cover Printer: The Lehigh Press, Inc.
Compositor: Thompson Type
Printer: Von Hoffmann Corporation

Printed in the United States of America
1 2 3 4 5 6 7 07 06 05 04 03

For more information about our products, contact us at:
Thomson Learning Academic Resource Center
1-800-423-0563
For permission to use material from this text, contact us by:
Phone: 1-800-730-2214
Fax: 1-800-730-2215
Web: http://www.thomsonrights.com

Library of Congress Control Number: 2003108206

ISBN 0-534-58140-4

Wadsworth/Thomson Learning
10 Davis Drive
Belmont, CA 94002-3098
USA

Asia
Thomson Learning
5 Shenton Way #01-01
UIC Building
Singapore 068808

Australia/New Zealand
Thomson Learning
102 Dodds Street
Southbank, Victoria 3006
Australia

Canada
Nelson
1120 Birchmount Road
Toronto, Ontario M1K 5G4
Canada

Europe/Middle East/Africa
Thomson Learning
High Holborn House
50/51 Bedford Row
London WC1R 4LR
United Kingdom

Latin America
Thomson Learning
Seneca, 53
Colonia Polanco
11560 Mexico D.F.
Mexico

Spain/Portugal
Paraninfo
Calle Magallanes, 25
28015 Madrid, Spain

■

Geri dedicates this book to her parents, and her family,
without whose continuous love and support
she would not have attempted to write,
let alone complete, this book project.

Carole dedicates this book in memory of her mother, Arlene,
who passed away this year,
and to her husband, Don, and children, Sierra, Josh, and David.
Their continued support and encouragement
helped to make this project possible.

Brief Contents

Contents

Part II
Method Responses in Communication Research: How to Conduct Communication Research

Foreword

Imagine an island archipelago in the vast, uncharted sea of science. Long ago intrepid explorers from a nation state far, far away settled the islands of this archipelago. Once the various islands were settled, the peoples found themselves separated by shark-infested waters, treacherous reefs, and inaccessible ports. Consequently, little commerce today occurs between natives of these separate islands. Over time, the peoples developed alternative customs, rituals, religions, values, dialects, and modes of exchange.

Because each island produces slightly different desirable natural resources, the various peoples of these islands face a fundamental choice: do they compete to take the territories across the waters by force, or do they find sufficient commonality to negotiate normative and mutually compatible relations for continued commerce? Conflict is costly, but may be seen as a means to possess the entire archipelago, the entire territory with all the resources and power entailed by the success of such a conflict. In contrast, a negotiated cooperative arrangement may reduce the total resources available to each individual island, but enable greater benefits by avoiding the costs of waging war and arranging complementary exchanges of the best each culture has to offer. Conflict can make a group stronger by steeling the motives to pull together against the external enemies, yet it can also reveal the weaknesses and fractures of a given group, and potentially, the entire overthrow of one's own cherished culture.

The methodological "cultures" of social scientists are like these separate island cultures. They each have their rules, customs, beliefs, and values. Each knows the others exist, but they engage in relatively little commerce, and often view each other with suspicion and incredulity. Conflict occurs more often than cooperation.

Social science began in the ancient, perhaps primal, desire to understand the world around us. Long ago, eastern and western traditions evolved across and into various eras, cultures, and locales of enlightenment. As it was increasingly realized that scientific methods for understanding the world could be cumulative and increasingly valid, the approaches to understanding the physical world were increasingly extended to investigating the social world.

These scholars eventually evolved into "tribes" of methodological and theoretical disciplines and associations. These tribes settled distinct islands of academe, often only dimly aware of the practices and beliefs of the tribes occupying the academic programs across continents, universities, colleges, departments, and even hallways and faculty room tables. The methods by which these tribes became acculturated and accustomed became claims to their natural resources of "truth" and the academic prestige implied by successful claims to this domain. Over time, these different methods have more often fomented divisive conflict rather than negotiated cooperation. Scholars peer derisively at the alien practices of the heathen tribe across the methodological divide, and chant the righteousness of their own personal beliefs and customs.

The domain of truth is often viewed as a limited resource, and any successful claims by other tribes result in territory no longer available to conquer except through renewed conflict. These territorial skirmishes often strengthen resolve and sometimes eliminate more destructive or flawed cultural customs of certain tribes, but often the ongoing battles serve no higher purpose than to fuel the conflict itself. The destructiveness of the conflicts is typically exacerbated by the tendency of the different cultures to employ distinct symbols, vocabularies, and dialects. Misunderstandings become rampant, even when negotiation efforts are pursued in the interest of cooperation.

Social scientists have developed different methodological idioms of scholarly inquiry. These methodological practices represent distinct cultures, sometimes cooperating, but more often competing, to claim the larger territory of social science. Even when representatives of these distinct cultures claim publicly the importance of "getting along," in private conversations with those of their own tribes, the rhetoric generally becomes incendiary and resentful of the others' intrusions into territories more "rightly" reserved for one's own endeavors.

Competition for the sake of competition may have reached the limits of its evolutionary value. Two millennia have helped hone a verdant array of methodological islands. Productive progress in the future may well require more than a mere truce. Instead, the academic archipelago of social sciences may need a common bill of rights, a common sense of collective purpose, and a common recognition of each other's contributions. Unfortunately, such a revolution is not in the immediate offing. However, before such a revolution can occur, bridges must be forged between and among the academic islands. This textbook lays the preliminary pontoons, in two important ways: First, by locating the nature of methods in the nature of argument, and second, by representing the broader scope of methods currently employed by the communication discipline.

By locating the central underlying architecture of all methods in the structure of arguments, this text helps decode the Rosetta Stone of methodological languages, the symbolic intersection through which negotiations for collective commerce in the pursuit of knowledge must progress. No matter what else a method attempts to accomplish, it must rely upon, and establish the validity of, its practices through argument. Every method guides the production, collection, and analysis of data. But data alone prove nothing. Data only become meaningful in the crucible of argument, which connects the data through warrants to claims. Warrants contextualize the reasonableness of the data in connection with a claim, which is the premise through which advancements in further arguments can be constructed. Warrants are the bridges between data and claim, and claims so established serve as bridges to further arguments.

For example, let's say that in meticulously observing everyday conversation, you recognize a highly complex process through which people navigate social life. That is, apologies, compliments, requests, and the "events" of everyday life are accomplished through a subtle choreography of behavioral move and countermove. In such a dance, thoughts, values, and beliefs are actually irrelevant to uncovering the structure of such accomplishments. For example, although an interactant cannot peer into your mind during a conversation, he or she can recognize an apology through the structure of the behavior observed. Therefore, such behavior is also observable by a researcher. The data of everyday accomplishments exists in behavior. If this is accurate, then it seems reasonable that all inferences about what conversationalists are attempting to achieve through interaction is exclusively "available" to others through their behavior. Several arguments could be derived from this rationale, but consider for the moment the following:

Data: Everyday conversation is accomplished exclusively through mutually observable behavior

Claim: Subjective thoughts of interactants are irrelevant to understanding how interaction is accomplished.

Warrant: Interactants have no access to others' subjective thoughts, yet accomplish everyday interactions.

In contrast, any given interactant makes judgments about the behaviors of others. In so doing, sometimes making one attribution rather than another may be an important determinant of how a person behaves in response to these behaviors. For example, if you think you deserve an apology from someone, and that person provides an apology that seems cursory and inappropriate, you are likely to devalue the apology. And if you think this person provided an insincere apology because he or she thought you didn't deserve an apology at all, you might begin disliking this person. Further, you might respond by seeking further apology, or you might avoid interactions with this person in the future. In short, your attributions, or subjective thoughts, about this person's behavior directly influence your interactions with this person. Consequently, an argument can be derived as follows:

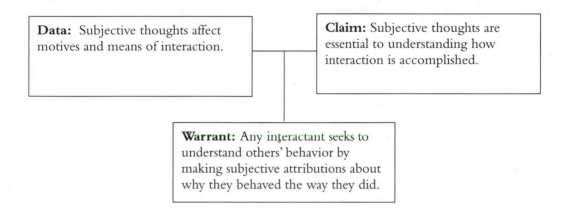

Data: Subjective thoughts affect motives and means of interaction.

Claim: Subjective thoughts are essential to understanding how interaction is accomplished.

Warrant: Any interactant seeks to understand others' behavior by making subjective attributions about why they behaved the way they did.

These two arguments, reflecting the conversation analytic and survey methodologies respectively, lead to very different claims (i.e., methods) of understanding social interaction. In the former, only behavior counts as data, while in the latter both thoughts and behaviors count as data. It follows that what counts as a theory differs radically across these approaches. In one, behavior explains behavior, whereas in another, perceptions and feelings explain behavior. Conversation analytic researchers don't see the relevance of the findings of survey researchers (i.e., the first argument above), and survey researchers have difficulty seeing how to generalize the conclusions of conversation analysts without a cognitive theoretical context (i.e., the second argument above). So it is with all methodological arguments—they are the ways we know, and the ways we choose to know often seem to preclude other ways of knowing.

So the islands upon which these researchers dwell are isolated by the arguments they make. But maybe, just maybe, if they recognize this fact, they can begin to understand why they reside on different islands in the first place, and how their respective tribes differ. Maybe they can begin to see how their arguments relate to each other, and begin a dialogue through which cooperation, rather than conflict, can be begun. This textbook, by excavating the underlying basis of these differences, lays the initial bridges (and warrants) for this dialogue to begin.

This dialogue is facilitated to the extent the interlocutors are known. Arguments are most competent when adapted to their audiences, including those with whom we argue (i.e., other practitioners), as well as other interested parties (e.g., granting agencies, foundations, the media, etc.). Another strength of this text is a fair representation of the domain of the discipline. Few survey textbooks, for example, do justice to conversation analysis, or only give shallow consideration of critical and rhetorical methods. In contrast, this textbook recognizes the legitimacy of these methods as equivalent because their endeavors are predicated on the same discourse of argument. As Walter Fisher (1978) claimed, all arguments are ultimately erected on the foundations of underlying values, and "no analytically grounded hierarchy of values will ever claim universal adherence" (p. 377). Nevertheless, having an understanding of the multiple cultures of values with which one may seek congress, the better the dialogue can become in the service of that engagement.

Nowhere is this dialogue more important than in the initial enculturation of students, beginning your own intrepid voyages into the often turbulent waters of the communication discipline. Just as it is easier developmentally to learn multiple languages early in the process of language learning, so it is easier to accept multiple methodologies before any single methodological argument has fortified its armaments and defenses against the other scholarly cultures with which it competes. Distinct cultural groups need not engage in similar practices to reap the benefits of mutual understanding and cooperation.

Therefore, go forth, and may you find the value of the voyage worthwhile. And for the few of you who will ever get the privilege of applying such arguments in the service of knowledge, may you get some glimpse of the excitement that derives from knowing something no one else knows, of discovering something no one else has discovered, or of seeing further than anyone else has previously seen. The risks of being wrong are great, but the potential of charting new routes or discovering new islands, or even building new bridges, holds its own rewards for those willing to venture forth with a spirit of scholarly adventure. This text will help you greatly along your way, providing as it does the charts and compass needed for the voyage ahead.

BRIAN H. SPITZBERG
SCHOOL OF COMMUNICATION
SAN DIEGO STATE UNIVERSITY

Preface

This book started in conversations between two teacher-scholars. As both researchers and educators, we share a commitment to multiple ways of knowing, the idea that different research methodologies are useful for exploring different questions about communication. We both felt that the implicit valuing/devaluing of particular methods, which students sense from their teachers, contributed to their premature evaluations of the worth or potential of particular methods or paradigmatic assumptions, before they fully understood those concepts. We have conducted research using multiple methodologies ourselves, and we love teaching research methods courses. Each year when we attend the meetings of our national and regional professional associations, we talk about teaching, the books we are using and those we have reviewed, their relative strengths and weaknesses.

Our professional acquaintance and personal friendship began when we were graduate students together at the University of Washington around 1990. Like most graduate students at Washington at that time, we took courses in both quantitative and qualitative research methods (i.e., experimental design, univariate and multivariate statistics, conversation analysis, ethnography of speaking, interviewing, and rhetorical criticism).

We each took our turn teaching the undergraduate research methods course at Washington, where we used Mary John Smith's (1988) text, *Communication Research Methods*. Since then, we have taught undergraduate re-

search methods courses at San Francisco State University (Merrigan) and the University of San Diego (Huston). Carole has taught both qualitative and quantitative methods courses for undergraduate students, and Geri has taught undergraduate and graduate courses in quantitative and multiple methods. Together, we have amassed 42 semesters' teaching experience with over 1200 research methodology students.

In the early years of our teaching research methods, we never considered writing a textbook. We used the Smith text until it went out of print. Then we shopped around, looking for books that we felt represented current developments in our field, especially noting the increasing reliance on and respect for multiple methodologies. We watched new Ph.D.s enter our field who practiced qualitative research, and we saw more of that research being published in our journals, along with the quantitative research and rhetorical and media criticism that was already present in those journals. We watched students enroll in one of three methodology courses (i.e., quantitative, qualitative, criticism), and we watched them complete those courses, often with a skewed perception of what constituted communication research in our field.

We developed this book to reflect the changes we saw, changes that happened over the past 50 years, from a predominance of persuasion and media effects studies in the 1950s to the current critical ethnographies and textual deconstruction research. This book locates quantitative, qualitative, and critical research methods within this context, and highlights the role of multiple methodologies for making different types of research arguments. The book is designed to introduce undergraduate and introductory graduate students to a range of contemporary communication research methods. The students should be upper-division majors in Communication, who have completed their University's breadth requirements in critical thinking, mathematical reasoning, and information competency or library requirement, if such requirements exist. However, no other prerequisite background knowledge or skills are assumed (e.g., communication theory, statistics, or specific computer programs).

THE RESEARCH-AS-ARGUMENT MODEL

Because many departments still require one research methods course for students majoring in Communication, this book treats communication research comprehensively. We organize our book around three epistemological paradigms, or responses to the question, "How can we know about communication?" These include discovery, interpretation, and criticism. If you are an experienced teacher of research methods, you will find the concepts you are used to teaching in this book, but you may find that those concepts are presented in a different order, or organized somewhat differently, than you have encountered in other textbooks.

Part I of this book gives students an overview, "Some Essential Questions in Communication Research: Why and What to Study?" Chapter 1 introduces the claim-data-warrant model of research as argument, and develops the three paradigms for communication research: discovery, interpretation, and criticism. We have used the Toulmin model of argument, which we have always believed to be applicable to a variety of research endeavors. Some of our reviewers questioned our use of the Toulmin model and felt that its applications were limited to rhetoric. On the contrary, the research-as-argument model is embraced by scholars in a variety of disciplines and is amenable to quite different research methodologies. Here is what a Yale statistics professor with 42 years of teaching experience wrote about the approach:

> Rather than mindlessly trashing any and all statements with numbers in them, a more mature response is to learn enough about statistics to distinguish honest, useful conclusions

from skullduggery or foolishness. . . . My central theme is that good statistics involves principled argument that conveys an interesting and credible point (Abelson, 1995, *Statistics as Principled Argument,* pp. 1–2).

In their textbook, *The Craft of Research,* published by the University of Chicago Press, Booth, Colomb, and Williams (1995) wrote:

> People usually think of arguments as disputes. . . . But that is not the kind of argument that made them researchers in the first place (p. 86). When you make a claim, give good reasons, and add qualifications, you acknowledge your readers' desire to work with you in developing and testing new ideas. In this light, the best kind of argument is not verbal coercion but an act of cooperation and respect (p. 93).

Both of these quotes mirror the way we are using the Toulmin model to teach research methods as a process of making claims about communication and supporting those claims with evidence and reasoning. The reasoning is always based on the values of a particular paradigm, whether that paradigm is discovery, interpretation, or criticism.

In Chapter 2, we outline the different kinds of claims made by communication researchers. In Chapter 3 we introduce students to various sources, settings, and strategies for collecting and analyzing communication data or evidence, as well as the notions of conceptual and operational definitions, and research design, since these are central concepts of evidence in the discovery paradigm. We also present an overview of research triangulation strategies in Chapter 3. Finally, in Chapter 4 we provide an extensive treatment of the ways that discovery, interpretive, and critical researchers warrant the value or worth of their studies.

Part II of this book consists of nine chapters, each concerned with how to conduct research using specific methodologies. Although hard-and-fast distinctions are impossible, this part of the book is roughly organized by the three epistemological paradigms. Chapters 5–9 concern the methods most often associated with the discovery paradigm, including survey research, experimental design, and content and interaction analysis, followed by descriptive statistics and hypothesis testing, then inferential statistics for testing significant differences and relationships. All of the Part II chapters except Chapters 8 and 9 are organized in parallel fashion, using the elements of research as argument (i.e., claim, data or evidence, warrant). Chapters 8 and 9 specifically address data analytic techniques used in discovery research, or the elements of evidence and warrant shared in common for survey, experimental, and content/interaction analytic methods. For that reason, Chapters 8 and 9 have their own internal structure.

Chapter 10 addresses the methodologies of conversation and discourse analyses and ethnomethodology. We present these methodologies as a bridge between the discovery and interpretive paradigms, and we show how some scholars who use these methods adhere more closely to one or the other paradigm's assumptions. Chapter 11 addresses the interpretive methodology, ethnographic research, and also presents critical ethnography as a method that bridges interpretive and critical paradigm values and assumptions. Chapters 12 and 13 address neoclassical, dramatistical, mythical, genre, and narrative rhetorical criticism, as well as critical studies.

Finally, a chapter-length appendix (Appendix A) introduces students to likely audiences for communication research in the form of professional association meetings, scholarly journals, trade journals, and popular press publications. This appendix provides students with instructions for writing research reports and critical essays. We designed the appendix as an optional element of the book, since not all research methods courses require students to conduct research and write manuscripts.

FEATURES OF THIS BOOK

The style of presentation and writing in this book is similar to that modeled in other research methods texts currently available. Each chapter begins with an abstract and chapter outline, and concludes with a summary of main points, discussion questions, and exercises. Each chapter also includes a section about the relationship of technology to that aspect of communication research, including the ways that technology is impacting how we conduct communication research, as well as computer-mediated communication (CMC) and other new media as a topic of study. We used headings and sub-headings to outline each chapter, and we highlighted key concepts with bold

font, as well as providing a list of key terms at the end of each chapter. The key terms are defined in the Glossary at the back of this book.

Each chapter provides students and teachers with extensive examples from contemporary research published in communication journals, along with the citations to those studies. The currency of the research cited is vital so that the examples and illustrations given in a textbook complement what students are learning in their other major courses. Our reviewers have said that our examples are accurate, current, and readable. We have also integrated unique experiential activities throughout the book, with "Try It!" Activities, including The Great Debates, and Designing Studies.

In Part I, each chapter includes an activity that we have called, "The Great Debates." These exercises, designed to be completed by groups of students both in and outside the classroom, encourage students to participate in some of the current conversations that are occurring among communication scholars, conversations about paradigm commitments, the role of the researcher in communication scholarship, the values that researchers embrace and prioritize, and ethical dilemmas in communication research. In both Parts I and II, each chapter includes "Try It!" Activities, exercises that encourage students to apply the concepts and skills of each methodology to topics of their own or their teacher's interest. These activities teach students to be critical consumers and practitioners of research as argument, as they identify key concepts from published communication research, develop research questions, design research projects, and analyze communication content, interactions, and texts.

TEACHING AIDS

We have seen the pedagogical methods for communication research methods courses change from almost exclusive reliance on lecture and examinations to more participatory teaching strategies and projects designed to demonstrate students' grasp of and ability to apply key concepts. We know that experiential learning and teaching methods are challenging in the face of increasing class size and multiple methodologies. In addition, changes in the technology available to students over the past 10 years impact our teaching strategies: Classroom instruction more often now includes computer laboratories, and even when a class does not meet in a lab, students have access to word processing, and even data analysis programs like Excel or NUD-IST. Furthermore, literature search capabilities on the Internet and online databases have exploded, and students are increasingly able to access and use these resources to supplement their learning about communication research methods. We have incorporated many of these technological changes directly into each of the chapters by illustrating their applications in examples of current research, by discussing the interface between technology and communication as the subject of research and the means by which it occurs, and by encouraging students to explore those applications on their own through the Discussion Questions and "Try It!" Activities that appear at the end of every chapter. Furthermore, this material is found in the text itself (with supplemental activities provided in the instructor's manual). For example, one "Try It!" Activity will direct students to a Web site where they can download a data set to use in calculating descriptive statistics.

This book includes a printed *Instructor's Manual,* as well as data-samples and practice test questions on the Internet, a definite plus for teachers who are less experienced in the full breadth of communication research methods, or who are novice teachers of research methods. The instructor's manual contains an array of in- and outside-class activities and a bank of sample test questions, as well as ways of accessing the Internet for research applications. Exercises for the statistics chapters are presented with easy data sets for students to solve with a calculator. The same exercises are presented as detailed computer laboratory instructions for using SPSS 10.1. A brief comparison of SPSS and MS-EXCEL is explained along with detailed examples of the data and output files for each program.

The IM also includes a checklist for reviewing communication research studies and preparing abstracts, or research summaries; two different formats are presented, one for reports based on self-, other-report or behavioral observations (or some combina-

tion of these data sources), and another for essays based on textual analysis and criticism. This distinction is also introduced in the book's appendix on writing research reports and critical essays. We hope to motivate students to pursue reading the research cited in the text, or research encountered in their other major courses, in order to develop awareness of and appreciation for multiple ways of knowing about communication.

ACKNOWLEDGMENTS

To all our students and teachers: We have learned from you, and we will continue to learn from you. We are grateful for the support of our families and friends over the three years we have worked on this project. We also appreciate and have benefited from the expertise of our reviewers hired by Thomson Learning: Kumiko Aoki, Boston University; Mark Bergstrom, University of Utah; Robert M. Brady, University of Arkansas; Joseph A. Bonito, University of Arizona; Connie Bullis, University of Utah; Guo-Ming Chen, University of Rhode Island; Natalie J. Dollar, Oregon State University; Alan Fried, University of South Carolina; Gary Layne Gneiting, Arizona State University; Terilyn J. Goins, University of Wyoming; Pamela Kalbfleisch, University of Wyoming; Pradeep Sopory, University of Memphis; Laurel Traynowicz, Boise State University; and Harry Weger, Indiana University–Southeast. We'd also like to thank our colleagues, who read chapters, suggested resources, and encouraged us in the writing of this book. We value the contributions made by Brian Spitzberg, both as a reviewer and critic and for writing the Foreword to this book. Finally, we are again grateful to Brian, and to Charlene Berquist and her colleagues at Southwest Missouri State University, along with their students, who piloted this book in their Fall 2003 research methods classes. Any errors or omissions remain our own, however.

About the Authors

GERIANNE MERRIGAN

Gerianne Merrigan is a Professor and presently the Chair of the Department of Speech and Communication Studies at San Francisco State University. She received her doctorate from the University of Washington in 1992. She holds Bachelor's degrees in Radio-T.V.-Film and in Elementary Education, and she is actively involved in teacher training through the Liberal Studies major at SFSU, and with her department's graduate teaching assistant training program. Her various published articles and book chapters in organizational and instructional communication are connected to her interests in communication and empowerment. She has also published two book chapters on research methodology (on ethnography and on focus groups). She has taught quantitative research methodology at the undergraduate and M.A. level for 11 years, and she has supervised thesis projects using survey, experimental, ethnography of speaking, analytic induction, and content analytic methods. In 1996–98, she served on a California State University committee charged with developing assessment measures for quantitative learning outcomes in general education.

CAROLE LOGAN HUSTON

Carole Huston is a Professor of Communication Studies at the University of San Diego. She received her doctorate from the University of Washington in 1990. She is currently the co-director of the Gender Studies program and previously served a four-year term as the chair of the Communication Studies Department. She has authored several papers and publications in interpersonal communication, communication theory, and rhetorical criticism, and co-authored an interpersonal communication textbook with John Stewart, *Together: Communicating Interpersonally.* In addition to collaborating on the *Communication Research Methods* textbook with Gerianne Merrigan, Professor Huston is currently engaged in several research projects investigating interpersonal and relational competence, information-seeking strategies of new employees, and family business communication. Professor Huston has been teaching research methods for over 15 years. Her experiences as a member of a research internal review board and a faculty statistics committee have given her additional insights into the research process. She lives in a suburb of San Diego with her husband, Don, and her son, David.

1

The Claim-Data-Warrant Model

ABSTRACT

This chapter begins by providing a classical model of argument as the basis for understanding communication research methods. The model is designed to help you learn to distinguish commonsense approaches to knowledge from the more rigorous forms applied to research analysis in our field. With the claim-data-warrant model, you will be provided with an overview of three paradigm approaches to knowing about communication: discovery, interpretation, and criticism. Each of these paradigms is a response to the question, "How can we know about communication?" The last section of this chapter outlines the philosophical perspectives that contributed to each of the three paradigms. The chapter also considers how the differences in the paradigms have led to noticeably different methodologies in communication research. You will find, as you read this chapter, that the boundaries between the various paradigms and methodologies are often fuzzy; a growing number of research studies cannot effectively be placed in just one paradigm. Moreover, advances in technology considered in this chapter have widened the boundary of communication itself, both in terms of how we define it and in terms of how we can analyze it. The model and the paradigms you will learn to use throughout this book will help you to understand why researchers have chosen to study communication in distinctively different ways.

OUTLINE

One of the first questions you may be asking yourself when you take this class is why you need to have a special class for learning about methods in communication research. You would not be alone. Methods in communication research take on many forms. Some of them, for instance, separate methods from the theories they are designed to test. But other researchers in our field see theories and methods as thoroughly intertwined so that theory and method are presented together in courses like rhetorical or media criticism. Neither approach is wrong, but the difference highlights the fact that there is no one uniform approach to methods in communication research. This textbook will help you begin to understand why treating methods as if there is just one way of thinking about them is no longer an effective way of understanding communication research.

These differences in methodologies come from profoundly different ways of thinking about what we know, what we believe communication is, and what we do as researchers when we study it. Each perspective represents a particular point of view, and this point of view is a focal point in the continuing debate across all social sciences about what constitutes good research. Frequently, when you are a researcher, you may simply come up with an idea for a study that answers a question you want to know about communication, like studying what makes someone really persuasive, without ever once thinking about the merits of one particular methodology over another. But by actually choosing a methodology, you can't avoid tapping the underlying assumptions that go with it.

Because it is impossible to do methods without representing a point of view, we are going to use a model that will allow you to see how changing your methods will also reflect a change in your point of view. We are not the only authors that approach studying methods as ways of constructing arguments (Jackson, Jacobs, Burrell, & Allen, 1986). In fact, a well-known professor of statistics at Yale University, Robert Abelson (1995), believed that methodological analysis was thoroughly grounded in making a good argument; it "should make an interesting claim; it should tell a story that an informed audience will care about, and it should do so by intelligent interpretation of appropriate evidence . . ." (p. 2). In this chapter, we will begin by introducing you to a classical Western model of argument (Toulmin, Rieke, & Janik, 1984). The model will serve as a foundation for helping you to distinguish forms of thinking in re-

search from other types of knowing. It will also provide a means for explaining how each of the paradigms in our field operates with different sets of basic assumptions. The remaining three chapters of Part I will explore each of the model's components in detail.

RESEARCH METHODS AS ARGUMENT

The model of research as argument is one that we simplified based on Toulmin's extended form (Toulmin et al., 1984). It is represented by Figure 1.1. Every argument contains at least these three elements as its basic structure. Whenever we make an argument, it is always based on some central assertion or premise. This premise is called the **claim** (p. 25). For example, a very simple claim would be "This is my bicycle." As you will see in Chapter 2, "Making Claims," research claims can take many complex forms in our field; they can be constructed as specific claims about the relationships between various communication phenomena, such as predicting that women will use different conflict strategies than men. Or claims can represent the general purposes or goals of the research, such as claiming that the study of communication in one group will help us better understand what is happening in other groups. The various forms of claims will be illustrated in each of the chapters of Part II.

Data, the second term in the model, refers to the evidence or grounds for a claim (p. 26). Using our earlier example, you could say, "I have the receipt for the bike's purchase right here in my wallet." The receipt is direct evidence of your claim. In Chapter 3, "What Counts as Communication Data?" you will learn about many forms of evidence for research claims that are generally accepted in our field. For example, data can be represented by a set of numbers analyzed statistically. Or data may take the form of extensive field notes gathered by a researcher interested in explaining how various groups of people talk to each other. Or data may also refer to rhetorical texts that are analyzed for the speakers' motives or effects on audiences. You will learn about each of these approaches to data in the chapters of Part II.

The third element, **warrant,** is the primary means of linking the claim to the data. Warrants are reasons for making a particular claim in view of spe-

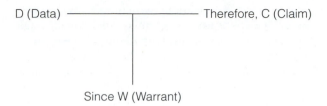

FIGURE 1.1 The claim-data-warrant model.

cific evidence; they are standards for evaluating the claim in light of the evidence. The reasons themselves can take the form of rules, laws, principles, or formulas (Toulmin et al., 1984). **Rules** are described as "rules of thumb," or reasons that you, and any other person living in our society, would be likely to accept as a basis for some action. **Laws** are briefly defined by Toulmin and his colleagues as immutable, physical laws of nature, and **principles** refer specifically here to legal rules and statutes. Finally, **formulas** refer specifically to mathematical principles used in physical and applied sciences (p. 26). In short, warrants enable you to apply standards of evaluation to the data as evidence of the claim you wish to make.

So in the bicycle example, you can make a claim of ownership based on the evidence you have provided, the receipt, because of the "receipt rule" we have in our society. This warrant will also depend upon a large body of information that clarifies how the rules are to be understood, applied, and relied upon as the worth or strength of an argument as its backing or support (p. 26). For this bicycle example, the rule of ownership based on printed receipts relies on a larger set of rules and beliefs we have generally about what constitutes legitimate ownership in our society. Chapter 4 presents uniquely different ways of establishing warrants for particular types of claims and data as they are applied in communication research. In each of the chapters of Part II, we will show you specific ways that warrants are defined and applied with specific methodological approaches.

In this chapter, we will begin by considering the ways you know what you know. The claim-data-warrant model is a useful way to distinguish the general kinds of reasoning that you would use to do research from the types of knowing you use ordinarily every day. It may surprise you that we use some of the same types of reasoning and rules when we use ordinary common sense. Although everyday thinking is similar in some ways, it is not applied with the same systematic

rigor characteristic of methodological inquiry. Moreover, it will frequently include elements of thinking that are not used in research. You will need to learn about these common ways we all think about things in everyday life before you explore the characteristics of methodological inquiry.

GENERAL WAYS OF KNOWING

If this is not your first communication course, you may recognize a struggle that is familiar to all communication scholars—the problem of meaning and the challenge of translation. As a student of communication, you must practice communication at the same time you are attempting to learn about it. Doing it and knowing about it are inseparable. Ultimately, you will decide what you think communication means. Perhaps less apparent to you is the idea that how you define communication influences what you believe you know about it, just as what you believe about communication will also influence the questions you will want to ask. This is true whenever you think about things that occur just ordinarily.

A philosopher by the name of Charles Sanders Peirce was interested in explaining the various ways we accept that we know things. He believed that everyday common sense could be distinguished from the methods of knowing we apply more rigorously in philosophy and the sciences. He identified four basic ways of knowing: tenacity, authority, a priori, and the method of science (Kerlinger, 1986).

Knowing by tenacity relies on customary knowledge; that is, you know something is true because it is commonly held to be true. For example, prior to the Renaissance, people in Western Europe believed the earth was flat and at the center of the universe before there was physical evidence to the contrary. You may believe common assertions are true, such as moon phases affect human moods and behavior. Or planetary alignment at the moment of a person's birth can forecast the personality dispositions that appear later in that person's life. Today, beliefs in lunar influence and astrology are commonplace; some people see them as superstitions or hoaxes, but many people accept them as unquestionably true.

Sometimes, your beliefs about reality can be influenced by what you hear and see around you. For example, media portrayals of crime or world events may lead you to think that you are more likely to be a victim of crime or that Americans make up a larger proportion of the world population than they actually do. Studies by Gerbner and his associates (summarized in Gerbner, Gross, Morgan, & Signorelli, 1986) have actually tested the various ways media can cultivate or influence viewers to adopt certain perceptions of reality like those we mentioned. The media, in effect, create the perception that certain beliefs are commonplace. Once a view of the world is accepted as the usual or ordinary pattern, it is accepted tenaciously. This means that even when we are shown quite strong evidence contradicting some of our basic assumptions, we are still unwilling to change our beliefs. Even though tenacity is difficult to shake as grounds for knowledge, this method is the weakest since it relies purely on belief without considering evidence. Because it is grounded in belief, it cannot be questioned or challenged as a method. It also cannot be verified.

The second way of knowing things is accepting the truth or value of **knowing by authority.** We believe something is true because someone we regard as an expert thinks it is true, such as listening to Dr. Dean Edell on ABC network news give advice on the latest diet or nutrition fad because of his medical expertise. Because we cannot develop an expertise in every area of specialized knowledge, we often do rely heavily on the testimony of experts. Building inspectors tell us when it is or is not safe to enter a building after it has been damaged in a storm or earthquake. Pharmaceutical researchers tell us which drugs to take to treat a physical condition. We pay our doctors to give us a diagnosis and lawyers to represent us knowledgeably in legal contexts. Every time we get into our cars and drive through an intersection, we depend on automobile and urban design experts to competently provide us with the means of getting from one point to another.

Knowing by authority is a trustworthy way of knowing things as long as your experts are correct, but what if they are wrong? There have been many cases of people who were prosecuted for claiming to be experts and misleading the people who trusted them; you don't have to look far to find a firm like Arthur Andersen, who misled many stockholders who trusted them to report their findings about businesses like Enron accurately.

Sometimes, experts will give you advice in areas where they have just customary knowledge, but you attribute greater weight to what they have to say because of who they are. For example, people who are celebrities in entertainment may use their public stature to advertise cars or medicine even though they have no specialized knowledge of these products. You may trust a teacher's knowledge not only about his or her area of expertise, but also, because you may admire them, you find what they have to say about other topics influential as well. Though you could not get along in life without relying on expert opinion, you will have a difficult time determining when the experts are wrong and avoiding potentially harmful consequences as a result.

Another way you acquire knowledge is on **a priori** grounds. This approach tests claims against standards of reasonableness. You may use the established logical processes of knowledge like deduction and induction, or you may establish other reasonable criteria, based upon moral or metaphysical standards for determining justifiable actions, or on aesthetic or artistic merits. The problem with this method is determining what constitutes a "reasonable" action. For example, using the electoral approach in presidential elections may satisfy the grounds of reasonableness in one election where margins between the candidates were wide; it may seem very unreasonable in an election where the margin of difference in votes between the two candidates, like Bush and Gore, was very small. In later chapters, you will learn about those methods in communication research that rely heavily on implementing standards of reasonableness and acceptability in the interpretation of what can be known about communication.

The final way we know things, according to Peirce (1992), is through the **method of science.** Like the a priori approach, the scientific method requires establishing standards by which any claim can be tested for its reasonableness. But in addition to logical consistency, researchers must also test their claims through observation and experience. Peirce identified the following properties of reasoning in science: observations, experimentation as "systematic analysis," and generalization as "probabilistic inferences" (pp. 182–192). The terms Peirce used came out of a very specific paradigm of thought that represents just one approach to understanding science. Before you can understand how Peirce meant to apply his terms, you will need to learn about all of the paradigms of knowledge that underlie the methodological approaches in communication research.

Researchers call different ways of knowing **paradigms.** Sometimes, researchers separate paradigms into two types: epistemological and ontological. Epistemological paradigms address the question "How can a thing be known?" Ontological paradigms address the question "What is the thing?" Because this is a methods book, we will focus on ways of knowing; that is, we will emphasize how and why we study communication the way that we do rather than focusing on the nature and substance of communication.

METHODOLOGICAL WAYS OF KNOWING

It might be well for all of us to remember that while differing widely in the various little bits we know, in our infinite ignorance we are all equal. (Popper, 1962)

Think of one thing that you know. How do you know this thing? Did you discover this by making observations about the world around you (i.e., touching, tasting, seeing, smelling, hearing)? Do you think that your observations are in some way unique to you (i.e., interpretations of your own experiences)? Do you think that there are things you know that can change the world? Whatever it is you think you know, it's wise to begin with Popper's humbling quote, that "in our infinite ignorance we are all equal." Your struggle to know something is an attempt to make sense out of the world; as you have probably already experienced, your sense-making processes can be very different from other people you know, and the conclusions you reach as a result of those processes are just as likely to be distinctive. Even so, some verifiable, agreed-upon things can be known.

Let's consider an example. Let's say that you know a tattoo is an identity marker, a way of expressing who you are. Did you know this by seeing and hearing about tattoos? Maybe you know some people with tattoos, or maybe you've read about tattoos in magazines or seen them on television. Maybe you have a tattoo yourself, and so you have firsthand experience in knowing how to get a tattoo. If you have a tattoo, it may mean something unique to you. You may interpret the meaning of your tattoo as a statement about who you are, but others may see it as a rejection of who they are. Or you may see your tattoo as purely decorative. Maybe you chose to locate your tattoo in a place where others can easily see it because you believe society needs to learn to accept people the way they are. For example, you tattoo a chain on your wrist to show how women are imprisoned by this culture. What you think your tattoo means is influenced by the way you know about it.

Even with our simple example of a tattoo, we can illustrate the three main paradigms of knowledge we introduce in this chapter. We may see it in terms of its physical properties that we can categorize and count; we will call this approach the discovery paradigm orientation. Or we may see it as a symbol with multiple and equally valid interpretations, the orientation reflected in the interpretive paradigm. Or we may see it as a sign of liberation and voice for a group marginalized by a dominant society, a view represented by the critical paradigm orientation. How we choose to study communication depends upon the assumptions inherent in the paradigm from which our methodology of choice is derived. What, then, do these paradigm assumptions entail? In the next section, we intend to provide you with an encompassing view of the major paradigmatic changes happening in our field, especially as they affect our communication research methods.

Knowing by Discovery

Some researchers believe that knowledge is obtained through the process of discovery. To **know by discovery** implies there is a reality outside of our personal experience that can be known by any observer. From the perspective of the researcher as discoverer, objectivity is an important part of this knowledge process. We discover knowledge by making precise, systematic, and repetitive observations of some event or thing. When we use the term **precise,** we mean being careful for the purpose of ensuring accuracy. For example, in their study of accounts and attributions, Mongeau, Hale, and Alles (1994) provided very specific definitions of what it means for a communicator to give an account and how communication behaviors like refusals and justifications are defined. Being **systematic** means that we follow clear, known procedures. Most discovery-based research begins with a general claim constructed from the evidence collected in many previous studies. Out of past evidence, we develop a prediction that will be tested through a series of observations (new evidence). Finally, when we are **repetitive** in research methods, it means that we make careful, systematic observations, over and over, to ensure that our findings are verifiable.

Though you do not usually scrutinize your surroundings in the same way that researchers do, you can perform similar kinds of investigations on the symbols you find in everyday life. For example, you can discern what a tattoo means by observing the shape, color, size, and content of the tattoo; its location on the body; what type of person is wearing it; and other people's reactions to it. *Precise* observations of a tattoo's shape, color and size may help us to discover precisely what that tattoo means. *Systematic* observations of hundreds of tattoos, over time, would help us discover similarities and differences among different types of tattoos. And *repetitive* observations of tattoos at different times and places, and on different people, would help to ensure that our initial conclusions about similarities and differences were valid, or accurate.

When you are conducting communication research, each of these properties is evident in the way you would define your terms and construct your study design. For example, Berry and Gray (1999) tested the effects of film violence on audience perceptions. In their experiments, they carefully constructed both the film clips that audience members would see to represent varying levels of violence as well as the series of questions they then asked the participants regarding how much they enjoyed or felt anxious about the film clips. Berry and Gray were *precise* in the way that they constructed their tests, using the same film format and questionnaires with all participants. They were *systematic:* the researchers were careful to show various versions of the film clips to separate groups to test how each version affected the audience viewing it. The authors were also *repetitive*, conducting not just one but three separate experiments to make sure that it was the degree of violence affecting audience perceptions and not some other factor. You will learn much more about these characteristics of communication research methods in later chapters.

Part of the discovery process is also putting objects into categories based on observed similarities and differences. Grouping objects together allows you to **generalize** (e.g., tattoos wearers are artsy). Sorting objects by their differences allows you to **discriminate** (e.g., bikers wear different tattoos than surfers). By the processes of generalization and discrimination, you could develop both a general meaning for tattoos, and multiple specific meanings for particular tattoos.

To illustrate how the process of generalization works in communication research, consider the study by Rubin, Rubin, and Jordan (1997). They examined the effects that a basic public speaking course had on students' communication competence (communication skills) and communication apprehension (fear of communicating with others). Over 800 students were surveyed at the beginning and end of one semester; the results showed that the basic course increased students' competence and decreased their apprehension. The researchers analyzed this group of students to *generalize* their findings from this study to other college students at other universities so that effective courses could be prescribed for students who have problems with communication competence and apprehension.

Researchers also wish to use knowledge in discriminating ways; that is, they often try to discover what kinds of differences they are seeing in the observations that they make. In a study of televised sports, Hallmark and Armstrong (1999) wanted to see if the media represent women's and men's basketball championship games in different ways. Previous studies had revealed a variety of sex differences across broadcasts of men's and women's sports. For example, Hallmark and Armstrong noted past observations that men's sports generally occupied more airtime than women's sports, that women's team sports have been virtually ignored except for tennis and golf, and that announcers tended to make negative comments significantly more frequently during women's games than during men's.

Although the authors cited progressive changes in media coverage of women's sports, Hallmark and Armstrong wanted to explore whether some gender biases might be subtler, requiring a different level of *discrimination*. They focused on more specific features of media presentation: camera shot variation, the length of a shot, and the type and frequency of graphics in each broadcast of women's and men's basketball games during a championship division playoff. By refining their conceptualizations of media presentation, they were able to make finer discriminations about the types of sex differences that exist in sports media coverage.

In each of the study examples above, it is clear that the researchers emphasize discovery as their central way of knowing. Their primary purpose is to draw various conclusions about their observations using the kind of careful, systematic, and repetitive procedures we have discussed in this section. Their conclusions will allow them to apply the processes of generalization and discrimination as the means for exploring what can be known from the discovery paradigm perspective. This perspective has at its core the assumption that knowledge is gained by objectivity; that is, any researcher who uses the same definitions and same procedures will observe the same pattern of results in the tests of the research claims. Knowledge is expanded not by understanding the subjective viewpoint of the researcher, but by being discovered through observable means that are precise, systematic, and repetitive.

Knowing by Interpretation

Knowing by interpretation is a very different process than knowing by discovery. As a clear contrast, this paradigm's central assumption is the claim that there is more than one reality that can be known. The knower is inseparable from the known, and so the knower's perceptions and values affect what is seen. Subjectivity is embraced wholeheartedly, and the researcher often becomes an active participant in the research context. Since there is more than one reality, there can be multiple interpretations. Therefore, the emphasis is on how people construct their meanings, and the process is one of rich description, not categorization. Classifying meanings into categories may be part of this process, but it is not the central point. Rich description is the primary method of understanding the whole context out of which meanings are constructed.

Let's return to the tattoo example we have been using in previous sections. You probably know that tattoos have many meanings. A single tattoo can mean more than one thing to its wearer. For example, the daughter of one of the authors of your text described her tattoo of the Little Prince, located on her right shoulder and chest, in the following way: "It's a kind of shorthand. People who've read that book 'get it' right away. It's also pretty. It's an invitation, 'Maybe we can talk about my art'" (S. L. Logan, personal communication, June 1999). The same Little Prince tattoo can mean something quite different to the people who observe it. One person may appreciate the intricate artwork, but another may negatively evaluate all tattoos on young women.

As observers we took this tattoo to mean that Logan was a literate person, because at age 20, she had read and appreciated *The Little Prince*. It is not important which interpretation is more correct. Instead, it is important to reflect the full range of sensible interpretations and to show how these interpretations were constructed. This emphasis is central to the interpretive paradigm of research.

In an ethnographic study, Dollar and Zimmers (1998) presented accounts of houseless young adult street speakers about how they had come to be where they were, living on the street in Portland and Seattle. The authors coined the term *houseless youth* in order to avoid the term *homeless*, since many of these youth had homes, where they refused to go at night. The article analyzed the ways in which the community at large and street youth are at odds in those cities because of conflicting definitions of youth identities. The authors showed that "youth and young adult street speakers rely on membership sets that conflict with those employed by parents, legislators, and other community members" (p. 596). For example, street youth see themselves as community members because they sleep consistently in the same area and shop in the local stores; they see cops as defining *community* differently, as those who own or rent a home, or have a business in the area. Dollar and Zimmers provide an interpretive view of how these participants construct their contextually situated meanings of everyday events.

In another ethnographic study, Miller (1995) as the researcher also became an active participant in the households where she was collecting research on mother-daughter communication and how it was related to suicide attempts. The interpretive researcher's role as participant is frequently the access that provides an insider view of what is occurring. Through analyzing observations, journals, and interview data, Miller identified 11 themes and proposed a gender-specific model of family interaction. Each theme represented a different construction or interpretation of the event. One theme was not more or less truthful. Each captured a different focus of meaning for the participants. The interpretive paradigm is also reflected in many forms of rhetorical criticism. The rhetorical critic often selects one or more interpretive frameworks as a basis for the analysis of communication. For example, by combining theories of organizational culture and Kenneth Burke's redemptive cycle as a dramaturgical framework, Scheibel (1999) analyzed the rhetorical and social significance of the college rumor "If your roommate dies, you get a 4.0." He showed how students' interpretations regarding the death of a dormitory roommate functioned to emphasize the power hierarchy and resulting distance between themselves and the university administrators. Scheibel also claimed that the students' interpretations were ways to legitimize their aggressive thoughts about roommates, and they gave a sense of cohesion to students during stressful periods (e.g., finals week). Combining rhetorical and organizational analyses enabled Scheibel to provide a unique view of significant elements in students' lives.

In another rhetorical analysis, Lindsay (1999) examined the Waco, Texas, tragedy using Burke's interpretive dramatism. By extending Burke's dramatistic analysis, Lindsay claimed that the Waco tragedy could have been averted, in effect, if the negotiators had been able to enter the "apocalyptic reality" of David Koresh. As Lindsay noted, "Points of agreement between Koresh and the negotiators would have and did allow Koresh to 'identify' with the negotiators," which could have enabled them to find an acceptable, peaceful solution in time (p. 281). But in Waco, Koresh and the negotiators ran out of time. Lindsay's central purpose was to show how redefining critical events would enable opposing sides on an issue to see the possibility of alternative interpretations and solutions. He asserted that people in similar social contexts could solve a social problem without the magnitude of the Waco tragedy. He made the point poignantly that there are multiple realities of the same events constructed and shared by specific social groups.

Knowledge by interpretation means that you wish to understand the points of view expressed by the people you are observing or the texts you are reading. By contrast, the discovery paradigm researcher defines and measures what will be observed, and the conclusions that are derived from these observations; alternatively, the interpretive researcher uses observations to help guide in understanding the perspectives of those observed or texts that are read. Interpretive researchers often fully acknowledge their roles in becoming active participants in the research process. They act as instruments describing their observations in rich detail, permitting interpretation of the patterns that emerge out of those descriptions. You will learn much more about this interpretive process of knowing in later chapters.

Knowing by Criticism

Those who seek to know through the process of criticism believe not only in multiple realities, but that these realities are culturally and historically situated. **Knowing by criticism,** then, means that everything that we know is shaped by our social, political, economic, ethnic, gender, sexual orientation, and ability values. The main agenda for critics is first to use knowledge to make people aware of the reality that society constructs for each of us. Then for some critics, the next step in this awareness is to bring about social change. The process depends on identifying what situated factors contributed to the status quo (e.g., historical, social, economic, etc.), especially as these factors relate to privilege and oppression.

In our tattoo example, some people who display their tattoos publicly are pushing for social change. They could elect to tattoo a body part that is typically covered by clothing, but they have chosen to make it easily visible instead. They want their tattoo to be seen by others because they want to live in a society that accepts them the way they are. By displaying their tattoo to others, they instigate the opportunity for change. In the same way that some people use their tattoos as triggers, scholars from the critical paradigm believe that research should flag an issue for social attention.

Critical researchers work to reveal the existing social structure, which grows out of social, historical, political, and economic realities, as well as ethnicity, gender, and abilities. Consider the following examples. A Vietnam vet sports a tattoo of a panther on his biceps to signal his membership in a specialized group of sharpshooters. A skinhead features a network of spider webs down one arm as a specific sign of the number of black people he has killed. A Jewish grandmother bears the mark of her internment in the Nazi concentration camps as a series of numbers on her forearm. A teen who listens to *emo* songs has a beautiful Chinese character for music tattooed on his upper back. Each of these examples reflects the wearer's membership in social, historical, political, and economic groups; it may also suggest the kinds of change the wearer desires.

In a recent essay, Allen (1996) argued that few scholars have applied feminist theorizing in organizational communication contexts. Allen recounted some of her experiences at a predominantly white university, in order to show how the view of an *out-*

sider within can provide insights that have been overlooked by traditional scholarship on a topic. She argued that the views of women of color should be solicited and incorporated into theories of organizational communicating. Women of color experience "dual oppression," by both their gender and race, so "they are uniquely positioned to identify patterns and behaviors that are difficult for those immersed in the culture to discern" (p. 258). In this case, women of color can identify how "normal practices" used to socialize new organizational members are based on the lives and needs of white men. Making everyone aware of how these practices may disadvantage women, or persons of color, is the first step to changing those practices, to ones that work for all employees, regardless of race, gender, or some equally distinguishing group membership.

From the perspective of this last paradigm, then, knowing by criticism means that the researcher not only reveals his or her subjective view. As a critic, the researcher is obliged to reveal the existing social hierarchical structure and, in some cases, to become an advocate for social change. If scholarship does not emphasize how the dominant social structure silences marginalized groups and classes, then the research community is as guilty of perpetuating the existing hierarchy as the rest of society. In order to reveal that social structure so that it can be changed, critical analysis must focus on the historical, political, and economic contexts that continually reinforce it.

In this section, you have learned about three epistemological paradigms: knowing by discovery, knowing by interpretation, and knowing by criticism. The next section of this chapter outlines the philosophical perspectives that contributed to each of these three epistemological paradigms. As part of understanding and appreciating the diversity of methods in our field, it will be important for you to see how the differences in the paradigms have often been at the core of the most heated controversies in communication research. In some cases, proponents in each separate paradigm have gone so far as to say that the differences are incompatible and irresolvable. Exploring the philosophical bases of these paradigms will help you to understand why epistemological distinctions have occurred, and how these have been applied to specific methods of research in our field. It will also help you to see that as researchers develop an appreciation for multiple methods and perspectives, the boundaries between the various perspectives are becoming fuzzy, and a growing number of research studies bridge the paradigms.

PHILOSOPHICAL PERSPECTIVES OF THE THREE PARADIGMS

The three types of knowing represented in three separate paradigms are supported by different philosophical traditions. Historically, the epistemological paradigm of knowledge by discovery came first and gave rise to the development of the other two paradigms. But its chronological precedence does not imply that you should value it or the philosophical perspectives associated with it any more than the others. Nor should you value the others intrinsically as better than the first simply because they are more contemporary. Each paradigm is a way of knowing that stands on its own merits. And every philosophical perspective within each paradigm brings a new facet to your understanding of how you might study communication. Table 1.1 provides an overview of the many perspectives that have contributed to each paradigm.

The categorization of perspectives leads to another general problem of classifying schemes. The categories represented in Table 1.1 are not mutually exclusive; that is, some philosophical perspectives can be placed in two categories because they represent bridges or transition points in the development of the next paradigm. For example, the writings of some modernists like Perelman reflected more of the discovery paradigm assumptions; other modernists like Richards, Weaver, and Burke revealed more of the assumptions found in the interpretive paradigm (Gill, 1994). The problem of placement is especially acute in a field like ours that borrows from many philosophical traditions—classical philosophy, the social sciences, linguistics, and literary criticism, to name just a few of our sources. As one philosophical tradition collides with another, it is easy to become confused about epistemological bases, their defining assumptions, and the methods of research associated with each.

Confusion, however, is not an excuse for lumping together willy-nilly any combination of methods you particularly favor in the name of fuzzy boundaries. As you will see, researchers with discovery-paradigm orientations may have preferences for controlled environments like laboratories when studying

Table 1.1 Philosophical Traditions Associated with the Epistemological Paradigms

Knowledge by discovery	Knowledge by interpretation	Knowledge by criticism
Rationalism	Hermeneutics	Critical theory
Empiricism	Phenomenology	Semiotics
Logical positivism	Symbolic interaction	Late structuralism
Behaviorism	Constructivism	Postmodernism
Realism	Naturalism	Poststructuralism
Early modernism	Early structuralism	Deconstructivism
	Late modernism	

Note. Adapted from Bogdan and Biklen (1982), Gill (1994), Mertens (1998), and Smith (1988).

communication behavior; researchers with interpretive-paradigm orientations will choose to make observations in natural settings. Instead of engaging in a theoretical battle of which side is more right, we present you with three points of view with three supporting rationales to increase your understanding of the differences. When you understand the discovery and interpretive paradigm preferences, for example, you may better appreciate studies with research laboratory settings that are constructed to make them more natural, or studies in natural settings that are designed to provide greater accuracy in their observations. *Understanding the differences among the three paradigms is essential to careful integration across them.* And that is precisely why we believe it is so important to provide you with an overarching view of all the various approaches to research currently practiced today. As such, we are only providing a thumbnail sketch of whole philosophies, but it will provide you with a basic vocabulary to understand the contributions that each philosophical perspective made.

Discovery Paradigm Perspective

The first paradigm, knowledge by discovery, has been the dominant paradigm in science and philosophy for many years. The philosophies of rationalism and empiricism were around since the time of the Greeks in the writings of Plato and Aristotle. **Rationalism** stressed reliance on the mind for a discoverable logic of objective reality. **Empiricism's** central assumption emphasized the way to objective reality was through observing and explaining sensory information. By combining these two perspectives, the process of science became associated with the three emphases we

identified earlier: (1) clarity or precision, (2) systematic inquiry, and (3) repetition for the purposes of verification (Mertens, 1998, pp. 6–10; Smith, 1988, pp. 307–309).

Logical positivism and **behaviorism** were later developments of empiricism. Both embraced an objective reality knowable through observational or empirical processes rather than through rational thought. Behaviorists sought to discover causal links between external factors and an individual's responses. Logical positivists believed precision was better served as a goal if they identified related rather than caused events. They also believed they could increase precision by identifying how scientists should classify objects and procedures and what exactly would constitute empirical evidence (Bogdan & Biklen, 1982, pp. 45–48; Denzin & Lincoln, 1998, pp. 13–15; Smith, 1988, 308–310). Many of these later approaches were realist attempts to ground scientific argument in empirical evidence as a basis for knowledge (Denzin & Lincoln, 1998, pp. 16–17; Lechte, 1994, p. 3).

The philosophical perspectives of modernism, realism, and structuralism are focused on a discoverable reality separate in some sense from the knower or perceiver. **Modernism** has been essentially described as "positivistic, technocentric, and rationalistic" (Harvey in Gill, 1994, p. 171). Modernism elevated science to the pursuit of a shared and objective truth. As Gill described this perspective, "A key element in the modern worldview was belief in progress, of movement toward truth in all areas of life; knowledge could be standardized and social orders planned" (p. 171). In **realism,** the goal is to accurately represent reality by distinguishing it from the preconceptions of the perceiver; reality can only be understood after transcending subjectivity (Hammersley, 1992, pp. 50–51).

Structuralism represents the third perspective. Early structuralists like Bachelard and Bakhtin identified the discoverable reality in the patterns or relationships between objects, events, or people, rather than in the truthfulness of the objects themselves. They were interested in how form became manifested in observations. Structuralists attempted to identify the various forms of thought, language, and experience by finding evidence of rules for explaining human interaction. The goal of the early structuralists, then, was to discover the embedded *rules* or *laws* grounded in observation and experience (Denzin & Lincoln, 1998, pp. 16–17; Lechte, 1994, pp. 3–11). In its essence, this early form of structuralism became a means of combining rationalism (ideation)

Table 1.2 Defining Assumptions of the Epistemological Paradigms

	Knowledge by discovery	Knowledge by interpretation	Knowledge by criticism
Nature of reality	There is one knowable reality that can be discovered.	There are multiple realities that are socially constructed.	There are multiple realities that are socially constructed.
Role of knower	Reality can be known by any knower.	Reality is interpreted from the standpoint of a knower.	Reality is shaped by the knower's social, political, economic, ethnic, gender, and ability values.
Role of context	The method of knowing is detached and decontextualized.	The method of knowing is subjective and contextual from the participants' perspective.	The method of knowing is subjective and broadly contextual.
Process characteristics	The process of knowing is precise, systematic, and repetitive.	The process of interpretation is creative and value laden.	The process of interpretation is revelatory.
Purpose	The purpose of research is to accurately represent reality.	The purpose of research is to understand how meaning is created.	The purpose of research is to reveal hidden structures and instigate social change.
Goal accomplishment	Accurate representation is accomplished by classifying objects and identifying universal rules or laws.	Understanding meaning is accomplished by describing participants' perspective as contextually situated.	Instigating social change is accomplished by identifying historically and culturally situated hidden structures, especially as they relate to oppression.

Note. Adapted in part from Bogdan and Biklen (1982), Mertens (1998), and Smith (1988).

and empiricism (tangible experience). Later bridge developments in structural theories and semiotics reappear in the interpretive paradigm. They will again be addressed in the discussion of that paradigm.

When taken together, the philosophical perspectives contributing to knowledge by discovery were combined to form several defining assumptions: there is an objective reality that can be known by any observer; the method of knowing is detached and decontextualized; the method depends on precise, systematic, and repetitive procedures; and the purpose of research is to represent reality accurately through classifying objects based on their similarities and differences, and by identifying essential and universal structures. These defining assumptions appear in Table 1.2. Many of the assumptions underlie certain types of studies in our

field. For example, you can find experimental studies, survey studies, content analyses, and classical rhetorical analyses that all derive their central assumptions from the knowledge by discovery paradigm. So, for example, you may find communication studied as quantifiable data in an experimental design, or as a speech text in a neoclassical rhetorical theory. In either case, the grounding assumptions will be shared.

The types of studies most frequently associated with the first paradigm include experimental and survey research, content and interaction analysis, and neoclassical approaches to rhetorical criticisms; these are listed in Table 1.3. The method or methods that researchers use were derived primarily out of the paradigm assumptions about what constitutes knowledge, claims, data, and warrant, as you will learn in Chapters 2, 3, and 4

Table 1.3 Communication Research Methods Affiliated with Paradigms

Discovery	Interpretative	Critical
Survey research and network analysis	Discourse analysis	Critical ethnography
Experimental research	Ethnography	Marxist criticism
Content analysis	Narrative and mythic rhetorical criticism	Feminist criticism
Interaction analysis	Metaphoric rhetorical criticism	Cultural studies
Neo-Aristotelian rhetorical criticism	Dramatism in rhetorical criticism	Postmodern criticism
Historical case studies	Fantasy theme analysis in rhetorical criticism	Poststructural criticism
Biographical studies in rhetorical criticism		Postcolonial criticism
Classical genre rhetorical criticism		Genre reform criticism
Conversational analysis		

in this first part of the book. Often, researchers do not consciously think about the assumptions associated with each paradigm, but they are there nonetheless.

It is crucially important that we point out that not all studies of one particular type of methodology will always come from the same paradigm. A growing number of studies are attempts to integrate several methods common to different paradigms. For instance, not all network analyses use discovery as the only epistemological paradigm. In a representative study, Tardy and Hale (1998) described their study of "stay-at-home Moms" as a combination of approaches: "The methodology in this study was ethnographic and involved participant observation, personal interviews" (p. 341). These methodologies are usually associated with the interpretive paradigm. In the same study, they also used questionnaires and a descriptive statistical procedure called "multidimensional scaling analysis" in order to develop a series of sociograms (pp. 343–344). These are methods usually associated with the paradigm of discovery. However, many studies in each of the methodologies in the first column of Table 1.3 can frequently be grouped under the first paradigm.

Interpretive Paradigm Perspective

The second paradigm of knowledge by interpretation is associated with a number of philosophical perspectives. The first of these, **hermeneutics,** has been defined as the "study of interpretive understanding or meaning" (Mertens, 1998, p. 11). It began as the pursuit of several German phenomenologists, Husserl, Dilthey, and Weber, and emphasized understanding or **Verstehen,** a term that referred to interpretation as a process that grew out of a historical and cultural perspective. **Phenomenologists** believed that interpretation of experience was only possible by understanding the perspective of the participants engaged in interacting.

Symbolic interactionism was an approach to sociology developed primarily by Mead and his students at the University of Chicago. Initial attempts to ground its claims came first from the discovery paradigm arising out of an empirical phenomenology. Over the years, the main purpose of the approach was to understand how people construct and interpret the meaning of their experiences. The process was centered in the interaction that each individual has with other people and became increasingly interpretive. New emphasis on the individual illustrated a shift in understanding that what may be true in one context is not true in another. Reality is best understood as multiple constructions of the experiences that individuals have in interaction, as understood in the perspectives of **constructivism** and **naturalism.** Constructivism had at its core the belief that there are multiple realities that are socially constructed. Naturalism was a professed adherence to studying people in their everyday lives as played out in their natural settings. Understanding meaning from the perspective of the people selected to be studied means adopting their frame of reference in the field (Bogdan & Biklen, 1982, pp. 10–14; Mertens, 1998, pp. 11–15; Smith, 1988, pp. 310–311).

As a bridge from the more traditional paradigm of discovery, structuralism begins with more formal and universal emphases in the work of Foucault in philosophy and psychology, Levi-Strauss in anthropology, Freud and Lacan in psychoanalysis, and Saussure and Chomsky in linguistics (Blanchard, 1980, p. 10; Gill, 1994, pp. 173–186). Many of these theorists were trained in both science and the humanities, and so their bridge roles were natural developments. The structure of human interaction becomes a system or construction embedded in a sociocultural and historical context (Lechte, 1994, pp. 148–152). For the first time in a Saussurian view of language, the linguistic codes have "no necessary relation to an external reality and, thus, no relation to an absolute and abiding truth"; yet they are relatively stable structures, and so exert "enormous influence over human action and understanding" (Gill, pp. 174–175).

The knowledge by interpretation paradigm is defined by the assumptions we explained earlier, including the belief that there are multiple realities and these are socially constructed from the interaction experiences of the individual, and to some extent, the experiences of the group. The process of interpretation happens when the researcher understands how participants construct meaning. It is critical that the researcher understands the participants' perspectives since all meaning and interaction is "contextually situated" (Denzin & Lincoln, 1998, pp. 16–17; Mertens, 1998, pp. 11–15).

Typical research studies in this second paradigm include ethnographies, fantasy theme analysis, mythic rhetorical criticism, dramatism, and narrative analysis. You will learn about each of these methodologies in depth in later chapters. *But as we noted in the previous paradigm, one type of methodology does not ensure one paradigmatic view.* For example, a number of researchers in our field conduct critical ethnographies (for example, Conquergood, 1991). They often use procedures identified originally with the interpretive paradigm, but the central goal of the research has shifted to reveal the oppression of a group marginalized by society and, in some cases, to instigate social change. In rhetorical criticism, Murphy's (1997) study of two speeches, one by Clinton and one by Martin Luther King, Jr., revisits classical rhetorical concepts

of *style* and *authority* from interpretive and critical perspectives. Generally speaking, however, studies using the methodologies identified in the second column of Table 1.3 are most likely to adopt an interpretive paradigm perspective.

Critical Paradigm Perspective

The last paradigm, knowledge by criticism, is associated with the most recent changes in communication research. The paradigm has its origins in the philosophies of critical theory, semiotics, deconstructivism, postmodernism, and poststructuralism. Denzin and Lincoln claim that the emergence of this paradigm stems from two crises: (1) the crisis of representation and (2) the crisis of legitimation (1998, pp. 19–22). These two crises are centered in the problem created by the subjective view of the researcher. In the past, the report or study has been represented as *the* scientific authority, but Denzin and Lincoln argued that every research study represents the "subjective view" of the researcher because of the way claims were constructed and because of the choices the researcher made in choosing specific methods to investigate them.

Common to the philosophies above is the understanding that evaluation and criticism are not only impossible to avoid, but they are desirable ends. Since the researcher cannot escape the subjective and interpretive view of reality, then this standpoint should be made explicit and clear. Otherwise, the researcher misrepresents research as objective when it simply reinforces the existing privileged hierarchy of power. The feminist, ethnic, Marxist, and cultural studies models of research explain how privileged groups exercise oppression of marginalized groups (like women, minorities, politically disfavored groups, etc.).

From the critical paradigm perspective, the purpose of research often takes the form of identifying the implicit and dominant social structures of power so that real change in the sociocultural, political, and economic bases can be instigated. Some researchers may approach these social structures as material and verifiable; other researchers consider them experiential and subjective. Often, poststructural studies demonstrate that social text in many forms continues to represent the dominant paradigm of thought and communication in ways that do not permit experiences of marginalized groups to be even minimally represented. Some feminist scholars, for example, have argued that new codes and interpretive schemes must be developed in order for the experiences of women to be fully voiced or acknowledged as participants in a patriarchal culture (Foss & Foss, 1988, pp. 151–160; Gilligan, 1982).

Just as we have discussed in the other paradigms, there are many studies that fit some elements, but not all, of what we have described here as the critical paradigm. Some may have more of an interpretive emphasis and be less politically motivated. Others may press exclusively for radical social change. Moreover, scholars in the communication field continue to debate the major tenets and assumptions common to all three perspectives. We are always in a state of flux as researchers, as theorists, as philosophers, as students, and as teachers! The discussion in this section was intended to provide you with an encompassing view of the major paradigmatic changes happening in communication research and, more specifically, in our methodological approaches. In choosing to conduct research, we select methods that have, at their core, basic assumptions about how we are acquiring knowledge. This chapter is designed to help you identify the epistemological assumptions common to the methods applied in communication research. The assumptions of each paradigm provide different answers to how researchers make claims (Chapter 2), what counts as communication data (Chapter 3), and how researchers should warrant their claims (Chapter 4). Before proceeding on to these chapters, however, we must consider another dramatic area of change: various technological advances have fundamentally revised the definition of communication as well as the tools we use to study it.

COMMUNICATION AND TECHNOLOGY

Undoubtedly, one of the greatest changes (if not *the* greatest) to our everyday lives in the 1990s was from the field of electronic communication. Words like the *Internet, World Wide Web,* and *email* have become commonplace. We are now dealing with computer-mediated communication (CMC) in many new forms, in commerce, for example, and in interpersonal relationships. We wonder about new possibilities for meaning like virtual realities, hyperspace, and cybersociety (Jones, 1998a).

The new advances in the technology of communication have affected our methodologies in two major ways. First, they have altered the way we define communication. We can do new things with communication like join groups for discourse online through Internet Relay Chat (IRC) or Multi-User Domains, otherwise known as MUDs. We can become group members by listservs, and we can "surf the Web" for information or services. We have, in many senses, become what Jones has called the "electronic community" (Jones, 1998a, p. 3). In a recent collection of essays, communication scholars explored a variety of new topics, such as how online communities emerge, how gender is constructed in cybersociety, how teens date on the net, how people form a "virtual ethnicity" by electronic group membership, and how online communities can lead to problems with identity formation and connections to social contexts, or spaces and places for discourse (Jones, 1998a).

An increasing number of studies specifically focus on how the electronic communication process is different than more conventional forms. For example, Hacker and Wignall (1997) identified several critical factors, such as the importance and relevance of information provided by CMC for students, that predicted greater success in accepting CMC as an alternative to face-to-face interaction in the classroom. In another study, Patterson and Gojdycz (2000) found no relationship between communication anxiety and CMC use. They did, however, find that *computer* anxiety significantly predicted use of email, chat, and the Web. As a final example, a study by Waldeck, Kearney, and Plax (2001) examined how teachers' strategies in their email messages influenced students' willingness to communicate with their teachers online. The examples provided here barely scratch the surface of the large number of studies now investigating electronic communities. Throughout the remaining chapters of the book, you will learn how technology has created a new interface for defining and analyzing the boundaries of communication, in ways that are relevant to the methods listed in Table 1.3.

A second way that research methods have been impacted by the technological advances in electronic communication is in the development of new analytic tools. Researchers can now collaborate easily online, creating a virtual space where they can mutually construct a study of communication. The widespread use of word processing programs and scanners has made the data collection and analysis phases more streamlined and accessible to the entire research team, publication editors, and ultimately to the targeted audiences. Finally, there are software programs that directly support the analysis of communication. In later chapters, you will learn about software like SPSS (Statistical Package for Social Sciences) for studies with quantitative data analyses and NUD★IST (Nonnumerical Unstructured Data ★ Indexing Searching and Theorizing) for studies employing qualitative data analyses. These are just two of the many new analytic tools available to communication researchers.

In studying communication research methods, it will be impossible for you to avoid how technology has impacted the field and ultimately your own experiences. We encourage you to use the various forms of electronic communication if you haven't already.

In each of the chapters of this book, we will provide you with a focus on how technology has changed our study of communication. We will also include some exercises to help you find ways to apply what you are learning about methods to several areas of electronic communication technology. As you read, you will probably be able to think of many more ways to investigate communication. The new technologies have opened up new areas of exploration where "the fronts are on our computer screens, beckoning us to go from a place, a 'where' of our own boundaries to a less palpable site, a 'who knows' that, like any new frontier, is colonized first by our imagination and thought" (Jones, 1998a, p. xvii).

SUMMARY

This chapter introduced the research-as-argument model based on Toulmin's conception of three elements: claim, data, and warrant. You learned that, as applied to research contexts, claims can be understood as basic propositions, data as evidence, and warrants as standards of evaluation. Commonsense approaches to knowledge were then distinguished from methodological ways of knowing. You were introduced to three basic epistemological paradigms: knowledge by discovery, knowledge by interpretation, and knowledge by criticism. These were further explained by considering the philosophical perspectives that contributed to each of the three paradigms. We concluded this chapter by considering two ways technology has impacted the study of communication: by redefining and expanding the concept of communication, and by equipping researchers with new tools to analyze communication. This chapter provided a foundation for the first part of the book: Chapter 2 explores the nature of claims in communication research, Chapter 3 is a discussion of what counts as communication data, and Chapter 4 provides an exploration of warrants as standards of evaluation applied across the three paradigms.

KEY TERMS

Behaviorism

Claim

Constructivism

Data

Discrimination

Empiricism

Formulas

Generalization

Hermeneutics

Knowing as a method of science

Knowing by authority

Knowing by criticism

Knowing by discovery

Knowing by interpretation

Knowing by tenacity

Knowing on a priori grounds

Laws

Logical positivism

Modernism

Naturalism

Paradigms

Phenomenology

Precise, systematic, and repetitive observations

Principles

Rationalism

Realism

Rules

Structuralism

Symbolic interactionism

Verstehen

Warrant

DISCUSSION QUESTIONS

1. From the common forms of knowing, what is the difference between knowing by tenacity and knowing by authority? Describe the strengths and weaknesses of both.

2. In beginning this chapter, we asked you to identify one thing that you know. Write it down here. Try to identify which epistemological paradigm presented in this chapter best describes the way you came to know this.

3. Some people may argue that research that comes from a paradigm other than their own is not *good* research. What are some of the points you can make to counter this argument? What would make research *bad*?

4. Throughout this chapter, we have used a number of tattoo examples. For example, we identified a wrist chain tattoo on a young woman and the Nazi internment camp code on a Jewish grandmother. Explain how these may represent the economic, ethnic, gender, or ability-based realities of the wearers. Think of a tattoo you have seen. How does it reflect these same factors?

"TRY IT!" ACTIVITIES

The Great Debates: I

One way to develop an appreciation for the differences between the paradigm of discovery and the other two paradigms is to construct a debate centered in the claims from one paradigm. Try selecting two groups of students. One group will represent researchers from the first epistemological paradigm, knowledge by discovery. They should develop an argument that supports the following claim: "There is one objective reality. Our research provides support for developing a set of verifiable rules or laws of communication. Some of these will be universal laws, common to all humans." The other group should develop an argument that supports the alternative claim: "There are many socially constructed realities. The purpose of our research is to describe one of these distinct realities to acquire an understanding of an insider perspective. Any preconceptions a researcher may have before entering the field should be abandoned so that alternate views can be fully understood."

Following the debate, the class should discuss the implications each set of assumptions carries. The instructor should probe students to extend their thinking. For example, students may discuss whether it is possible to use both discovery and interpretation as two epistemologies. If they say "yes," ask them to figure out whether they peacefully coexist side by side, or whether they can actually be integrated.

The Great Debates: II

Another way to distinguish between the interpretive and critical paradigms is to debate an essential difference in assumptions. Try selecting two groups of students to represent these differing views. One group will represent researchers from the second epistemological paradigm, knowledge by interpretation. They should develop an argument that supports the following claim: "There are many views of reality. Each is specific to its cultural and social context. The researcher's task is to become immersed in the group studied and to provide a rich description of the activities and interaction of that group. This level of understanding is necessary to develop a clear representation of any group studied." Another group of students should support this claim from the critical paradigm: "You will never be able to absent your perspective from the group you are studying. Everything you decide to record represents *your* perspective, not theirs. It is much better to identify your own standards of evaluation and apply these openly as criticism. By this approach, you will be able to work as an advocate for social reform."

The Great Debates: III

This last debate contrasts the claims from the critical and discovery paradigms. Establish two groups of students. One group will represent researchers from the last epistemological paradigm, knowledge by criticism. They should develop an argument that supports this claim: "The purpose of research should be to advocate for social reform. We should use our methods of analysis to reveal hidden social structures of power that continue to dominate and oppress marginalized groups." A second group of students should counterargue the following claim: "Researchers cannot allow themselves to become adherents to social causes. Such fanaticism blinds all people to 'balance' in perspectives and will lead to the same kind of domination they supposedly eschew. Researchers should remain as detached as possible from the research setting and participants; they should embrace skepticism about all beliefs as a way of imposing a correcting influence on their thought processes."

Review Actual Communication Studies

Use actual studies conducted by communication researchers in your answers.

1. Review a study that investigates communication as an observable and quantifiable phenomenon. By adopting an empirical and rational approach to communication, researchers use methods common to the knowledge-by-discovery paradigm. For example, you could explain how Kline and Clinton investigated the rules of children in a day care setting through empirical, quantitative methods (Kline & Clinton, 1998).

2. Review a study that describes communication within a specified cultural group for the purposes of understanding what is occurring from the perspectives of its members. This approach is central in the knowledge-by-interpretation paradigm. For example, you could explain how Baxter and Goldsmith studied the specialized talk and practices of an adolescent clique at a local high school (Baxter & Goldsmith, 1990).

3. Review a study that describes and critiques how marginal groups are co-opted by the dominant social group as one of the central assumptions of the critical paradigm. For example, you could explain how Tretheway explores the ways marginalized groups express "resistance, identity, and empowerment in a human service organization" (Tretheway, 1997).

4. Find a study that uses CMC (computer-mediated communication) in some form (for example, email). Using the information in this chapter, and Tables 1.1 and 1.2, see if you can identify the paradigm and the methodology associated with the study you have selected. Explain your answer.

2

Making Claims

ABSTRACT

In this chapter, you will learn about the first component, the claim, of the "research as argument" model we identified in Chapter 1. The claim in research is the central assertion or premise on which the analysis is based. There are six different types of claims: descriptive, explanatory, predictive, interpretive, evaluative, and reformist. We will describe each type and apply it to different communication research methodologies across each of the three epistemological paradigms: discovery, interpretive, and critical. Our discussion in each section will show that research often combines several different types of claims into one analysis. Explanatory and predictive claims are typically combined, and evaluative claims are either implied or made explicit along with reformist claims. Moreover, how we as researchers understand and use one type of claim depends upon our paradigmatic assumptions. This chapter concludes with a suggested "Great Debate" activity by discussing the merits and drawbacks to applying the ethical principle of "disinterestedness" to the researcher's role.

OUTLINE

The first step toward doing research very often involves thinking about some aspect of communication that is problematic in some way or that piques your curiosity. You may not know why some friends regard "teasing" as a fundamental part of their relationship, and yet others try to avoid it. Or perhaps you would like to know how to create a more favorable impression during a job interview.. Or you might want to understand what makes some television commercials more persuasive than others. Or maybe you are socially concerned that violence in visual media really is adversely affecting us as audience members.

THE PROCESS OF MAKING CLAIMS

Our interests guide our decisions to conduct research. From these, we form a **claim,** or central assertion or premise of a research study. But even in the most formal research contexts, scholars don't sit down and consciously decide to do an ethnographic study, an experimental study, or a rhetorical analysis because of their values from the three paradigms we described in Chapter 1. You wouldn't say, for instance, "I want to do an experiment on the effects of three types of messages because I believe there is a discoverable objective reality, that my purpose is to accurately represent reality, and that I will do so by precise, systematic, and repetitive methods." Instead, what you would consciously think about is something about communication that you want to study. You would think of a question about communication that you want to answer.

Nevertheless, the process of thinking about communication, what your questions are and how you would study them, is implicitly informed by the three paradigms we described in Chapter 1—whether you are aware of this or not. For example, if you value the assumptions of the paradigm of discovery, then you will tend to construct research that achieves certain goals and not others. You will think of research designs that often begin with constructing testable claims, describing precise procedures for measurement, and reporting results of testing those predictions.

To illustrate this process of beginning with a claim that is measured and tested against observations, Bachman and Zakahi (2000) conducted a survey study to test the relationship between strategies relational partners used to initiate romantic relationships and their attachment styles, called love schemas. The researchers in this study began by identifying claims about the different ways people think about and express their love and how these affect the kinds of strategies they use with their romantic partners. Bachman and Zakahi thought first about the claim they wanted to make and then tested it against their observations. We will have more to say about these types of studies in Chapters 5 through 7.

If you value the assumptions of the interpretive paradigm, however, you would think of communication problems in a very different way, beginning with the first step of research. Frequently, you would not even know what your specific claims are until you explored and described in depth your observations of a particular social setting or situation. The goal of your study may be to faithfully represent that culture by describing its members' perspectives of their roles and practices, but you may not even know how to adequately describe the culture, community, or group you are interested in studying before you begin. Examples of such speech communities are found in Dollar and Zimmers' (1998) study of identity and communicative boundaries in street youth, Braithwaite's (1997a) study of Vietnam veterans' "ritual of legitimacy," and Philipsen's (1975) study of male communication patterns in an urban setting. We will focus on these studies and others reflecting the methodology of ethnography in more detail in Chapter 11, "Ethnographic Research." You might even want to know how people from more than one group or community switch their styles of speaking in various contexts, a question you could explore with conversation or discourse analysis, which we will cover in Chapter 10, "Conversation and Discourse Analysis."

Rhetorical critics who share the interpretive paradigm with ethnographers often begin by applying an interpretive framework to some type of rhetorical text. In the process, they make the claim that the framework they have selected will reveal something about the text's social significance. For example, Kenny (2000) used a Burkean conceptual framework to explore the rhetoric of Jack Kevorkian, a physician who helped several of his patients commit suicide. The Burkean framework is one way rhetorical critics interpret texts. This rhetorical framework and others will be explored more fully in Chapter 12, "Traditional and Interpretive Methods of Rhetorical Criticism."

EXHIBIT 2.1   Characteristics of Descriptive Claims

General function: Description is definitional; descriptive claims generally define what is occurring.

I.   **Discovery paradigm:** Function of descriptive claims is to represent reality accurately.

II. **Interpretive paradigm:** Function of descriptive claims is to reveal the underlying structure of meanings of communication processes.

III. **Critical paradigm:** Function of descriptive claims is to reveal the existing framework or foundation of observations.

Sometimes the central question we are formulating requires a different type of an answer than can be provided by either a discovery-paradigm perspective or an interpretive-paradigm perspective. You may want to know an answer to the question you have about communication that only the critical paradigm can address. If you value the assumptions of the critical paradigm, you might begin by looking for those political and social practices that reveal the oppression of marginal groups, and you might feel very strongly that your study has an obligation to instigate some form of social change. For example, the central message in Goldzwig and Sullivan's (2000) analysis of racialized discourse in Milwaukee was to expose how local "talk" was ignored because it was outside the mainstream of general social discourse. The authors believed very strongly that rhetorical critics are obliged to focus their analytic skills on the rhetoric of marginalized groups to help bring about social change. We shall explore the many types of communication phenomena from the critical-paradigm perspective in Chapter 13, "Critical Studies."

By understanding how the paradigms we described in the first chapter guide us in making claims, it becomes increasingly clear that we cannot tell you all communication research has the same, systematic set of practices that constitute the method process. Not all research begins with establishing a claim, testing that claim with data or evidence, and verifying that process with warrants. Some research begins with a claim, some with data, some with describing the existing social warrants and backing of specific social practices. In fact, the same terms, like *description, explanation,* and *interpretation,* are sometimes used across the paradigms, but they mean different things in each paradigm. Exhibit 2.1 shows a clear distinction in how descriptive claims function across the three paradigms.

Methods and their paradigm assumptions do not have equivalent components and processes; therefore, we don't believe all communication research methods can be explained by the same stages, phases, or any other linear sequence of steps (Philipsen, 1977). We chose to start our explanation instead by considering how various claims reflect the paradigmatic assumptions. We are not trying to accentuate the differences for effect; we are simply trying to explain the differences you are likely to find when you look at communication research.

Definition of Claim

We will begin with the concept of claim as a rather traditional approach to unpacking the model of research we presented in the first chapter. There, we defined **claim** as the central assertion or premise of a research study. It often, at least implicitly, represents the study's purpose or goal as well. We identify the six types of claims made in research as descriptive, explanatory, predictive, interpretive, evaluative, and reformist (adapted from Smith, 1988, and Littlejohn, 1996). Not every type of claim can be found in every paradigm, nor is every type mutually exclusive. Descriptive claims can be found across all three types of paradigms. Explanatory and predictive claims are concentrated in the discovery paradigm. The interpretive paradigm emphasizes interpretive claims obviously. And the critical paradigm focuses on evaluation and social reform. The types of claims by paradigm are illustrated in Table 2.1. There are no doubt exceptions to these distinctions, especially in the fuzziness of paradigm boundaries. But generally the paradigm perspectives emphasize certain types of claims over others.

Table 2.1   Types of Claims Emphasized Across the Paradigms

Type of claims	Discovery paradigm	Interpretive paradigm	Critical paradigm
Descriptive	Yes	Yes	Yes
Explanatory	Yes	No	No
Predictive	Yes	No	No
Interpretive	No	Yes	No
Evaluative	No	No	Yes
Reformist	No	No	Yes

Types of Claims

Descriptive claims If you are interested in making assertions about how to define some particular communication phenomenon, you are making **descriptive claims.** Description is a process that appears across all three paradigms and across a variety of methodological approaches. Its focus is on what some part of communication is, not why it happens, or whether it is positively or negatively valued. The specific types of descriptive claims you make and how you put them to work will depend on your paradigmatic assumptions.

From the discovery paradigm, the purpose of descriptive research claims is to accurately describe reality (refer to Exhibit 2.1 again). The goal of description remains the same throughout the discovery paradigm whether researchers are conducting an experiment, administering a survey, analyzing message content, or explaining the components of argument present in a text from a neo-Aristotelian rhetorical perspective. Experiments, surveys, and content analyses are **empirical methods** that rely on measuring quantitative or numerical data; rhetorical critical methods from the discovery paradigm, however, retain textual data in its qualitative and verbally descriptive form.

Rhetorical critics from the discovery paradigm use description in at least two ways (Foss, 1996, pp. 17–18). First, they must accurately describe communication texts or messages when they give overviews or summaries of the main features or elements of the text they have selected to study. Second, description occurs whenever the rhetorical critic makes a rational argument for selecting a specific method of analysis. For example, Hill (1972) argued that the structure of a speech is best represented by the five canons of rhetoric. His claim that the speech illustrates these structural components is a descriptive claim.

Description is equally essential in survey studies, a type of empirical research, whenever researchers construct conceptual measures to use in interviews or questionnaires. To illustrate this process, Mikesell and Messman (1994) used open-ended questions in their interviews to obtain descriptions of the ways romantic partners compete with each other. The descriptions were analyzed and found to contain 40 different categories of competition! In a follow-up study, Messman and Mikesell (2000) used those content categories to explore the relationship between competition and the strategies that couples use in their conflicts. Gow (1996) also asked descriptive research questions when he wanted to discover what lead and supporting roles women and men occupied in MTV videos. After many observations, he was able to construct a description of all the various types of roles he found in the MTV videos.

Within the discovery paradigm, problem statements for empirical studies usually take the form of research questions (Smith, 1988; Mertens, 1998). **Research questions** (RQs) ask how a concept chosen for study can be classified, or they ask what relationship exists between various types of communication variables. **Hypotheses** (Hs) are considered more precise since hypotheses make specific predictions about relationships between communication variables. You will learn more about RQs and Hs in Chapters 5 through 7. Some examples of descriptive research questions from published communication research literature are shown in Exhibit 2.2.

Empirical methodologists from the discovery paradigm often make it a point to separate descriptive claims from explanatory claims; explanatory claims are described in detail in the next section but are introduced here for contrast. With a purely descriptive focus, a researcher "begins with a well-defined subject and conducts research to describe it accurately.

EXHIBIT 2.2   Descriptive Claims as Research Questions in the Discovery Paradigm

RQ$_1$:   What kinds of roles are occupied by women in popular music videos aired on MTV in 1990 compared to 1995? (Gow, 1996)

RQ$_2$:   Are there turning points that characterize and define postdivorce relationships? (Graham, 1997)

RQ$_3$:   What levels of communication apprehension, intercultural communication apprehension, and intercultural willingness to communicate exist in international teaching assistants? (Roach & Olaniran, 2001)

RQ$_4$:   What is the typical length of a contemporary daytime fringe commercial? (Dahlberg, 2001)

RQ$_5$:   What proportion of Web sites for children collect personal information from children? (Cai & Gantz, 2000)

The outcome of a descriptive study is a detailed picture of the subject" (Neuman, 1994, p. 19). Examples of descriptive claims might include describing the proportion of Web sites for children that collect personal information from them (Cai & Gantz, 2000), and the proportions by type of experts (e.g., expertise from education versus expertise from experience) who appear on television talk shows (Johnson, Smith, Mitchell, Orrego, & Yun, 1999). By contrast, explanatory claims are assertions about why one communication characteristic or behavior influences another. An explanatory claim moves beyond what a descriptive claim is intended to do.

Descriptive claims often require the development of a categorizing scheme or **taxonomy** for communication behaviors, events, and messages. The study we cited earlier by Messman and Mikesell (2000) found that romantic couples identified many different types of competition they experienced in their relationships. Competition was defined as "attempts to 'out-do' or 'keep up with' your partner" (p. 26). Couples reported feeling competitive in about 40 different areas. One area reported by the researchers was "control over the relationship. For example, who gets their way, who makes decisions, and/or who is in the dominant role" (p. 26). One of the purposes of this study was to verify the taxonomy or classification system they had developed for areas of competition between romantic partners from an earlier study (Mikesell and Messman, 1994) so that they could refine the way they were measuring it.

Researchers with similar types of descriptive goals study different types of communication phenomena. One study reported a taxonomy for the types of turning points that characterize postdivorce relationships (Graham, 1997); another study identified a taxonomy of motivations that Chinese students identified for communicating with family and friends (Anderson, Martin, & Zhong, 1998).

If you view description as a preliminary step toward theoretic explanation as many discovery paradigm researchers do, then research never ends in description. You will typically adopt a deductive method of inquiry; that is, you will begin by making a descriptive claim, and then test your claim against observations. Your ultimate goals are explanation and prediction. Descriptive studies are initial attempts to map out conceptual territory for empirical study.

As we noted earlier, descriptive research often begins with the claim as a research question; for example, Wagoner and Waldron (1999) asked what types of face-protecting or face-threatening strategies subordinates used in organizational contexts. Results from this study permit you to eventually move to more specific claims that are usually worded as explanatory predictions or hypotheses; from the example above, you can test the relationship between subordinates' feelings of liking/disliking their superiors and their use of face-saving strategies in various organizational contexts. In this case, you could assume that how subordinates feel about their supervisors will influence the types of strategies they adopt to help them save face. In empirical research, you will advance descriptive and explanatory claims as a way of preparing to achieve more accurate and precise explanations and predictions.

Although scholars from the discovery paradigm tend to view observing and describing communication phenomena as just the first step of research, scholars from the interpretive paradigm view description much more broadly. In interpretive communication studies, description is a complete process. It is not meant to be backgrounded as some preliminary process. Interpretive researchers move back and forth between what they are observing and their descriptions, modifying these as they attempt to uncover emerging patterns as communicative behavior. For example, in ethnographic or discourse analytic research, your descriptive claims will emerge and will change throughout the research process; by contrast, in a survey study, you will use the deductive method of constructing claims ahead of time and keeping them fixed during the study as we described earlier. The interpretive researcher's goal is "to discover the meanings communicators have in mind when they talk with others in particular contexts" (Smith, 1988, p. 9). Interpretive paradigm researchers tend to view description as reflecting a socially agreed upon reality rather than some physical, external reality as it is viewed in the discovery paradigm.

When using description in the interpretive paradigm, you will typically focus on three sets of observational descriptions as the method of collecting data: the observational domain, the interpretive schemes, and relations between observations (Smith, 1988, p. 9). Each set of observational descriptions reveals a distinct type of claim. In the first case, you can make a claim about *what* is occurring in communication— verbal/nonverbal, face-to-face/mediated, ritualized/ unscripted, and so forth. For example, Robinson (1998) investigated verbal and nonverbal practices between doctor and patient in the conversational openings of medical consultations. He claimed that verbal and nonverbal behaviors are mutually constructed between both interactants.

In the second set, you can construct descriptive claims about the interpretive schemes that communicators use to arrive at meaning. To illustrate, Robinson's claims about the coordinated conversational patterns he observed revealed two interactional problems: (1) how conversational partners accomplished noncollaborative acts while collaborating on talk, and (2) how each partner determined the other's readiness to discuss the chief problem (1998, p. 12). The third set of observations leads to descriptive claims about how actual observed responses are connected through an interpretive scheme shared by the participants. Robinson showed how the actual nonverbal behaviors of both doctors and patients served as cues to help bridge periods of noncollaboration

(closing the door, situating belongings, getting undressed/dressed, etc.).

In later chapters, you will learn how descriptive claims are made in a variety of methodologies from the interpretive paradigm. At this point, you need only to know that description in the interpretive paradigm provides a shared basis of understanding whether you conduct an ethnographic study, a discourse analysis, a metaphorical analysis, or an interpretive dramatistic account of a communication text and its creation.

You can also distinguish description in critical paradigm research from description in discovery and interpretive paradigm research by its underlying assumptions. Your purpose in using description in critical research is to provide a framework for instigating social change. Critical researchers have recognized that any use of description reflects the standpoint of the researcher and is, therefore, value laden. Even the most basic of taxonomies represents the way in which you, the researcher, view the hierarchy or layers of classification rather than representing some "true" intrinsic structure. Your goal in description gives you a framework for evaluating social structure without implying that structure is externally valid in any decontextualized sense. Your research should satisfy this basic common goal regardless of conducting analyses in critical ethnography, in cultural studies, or in critical studies of social movements.

To illustrate this form of description, Thomas (1993) stated that critical ethnography deviates from conventional ethnography in that conventional ethnographers "study culture for the purpose of describing it" while critical ethnographers "do so to change it" (p. 4). Your goal is not only to explain how members of a culture share their interpretations of reality, but you would also be concerned with giving voice to and representing members of marginalized cultures who are otherwise not represented (p. 34). The entire purpose of describing how social groups are marginalized makes the process of description in the critical paradigm one that has the potential to reveal and reform various social practices. Thomas's (1993) study of prisoners revealed not only the way inmates use violence and the legal system, but illustrated clearly the need for general prison reform. We will say more about these specific goals in later sections of this chapter.

Remember that the function of a term often changes as we move from paradigm to paradigm. We will explore how this happens in more depth in Chapters 3 and 4. However, as you read this section, it should already be apparent that as we have switched our discussion from the discovery paradigm to the interpretive and critical paradigms, the function of description actually changes. Refer again to the differences in how descriptive claims appear in each of the paradigms as explained in Exhibit 2.1. Whatever we *see* as researchers has already been heavily influenced by our existing beliefs about what we expect to be seeing. A conversational analyst from the interpretive paradigm will see a very different event when two people are arguing than will an empiricist attempting to classify compliance-gaining strategies people use in arguments. In the former instance, description is used to reveal the interpretive schemes conversational partners use in having arguments, and in the latter instance, description functions to classify behavior as a preliminary step in building compliance-gaining theories about arguments.

Explanatory and predictive claims When they occur together, explanation and prediction are terms often associated with the discovery paradigm. As we noted in the previous section, **explanatory claims** explain the relationships between various communication phenomena, often by identifying reasons or causes for communication phenomena. In empirical research, explanatory claims are frequently worded as research questions or predictions in the form of hypotheses. **Predictive claims** identify the causal connections you would expect to test based on the communication phenomena you are studying.

Explanation and prediction are the means by which you can make causal arguments. Making causal arguments is the crux of the discovery paradigm view, which assumes knowledge is objective and that reality is discoverable. You would expect to find such claims in experimental and survey research, in content and interaction analysis, even in the more classical approaches to rhetorical criticism, but you will not find them in interpretive and critical paradigm research (see, for example, Silverman, 1993, and Thomas, 1993).

In discovery paradigm research, you will attempt to discover what rules or laws *explain* whatever you observe happening between one set of communication behaviors and another. As an empiricist, you will tend to see research as a five-part process: (1) development of theories, (2) testing of theories, (3) control

of alternative explanations, (4) nature of relationships, and (5) testing theories with observable evidence (Kerlinger, 1986; Watt & van den Berg, 1995). You will see theories as explanations that allow you to make certain causal predictions.

When the claim you construct *predicts* that a change in one communication phenomenon, usually called the **dependent variable**, is preceded and influenced by a change in the other, usually defined as the **independent variable**, you have made a **causal claim**. We will have more to say about variables and the nature of causality in Chapters 3 through 6. For now, it is important that you realize explanatory claims are formulated as predictions in the discovery paradigm. They are not separate types of claims.

As we said before, explanatory claims about the relationships between communication variables can take the form of either research questions or hypotheses. Typically, you will use research questions when past research is not very extensive or when results from different studies appear to be contradictory. As an illustration, consider a study by Ragsdale (1996). He posed the following research question: Is there a positive, linear association between one's relational satisfaction level and the frequency of relational maintenance strategy use? By making a claim in question format, Ragsdale indicated a need for generally exploring the types of strategies people used in their interpersonal relationships and whether these were linked uniformly with relational satisfaction.

Expecting these two communication variables to occur together is also a claim of **association**. Although it is not sufficient as grounds for a causal argument, it is one of the conditions of causality we will be discussing later on. More generally here, a claim of association can be predictive as well. That is, you can predict that as one variable (like relationship satisfaction) changes, the second variable (the types of strategies people choose) changes as well. But associative, noncausal claims will not tell you which of these two variables is predicted to be the cause of change in the other variable.

In the study example above, there was enough depth and consistency in the findings to also allow Ragsdale to construct a specific hypothesis: Married females use more relational maintenance strategies (positivity, openness, assurances, network, tasks) than their male partners. In this case, Ragsdale constructed a causal claim to predict how marital status and biological sex would influence the selection of relational

---

EXHIBIT 2.3   Explanatory Research Questions and Hypotheses from Empirical Studies in the Discovery Paradigm

RQ$_1$: Will friends with similarly low levels of communication skills be less satisfied with their relationships (i.e., more lonely) than friends with similarly high levels of communication skills? (Burleson & Samter, 1996)

RQ$_2$: What are the specific relationships between levels of interaction involvement and types of alignment strategies across conversational partners? (Adapted from Chen, 1997)

H$_1$: Married females use more relational maintenance strategies (positivity, openness, assurances, network, tasks) than their male partners. (Ragsdale, 1996)

RQ$_3$: Is there a positive, linear association between one's relational satisfaction level and the frequency of relational maintenance strategy use? (Ragsdale, 1996)

RQ$_4$: What are Latino, Asian American, African American, and Anglo close friends' individual and joint impressions of general conversational rules in their friendship? (Collier, 1996)

H$_2$: Employees who believe that they are being observed by the administration will report significantly lower levels of workplace communication than will employees who do not believe they are being observed. (Adapted from Botan, 1996).

---

maintenance strategies. More examples of explanatory research questions and hypotheses can be found in Exhibit 2.3.

One general line of research is undertaken solely for the purpose of its more practical and applied outcomes rather than to develop theory or increase epistemological understanding. It is sometimes called **action research** (Taylor & Bogdan, 1998, pp. 260–261); it seeks to evaluate some communication problem, and what may be done to find a practical solution. If, for example, you were a researcher interested in testing the effectiveness of early intervention programs with students who are communication apprehensive, you would be engaged in this type of research. Although specifically designed to find solutions for short-term effects, this research can also impact theory development about communication apprehension. Program evaluations and assessment projects are other types of action research and, because of their goals, often blur the boundary between explanatory research and evaluative-reformist research.

Bogdan and Biklen (1982) defined action research as "the systematic collection of information that is designed to bring about social change" (p. 215). When you conduct action research, you will collect and analyze data as evidence of negative effects from some current social problem. Researchers use both qualitative and quantitative methods to make specific recommendations for change. Bogdan and Biklen cited numerous action research examples, including

studies designed to change the negative ways females are depicted in texts used by schools, advocating for the rights of disabled students, exposing negative conditions and practices at government institutions for ethnic minority clients, and unethical treatment of prisoners.

Even though action research may identify practical needs and their solutions, Bogdan and Biklen explain that it is frequently considered unacceptable because it violates two assumptions some discovery paradigm scholars hold dear: (1) Researchers should be academically trained only and not conduct research in applied contexts, and (2) research should always be nonpartisan (p. 214). Because action research goes beyond purely descriptive and explanatory claims, it has been negatively evaluated. But research that blurs paradigm boundaries is often research that engages us creatively and constructively, as we will see in many instances throughout the book.

For the most part, the ability to make accurate predictions is a major characteristic of empirical science from the discovery paradigm (Frankfort-Nachmias & Nachmias, 1996, p. 10). However, if you were interested in rhetorical criticism, you could also identify your work as theoretical, explanatory, and even predictive. Andrews, Leff, and Terrill (1998), three contemporary rhetorical critics, list "development and refinement of theory" as one of the main critical functions. They claim that rhetorical theories help us to understand patterns or principles that "explain a complex set of facts or phenomena" (p. 19). In fact, they describe all rhetoric as theoretical:

> The more we learn about what happened in one particular situation—that is, the more information bits that can be adduced—the better able we will be to generalize a pattern of rhetorical behavior. As these patterns are formed, and compared and contrasted with other patterns, a basis for predicting what will happen in similar cases is established (pp. 19–20).

In one study, for example, McGee (1998) used the theory of *ethos* or speaker's credibility to explain a change in the rhetoric of David Duke, a one-time leader of the Ku Klux Klan and self-proclaimed white supremacist. McGee showed that Duke's bid for governor was couched in new sloganlike phrases borrowed from the rhetoric of a "born-again" Christian. Frequent use of these terms throughout a half-hour gubernatorial campaign film predicted that Duke's transformation and renunciation of his former affiliations would seem more plausible and acceptable to his voter audiences.

Andrews, Leff, and Terrill also warn that not all rhetorical criticism is explicitly theoretical, explanatory, and predictive; that is, your intention may not be to develop a set of generalizations that allow future critics to predict certain sets of results. Rather, you may be more concerned with simply illuminating a particular speaker's motive or situational constraints to increase our understanding of existing rhetorical texts or acts. These claims are more interpretive than explanatory.

If you are a researcher from the interpretive and critical paradigms, you will not tend to use the language of explanation and prediction. From these two paradigms, you will assume reality is socially constructed and knowledge is intersubjective, and because of these assumptions, the types of claims you will create will be interpretive, evaluative, and reformative for the most part. You will not believe that explanation can be objectively detached from your own subjective standpoint, and you will not interpret your job as a researcher as one in which you simply "announce the facts." You will instead explicitly assert that any claim implies "an evaluative judgment of meaning and method in research, policy, and human activity" (Thomas, 1993, p. 18). Therefore, unlike the discovery paradigm researchers we have been discussing, constructing interpretive claims will be central to your goals.

Interpretive claims If you wish to show how communicators create meaning, you are engaged in making **interpretive claims**. As a researcher from the interpretive paradigm, you will share the goal of broadening understanding among all researchers. You will achieve this goal by describing and interpreting how meaning is accomplished from the participants' perspectives, and those perspectives are situated in the contexts of communication that you will be studying.

Interpretive claims are not only found in ethnographic studies, but in conversational and discourse analyses, and some forms of rhetorical criticism. If you take an interpretive approach, your emphasis will be on interpreting meanings and identifying cultural patterns, in contrast with reporting behaviors and pursuing scientific laws as you would do from the discovery paradigm perspective (Hammersley, 1992, pp. 48–50). Scholars have defined interpretation as a way of seeing or an understanding of some phenomenon (Jorgensen, 1989, p. 16). Specifically, any theory that advances interpretive claims "differs from conceptions of theory aimed at explanation, prediction, and control of human phenomena. . . . Explanatory theories are composed of logically interrelated propositions" with an emphasis on testing these through a "logic of verification" (Jorgensen, 1989, p. 17). Altheide's (1985) theory of news bias and Goffman's (1961) view of institutions are examples of well-known and widely used theories supporting interpretive claims.

In some cases, it may be important to distinguish between studies that emphasize descriptive claims and those that are more theoretically interpretive (Taylor & Bogdan, 1998). The main difference in the interpretive paradigm is that descriptive studies focus primarily on data description while interpretive studies emphasize how various theoretic concepts are illustrated by the data. Taylor and Bogdan identify some ethnographies as typical of descriptive studies:

> In ethnographies, researchers try to paint a picture of what people say and how they act in their everyday lives. Descriptive ethnographies are marked by minimal interpretation and conceptualization. The researcher tells the story not through concepts but through descriptions of events. . . . readers are free to come to their own interpretations and draw their own generalizations. (p. 135)

These types of descriptive interpretive claims were characterized in Exhibit 2.1.

EXHIBIT 2.4   **Descriptive and Interpretive Research Questions**

1. Where in the public environment do teenagers (boys and girls) congregate? What characterizes these places? How do these places relate to the housing area and to the city as a whole?

2. In what kind of activities and actions do the teenagers engage in these places? Why do they seek

out these places? Are there any differences in the ways boys and girls use public places?

3. What symbolic significance do public places have for boys, and what symbolic significance do they have for girls?

(Lieberg, 1995, p. 723)

By contrast, you can also use studies from the interpretive paradigm to develop theories. For example, Glaser and Strauss (1967) advise using the **grounded-theory approach** to generate theory. We will have more to say about this approach in Chapter 11, "Ethnographic Research." To illustrate briefly, Lieberg (1995) constructed three descriptive and interpretive claims through the development of guiding research questions, participant observation, and interviews. Her analysis used the theoretic concepts of *cultural release* and *individuation* as an interpretive framework for showing how teens use public space for "retreat and interaction." Examples of Lieberg's interpretive theoretical research questions can be found in Exhibit 2.4.

There are a variety of methods you can use in rhetorical criticism that also rely on interpretive claims. Deciding which elements of a communication text to describe and how to represent a particular critical method are often considered to be interpretive decisions (Foss, 1996, pp. 11–12). You will also be making an interpretive claim about a text if you explore its meaningfulness. In one study, Phillips (1999) analyzed the "rhetoric of controversy" by offering an interpretation of the controversy surrounding the African Burial Ground in New York City. Rather than evaluating the rhetorical texts of this specific controversy or using them to initiate social change, Phillips's primary purpose was to further our understanding of controversy in general. He interpreted the concept as a series of "moments" in which "time, space, and identity become disoriented, disrupted, and displaced" (p. 507).

Phillips offered a unique perspective on a conceptual field rather than arguing that one explanation is more justified or accurate than another. In other words, when you adopt the role of rhetorical

critic, you are "not concerned with finding the one correct interpretation of the artifact because the critic recognizes the artifact does not constitute a reality that can be known and proved"; you can never "know what the artifact 'really' is" (Foss, 1996, p. 18). Instead, as an interpretive critic, you will argue for what a communication text means socially, culturally, and politically. More examples of interpretive rhetorical claims can be found in Exhibit 2.5. When you move beyond interpretation to claims of evaluation and reform, your emphasis on the significance of communication changes from the interpretive to the critical paradigm.

Evaluative and reformist claims When you make **evaluative claims,** you establish a set of criteria or standards and render judgments about how well or how poorly some communication phenomenon meets those standards. **Reformist claims** are not only evaluative; they identify negative consequences of the existing social system as a way of instigating change. Because evaluative and reformist claims require you to make explicit value judgments, they are associated only with the critical paradigm. By contrast, the underlying assumptions of the discovery paradigm require you to find and maintain a detached and objective perspective when observing communication. In the interpretive paradigm, you will value subjectivity, and your focus will be to identify emergent patterns in the communication text or in the observations of various cultures without evaluating the communication as effective or ineffective, constructive or destructive.

Because of the underlying assumptions of the discovery and interpretive paradigms, evaluative and reformist claims are found primarily in the methods of the critical paradigm, that is, in some forms of rhetor-

---

EXHIBIT 2.5   Interpretive Rhetorical Claims

1. "Specifically, given Duke's need to deal with his own past as a vituperative racist, I argue that examining Duke's discourse will help us understand both how one might construct a new ethos for oneself and how history can be used as a rhetorical resource in the current milieu" (McGee, 1998, p. 3).

2. "My purpose is to explore how the discourses on computer use—specifically 'computer-phobia' and 'computer addiction'—function toward the process of computers 'becoming' a (social) technology" (Reed, 2000, p. 163).

3. "In this essay I use Burke's conceptions of the pentad, his terms for order, and his characterizations of the dramatic genres of tragedy and comedy to analyze and interpret the significance of [a] shift in the forms of [Martin Luther] King's language. . . . Burke's constructs help explain the declining influence King experienced in his last year and also the tragic grandeur and enduring power of King's life and rhetoric" (Appel, 1997, p. 381).

---

ical criticism and critical studies, including critical ethnographic and discourse analytic research. As a critical researcher, you will emphasize both evaluation and reform, openly acting as an advocate for your cause. You will make the general argument that no research can ever be value-free. Moreover, you may go so far as to say that scholars have an ethical obligation to improve social conditions through their efforts (Campbell, 1974; Foss & Foss, 1988; Thomas, 1993). In a recent study, Watkins (2001) explored how the discourse of hip-hop nationalism gave voice to the "growing discontent of a generation of young black Americans who were either disillusioned by the racial hostilities brought on by participation in the societal mainstream or dislocated from the center of social and economic life altogether" (p. 381). Hip-hop artists like Chuck D, KRS-One, and Sista Souljah have become mentors and spokespeople for many black youth who have felt disenfranchised from mainstream society.

When you come from the critical paradigm perspective, you must decide not only whether your argument is logical, but whether it also makes a positive contribution to society. Effectiveness becomes an ethical value judgment rather than a precise measure of a rational claim (Foss, 1996, p. 19–20). As one brand of critical paradigm research, feminist criticism is often based on the assumption that society must be reorganized "on the basis of equality for the sexes in all areas of social relations" (Foss, Foss, & Griffin, 1999, p. 2). A prominent rhetorical critical theorist, bell hooks, has argued that resisting dominance is a central part of learning to think and speak freely, an essential quality of a truly democratic society (hooks, 1989, 1994, 2000). She refused to conform to capitalizing her name in the conventional way as one of her many forms of personal protest. We will discuss in Chapter 13, "Critical Studies," that your focus as a critical researcher will be to determine how various forms of communication perpetuate the dominant social order, marginalizing any voices in the minority, and how various social texts signify resisting dominance and reconstructing a new society.

Studies that contain evaluative claims do not necessarily include reformist claims. But all studies that make reformist claims must also at least imply some evaluation. As Brock, Scott, and Chesebro (1990) have pointed out, the appeal for reform is often made on moral or ethical grounds. In one analysis critiquing social practices, Mitchell (2000) claimed that the Pentagon organized a "campaign of strategic deception" to mislead audiences regarding the accuracy of the Patriot missiles used in the Persian Gulf War. They discussed implications for continuing this deception if the Pentagon fails to see current policy as "normatively bankrupt." Other critical paradigm rhetorical perspectives will be explored in more detail in Chapter 13, "Critical Studies."

Claims of reform are not exclusive to rhetorical criticism. From a different tradition, Thomas (1993) conducted a critical ethnography on prisoner litigation and prison violence. By exploring the culture of prison life, Thomas illustrated its *organizing themes* by showing how the prisoners used the legal system as a form of rebellion and violence as a means of expressing power and identification. In the illustration of

---

EXHIBIT 2.6   Examples of Critical Claims

1. "We believe this particular case study of McGee will draw attention to the importance of studying rhetoric considered alien to and counter-normative of the public sphere. Furthermore, the case study will allow us to describe, analyze, interpret and evaluate an interesting intersection of local politics, rhetoric, print-media coverage, and racial ideology. . . . Because McGee . . . was an 'out-law,' using 'a local logic that, when translated into the dominant system of judgment, [was] deemed illegal, and immoral' (Sloop & Ono, p. 51), his views were dismissed in local mainstream media accounts" (Goldzwig & Sullivan, 2000, p. 217).

2. There is gender and class-based oppression in naming practices in Chinese cultures (Lee, 1998a, p. 283).

3. We use thematic analysis to illustrate concretely how these strategies work ideologically to produce a depoliticized romantic adventure. Pollack employs these strategies to move to the margin, or to mute altogether, pivotal elements of Dinesen's texts, including her complex voice and unconventional beliefs (Cooper & Descutner, 1997, p. 230).

"how people recognize and mediate an oppressive culture," it implicitly raises the more complex issue of general prison reform (pp. 48–55).

In a similar vein, a study of two high schools examined how ethnic identities were constructed. Perry's (2001) analysis revealed that white students in both high schools asserted "racial superiority by claiming they have no culture because to be cultureless implies that one is either the 'norm' (the standard by which others are judged) or 'rational' (developmentally advanced)" (p. 56). More examples of specific critical claims appear in Exhibit 2.6.

From the critical paradigm perspective, your research will always be multifaceted. It is descriptive and interpretive, evaluative and reformist, with these goals thoroughly intertwined. Before we leave our general discussion in this chapter, we will address how the rapidly developing fields of technology have impacted the process of constructing claims.

THE INTERFACE OF TECHNOLOGY AND CLAIMS

As we pointed out in Chapter 1, technology interfaces with communication research in two different dimensions. First, it enables you to actually conduct the business of doing research in collecting and analyzing data in a functional sense. Second, with every technological inroad into our daily lives, it becomes the content subject matter as we explore how technology has changed communication. In this chapter, we focus on how claims imply the use of technology in the research process, and we will examine a few of the claims that specifically target new areas of technology as their main topic of investigation.

Using Technological Applications

We identified descriptive claims early on in this chapter as bridging the paradigms. It is certainly true that the term *description* appears in many methodologies across the three paradigms, but as we explained before, the term means different things in different studies. We used Gow's study of leading and supporting roles in MTV videos to illustrate descriptive claims used in a content analysis. One of the claims was phrased as a research question: What kinds of roles are occupied by women in popular music videos aired on MTV in 1990 compared to 1995? (Gow, 1996; see also Exhibit 2.2). As we illustrate in Chapter 7, "Content and Interaction Analyses," descriptive claims in empirical research lead to using a variety of statistical tools for warranting claims and collecting, coding, and analyzing the data. Other similar tools are used in network analysis, which we will explore in Chapter 5, "Survey Research." These statistical tools come in a variety of software packages, which we will discuss in more detail later on.

Like descriptive claims, explanatory and predictive claims in empirical research are made with the same implied assumption that the data will be warranted and analyzed statistically. The type of relationship between the communication variables that is described in the research question or hypothesis also implies certain types of statistical analysis will be favored over others. One of your tasks as a student of research methods will be to develop an appreciation for *how* technology has made the various statistical tools and procedures much easier to use and apply to your own research study. Another goal will be to decide *when* to use various statistical tests. We will see more precisely how this occurs when we discuss survey research in Chapter 5 and experimental research in Chapter 6, and the statistical procedures themselves in Chapters 8 and 9.

The use of technology in the research process has expanded enormously. In this chapter, we explored descriptive and interpretive claims typical of research methodologies from the interpretive paradigm. For example, Fisherkeller (1999) conducted an ethnographic analysis of how urban teens interpret TV culture. Her main claim identified television's central role in "enabling young adolescents to learn more about their identities, success and social power relations in the culture of the United States" (p. 187). She examined how teens used television (one form of technology) by taping and analyzing their interview responses (another form of technology). Other interpretive paradigm research may use software programs that make word or thematic searches much easier to perform. We will have more to say about these applications in the next chapter, "What Counts as Communication Data?" and in the chapters on conversational and discourse analysis (Chapter 10), ethnography (Chapter 11), and rhetorical criticism (Chapter 12).

Field researchers from the critical paradigm may use as many technological resources as their interpretive paradigm counterparts. Data is often collected and analyzed with the help of a variety of new technological tools. Perry's (2001) claim that white students' identity constructions are "cultureless" was supported by tape-recording and transcribing her interviews. Watkins (2001) used mediated messages of hip-hop culture as texts, and Stewart, Shields, and Sen (1998) explored their claim that online communities exclude diverse populations by collecting and transcribing the complete listserv discussion from a communication class for an entire semester (over 300 messages). They also used a variety of tabulations such as frequency counts and message length as part of their analyses. In this type of a study, the interface of communication and technology is present in both its

implied use during the research process and as a targeted topic. In the next section, we will examine just a few of the increasing number of claims about technology as a topic of communication research.

Constructing Claims About Communication and Technology

It does not take a degree in rocket science to appreciate the explosion of technology in our everyday lives. Technology has impacted the way we develop our closest relationships with each other, the way we socialize with our friends, our sense of "community," how we get through our workday, how we navigate our ways around each other in urban planning, international institutional frameworks, and global environmental conditions. We cannot think of a facet of living that has not been dramatically impacted at some level by technological change. The number of studies whose central claims involve technological features of communication has sharply increased. Studies have described, explained, predicted, interpreted, and critiqued the role of technology in contemporary society. We will identify just a few of the more recent ones.

From the discovery paradigm, a survey study by Perse and Ferguson (2000) of Web surfing explored a variety of claims regarding the potential benefits of Web use. They discovered that Web users most frequently ranked learning, "passing the time," entertainment, relaxation, escape, excitement, and companionship as the benefits of Web use. Time and effort spent Web surfing were only perceived as costs at lower levels of user expertise and computer speed. In a related study, Eveland and Dunwoody (2001) reported results from their experiment in support of one of their claims that "hypermedia presentations may reduce learning compared to traditional print" (p.19). These two researchers were careful to construct differences only in the forms of the mediated messages rather than in the actual content of the messages, and their research design led them to conclude that the reduction in learning from the Web material was because participants "selectively scanned" more of the Web-based message, and tended to miss some of the more important information as a result. Participants who had more Web expertise learned equally as well from print and Web messages, which indicated that expert Web users could do a better job of screening out irrelevant and distracting features while retaining essential information. Perhaps you should keep this study in mind when you are working on finding material for your next class assignment!

A recent study from the interpretive paradigm (Stroud, 2001) explores the story of the hero quest in the movie *The Matrix*. In a complex network of interconnections revealed throughout the film, Stroud claimed that the hero, Neo, maintained his individuality because he could use his technological expertise to stay free from the technologically trapped members of a futuristic society. Stroud used narrative theory as support for his claim that the film was "shown to be a powerful myth for alienated and disempowered individuals in technologically driven communities" (p. 416).

From the critical paradigm, a study by Stewart, Shields, and Sen (1998), mentioned earlier in our discussion, claimed that online discussions exclude marginalized voices. Though the group they studied was small, the pattern of results found in their study of listserv discussion messages repeated patterns found elsewhere in the research literature. They found evidence that men sent longer and more frequent messages than women (more than twice as many even though there were 11 women and 9 men), and Whites sent more messages than other cultural groups (Whites sent slightly more than the combined minority groups, but there were only 6 Whites in a group of 20) (p. 5). They also found that men were more willing to adopt the technology than women (earlier start times in the discussion), and Whites adopted the technology earlier than other minority group members (p. 7).

In another study, Ott and Aoki (2001) advanced evaluative and reformist claims in arguing that the *Star Trek: The Next Generation* series perpetuates the vision of the current dominant social order in "its representations of race, gender, and sexuality" (p. 393). The series reflects a technologically advanced social utopia whose values have not really evolved passed contemporary stereotypes. Ott and Aoki "demonstrated that the utopian appeals of *The Next Generation* affirm and re-center White heterosexual masculinity in U.S. popular culture" (p. 410). They ended their article by encouraging educators to "offer valuable insights into how individuals think about their world, social change, and themselves" and by challenging the "producers of cultural texts" to not "allow our collective visions of the future to be reduced to existing codes of injustice simply because they are familiar and comfortable" (p. 411). How technology is valued in society affects the roles it will play and the measure of their influence; technology is also affected by how it is represented to its members. Critical research plays a foundational role in exploring those elements.

Regardless of the paradigm, you can see that the interface of technology and communication is pervasive. As a researcher, you will move continually between using technology as a fundamental part of the research process and critiquing the role of technology in contemporary life. In this chapter, we have explored how each of these functions is expressed in constructing claims about communication. In subsequent chapters, we will examine how technology both informs the research process and is the target of its investigations.

SUMMARY

In this chapter, we have defined and applied the first component of our research-as-argument model, the *claim*. The claim refers to the central assertion or premise on which a specific analysis is based. There are six different types of claims: descriptive, explanatory, predictive, interpretive, evaluative, and reformist. We illustrated each by applying a variety of methodologies spanning the three epistemological paradigms we discussed in Chapter 1. We also explored the role of technology as it contributes to the general research process and how it is beginning to impact the process of constructing claims about communication.

How we as researchers understand the types of claims we construct depends in a large part on the paradigmatic assumptions we make when we engage in the research process. So, for example, it is very likely that you would find explanatory and predictive claims presented together, and evaluative and reformist claims appear just as frequently in combination. Many empirical researchers, who see their studies as descriptive, explanatory, and predictive, do not share the same goals of or assumptions about research with rhetorical critics, who see their analyses as descriptive, interpretive, evaluative, and reformist. We do not present these differences here in order to make you take sides, but to help you understand why they exist as you begin to read through the many different types of studies in our field. You will have an opportunity to explore the differences in assumptions and goals in the "Great Debates" activity at the end of this chapter.

KEY TERMS

Action research

Associative claim

Causal claim

Claim

Dependent variable

Descriptive claim

Empirical methods

Evaluative claims

Explanatory claims

Grounded-theory approach

Hypotheses

Independent variable

Interpretive claims

Predictive claims

Reformist claims

Research questions

Taxonomy

DISCUSSION QUESTIONS

1. Why do you think descriptive claims are found across all three paradigms? Do they have the same function across all three paradigms?

2. What assumptions are made in the discovery paradigm that make explanatory and predictive claims more likely than interpretive or evaluative claims?

3. In what ways are evaluative and reformist claims different than descriptive and interpretive claims?

"TRY IT!" ACTIVITY

The Great Debate

We have been addressing the role of the researcher in making claims to achieve certain goals across the three paradigms. As we have stated before, the claims we make depend on the assumptions and beliefs we have about what constitutes research. The concept of "disinterest-edness" refers to the belief by some researchers that we should try to remain objective and free from bias in the research process. Other researchers believe expressing "disinterestedness" is impossible, and still others believe it is not even desirable.

To gain a better appreciation of how different these points of view are, we will explore how applications of these three might occur in a "real world" setting. Suppose you went to work for the juvenile justice system as a program analyst. The warden of Juvenile Hall asked you to evaluate the methods employed in a film from a research perspective. The film, *Walk the Talk,* is part of a training program that corrections officers receive before they go to work in a juvenile detention facility, but any training film could be used for this activity. (This particular film used role reversal and an experientially based training method.)

The warden doesn't realize, of course, that you were trained to analyze problems in a particular way. You will be assigned to a group representing one of the paradigms. Your task will be to decide what is important to study (i.e., what claims you want to make) based on your paradigm-oriented point of view.

Proponents of the discovery paradigm should argue that the researcher should devise claims to describe, explain, and predict communication phenomena without interjecting his or her subjective point of view. You should explain why remaining objective allows a researcher to achieve those goals, that personal biases would make it impossible to devise careful, systematic descriptions, explanations, or predictions. Apply these assumptions to ways you could evaluate the type of training you see occurring in the film.

Proponents of the interpretive paradigm should argue that the researcher should allow claims to emerge from observations of the community or text for the goal of understanding participants' significant practices or textual meanings. In representing interpretive scholars, you should realize that the researcher's perspective cannot be eliminated; its presence should be acknowledged while carefully allowing participants' perspectives to be foregrounded. The goal of understanding can only be achieved when researchers enter the interpretive process with no preformulated or preconstructed explanations or predictions about what they will see. Apply these assumptions to analyzing the value of the training you see occurring in the film.

Proponents of the critical paradigm should argue that maintaining any kind of detached persona is a pretense. You should not only acknowledge your personal perspectives as part of the research process, but you should also use these perspectives to evaluate the social system that creates a need for the type of training you see occurring in the film, and use it as an example of why we need to actively seek social reform.

Some of the questions you may consider regardless of your paradigm include the following:

1. Is this type of training generally useful or effective?

2. How could its utility or effectiveness be determined?

3. Do you think both juvenile detainees and officers would perceive this training as effective?

4. Will this type of training lead to productive changes in the juvenile correctional system, and to society in general?

5. Explain why the training would or would not lead to productive changes.

3

What Counts as Communication Data?

ABSTRACT

In this chapter you will learn about the second element of the research-as-argument model, the data. We will first outline some typical sources, settings, and strategies for collecting communication data, emphasizing the relative value of each of these for supporting particular types of research claims. We will then introduce the ideas of research design and triangulation, both abstract processes used in different ways in discovery, interpretive, and critical research studies. Finally, we will discuss the role of technology in the collection and analysis of communication data, and we will present a variety of ethical issues regarding the treatment of research participants as data sources and the analysis and use of research data.

OUTLINE

FIGURE 3.1 Evolution of data.

This chapter deals with the second component of the research-as-argument model, the data or evidence used to support a research claim. You will learn about a variety of sources for communication data, settings in which data are collected, and strategies that you can use to collect data. In addition, you will learn about two more abstract ways that researchers manage the quality of their data collection settings and strategies: research design and triangulation. *Research design* is a general term intended to cover many specific strategies for carefully controlling all the various aspects of data collection, such as the selection of people or messages to be included in a research project, the location where the data are to be collected, and so on. We will introduce the concept of research design in this chapter, and you will learn more about specific strategies in Part II of this book (e.g., survey and experimental research design are covered in Chapters 5 and 6). *Triangulation* is a general term for the use of several different kinds of evidence to support a research claim.

It is important for you to know about these general and specific issues of communication research data in order to conduct research yourself, and to critically evaluate research conducted by other people. Figure 3.1 illustrates the evolution of data into wisdom: the data are at the lowest level of the hierarchy, and wisdom is at the top of the hierarchy. When you select data as evidence for a research study, you are narrowing down the information you want to see. If you combine two or more groups of data, you can

make comparisons from one to the other. We all use rules and make decisions in order to analyze information; when we break things down into parts and analyze the relationships among those parts (i.e., compare and contrast), we are gaining knowledge. As students of communication, we increase our wisdom by combining the data, information, and knowledge gained through our experiences, research, and course work in unique, sometimes unforeseen ways. Thus, data are fundamental to a research argument. "In the hands of the falsifier, mean-spirited, or gullible, they can become an awesome weapon of control, power, or mayhem" (Getis, 1995, p. 24).

Some of the data collection sources, settings, and strategies we will discuss in this chapter are more likely to be associated with the discovery research paradigm; others are more likely to be associated with the interpretive and/or critical paradigms. The same observation is true for data analytic strategies (i.e., some ways of analyzing communication data are more likely to be used in discovery research, or interpretive studies, or critical scholarship). Indeed, some critical studies scholars object to the very idea of data itself: "Postmodern theorizing challenges the very notion of a common ground. In particular, postmodernists warn against any totalizing narrative . . . " (Stablein, 1996, p. 510). One reason that critical scholars might object to data is the difficulty (some would argue, futility) of representation. You will read more about representation in Chapter 13, "Critical Studies." Briefly though, critical scholars believe that any time we use a symbol to represent some thing, power relations are implicated, because we raise the question, Who can decide which symbols are used to represent anything?

We agree that universals, or categorical definitions, tend to fall apart easily when one considers individual cases of phenomena. For example, there is no average person, no ordinary man or woman. Nonetheless, we will define, in this chapter, some of the usual sources, settings, and strategies for data collection in communication research. Generally, the categorical distinctions we outline here for clarity's sake blur upon close examination. However, in Part II of this book, you will learn more about *how* data sources and settings are selected and *which* data collection and analytic strategies are preferred in particular research methodologies. For now, we will begin with basic definitions and examples of data collection sources, settings, and strategies.

DATA COLLECTION SOURCES

By **data collection sources,** we mean the points from which the data originate. Communication data can originate from four possible points: (1) observations of communicative interactions; (2) self-reports of communicative behaviors, beliefs, and/or characteristics; (3) other-reports of communicative behaviors, beliefs, and/or characteristics; and (4) texts. Although it may seem obvious to you what each of these sources is, we will briefly differentiate each one, before we move on to consider the settings where these sources can be studied, and the means used to capture each source so that it can be used in a research project.

Observations of Communicative Interactions

If you are dealing with **observed interactions** between people, you can be sure you are studying communication (Patterson, Neupauer, Burant, Koehn, & Reed, 1996). You may be interested in observing the verbal and nonverbal messages themselves, or the communicators who construct and interpret those messages, or the channels through which an interaction occurs. Either way, audio-and/or videotaped recordings of communicative behaviors provide the most exact replications of the original behavior (Amidon, 1971). Observing behaviors that have been tape-recorded and rating their characteristics provides a representation and evaluation of the behavior (i.e., interpretations). Researchers can observe communicative behaviors immediately (i.e., live and in real time), or they can employ tape recordings, depending on the availability of observational equipment and trained observers (see, for example, Tracy & Tracy's 1998 case study of two telephone calls to a 911 center in a large city). Specific decisions about what or whom to observe, how to observe, and when to observe are all important aspects of research design that you will learn much more about in Part II of this book.

Physiological responses, like heart rate, pupil dilation, or blushing, are another possible way to observe communication behavior (Smith, 1988). Collecting physiological responses is a way of observing communication without actually participating in the creation of those behaviors. Sometimes researchers who observe communicative interactions are also helping to create the interactions they observe (i.e., they are participant-observers).

As a communication researcher, you may be interested in observations, participant observations, or some combination of all these things, and your interests may be based on any of the six research goals outlined in Chapter 2, "Making Claims" (i.e., describe, explain, predict, interpret, evaluate, reform). Whatever specific focus and reasons you have for observing communicative behaviors, observations are a fundamental source of data for communication research.

Self-Reports of Communicative Behaviors, Beliefs, and Characteristics

A second source of data for communication research is to ask people to report their own behaviors, beliefs, or characteristics related to communication. If you want to know what people feel and how they think, **self-report** data will probably be your first preference. At first glance, it may seem that this data source is most prevalent in survey questionnaires, but in fact, self-report data are also used whenever the researcher interviews key informants (e.g., Varallo, Ray, & Ellis, 1998).

From the point of view of the discovery researcher, self-report data is subject to some standard biases, or systematic sources of error. For example, humans tend to overestimate their own positive qualities and behaviors, and underestimate their negative qualities and behaviors. Depending on the research topic, their relationship with the researcher, and many other factors, people may not report all of their thoughts and feelings. Memories can be incomplete, inaccurate, and so on. Despite these well-known limitations, self-report data continues to be prevalent in communication research. Network analysis scholars have examined some of the ways that informant accuracy varies in conjunction with the informants' placement in a social network structure (see Bernard & Kilworth, 1977; Bernard, Kilworth, & Sailer, 1980, 1982, for more details on this line of argument). In addition, the feelings that people report having, or the behaviors they say they perform, may be as important and informative (if in a different way) as the behaviors that they actually do perform (which could be documented by some more objective data source).

Other-Reports of Communicative Behaviors, Beliefs, and Characteristics

Asking individuals to report their perceptions of other people's behavior, beliefs, or characteristics is a third, and slightly different, source of communication data. Communication researchers routinely use **other-report** data in at least three ways, each for a different purpose. The first way that other-reports are used is when a researcher wants to know how a certain communicative act affects those who receive it (i.e., people who are not the source or creator of that act). For example, studies of audiences' reactions to mediated messages, or to public speeches, often rely on other-report data. The second way that other-report data gets used is when a researcher wants to compare self-perceptions of a communicative act with other-perceptions of the same act. For example, interpersonal competence scholars have learned that people typically think of themselves as more competent, attractive, and so on than others do (e.g., Spitzberg & Hecht, 1984). Finally, other-report data is sometimes used for verification purposes; almost like voting by majority rule, other-reports are used to show the truth as more than one person sees it.

Texts

A fourth source of communication data, and one that has grown immensely in popularity over the past decade or so, is the use of existing texts. You may think of **text** as written or spoken words, and we do mean to include those texts in this data source. But we also mean to include texts that are symbolic, performed, and purely visual/pictorial, as well (Bowman, 1996; Jarmon, 1996). For example, Lewis (1997) examined the ideologies of professional wedding photography, considering as texts the photographic images that producers and consumers together negotiate to represent the social and cultural reality of a wedding. Stablein's (1996) description of the potential data used by students of organizational reality suggested the breadth of the term *texts* as it is currently used in communication scholarship more generally:

> All data are representations. Respondents' questionnaire answers, experimental subjects' behaviours, employee records, financial records, boardroom conversations, production records, shopfloor humour, corporate balance sheets, informants' expressions, participant or nonparticipant observations and emotional reactions, annual reports, acetylcholine blood levels and pulse rates, photos, videos, corporate architecture and the products of earlier research may all be used by organization students to represent aspects of organizational reality (p. 511).

Researchers in the interpretive and critical paradigms of communication research, building on work done in literary, art, and dramatistic criticism, have extended the functional meaning of text well beyond its traditional association with the written word—or even with words at all (Bowman, 1996; Bowman & Kistenberg, 1992). Whereas interpretive researchers see text as representations of reality, " . . . the postmodernist treats the text as the empirical reality to be studied. . . . For the postmodern researcher the text is data which represent and constitute multiple realities. However, the representational process of *deconstruction* is required to reveal those realities" (Stablein, 1996, p. 521). For more on deconstruction, refer to Chapter 13, "Critical Studies."

An endless variety of texts, then, can be analyzed by communication scholars, including census documents, class notes, diagrams, diaries, email messages, journals, maps, memos, magazine and newspaper articles, photographs, poetry, prose, and policy statements, to name several (Lofland & Lofland, 1984; Morse, 1998). The above list does not even include symbolic texts like gestures or signs, nor does it include artifactual texts, like clothing, hairstyle, jewelry, types of automobile or other possessions, and so on. As you can see, the range of texts that can potentially be studied by communication scholars is theoretically endless!

DATA COLLECTION SETTINGS

Data collection settings are the places where observation, self-report, and other-report data are gathered or found. The issue of a data collection setting is less relevant when textual data are used to support a research claim; in that case, an archive may be the setting in which we actually collect our research evidence. An **archive** is a preexisting collection of textual data or evidence. Examples of archives include the library, an online database, the county clerk's office where birth and marriage certificates are recorded, and so on. However, for nonarchival communication data that are collected via observation or people's reports, there are essentially two possible settings, either in the field or in the laboratory (Smith, 1988).

Most interpretive communication research takes place in the **field settings** where communicative interactions occur naturally. By contrast, in **laboratory settings,** the researcher selects and controls the setting for interaction, and induces the communicative phenomena of interest to occur. In other words, the researcher controls what interactions occur, when, and with whom. But the researcher's control of the data collection setting is the only analog to the sterile, steel and glass settings you might imagine being used for scientific research. Communication research labs are more often rooms in academic buildings that are contrived to resemble the settings where communicative interactions occur naturally (e.g., classrooms, living rooms, waiting areas). Communication laboratories sometimes contain one-way mirrors, so interactions can be observed without participants' knowledge. They may be equipped with audio or video recording equipment, which is less obtrusive than simply placing a tape recorder or camera in the room.

Because we Americans have a scientific image of the laboratory, we see lab settings as somewhat artificial—no matter how cleverly data collection equipment is hidden and natural settings are emulated. So the *rigor* provided us by a laboratory setting often comes at the cost of decreased *relevance* of our research findings to people who are operating in their natural environments. The benefit of rigor is typically to realize a higher degree of control over variables that are part of a causal argument. The degree to which research participants are aware of and change their behaviors during data collection will be of grave concern to you if you are making explanatory and predictive claims.

We will return to the issues of laboratory research settings more in Chapters 5 and 6, and we will elaborate on field research settings in Chapter 11. Evidence you collect in archival settings may be useful to you in these methodologies, as well as in content analysis, conversation and discourse analyses, rhetorical criticism, and critical studies (Chapters 7, 10, 12, and 13, respectively). Of course, archival research is always relevant when conducting a literature review, as is the case for any communication research project.

DATA COLLECTION STRATEGIES

Data collection strategies have to do with how data for a study are gathered, whereas data sources refer to the people or messages from whom the data are sampled, and settings refer to the physical location in which the data are actually collected. For example, self-report data can be captured using oral interviews, written surveys, or written diaries. Other-report data (i.e., perceptions about other people's behavior or attitudes) can be collected using interviews, surveys, or existing documents (e.g., written performance appraisals). Behavioral observations may be gathered by taking field notes, but can also be preserved using audio- or videotapes. Obviously, all three of these sources of data (self- and other-reports, and observations) may be archived, once collected, in textual forms, and then used for similar or different purposes in subsequent research projects.

We will first discuss the general concept of **selection,** or how researchers decide which people or messages to include in a particular research study. Selection is an issue that receives much more attention in some communication research methodologies than in others (e.g., experimental research vs. rhetorical criticism). It all depends on the claim you are trying to support. Whatever the claim, though, all scholars "select and interpret data for their audience in the attempt to achieve their purposes" (Stablein, 1996, p. 511). You will learn more about how selection decisions are made and implemented in the particular methodologies in Part II of this book.

Selecting Data Sources

We have said that *data sources* refer to the people or textual messages from which data are selected. The question is, How do researchers pick the people whose behavior will be observed, or who will be asked to report on their own or others' behaviors, beliefs, or characteristics? If the data are to consist of verbal and/or nonverbal messages, how are the particular messages to be analyzed chosen for inclusion in that study? These are the issues of data selection.

Although paradigm boundaries are fuzzy when looking at the process of selecting data or evidence on which to base research claims, some distinctions exist. In general, random selection methods are preferred in the discovery paradigm, whereas nonrandom

---

EXHIBIT 3.1   Types of Sampling Methods

Random sampling methods	*Nonrandom sampling methods*
Simple random sampling	Convenience sampling
Systematic sampling with a random start	Purposive sampling
Stratified sampling	Network or snowball sampling
Multistage cluster sampling	Quota sampling
	Maximum variation sampling
	Deviant case sampling

---

selection methods are preferred in the interpretive paradigm. Critical researchers approach the whole issue of selection quite differently than do researchers in either the discovery or interpretive paradigm; we will consider the selection processes involved in critical studies last in this section.

In fact, the methods of selecting, collecting, and analyzing published communication research data are consistent with what you might expect, given the assumptions and values of the discovery, interpretive, and critical paradigms (Fink & Gantz, 1996). Fink and Gantz specifically looked at mass communication research, not all areas of communication studies: "All told, mass communication researchers conformed rather highly to expectations. Interpretive researchers were more likely to adhere to their tradition's assumptions than were social scientists or critical scholars" (p. 125).

In the discovery paradigm, the issue of selection is referred to as **sampling,** "the process of selecting a set of subjects for study from a larger population" (Fink & Gantz, 1996, p. 117). Sampling is a social scientific term, meaning "to select a relatively smaller number of cases in order to represent some larger group of cases or instances of phenomena." The larger group of cases or instances the researcher is attempting to represent is called the **population.** A research population is a "comprehensive and well-defined group (a universal set) of the elements pertinent to a given research question or hypothesis" (Smith, 1988, p. 77). For example, the population of the United States of America can be theoretically specified in a number of ways, such as all the persons who are U. S. citizens, or all the persons residing within the borders of the nation. Notice how these two specific definitions of population would include somewhat different groups of people. Populations are always theoretic in this way. Discovery researchers try to select a sample that well represents the population they seek to describe or explain, or about which they hope to make accurate predictions. Therefore, when you are conducting survey, experimental, content, or interaction analytic research, you will want to use procedures for selecting samples that are most likely to represent a population, within the limits of chance or random error. These are called **random selection methods,** or sometimes, probability sampling methods (Smith, 1988). Randomizing data selection introduces some element of chance as to the people or texts included in a study, which will help you eliminate **bias,** specific sources of error, in selecting data.

Random selection methods In this section, we will outline four different random selection methods: (1) simple random sampling; (2) systematic sampling with a random start; (3) stratified sampling; and (4) multistage cluster sampling. These methods are listed in Exhibit 3.1.

Chief among random selection methods is the **simple random sample,** in which each person (or text) in the population has an equal chance of being selected for inclusion in a study (Babbie, 2001). Thus, simple random sampling occurs when a subset of the population is randomly chosen from a sampling frame. A **sampling frame** is a list of all the members of the population. For example, if we are interested in obtaining a random sample of students from our university, the registrar's list of currently enrolled students is one possible sampling frame for that population. Likewise, the telephone book is one sampling frame for the population of a city. As you can imagine, sampling frames need to be as complete and accurate as possible if the people or texts selected from those frames are to represent the population well.

The second random selection method is **systematic sampling with a random start.** Systematic sampling is easier to implement, and thus used more frequently than simple random sampling. Babbie (2001) described systematic sampling as selecting "the first element at random" and then "every *k*th element in the total list is chosen (systematically) for inclusion in the sample" (p. 197). He illustrated with this example: "If a list contained 10,000 elements and you want a sample of 1,000, you would select every tenth element for your sample" (p. 197). Since it is now fairly well established that simple random sampling and systematic sampling yield virtually identical samples, most researchers opt for using systematic sampling as the easier of these two methods (Babbie, 2001).

However, a problem with systematic sampling is **periodicity**—a recurring pattern or arrangement that exists naturally in the sampling frame. Once again, using Babbie's example, imagine that you want to obtain a random sample of apartments in a large complex. The units might be arranged in such a way that sampling, say, every 10th apartment would lead to the selection of "only northwest-corner apartments or only apartments near the elevator" (Babbie, 2001, p. 200). Obviously, such patterning could lead to a biased sample, not a representative one.

Stratified sampling is the third type of random selection method. Stratified sampling is a more refined and complex selection method than either simple random selection or systematic sampling. Stratified sampling "organizes a population into homogeneous subsets and selects elements in each subset, using either systematic or simple random procedures" (Smith, 1988, p. 82). The researcher obtains a sampling frame, but knows in this case that some characteristics or variables exist in the population that form homogeneous subsets (e.g., groups that share a common characteristic). For example, we may know that two-thirds of our university's student population is female, and one-third is male. We can stratify the population by selecting out all males and then all females, then randomly select from each subset until our sample has the approximate proportions of the sexes as represented in the population. We could also stratify the population on the basis of academic class level, randomly selecting proportionate subsets of first-year students, sophomores, juniors, and seniors. Large polling companies like Gallup frequently stratify voters on the basis of geographic location in order to increase sample representativeness in terms of ethnicity, social class, urban and rural differences, types of occupations, and so forth. One company, called Survey Sample, Inc. breaks, the United States down into eight discrete geographic regions based on past survey results across a variety of marketing and political variables. Generally, if you are measuring a number of variables, you are more likely to achieve greater representativeness if you use stratified samples than if you use simple random sampling (Babbie, 2001).

Random selection methods become more complex when a sampling frame or list of all population members is not readily available. For example, it is not feasible to obtain a list of all males or females in the United States, all university students in Japan, all elementary school children in Western Europe, and so forth. In such cases, **multistage cluster sampling** is the alternative method. Cluster sampling occurs in multiple stages, using two basic types of procedures, listing and sampling. For example, it may be impossible to obtain one list of all employees in a particular city, but possible to obtain a fairly comprehensive list of all the for-profit companies in that city through the Chamber of Commerce or the Office of Records in City Hall. The first step would entail creating a list of all companies available, which would serve as the sampling frame. Then, you would randomly sample a targeted number of companies from that list. This listing and sampling of companies makes up the first stage of cluster sampling. Next, you may decide to list departments within companies or businesses from which a second stage of sampling will be drawn. Finally, you can compose a list of employees from each randomly selected department to use as a basis for a third stage of sampling. Because the number of stages can vary depending on the desires of each research team, this technique is just referred to as multistage cluster sampling (Babbie, 2001; Smith, 1988). Sometimes, in order to draw a sample that fairly represents a population, you may have to use even more complex variations of multistage cluster sampling.

Regardless of the specific type of sampling you use, all random selection methods have in common an interest in sample representativeness. If a sample adequately represents its parent population, then the results of the study will be generalizable to all other members of the targeted population. We call this ability to generalize findings to a parent population *external validity*. Since generalizability is a warrant for causal arguments, we will develop this concept further in Chapter 4, "Warrants for Research Arguments." But for now, let's contrast random selection methods with nonrandom selection methods.

Nonrandom selection methods   Selecting people and texts in ways that do not ensure that the resulting data sample represents some theoretic population are called **nonrandom selection methods.** There are actually two reasons for choosing nonrandom selection methods. In the first case, you may desire to represent a population but be unable to use one of the random selection methods, either because you have insufficient time or money, or because constraints of the setting make random selection untenable (Fink & Gantz, 1996; Stake, 1998). In such cases, you might employ either convenience sampling or quota sampling as alternatives to a random selection method. We will define both convenience and quota sampling below. Whether your reason for using convenience sampling is lack of time, money, or setting constraints, choosing that nonrandom selection method will weaken your ability to claim that your sampled results apply to some larger population, or that your sampled results adequately represent phenomena in a specific context. So purely convenience sampling is undesirable for any research paradigm.

A second reason for using nonrandom data selection methods, though, is when you do not endorse discovery paradigm assumptions, but instead rely on interpretive or critical paradigm assumptions. Interpretive and critical scholars treat data selection quite differently than do discovery scholars. Interpretive researchers, in particular, are likely to prefer nonrandom selection methods because interpretive research claims are more likely to be based on representing communicative phenomena within a specific context. In this case, we do not need to use a small sample of data to represent some larger population (Fink & Gantz, 1996). After reading Chapters 1 and 2, you should be able to articulate some claims that do not require random samples for their support.

If you want to preserve participants' subjective realities and richly describe a specific communication context, you are likely to prefer one of the nonrandom selection methods that we outline here, except for convenience sampling. We will elaborate some rationales for using nonrandom selection as we discuss these six types of nonrandom selection methods: (1) convenience sampling; (2) purposive sampling; (3) network or snowball sampling; (4) quota sampling; (5) maximum variation sampling; and (6) deviant case sampling (see Exhibit 3.1).

The first nonrandom selection method is called **convenience sampling**. Convenience samples are comprised of whatever data is convenient to the researcher (e.g., people who volunteer to fill out a questionnaire, messages that are readily available, behaviors that the researcher had already captured for other purposes, etc.). As we emphasized already, convenience sampling is less than desirable for research in any paradigm. Let's consider why in two specific examples.

First, imagine that you are a survey researcher and that you use convenience sampling to recruit participants who are easily obtainable. In academic contexts, the participants are college students, typically those enrolled in large, undergraduate introductory communication courses. The fact that they are college students is irrelevant, since they are not chosen for any particular reason other than their accessibility. Because your selection process is nonrandom, the sample does not represent the population of either college students or people in general. Factors like the type of course it is, the time of day, and the geographic region of the university are all likely to introduce biases that threaten the sample's ability to represent the population of interest.

As a second example, imagine that you are a conversation analyst who uses convenience sampling to select messages that are readily available. Here, your problem may be the ability to represent a message population if you intend to generalize beyond those conveniently accessible messages. But if you aim to *interpret* the ways that messages are used in a particular context, then a convenient sample of messages also is likely to be inadequate. If your research question deals with particular types of people, or messages, or behaviors, then a purposive sampling strategy will be the most appropriate choice.

Purposive sampling, then, is the second nonrandom selection method. When your research *purpose* requires that particular messages or behaviors or people be studied, you are not interested in generalizing your findings to an entire population of messages, behaviors, or people. Instead, you need particular cases to test your claim. Therefore, **purposive samples** "intentionally focus on the target group to the exclusion of other groups" (Smith, 1988, p. 85). For example, Frey, Adelman, Flint, and Query (2000) studied residents of Bonaventure House in Chicago because they had all been diagnosed with AIDS. The purpose of this study was to examine how residents constructed a sense of community through their communicative practices. The researchers asserted that because of the unique identities of each member, their combined contributions in constructing a community made it a singular event. So participants selected on this purposive basis served as a case study, rather than a representative sample whose findings could be generalized to the population from which they were drawn (Stake, 1998).

Purposive sampling methods lack representativeness, just as do other nonrandom selection methods. However, randomization may not be a practical or desirable way to collect evidence about some research questions. To illustrate, Kassing and Infante (1999) asked athletes to report on their coaches' verbal and physical aggression. They had limited access to certain types of athletes and virtually no access to their coaches. They used a purposive sample of athletes to report their perceptions of coach behavior.

Similarly, if you wanted to target elementary school students, you might first restrict the sample frame to several classrooms, then further restrict participation by requiring parental permission. Purposive sampling lets you access just the right people or texts for your study. For example, Chung and Ting-Toomey (1999) targeted Asian Americans in their study of ethnic identity and interpersonal relationship expectations. Since obtaining a random sample of this ethnic minority would have been extremely impractical, Chung and Ting-Toomey purposively selected Asian American participants from as many diverse settings as possible.

For similar reasons, researchers often use snowball or network sampling, the third type of nonrandom sampling (Lindlof, 1995). **Network sampling** is sometimes called **snowball sampling** because the data sample is collected in much the same way that snow is collected when you roll a snowball down a hill. Just as each snowflake picks up other snowflakes,

each subject in a snowball sample solicits additional subjects to participate in the study (e.g., Bruess & Pearson, 1997; Hinkle, 1999). Bruess and Pearson (1997) asked marital partners and their friends to recommend others whom they knew as potential participants. Hinkle (1999) used the same approach to select marital partners for her investigation of nonverbal immediacy and liking. Often, snowball sampling is also purposive. Participants are selected because of a particular characteristic and are therefore more likely to know others who share the same characteristic.

The fourth nonrandom selection method is called **quota sampling.** Quota sampling used to refer to developing a "complex sampling frame called a quota matrix to divide a target population into all its relevant subclasses . . . . [The researchers] must accurately determine the proportion of population members falling into each relevant subclass or cell of the quota matrix" (Smith, 1988, p. 85). Quota sampling by matrix was used more frequently before the advent of random selection methods. It was an extremely cumbersome process. As a general rule, it has been replaced with easier random selection methods that permit estimates of sampling error, or the degree to which the sample does not represent the population (see Chapter 5, "Survey Research," for more on sampling error).

However, quota sampling is still used when target populations are relatively small and their characteristics are well known. For example, Kirkman and Shapiro (2000) sampled employees from a Fortune 500 insurance company. They solicited participants until they achieved a demographic profile of the sample that matched the demographic profile of the entire organization. **Demographics** are the general characteristics common to any group of people, such as age, biological sex, socioeconomic class, level of education, ethnicity, and so forth. Kirkman and Shapiro were attempting to achieve a sample of voluntary participants that represented the insurance company. They were interested in team members in this particular context, not all team members in every organization, or even every similar organization.

In interpretive communication research, rich descriptions are prized for the purpose of understanding, rather than for the purposes of verifying, explaining, and predicting phenomena. When you seek to enrich your existing descriptions of phenomena, two additional nonrandom selection methods, maximum variation sampling and deviant case sampling, will be useful.

Maximum variation sampling attempts to represent the broadest range of cases in a particular category or setting (Lincoln & Guba, 1985; Morse, 1998; Patton, 1990). For example, Graham (1997) recruited 35 divorced individuals to participate in a study of the turning points in subjects' postdivorce relationships with their former spouses. All of the subjects in Graham's study had to meet three criteria. They must (1) have been divorced one year; (2) be a parent of at least one child; and (3) be actively involved with the former spouse in parenting that child. Maximum variation sampling allowed Graham to examine a number of rich cases of an abstract concept, in this case, the postdivorce relationship participants had with their former spouses, and to observe similarities across those cases.

By contrast, you might want to use **deviant case sampling** (also known as extreme case sampling) to represent cases that are different from those you have already analyzed. One reason to seek out extreme cases—those that deviate from the norm for the topic of study—is to find examples that do not fit the pattern that you have already identified, if such examples exist (Patton, 1990). Deviant case sampling also allows you to select cases that exemplify particular characteristics (Morse, 1998). For example, if you have already collected many instances of cultural rule violations that were followed by some sort of sanction, or negative consequence, for the violator, you might explicitly seek out some instances of rule violations for which there was no sanction, or negative consequence.

Selection in critical studies Published reports of critical scholarship rarely address the selection of cases for analysis in any explicit way. But even though they do not usually address the selection of research participants or texts, critical researchers do emphasize the issue of selection when selecting a topic or case to study. However, ". . . topic selection usually begins with only a vague idea of some broad question or issue. It may not be narrowed down until well into data collection" (Thomas, 1993, p. 34). Notice how differently the whole concept of selection is framed in critical studies. Instead of selecting data to support particular claims, critical scholars engage in data gathering until the questions that are most interesting emerge, as a visual figure emerges from a chaotic background. Notice, too, that the critical scholar's very topics, not just the particular data sources to be studied, are unspecified at the outset of the research project because "the focus of attention often lies in areas at first glance unnoticeable and within data sources possessing mechanisms to conceal, rather than reveal, their secrets" (Thomas, 1993, p. 35).

Nevertheless, as a critical researcher you might select a case of "some typicality, but leaning toward those cases that seem to offer *opportunity to learn*" (Stake, 1998, p. 101). Even once you have selected a case, the sampling of persons, places, and events to observe within the case is another factor you will need to consider. At this stage, variety, rather than representativeness, should guide your selection decisions on these points, since the principal criterion is the opportunity to learn (Stake, 1998).

As we mentioned earlier, Fink and Gantz (1996) performed a content analysis of the extent to which published mass communication studies conformed to the expectations of the discovery, interpretive, and critical research traditions. They concluded: "Researchers using the critical tradition nearly always (92%) used data collection procedures that were 'nonfiltered, unobtrusive, and noninteractive'" (p. 123). Let's define each of these terms as a way of unpacking some selection issues you will need to think about if you are conducting critical studies.

Nonfiltered data collection procedures employ information directly from either research participants or existing texts. **Filtered data collection procedures** are ones "in which the researcher approaches the subject of study with an *a priori* categorization of desired findings" (Fink & Gantz, 1996, p. 118).

Unobtrusive data collection procedures "are those in which the researcher's presence is not known" (Fink & Gantz, 1996, p. 118). **Obtrusive data collection procedures** make the researcher's presence known to participants, which may affect the observations or reports collected as evidence in support of a claim.

Finally, **noninteractive data collection procedures** are used when you do not want to influence the data beyond focusing the topic for your participants. Otherwise, **interactive data collection procedures** are used. As the name implies, interactive techniques involve you as "an active participant in the situation being studied and purposely influences the data" (Fink & Gantz, 1996, p. 118). If you want to conduct a critical study, consider whether the case(s) you are selecting for study is more or less typical, and what you will be able to learn from analyzing the case(s). Once you have selected the case(s) for critical analysis, consider how you can access textual evidence related to the case(s) that is "unfiltered, unobtrusive, and noninteractive" (Fink & Gantz, p. 123).

Now you have an overview of random and non-random selection methods, and some sense of how to approach *selection* for critical studies. Let's next consider some specific data collection *strategies*, beginning with ways to collect observations of communicative interactions.

Capturing Observed Interactions

Whether you are interested in studying human interactions as they occur in their natural contexts (i.e., field settings) or in a more controlled laboratory setting, you will have to devise some means of capturing all the information you sense, in order to study those data systematically. The means of capturing communication research data are highly biased to our senses of sight and sound, although performance studies scholarship is one segment of communication research that pushes the means of capturing observed interaction well beyond visual and auditory boundaries to include touch and movement, for example. But sight and sound are still the primary senses used to record observed interactions in communication studies (Lindlof, 1995). In this section, we will outline some of the means used to capture data by sight, sound, and the combination of sight and sound.

Sight records Data captured by visual means often consist of written words, but may also consist of visual images. In terms of written words, field notes, transcripts, archival documents, and existing written texts such as books and road signs all provide visual means of capturing data we sense by sight. In his seminal book, *The Interpretation of Cultures*, anthropologist Clifford Geertz (1973) noted that ". . . what we call our data are really our own constructions of other people's constructions of what they and their compatriots are up to" (p. 9). In his book, *Tales of the Field: On Writing Ethnography*, Van Maanen (1988) wrote: "Only in textualized form do data yield to analysis. The process of analysis is not dependent on the events themselves, but on a second-order, textualized, fieldworker-dependent version of the events" (p. 95).

However, some visual data records do not consist of written words, such as photographs, objects or artifacts, paintings, line drawings, graphs, and charts. Any of these sight records also may constitute data for communication research. Our purpose here is not to delineate certain ways of capturing data as belonging to certain methodologies; rather, we intend to stimulate (and perhaps broaden) your thinking about how data can be temporally fixed for systematic study.

Sound records Audiotape recordings are the primary means of capturing data sounds (i.e., via hearing). Typically, audiotape is transcribed or converted to sight records by producing written words that represent all the sounds on the tape. You will learn more about transcription in Chapters 10 and 11. For some methodologies, audiotaping is merely a means of capturing the data; the transcript, rather than the audiotape, is actually the object of data analysis. For other methodologies, both the tape and the transcript together are the objects of analysis.

Sight and sound records Videotape recordings, films, and digital sight-and-sound records like Web sites and some chat rooms capture both visual and auditory sensory data simultaneously. Sight and sound records are increasingly popular and available. Sight and sound means of capturing communication data increase the reliability and validity of data collection, provide a tool for training observers, give a permanent record of the research data, increase the number of possible observers through replay and remote broadcast, and allow self-observation and analysis (Amidon, 1971). In addition, sight and sound records also provide a basis for supervisory diagnoses and evaluations. For instance, telephone service calls often are recorded in order to facilitate the training and development of employees' customer service and selling skills.

However, audio- and videotaping interactions require specialized equipment and facilities. Even a videotape camera does not pick up every behavior in a context because the researcher has to choose a camera angle and range. In addition, the means of analyzing the complex data provided by both sight and sound records have yet to be codified or fully exploited. Although conversation analysts acknowledge that it is just as important to study the structure and function of nonverbal messages as verbal messages, very little published conversation analytic research addresses nonverbal data (Patterson et al., 1996). One reason is that coding schemes for categorizing nonverbal messages are less readily available

Table 3.1   Linking Data Collection Strategies to Research Questions

Data Collection Strategies	Type of Research Question
Audiotaped conversations Written anecdotes of personal experiences Phenomenological literature (e.g., poetry)	Meaning questions aimed at eliciting the "essence of experiences"
Unstructured interviews Participant observation Field notes Documents, records, photographs, maps, diagrams	Questions aimed at describing group values, beliefs, and practices
Interviews Participant observation Diaries	"Process" questions involving experience over time, especially changes in phases or stages.
Dialogue (audio/video recorded) Observations Field notes	Questions regarding verbal interaction and conversational behavior
Interviews Photography Observations Field notes	Questions about macro-level behavior

Note. Adapted from Morse (1998).

than are schemes for categorizing verbal messages (Patterson et al., 1996; Sigman, Sullivan, & Wendell, 1988). Moreover, replay of audio- and/or videotaped data may prove threatening to participants, especially if the taped records are available to people in authority positions. Granted, Amidon (1971) has published a coding scheme for analyzing nonverbal interactions in classroom settings.

Capturing Self- and Other-Reports

As we pointed out earlier in this chapter, some communication research uses data from sources other than observed interactions. Two other data sources for communication research are asking people to report their own behaviors, beliefs, and characteristics (self-report), and asking people to report about other people's behaviors, beliefs, and characteristics (other-report). Two of the most frequently used ways that you might capture self- and other-report data are by interviewing people or distributing survey questionnaires, orally or in writing. We will discuss questionnaires in more detail in Chapter 5, "Survey Research," and we will talk more about interviewing in Chapter 11, "Ethnographic Research." Another, less frequently used way to capture self- and other-reports is by asking people to complete some sort of task, such as rating behaviors, explaining observed be-

haviors, or sorting written records of observed behaviors into categories (e.g., coding tasks). Table 3.1 shows how particular data collection strategies may be linked to different types of research questions.

As we mentioned earlier in this chapter, critical scholars treat the process of selecting evidence upon which to base their claims quite differently than do scholars in either the interpretive or discovery paradigms. The next section of this chapter applies specifically to the discovery paradigm. If you are conducting discovery research, then you will need to specify the communication concepts you want to study, and your ways of measuring those concepts, before you can collect observations of communicative interactions, or self- or other-reports of beliefs, attitudes, and values. To do this, you will have to identify both conceptual and operational definitions.

CONCEPTUAL AND OPERATIONAL DEFINITIONS

Whether your data source for a discovery paradigm study is observation, self-report, or other-report, you will need to define just how your topic will be observed or reported on (i.e., how things will be measured). Some communication phenomena are concepts that can only be observed indirectly. For example, you cannot cut open a person's head and see if they are intelligent. You can only observe indirect indicators of a person's intelligence.

When phenomena that can only be observed indirectly are selected for study, we call them **constructs** (Babbie, 2001). Verbal aggressiveness, communication competence, communication apprehension, and verbal immediacy are a few examples from our field. Each of these constructs refers to an abstract and internal condition of a person, and each of these constructs can be studied by collecting observations of behavior, self-report data, or other-report data. The first step in the process of trying to study constructs is to develop a conceptual definition.

Conceptual definitions map out the territory of a construct by denoting "its essential qualities and excluding nonessential ones" (Smith, 1988, p. 33). Conceptual definitions describe a construct by relating it to other abstract concepts. For example, verbal aggressiveness can be conceptually defined as a predisposition to attack the self-concept or self-esteem of another individual; the original conceptualization of this construct included attacks on another person's character or competence, insults, teasing, ridicule, profanity, and threats, whether those were made verbally or nonverbally (Infante, 1987, 1989). Of course, all these terms being used to conceptually define verbal aggressiveness are abstractions as well. They do not provide a definition that enables empirical measurement of the construct. In order for verbal aggressiveness to be measured, it must be operationally defined, a process we shall discuss in a moment.

First, though, it is important to notice that not all communication phenomena need be conceptually defined. Some variables have essential characteristics that are directly observable. There is no need to conceptualize them further. Empirical indicators that are observable and measurable already define physical characteristics and behaviors. For example, we accept biological sex as a given, as well as common behaviors like smiling, without having to define them (Smith, 1988).

Constructs that have generally agreed-upon meanings (like biological sex) are defined by **primitive terms** (e.g., male, female). Constructs, like verbal aggressiveness, that are defined by other constructs, like predisposition to attack others, make use of **derived terms**. Any construct defined by derived terms is therefore conceptually defined. Either way, once the construct is conceptually defined, it must

also be operationalized before it can be reduced to its observable features.

Operational definitions specify as precisely as possible every operation, procedure, and instrument needed to measure a construct. Once constructs are operationally defined, they can take on numerical values, becoming variables. For example, Infante and Wigley (1986) created the Verbal Aggressiveness Scale (VAS) to operationalize that variable. The VAS is a written survey measure that consists of 20 statements about how individuals try to get others to comply with their wishes (e.g., "If individuals I am trying to influence really deserve it, I attack their character," or "I refuse to participate in arguments when they involve personal attacks"). Five response choices are provided for each item, from 1 = "almost never true" to 5 = "almost always true." You will learn more about this kind of written survey measure, called a Likert scale, in Chapter 5, "Survey Research."

When you conduct your own research, you may need to explain how some communication behaviors will be measured even if they are already defined in primitive terms. For example, in a survey of children's television-viewing habits, Abelman and Atkin (2000) measured children's recall of television station channel numbers, call letters, and network affiliations. They described in detail how each incidence of recall was counted:

> [T]he number of generated correct responses out of the total possible correct responses was used to classify 'low awareness' (0–33% correct), 'moderate awareness' (34–66% correct), and 'high awareness' (67–100% correct). In all cases, a point was awarded for each correct response and no point was awarded for each wrong response or nonresponse (pp. 146–147).

The process of **operationalization,** then, is the process of specifying the operations, procedures, or instruments used to measure various communication phenomena (Smith, 1988, p. 39). When the construct is operationally defined so that it can take on an array of numerical values, it becomes a **variable** (Smith, p. 29). Some variables are used so frequently that there is no need to explain how they are operationally defined. For example, biological sex is typically measured by assigning a "1" to males and a "2" to females, or vice versa. Since most researchers conducting statistical analyses know this is the standard procedure, the variable does not need to be conceptually or operationally defined.

RESEARCH DESIGN

In the broadest sense, a **research design** is the logical sequence that connects a researcher's claim, data or evidence, and warrant. So research designs are part of the backing we outlined in Chapter 1, "The Claim-Data-Warrant Model." But, as we noted earlier about the term *description,* the words *research design* are used very differently by different kinds of researchers, often without any explicit recognition of the existence of these different meanings.

Design as a Bypassing Term

In this section, we will highlight a problem that has its inception in the evolution of research methods for communication studies. Over the past 20 years, as communication scholars have increased the number and variety of methods they use to conduct research, terms from one paradigm have come to be used in quite different ways by practitioners of other paradigms. As we just mentioned, researchers operating in different paradigms sometimes use the same terms without explicitly recognizing that they hold quite different meanings for these terms. Misunderstandings based on divergent meanings for the same terms are often the root of conflicts between researchers operating in different epistemological paradigms. Of course, clearly understood value differences are also the root of some conflicts.

From the traditional perspective of the discovery paradigm, the term *research design* encompasses many specific strategies for carefully controlling the selection of the people or messages to be included in a study, the setting in which the data will be collected, and the strategies for capturing those data. Claims of explanation and prediction are best supported by true experimental designs, which are highly standardized ways of collecting research data in order to provide evidence for causal arguments. (See Chapter 4, "Warrants for Research Arguments," for a full explanation of causal argument and Chapter 6, "Experimental Research," for detailed coverage of a true experimental design.) By *design,* experimental researchers eliminate an array of competing explanations for the observed set of effects on outcome variables, thereby establishing a strong case for causality.

For example, in one experimental study, Floyd and Burgoon (1999) manipulated verbal and nonverbal behaviors associated with liking and disliking as they trained confederate participants to interact with their partners. By controlling various design features, the researchers argued that the pattern of effects they observed were due to those features they manipulated, rather than to extraneous factors they could not control. In similar fashion, Grabe, Lang, Shuhua, and Bolls (2000) constructed an experiment to test how varying level of education affected participants' levels of attention, memory recognition, and arousal as they viewed television news stories. In both of these studies, the force of the argument the researchers constructed for explaining the changes in their observations depended upon their ability to control the factors that influenced those changes either by strategic manipulation or by holding them constant.

As we mentioned in Chapter 2, "Making Claims," not all claims from the discovery paradigm can be considered arguments of causality through experimental manipulation. For many years, communication researchers have looked at how various characteristics or behaviors are associated. Studies of this type do not describe design procedures that permit experimental manipulation of these characteristics or behaviors. Instead, researchers focus their attention on the *design* of the survey instrument as a basis for arguing the level of relatedness.

For example, Hsu (2002) constructed a survey designed to measure the relationship between levels of communication apprehension and participants' perceptions of their families. Hsu used measures whose reliability and validity had already been established, and the strength of her argument rested specifically in the strength of her instruments.

So, even within the discovery paradigm, the term *design* has different meanings, depending on whether you are conducting an experiment or administering a survey. In conducting experiments, you will refer to research design when you vary procedural features such as random selection of data sources, exposure to a carefully manipulated variable, or assessment of baseline levels of the variable(s) of interest. In conducting survey research, you will refer to research design as the structure of a questionnaire or interview schedule, and the timing of its administration to research subjects.

Both experimental and survey research designs will require you to specify data settings and selection methods before you begin to collect the data. But interpretive researchers use the word *design* to indicate the emerging or unfolding process of doing research, including data collection and analysis. For interpretive studies, research design is not, by any means, a reference to the way the researcher has constructed measures of the communication phenomenon under investigation prior to ever entering the research setting. Philipsen (1977) wrote that "naturalistic inquiry is characterized by a weak commitment to make such advance specifications, and having made them, to follow the plans as drawn" (p. 42). Instead, he argued, "the ethnographer of speaking must allow for, even exploit, non-linearity in research design" (p. 45). Your interpretive research design is more likely to be changed during the data collection and analysis than a discovery research design (Janesick, 1998). In interpretive research studies, design includes attention to the identification and selection of key informants, development of interview questions and perhaps observation schemes, and sampling techniques for data collection. For example, your decision to return to the field setting and conduct deviant case sampling (a nonrandom selection method discussed earlier in this chapter) is a design decision that can be made only after your initial data collection and analysis are completed.

To summarize, the term *design* is an instance of bypassing because people use the same term to mean very different things across paradigms and types of research claims. Nonetheless, in the most basic sense, a research design is your plan for exploring a research question or testing a hypothesis. Some research methods that you will study in Part II of this book place a great deal of emphasis on research design (e.g., survey and experimental research). Other methods treat design differently (e.g., ethnography and ethnomethodology), and some methods do not use the term *research design* at all (e.g., rhetorical criticism and critical studies). When research design is an explicit element of a study, the two basic types are the cross-sectional and the longitudinal design.

Cross-sectional and Longitudinal Research Designs

Cross-sectional research designs are the most simple and common form of design used in communication studies. In cross-sectional research studies, a sample of data collected at one point in time is used to draw inferences about the research question. Just as a tree stump shows a cross-section of the tree's life, evidenced in the growth rings, a cross-sectional study gives the researcher a snapshot, one perspective on the phenomenon of interest, at one point in time.

You might design a cross-sectional survey study by administering written questionnaires to a sample of people drawn from one population at one point in time. For example, you might poll junior high students to see how many hours of television they are currently watching per day. You could also poll elementary school and high school students as multiple samples; but if your survey is administered only once, the design of your study is still cross-sectional (Mertens, 1998; Smith, 1988).

Longitudinal research designs are more complex and less common. Longitudinal research studies are those in which you collect data at several different points in time. There are three types of longitudinal research designs: trend, cohort, and panel studies (Frey, Botan, & Kreps, 2000, p. 208; Mertens, 1998, p. 108). **Trend studies** are conducted by examining several different representative samples from the same population at different points in time. For example, when Gallup conducts a nationwide opinion poll in March, June, and September, the company has selected three representative samples of different voters at each point in time, in order to show changes in voter opinion over the course of a political campaign. In **cohort studies,** members of two or more groups are sampled at two or more points in time. For example, all of the entering students at your university this year might be included in a cohort study as follows: Half of the entering students would be required to see an academic advisor once per semester; the other half would not have any required advising. Both groups (or cohorts) would be asked to fill out annual surveys, thus allowing the researcher to follow the academic progress of each group. Finally, **panel studies** examine the same sample of individuals over time. For example, Parks and Roberts (1998) administered two separate surveys to their online participants in two distinct phases of data collection. Panel studies can help you to see how one group's responses have changed over time.

It is important for you to notice that even though these research design *terms* are most likely to be used in conducting survey and experimental studies, the *concepts* of cross-sectional and longitudinal research design, specifically data collection, apply much more broadly to communication research in all three paradigms. For example, collecting data over a long period of time is one of the defining characteristics of ethnographic research, whereas sampling data from one point in time is more common in content analysis.

TRIANGULATION

Originally, the concept of **triangulation** came to social science research from military navigation, where using more than one reference point enabled navigators to pinpoint an object's exact location (Newman & Benz, 1998). Over the past half century, the notion of triangulation has been elaborated to include using multiple data sources, settings, collection and analytic strategies, and investigators (e.g., Denzin, 1978; Janesick, 1998; Lindlof, 1995; Lofland & Lofland, 1984; Miles & Huberman, 1994; Morse, 1998; Newman & Benz, 1998; Seale, 1999; Stage & Russell, 1992). As you just learned about research design, the term *triangulation* can also have different meanings for discovery, interpretive, and critical researchers.

The basic assumption that discovery researchers make about triangulation is that using multiple data sources, settings, data collection strategies, and so on will compensate for the inherent weaknesses of each individual method, thus contributing to verification, that is, the attempt to accurately describe one, knowable reality (Matthison, 1988). "Triangulation used in this way assumes a single fixed reality that can be known objectively through the use of multiple methods of social research" (Seale, 1999, p. 473). In addition, Seale argued, triangulation has a place within a variety of paradigms.

When you use multiple data sources, settings, and so on to support interpretive or critical research claims, triangulation is not intended to verify one true reality (Denzin & Lincoln, 1998). Rather, using more than one data source, setting, or investigator can enrich the range of subjective participant views available to you. In this way, inconsistencies or "contradictory findings may actually help to understand the richness of what is being studied" (Stage & Russell, 1992, p. 489).

Even though triangulation refers to the use of more than one data source, setting, data collection or analytic strategy, or investigator within a single study, the expected benefits of triangulation vary depending on the kind of research claim and the epistemological stance of the researcher. For all that, the advantages of reading and incorporating insights from multiple studies, using different data collection sources, settings, and strategies, simply extend the idea upon which triangulation is based (Miles & Huberman, 1994). Consider the concept of triangulation being applied to a program of research, as you come to understand a topic or problem from more than one vantage. For example, insights from the discovery, interpretive, and critical communication research paradigms have all contributed to our current understandings of, and knowledge about, intercultural communication, interpersonal communication, and organizational communication. In the following sections, you will learn about some of the ways that triangulation can be accomplished within a study, or across several studies, including multiple data sources, settings, collection and analytic strategies, and investigators.

Multiple Data Sources

Observed behaviors, textual data, and people's reports of their own or others' behavior and meanings are all *sources* for communication data (Frey, Botan, & Kreps, 2000). Physiological responses, like heart rate, pupil dilation, or blushing, are another possible source of communication data (Smith, 1988). Multiple data source triangulation means that you compare data from more than one source, usually in the same study or in the course of conducting a program of research that involves more than one study (Denzin, 1978; Lindlof, 1995). For example, self-reports of communication competence have been compared with other-reports and with behavioral observations, in the interpersonal communication competence literature (e.g., Spitzberg & Cupach, 1984) and in studies designed to evaluate the effects of presentational skills training programs (e.g., Kessler, 1995; Seibold et al., 1993). In ethnographic research, it is quite usual to employ multiple data sources, such as the observed behavior, textual data, and self-report data gained in in-depth interviews (e.g., Browning & Beyer, 1998; Lindsley, 1999; Tardy & Hale, 1998).

Multiple Data Settings

Besides multiple data sources, another way to use triangulation is to examine a single phenomenon at multiple settings or data collection sites. Using multiple data collection sites for verification helps increase generalizability by reducing the effects of one setting (or one group of participants) on the researcher's interpretations of those phenomena (Newman & Benz, 1998). In addition, choosing underresearched groups or settings can help to counteract the unique effects of one setting and can contribute to a richer description of the phenomena being studied (Frey, Botan, & Kreps, 2000; Newman & Benz, 1998). So using multiple data settings is a good triangulation strategy whether you adhere to the discovery, interpretive, or critical research paradigm.

Multiple Data Collection Strategies

Recall that multiple data collection strategies have to do with *how* data for a study are gathered, whereas data sources and settings refer to the people and places *from whom* or *where* the data are sampled. For example, self-report data can be collected using oral interviews, written surveys, or written diaries. Other-report data (i.e., perceptions about other people's behavior or attitudes) can be collected using interviews, surveys, or existing documents (e.g., written performance appraisals). Behavioral observations may be collected live, face-to-face, but may also be preserved using audio- or videotapes.

Obviously, there are many ways you might accomplish data collection strategy triangulation. We think it is good practice to use several kinds of evidence to support a claim, although, as we pointed out earlier, the specific benefit of triangulation will vary across the paradigms for communication research. If you are interested in verifying one knowable reality, then you might combine other-report data collected from interviews and existing documents and only use reports that are confirmed by both means of data collection.

However, imagine that, instead of verifying one knowable reality, you are interested in interpreting multiple realities. For example, you may want to understand how compliments are handled within a particular cultural group. In that case, collecting self-reports with a combination of oral interviews and written diaries should help to enrich the range of interpretations you gather from members of that culture. Rather than throwing out interpretations that are reported by some (but not all) members, you will probably want to explain why compliments are handled differently by different members of a group. Instead of viewing inconsistencies in the data as problematic, "data from the complementary method can enrich, or impose qualifications on, explanations arising from the primary one" (Lindlof, 1995, p. 239).

Multiple Data Analytic Strategies

So far you have learned how to use more than one data source, setting, or collection strategy. But you may also want to use more than one data analytic strategy as a form of triangulation. The most obvious form of data analytic triangulation is to combine some version of quantitative and qualitative data analysis. Quantitative data analysis involves the use of numbers to indicate the amount, degree, or frequency of some variable(s). Quantitative data analysis may further involve exploring the relationships and differences among those variables to explain their causes (or effects) and to predict their future occurrences or changes. Qualitative data analysis involves inferring meanings from data, usually without using numbers. Let's consider two sample studies.

Kim, Lujan, and Dixon (1998) combined quantitative and qualitative data to analyze the identity experiences of American Indians in Oklahoma. Their quantitative questionnaire data measured participants' degree of communicative involvement with in- and outgroup members (i.e., the number of friends they reported who were Indian versus friends who were White), as well as the participants' income, education level, and so on. The qualitative data that Kim et al. analyzed addressed these participants' "lifestyle and acculturation indicators. . . interpersonal and organizational communication patterns. . . mass media consumption patterns" (p. 258). Thus, Kim et al. used data analytic triangulation to articulate both matters of degree (quantitative) and meaning (qualitative) in describing these participants' intercultural identities.

In a second example of data analysis triangulation, Pittman and Gallois (1997) analyzed college students' language strategies for attributing blame about the transmission of HIV and AIDS. First, they performed a quantitative analysis by *counting* blame instances (i.e., the number of times members of particular groups were blamed for spreading HIV and for contracting HIV). Then, they conducted a qualitative analysis by examining the levels of responsibility for which ingroup and outgroup members were blamed. They found that outgroup members, people different from the students involved in the discussion groups, were seen as unsuspecting victims, whereas ingroup members were more likely to be seen as careless or irresponsible when they contracted HIV. Based on the quantitative and qualitative data analyses, Pittman and Gallois discussed ways that college students position themselves vis-à-vis HIV and AIDS. Whenever you use some combination of numerical and meaning-based procedures to make sense of your communication research data, you are practicing data analytic triangulation.

Multiple Investigators' Viewpoints

The last form of triangulation we will describe in this section is particular to interpretive research, more so than to discovery or critical communication studies. Interpretive researchers frequently incorporate multiple researcher viewpoints throughout a study, either by arranging some form of collaboration among two or more researchers, or simply by recognizing one researcher's multiple roles in the setting under study (Denzin, 1978). For example, Ellingson (1998) used her "multiple identities as a cancer survivor, researcher, and pseudo-staff member" to aid her understanding of an oncology clinic for cancer patients.

Discovery researchers do triangulate investigator viewpoints when they assess interrater and intercoder reliability levels (Patterson et al., 1996). In this case, triangulating the observations of more than one person is used to insure observational validity and decrease the possibility of observer bias (Amidon, 1971). However, unlike interpretive collaboration throughout the course of a study (i.e., planning the research, collecting and analyzing the data, writing up the report), triangulating investigator viewpoints for assuring coding reliability, for example, only occurs in the earliest stage of data analysis. You will learn more about intercoder and interrater reliability in Chapters 5 and 7.

When your claim is interpretive, you may want to use multiple investigators in order to "compensate for their individual biases, or shortcomings, or to exploit their specific strengths" (Douglas, 1976, as cited in Lindlof, 1995, p. 239). Perhaps you might deploy more than one researcher in the same setting, or you might work with another researcher to analyze themes from interview data, for example. Or, you may want to check the soundness of a category you have identified by talking it over with a person who is a participant in your data collection setting or a content expert on the topic (e.g., your professor). In fact, team research offers several advantages for making interpretive claims. "Two or more observers or interviewers can simultaneously be looking, listening, and/or asking in different places with different people, generating a potentially broader and richer data log in a shorter period of time" (Lofland & Lofland, 1984, p. 50).

One form of team research is **collaborative ethnography,** which uses more than one researcher to provide multiple viewpoints on a setting, or on similar settings (e.g., May & Pattillo-McCoy, 2000). Collaborative ethnographies can increase the body of data used to describe and understand the social setting or phenomena under study. Furthermore, juxtaposing your field notes against the notes taken by another student working on the same project will reveal the angles at which each of you is viewing the subject of your study.

As a case in point, May and Pattillo-McCoy (2000) conducted a collaborative ethnography of Chicago neighborhood recreation centers, and they advocated that collaborative researchers intentionally induce diversity into their research teams, such as having researchers from different age groups, races, cultural backgrounds, or disciplines. They argued that it is very likely that such diverse research teams would lead to radically different field notes taken in the same settings, and that such "conflict might improve the final narrative by pushing the field-workers to gather more data that might inform those discrepancies" (p. 85).

But collaborative research teams need to be managed to be effective. Their advantages are balanced by difficulties that arise from the sheer quantity of data and intensified problems getting along in the field, since more than one researcher must establish and maintain relationships with participants (Lofland & Lofland, 1984). Obviously these problems are lessened when the method of data collection is primarily document analysis, as in interpretive rhetorical studies. Even so, Miles and Huberman (1994) advised avoiding "sharp senior-junior divisions of labor, such as having juniors do the fieldwork and the seniors do the analysis and writing" (p. 46). Instead, it is important to have strong relationships within the staff of a team research project—relationships that will last over time and through adversity.

Sometimes, more than one type of triangulation is used in a single study. Recall our first example of data analytic strategy triangulation, Kim et al.'s (1998) study of American Indians' identity experiences in Oklahoma. During the *data collection* phase, the researchers employed multiple data collection strategies, sources, and settings: They conducted individual interviews with 182 American Indians at six different research sites in Oklahoma, at the same time, collecting observational data and testimonials from community members. During the *data analysis* phase, the researchers applied two coding schemes to the data, one qualitative and thematic, the other numeric or quantitative. They first grouped their interview data into thematic clusters that represented American Indians' different ways of responding to identity dilemmas. Then they applied a numerical rating scale to assess these American Indians' view of their own cultural-intercultural identities. Finally, the study was conducted by *multiple investigators*: "The six-member research team consisted of three members who had Indian backgrounds and were long time residents of Oklahoma. . . . The other three non-Indian members were of Asian, Black, and Irish backgrounds" (p. 259). In short, Kim et al. employed all five types of triangulation that we have introduced in this chapter: multiple data sources, multiple data settings, multiple data collection strategies, multiple data analytic strategies, and multiple investigator viewpoints. Kim et al.'s study shows how triangulation can be used in practice and suggests the potential benefits of fully integrating triangulation in designing communication research.

TECHNOLOGY AND COMMUNICATION DATA

Technology is changing the sources, settings, and strategies for collecting and analyzing communication data. As we mentioned earlier, the means of capturing evidence for communication research are highly biased toward sight and sound; computers won't alleviate this bias, since computers are also highly visual media, with a secondary emphasis on sound. But the Internet and a proliferation of computer software programs are impacting the ways that you will learn about research methods, the archival databases you can use to conduct literature reviews, and the ways that you will actually conduct communication research.

The first way that communication data is affected by technology may be the least obvious. That is, simply, with the increasing presence of technology in all our lives, it becomes an ever-more-taken-for-granted part of all that we do, including conducting research. Think about your own familiarity with digital technology. Chances are good that you have been using a personal computer since elementary school. Perhaps you carry a mobile phone, own a video camera, pay bills online, check email with your PDA, and so on. Your ease with the presence and use of digital tech-

nology in all aspects of daily living might make the use of some technology in collecting communication research data more or less seamless.

As a research participant, you are more likely now to respond to prerecorded telephone or email surveys in the some of the same ways that you respond to real time, face-to-face interactions with another person. You may be comfortable being recorded on video- or audiotape, although one colleague to whom we suggested this idea thinks that you may be more of a "ham" whenever you know that there's a camera present. The point is, when participants are very comfortable with a particular form of technology, then the use of that technology in collecting communication research data may facilitate, and not threaten, the researcher's aims. Some of the effects of technology on communication data collection are empirical questions that can be answered by observation.

The increasing assortment of mass-mediated data sources, like television shows, films, and Web sites, are also topics and data sources for communication research. To cite just two recent examples, Chan-Olmsted and Park (2000) analyzed the content of broadcast TV stations' Web sites, and Bakardjieva and Smith (2001) conducted an ethnographic study of the Internet in everyday life in Vancouver, British Columbia, especially focusing on how users' daily practices are shaping the Internet as a communication medium. Just as communication is both a means of doing research and a topic of study, technology is also implicated in the topics and methods of communication research.

As a researcher, digital technology will greatly impact your data collection and analytic strategies. Whether you are conducting interviews or observations in real time, face-to-face with your research participants, or receiving their responses electronically via email, the Internet, videotape, and so on, your means of getting, storing, and accessing those data will be inherently tied to computers. And your agility with the ever-changing proliferation of computer software programs designed to aid in data storage, retrieval, and analysis will greatly impact your efficiency as a researcher. You will hear more about some of those computer software programs in Part II.

Digital technology also helps to facilitate team research because of the ways that it breaks down what were formerly time and space barriers. If you want to conduct collaborative ethnography, for example, technology will help you do that with people who are geographically distant. Email and file sharing will allow you to interact with members of your research team in asynchronous time, a matter of considerable convenience.

ETHICAL ISSUES AND COMMUNICATION DATA

Collecting communication data raises ethical concerns about the treatment of research participants (Jaksa & Pritchard, 1988; Scanlon, 1993). Some of these ethical issues are sourced in a tension that exists between an individual researcher's goals and the social goals of a society. In this section, we will introduce some general principles of research ethics that are consistent with the guidelines to which committees charged with the protection of human subjects in research adhere. These committees are called **Institutional Review Boards** (IRBs). IRB guidelines in the United States were originally based on the Nuremberg Code, which was composed from the *Trials of War Criminals Before the Nuremberg Military Tribunals,* and which is available from the U. S. Government Printing Office in Washington, D.C. The Nuremberg Code specified 10 ethical principles for the treatment of human subjects involved in research experiments:

1. The voluntary consent of human subjects is absolutely essential.

2. Experiments involving human subjects should yield good for a whole society that is unprocurable by other methods.

3. Experiments involving human subjects should be designed and based on the results of animal experimentation first.

4. Experiments should avoid inducing unnecessary physical and mental suffering and injury upon human subjects.

5. If there is an a priori reason to expect that death or disabling injury will occur, the experiment should not be conducted.

6. The degree of risk to be taken should never exceed that determined by the humanitarian importance of the problem to be solved by the experiment.

7. Human subjects should be protected against potential injury, disability, or death.

8. Experiments should be conducted by scientifically qualified persons.

9. The human subjects should have the opportunity to cease participating at any time during an experiment.

10. The researcher must be prepared to terminate an experiment at any time his or her "good faith, superior skill, and careful judgment" suggest that a "continuation of the experiment is likely to result in injury, disability, or death to the experimental subject."

As you can see from these 10 principles, the primary goal of IRBs is the protection of human subjects involved in research. Some of the specific concerns you will read about in later chapters of this book include informed consent (as well as reasons for and against deceiving research subjects during the course of a study), privacy, confidentiality or anonymity, and weighing potential research benefits against potential harm to participants.

Although these issues may seem simple to you at first glance, some of them actually are quite complex. For example, inducements to participate in a research study, from cash to extra-credit points, may threaten the principle of voluntary consent. Experiments in which the effects of a treatment program are tested by comparing people in the treatment program with a control group of subjects who do not receive the same treatment raise ethical concerns both about the injustice of denying potentially beneficial treatment to a group of people and about deception. At the same time, such experiments afford control over competing explanations about causal variables, and all of us have benefited from this type of research. Medical examples like the polio vaccine are obviously beneficial, but we also benefit from experimental communication research (e.g., treatments for communication apprehension or advice regarding deception detection).

Similarly, **anonymity,** taking steps to protect the identity of people involved in research studies, has both costs and benefits. It is up to you, the researcher, to weigh potential gains and harms from the ways that research participants are treated, and to decide what degree of anonymity to promise participants. Sometimes, confidentiality, rather than anonymity, is protected. Anonymity means that you won't know participants' identifying information (e.g., name, social security number, etc.); **confidentiality** means that you will know this information, but you will not share identifying information with anyone else, such as other researchers, people the participants know, or the readers of your research report.

For example, Amason, Allen, and Holmes (1999) conducted interviews with employees in a multicultural organization about their experiences seeking social support at work. Some of the interviews were conducted with Hispanic employees who spoke in Spanish:

> When the interviews were conducted with Spanish speaking employees, a translator (not affiliated with the organization to protect employee confidentiality) was used. Translators were native Spanish speakers who either taught Spanish at the university level or provided translation services for the community through a local social service agency (p. 316).

Whether you decide to protect anonymity or confidentiality, protecting participants' identities is just one kind of agreement you might make with your research participants. Beyond individual assurances of confidentiality or anonymity, you will need to carefully consider your research purpose and make decisions about ethical conduct that can accomplish your goals. For instance, Miles and Huberman (1994) suggested several possible purposes for doing field research: You may want to tell the participants' stories (for them or with them); you may also want to collaborate with them in solving a social problem. However, your purpose could be merely to use them as informants for *your* research interests. The nature of the agreements that you make with your research participants will vary, depending on these types of goals. As the researcher, it is your responsibility to consider the ethics of your actions for yourself and your participants.

Indeed, status differentials among participants, or between participants and you, can open the way for potential power abuses (Scanlon, 1993). **Status differentials** occur whenever one party to an agreement has more power resources than the other(s). Power resources may be money, time, expert knowledge, skills, and so on. In the same way, a potential for power abuse exists in groups that are formed purely for research purposes, and in interviewing situations that violate privacy or other cultural norms (e.g., Miller, Creswell, & Olander, 1998). Even conducting textual analysis and making post hoc judgments about historical contexts from a different point in time, and from a different group membership, can raise ethical concerns for rhetorical critics.

You should always assess the potential consequences that the conduct and publication of your research has for yourself and for others. Communication research projects can have potential positive and negative consequences, and the decision to pursue (or not pursue) research projects that lead to those consequences also has ethical implications.

In Part II of this book, we will elaborate on these ethical concerns as you learn how to conduct communication research using survey, experimental, content analytic, conversation analytic, ethnographic, classical and contemporary rhetorical criticism, and critical communication studies. In all of these methods, the protection of human rights for those involved in the research is paramount. "The value of the best research is not likely to outweigh injury" to a person harmed by the project (Stake, 1998, p. 103). Therefore, in Part II we also will touch on ethical issues related to the analysis and reporting of research data, and the use of research findings.

SUMMARY

In this chapter, we outlined the second element of the research-as-argument model, the data or evidence presented in support of a research claim. We began by discussing the typical sources, settings, and strategies used by communication scholars for collecting research data. We introduced the general notion of selection, the means by which people or messages are picked for inclusion in a study; within this subsection, we outlined four random sampling methods and six nonrandom sampling methods. We also introduced strategies for capturing observations, self- or other-reports, and textual data.

Throughout this chapter, we have stressed the relative value of different data collection sources, settings, and strategies for supporting particular research claims. We hope that our approach will help you begin to appreciate some of the key differences in the communication research conducted by discovery, interpretive, and critical scholars, as each of these research paradigms contributes valuable insights to the field of communication studies.

Because researchers in our field use terms like *data, evidence, research design,* and *triangulation* differently, we also included sections that introduce conceptual and operational definitions and research design in this chapter, even though these ideas lead into the warrants and backing elements of our research-as-argument model. Conceptualizing and operationalizing research variables are endeavors traditionally associated with discovery paradigm assumptions. Like research design, as paradigm differences have developed in our field, these terms have become problematic because they are used in very specific ways by survey and experimental researchers, in different ways by interpretive researchers, and are not used at all in critical studies. A second difference is that discovery researchers are most likely to commit to their design specifications (including conceptual and operational definitions of variables) before they begin collecting data. Researchers operating within the interpretive paradigm are more likely to allow definitions, meanings, and design decisions to emerge and to be guided by what happens during data collection and analysis. Our extensive overview of research triangulation in this chapter should further enrich your ability to think broadly about research design.

Our section on technology and communication data highlighted some of the sources and data collection strategies made possible by computers and the Internet, in particular. Of course, technology not only expands the sources for communication data, and the means of collecting that data, but it also facilitates data analysis in so many ways that we now take for granted. Some of these ways include ease and speed of data entry, storage, and analysis—topics you will learn more about in Part II of this book.

Finally, we presented an overview of some ethical issues regarding the treatment of research participants as data sources and the analysis and use of research data. The "Great Debate" activity at the end of this chapter should help you appreciate the complexities of these ethical issues in practice.

KEY TERMS

Anonymity

Archive

Bias

Cohort studies

Collaborative ethnography

Conceptual definitions

Confidentiality

Constructs

Convenience sampling

Cross-sectional research design

Data collection settings

Data collection sources

Data collection strategies

Demographics

Derived terms

Deviant case sampling

Field settings

Filtered data collection procedures

Institutional Review Boards (IRBs)

Interactive data collection procedures

Laboratory settings

Longitudinal research designs

Maximum variation sampling

Multistage cluster sampling

Network sampling

Nonfiltered data collection procedures

Noninteractive data collection procedures

Nonrandom selection methods

Observed interactions

Obtrusive data collection procedures

Operational definitions

Operationalization

Other-report

Panel studies

Periodicity

Population

Primitive terms

Purposive samples

Quota sampling

Random selection methods

Research design

Sampling

Sampling frame

Selection

Self-report

Simple random sampling

Status differentials

Stratified sampling

Systematic sampling with a random start

Text

Trend studies

Triangulation

Unobtrusive data collection procedures

Variable

DISCUSSION QUESTIONS

1. Academic research is frequently conducted using college students as "subjects" or "participants." Considering the random and nonrandom sampling methods outlined in this chapter, discuss what kinds of communication research projects could be appropriately conducted using students in college classrooms (even communication classes, more specifically) as research samples. When or why should researchers move beyond using college students as participants in communication research?

2. What are the differences between trend, panel, and cohort studies (i.e., the three longitudinal research designs)?

3. How might triangulation contribute to the worth of a research project given the different values and forms of argument used in discovery, interpretive, and critical communication research? It may help to consider this question in terms of the different forms of triangulation described in this chapter.

4. Why do researchers need to be concerned about status differentials, or different levels of expertise, skills, time, or financial resources between researchers and participants (or even among participants) when conducting communication research?

"TRY IT!" ACTIVITY

Collect instances of ordinary uses of the word *data* from magazines and newspapers, your workplace, the Internet, or other sources. See what meanings of the word *data* are reflected by the research we do in communication studies. What parts of the research we do are not reflected in these ordinary meanings of the word *data*?

The Great Debate: Ethical Dilemmas in Communication Data

Working in small groups, identify at least one ethical dilemma in each situation given below. Discuss with your group members the potential harms and benefits of this dilemma, and develop a position statement that specifies the ethical standards you, as the researchers, would attend to. Identify the ethical behaviors you would select in this case as well as the potential harms that could ensue if you do not behave ethically:

1. You are collecting observational and interview research data at a clothing manufacturing company. You are given hundreds of dollars worth of free clothing during your data collection. You really like the clothes and wear them proudly, but you don't know whether to tell people they were free or keep that a secret.

2. You discover information during data collection that could hurt the research participants if you disclose it (e.g., either the participants are engaging in illegal behaviors, like underage drinking or the use of controlled substances, or they are behaving in ways that will be called to moral account by others, like committing certain sexual acts or making racial slurs).

3. You want to conduct research in a group of which you are a member, but for your own personal reasons, you don't want to disclose your membership status (e.g., HIV positive, incest survivor, recovering alcoholic or drug addict).

4. You have developed a treatment program for communication apprehension, based on visualization and systematic desensitization. You would like to see whether students in your department's basic course would benefit from your training program by providing your treatment program to some students and comparing their course performance against students who did not take your treatment program.

5. You are interested in studying people's responses to communication rule violations in cross-cultural interactions. You want to collect actual instances of rule violations and responses from several different cultural contexts.

6. As a way to insure plausible interpretations, you return to check your interpretations with your participants/informants, and they disagree. Should you publish your interpretations, with or without mentioning that you checked the interpretations with the participants?

Adapted from Braithwaite, Dollar, Fitch, & Geist (1996).

4

Warrants for Research Arguments

ABSTRACT

In this chapter, you will learn about the third element of the research-as-argument model, the warrants and backing. Warrants are the standards we use to evaluate whether particular evidence is a good way to support a claim. We stress the inherent relationship between the values and forms of argument used in the discovery, interpretive, and critical research paradigms, and the different standards used to evaluate evidence in those paradigms. First, we will present the values and forms of argument (or the backing) preferred in each paradigm, and then we will show you how to develop the warrants for each type of argument, based on those values, or standards. We conclude this chapter by comparing three different possible views of truth, implicated by the warrants for each paradigm's form of argument.

OUTLINE

Discovery Paradigm Warrants

Scientific Values: Precision, Power, and Parsimony

Form of Argument: Demonstrating Causality

Reliability as a Standard for Evaluating Evidence

Validity as a Standard for Evaluating Evidence

Interpretive Paradigm Warrants

Interpretive Values: Subjectivity and Rich Description

Form of Argument: Demonstrating Multiple Realities

Researcher Credibility as a Standard for Evaluating Evidence

Plausible Interpretations as a Standard for Evaluating Evidence

Transferable Findings as a Standard for Evaluating Evidence

Critical Paradigm Warrants

Emancipatory Values: Voice and Liberation

Form of Argument: Demonstrating Ideological Need for Change

Researcher Positionality as a Standard for Evaluating Evidence

Three Views of Truth

Critical Paradigm

Interpretive Paradigm

Discovery Paradigm

Technology and Warrants for Research Arguments

Summary

Key Terms

Discussion Questions

"Try It!" Activity

The Great Debate: "How Should We Prioritize Research Values?"

If you look up the word *warrant* in the dictionary, you will find that it is "something that serves as an assurance, or guarantee, of some event or result" (Guralnik, 1986, p. 1602). To warrant is to authorize the doing of something, to give formal assurance or guarantee to someone for something. The colloquial meaning of *warrant* is to state with confidence. In the research-as-argument model, warrants allow you to state with confidence that your evidence (or data) supports your research claim (Booth, Colomb, & Williams, 1995). Because each of the three paradigms for communication research that you learned about in Chapter 1 has its own values, each of the following sections is organized by first discussing the values embraced in that paradigm.

Values guide the way that you will frame research problems, what will count as data, and the strategies you will use to collect, analyze, and estimate the worth of your evidence and conclusions. Think of research values the way you think of cultural values. Different values are embraced by members of different cultures. Some values are seen as better, worse, or just different, depending on how strongly you adhere to your own cultural values, and on how similar or different particular values seem from your own values.

For example, we are both white women who were raised in the United States. When we started teaching research methods, we shared the expectation that students would show us respect in the classroom by looking directly at our faces when we were speaking to them. However, we now understand that students from Chinese or Japanese cultures are likely to show their respect by avoiding direct eye contact with a teacher who is speaking to them. For us to judge those students as disrespectful because they do not show respect in the way that our cultural norms prescribe is ethnocentric. Just so, evaluating the worth of research that has been conducted in one epistemological paradigm by applying the normative standards of another paradigm is also ethnocentric.

We do not believe that you must adopt one research paradigm and reject the others. To the contrary, we prefer a view of all three paradigms coexisting in the world of inquiry, if not in one person or in one study. If you want to fully understand a communication topic, we believe you can benefit from knowledge gained in all three paradigms. Furthermore, we feel that the best research on a topic is acquired through the use of multiple methods. Within any one particular study, we agree with Newman and Benz (1998), who wrote: "The better paradigm is the one that serves to answer the specific research question" (p. 11).

But the paradigm from which you approach a research project will likely influence the research questions you ask, and those you choose to ignore. So, instead of paradigm allegiance, we prefer that you develop **methodological awareness,** which "can be acquired by exposure to almost any intelligent methodological discussion" (Seale, 1999, p. 465). To use Seale's metaphor, reading and discussing methodological ideas builds your intellectual muscles and makes you a stronger, more alert practitioner of research methods. Methodological awareness will serve you well in your other major courses and in your interactions with research outside your college classes.

DISCOVERY PARADIGM WARRANTS

Recall from Chapter 1 that the discovery paradigm has its origins in the philosophical traditions of rationalism and logical positivism. Rationalism emphasizes "a common reality on which people can agree" (Newman & Benz, 1998, p. 2), and logical positivism emphasizes precision. So, warrants in discovery research necessarily address issues of agreement and scientific values of precision and accuracy. In the next section, we will describe three scientific values and illustrate their use in discovery paradigm communication research. After that, we will outline the basic form of scientific argument, attempts to demonstrate causality. Finally, we will examine two specific warrants, or standards for evaluating evidence in discovery research, namely, reliability and validity.

Scientific Values: Precision, Power, and Parsimony

You can use alliteration to remember the scientific values embraced within the discovery paradigm. Just remember the three *P*s—precision, power, and parsimony. Each of these values guides discovery research, from the way that research questions and hypotheses are framed, to the type of data and how it is collected, the strategies used to analyze those data, and of course, the procedures used to estimate how well that data supports the research claim.

Precision refers to detailed accuracy in defining and measuring communication variables. Precise definitions specify what the concept is and what it is not. Precise measurements are informative because they show how a variable can be differentiated from other variables. Precision also connotes agreement. For example, you may think that your research methods teacher talks too fast during class lectures. But what does that mean, precisely? A rate of speaking that is too fast for one student may be perfectly acceptable to another student. Discovery communication research aims to use descriptions that are precise and that are likely to be agreed upon by more than one person. In this case, you could count the number of words your teacher speaks in 60 seconds: A teacher who speaks 80 words per minute is speaking faster than a teacher who speaks 50 words per minute. A group of 40 students could probably agree on a range of words per minute that is too fast for comprehension or for note-taking purposes. Of course, a number of other factors would be relevant to this evaluation of speaking rate, such as clear enunciation by the teacher, and the listeners' motivation and skill levels. But the value of precision is that we "can differentiate the event much more precisely from other events, and different individuals can more readily agree on the accuracy of the description" (McCain & Segal, 1988, p. 49).

The second value embraced in discovery communication research is **power**—the scope of a definition or measurement used in discovery research. For example, a flashlight is more powerful when it shines a brighter light on a larger area of darkness. In the same way, a measurement scheme is more powerful when it captures more detail or the broadest aspects of a concept, than when it captures less detail or only the more narrow aspects of a concept. Similarly, a data selection technique that better represents the population under study is considered more powerful than a technique that is less likely to represent the population. The ability to accurately represent a broader segment of the population is powerful because it allows you to generalize from the people or messages you study to those you did not specifically study.

If you think about the flashlight analogy, you can see another aspect of power: how likely are you to mistake what you see when you point the light into a dark place? Under the beam of a weak flashlight, a dusty floor may be mistaken for a clean floor. Similarly, when using a low-power statistical test in discovery research, a small effect may be mistaken for no effect. (This mistake is called a type II error, which you will learn more about in Chapter 8, "Descriptive Statistics and Hypothesis Testing"). Statistical techniques that deal with cause-and-effect explanations of several variables at once are thought to be more powerful than data analytic techniques that deal with fewer variables, so those multivariate statistics are prized in discovery research.

Finally, **parsimony**—the combination of precision and power—is highly valued in discovery research. A parsimonious study of communication is both accurate in detail and covers a broad or important concept. In other words, a parsimonious explanation of communication behavior or processes offers a bright light in a dark area. Discovery paradigm adherents appreciate data collection and analytic strategies and research studies that say a lot in a succinct way (i.e., that are parsimonious).

Form of Argument: Demonstrating Causality

Causal arguments are the basis of discovery research. Although not all discovery research studies offer full causal accounts of communication phenomena, most discovery research is concerned, at least in part, with some aspect of cause-and-effect patterning. In scientific notation, X is used to denote the cause, and Y is used to denote the effect. There are three well-agreed-upon types of evidence for supporting a causal argument, or the idea that "X causes Y": (1) time order, (2) covariation, and (3) control over rival hypotheses. Exhibit 4.1 shows how each type of evidence is defined in discovery research (Babbie, 2001).

The best way to demonstrate causality is to use a true experimental design, a strategy that you will learn about in Chapter 6, "Experimental Research." Experimental designs provide evidence that can be used to test the claim that "X causes Y." Such evidence is evaluated based on the standards of reliability and validity, to which we will turn later in this chapter. The main function of an experimental design is to control extraneous influences on the hypothesized causal variable. In other words, the experimental researcher wants to show that variable X, and not some other factor, is the best possible explanation for changes in variable Y.

Experimental research fits with the values of the discovery paradigm. When you conduct an experiment, you are not interested in developing your subjective

---

EXHIBIT 4.1 Evidence Needed to Support a Causal Argument

Time order: X changed (or occurred) first, then Y changed (or occurred).

Covariation: When X changed (or occurred), Y also changed (or occurred).

Control over rival hypotheses: Change in (or occurrence of) X is the best possible explanation for the change in (or occurrence of) Y.

---

interpretations of events, nor do you offer evaluative critiques of communicative practices. Instead, explanation, prediction, and control are your goals in doing communication research.

As you will learn in Chapter 6, claims of causality begin as theoretic explanations for patterns of communication you have observed (Smith, 1988). Causal claims are constructed in the form of hypotheses, which predict the effects that causal variables will have if those variables are manipulated. Next, the hypotheses (or predictions) are tested by designing experiments in which the effects of varying X can be systematically observed. Those observations are then used to support (or refute) the researcher's causal argument.

Experimental research designs address several standard rival hypotheses, or competing explanations about the cause of X, which you will learn about in much detail in Chapter 6. But there are two basic conditions for causal explanations that we do want to cover here—necessity and sufficiency. A cause is necessary if the effect that occurs when it is present does not occur when it is absent. For example, as the old saying goes, you can't win the lottery if you don't buy a ticket; buying a ticket is a necessary condition for winning the lottery. Necessary conditions *must* be present for the effect to occur. However, a cause is sufficient when it is the best possible explanation, without any additional explanations, for the effect under study. Buying a ticket is a necessary, but in most cases insufficient, condition for winning the lottery. Babbie (2001) pointed out that "the discovery of a cause that is both necessary *and* sufficient is, of course, the most satisfying outcome in research" (p. 79). But he also noted that in scientific research, "demonstrations of either necessary or sufficient causes—even imperfect ones—can be the basis for concluding that variables are causally related" (p. 80).

You can evaluate the merit of any causal argument by using two basic standards, reliability and validity, described in the following sections.

Reliability as a Standard for Evaluating Evidence

A good synonym for the **reliability** standard in discovery research is consistency. Reliable measuring instruments are consistent; they are free from random variations. For example, on a reliable bathroom scale, a 5-pound bag of flour should weigh 5 pounds every single time. On an unreliable bathroom scale, a 5-pound bag of flour may weigh 4.9 pounds the first time you weigh it, and 5.1 pounds the next time you weigh it. If your bathroom scale is unreliable in this way, you should never believe the results when you weigh yourself! Just as in discovery research, if your measuring instrument does not yield consistent results, you should not believe the conclusions that instrument leads you to make about communication variables.

Measurement reliability means that your research observations are consistent over time, across settings, subjects, and instruments. Before we specify all these different ways that you can demonstrate measurement reliability, let's take a closer look at the problem of inconsistent measurement.

Noise: A threat to consistent measurement Because consistency is a synonym for reliability of measurement, random error is the source of unreliable measurement. Random errors in measurement are sometimes called *noise* because they attenuate measurement reliability, the way that static noise attenuates a radio or telephone signal. When there is too much noise on the line, you have trouble hearing the voice you tuned in to hear.

Three different sources of random error contribute to inconsistent measurement: random individual differences, lack of instrument clarity, and errors in data processing (Smith, 1988). **Random individual or situational differences** simply means that every person or situation is unique. People experience transient states of being, like moods, illness, or fatigue, that change randomly. Of course, situational characteristics also vary, such as lighting, temperature, and so on. Random measurement errors caused by lack of **instrument clarity** can come from ambiguously worded questions (e.g., on a survey questionnaire or in an interview) or from unclear instructions to research participants, either of which might lead participants to respond inconsistently. Finally, **errors in data processing** occur when data are being translated from one form to another. For example, an error may be committed when data from the hard copies of a survey questionnaire are entered into the computer, or when interview responses are being transcribed from audiotapes into a word processor. All of these are sources of error that result in inconsistent measurement, and therefore lower measurement reliability.

Types of measurement reliability Reliability is an ideal in measurement. In practice, we never achieve perfectly consistent measurement because it is impossible to completely eliminate random errors like the ones we just described. Instead, measurement reliability is estimated in different ways, depending on the type of consistency you are trying to achieve (e.g., consistency over time, across subjects, settings, etc.). Measurement reliability can be estimated through three approaches: stability, homogeneity, and equivalence. When relevant, we will introduce you to variations on these basic forms as you will need them to use a particular methodology.

Stability of measurement is achieved when the results obtained by one measuring instrument remain consistent over time. For example, if you want to measure how a group leader impacts the decision-making process in their group during one semester, you might administer a leadership scale at various times, in order to illustrate the stability of the leader's role. This method of demonstrating reliable measurement is sometimes called the **test–retest method** (Babbie, 2001, pp. 141–142). If you want to establish measurement stability, you must use the same measuring instrument each time. Providing group members with one scale to assess leader impact initially, and then changing the way the leader's impact is measured the next time, will not ensure stable measurement across time. In Chapter 6, you will learn more about how to demonstrate stability in measurement and about some predictable types of instability in measurement.

The second form of measurement reliability also concerns the consistency of measurement for self- and other-report data. **Homogeneity,** also known as **internal consistency,** means that all the items used to measure a concept yield consistent responses from subjects, so that each item in the measuring instrument consistently refers to the same underlying concept. Internal consistency is demonstrated when scores on one self-report item, for example, are similar to scores on the other self-report items that make up one survey instrument. Another way to show internal consistency is to see whether subjects at one end of a variable continuum score similarly to one another, and differently from people at the other end of that same continuum. If, for example, a communication anxiety measure has a high degree of internal consistency, as does McCroskey's (1982) Personal Report of Communication Apprehension (PRCA), then people who are highly anxious should respond similarly to one another on each item, and differently from people who are only slightly anxious.

The third form of measurement reliability is called **equivalence.** Just as you can assess self-report data for its consistency across time, using test–retest reliability, you can also evaluate self-report data for consistency across measures or across researchers, who are in this case known as coders. Equivalence across different measures is called the **alternate forms method.** It is used when self-report data are already quantified, or given in numeric form. When self- or other-report data are qualitative, as in the cases of responses to open-ended survey questions, or participant observations, then you can verify the consistency of measurement by checking the equivalence of different people's interpretations. This method of demonstrating equivalence is called **agreement among judges.**

For example, imagine that you want to demonstrate the equivalence of your quantitative self-report data. You may want to use the alternate forms method (Smith, 1988, p. 47). Whenever we use two different forms of a single instrument to measure the same variable, we want to show that the scores yielded by one measure are consistent with the scores yielded by the other measure. For example, we might want to shorten a lengthy pen-and-paper survey questionnaire by reducing the number of items from 40 to 20. If so, we should give both measures to a single group of people at the same time, then check to see that people who earned high scores on one measure also earned high scores on the other measure. If so, we have established that the short and long form produce equivalent results.

You can also assess equivalence using multiple measures that are all designed to measure the same construct. For example, if you used two scales to measure the degree of loneliness that individuals are experiencing, then those two measures should yield consistent results. The greater the degree of similarity between the two sets of resulting scores, the higher the equivalence between the two measures. However, it is difficult to find two separate instruments that measure the same social construct with high levels of consistency.

If you want to establish the consistency of measurement for qualitative self-report, other-report, or participant observation data, you will need to establish a different type of equivalence—the equivalence of measurements made by more than one researcher. Agreement among judges is verified whenever two or more researchers categorize audio- or videotaped communication behaviors or transcribe interactions, and when they agree about which behaviors fit into which categories. **Interrater reliability** concerns the agreement among either research participants or researchers who rate communication characteristics of a single target, and **intercoder reliability** concerns the agreement among two or more researchers who are categorizing messages. You will learn more about these two specific forms of agreement among judges in Chapters 6, 7, and 10.

[handwritten note in margin: More than one person doing rating.]

Finally, agreement among judges is confirmed whenever two independent transcribers agree about the content of a source audio- or videotape, called **intertranscriber reliability** (Patterson, Neupauer, Burant, Koehn, & Reed, 1996). You will have an opportunity to practice conducting this kind of reliability assessment in the "Try It!" Activities included with Chapter 10, "Conversation and Discourse Analysis." But now that you have a sense of all the ways to evaluate measurement reliability, let's consider the standard of accuracy, also known as **validity.**

Validity as a Standard for Evaluating Evidence

Valid measurement is accurate, so valid measuring instruments measure precisely what they claim to measure. Remember the example we used earlier of the reliable bathroom scale? A valid bathroom scale reports the weight of that 5-pound bag of flour as precisely 5 pounds, not 4.9 pounds, or 5.1 pounds. If a bathroom scale is *both reliable and valid,* it will report the same weight for that bag of flour every time the bag is placed on the scale. All good measuring instruments need to be both reliable and valid, or consistent and accurate. It is possible for a measuring instrument to be reliable but not valid (i.e., consistently inaccurate). But if a measuring instrument is very accurate, it should also be very consistent.

Just as consistent measurement within each study, and replication across studies, is prized in discovery research, so too the discovery scholar is concerned about validity within and across studies. Efforts to assure **internal validity** warrant the factual accuracy of measurement within a research study; whereas efforts to assure **external validity** concern the accuracy of applying conclusions from one study to another setting or to other people. Before we look at all the ways to establish validity, let's consider the source of inaccurate measurement, bias.

Bias: A threat to accurate measurement Bias is a constant source of error in measurement. When bias is present, it is impossible to accurately measure anything. You are probably familiar with the idea of bias. You may have thought, for example, "My math teacher is biased against Speech majors." Your math teacher may be unable to accurately measure your performance in class if he or she is biased against Speech majors. In the same way, measuring instruments that are contaminated by bias do not accurately measure communication variables. In discovery research, we are trained to guard against several standard biases, which are sometimes collectively referred to as *rival hypotheses.* For example, biased findings may result from selecting only a particular type of research participants, or from participants reacting to the researcher's personal attributes. You will learn about a number of standard biases, or rival hypotheses, in Chapter 6. For now, it is enough to know that constant error patterns can threaten the accuracy of measurement. Let's look now at three ways to ensure that your research measurements are free of bias, or accurate.

Types of measurement validity Since measurement validity refers only to the accuracy of measurement within one study, all three types of measurement validity that we introduce in this section (face validity, criterion validity, and construct validity) can be grouped under the same heading, internal validity.

Face validity, sometimes also known as **content validity,** is the most basic way to establish measurement accuracy. It means that a measuring instrument appears to be valid in at least two ways: It is rich and it passes the test of public scrutiny. First, a content valid measure captures the richness of the concept it was intended to measure. Measuring instruments that capture more inclusively the broadest meanings of a concept are considered richer and more accurate (Smith, 1988). For example, if you measured aggression on the school playground by counting the number of times children hit each other, you will probably not capture the richest sense of the aggression concept. Instead, if you also include observations of verbal aggression, such as name-calling, and other physical manifestations of aggression, like making faces or shoving, you will broaden your measurement of aggression.

Second, all measuring instruments should be subjected to **public scrutiny** of people who are experts on the topic to be measured. If people with considerable training and experience agree that your measure seems likely to yield accurate data, then your measure has passed the test of public scrutiny. Whenever researchers report that a measuring instrument was used in prior research and was there found to be valid and reliable, they are assuring us that the measure has passed the test of public scrutiny and should therefore be accepted on the strength of that test. If links to previous researchers' measures are your only basis for demonstrating measurement validity, you will have advanced a fairly weak argument, that we should accept your definition on face value, with no further evidence.

You can make a stronger case for content validity by explicitly submitting your variable definitions to a **panel of judges.** For example, when Bradford, Meyers, and Kane (1999) asked Latino focus groups to define communication competence from their particular and knowledgeable cultural perspective, they asked open-ended questions so that the focus

groups would define communication competence in their own terms. If the authors created a quantitative measuring instrument on the basis of those focus group discussions, they would have made a strong case for having defined communication competence from a Latino/a cultural perspective.

It is possible, and desirable, to establish accurate measurement beyond content validity. If you can relate your measuring instrument to other instruments that have already been shown to be valid, you will have an even stronger case for measurement validity. The other, already-established measuring instrument becomes the criterion by which the accuracy of your measure is established. Therefore, the second type of validity is called **criterion validity.** Criterion validity can be further distinguished as one of two types, **concurrent** or **predictive validity.**

If you present an existing measuring instrument as validation of a newly created instrument, you are using concurrent validity to warrant the accuracy of your new measure. For example, imagine that you want to create a new scale to assess intelligence. You could compare the results obtained with your measure to the results from the same group of participants using an existing standardized test of intelligence.

In a recent communication research example, Kremar and Valkenburg (1999) attempted to establish concurrent validity. They compared children's responses on their new Moral Interpretation of Interpersonal Violence Scale with the short form of another instrument, the Sociomoral Reflection Measure. Ostensibly, both instruments measure children's moral reasoning. If the results from Kremar and Valkenburg's new measure showed a pattern similar to the results from the other test, the new measure would be seen as accurate. Unfortunately, Kremar and Valkenburg could only validate some portions of their new scale with this procedure. It is likely that the conceptual territories of the two measures had areas that did not overlap.

Another way to demonstrate criterion validity is to show that your measure predicts scores on some other variable in the way that a theory predicts it should work. To do this, we usually find some way of identifying the communication behaviors associated with someone who would score at the high end of our scale and someone else who would score at the low end of the scale. For example, Burgoon et al. (1998) asked one group of college students to compare statements constructed to reflect a dominance-submission continuum to the one person in their circle of friends who was the most dominant. Burgoon et al. then asked a second group of college students to compare the same items to the person in their circle of friends who was the least dominant. Ideally, Burgoon et al.'s measuring instrument should discriminate between those friends at each end of the continuum. This approach to predictive validity is called the *known-groups method* because the scales are validated by groups of people known to possess the construct's characteristics (Smith, 1988, p. 49).

The third type of measurement validity, called **construct validity,** is the strongest way to assure accurate measurement because it represents a comprehensive attempt to identify and validate the structure of a particular measuring instrument. The processes of convergence and divergence are used to establish construct validity (Watt & van den Berg, 1995).

Convergent validity is established when the results of one instrument's administration are compared with the results of another measure of the same concept, provided that the second measuring instrument has already been shown to be accurate. Communication researchers sometimes administer two different forms of a measuring instrument to a group of subjects at the same time in order to validate a new instrument, by comparing its results to those achieved using a previously proven measuring instrument. For example, you might measure the subjects' heart rate at the same time you have them fill out a self-report survey of communication anxiety. If subjects who have a fast heart rate also report high anxiety, and those with lower heart rates report lower feelings of anxiety, then your self-report measure would be said to have demonstrated convergent validity.

[margin note: related = correlate]

Divergent validity is established when the results of one measuring instrument are shown to be unrelated to the results of another measuring instrument, provided that the concepts these two instruments purport to measure are theoretically unrelated. The relationships between scores for two measuring instruments can be determined using a statistic called **correlation,** which you will learn more about in Chapter 9, "Testing Differences and Relationships." The concept that undergirds the correlation statistic is covariation, one of the three criteria for causal argument. Recall that when two things covary, they change at the same time (e.g., in San Francisco, many people's moods covary with the weather; when it's

[margin note: unrelated = don't correlate]

sunny outside, we feel happy, but when the fog falls over the city, our moods also drop). When two things are unrelated in theory, the results of their measurement should also be unrelated.

Together, the processes of convergence and divergence provide a thorough conceptual analysis by comparing measures that are assumed to be related to, or convergent with, the variable under study, or by contrasting measures assumed to be distinctly different, or divergent from the variable. All three ways of establishing internal validity (face, criterion, and construct validity) refer to the accuracy of measurement within one study. If the results of a study are both accurate and consistent (i.e., valid and reliable), we may want to generalize them or apply the results to some other setting or group of people. If we are interested in generalizing results in this way, we have to consider the matter of external validity.

External validity   External validity refers to the accuracy of applying conclusions from one research study to another setting or another group of people or messages. The most common way this happens in discovery research is when we apply results from one sample of people or messages to an entire population of people or messages. For example, election pollsters survey a few hundred people in order to say something about the likely voter behavior of thousands or even millions of people. When you want to generalize from one data sample to a larger population, external validity is a very important concern.

But researchers also sometimes wonder whether results from one study may be accurately applied to the same subjects in another setting. In this case, we are concerned with a special form of external validity called **ecological validity**—the relationship between the data in a research study and the larger environment of which that data is a part. Ecological validity is usually a concern in laboratory studies of communication behavior because researchers know that their participants may behave differently in the lab setting than they might behave when they are not participating in a research study. The lab offers the researcher control over important features of the setting and communication situation, but that control may reduce ecological validity.

As a general rule, tighter control over the variables of interest increases internal validity, but that usually comes at the cost of external validity. So even though a study may have excellent internal validity, it could be inaccurate to apply the conclusions from that study to people, messages, or settings beyond those included in the study. If the data for a study do not represent the larger population because there was some form of bias in the selection of research participants, then external validity will be threatened (i.e., generalization may not be warranted). If the setting in which the data were collected somehow biased the subjects' responses, then ecological validity is threatened.

In the next section, we will turn to the values of the interpretive paradigm in communication and to the specific warrants that interpretive scholars use to evaluate the merit of their research claims and data.

INTERPRETIVE PARADIGM WARRANTS

As you know from Chapter 1, interpretive research is rooted in philosophies that include the idea of multiple realities, where multiple, equally valid interpretations are socially constructed in communication among actors. Reality is best interpreted from the standpoint of the knower, and the ways of knowing most valued are subjective and situated, or contextualized, from the participants' perspectives. The purpose of interpretive research is to understand how meanings are created, maintained, or changed by participants. Therefore, the warrants for interpretive communication research address the researchers' ability to capture and represent multiple realities. Because interpretive researchers value subjectivity and rich description, the warrants for interpretive research are quite different than the warrants for discovery research: The discovery research argument rests on concerns for validity and reliability, but in interpretive research, these concerns shift toward researcher credibility, plausible interpretations, and transferable findings. Before we consider each of these warrants, let us describe in more detail the values embraced in interpretive communication research.

Interpretive Values: Subjectivity and Rich Description

Just as precision, power, and parsimony guide the discovery research project from start to finish, a preference for subjectivity and rich description guide interpretive researchers' choice of topics and research questions, data collection and analytic strategies, and standards for judging the worth of a research project. Like all cultural values, the values associated with interpretive communication research influence what counts as good data collection and analysis, and whether interpretive research is considered believable and important.

Subjectivity refers to our human ability to know using our minds, based on our thoughts and feelings. Subjectivism is the philosophy that all knowledge is subjective and relative, never objective. Subjectivity has to do with the idea that perception of reality is as important as, or more important than, any reality that exists independent of human perceptions. The issue of subjectivity and its role in interpretive communication research is huge. Interpretive researchers have taken a stance on the side of valuing subjectivity, whereas discovery researchers tend more toward valuing objectivity (i.e., the ability to know about something outside one's own perceptions, thoughts, and feelings).

One way that interpretive researchers often show that they value subjectivity is to privilege instances of communication as they normally occur, in contexts outside research projects. Interpretive researchers typically prefer natural observations and interviews, especially unstructured conversations between researchers and participants, over other methods of data collection such as written surveys (Newman & Benz, 1998). The preference for direct observation is linked to epistemology, specifically, the belief that face-to-face participation with other humans is needed to acquire social knowledge (Lofland & Lofland, 1984).

Valuing subjectivity goes beyond preferring participant views and natural settings, however. It extends to the researcher's thoughts and feelings as well. Peshkin (1988) argued that "researchers should systematically seek out their subjectivity, not retrospectively when the data have been collected and the analysis is complete, but while their research is actively in progress" (p. 17). Interpretive researchers are more likely than discovery researchers to acknowledge their initial reasons for being interested in a project because interpretive researchers see their subjective interests as important and legitimate. They value, rather than discount, the relationship between their interests and their research activities. In this way, Peshkin noted, researchers can see "how their subjectivity may be shaping their inquiry and its outcomes" (p. 17).

Rich description is the second value that best characterizes interpretive communication research (Lofland & Lofland, 1984; Miles & Huberman, 1994):

Your overall goal is to collect the *richest possible data*. Rich data mean, ideally, a wide and diverse range of information collected over a relatively long period of time. And for the naturalist, that data collection is achieved, again ideally, through direct, face-to-face contact with, and prolonged immersion in, some social location or circumstance (Lofland & Lofland, 1984, p. 11).

The interpretive paradigm value of rich description extends from the type and amount of data collected to the way that interpretive researchers typically depict their data in a research manuscript. Rich descriptions address every aspect of a social situation or text, such as the setting, the participants, their actions, relationships, and roles (Geertz, 1973). Rich descriptions are best achieved when the researcher is immersed in a social situation or the analysis of a text for a long time. Or if the researcher analyzes a social situation, rich description is enhanced by extensive face-to-face contact with the participants over time. Therefore, rich description serves at least two purposes: First, it allows the researcher to understand one text or social situation as fully as possible. Second, rich description helps the researcher be able to compare one text or social situation to another.

So rich description is important to interpretive researchers, whether they are studying participants' communicative behaviors in natural settings or conducting rhetorical analysis of communicative texts. The ethnographer or ethnomethodologist tends to use rich description to capture and depict the full range of participants' meanings. The rhetorical critic uses rich description to elaborate his or her multiple readings of the text. In any case, when your purpose is to describe one or more social situations or texts in detail, valuing rich description will guide you to several helpful data collection and analytic strategies. In the next section, we describe the general form of argument used in interpretive communication research to achieve rich descriptions. You already learned about this form of argument in Chapter 3. It is called triangulation.

Form of Argument: Demonstrating Multiple Realities

Because the philosophy of the interpretive paradigm includes the ideas of multiple realities and multiple valid interpretations of any reality, one standard for evaluating the merit of interpretive research is triangulation. We've chosen to reiterate the concept of triangulation here because it is a practice common to interpretive communication research. As you already know from Chapter 3, triangulation involves the use of multiple data collection sources, settings, analytic strategies, or investigator viewpoints. So you should already have some basic grasp of triangulation as a general research strategy for demonstrating multiple realities. We will now turn to three specific standards that interpretive researchers use to evaluate claims and data: researcher credibility, plausible interpretations, and transferable findings.

Researcher Credibility as a Standard for Evaluating Evidence

Researcher credibility means many things, and it is important in all research paradigms. But for interpretive communication studies, researcher credibility is an especially important standard because the *researcher* is the instrument through which interpretations are made, whether by interviewing, participant observation, or textual analysis (Patton, 1990). In this section, we will explore three aspects of researcher credibility: the researcher's training and experience, his or her degree of membership in the social situation under study, and faithfulness.

Training and experience   The researcher-as-instrument is a familiar concept among interpretive communication scholars. Interpretive methods for collecting and analyzing communication data rely on the researcher's skills and abilities to a somewhat greater degree than in discovery research, where some of the measurement can be warranted by an instrument outside the researcher, as we discussed in the case of criterion and construct validity. Interpretive researchers' instruments are their own skills at observing, interviewing, and analyzing texts.

Consider some of the skills you will need to be a successful participant-observer. You will need to be able to enter the field of observation in the least intrusive way. You will need to know how and when to blend in versus when to be openly in the learning role, or when to appear competent in the participant role. You will need to be adept at recalling and taking notes about what you see, hear, feel, touch, and smell. And this list is really just the tip of the iceberg!

Interviewers also need particular skills. As an interviewer, you will need to develop and ask questions;

know when and how to probe for additional information; know how to recognize and interpret evasions, avoidance, and lies from participants; be experienced in using audio or video recording equipment; be familiar with the practices of transcribing taped material to written form; and so on.

A similar list of learned skills can be named for textual analysts and rhetorical critics, who must select a focus of criticism, develop a theoretical and critical vocabulary, select perspectives from which to approach their work, and so on (Brock et al., 1990). And regardless of whether you are using participant observation, interviewing, textual criticism, or some combination of these methods, you will need both methodological awareness (Seale, 1999) and theoretical sensitivity (Strauss & Corbin, 1998). Both of these terms suggest highly developed knowledge of, and experience with, communication research methods and theories.

You already know a little bit about methodological awareness from the beginning of this chapter. **Theoretical sensitivity** is a similar concept, except that it connotes experience with and knowledge of communication theories, rather than research methodologies. Although interpretive researchers often enter the field of data collection without hypotheses, and sometimes without explicit research questions, they are not blank slates onto which the lived experience of participants can be written. Strauss and Corbin (1998) emphasized the "unquestionable fact (and advantage) that trained researchers are theoretically sensitized. Researchers carry into their research the sensitizing possibilities of their training, reading, and research experience, as well as explicit theories that might be useful if played against systematically gathered data" (p. 167).

Thus, the more developed your awareness of method and theory, the better tuned you will be as a research instrument, and the better choices you will be likely to make as you conduct your research. Think about one thing that you know how to do very well: Let's say it's dribbling a basketball. When you first learned it, you probably had to concentrate more than you do now, and you probably did it more slowly at first. But once you know something very well, you do it more effectively, faster, and with less exclusive concentration. The skills associated with researcher-as-instrument are something like that: It takes some specific knowledge of procedures (which we get from training) and some practice in context (which we get from experience) in order to be effective. Even highly trained and experienced interpretive researchers must think about their degree of membership in a social setting in order to develop good claims and evidentiary support for these claims.

Degree of membership Well-trained, highly experienced researchers are not automatically guaranteed interpretive credibility. One way that interpretive researchers gain credibility is to study social groups to which they already belong. A researcher's **degree of membership** in a social group can provide a number of advantages. First, members can sometimes gain access to the sites of study more easily than can nonmembers (Ellingson, 1998; Lindlof, 1995). Second, members can recognize and enact a range of communicative features, patterns, practices (and blunders in the enactment of these practices) in ways that nonmembers cannot (Dollar, 1995). Third, members ask different questions about a situation than do nonmembers; but even more importantly, members understand how social relationships and actions are constructed differently than do nonmembers.

For example, Ellingson (1998) described how her experience as a cancer survivor shaped her ethnographic research in an oncology clinic, and how the research influenced her own understanding of her personal experiences with cancer. "I believe I was more easily trusted and was afforded greater credibility by patients who knew I had survived cancer" (p. 500). In addition, "I could not have understood it intellectually, I don't think, if I had not experienced it emotionally" (Rothman, 1986, p. 53, as cited by Ellingson).

Membership is partly a matter of knowing the cultural rules of the situation you intend to study: You may know the cultural rules before you begin the study if you are a member, or you may intend to learn as you go if you are an outsider. Anthropologists call these emic and etic views of culture, respectively (Anderson, 1987). An **emic view** holds that the participants' understanding of what they are doing in the situation is the most useful or important. An **etic view** prefers the patterns of behavior that are available to the outside observer. Think back to Kim, Lujan, and Dixon's (1998) analysis of identity among American Indians in Oklahoma (from Chapter 3). Kim et al. combined emic and etic perspectives, as their six-member research team consisted of "three members who had Indian backgrounds and were longtime residents of Oklahoma. One of the three was an active, full-blooded Kiowa. The other three non-Indian members were of Asian, Black, and Irish backgrounds" (p. 259). In addition to the research team, 26 Indian students served as interviewers and coders, and 17 Indian residents served as community informants.

If your research claim concerns the rules that participants in a social situation use to construct and interpret their own and others' behaviors, then the emic, or insider perspective, may be your best choice for studying culture and communication. After all, insiders possess at least two kinds of cultural knowledge: **Explicit cultural knowledge** is used to interpret experience, or to read cultural artifacts, physical environments, and behavior and events (Spradley, 1980). **Tacit cultural knowledge** is used to generate behavior in culturally intended ways, including taking actions, feeling, and using cultural artifacts (e.g., what to wear, buy, eat, etc.).

However, not everyone agrees that membership status necessarily confers additional credibility on the interpretive researcher/participant/observer. A greater degree of membership may actually blind the researcher to "the peculiarities he is supposed to observe" (Newman & Benz, 1998, p. 59). In that case, using multiple observers, whose degree of membership in the situation being studied varies, may enrich the collection and interpretation of participant observation data.

It is also important to consider the collaborative relationships that interpretive researchers develop with participants, particularly when the researcher is not a member of the situation under study (Adelman & Frey, 1994; Frey, 1994a; Lindsley, 1999). In fact, multiple issues are associated with a researcher's degree of membership in any social situation. For example, culture-same pairings, such as women studying women, "smooth the way initially, promote empathy, and lead to better field relations and quality of data" (Lindlof, 1995, p. 140). The staff of the clinic where Ellingson conducted her observations were all women, except for the male physician who headed the program. "Being a woman undoubtedly helped me fit in with this group" (p. 501). But it is possible that differences between researchers and participants can be equally helpful, if for different reasons. Consider what barriers and advantages exist for the degree of fit (or lack of it) between your background and the participants' characteristics (Lofland & Lofland, 1984).

No matter whether you are an insider or an outsider in an interpretive research situation, you will need to make the familiar unfamiliar, and vice versa. Fred Davis (1973) described two roles you might take toward what you are studying, the Martian and the Convert. The Martian tries to make everything strange, in order to grasp it without imposing his own cultural knowledge, whereas the Convert tries to make it all familiar.

> Davis's metaphorical creatures represent very real methodological preferences and debates about those preferences within the social sciences. More profoundly, however, they symbolize a tension which many researchers feel *within themselves.* To ask questions of, to "make problematic", to "bracket" social life requires distance (Martian). To understand, to answer questions, to make sense of social life requires closeness (Convert). The sensitive investigator wishes not to be one or the other but to be *both* or *either* as the research demands (Lofland & Lofland, 1984, p. 16).

If you have accrued adequate training and experience to be a credible researcher and you have considered the issue of your degree of membership in the situation you are studying, you are ready to apply the third standard used to link interpretive research claims to data—faithfulness.

Faithfulness In interpretive research, **faithfulness** means both doing things right and doing the right things. To be faithful means to remain constant or steadfast. An interpretive researcher's faithfulness is demonstrated in a number of ways. Prolonged engagement in the field or topic of study is the hallmark of faithfulness. For instance, Spradley (1980) noted that "immersion is the time-honored strategy used by most ethnographers. By cutting oneself off from other interests and concerns, by listening to informants hour on end, by participating in the cultural scene, and by allowing one's mental life to be taken over by the new culture, themes often emerge" (p. 145).

Morse (1998) expressed a similar observation:

> Good qualitative researchers must be prepared to learn to be trusted in the setting; they must be patient and wait until they are accepted by informants; they must be flexible and resilient. . . . Good researchers are meticulous

about their documentation, file methodically, and keep notes up-to-date. . . . Good researchers revel in the intellectual work of making sense of their data . . . on being haunted by the puzzle of their data (p. 67).

As you can see from the above passages, interpretive researchers engage in detailed hard work, which is another reason that makes faithfulness an important warrant for interpretive research. A faithful researcher will steadfastly do the right things, even when those things are difficult.

Faithfulness comes, in part, from researchers remaining very close to the data they collect. Doing your own fieldwork, transcription, filing, coding, and writing are some specific and practical ways that you can practice faithfulness. Another aspect of faithfulness comes from identifying your own assumptions about a research topic, setting, or participants at the outset of your research project. Finally, faithful researchers acknowledge their limitations honestly and forthrightly, not only in terms of the data, but also in terms of themselves as research instruments. For instance, Witmer (1997) disclosed that a legal secretary with professional transcription experience transcribed the speaker tapes for her study into computer text files.

Plausible Interpretations as a Standard for Evaluating Evidence

Because interpretive researchers usually believe that there are many potentially legitimate interpretations of any social situation, their task is to develop plausible, rather than correct or accurate, interpretations of a situation. In this section we will present three aspects of developing plausible interpretations: adequacy of evidence, coherence, and negative case analysis.

Adequacy of evidence "**Adequacy** refers to the amount of data collected, rather than to the number of subjects, as in quantitative research. Adequacy is attained when sufficient data have been collected that saturation occurs and variation is both accounted for and understood" (Morse, 1998, p. 76). The interpretive researcher must overlap tasks of data collection and analysis, in order to make good decisions about when adequate evidence has been collected.

You will cease to collect interpretive research data when the data you have accrued is adequate to test your claim. Here are a couple of tests by which you can

determine adequacy. First, you may elect to exit the field of data collection when you sense a taken-for-grantedness, when everything in that situation seems routine, and nothing surprises you anymore. Second, you may recognize **theoretical saturation,** when any new data that you collect adds little that is new or useful to the explanation or categories you have already generated (Snow, 1980).

Lindlof (1995) advised that interpretive researchers complete three tasks on their way toward quitting the field. These tasks were to check out questionable hunches, evaluate the credibility of informants, and settle any "outstanding moral and material debts to informants and others . . . leave on good terms" (p. 242). All of these tasks will help you to ensure that you will have collected adequate evidence to elicit plausible interpretations.

Coherence For many communication researchers, the concept of **coherence** in interpretive research has gradually replaced a concept that was more directly linked to discovery research, that of internal validity. For example, in 1982, LeCompte and Goetz argued that ethnographic methods had superior internal validity, but at the expense of external validity (i.e., generalizability). Internal validity, they argued, came from four features of the ethnographic method: First, due to membership and sustained participant observation, the ethnographer can refine interpretations over time. Second, interviews with informants use the participants' phrasing and vocabulary, increasing the chance of tapping the data the researcher seeks (the emic view), whereas survey items are in researcher language, and may be misinterpreted by participants. Third, the natural settings within which participant observations occur may increase the validity of observed behaviors, relative to more contrived researcher settings. Fourth, the researcher's self-monitoring process in data analysis requires continual questioning of the data (LeCompte & Goetz, 1982, p. 43).

Miles and Huberman (1994) identified some specific steps you might take to achieve coherent interpretations, including noting patterns or themes; clustering similar concepts together; making metaphors; counting; drawing comparisons; subsuming particulars into a general interpretation; and building a logical chain of evidence. Although space limitations prevent us from giving more detailed explanations of each of these techniques, we hope you can see that each one is a way of synthesizing particular observations or bits of data into broader interpretations. Coherent interpretations of this sort convey the researcher's detailed understanding of a social situation to people who have not lived in that situation.

But in order for such a contribution to be valuable, your coherent interpretations must be internally consistent. Deetz (1982) added that internal consistency is, in part, "more what would have to be denied if the understanding were not accepted than what it claims if accepted" (p. 148). If you have collected adequate evidence and developed a coherent interpretation of the social situation or text, you are ready for one final means of ensuring plausible interpretations, negative case analysis.

Negative case analysis Negative case analysis is a conscientious search for counterexamples, that is, instances of data that do not fit your categories or explanations of a social situation (Lindlof, 1995; Jackson, 1986). If instances of data are found that do *not* fit your interpretations, then you must "redefine the hypothesis to accommodate the data. The analyst keeps considering new data, and revising the hypothesis, until there are no more negative cases to account for. Ultimately, negative case analysis results in a highly confident statement about a phenomenon" (Lindlof, 1995, p. 240).

In the normal course of interpretive scholarship, you will develop an initial claim using some inductive process. **Inductive reasoning** involves generalizing from particular cases, whereas **deductive reasoning** involves "moving from the general to the particular" (Bulmer, 1979, p. 660). In an interpretive research project, you are more likely to operate in an inductive, rather than a deductive, fashion because inductive reasoning will help you "to maintain faithfulness to the empirical data while abstracting and generalizing from a relatively small number of cases" (Bulmer, 1979, p. 661).

Conversation and discourse analysts, and some rhetorical critics, refer to this reasoning process as **analytic induction.** Sally Jackson (1986) outlined the method of analytic induction in her essay titled, "Building a case for claims about discourse structure":

> The process of analytic induction begins with collection of a set of examples of the phenomenon being studied. The examples are used to build, inductively, a hypothesis. The hypothesis may be about the properties

of a class, the rules that generate a pattern of interaction, the sequential characteristics of a kind of interaction, or some other empirical issue. An initial test of the hypothesis is its adequacy as an account of the examples. But this is only a preliminary step. The method of analytic induction is driven by a falsificationist attitude, which subjects any hypothesis about discourse structure to critical examination. The method of analytic induction requires that empirical claims be tested through active, procedurally diverse search for counter-examples (p. 129).

Thus, for ethnographers and ethnomethodologists, negative case analysis is a way of evaluating the interpretations developed in the field, by analyzing participant observations, interviews, and field notes, and sometimes by collecting additional data to back up or test initial interpretations. For conversation and discourse analysts, the search for counterexamples is a more central aspect of data analysis, rather than a standard used to warrant its worth (Pomerantz, 1990; Jacobs, 1990).

Transferable Findings as a Standard for Evaluating Evidence

So far, we have considered the interpretive standards of researcher credibility and plausible interpretations. One additional test of the worth of interpretive research is **transferability**—the ability to transfer insights from one study to other settings, participants, or texts. Transferability is related to, but not the same as, **generalizability** as it is used in the discovery paradigm. In discovery research, a study is generalizable if the sample selected adequately represents the population of interest (Kerlinger, 1986). If a sample well represents the population, then findings based on a small sample of subjects can be trusted to apply to all those people who were not studied, but who are members of the same population.

Because of the contextual nature of the phenomena studied by interpretive researchers, phenomena that are situated in time and place, "the move to generalize in the traditional sense is neither warranted nor particularly desirable" (Lindlof, 1995, p. 238). Transferability is less direct than generalizability. It means that an interpretive insight is heuristic, or useful in another way, even though it cannot be directly applied in another setting or with other participants, the way that generalizability implies. In order for an interpretive insight to be of use in some other setting, or with other texts or participants, it must be both confirmable in the original study and relevant. We will describe each of these aspects of transferability in more detail.

Confirmability The discovery researcher's quest for accuracy, or valid research findings, rests on the assumption of *one* observable reality. Since interpretive researchers presume multiple subjective realities, they seek findings that are confirmable, rather than accurate, per se. The question of accuracy in interpretive research might better be phrased as "accurate for whom?" Member checks and audit trails are two strategies you may use in order to establish confirmability.

Member checks can be used to verify the interpretations that you have attributed to members in the course of doing fieldwork (Janesick, 1998; Lindlof, 1995; Miles & Huberman, 1994; Strauss & Corbin, 1998). Member checks involve allowing your research participants to review some or all of the materials that you have prepared, such as field notes, interview transcripts, and narrative research reports (Lindlof, 1995). The persons who participate in member checks need not be key informants or people with whom you have had any prolonged engagement. Member checks can be informal, even spontaneous. For example, you might perform member checks with people who have been, up until that point, insiders to the culture but outsiders to the research project (Lindlof, 1995). However, consistent with the interpretive research value of subjectivity, "no participant is a dispassionate, fully informed member of his or her culture. A person's alliances and passions about certain things, and disinterest about others, surely affect what he or she can authenticate" (Lindlof, 1995, p. 241).

Carbaugh (1988) used **performance tests,** another form of member checking. Carbaugh conducted participant observations and interviews at a television station and developed interpretations about how the employees there viewed themselves and their workplace. He tried out his interpretations by returning to the scene and using the categories (types of persons) that he had developed while talking with the employees. Then he would take note of their reactions to his usage of the categories. For example, if the employees affirmed his usage or if the interaction was seamless (that is, there was no indication that the employee disagreed with his interpretation), Carbaugh considered his interpretations confirmed.

Douglas (1976) used the term **fronting** to describe participants' attempts to avoid telling the whole truth when being interviewed. Fronting includes not only telling outright lies, but also half-truths, evading answering a question, and so on. The term comes from a dramatistic metaphor, where the aspects of a situation that can be seen by an audience are considered frontstage. Other aspects, also important to the situation, are not seen by the audience and so are backstage. Fronting is probably most likely in public settings, with people who have or desire power to maintain face or, because of ulterior motives, either to thwart or please the researcher (Lindlof, 1995).

Obviously, fronting is a concern in performing member checks, just as it can be a concern in conducting interviews in the first place. Interview participants use fronting to deceive researchers and themselves. But fronting can give you valuable clues toward understanding the participant's world, if you see it occur (Van Maanen, 1988). So fronting is not a threat to your ability to develop plausible interpretations. Rather, fronting adds a layer of complexity in understanding your participants' subjective realities. You may detect fronting when performing member checks, or it may be just a suspicion that you log into field notes and that later develops into part of an interpretation about the communication in that setting. Such notes will be useful later if you maintain a careful audit trail.

An **audit trail** is your best way of documenting the development and progress of an interpretive research study. It is important because of the massive quantity of data that is generated in interpretive research; without the audit trail, you may end up with a warehouse of information of which no sense can be made. Notes from participant observations and interviews, plus expanded accounts, journal entries, analysis, and interpretation notes, all need to be retrievable as you write up your interpretive research report. You may have encountered ethical problems, for example, and want to write about your response to those problems later (Spradley, 1980). Carefully documenting the conceptual development of a project helps you retrace your steps when reporting how your interpretations were developed.

A good audit trail also provides evidence that interested parties (like your research methods teacher) can use to reconstruct the process by which you reached your conclusions. An audit trail consists of several types of documentation, including (1) raw data; (2) data reduction and analysis products like category lists or classification schemes; (3) data reconstruction and synthesis products; (4) process notes related to the setting, including permission agreements with participants; (5) materials relating to the researcher's intentions and dispositions; and (6) instrument development information such as interview guides (Lincoln & Guba, 1985; Miles & Huberman, 1994; Morse, 1998). Your audit trail will help you document the relevance of specific interpretations, should you want to transfer those interpretations to another setting, participant, or text.

Relevance In order for an interpretive finding to be transferable, it must not only be confirmable in the original setting or text, but it must also be relevant to the setting or text in which its insight is expected to contribute. This kind of relevance involves a translation of sorts: "A translation discovers the meanings in one culture and communicates them in such a way that people with another cultural tradition can understand them" (Spradley, 1980, p. 161). It is possible for you to do a good job of discovering cultural meanings, but a bad job of communicating those meanings to another audience. In Appendix A, "Writing Research Reports and Critical Essays," you will learn about some other ways that you can make your interpretive findings relevant, and thus more transferable, to others outside your project.

CRITICAL PARADIGM
WARRANTS

As we said in Chapter 1, the critical studies paradigm is associated with the most recent changes in communication research. Whereas the subjective views of the researcher and the participants are something to *control for* in discovery research, and are acknowledged as *legitimate* in interpretive research studies, the critical researcher *embraces* subjectivity. In ideological arguments, the researcher's subjective evaluation and criticism of the text, or other evidence upon which claims are based, is desirable and valuable. If other people disagree with a critical scholar's evaluations or ideas about what social practice ought to be changed,

they are free to resist those ideas in a variety of ways or to ignore them altogether. "In a way, this suits critical theory, because of the common belief in the existence of contradiction. Society is filled with contradictions, so why should critical studies be any different?" (Littlejohn, 2002, p. 230) In fact, a growing number of critical social science studies are now being published in communication journals, and Littlejohn (2002) noted: "Although critical theories borrow liberally from relevant concepts of other traditions . . . they also constitute an oppositional critique of many of these other traditions" (p. 229).

Critical scholars, then, "are not expected to engage in any formal, intra-study verification" (Fink & Gantz, 1996, p. 119). Fink and Gantz (1996) noted that 98% of the critical studies they analyzed, which were published between 1990 and 1992, reported no verification procedures. That is to say, the authors of those studies did not explicitly reference in their reports any effort to formally verify their data, instruments, or results. "It can be argued that a good literature review serves as verification for a study by positioning that study appropriately in the context of a given research history" (Fink & Gantz, 1996, p. 128). In this sense, the data and conclusions of critical studies may be verified by the context into which they are placed, given the literature review that accompanies a particular critical analysis.

Contrast the view of warrants for critical arguments presented by Fink and Gantz (1996) with the view provided by Newman and Benz (1998), who pointed out that scholars from various methodological camps have tried to legitimize qualitative research strategies, and that two such attempts are related to the critical paradigm. First, Newman and Benz noted, postmodernists claim that "there can be no criteria for judging qualitative research" (1998, p. 18). Moreover, they asserted that critical poststructuralists believe that new criteria, completely different from those of both the positivists and postpositivists, need to be developed. However, the development of any new criteria is always problematic because any new criteria will still need to rely on some ideological authority in order to be accepted (Newman & Benz, 1998).

This is a good point at which to reemphasize that methodologists' *descriptions* of communication research methods, as well as their *practices* in conducting research studies, are informed by their paradigmatic commitments. We strongly believe in the value of multimethod communication scholarship. We have tried very hard in this book to portray all three paradigms evenhandedly, but you will probably detect our own framings of certain methodological issues.

Emancipatory Values: Voice and Liberation

Two values undergird the methodology of critical studies in communication: voice and liberation. The *Western Journal of Communication* published a series of a dozen or so essays on **voice** in 1997, essays that "grapple[d] with the theoretical, personal, social, and political issues related to the voices in which we write and the voices of those we study and about whom we write" (Vande Berg, 1997, p. 87). Voice is related to existence and participation in our democratic society because one of the ways that we participate is by making our voice heard. If our voice is never heard, it's as though we don't exist. Ellingson (1998) illustrated the function of voice in her ethnography of an oncology clinic: "I feel a powerful urge to be heard. When I tell my story and others' stories, I seek acknowledgment (from myself and others) of what we suffered" (p. 510).

Making your voice heard is the first step toward **liberation,** which can be defined as the "securing of equal social and economic rights" (Guralnik, 1986, p. 814). If you prefer, you could use the word **emancipate,** which means "to set free, release from bondage, or from constraint" (Guralnik, 1986, p. 455). Both these words point toward the critical scholars' emancipatory values. Critical scholarship aims to give voice to people who are underrepresented in the current societal discourse, and to liberate those people from the bonds of ideological oppression (i.e., liberation through awareness). The claims and evidence of critical scholarship are evaluated by considering the researcher's position in relation to the topic, and the basic form of argument that is used is to demonstrate the need for ideological change.

Form of Argument: Demonstrating Ideological Need for Change

Because critical communication studies emphasize claims of evaluation and reform, the basic argument made in these studies is that there is a need to change some existing ideology. As we will discuss in more detail in Chapter 13, "Critical Studies," **ideology** is "a set of ideas that structure a group's reality . . .

a code of meanings governing how individuals and groups see the world" (Littlejohn, 2002, p. 211). Awareness of a need to change, or perhaps dissatisfaction with some present view or circumstance, is the first precursor to change itself. In critical studies, ideological changes are typically attempted first by the researcher's efforts to raise awareness of unjust power relations (e.g., Pearce, 1998).

Hegemony occurs "when events or texts are interpreted in a way that promotes the interests of one group over those of another" (Littlejohn, 2002, p. 211). Thus, the basic form of argument for critical communication research is to demonstrate the ideological need for change, due to hegemonic oppression, and to assert that all members of a society should share equal rights and privileges:

> The growing prominence of critical perspectives on communication influences and is influenced by the concurrent general awareness of inequities in the prevailing social order. . . . Scholars, like people in other walks of life, are not immune to growing awareness of disadvantage and social injustice. Yet scholars cannot fully respond to these problems within traditional theoretical frameworks that emphasize scholarly detachment and objective attitudes. . . . Although experimental, quantitative studies continue to be conducted and add to knowledge, there is clearly increasing support for qualitative, interpretive research and the deep understandings it fosters. . . . Taken together, critical and interpretive impulses are enlarging the terrain of scholarship and the means by which scholars go about their work (Wood, 1997, pp. 361–362).

In order to argue a need for ideological change, critical scholars highlight such factors as the stability of the dominant ideology. If the dominant code of meanings (or worldview) is very stable, then power relations are heavily entrenched and resistant to change. If there are already competing ideologies at work in a social situation, then multiple interpretations of power relations, and change, may be more likely (see Dow, 1990, and Shugart, 1997, for examples of this line of argument).

Kim's (1999) critique of the Western view of communication avoidance solely as a deficiency is one example of critical communication scholarship aimed at raising awareness of hegemonic oppression and encouraging change in a familiar and, until now, relatively stable ideology. Kim pointed out that the motivation to approach, rather than avoid, communicating with others (and thus, asserting oneself) has been privileged by Western theorizing and research, due to a philosophical bias toward individualism. That bias privileges assertiveness over avoidance. For instance, students in U.S. classrooms are taught that they must speak up to get what they need and that if they do not speak out, then the fact that their needs may be overlooked is, at least in part, their own fault.

Researcher Positionality as a Standard for Evaluating Evidence

Because critical scholars value voice and liberation, they place great emphasis on their own subjective positions in relation to the topics that they select to study. We use the term **researcher positionality** to include both the researcher's standpoint and his or her reflexivity. Let's first consider each of these terms.

Standpoint theory "argues that the material, social, and symbolic circumstances of a social group shape what members of that group experience, as well as how they think, act, and feel" (Wood, 1997, p. 384). Your standpoint as a researcher will affect the topics you believe are worthy of study, the views of a topic you elect to present or to ignore, and the kinds of reform you work to effect. Our standpoints depend on our membership in various social groups because what we see of the world depends on where we are standing as we view it. For example, "standpoint logic would suggest that whites are less likely than people of color to recognize the continuing legacy of racism and discrimination" because people of color have conscious experiences of being discriminated against, whereas white people living in the United States have likely benefited from racism in ways that are invisible, or unexamined (Wood, p. 255).

Yep's (1997) essay, "My three cultures: Navigating the multicultural identity landscape," described his standpoint as an "Asianlatinoamerican":

> Although I have never been to China, I am racially what my parents describe as "100% pure Chinese." During my formative years, we lived in Peru, South America and later moved to the United States. . . . I am trilingual (English, Spanish, Chinese), and I speak all three languages with a slight accent. I used to be concerned about the accent in my speech, but in recent years I have adopted a different attitude: My accent might simply be an indication that I probably speak more languages than my conversational partner (p. 43).

All three of Yep's cultural memberships, "Asianlatinoamerican," contribute to his standpoint, which he views as connected and unified, although not "necessarily harmonious and free of tension" (1997, p. 54). Yep's awareness of how each culture contributes to his thoughts, actions, and feelings in communicating with others, and to his scholarship, is called **reflexivity.**

Reflexivity is a process by which researchers recognize that they are inseparable from the settings, contexts, and cultures they are attempting to understand and represent. Critical scholars use reflexivity to question their own interpretations and representations of social situations (e.g., May & Pattillo-McCoy, 2000; Nakayama & Krizek, 1995).

Quite often, critical scholars will consider one particular social situation, or one case in which they have some intrinsic interest. "Perhaps the simplest rule for method in qualitative casework is this: Place the best brains available into the thick of what is going on. The brainwork ostensibly is observational, but more basically, reflective" (Stake, 1998, p. 99). If you are considering a particular case in which you have some interest, reflexivity becomes very important. For instance, you might select a case of "some typicality, but leaning toward those cases that seem to offer *opportunity to learn*" (Stake, 1998, p. 101). Once you select a particular case to study, sampling people, places, and events to observe within that case is also a factor on which you should reflect. Here, variety, rather than representativeness per se, should guide your selection decisions. The primary criterion is the opportunity to learn (Stake, 1998; Frey, 1994a). For example, Frey (1994a) urged communication researchers to study underresearched populations and groups because they offer an opportunity to learn something that is not represented in existing published communication research.

Perhaps we can further illustrate researcher positionality as a warrant for critical scholarship by considering the method of historical criticism. Historical criticism is primarily accomplished by analyzing existing texts, or documents, but some historical critics also employ case studies and interviews (e.g., Carpenter, 1999; Lewis, 1997; McLaughlin, 1991). In either case, "the interpretation of history varies with the subjective social experience of the historian" (Newman & Benz, 1998, p. 73). Furthermore, historical methods sometimes require the researcher to "reconstruct the facts from unverifiable sources. These facts are based on their plausibility and can only be inferred" (Newman & Benz, 1998, p. 70, citing Mouly). It is at this point that historical criticism bridges the interpretive and critical paradigms. Historical critics' explicit reliance on their subjectivity is consistent with critical scholarship, and the plausibility of inferences is consistent with interpretive scholarship. In fact, some communication researchers refer to their work as *critical-interpretive* research (e.g., Deetz, 1982; Scheibel, 1994, 1996).

THREE VIEWS OF TRUTH

So far in this chapter, we have looked at the values, forms of argument, and standards for evaluating evidence in three paradigms for communication research. In the research-as-argument model, all of these elements together comprise the warrants for communication research. Each paradigm has different warrants, in part, because the very nature of truth itself is viewed differently in each paradigm.

In the following sections, we will present three views of truth, each one associated with one of the three paradigms of communication research. It is likely that you will find yourself strongly identifying with one paradigm's view of truth and want to reject the other views of truth. Since we are trying to present these paradigms fairly and not lead you to accept one or reject another, we will let these views of truth be represented by the authors of published research in each paradigm. We begin with the most recent, and perhaps most radical view of truth, that adopted by communication researchers from the critical paradigm.

Critical Paradigm

Communication researchers who embrace the critical paradigm tend to believe that truth is individual and fragmented at best; no one thing is true for all people, at all times, in all places. Rather, because people have different standpoints, truth is subjective and

political (power-related). Strauss and Corbin (1998) summarized the relationships among power, ideology, and truth as follows:

> Power certainly affects the ability to convince audiences, including probably oneself, if one takes one's power seriously. Ideologies we all have—we all have political and other positions. . . . The feminist critique of the objective biases of traditional science seems to us correct insofar as some scientists may assume they are just human instruments reporting on nature. . . . Contemporary physical and biological scientists seem to understand quite well the naivete of such a position . . . (p. 180).

Denzin and Lincoln (1998) called the idea that there is no one knowable truth a "postmodern sensibility" (p. 9). However, the debate over *truth* is more specific and discrete than whether one knowable truth exists or more than one. Thomas (1994) pointed out that the contested meanings in content analysis are not about which messages fit into which categories, as warranted by estimates of intercoder reliability. "For instance, if there is a count of words or a coding of characters' hair color, or even noting violent acts (as explicitly defined), few would argue that these measurements alone are sites of contested meaning" (Thomas, 1994, p. 693). Rather, what is likely to be contested is whether particular categories should even be counted in a study, or whether the distribution of categories means what the researcher thinks it means.

Moreover, some critical researchers have condemned all statistical analysis of communication data as reductionist and fragmented. Again, Thomas (1994) argued that people don't like to place human behaviors into categories, for two reasons. First, "we may believe that our species is too complex and sophisticated to respond to the same techniques of observation acceptably applied to many other phenomena," like weather patterns, chemical reactions, and so forth (p. 692). Second, many people oppose stereotyping, or treating people *like numbers* (i.e., interchangeably). In that case, we might equate research that categorizes communication behavior in numerical terms with stereotyping humans. Thomas concluded:

> I would like to point out here that verifying a finding through statistics is (logically) no more positivist than verifying it through detailed

verbal explanation. It should not be discounted that the fear and loathing many individuals have toward numbers, math, and statistics may also be guiding their methodological philosophies (and, on a larger scale, career choice) (p. 692).

Indeed, McCain and Segal (1988) pointed out that "although science plays a dominant role in our society, only a small minority has any serious understanding of it" (p. 9). They characterized hostility as one attitude that people have toward science, including social science:

> We all have belief systems that require certain statements to be true, and we won't accept denial of those truths from anyone. . . . we become emotionally involved with our beliefs, and woe to those who challenge them, no matter what the argument or evidence. Thus, the social sciences, which often challenge our personal beliefs, are applauded when they agree with us and scorned when they disagree (p. 18).

It is very likely that critical communication studies are being met with these same emotional reactions. When we agree with the author of a critical essay, we applaud that person's progressive contribution; when we disagree, we scorn that author, that study, or perhaps the entire paradigm.

Interpretive Paradigm

In the interpretive research paradigm, truth is viewed as subjective but not wholly personal. Rather, some collective truths can be ascertained by social agreement, which may be relatively stable or unstable. Even so, Denzin and Lincoln (1998) pointed out that interpretive and critical research is often seen as "an attack on reason and truth" (p. 7). Here, reason and truth are represented by positivist scholarship as it is practiced in the hard sciences, like physics, chemistry, or economics. "At the same time, the positive science attack on qualitative research is regarded as an attempt to legislate one version of truth over another" (Denzin & Lincoln, 1998, p. 7).

For the interpretive communication researcher, truth is subject to the interpretations of human actors who participate in *and* who conduct academic research, which is one reason interpretive researchers work to systematically include multiple perspectives

in their research. As Strauss and Corbin (1998) pointed out: "Perhaps not every actor's perspectives can be discovered, or need be, but those of actors who sooner or later are judged to be significantly relevant must be incorporated. . . . These are *also* interpreted conceptually by the researcher" (p. 172).

May and Pattillo-McCoy (2000) also addressed the interpretive view of *truth* in their collaborative ethnographic study of a neighborhood community center. "Indeed, most academic writing (primarily journals and books) requires that there be some suggestion that the author is offering the 'truth' about the field he or she studied. What our experience taught us was that there is neither one truth nor one reality" (May & Pattillo-McCoy, 2000, p. 67). The authors emphasized that collaborative ethnography offered several advantages, such as increasing detail in field notes, pointing out inconsistencies, and revealing the subjectivity of each researcher due to background, experience, race, class, gender, and so on. Yet they cautioned, "We do not believe that if we just had enough people in the field, then we might have got at some reality that is more true than the one we recorded" (p. 84).

Furthermore, what any one researcher or participant sees, at any one moment, in any social setting is bound to look slightly different at another moment in that same setting:

> All interpretations are temporally limited— in a dual sense. First, they are always provisional, they are never established forever; their very nature allows for endless elaboration and partial negation (qualification). Second, like many other kinds of knowledge, theories are limited in time: Researchers and theorists are not gods, but men and women living in certain eras, immersed in certain societies, subject to current ideas and ideologies, and so forth (Strauss & Corbin, 1998, p. 171).

The provisional, temporal nature of interpretive truths is also relevant in rhetorical criticism. For example, Brock et al. (1990) allowed that rhetorical critics adhere to authority and tradition as criteria for evaluating the effectiveness of persuasive appeals *because* the dictates of authority and tradition have already shown themselves to be logical and coherent. Even if a rhetorical scholar rejects a tradition, "she or he will probably do so either because it fails to do what it promises or because the critic appeals to standards that are outside the tradition" (Brock et al.,

1990, p. 19). In either case, accepting authority and tradition as guidelines, or rejecting those guidelines for criticism, involves an appeal to subjective truths.

Discovery Paradigm

Adherents to the discovery paradigm agree that truths exist that can be objectively verified. The standard design features and controls for rival hypotheses common to quantitative research (and which are the focus of Chapter 6, "Experimental Research") link quantitative research questions and evidence to their truth values (Newman & Benz, 1998). As you already know, validity means accuracy in measurement of variables, and appropriate attempts to generalize findings from one study to another setting, group of participants, and so on. To the degree that variables are reliably and validly measured, findings are confirmed as *true,* or empirically verified.

Newman and Benz (1998) asserted that "science, as reflected in the scientific method, is the only defensible way of locating and verifying truth" (p. 10).

As we mentioned earlier, with respect to the critical paradigm's view of truth, science has been the subject of some hostile backlash in recent years, in many disciplines. Robert Abelson (1995), a statistics professor at Yale for 42 years, wrote:

> The field of statistics is misunderstood by students and nonstudents alike. The general public distrusts statistics because media manipulators often attempt to gull them with misleading statistical claims. . . . Suspicion of false advertising is fair enough, but to blame the problem on statistics is unreasonable. . . . Rather than mindlessly trashing any and all statements with numbers in them, a more mature response is to learn enough about statistics to distinguish honest, useful conclusions from skullduggery or foolishness (p. 1).

TECHNOLOGY AND WARRANTS FOR RESEARCH ARGUMENTS

As we said in the first three chapters, technology influences communication research in two important ways. In the first instance, technology is a topic for communication researchers, who examine how technologies are changing and shaping and are shaped by human communication processes. In the second instance, technology is changing the means of doing research, as it is used to assist researchers in the collection, analysis, presentation, and dissemination of research evidence. In this chapter, technology is most relevant as it relates to the values embraced by discovery, interpretive, and critical communication researchers, and as it impacts the way we link research evidence to claims (i.e., warrant research).

The values implicit in conducting research are changing right along with the technological shifts that are altering all our lives. The values of all three paradigms are implicated in these changes. Just as digital technology can increase precision and power, it can also enhance rich description and, potentially, can be a means of liberation as well as a potential means of oppression. The precise nature of these value shifts, in relation to particular technologies, is a great topic for communication research (e.g., Tardy & Hale, 1998).

Further, technological innovations are already affecting, and will continue to affect the means by which we all warrant communication research. For example, it's likely that you will present findings using technological means, whether that means showing charts and graphs to an audience using PowerPoint, playing some videotaped interaction at a conference, or conducting member checks over email with your research participants. The potential of digital technology for storing, retrieving, and disseminating communication evidence has hardly even begun to be realized. For example, a CD-ROM can hold the amount of data that once took up whole file cabinets, but a CD-ROM can be carried, copied, and digitally searched in ways that file cabinets cannot.

Computer software programs are becoming more user-friendly and more ubiquitous, which could result in the means of collecting and analyzing research data being accessible to a broader audience of users (i.e., not just academic researchers). It's now not unusual to expect college graduates to use spreadsheets and conduct simple quantitative analyses of data—activities that were once the province of professional researchers. Ten years ago you needed a specialized software program to analyze numerical data collected from 100 or more surveys; now Excel (or similar programs) will do that analysis, and most personal computer users can navigate the program.

Finally, technological changes will continue to transform all our contexts for communicating (e.g., work, home/family, community), so that whether you are a researcher or not after college, you will have to evaluate technology, use it, and negotiate the ways that it changes your communication. Just as we linked paradigm values to the standards by which you can judge whether particular evidence supports a research question, you will need to link your values to the standards by which you judge technology in all these contexts. Research from all three paradigms can help us all figure out the degree to which technology changes are fulfilling their potential (e.g., more equal access to information and participation in decision-making for everyone).

SUMMARY

In this chapter, we have outlined the third element of the research-as-argument model, the warrants and backing. We cannot begin to include all the backing (i.e., social, cultural, and procedural rules and knowledge) that experienced researchers bring to bear on their assessments of a study's merit. Knowing this, we elected to begin the description of warrants for each epistemological paradigm by presenting some of the values embraced by researchers in that paradigm. We also presented a basic form of argument for each paradigm. Discovery researchers typically seek to demonstrate causality, interpretive researchers seek to demonstrate multiple realities, and critical researchers seek to demonstrate the ideological need for change.

For each of these three paradigms, we have presented some of the standards by which you can assure the value of your data collection and analytic sources, strategies, and settings. These standards link particular research claims to evidence (or data). In the discovery paradigm, the warrants ensure consistent and accurate measurement of variables, as well as accurate attempts to apply the results of data analysis from one study to another group of people or messages. In interpretive research, the warrants assure the researcher's credibility as an interpreter of the data, and they also specify when it is and is not appropriate to transfer the results of data analysis from one setting to another. Finally, in the critical paradigm, the warrant reveals the positionality of the researchers, both their standpoint and the degree to which they are reflexive (i.e., aware of their own position). Revealing your own position will allow others to more freely consider the source, and choose to accept or to reject your ideas.

As we said in Chapter 1, backing for any argument rests on a large body of information that clarifies how the warrants are to be understood, applied, and relied upon. Ultimately, the backing or support for any warrant depends on the researcher's conceptualization of truth. Hence, we concluded this chapter by comparing three possible views of truth; we argued that these views are associated with these three ways of knowing about communication.

KEY TERMS

Adequacy	Correlation	Etic view of culture
Agreement among judges	Criterion validity	Explicit cultural knowledge
Alternate forms method	Deductive reasoning	External validity
Analytic induction	Degree of membership	Face validity
Audit trail	Divergent validity	Faithfulness
Coherence	Ecological validity	Fronting
Concurrent validity	Emancipate	Generalizability
Construct validity	Emic view of culture	Hegemony
Content validity	Equivalence	Homogeneity
Convergent validity	Errors in data processing	Ideology

Inductive reasoning

Instrument clarity

Intercoder reliability

Internal consistency

Internal validity

Interrater reliability

Intertranscriber reliability

Liberation

Measurement reliability

Member checks

Methodological awareness

Negative case analysis

Panel of judges

Parsimony

Performance tests

Power

Precision

Predictive validity

Public scrutiny

Random individual or situational
    differences

Reflexivity

Reliability

Researcher positionality

Rich description

Stability

Subjectivity

Tacit cultural knowledge

Test-retest method

Transferability

Theoretical saturation

Theoretical sensitivity

Validity

Voice

DISCUSSION QUESTIONS

1. Think back to the one thing you said you knew for sure, when you first read Chapter 1. We asked you to make some argument for how you knew that thing. Was your argument a causal argument, an argument about your own (or another person's) subjective reality, or an argument about something that needs to be changed?

2. Which paradigm's view of truth that we outlined in this chapter seems nearest to your own current view of truth? Why?

"TRY IT!" ACTIVITY

The Great Debate: How Should We Prioritize Research Values?

Along with your classmates, form two small teams of about 4 or 5 people each. Select one of the following research topics: (1) What is the relationship between media consumption and violent crime in the United States? (2) What is the relationship between judicial process and racial/cultural membership? Develop a position, with your team, as to the rank order of the following research values (i.e., rank the most important value first, the next most important value second, and so on, until you have identified the least important value on this list):

1. Liberation
2. Parsimony
3. Power
4. Precision
5. Rich description
6. Subjectivity
7. Voice

5

Survey Research

ABSTRACT

In this chapter, you will learn how to conduct survey research in communication, beginning with developing descriptive, explanatory, and predictive *claims*. Then, you will learn about survey *data* collection sources and strategies, including cross-sectional and longitudinal research designs, sampling techniques, interviews and questionnaires, and instrumentation. Three *warrants* for survey research are presented, including assessment of response rate, and measurement reliability and validity. You will see how each of these is applied. Additionally, you will explore how recent developments in technology have impacted survey research.

OUTLINE

Survey Research Claims

Descriptive Claims

Explanatory Claims

Survey Research Data

Sources for Data Collection

Settings for Data Collection

Survey Research Design

Data Sampling Strategies

Capturing Self- and Other Reports

Instrumentation and the Measurement of Survey Data

Survey Research Warrants

Response Rate as an Essential Contributor to Validity and Reliability

Establishing Valid Measurement

Establishing Reliable Measurement

Surveys and Technology

Summary

Key Terms

Discussion Questions

"Try It!" Activities

SURVEY RESEARCH CLAIMS

In Chapter 2, we identified claims as general premises or propositions. Survey research generally makes use of claims from the discovery paradigm about empirical or observable and quantifiable data. Because of the underlying assumptions of this perspective, claims in survey research are most frequently stated in the format of research questions and hypotheses. You may recall from this discussion that *research questions* often ask how a variable (or concept) can be classified; or they may ask what relationships exist between various types of communication phenomena. *Hypotheses* make more precise and specific predictions about relationships among communication variables. A **variable** is one communication phenomenon with a set of characteristics or groupings or scores. Biological sex is a variable with two characteristics: female and male. Scores on an aptitude test make up a variable of aptitude levels. Because each of the characteristics can be assigned a numeric value, it is called a variable (a communication phenomenon with varying values).

There are two general types of claims in survey research: descriptive and explanatory. Descriptive claims attempt to define the characteristics of a population based on one or several samples drawn (Smith, 1988, p. 219). We have previously discussed selecting samples from populations in Chapter 3, "What Counts as Communication Data?" We will discuss sampling methods again in more detail later on in this chapter and in Chapter 7, "Content and Interaction Analyses." Explanatory claims in survey research include both associative and causal claims. Recall our discussion in Chapter 2 when we distinguished between *associative claims,* which predict phenomena that will occur together, and *causal claims,* which predict the influence of one phenomenon on another.

Descriptive Claims

Descriptive claims in communication survey research are often posed as research questions used to identify characteristics of a particular group or category of people that the researcher believes will be unique to that specific population. For example, Graham (1997) asked survey respondents to indicate what types of turning points, or critical events, characterized postdivorce relationships. In this study, the researcher was interested in identifying the turning points (as the variable of interest) that uniquely characterize a certain type of personal relationship.

In another study, Barnes and Hayes (1995) used a survey to find out what type of demographic characteristics describe high school teachers of English who also teach speech in their classrooms. **Demographic characteristics** are those items that provide background information, such as age, sex, education, socioeconomic class, about the study's participants. Survey research typically focuses on characteristics of individuals or groups of people rather than specific message characteristics.

In some cases, descriptive claims are used in survey research to map out specific conceptual territory. You may wish to explore a new concept to find out what types of opinions, attitudes, feelings, or behaviors people identify with a particular communication variable. For example, in a recent study, Kruml and Geddes (2000) explored the dimensions of *emotional labor* as their variable of interest; emotional labor refers generally to the work an employee of a business must engage in when deciding to either express, disguise, or, in some other way, manage feelings while interacting with customers either face-to-face or voice-to-voice. First they collected descriptions of emotional labor from past studies and interviewed additional employees about this variable. From these, Kruml and Geddes constructed a survey questionnaire containing 63 descriptive statements as items that they believed adequately reflected the conceptual field of emotional labor (see Exhibit 5.1). In later sections, you will learn how such questionnaires are constructed, what type of data emerges, and what warrants are established for developing criteria to evaluate the content and structure of the questionnaires. But first, you will see how claims are also explanatory in survey research.

Explanatory Claims

When surveys are used to support explanatory claims, there is a shift in emphasis from describing one concept or variable to exploring the relationship between two or more concepts or variables. Explanatory claims can be associative or causal, and are typically advanced as research questions or hypotheses. Associative claims are more traditionally aligned with survey research. Surveys differ from experiments in that they do not involve any manipulation or controlled change in one of the variables or concepts

---

EXHIBIT 5.1   Descriptive Claims in Survey Research

RQ$_1$: Are there demographic features that describe high school English teachers who teach oral communication? (Barnes & Hayes, 1995)

RQ$_2$: What are the dimensions of emotional labor? (Kruml & Geddes, 2000)

---

studied. Simon, a social scientist (in Berger, 1998), described this difference: "The important distinction between the survey and the experiment is that the survey takes the world as it comes, without trying to alter it, whereas the experiment systematically alters some aspect of the world in order to see what changes follow" (p. 35). *Associative claims* simply predict that two or more concepts or variables are associated with each other, or that changes in one variable are accompanied by changes in the other. They are assertions about the contiguous nature of change in the variables rather than implying a causal direction.

Purely associative claims do not satisfy conditions for accepting a causal claim. For example, Bachman and Zakahi (2000) examined the level of association between love schemas, or attachment styles, and affinity-seeking strategies. Similarly, Chesebro (1999) investigated the relationship between listening styles and conversational sensitivity. The researchers were not interested in predicting which variable caused or influenced changes in the other. They merely assumed that the variables changed together.

Associative claims express contingency relationships or **correlations**—changes in variables that occur together in time. If the variables increase or decrease together, the type of association is said to be **positive** (see Exhibit 5.2). In the above examples, Bachman and Zakahi hypothesized that two types of love schemas would be positively related to the use of affinity-seeking strategies; that is, the higher one scored on the test for those two types of love schemas, the more likely one would be to engage in affinity-seeking strategies (p. 13). Similarly, Chesebro hypothesized that there would be a positive association between the People listening style and conversational sensitivity (p. 235).

If one variable decreases as the other increases, or vice versa, the relationship is identified as a **negative correlation** (see Table 5.2). Bachman and Zakahi predicted that those scoring high on the Casual

schema would be less likely to use affinity-seeking strategies (p. 13). Chesebro hypothesized individuals with an Action listening style would score lower on the conversational sensitivity measure (p. 235). Sometimes, the relationship is expected to be even more complex, changing several different directions. This type is called a **curvilinear relationship.** For example, Behnke and Sawyer (1999) found a curvilinear relationship between important speech preparation events over time and anticipatory anxiety patterns. You will learn more about these relationships in Chapters 8 and 9, where you will discover how to test them statistically.

Unless you specify a causal direction for the change between variables, it is not clear how one variable is expected to influence the other. For instance, do you develop conversational sensitivity first and then a corresponding listening style? Or do you learn to listen in a particular way that leads to increasing conversational sensitivity? Or does some third variable, like your gender or interpersonal perception, explain the changes that occur in both listening styles and conversational sensitivity? When you do not consider how to justify what influences what, you have omitted grounds for causal arguments (Babbie, 1995, p. 70).

Purely associative claims are traditionally considered to be more descriptive or exploratory because they do not predict change as a result of an experimental manipulation, and because more complex data analysis techniques, like regression and path analysis, have only been possible with technological advances in statistical methods. Causal claims must go several steps further by showing that a change in one variable precedes and influences change in the second variable and that the change is not likely to be explained by the influence of any other variable. As we mentioned in several other chapters, the variable of influence is called an *independent variable;* the one that is influenced or changed by the other is called the *dependent variable.*

EXHIBIT 5.2   Two Types of Explanatory Claims in Survey Research

ASSOCIATIVE CLAIMS

1. **Positive correlation**: variables change together:

   H_1:   Scores on the secure schema will be positively related to the likelihood of using affinity-seeking strategies. (Bachman & Zakahi, 2000)

   H_2:   A positive relationship exists between the People listening style and conversational sensitivity. (Chesebro, 1999)

2. **Negative correlation**: variables change in opposite directions.

   H_3:   Scores on the casual schema will be negatively related to the likelihood of using affinity-seeking strategies. (Bachman & Zakahi, 2000)

   H_4:   A negative relationship exists between the Action listening style and conversational sensitivity. (Chesebro, 1999)

CAUSAL CLAIMS

RQ_1:   Among those who use MOOs (Multi-user dimensions, Object Oriented), what factors differentiate people who have started personal relationships online from those who have not? (Parks & Roberts, 1998)

Independent variable: Type of relationship initiation (online vs. offline)

Dependent variables: Relationship duration, frequency of contact, breadth, depth

RQ_2:   What are the roles of ethnic identity and ethnicity of dating partner on Asian American relational expectations concerning interethnic and intraethnic dating? (Chung & Ting-Toomey, 1999)

Independent variables: Ethnic identity and ethnicity of dating partner

Dependent variables: Relational expectations

In a two-stage survey design, Parks and Roberts (1998), for instance, posed the following research question: "Among those who use MOOs (Multi-user dimensions, Object Oriented), what factors differentiate people who have started personal relationships on line from those who have not?" (p. 522). In other words, they were interested in finding out whether the type of relationship (online versus offline) as the independent variable could predict the presence of certain factors in people as the dependent variables (see Exhibit 5.2). To illustrate, they found that offline relationships were significantly greater in duration and in number of hours spent with one's partner. However, many of the characteristics investigated revealed no significant differences in the two types of groups; for example, they found that online and offline relationships were not different in the number of topics the two shared (breadth of communication) nor in the level of intimacy explored in each of those topics (depth of communication).

Another area of research in communication that often tests complex patterns of causality is network analysis. A typical example using this method is the study of communication patterns among coworkers belonging to the same organization. For example, Chang and Johnson (2001) recently explored the factors that influence the way network members belonging to the organization Cancer Information Service chose media to communicate within the network. Their study entailed examining complex pathways of influence in an attempt to explain the channels that network members selected.

Network analysis is unique in communication research because it is both a research method and a theoretical framework (Doerfel & Barnett, 1999). Its research methods are closely aligned with systems theories, in particular, which focus on holism and interdependence among the component parts of a system. **Network analytic research** aims to describe and explain communication processes and structures by collecting data about relationships among people, symbols, or groups. "At its core lies a substantive focus on the structure of social relationships and an epistemology that seeks explanation, not in the attributions of individual actors (persons, groups, organizations), but in the patterns of ties that relate them to one another" (Lincoln, 1990, p. 746). Thus, network studies have claims that are also frequently descriptive and explanatory as they attempt to account for how various components of network structure and function are interrelated.

As a general comparison, surveys have traditionally been thought of as a weaker form of study design because variable changes are not controlled in order to test patterns of effects as they are in experiments. However, as understanding of variable measurement changes along with the types of analyses that are available, data collected from surveys will permit you to test more complex sets of causal relationships that exist naturally in the environment. Making descriptive and explanatory claims using surveys is only the initial step in this research process. Collecting and analyzing the data are the next steps of survey research.

SURVEY RESEARCH DATA

Data treatment in survey research entails a lengthy process of preparation before the survey is ever administered. As part of this process, you must make decisions and take the following steps:

1. Identify data sources and settings.
2. Select a general survey design.
3. Decide on sampling strategies.
4. Identify data collection format as interviews or questionnaires.
5. Construct the interview and questionnaire format.
6. Develop data collection procedures as instruments.
7. Assess the validity and reliability of the data collection instruments.

These steps are conducted prior to actual data collection, analysis, and interpretation of the results.

Sources for Data Collection

Surveys are a very common form of collecting data in communication research. They usually take the form of questionnaires either administered to oneself (by research participants) or administered by a member of the research team through an interviewing process. As you learned in Chapter 3, "What Counts as Communication Data?" you can ask respondents to report on themselves, called *self-report data,* or on others they know, or *other-report data.* Surveys typically assess characteristics or attributes of individual persons or groups to investigate how those characteristics are related to the communication process. These attributes or characteristics can refer to factual or observable features such as sex or age or birthplace. Or they can be composed of ideas, attitudes, opinions,

and emotions. Whether in questionnaire or interview format, surveys are useful ways to find out information from a sample of people when the general population is too large to observe or test every member.

Settings for Data Collection

Laboratory and field settings The data collected from surveys can either be obtained in *laboratory* settings or in *field* settings. As you learned in Chapter 3, "What Counts as Communication Data?" laboratories in communication research are seldom like the sterile environments portrayed in stereotypes of research facilities. They are very often offices or conference rooms or even classrooms in the academic department at the university where one of the researchers is a professor. The role of the researcher varies depending on the paradigm assumptions that underlie the method of choice and depending on the type of survey used as well. We shall discuss this role in more detail in a subsequent section. Generally, the function of using a laboratory setting is to provide a more controlled environment and to facilitate the collection of data.

Survey data may also be collected in the field. In Chapter 3 you learned that field research is any research that investigates communication in the setting where the communication would most naturally occur. For example, Richmond and McCroskey (2000) recruited volunteers to distribute questionnaires to individual employees in 46 different organizations, and Parks and Roberts (1998) went online to recruit survey volunteers from various MOOs, or Internet venues that allow participants located around the world to engage each other in conversation (p. 518). In the past, selecting the data collection setting was frequently dependent upon the type of analysis: basic or applied research.

Basic and applied research By design, surveys have traditionally been used as a research tool for collecting and analyzing data from natural settings. Experiments were conducted in the laboratory when a controlled environment was warranted; surveys were conducted in the field when researchers wanted to access groups and contexts not available through experimental research. By methodological tradition, field settings with survey instruments typified **applied research;** lab settings in academic institutions were associated with **basic research.** Basic research emphasizes investigating theoretic relationships among variables where practical outcomes in specific contexts may be implicit or unknown. Applied research focuses on satisfying practical outcomes in solving specific problems in field settings (Smith, 1988, p. 219).

Three types of applied survey research Applied research settings that use the survey method in communication research have been traditionally associated with political polling, consumer research, and action research.

    Political polling research refers to assessing political opinions and attitudes, often to predict voter preferences. You are probably familiar with the Gallup poll, still one of the most prominent in predicting success for particular candidates.

    Consumer research (also called market research) is designed to assess consumer attitudes and preferences for various products or services. Nielsen ratings, for example, help media and advertising organizations assess the characteristics and sizes of audiences who watch various television programming.

    As you learned in Chapter 2, *action research* is used to assess the performance of individuals within various programs or other organizational or institutional units. In action research, you conduct surveys for the purposes of evaluating and changing current practices. Recall that action research is reformative because its focus is on whether the change intended is actually achieved.

    In general, it is important to remember that survey research has the potential to provide important contributions to understanding communication whether it is collected in a laboratory or in the field, or whether its goals make a study more basic or more applied.

Survey Research Design

In Chapter 3, you learned that a *research design* is the structural plan for conducting a test of the researcher's hypotheses or research questions. It specifies the procedures for collecting and analyzing the data. Recall that there are two general types of survey designs: cross-sectional and longitudinal.

Cross-sectional surveys Cross-sectional surveys are the more prevalent of the two types of surveys in all communication research. Collecting data one time only is cheaper and less time-consuming. For these reasons primarily, survey research designs are typically cross-sectional, rather than longitudinal, although a few studies have been conducted that examine the changes in communication variables over time (e.g., White, 1999). Additionally, in cross-sectional designs, the researcher does not have to worry about loss of data over time as participants drop out or are lost from the original roster. But cross-sectional studies are limited in that they provide only a "snapshot" view of communication at a single point in time. Deciding to study complex phenomena may make it necessary to conduct a longitudinal study.

Longitudinal surveys Deciding what type of longitudinal survey study to conduct also depends on a number of factors. If the size of the population is very large, for example, the only feasible design is the trend study. The impracticability of surveying the same members of a large population, as you would do in a panel study, is fairly obvious. However, sometimes the claim a researcher wishes to test makes a panel study more advantageous. If you wanted to show, for instance, what types of networks individuals develop online over time, following the same group of individuals will allow the researcher to map out gradual changes in network development (Parks & Roberts, 1998).

    A final consideration in deciding what type of longitudinal study to use concerns the effects of mortality, or the dropout rate. You will learn more about this factor in the next chapter. If the research question or hypothesis poses a claim that is susceptible to this effect, selecting a panel format will not be advantageous. For example, if you wanted to see whether romantic couples' enrollment in a communication seminar influences relational satisfaction over the course of a semester, you need to assure that your sample will not reflect only those who continue to be couples and participants in your study. Those who break up are least likely to be satisfied but no longer qualify to be part of a study of couples.

    Once you have decided which design best matches your claims and population characteristics, you must then select the sampling method you will use to construct a sample of people you will contact to take your survey.

Data Sampling Strategies

Design issues specify how data will be collected over time. The researcher must also consider other collection strategies such as selection and collection formats.

Random selection methods As we stated earlier, the primary purpose of surveys is to examine the characteristics or attributes of interest to our study from a sample that is representative of a larger population. Sample *representativeness* is, therefore, a key issue in survey research generally. In Chapter 3, you learned about the general principle of representativeness. When a sample represents its population, you say it provides a very good picture of what the whole group looks like even though you cannot test every member. The best way to ensure representativeness is to use random selection or another probability sampling method. When you select population members randomly to make up a sample, you are ensuring that every member of the population has an equal chance of being chosen for the sample.

Because representative samples are such good pictures of the whole population, you can assume that the conclusions you reach about your observations have good external validity. In Chapter 4, "Warrants for Research Arguments," you learned that external validity is the ability to generalize beyond what you see in your sample to the population at large. With strong external validity, you can say, for example, that your samples of voters, teenagers, women, or television audiences—or whatever group you have selected—will allow you to make accurate predictions about what all voters, teenagers, women, or television audiences will generally do even though you cannot test or observe every member of the whole group.

Here's how simple random sampling actually works in a typical survey study. First you must decide on the total number of individuals selected for your sample. Let's say you wish to obtain a sample of 500 students from a sampling frame or list of 36,051 students, the total number enrolled at your university. Each of these students is assigned a number from 1 to 36,051. You can either use a computer program that will randomly select 500 numbers from 1 to 36,051 or you can use a table of random numbers like the one that appears in Appendix B. To select 500 students, you might start with the student whose number is 00130 as the first member of your sample, and 03167 as the second member, and 15070 as the third member, until using the table of random numbers, you have selected 500 students from the population to comprise our sample.

Survey researchers may use any of the random sampling methods identified in Chapter 3; simple random sampling, stratified sampling, and cluster sampling are among the most frequently chosen. Usually, researchers will select the method that is most cost effective and will satisfy the goals of obtaining a representative sample. For example, one set of researchers used "stratified systematic random sampling" to obtain a sample of adolescents from grades 8 through 12 to assess the effects of an antidrug media campaign (Stephenson, Palmgreen, Hoyle, Donohew, Lorch, & Colon, 1999). They recruited about 100 participants each month from each county across two states until their final sample consisted of 1,601 people. Even though the number of states represented was small, these researchers spent a considerable amount of time and money to gain greater representativeness in their sample than you would ordinarily find in most survey research.

Many telephone survey studies make use of a procedure called **random digit dialing** (RDD). This procedure randomly identifies areas of a region to be sampled with their corresponding area codes and exchanges (first three numbers). Then, the last four digits of the telephone number are randomly generated. This procedure also enables you to access unlisted numbers. In a recent study, Dimmick, Kline, and Stafford (2000) used RDD to obtain a representative sample of email users in a pilot survey of reasons people identified for using email. RDD can also be adjusted to account for areas that have greater or lesser concentrations of various minority groups or other socioeconomic stratifications (Mertens, 1998, p. 114). In some cases, survey researchers depend on samples previously drawn to recruit participants for new studies. For example, Valkenburg, Cantor, and Peeters (2000) randomly sampled 314 Dutch children from a nationally representative data bank of 10,000 families who had previously agreed to participate in telephone surveys.

Random sampling methods enable you to estimate how far your sample characteristics (statistics) are likely to deviate from population characteristics (parameters). You will learn about this process in more detail in Chapter 8, "Descriptive Statistics and Hypothesis Testing." For the time being, we want to identify the assumptions you will make in attempting to establish external validity:

1. Hypotheses are claims developed about relationships between population characteristics.

2. Researchers should specify the probability of error associated with sample characteristics (statistics).

3. The probability of error permits researchers to establish a decision rule for rejecting or accepting a hypothesis (Smith, 1988).

These assumptions are grounded in random sampling, and they are inherent in most survey research. Why, then, would you choose a nonrandom sampling method?

Nonrandom or purposive selection methods
One reason for choosing nonrandom sampling methods in survey research is because you cannot afford to use one of the random selection techniques, or constraints of the setting make random selection impractical (Fink & Gantz, 1996; Stake, 1998). This rationale weakens your ability to generalize study results to the population if the study is based on the "logic of hypothesis testing." To compensate, you may take steps to help ensure representativeness in other ways. For example, Trost, Langan, and Kellar-Guenther (1999) surveyed a sample of students ($n = 2,166$) from 31 junior high schools in a large southwestern city. Because they could not randomly sample students, they were careful to make sure their sample was large and ethnically diverse, and therefore more representative of the general population of junior high school students. In another study, Nathanson (1999) obtained a sample of elementary school children from two communities outside of the university community to try to increase the variety of participants in her sample. As Nathanson pointed out, samples within the university community were more likely to be "practiced" research participants and be more educated, two factors the author believed might interfere with her investigation of parent mediation (control of and commentary about their children's television programs) and children's television-viewing habits.

In some cases, survey research questions specifically call for a nonrandom sampling method. For example, network studies emphasize the uniqueness of each network as a whole system. In such studies, the selection method for network analysis is almost always purposive or snowball sampling, rather than random, because the network researcher aims to describe the entire social system. In other network studies, however, representative sampling techniques can be used to select a subset of participants from a very large, loosely structured social network (e.g., McLeod, Scheufele, Moy, Horowitz, Holbert, Zhang, Zubric, & Zubric, 1999).

Communication researchers typically employ purposive sampling in two types of network analysis: semantic network analysis and ego-centered network analysis. **Semantic network analysis** is a method for studying relationships among the parts of a system, based on the ways that members of the system share symbolic meanings. For example, Doerfel and Barnett (1999) described the structure of the International Communication Association, a professional association for communication scholars, by comparing the divisions of the organization (e.g., Interpersonal Communication, Political Communication, Health Communication) with the content of the paper titles that were presented at the association's 1991 annual meeting. Semantic network analysis focuses on the *content* of communication in a social system.

In semantic network analysis, textual data are purposively sampled from a population of messages in order to draw conclusions about the degree to which communicators' use of symbolic concepts overlap. In the example above, the messages are the collection of titles of the set of professional papers presented at the annual conference. Instead of survey methods, content analysis of this data can often help to determine which symbols are used most frequently. You will learn about this method in more detail in Chapter 7, "Content and Interaction Analyses."

Whereas semantic network analysis focuses on the extent to which people's symbol usage overlaps, general network analysis focuses on the relationships, called **links,** among communicators. **Ego-centered network analysis** aims to describe a system of social relationships from one individual communicator's point of view. Involvement in ego-centered networks is thought to impact many other aspects of everyone's lives. For example, network researchers have shown that "level of connectedness in each other's networks was a significant predictor of the development and stability of a relationship" (Monge, 1987, p. 269). As you become more deeply involved with a romantic partner, you tend to withdraw from your individual network and forge joint networks with your partner. Parks and Aldeman (1983) showed that "respondents experienced less uncertainty about their romantic partners and were less likely to break up" when they had greater contact with their partner's friends and family, "received greater support for their romantic relationship from family and friends, communicated more often with their partners, and perceived greater similarity to their partners" (p. 55).

In ego-centered network analysis, you would use purposive sampling to collect each person's egocentric view of the network. This permits you to compare different people's views of the system with one another, and to look for areas of confirmation and disconfirmation. For example, Sally may report that she has friendships with Tito, Josh, and Natasha. Perhaps Tito and Josh will confirm that they are friends with Sally, but Natasha will not report that she has a friendship with Sally. As a network researcher, you will be interested in both patterns (i.e., confirmation and disconfirmation). Confirmed links are sometimes called **reciprocated** links, whereas disconfirmed links are called **nonreciprocated.** In this type of network analysis, purposive sampling is essential.

Some survey research uses other forms of nonrandom sampling. For example, Morton and Duck (2000) used a modified snowball sampling technique to recruit gay men for their sample. They asked a group of gay men to refer other gay men through personal contact; the researchers also solicited study participation from gay men through university campus groups. Morton and Duck used this procedure because they were interested in studying the effects of media dependency on gay men's attitudes toward safe sex practices. As the authors pointed out, if they had recruited their sample through mass-mediated sources, they may have obtained a sample already biased toward media dependency.

To summarize, the sample selection process for survey research can be accomplished by using either random or nonrandom sampling techniques. If you are interested in obtaining a sample that is a representative subset of its population, then random methods are preferred. If you are not interested in generalizing the study's findings beyond the particular communication context, or if there are special constraints on sampling imposed by the context, then you may select a nonrandom method.

Capturing Self- and Other-Reports

As you discovered earlier, survey research is based on reports individuals give of their own or others' ideas, attitudes, beliefs, emotions, behaviors, or demographic characteristics. Gathering this information can be completed through interviews or by questionnaires. In the following section, you will learn about the types of interviews you may conduct and how these differ from administering questionnaires.

Types of survey interviews When you collect survey data by interviews, you must make several decisions. The first decision concerns the setting for data collection. You can choose to meet participants face-to-face either in a laboratory setting or in the field. If a field setting is selected, you can intercept participants in a general public setting like a shopping center or mall, or you can solicit interviews over the telephone. You can meet with individuals, or in groups, or even conduct extensive interviews of whole networks. Second, you must decide what to ask during the interview. The format of questions can vary as well as your role as the interviewer. In preparing for the interview process, you must decide how structured the format will be, the degree of participation you will take as the interviewer, and how much training it will be necessary for you to receive. Each of these decisions comes with a set of distinctive advantages and disadvantages.

Interviews can be arranged with individual participants, couples, or groups **face-to-face** in a field setting or in a laboratory setting. For example, Kremar and Valkenburg (1999) interviewed children in their homes and in a day care setting to assess their perceptions of whether violence in television programs should be considered justified or unjustified. By contrast, Le Poire, Shepard, and Duggan (1999) brought romantic partners into a lab setting and separated them following a videotaped interaction for the purposes of interviewing them about the direction they thought their relationship was taking. Interviews that take place in natural settings are less likely to produce artificial effects due to the setting itself, but they are usually less controlled environments. Le Poire et al. tried to minimize the negative effects and maximize the positive effects of both settings by bringing romantic partners into the lab but creating an environment that resembled the sort of setting where such interactions might naturally occur.

Face-to-face interviews with individual participants, also called *personal interviews,* pose some unique advantages. It is much easier to establish a rapport and climate of trust between the interviewer and the participant if they meet personally than if they talk over the phone or by mailed questionnaire. Plus it is also more difficult not to answer all items, and so response rates are typically higher. You will also have access to more information from participants; you can probe for more in-depth responses, and you can easily monitor participants' nonverbal reactions for any expressions of confusion or concern. This ability is especially important when participants cannot read fluently because, for example, English is not the participant's native language, or when the questions are especially complex or need further explanation (Mertens, 1998).

Additionally, you can combine interview questions with some other form of media as part of the questioning, as when participants are asked to look at pictures or watch videotapes of interaction in order to then probe for a greater depth of information. Sometimes, face-to-face interviews can lead to more apprehension, especially when researchers are asking to enter participants' homes (Watt & van den Berg, 1995). Depending on the nature of the study, it may be easier to interview participants collectively.

An interviewing strategy used with increasing frequency is the **focus group,** a small group of respondents (between 4 to 10 participants) who are selected by convenience, purposive, or snowball sampling methods. The format of the interview is generally loosely structured so that a wide range of information may be collected about a particular subject (Krueger, 1994; Morgan, 1988; Watt & van den Berg, 1995). For example, Valkenburg and Janssen (1999) used focus groups to explore what children from ages 6 to 11 value about television programs. As the authors pointed out, focus groups frequently help young children feel at ease with adult interviewers.

In a similar vein, Kramer and Pier (1999) used focus groups of college students to discuss behaviors of teachers they considered to be effective and ineffective. The authors claimed that focus groups are an especially effective means of collecting data from a population "because ideas that would not otherwise have been considered are generated through group interaction, and the small size allows for all group members to participate" (p. 19).

In their study of Latino expectations of communicative competence, Bradford, Meyers, and Kane (1999) listed three advantages of using focus groups. They noted that the "interactive effects of group settings" help to focus on participants' perceptions, attitudes, and behaviors to explore a specified concept from the perspective of the participants rather than the researcher. Focus groups may also increase the level of self-disclosure for participants from cultures that are more collective than individualistic. In this case, participants' responses are seen as parts of a whole group discussion rather than singular expressions. A final advantage they identified is that focus groups facilitate brainstorming around a specific concept or topic. The authors noted that "people are more inclined to disclose information amid the security of others similar to themselves" (p. 105).

Face-to-face interviews with individuals or focus groups can probe participants for information about themselves, about others, about groups to which they belong, or even about whole networks of which they are members. Network studies frequently make use of questionnaires and interviews. Because researchers are often looking for complex responses, combining face-to-face or even telephone mediation with a fairly structured set of questions often yields the richest form of network data.

One of the disadvantages of face-to-face interviews for any study including network analyses is that they are the most expensive form of data collection in terms of money and time. They also frequently require the most intensive form of interviewer training. Because using personal interviews means also relying on nonrandom sampling methods, the sample obtained is often less representative and poses greater threats to external validity. The relative advantages and disadvantages of personal interviews and focus groups are listed in Exhibit 5.3. Because of the disadvantages, many researchers decide to use mall intercept surveys or telephone surveys instead.

Mall intercept surveys, in which you find your participants at a shopping mall, are less costly than personal interviews, and they provide relative anonymity to participants. The public setting reassures both participants and researchers about privacy and safety issues. However, some malls strictly prohibit administering surveys, shoppers are frequently pressed for time, and you must still be concerned about threats to external validity. You must take steps to ensure that the study's purpose will be addressed adequately by samples typically found in shopping malls, and sampling should be scheduled across times and days the mall is open. For these reasons, telephone surveys may be more advantageous (Watt & van den Berg, 1995).

Telephone surveys provide you with some distinct advantages. First of all, you can obtain more representative samples. Recall the random digit dialing procedure you learned about in the previous section. Telephone interviews also eliminate many privacy and safety concerns. Respondents may be more honest if the interviewer does not confront them personally, and the interviewer's appearance cannot influence

> **EXHIBIT 5.3   Advantages and Disadvantages of Face-to-Face and Focus Group Interviews**
>
> **ADVANTAGES**
>
> *Face-to-face personal interviews:*
>
> 1. Easier to establish a rapport and climate of trust.
> 2. More difficult to avoid answering any item.
> 3. Can probe for more in-depth responses.
> 4. Can monitor participants' nonverbal reactions.
> 5. Can help to clarify any questions for participants.
> 6. Can combine interview questions with some other form of media as part of the questioning.
>
> *Focus groups:*
>
> 1. Loosely structured format for collecting wide range of information.
> 2. May help young children feel at ease with adult interviewers.
> 3. Group formats stimulate a greater variety of ideas.
> 4. Help to explore a specified concept from the perspective of the participants rather than the researcher.
> 5. May also increase the level of self-disclosure for participants from cultures that are more collective than individualistic.
>
> **DISADVANTAGES**
>
> *Personal interviews and focus groups:*
>
> 1. Can lead to more apprehension with sensitive questions.
> 2. Greater risk entering subjects' home.
> 3. Most expensive forms of data collection in terms of money and time.
> 4. Require the most intensive form of interviewer training
> 5. Samples often less representative, posing greater threats to external validity.
> 6. Some groups may exert conformity pressure over individual responses.

the way in which questions are answered (Babbie, 1995). Generally the use of telephones can enhance interviewer consistency. Interviewers are often located at a research center where supervisors may be available to answer any questions interviewers may have as they interact with participants. Finally, telephone and in-person interviewers are making more frequent use of computers to aid in data collection. You will learn more about computer-assisted and computer-mediated interviews in the technology section of this chapter. The actual interview format undoubtedly influences the effectiveness of the type of interview selected. The relative advantages and disadvantages of mall intercept and telephone surveys are listed in Exhibit 5.4.

Once you have decided on the type of survey interview you will conduct, you must then select a format that will determine how questions are asked and what their content will look like.

Formats for survey interviews Interview formats can vary in three ways: structured, semi-structured, or unstructured. **Structured interviews** have protocols or schedules that dictate what questions to ask when. They are defined by the following criteria:

1. The number of questions and their wording remains identical for all participants.
2. The questions are presented in the same order.
3. Researchers do not attempt to clarify or explain any question, even when asked, at any time during the interview process.

The rationale for such strict requirements is that any change can then be attributed to the respondents and not to the interviewing process (Frankfort-Nachmias & Nachmias, 1996).

Semistructured interviews are also called focused or "non-schedule-structured" interviews (Frankfort-Nachmias & Nachmias, 1996, p. 234). This second type of interview format has four characteristics:

1. It asks respondents to reflect on an experience or a concept that they all have in common.
2. It refers to situations or constructs that have been analyzed and often defined prior to the interview.

EXHIBIT 5.4   Advantages and Disadvantages of Mall Intercept and Telephone Surveys

ADVANTAGES

Mall intercept surveys:

1. Less costly than personal interviews.
2. Provide relative anonymity to participants.
3. Public setting reassures both participants and researchers about privacy and safety issues.

Telephone surveys:

1. Provide more representative samples.
2. Eliminate many privacy and safety concerns.
3. Respondents may be more honest if they are not confronted personally by an interviewer.
4. Interviewer's appearance cannot influence the way in which questions are answered.
5. Interviewers are often located at the research center where supervisors may be available to answer any questions interviewers may have.

DISADVANTAGES

Mall intercept surveys:

1. Some malls strictly prohibit surveys.
2. Shoppers frequently pressed for time.
3. Samples still not representative.

Telephone surveys:

1. Respondents may actually become less willing to disclose information because of less personal format.
2. Interview length cannot be as long as those conducted in person.
3. Greater distrust of telephone surveys as veiled marketing devices.
4. Respondents frequently use their answering machines to screen callers.
5. Can break it off at any point just by hanging up.

---

3. It requires the interviewer to use a guide that specifies topics of interest, rather than an interview schedule.
4. It focuses on the participants' understanding or meaning of a particular concept or experience.

Bradford et al. (1999) used a semistructured interview format to explore Latinos' perceptions of communication competence. The interviewer presented focus groups with four scenarios constructed in a previous study. Then each group was asked an open-ended question: "You want to make a favorable impression on this person, be seen as a competent communicator. What do you do?" (p. 107). The scenarios and the question for each scenario were meant to serve only as a guide to stimulate discussion. After the third group had been interviewed, it was clear from the responses that the scenario and question had provided enough of a focus to establish consistencies in responses.

Unstructured interviews have the greatest amount of flexibility (also called the nondirective interview). In this type of interview, you will not have any prespecified set of questions; you will rely entirely on the participants to identify experiences and events that seem significant or meaningful. You may also use initial interviews to help construct questions as probes for subsequent interviews.

The purely nondirective approach to interviewing is more likely to be associated with more interpretive and critical methods such as conversational and discourse analyses and ethnography (see Chapters 10 and 11). From these paradigm perspectives, you are concerned with presenting the subjective points of view that the participants express; it would not be important to you therefore to keep the structure of the interview uniform for every participant. You will learn more about these differences in the last section of this chapter. At this point, however, we will explore the role of the interviewer and the amount of training required, which varies depending on the type of interview and the format selected.

Training survey interviewers   Survey researchers who come from the discovery paradigm perspective have traditionally preferred structured interview formats. This type of interview requires extensive training, and the following set of rules usually applies:

Intrude in the research process as little as possible. This means that the interviewer should never direct the respondent toward an answer, should never be judgmental, should not interpret the respondent's answers according to his or her own beliefs or values. The interviewer must be consistent in his or her communication style and language, so that each respondent is exposed to the same kind of measurement environment (Watt & van den Berg, 1995, p. 359).

These authors detailed a thorough training program in which interviewers are given very specific sets of instructions on how to approach each participant and what to ask them. Then, interviewers are usually required to complete practice interviews so that their performance can be thoroughly evaluated by the research team. Finally, the interviewer is required to repeat the practice trials until the researcher "is convinced that the interviewer is sufficiently low-key and consistent and will not bias the results" (Watt & van den Berg, p. 359).

Essentially, many survey researchers believe that the interviewer should be a neutral medium and not affect responses in any way. This form of survey research is based on the assumption that every question will mean exactly the same thing to each participant, and that the "interviewer's presence should not affect a respondent's perception of a question or the answer given" (Babbie, 1995, p. 264). The assumption of complete neutrality on the part of interviewers necessitates they play the role of detached observer. Even probes for more information or answers to respondents' requests for clarification must be carefully constructed so that they remain neutral and cannot "in any way affect the nature of the subsequent response" (Babbie, p. 267).

In semistructured and unstructured formats, interviewers are concerned with using preconceived questions as guides only; precision and consistency of wording are generally not as important as they are in structured interviews, and in the second main form of capturing self- and other-reports in survey data, the questionnaire.

Questionnaires The second most common way of capturing survey research data is the **questionnaire,** the written form of self- and other-report data collection. Questionnaires can be read in structured interview settings with or without telephone and computer mediation, mailed out to participants, or administered through email lists or Internet Web sites. When using a questionnaire, you must also decide what the structure of the questionnaire should look like, and how questions should be asked. Every decision about using questionnaires has advantages and disadvantages, just as interview decisions have.

General structure of questionnaires The term **questionnaire architecture** has been used previously to capture the general structure of the questionnaire (Watt & van den Berg, 1995, p. 368). This term focuses very nicely on the attention you should pay to the structure of your questionnaire. You must consider its general length, comprehensibility, and question order.

First, you should regard length as a critical factor. Questionnaires that are excessively long are fatiguing to individuals who may not complete certain items or who may decide not to complete the questionnaire at all because the task seems too demanding.

The second feature to consider is clarity. Because questionnaires often take the place of interviewers, both the questions themselves and the instructions to participants should be easy to understand and self-administer, or at least, easy for your research team to administer with little advance training. The survey questionnaire should come with a cover letter and/or set of instructions that identify the basic purpose of the study and how to fill out the questionnaire. These should be clearly worded and use a vocabulary appropriate for the age and education level of the respondents. For the potential effects of length and clarity, all questionnaires should be pilot tested before they are administered to the study's selected sample.

Because the structure of the questionnaire is important, you will often be concerned with the order in which the questions are presented. Questionnaires in survey research are designed to measure concepts. When researchers construct a questionnaire, they have to be especially careful of **order effects**—that questions asked early on will not adversely affect the way respondents answer later questions. For example, asking respondents to indicate whether they believe disclosures about their sexual histories are part of practicing safe sex will likely influence later attempts to ask questions about how truthful they are in disclosing information about their sexual histories to new partners (Lucchetti, 1999).

However, the pattern of order effects isn't always clear. For example, asking in general how religious a person is can affect later specific questions regarding church attendance, but asking the more specific question first is just as likely to affect the later general response. People try to respond in ways that make them appear to be consistent. Sometimes, question sequences are randomized to eliminate order effects. However, randomizing the order can make the questions appear chaotic to respondents who have to jump from one topic to the next, and it does not guarantee no order effects, just no control over them. Researchers should pay more attention to constructing an order that participants find easy, interesting, and topically consistent or logically arranged (Babbie, 1995, p. 151; Berger, 1998, pp. 40–42).

Formats for survey questions This section examines the various types of questions based on their functions and the guidelines you should use in constructing these specific questions. There are several general types of question formats that can change how questions function depending on the purposes of the research. First, questions can be open-ended or closed-format. **Open-ended questions** are defined as questions that ask respondents to provide unstructured or spontaneous answers or to discuss an identified topic. For example, Bradford et al. (1999) asked Latino focus groups to respond to open-ended questions about what makes a communicator competent across several types of situations. Messman and Mikesell (2000) asked romantic partners to identify areas of competitive behavior using open-ended questions. Open-ended questions ask respondents to report on an experience or concept in their own terms. Frequently, they are used in survey research as a means of exploring conceptual territory.

Closed-format questions (sometimes called forced-choice) ask respondents to "choose from a fixed set of alternatives or to give a single numerical value" (Watt & van den Berg, 1995, p. 366). Questions that specify all possible response alternatives are scaled items. You will learn more about these types of responses in the next section of this chapter. Briefly, examples of closed-format questions include those that ask respondents to identify their biological sex or to indicate their level of agreement with various beliefs or attitudes. Generally speaking, open-ended questions are harder to code and can lead to greater problems with consistency as a result. Closed-format questions are much easier to handle but may be less accurate reflections of the respondents' perceptions and interpretations. This issue will surface again when we consider warrants for survey research.

Network studies have their own versions of questions that are unique. The **roster method,** sometimes also known as the recognition technique, is most common for collecting ego-centered network data. It resembles closed-format questions in that par-

ticipants in the study are given a roster of all the members of their social system (e.g., all the employees in an organization, or all the members of a sorority) and are asked to respond to questions about all the other members with whom they regularly interact. In this way, the participants are given an opportunity to recognize the members of their ego-centered network. Alternatively, the **free-recall technique** may be used. In this technique, the participants are asked to list all the members of their social network, and then to answer a series of questions about each of those people.

Neyer (1997) explored the consequences of collecting network data using free recall instead of recognition. He studied the ego-centered networks of 479 young adults twice, over an 18-month period. In the first study, the subjects were asked to freely recall those with whom they interacted. In the second study, a recognition technique was used to collect the network data. Neyer concluded that the recall technique was useful for generating "high numbers of network members and strong activity, while free recall produces networks which are smaller and less active in comparison, but nevertheless can be identified as networks of significant others" (p. 305). If you are interested in reading more about relationship networks in adolescents and young adults, see Furman and Simon (1998).

Questionnaires can also make use of filter and contingency questions. **Filter questions** direct people to respond to various portions of the questionnaire. For example, the question "Do you own a DVD player? If yes, then skip to question #10" is a filter question. The **contingency question** depends upon responses to filter questions. In the above example, question #10 may ask respondents how long they have owned a DVD player as a contingency question.

In general survey research, questions can also ask for different types of information. Three types of information are commonly sought: (1) information that describes who participants are, called demographics; (2) information about behaviors that participants engage in; (3) information about participants' thoughts, feelings, beliefs, and attitudes. You will learn about each of these types of information in the rest of this section.

First, as a researcher, you may ask for descriptive information about the participants' demographics—personal characteristics of the respondents such as biological sex or ethnicity. You must learn to become very sensitive about the ways in which individuals identify themselves along lines of race, class, and disabilities. Mertens (1998) suggested broadening all of our classification codes and thinking generally about the way we use various categories like those that pertain to physical disabilities or learning disorders (pp. 121–122).

Second, you may want to know about participants' *behaviors.* When questions ask for information about specific behaviors or frequencies of behaviors, you should be aware of behaviors that respondents are likely to interpret as threatening as well as those behaviors that are not. Nonthreatening behaviors are those that are typical and easy to talk about, like the number of times a week a person watches the evening news or how frequently a person emails friends. Threatening behavioral questions make participants feel defensive. When constructing questions, you should *avoid using provocative language,* and make sure your questions are not leading. **Leading questions** direct respondents to answer in a specific way. Asking respondents "How many times a week do you abuse drugs?" is obviously provocative *and* leading. It will very likely encourage participants to give you socially desirable responses regardless of the truth about their behaviors.

Sometimes you might be asking much subtler leading questions without even realizing that you are doing so. Oliver (1992) illustrated a contrast between questions worded in ways that implicitly locate blame for a disability within the person versus questions that locate the cause elsewhere. For example, notice the difference between asking, "What physical condition causes your difficulty in holding, gripping, or turning things?" and "What difficulties in the design of everyday things make it difficult for you to use them?" Oliver argued that questions that appear to be neutral in tone could still reflect researcher biases. To avoid the use of potentially threatening wording, all questionnaires should be piloted with a sample of people representative of the population you wish to study.

When you construct a questionnaire, you can be extremely careful in your wording and still run into problems. Any questions that ask respondents to reveal the occurrence and frequency of undesirable behaviors, like questions about physical and sexual abuse, drug use, sexual behavior, or criminal activity, are often underreported. There are a variety of ways to minimize the threat inherent in these questions. Asking open-ended questions instead of closed-format questions that ask for frequencies is one way to obtain more accurate information. Wording the question in such a way that provides a rationale for its im-

portance or in a way that makes it all right to reveal the behavior asked for can circumvent tendencies to withhold information. For example, the question "Many people complain that tax forms are just too complicated to figure out and compute accurately. What do you think about this problem?" may elicit more truthful tax practices than asking people directly if they fudge on their taxes. Finally, assuring respondents of complete confidentiality makes it more likely they will disclose with greater accuracy when questions are threatening.

The third type of information you may want to find out about from respondents is about their *internal or mental states,* that is, their thoughts, beliefs, values, feelings, and attitudes, or their perceptions of these in other people they know. Sometimes, the questions you will use are open-ended questions designed to explore a particular communication concept. Such questions can be used alone or in conjunction with closed-format questions. For example, Emmers-Sommer (1999) asked college students three open-ended questions regarding their perceptions of negative events in their relationships. This part of the questionnaire was used to confirm an existing classification scheme for negative relational events. She also asked them to complete the closed-format Miller Social Intimacy Scale that "examines individuals' feelings of psychological closeness" (p. 290).

Ideally, all questionnaires are piloted to check for clarity of questions. In a study with Malcolm Parks, one of the authors of this book had the experience of constructing a question designed to tap the concept of interpersonal commitment. She asked respondents to indicate how much they agreed with the statement "I am afraid my relationship will end soon." In the pilot study, it became clear that this was an example of a **double-barreled question,** a question that asks two things simultaneously (Smith, 1988, p. 227). It asked respondents if they felt afraid about the relationship ending, and it also asked them if they expected the relationship to end soon. If she had not piloted the questions, this error would not have surfaced until the consistencies of the responses were checked—and then it would have been too late to correct.

To summarize, researchers should follow a few simple guidelines for questionnaire construction, listed in Exhibit 5.5. In the next two sections of this chapter, you will learn in detail how questionnaire items are constructed as instruments and how their use is validated.

EXHIBIT 5.5   Guidelines for Questionnaire Construction

1. Avoid making the questionnaire too lengthy.
2. Make the instructions and questions clear.
3. Make the instructions and questions easy to understand.
4. Consider the possibility of order effects, test for them, and make adjustments accordingly.
5. Avoid using provocative language.
6. Avoid leading questions.

7. Use open-ended questions and questions that provide support for answering truthfully when questions are potentially threatening.
8. Be sensitive to diversity issues when asking for information.
9. Avoid using double-barreled questions.
10. Pilot the questionnaire with a sample appropriate to the study.

Instrumentation and the Measurement of Survey Data

If you accept the underlying assumptions of the discovery paradigm, you will be interested in testing your hypotheses through the processes of operationalization and statistical analysis. In this section, you will explore the first process, indicating how survey data are defined and measured. This section will be followed by a brief explanation of what statistical analyses are appropriate in survey research, reserving most of our discussion for Chapter 9, "Testing Differences and Relationships."

Operationalization of variables In the beginning of this chapter, you learned that survey research traditionally relies on descriptive and explanatory claims associated with the discovery paradigm. From this perspective, the primary goal of research is to test the relationships posed in the claims as research questions and hypotheses by examining the data. Researchers who commit to the logic of hypothesis testing also commit to specifying the empirical characteristics of whatever communication phenomenon they have chosen to study. This process is called **operationalization.** Empirical indicators are observable and measurable. Recall that you learned about conceptual and operational definitions in Chapter 3. Conceptual definitions describe a communication construct by using other related concepts. Operational definitions specify the operations, procedures, and instruments needed to measure the communication construct. When you use empirical methods to test your evidence or data, how data are measured determines the kind of analysis that can be performed.

In the next section of this chapter, you will learn about the four levels of measurement that are used in operationalizing communication variables in surveys and other forms of empirical research.

Levels of measurement In order to transform constructs into variables, you may use any of four different levels of measurement. Very often, the natural structure of a variable will dictate how a variable is measured. Biological sex is this type of variable: its natural structure requires a measurement scale that will be able to identify its two values, male and female. Just as frequently, you will choose to create a variable with a format that will also dictate the level of measurement. In order to understand how variables in survey research are operationalized, you will need to look at the four possible levels of measurement.

Nominal level Variable values change. That is what makes a construct a variable. How they change is the crux of the differences in measurement scales. Variable data that is measured by discrete changes in categories is nominal level data. Discrete changes in categories mean that **nominal scales** assign one value of the variable for one and only one category or subgroup of the variable. Biological sex is expressed by the categories "female" and "male." Answers "true" and "false" are also expressed by just two categories. Both are examples of data measured with nominal scales.

In survey research, answers to interview questions or questionnaires can provide a nominal level of measurement. Questions may ask respondents to identify their naturally occurring characteristics. Membership in an academic class (junior, senior, etc.), academic

---

> **EXHIBIT 5.6   Examples of Organismic and Background Variable Survey Questions (Nominal Level of Measurement)**
>
> *Organismic variables:*
>
> 1. Circle whether you are male or female: M   or   F
> 2. Circle academic class standing: Fr   So   Jr   Sr
>
> *Researcher-constructed variables:*
>
> 1. Indicate the type of relationship you are using as a basis for your responses:
>
>   ____ Acquaintance ____ Friend ____ Romantic partner
>
> 2. Indicate the type of employee you are based on your length of employment:
>
>   ____ Newcomer (0 to 6 months)
>
>   ____ Transitional employee (6 months to 2 years)
>
>   ____ Veteran (2+ years)

---

major, and sex are just a few ways that categories of data occur naturally. When changes reflect the natural structure of the variable, they are called **organismic variables** because they represent organic or natural differences in the participants' internal characteristics, or characteristics that the participants have chosen for themselves (Smith, 1988, p. 199).

You can also construct the categories and ask participants to classify themselves according to these categories. For example, a survey of interpersonal relationship types may ask respondents to indicate whether they are involved in an acquaintance type, friendship type, or romantic type of relationship. Survey questions may also ask members of an organization to identify themselves as newcomers, transitional employees, or veterans, after each of these categories is sufficiently explained. Sometimes these are called **background variables** because they represent some characteristic of the participant that is already present before he or she takes part in the study (Vogt in Frey, Botan, & Kreps, 2000, p. 87). Examples of survey questions that tap information as organismic and background variables are found in Exhibit 5.6.

Sometimes, survey questions give participants just two alternative categories from which they must make their choices (e.g., asking yes/no questions or true/false questions). Responses based on two choices are called **dichotomous variables** (Frey et al., 2000, p. 42). For example, Lucchetti (1999) asked college students to indicate with a yes or no whether they were aware that "disclosing one's sexual history is a safe-sex practice," whether they were knowledgeable about specific safe-sex activities, and whether they were "truthful in disclosing their own sexual history" (pp. 305–306). In testing cultivation theory,

Gerbner, Gross, Morgan, and Signorielli (1986) developed the Mean World Index by posing a series of questions with dichotomized responses. The response format of their questions varied from the traditional yes/no or true/false type questions, but they were still dichotomized (see Exhibit 5.7).

There are two criteria that all nominal level measurements should satisfy. The variable categories must be exhaustive and mutually exclusive. Ideally, when you list the categories from which participants choose responses, it should be an **exhaustive** list; that is, all possible categories of the variable should be listed. See, for example, the questions in Exhibits 5.6 and 5.7. Answering any of those questions requires making a choice from a list of available alternatives. The risk you take in providing the list is that an essential category is overlooked. For example, we noted earlier that in constructing questions about ethnicity and disabilities, you should be very sensitive about the ways in which these groups classify themselves, especially as the distinctions between categories become more mixed or diffuse. One solution to omitting crucial categories is to use open-ended questions, as described in the previous section, so that classification schemes, or taxonomies, can be developed from participant responses. In this way, survey questions can be categorized at the nominal level once they have been obtained through another question format.

For example, Messman and Mikesell (2000) asked their subjects to respond to an open-ended question about areas of competition in romantic couples. From their responses, the researchers constructed 40 nominal categories. Similarly, Bradford et al. (1999) used focus group interviews to ask participants to identify

---

EXHIBIT 5.7   Examples of Dichotomous Responses to Survey Questions (Nominal Level of Measurement)

1. Do you think that most people would try to take advantage of you if they get a chance or would try to be fair?

   _____ Try to take advantage

   _____ Try to be fair

2. Generally speaking, would you say that most people can be trusted or that you can't be too careful in dealing with people?

   _____ Can be trusted

   _____ Can't be too careful

3. Would you say that most of the time people try to be helpful, or that they are mostly looking out for themselves?

   _____ Try to be helpful

   _____ Looking out for themselves

Note. These dichotomous variable examples come from Gerbner et al. (1986).

---

conflict strategy a person would be likely to use, and the list of possibilities should include only those behaviors that satisfy both conditions (i.e., a conflict behavior and a type of strategy). We would not want to include responses that identify persuasive strategies or conflict styles as well.

Variables measured at the nominal level are called **categorical,** discrete, or simply nominal. They have numbers assigned to each variable category. To illustrate this process, you may assign all "yes" responses the value of 1, and all "no" responses the value of 2. For marital status, all single people are assigned 1s, all married people are 2s, all cohabitants are 3s, all divorced people are 4s, and so on. The function of assigning numbers to the categories is that the number identifies or names the category (hence, the term *nominal,* coming from the Latin word *nomen,* meaning "name"). The numbers of each category are not mathematically related to each other. "No" responses are not twice as much as "yes" responses; females are not twice the value of males. This characteristic is a critical distinction of nominal measurement that we will return to repeatedly in Chapters 6, 8, and 9. As you will see, measuring categorical variables at the nominal level specifies what types of data analyses can be performed later on in your study.

competent communication behaviors in Latinos. Their responses were used to expand and confirm an existing classification system of nonverbal and verbal behaviors developed by Martin, Hammer, and Bradford (1994). Although it is encountered in survey research, this technique is more frequently used as a form of content analysis or interaction analysis, discussed in Chapter 7.

The second criterion of categories is that they be **mutually exclusive.** This requirement means that each response can be placed in one, and only one, category. For example, if you answer that you are male, you cannot also be placed in the female category. If you indicate that you are a sophomore, you cannot also be a senior. If you indicate you are a newcomer to an organization, you cannot also be classified as a veteran. Respondents should not be able to choose more than one alternative from the list.

The criteria of developing an exhaustive and mutually exclusive list of categories implies that you must decide what should be present as well as what should be excluded. Items should be topically relevant. For example, a question might ask what type of

Ordinal level The ordinal level of measurement provides some estimate of quantity; the numbers assigned to the variable are, in some sense, mathematically related. But how they are related is not precise. **Ordinal scales** measure rankings of various categories of variables. For example, a question may ask respondents to rank from 1 to 3 the frequency of media use as a source of news information, identifying the most frequent source with a 1 and the least frequent with a 3. Or respondents may identify their five favorite prime time sitcoms. Or *Rolling Stone* may report survey results identifying the top 10 songs of the decade.

At the nominal level, the numbers assigned to variable categories have no real mathematical value. Their main function is to identify a variable category. In ordinal scales, the numbers do express magnitude, but the units of measurement are not assumed to be equal. For example, suppose we ask Maria, Alex, and Julie to indicate their uses of media as news sources. They all may indicate television as their highest frequency, radio as their second, and the newspaper as their third; however, Maria's ranking of 1, 2, and 3 may represent very different actual frequencies of

---

EXHIBIT 5.8   Ordinal Measurement of Quantity

Indicate the media sources you use as a source of news information and rank each source starting with 1 as the most frequently used source:

Maria's response:

__1__ television (Maria watches television news about 8 times a week.)

__2__ radio (Maria listens to the radio for news about 5 times a week.)

__3__ newspaper (Maria reads a newspaper about 3 times a week.)

Alex's response:

__1__ television (Alex watches television news about 5 times a week.)

__2__ radio (Alex listens to the radio for news about 4 times a week.)

__3__ newspaper (Alex reads a newspaper about 3 times a week.)

Julie's response:

__1__ television (Julie watches television news about 7 times a week.)

__2__ radio (Julie listens to the radio for news about 2 times a week.)

__3__ newspaper (Julie reads a newspaper about 1 time a week.)

---

media use than either Alex's or Julie's, as shown in Exhibit 5.8. Even though they have indicated the same rankings, Maria's values of 1, 2, and 3 are not the same as Alex's 1, 2, and 3, or Julie's 1, 2, and 3. But an ordinal scale cannot detect those precise differences. Often, ordinal scales are used when "the distance between the different values of the variables is unknown or is known to be unequal and a rank ordering can be imposed" (Smith, 1988, p. 45). Ordinal scales give us more information about the variable than nominal level measures do, but they are not as precise as the next two types of scales.

Interval level Scales used to measure communication variables that express values of magnitude and have equal distances between each value are called **interval scales.** Many surveys use interval scales to assess communication constructs. The two types of interval scales most frequently used in communication research are the Likert scale and the semantic differential. In **Likert scales,** the construct is measured by providing research participants with statements assumed to reflect the presence or absence of the construct. Each statement is followed by a range of alternatives that allow participants to indicate a level at which they estimate the construct to either be present or absent.

For example, Behnke and Sawyer (1999) used McCroskey's Likert-type scale of communication apprehension and Tuckman's Likert-type scale of pro-

crastination to assess the relationship between these two variables. There is an example of the communication apprehension measure in Exhibit 5.9. Sutter and Martin (1998) used Infante and Wigley's (1986) verbal aggressiveness scale in assessing the relationship between that variable and several different types of disengagement strategies. An example of verbal aggressiveness also appears in Exhibit 5.9.

Variables measured with Likert-type interval scales can be either unidimensional or multidimensional. When the variable is **unidimensional,** it means that there are no subconstructs or factors that the variable can be broken down into; the conceptual field is uniform, and all of the items on the scale reflect this uniformity. Communication apprehension measured with the PRCA-24 and verbal aggressiveness measured with Infante and Wigley's (1986) scale are both unidimensional variables.

Sometimes, variables are **multidimensional**— several different subconstructs represent each of the different dimensions. For example, Montgomery and Norton's (1981) Communicator Style scale contains the following dimensions: friendly, impression leaving, relaxed, contentious/argumentative, attentive, precise, animated/expressive, dramatic, open, dominant, and communicator image. The questionnaire contains 51 items, of which 45 are scored (the rest are filler items). Certain items in the survey correspond to the different dimensions; for example, items 3, 6, 38, and 46 correspond to the friendly dimension;

EXHIBIT 5.9   Examples of Likert-Type Interval Scales

Personal Report of Communication Apprehension, PRCA-24 (unidimensional)

Directions: This instrument is composed of twenty-five statements concerning feelings about communicating with other people. Please indicate the degree to which each statement applies to you by marking whether you (1) strongly agree, (2) agree, (3) are undecided, (4) disagree, or (5) strongly disagree. Please just record your first impression.

___ 1. *While participating in a conversation with a new acquaintance, I feel very nervous.*
___ 2. *I have no fear of facing an audience.*
___ 3. *I talk less because I'm shy.*
___ 4. *I look forward to expressing opinions at meetings.*
___ 5. *I am afraid to express myself in a group.*

Verbal Aggressiveness Scale (unidimensional)

This survey is concerned with how we try to get people to comply with our wishes. Indicate how often each statement is true for you personally when you try to influence other persons. Use the following scale: 1 = almost never true, 2 = rarely true, 3 = occasionally true, 4 = often true, and 5 = almost always true.

___ 1. *When individuals insult me, I get a lot of pleasure in really telling them off.*
___ 2. *When individuals are very stubborn, I use insults to soften the stubbornness.*
___ 3. *When I attack persons' ideas, I try not to damage their self-concepts.*
___ 4. *When others do things I regard as stupid, I try to be extremely gentle with them.*
___ 5. *If individuals I am trying to influence really deserve it, I attack their character.*

EXHIBIT 5.10   Examples of Likert-Type Interval Scales Measuring a Multidimensional Variable

COMMUNICATOR STYLE SCALE (MULTIDIMENSIONAL)

The following scale is used for each item: YES! = strong agreement with the statement, yes = agreement with the statement, ? = neither agreement nor disagreement with the statement, no = disagreement with the statement, NO! = strong disagreement with the statement.

Friendly dimension:

3. I readily express admiration for others.
6. To be friendly, I habitually acknowledge verbally others' contributions.
38. I am always an extremely friendly communicator.
46. Whenever I communicate, I tend to be very encouraging to people.

Relaxed dimension:

8. I have some nervous mannerisms in my speech.
9. I am a very relaxed communicator.
15. The rhythm or flow of my speech is sometimes affected by my nervousness.
16. Under pressure I come across as a relaxed speaker.

Dominant dimension:

28. In most social situations I generally speak very frequently.
35. I am dominant in social situations.
41. I try to take charge of things when I am with people.
43. In most social situations I tend to come on strong.

---

items 8, 9, 15, and 16 correspond to the relaxed dimension; and items 28, 35, 41, and 43 correspond to the dominant dimension. These have been illustrated in Exhibit 5.10.

The second type of interval scale that appears frequently in our research literature is the **semantic differential.** This scale consists of a series of bipolar adjectives placed at either end of a continuum. The adjectives act as anchors for extremes; the respondents indicate where along the continuum between the extremes their perceptions lie. One communication construct that is often measured with a semantic differential type of scale is credibility. Credibility is a multidimensional construct applied across many contexts, including teacher credibility, news credibility, and speaker credibility (McCroskey & Young, 1981). An example of source credibility measured with this type of semantic differential appears in Exhibit 5.11.

EXHIBIT 5.11   Example of Semantic Differential Scale

SOURCE CREDIBILITY SCALE—15-ITEM SEMANTIC DIFFERENTIAL

This type of credibility scale is often used to assess respondents' attitudes toward public figures like political candidates. We used George W. Bush as the sample source here. Instructions: On the scales below, please indicate your feelings about President George W. Bush. Circle the number between the adjectives that best rep-

resents your feelings about George Bush. Numbers "1" and "7" indicate a very strong feeling. Numbers "2" and "6" indicate a strong feeling. Numbers "3" and "5" indicate a fairly weak feeling. Number "4" indicates you are undecided or do not understand the adjectives themselves. Please work quickly. There are no right or wrong answers.

Sociability:

Good-natured	1	2	3	4	5	6	7	Irritable
Cheerful	1	2	3	4	5	6	7	Gloomy
Unfriendly	1	2	3	4	5	6	7	Friendly

Extroversion:

Timid	1	2	3	4	5	6	7	Bold
Verbal	1	2	3	4	5	6	7	Quiet
Talkative	1	2	3	4	5	6	7	Silent

Competence:

Expert	1	2	3	4	5	6	7	Inexpert
Unintelligent	1	2	3	4	5	6	7	Intelligent
Intellectual	1	2	3	4	5	6	7	Narrow

Composure:

Poised	1	2	3	4	5	6	7	Nervous
Tense	1	2	3	4	5	6	7	Relaxed
Calm	1	2	3	4	5	6	7	Anxious

Character:

Unsympathetic	1	2	3	4	5	6	7	Sympathetic
Dishonest	1	2	3	4	5	6	7	Honest
Good	1	2	3	4	5	6	7	Bad

Semantic differentials can be used with unidimensional constructs as well.

An important feature of both types of interval scales is that they contain statements that reflect high and low levels of the construct under investigation. For example, in the Likert-type PRCA-24 measure, the statements "I talk less because I am shy" and "I am afraid to speak in a group" are statements that you would expect those people high in communication apprehension to express; statements like "I have no fear facing an audience" and "I look forward to expressing my opinions at meetings" are statements with which those low in communication apprehension are likely to agree. These are randomly interspersed throughout the scale.

When semantic differentials are used, both positive and negative ends of the polar attributes are named, and

the order in which they appear is randomly reversed. Moreover, if the construct is multidimensional, the order of the adjectives is frequently randomized so that the adjective pairs for each dimension are integrated. Some researchers even go so far as to eliminate the neutral position on these scales, making the number of response options an even number so that the response must indicate more of a direction. These procedures are recommended to avoid a **response bias,** sometimes called a response set, or the tendency for respondents to get into the habit of responding in a particular way so that they cease being mindful of their responses. Questionnaires that have all the same numbers checked (all 5s or all 3s) are usually discarded for this very reason. You will learn more about biases in the last section of this chapter and in the next chapter.

Social scientists have debated whether interval scales like those described in this section really have equal distances between their semantic points along the continuum from one end to the other. Is the distance between "strongly disagree" and "disagree," for example, the same distance as between "disagree" and "don't know/unsure"? Several serious attempts to test for any differences have found that, in most cases, Likert-type and semantic differential scales could be treated as true interval scales.

In some questionnaires, it may be necessary to obtain greater precision in scale construction, and then the researcher must select a much more difficult procedure like Thurstone or Guttman scaling to reduce the amount of error present in the data (see Frey et al., 2000, p. 93, and Watt & van den Berg, 1995, pp. 119–122, for a description). However, it is rare that you will find this procedure used in communication research.

Ratio level **Ratio scales** are like interval scales in that values represent points along a continuum separated by equal distances or intervals. The difference between the two is that a ratio scale has a true or absolute zero point. An absolute zero stands for an absolute absence of the variable in question. Ratio scales are used when you wish to determine the frequency of communication behaviors or time period durations. For example, you could ask how many hours per day the television is on at home, how many times a week a person emails family members and friends, or how many months two people have known each other. Each of these is measured with a ratio scale. You could also give participants a memory quiz and count the number of correct responses. Or you could ask how frequently a described internal state, such as a certain feeling about a relationship, occurs in participants, ranging from "never" to "always." This type of measurement also uses a ratio scale.

Ratio and interval scales are very powerful measurement tools. Unlike nominal and ordinal scales, they have precise measurement units. The value 2 is twice as much as 1, and 3 is half as much as 6; for example, 2 on a ratio scale measuring the number of contacts you have had with your employer is twice as many contacts as someone who answered with a 1.

These scales provide you with a great deal of information, and they enable the data to be analyzed with more complex tests of the hypotheses. As you will see in Chapters 8 and 9, ratio and interval measurements give an array of information along a continuum instead of requiring the use of just one value to represent a whole group or sequence of numbers. Because of this difference, it will be possible to make inferences that are not available when data are measured with nominal or ordinal scales. Constructs measured with interval and ratio scales are called **continuous variables,** sometimes also referred to as ordered or scaled variables. This level of measurement has serious implications for the types of analyses that researchers will choose to test their hypotheses.

As explained at the beginning of the section on survey data, a large amount of the work of survey research is done prior to the actual administration of the survey, unlike ethnographic studies or conversational analysis or many methods in rhetorical criticism. From a discovery paradigm perspective, analyses of the data in survey research are direct tests of the claims. Depending on the scales used to measure each of the variables, certain statistical tests will be selected. For example, when your survey variables are all categorical, tests called nonparametric statistics are frequently used. When they are all continuous, you may use a correlation statistic or a regression test to find out whether you can support your claims. We will reserve most of the discussion of statistical data analysis in survey research for Chapters 8 and 9.

Before statistical analyses can be performed, you must assess the validity and reliability of the sampling and data collection methods used in your survey to establish the worth of the data as evidence. Ideally, the assessment decisions are made before any data collection as separate tests of the instruments or measures. These often occur, in fact, in separate studies whose primary purpose is to validate the instrument. Validity and reliability assessments, as warrants in the research-as-argument model, are the last topic we shall consider in this chapter on survey research.

SURVEY RESEARCH
WARRANTS

As you learned in Chapter 4, validity is a concern for accuracy or precision. It can refer to the *internal validity* of a survey study, which is the ability of the survey to accurately test claims in the form of hypotheses or research questions. In survey research, internal validity is almost synonymous with measurement validity because surveys are generally based on data collection strategies, not data manipulation. Data collection strategies are aimed at maximizing response rates. In considering response rate, you will also become aware of the concern for *external validity* in survey research, which is the ability to generalize your results from representative samples to larger populations. *Measurement validity* specifically refers to the ability of a specific instrument or scale to accurately measure a variable. When you learn about experimental research designs in Chapter 6, you will explore how internal validity extends beyond measurement validity. In this chapter, you will examine the specific types of validity and reliability, and how these are assessed in survey research.

Response Rate as an Essential Contributor to Validity and Reliability

There are two types of response rates: total response rate and item response rate. The **total response rate** refers to the percentage of total surveys successfully completed and collected. The **item response rate** refers to the percentage of completed items on each individual survey. Missing data in the form of whole surveys or specific items can affect the validity and reliability of any survey. You can influence the response rates, to some degree, by manipulating the format of the interview or the questionnaire. The guidelines in Exhibit 5.5 will help you to maximize response rates.

If the survey asks participants to respond to very complex and emotionally sensitive information, then arranging a smaller number of personal interviews will probably result in higher response rates than conducting a telephone interview or mailing out questionnaires. Interviews of any type are more likely to increase response rates because, as the interviewer, you are present to clarify any questions that respondents may have about the survey, you can monitor respondents' nonverbal (or at least vocal) reactions, and you can probe respondents for more information. Increasing the amount of information collected usually increases the internal validity and reliability of the responses.

You must also consider the assurance of anonymity that a mailed questionnaire provides. It may be easier to return a survey privately than to be singled out at a school, for example, for an interview. Other considerations in questionnaire construction already mentioned can affect response rates. Incomplete surveys or total nonresponses are more likely when the questionnaire is too long, too complex, or too vague. Questions that are leading or provocative or are generally insensitive to respondents' diversity are also likely to diminish response rates.

Paying attention to these important factors will help to increase response rates as a function of the actual interview process. In the case of mailed questionnaires, you can also send out follow-up mailings to increase the total response rate. There are a number of studies that show significant increases in returns where follow-ups were used compared to no follow-ups used (Babbie, 1995, pp. 260–261). Adopting strategies like follow-up contacts to increase total response rates will also affect external validity. If you use a random sampling method, the higher the rate of return, the more likely the sample you obtain will be representative of the larger population.

How do you determine what return rate is acceptable? There are widely varying answers to that question, but the following is a useful guide:

> Even so, it's possible to state some rules of thumb about return rates. I feel that a response rate of at least 50 percent is *adequate* for analysis and reporting. A response of at least 60 percent is *good*. And a response rate of 70 percent is *very good*. You should bear in mind though that these are only rough guides . . . (Babbie, 1995, p. 262).

Babbie also added a caveat that a high response rate is not the ultimate goal; you should work for samples that are not biased by selection, and achieving a high response rate is only one means of achieving that end. Adopting strategies to increase item response rates also affects the measurement validity and reliability of a scale constructed to measure a variable as described earlier.

Establishing Valid Measurement

In Chapter 4, "Warrants for Research Arguments," you learned about several types of measurement validity that researchers from the discovery paradigm use as warrants for their arguments. Here, you will only consider two points that address *how* measurement validity is established in survey research.

Our first point is that measurement validity requires that you construct a rationale for how you have arrived at your definition of a variable. This is most closely related to the idea of *richness* as we presented it in Chapter 4. You may also establish *criterion validity* by appealing to past and current conceptual and operational definitions of a variable. You can do so, as explained previously, by using *predictive* and *concurrent* grounds. Finally, you will frequently want to assess *construct validity* by evaluating the structure of a variable; that is, by defining what a variable is and is not. There are a variety of techniques used to make these assessments, such as exploratory or confirmatory factor analysis and discriminant analysis, but these are beyond the scope of this book.

Second, validity assessments are companions to reliability estimates. Validity tests establish warrants for *accuracy* of a study's measures, whereas reliability estimates establish warrants for the *consistency* of measurement. Ideally, you will strive for instruments that have high levels of both accuracy and consistency. Babbie (1995) illustrated the relationship between the two with the visual analogy of shooting at a bull's-eye. Measures that are high in reliability but are not valid show all of the shots clustered together but off-center. The measures may be consistent, but they are consistently wrong. This type of error is called **constant error** or **bias.** Measures that are valid but not reliable are like shots that encircle the center but only diffusely. In this case, measures have small amounts of error that infiltrate from a variety of sources. This type of error is called **random error** or **noise.** And measures that are high on both dimensions show the shots dead-on the center and clustered closely together (p. 128). Measurements that are valid and reliable are not only accurate; they are consistently accurate. It is important, therefore, that we now consider the final element of this section, reliability estimates in survey research.

Establishing Reliable Measurement

Each of the three types of measurement reliability you learned about in Chapter 4 is relevant to survey research methodology. In this section, you will briefly explore how researchers establish stability, homogeneity, and equivalence in measurement.

You may recall that *test-retest reliability*, a form of stability, occurs when a self-report survey instrument that has been administered to a group of people is given again, to those same people, on a later occasion. To the extent that the same people achieve consistent scores over time, test-retest reliability has been achieved. In order to demonstrate test-retest reliability, you need to consider what interval of time would

be appropriate. If your measurement is repeated too soon, the participants may recall the items, and their scores may have not changed because of familiarity. But if too much time elapses before the second measurement, then real change on the variable being measured is likely to have occurred. Obviously, the appropriate time interval for demonstrating test-retest reliability will depend on the concept being measured. For example, children's reading ability is very likely to change over six months, but other variables are much more stable over time. So you will need to consider how much time to allow between your test and retest: Allow enough time that your respondents are not simply recalling the items on your survey. But do not wait so long that real change in the variable you are attempting to measure is likely to have occurred.

The second way to estimate reliability of a survey instrument is to assess the *homogeneity* (or internal consistency) of measurement. There are several methods used to check the patterns of response consistency in interval scales like the Likert-type and semantic differentials. One common technique is called the **split-halves technique**—one half of the items on a scale are randomly chosen and correlated with responses from the other half. Another more prevalent method is to calculate a **Cronbach's alpha.** This technique "randomly selects multiple pairs of subsets from an instrument, correlates each pair's scores, and then uses the composite correlation between all the paired subsets as an index" of consistency (Smith, 1988, p. 47). As with any correlation, the closer the values are to 1.00, the higher the consistency estimate. Cronbach's alpha is so commonly used it has many equivalent terms; whenever you see references to alpha reliabilities, reliability coefficients, alpha coefficients, *A,* or α the authors are most likely referring to Cronbach's alpha.

The final way survey researchers assess the consistency or reliability of variable measurement is to establish *equivalence*. Recall that equivalence can estimate consistency in two ways, depending on the data source: Intercoder agreement verifies the agreement among judges about how qualitative data are interpreted or categorized, and the alternate forms method verifies the consistency of measurement results yielded by more than one measure of the same construct. Whenever several coders are categorizing communication responses according to the operational definitions of the variables, we expect their re-

---

EXHIBIT 5.12   Advantages and Disadvantages of Computer-Assisted Interviews

ADVANTAGES

1. Have all the advantages of telephone interviews listed earlier.
2. Can provide greater consistency by prompting both interviewers and participants with the appropriate questions to ask at every phase of the interview.
3. May be preferred in longitudinal studies in the place of diaries especially when the same information is repeatedly collected.

DISADVANTAGES

1. Have all the disadvantages of telephone surveys listed earlier.
2. Are more likely to be seen as an impersonal intrusion.

---

sponses to be equivalent or to agree. Intercoder agreement can be expressed as a correlation between the values of +/-0.00 and +/-1.00. The closer the value approaches 1.00, the higher the level of agreement. Other estimates can be used as well. Scott's pi, Krippendorf's alpha, and Cohen's kappa are all assessments of intercoder agreement. For example, Bradford et al. (1999) used Krippendorf's alpha to determine consistency across coder judgments, which they estimated to be 80% (p. 107).

You should always provide some assessment of reliability and validity of your measures in order to establish warrants for connecting the data to your claims. As stated earlier, measurements that are valid and reliable are not only accurate; they are consistently accurate. Failure to estimate validity and reliability considerably weakens your argument that the instruments found in your survey will provide an adequate test of your study's claims. Before leaving the topic of survey research, it is important to consider how recent developments in technology have impacted this particular methodology.

SURVEYS AND TECHNOLOGY

There are two ways in which technology can be seen in survey research. It can be used as part of the research methodology itself, or it can be the main topic of the study's claims. You will briefly see examples of both.

Survey research routinely makes use of technology in collecting and analyzing data. You can use computer-generated random digit dialing programs to reach a broader and more representative sample of any population you have targeted for interviews by phone. Randomizing procedures of many types are usually constructed by various computer programs. Some generate mailing lists for sending questionnaires. Others are capable of assisting in or conducting complete interviews online.

Computer-assisted interviews are programs that can provide greater consistency by prompting both interviewers and participants with the appropriate questions to ask at every phase of the interview. There are other research situations in which telephone interviews are entirely conducted by computers. You may have already been targeted by this type of survey in various marketing strategies or polling surveys for political preferences. You are asked by a computer to indicate your preferences using the touch-tone keypad on your phone or by speaking a simple response clearly. Your response is converted into digitalized information to be read and measured as part of the same data collection program.

The disadvantages of telephone surveys increase the more computer-mediated they become. Respondents may actually become less willing to disclose information to a machine than a person. Interview length cannot be as long or as complicated as those conducted by a person. Many respondents distrust any telephone context as veiled marketing devices and frequently use their answering machines to screen calls, especially those that appear to be a "canned" sales pitch. Additionally, people who originally begin to participate in a computer-mediated interview can break it off at any point just by hanging up. However, there is recent evidence that when you must administer the same survey over several points in time to the same group of people (the panel design), the telephone or computer-generated interview may be more preferable as a data collection strategy than the common self-administered diary method typically used by research agencies like Nielsen who monitor television program ratings (Hoppe, 2000). Exhibit 5.12 lists a variety of advantages and disadvantages associated with computer-assisted and computer-mediated interviews.

An increasingly common means of obtaining information by surveys is through the Internet. Many media news groups, like the *New York Times* online, will give incentives to participants who agree to answer a variety of surveys from time to time, typically about their market preferences. Recently, several communication researchers have contacted one of the authors of this textbook to participate in an online survey as part of their data collection process. This trend is likely to increase since various listservs or emailing lists make contacting members of numerous groups and organizations very easy.

Technology has also impacted the data analysis process. In Chapters 8 and 9, you will learn about several computer programs that will enable you to examine your data for errors and as well as conduct tests of differences and relationships. In this chapter, you have been introduced to network analysis as a form of survey research. There are now many programs equipped to handle small and large data sets collected from networks. Of the many that are available, NEGOPY, FATCAT, and MultiNet are very common programs used in social network analysis.

In a recent study, Johanson (2000) explored the influence of communication networks on perceptions of job satisfaction, organizational commitment, and organizational culture. To calculate network measures, Johanson used Ucinet network analysis with Spacestat software, which allows network data to be transformed into complex equation models for analysis. Ucinet software was also used by Feeley (2000) in exploring employee turnover rates based on their positions and levels of commitment. Another study of networks by Chang and Johnson (2001) explored how organizational network members use media as channels for messages. They explored direct and indirect paths of influence for media usage by using a program called Burt's STRUCTURE. Each type of network analysis software has unique specifications that allow it to be applied in specific contexts. What these specifications are and how they are applied are clearly beyond the scope of this book.

The second way technology impacts survey research is as the focus of many newer studies. Research on computer-mediated communication (CMC) is on the rise as well as tracking media use generally in a variety of social contexts. A study mentioned earlier by Parks and Roberts (1998) explored interpersonal relationships online versus offline. Online communication chat rooms called MUDs or MOOs (Multi-User [Object-Oriented] Domains) and the IRC (Internet Relay Chat) allow participants to communicate simultaneously. Many have been in existence for some time and have developed cybercommunities. Another study by Parks and Floyd (1996) explored how online participants use additional media sources like the telephone or snail mail to extend their communication. Undoubtedly, as cybercommunities are established and develop, there will be researchers waiting to explore them, and survey methodologies will be among the tools they use.

SUMMARY

As you can see, when surveys are used in communication research, they require careful preparation and administration. In the preparation of surveys, you must decide what types of claims you wish to construct: descriptive or explanatory. Explanatory claims are further defined as associative or causal. Once your claims are identified, you must decide on the sources, settings, and design you will use in collecting the data. You must also carefully construct the instruments whether you are structuring questions for interviews or questionnaires. In operationalizing your constructs, you must decide on the levels of measurement you will use: nominal, ordinal, interval, and ratio. In administering the survey, you must establish warrants for the data collected in support of the study's claims by assessing the survey's validity and reliability. As you will see in Chapters 8 and 9, the specific tests of survey research questions and hypotheses are statistical analyses that require equal care in interpretation. These analyses are frequently conducted with computer software—one of the many ways technology has impacted survey research. Other ways include an extensive list of network analysis software programs and survey studies of online communities.

KEY TERMS

Applied research

Background variables

Basic research

Bias

Categorical variables

Closed-format questions

Computer-assisted interviews

Constant error

Consumer research

Contingency questions

Continuous variables

Cronbach's alpha

Curvilinear relationships

Demographic characteristics

Dichotomous variables

Double-barreled questions

Ego-centered network analysis

Exhaustive categories

Face-to-face interviews

Filter questions

Focus groups

Free-recall technique

Interval scales

Item response rate

Leading questions

Likert scales

Links

Mall intercept surveys

Multidimensional variables

Mutually exclusive categories

Negative correlation

Network analytic research

Noise

Nominal scales

Nonreciprocated links

Open-ended questions

Operationalization

Order effects

Ordinal scales

Organismic variables

Political polling research

Positive correlation

Questionnaire architecture

Questionnaires

Random digit dialing

Random error

Ratio scales

Reciprocated links

Response bias

Roster method

Semantic differential scales

Semantic network analysis

Semistructured interviews

Split-halves technique

Structured interviews

Telephone surveys

Total response rate

Unidimensional variables

Unstructured interviews

Variable

DISCUSSION QUESTIONS

1. Why are interviews taken "at random" on a street corner not really random?

2. Why do you think random sampling is essential from a discovery paradigm perspective and not essential from an interpretive or a critical paradigm perspective?

3. If you wanted to conduct a survey study of children's reactions to frightening movies, what should you consider in deciding to use interviews or questionnaires?

4. Would researchers from a discovery paradigm prefer structured or unstructured interview formats? Explain your answer.

5. Because survey research is traditionally a form of research situated in the discovery paradigm, how do the warrants of validity and reliability differ from those used in research from the interpretive and critical paradigms?

"TRY IT!" ACTIVITIES

1. Find a survey research report that identifies a descriptive claim and one that identifies an explanatory claim. The two can be taken from the same article. Explain the difference between these two types of claims. Identify whether the explanatory claim is associative or causal.

2. Suppose you want to conduct a survey of attitudes toward rap music. Explain the various types of research designs you could use (cross-sectional or longitudinal). Explain the advantages and disadvantages of each type.

3. Suppose you wanted to compare at-risk high school students with those not at risk for susceptibility to peer persuasive strategies. How would you go about defining and sampling both groups? What issues might require sensitivity to diversity?

6

Experimental Research

ABSTRACT

This chapter introduces you to experimental communication research beginning with causal arguments. *Claims* of experimental research aim to describe, explain, and predict changes in communication attitudes and behaviors. Next, elements of experimental *data* collection and pre-, quasi-, and true experimental research designs are added to the study formats presented in the last chapter. The *warrants* for experimental research are presented as validity and reliability assessments whose purpose is to eliminate or reduce the number of rival hypotheses or threats to the proposed cause-and-effect relationship between the variables. Finally, we will consider how the impact of technology has affected the process and content of experimental communication research.

OUTLINE

When you conduct experimental studies, you would not be interested in developing subjective interpretations of events nor would you construct evaluative critiques of communicative practices. Your primary goal is to build an argument for causality based on the warrants of validity and reliability. *Controlling extraneous influences on the dependent variable* is the main function of an experimental design; you want to show that variable *X,* and not *W* or *Z,* causes changes in variable *Y.* Explanation, prediction, and control are the desired goals of experiments in communication research, and knowledge by discovery is the dominant paradigm.

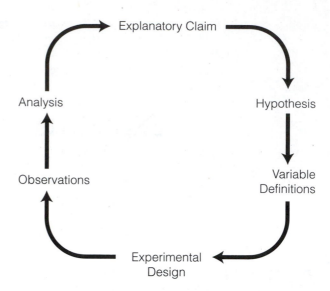

FIGURE 6.1 The deductive model of experimental research.

EXPERIMENTAL RESEARCH CLAIMS

Experiments are by their very nature designed to test the effects of one variable (or a set of variables) on another (or another set of variables); they are the classical method that researchers have used to advance causal arguments. Descriptive claims may set the groundwork to assess the conceptual field of a variable or explore the nature of the relationship between the variables, as we noted in Chapter 2, but these claims are only preliminary steps in designing an experiment that will test a causal relationship. Experiments therefore rely on predictive claims tested deductively as forms of causal arguments.

Deductive Process

Establishing causality in experimental research is essentially a deductive process. It begins with generating claims as "theoretical explanations for observed patterns of human communication" (Smith, 1988, p. 10). These are constructed in the form of hypotheses that predict that manipulating causal factors will account for observed effects on the dependent variable. You would then test the hypotheses by designing an experiment for observing those effects. The observations verify the explanatory predictions through precise and systematic analysis. This process is illustrated in Figure 6.1. Using our research-as-argument model, the deductive process begins with constructing claims that are verified through observations as data or evidence, and warranted through tests of va-

lidity and reliability. We shall explore each of the components—claim, data, and warrant—as they apply to experimental studies in our field.

In Chapter 5, you learned the difference between survey research and experimental research. Surveys assess the world as it is; the variables are "givens" and are assumed to occur naturally. Survey researchers do not create verbal aggressiveness; they simply design an instrument scale used to measure how this variable occurs in the general population. As an experimental researcher, however, you would be interested in exploring how verbal aggressiveness as a cause affects other variables. For instance, you might want to manipulate how verbally aggressive teachers versus nonargumentative teachers affect student learning, motivation, and satisfaction (Myers, 2002). By manipulating the independent variable, you can examine those sets of effects deductively, testing your claim against your observations. The deductive process is the key to constructing a causal argument.

Causal Arguments

There are three basic criteria for establishing causal arguments. First, the manipulation of the independent variable precedes the change or effect in the dependent variable. The order of effects is invariant; the changes in the dependent variable cannot precede manipulation of the independent variable. For example, Ayres, Heuett, and Sonandre (1998) constructed an experimental design to test the effectiveness of two different types of visualization in helping people reduce high levels of communication apprehension. Obviously, to test the effects of the visualization techniques, the researchers had to expose students to various forms of visualization techniques before their effectiveness on communication apprehension could be evaluated.

The second criterion for a causal argument is that variable changes must happen together; they are correlated. When the change in the independent variable occurs, it must be followed fairly closely in time by the change in the dependent variable. In the previous example, if too much time elapsed between the students' participation in the visualization exercises and the test that measured their communication apprehension, the causal link between these two would be considerably weakened. You could argue that students' apprehension levels were lessened just by the passage of time, or because the end of the school term was drawing near, or because the students who experienced the highest levels of communication apprehension had time to drop out of the experiment before they were tested. You will learn more about how causal arguments are strengthened or weakened in the section on warrants in this chapter.

The third criterion for causality is that the observed effects on the dependent variable can only be accounted for by the independent variable, not some third factor. Again referring to our earlier example, Ayres et al. (1998) constructed a design to demonstrate the causal link between visualization techniques and communication apprehension levels. The researchers had to take steps to effectively control for any rival explanations of cause and effect. They wanted to be sure that the pattern of effects observed were due to variations in the visualization techniques and not due to simply participating in an experiment. Some rival explanations are called **intervening variables,** which are other independent variables that produce effects in the dependent variable that are not controlled and so weaken the cause-and-effect relationship observed in the study (Smith, 1988, p. 199).

Experimental researchers spend a great deal of time and attention to detail in constructing a design as a fair test of the data based on these three criteria. In experimental research, claims are most often found in the form of research questions or hypotheses, veri-

fied by some sort of observation. In traditional experimental designs, predictions are phrased as hypotheses where at least one of the independent variables is manipulated while rival explanations are strictly controlled. This is the classic "wiggle" test. If we want to see what part of a machine causes changes in the other parts, we can wiggle each part systematically, eliminating every other possibility, until we can see what moves what.

In our earlier example, Ayres et al. (1998) constructed a careful design to test the effectiveness of visualization to help reduce communication apprehension. By taking certain steps to hold other factors constant (steps you will learn about later on), the researchers hoped to strengthen their claim that various types of visualization, and not some other factor, were the probable cause of change in the participants' level of communication apprehension. Additional examples of hypotheses from experimental studies appear in Exhibit 6.1. In each of these cases, the researchers presumed it was the manipulation of the independent variable that produced the observed effects in the dependent variable.

In experimental research, the distinguishing factor from every other type of research, then, is that the researcher intentionally manipulates the independent variable for the purposes of testing its effects on the dependent variable. The manipulation expresses control over the independent variable as the probable cause of change in the dependent variable. For example, Gorham, Cohen, and Morris (1999) tested the effects of teacher immediacy (how approachable they are) and teacher clothing style on student perceptions of the instructor and learning in general. The researchers varied the levels of immediacy (immediate vs. nonimmediate) and attire (formal vs. casual) as the independent variables to assess the influence of these factors on the dependent variables (students' perceptions and learning).

Not all causal arguments are tested with experiments. In the last chapter, you learned about a number of examples of survey studies that examined causal relationships. However, because of the central importance of establishing causal links in experimental studies, the strength of the causal argument that supports each hypothesis or claim rests in the design and analysis of experimental research data, and the warrants for those claims. We shall first examine experimental research data.

EXHIBIT 6.1   Explanatory Claims in Experimental Research

H₁: College students' perceptions of learning are influenced by instructor immediacy and, to a lesser degree, by instructor attire at both the initial meeting and at midterm (Gorham, Cohen, & Morris, 1999, p. 284).

- Independent variables: instructor immediacy and instructor attire
- Dependent variables: students' perceptions of learning

H₂: Highly involved pleasant communicators produce more positive and fewer negative reports of mood, arousal, and affect than less involved unpleasant communicators (Le Poire & Yoshimura, 1999, p. 4).

- Independent variables: involvement level changes and communication-relevant expectancies
- Dependent variables: affective ratings of mood, arousal, and emotions

H₃: Varying levels of nonverbal cues displayed by a witness during a videotaped deposition will influence participants' ratings of deceptiveness and nervousness of the witness (Henningsen, Cruz, & Morr, 2000, p. 3).

- Independent variable: nonverbal cues manipulated across three nonverbal cue conditions

- Dependent variable: participants' ratings of deceptiveness and nervousness of the witness

H₄: Viewers of scenes featuring rapid point-of-view movement on a large-screen television will be more aroused and will report a variety of more intense responses that indicate presence (sense of physical enjoyment, queasiness, excitement, involvement, affective enjoyment, and participation) than will viewers who watch these scenes on a small-screen television (Lombard & Reich, 2000, p. 82)

- Independent variable: television screen size
- Dependent variable: presence responses (physical enjoyment, etc.).

H₅: Children remember more from television news stories in a children's news format than from the same stories presented in print (van der Molen & van der Voort, 2000, p. 138).

- Independent variables: television vs. print, children's vs. adults' news, adults vs. children age groups
- Dependent variable: children participants' recall of the news stories

---

EXPERIMENTAL RESEARCH
DATA

The assumptions of causality and the requirements of experimental designs structure the data portion of the research model in some very unique ways. We will explore these by examining sources, settings, types of designs, data collection strategies, and data analysis.

Data Sources

Sources of data for experimental studies vary by the type of variable you have selected to study. In the last section, you learned that the independent variable is constructed and manipulated by the researcher. Its manipulation is observed to see what effects it will have on the dependent variable. The changes in the state or conditions of the independent variable are solely based on its manipulation. The dependent variable is then assessed by the data sources of observa-

tion, self-report, or other-report to see what changes have occurred.

For example, Armstrong and Chung (2000) wanted to test the effect of background noise on recall and recognition of information in newspaper articles. They manipulated the independent variable by varying the conditions under which noise was present (or not). In the first condition, they showed participants a television drama while requiring them to read one of two newspaper articles. Armstrong and Chung then tested the participants for recognition and recall in silence. In the second condition, participants read the articles in silence, but were tested for recall and recognition with the television drama program as background noise. In all, the researchers manipulated five conditions or variations of the independent variable. Each of these conditions is illustrated in Table 6.1.

After each group of participants had been exposed to one of the conditions, Armstrong and Chung

Table 6.1. Experimental Conditions as Manipulation of the Independent Variable

Armstrong & Chung study	Part I: reading articles	Part II: recalling and recognizing information
Condition #1	Television on	Television off
Condition #2	Television off	Television on
Condition #3	Television on (*ER* or *Party of 5* is background program)	Television on (same program, *ER* or *Party of 5,* is shown as in Part I)
Condition #4	Television on (*ER* or *Party of 5* is background program)	Television on (if *ER* on in Part I, then *Party of 5* is on in Part II; if *Party of 5* on in Part I, then *ER* is on in Part II)
Condition #5: control group	Television off	Television off

gave them a "cued recall format" test and a "multiple choice test assessing recognition for the same information" (p. 338). The independent variable, five conditions of background noise, served as a **stimulus variable**—a variable manipulated in order to provoke a targeted response—observed for its effects on recall and recognition as the dependent variables. The data sources for the dependent variables in this particular study were the self-report measures.

Independent variables in experimental studies are classically analyzed by examining differences between various treatment groups. But sometimes variable groups occur naturally as internal characteristics of the research participants; they vary by types of characteristics that cannot be controlled by the researcher. In Chapter 5, we called this type of variable an **organismic variable.** For example, Kaid and Holtz-Bacha (2000) assessed gender and country-of-origin differences for their effects on responses to political advertising. The independent variables of gender and country were intrinsic characteristics of the participants.

Some studies mix stimulus variables with organismic variables; the resulting design is called a **mixed model paradigm** (Miller, 1970, in Smith, 1988, p. 200). For example, Monahan and Lannutti (2000) varied levels of alcohol consumption as the stimulus variable with high and low levels of self-esteem as the organismic variable to test their effects on anxiety levels and self-disclosure. The researchers could manipulate the levels of alcohol as the stimulus variable, but they could not manipulate the varying levels of self-esteem (high and low). Self-esteem was the or-

ganismic variable because participants came to the research setting with their own characteristic levels of self-esteem already in place.

Data Settings

In Chapter 3, you learned that there are two basic settings: laboratory and field. The traditional setting for an experimental study is the laboratory. Lab settings permit researchers to exercise more control over environmental factors that might interfere with testing the causal relationship between the variables. Unfortunately, the control of extraneous factors achieved with the lab environment is sometimes offset by its artificiality. Participants often react in ways that they wouldn't ordinarily because there's just no place like home! Because of this problem, you might try to make the setting more natural. For example, in the study mentioned earlier, Armstrong and Chung (2000) set up the experimental area "like a living room, including lamp lighting. Participants sat on a small couch, with a low table immediately in front of them and a television and VCR at eye level approximately 45 degrees to their left at a normal viewing distance" (p. 342).

In some experiments, you might use a **cover story** that obscures the real testing situation so that the procedure will seem more natural to participants. Cover stories are deceptive strategies designed to reduce participants' reactions to the experimental situation. For example, Guerrero, Jones, and Burgoon (2000) employed a complicated ruse to mask the actual manipulation of the independent variable. They interjected a "short break" between conversations to give instructions to one group of **confederates** on changing their behavior. They were confederates because, unlike the other participants, they were "in on" the ruse and helped the researchers manipulate the independent variable.

The cover story was given only to the **target** (or true) **participants.** The short break between conversations was explained as necessary so that the confederate and target participants could complete a personality questionnaire in private. In actuality, the confederates went off to a room to get instructions on changing their behavior as part of the independent variable manipulation, while the target participants stayed in the original room and completed a bogus questionnaire, one that was not used at all in the experimental analysis. By using the cover story, Guerrero et al. hoped the target participants would react to the change in the confederates' behavior more naturally instead of attributing the change to the experimental situation (p. 332).

You will learn more about laboratory setting effects in the discussion of validity and reliability in the warrants section of this chapter. Before leaving the topic of setting, however, we want to point out that many experimental studies are conducted in the field. For example, McDevitt and Chaffee (2000) went out to schools in the San Jose unified school district and solicited students as participants who had been exposed to a particular curricular program on voting as well as student participants who had not been exposed. Adoption of the curriculum was not controlled by the researchers but by the teachers. The researchers were fortunate to find equally large groups of students who had and had not been exposed to the program.

The weakness of field studies is a direct contrast with lab studies. In field studies, you do not have to recreate a natural environment for the sake of validity as you may have to in a laboratory study. But as a result, you will have much less control over extraneous factors in the field. McDevitt and Chaffee had to conduct special analyses to make sure that students exposed to the curricular program on voting did not differ substantially in characteristics from those other students not exposed to the curriculum; they also had to ascertain whether either group had been exposed to any events outside of the study that might influence the study's outcome (p. 269). We will also elaborate on these potential setting effects when we discuss validity and reliability concerns in the warrants section.

Research Designs and Experimental Control

The research design of an experimental study enables you to construct an effective experimental manipulation of the independent variable. Its primary purpose is to establish a strong base for causality through **experimental control.** This objective is achieved by checking the manipulation of the independent variable for its effectiveness, and through controlling alternative rival explanations for the observed set of effects on the dependent variable.

To ensure that the manipulation of the independent variable has been successful, researchers will frequently use **manipulation checks**—procedures that directly test whether the participants perceived the independent variable the way it was intended to be. In a complex experiment, Afifi and Burgoon (2000) designed a test of five alternate theoretical explanations for the effects of violating the participants' expectations on the uncertainty they felt about a communication situation they were observing. The researchers used videotapes of two confederates, one female and one male, interacting with each other. These confederates were instructed to violate expectations in one of four ways, or to not violate expectations during the interaction. For example, one of the violation conditions required the confederates to move from a moderate level of involvement with each other to complete uninterest. To make sure that the confederates accurately portrayed each of the violation conditions, Afifi and Burgoon asked the participants to report any and all violations of expectations that occurred. In this way, the researchers could assess whether the confederates were successful in portraying an expectancy violation.

Frequently, measures designed as manipulation checks extend beyond the current study setting to determine how the independent variable is perceived. For example, Weaver, Lariscy and Tinkham (1999) tested the *sleeper effect* of attack and defensive messages in political commercials. The sleeper effect is defined as "the phenomenon characterized by increased impact at some point in time after a stimulus event occurs" (p. 14). In order to check the construction of attack and defensive messages, the researchers used a separate sample of 70 students to evaluate each message. This sample was drawn from the same college that was the source of the participants in the experiment and served as a preliminary testing group in assessing the political commercials. Both message types, attack and defense, were correctly identified by the majority of students in this separate sample.

Design elements Experimental control is acquired through three procedural elements: comparison groups, random assignment to independent variable conditions, and pretest–posttest administrations (Katzer, Cook, & Crouch, 1982, pp. 118–119).

Comparison groups **Comparison groups** refer to groups of study participants who are exposed to the manipulated levels of the independent variable. Researchers vary the levels or conditions of the independent variable to observe the results for each variation on the group of participants. In Armstrong and Chung's (2000) experiment mentioned previously, there were five experimental conditions. As we explained before, the first condition exposed subjects to a videotape of a dramatic television show played as background noise while the subjects read a newspaper article; recognition and recall were tested in silence. In the second condition, subjects read the article in silence and were tested with the background videotape. The third and fourth conditions played the videotape during both the reading session and the testing session, but the type of program was either the same or varied. Referring back to Table 6.1 should help to clarify each of these experimental conditions.

In the fifth and last condition, participants read the article and were tested with no exposure to the background videotape. When participants are not exposed to any variation of the independent variable, their group is called a **control group.** The group is held constant, with respect to the independent variable, as a baseline comparison for every other condition. Groups that receive some exposure to the manipulation of the independent variable are sometimes called **treatment** or **experimental groups.** Armstrong and Chung were interested in finding out if background television interfered with processing information during both the reading and the remembering phases. Their comparison groups permitted them to assess the effects of noise during each of the separate phases or with variations of noise during both phases.

When you use comparison groups, you are trying to ensure that the groups are equivalent in every way except for exposure to the various levels or conditions of the independent variable. Isolating this single difference helps to build a strong case for a causal relationship between the independent variable and its effects on the dependent variable. Control groups are placed in the same setting and are responding to the same environmental cues except for the manipulation of the independent variable.

Sometimes, researchers go so far as to fool group members into thinking they have received a treatment when they have not. The false treatment is called a **placebo** and is used extensively in medical research where many studies investigate the effectiveness of various medications. By administering a placebo, researchers hope to be able to distinguish between the psychological effects of believing medication has been ingested and the actual physiological effects of the drug. Occasionally, placebo groups are also used in communication research.

In a study mentioned earlier that tested the effectiveness of various treatments of communication apprehension, Ayres, Heuett, and Sonandre (1998) had both a control condition and a placebo condition in addition to treatment levels of the independent variable. Study participants were exposed to one of three treatment conditions: (1) a treatment condition in which a visualization technique was read by one of the experimenters; (2) a treatment condition in which they were given a booklet depicting a pictorial representation of the same visualization technique as the one read by the experimenter; or (3) a treatment condition in which they looked at the pictorial representation while the experimenter read the visualization script.

Some of the participants were exposed to the placebo condition, in which they were also read to by an experimenter but the excerpt was from an unrelated source of information. In the control condition, participants were left alone with no interaction with the experimenter. You will hear about the use of placebos and control groups again later on in this chapter when you learn about the various ways of eliminating or reducing potential threats to validity. Researchers use comparison groups to strengthen their causal argument, but simply having groups to compare is an insufficient test. Experimental designs can also employ random assignment to treatment conditions.

Random assignment **Random assignment** refers to a procedure in which the researchers select subjects on a purely random basis to participate in either treatment or control conditions. Random assignment is not the same thing as random sampling, which we discussed in Chapter 3. Recall that the purpose of random sampling is to select a representative sample or group from the larger population. After selecting the participants, the researcher may then randomly assign them to experimental or control groups. Randomizing this process ensures that every participant has an equal chance of being assigned to any of the comparison groups.

The main purpose of random assignment is to help establish equivalent groups at the beginning of the experiment. A sample that is not randomly assigned may lose representativeness through some type of selection bias, or characteristic present in one group but not the other. To return to our earlier example, McDevitt and Chaffee (2000) could not randomly assign students to classrooms. As a result, they had to demonstrate that the students who were exposed to the treatment could not be distinguished in any other way from students who were not exposed. You will learn more about this problem later in the chapter when we discuss threats to validity.

Pretesting When researchers administer a **pretest,** they are assessing baseline or naturally occurring levels of the dependent variable before the independent variable is manipulated. They administer the very same test as a **posttest** following the manipulation. By using a pretest-posttest procedure, researchers want to establish a precise comparison between the first measurement of the dependent variable as a pretest and the second measurement as a posttest. If the participants are exposed to the manipulation of the independent variable while other environmental factors are held constant, then researchers can assume any change between pretest and posttest levels of the dependent variable is due to the influence of the independent variable.

To illustrate how pretests are used, the study introduced earlier by Ayres, Heuett, and Sonandre (1998) that used various treatment levels of visualization techniques also made use of a pretest. Participants were given the public speaking scale of McCroskey's Personal Report of Communication Apprehension to first help the investigators screen those who had very high levels of communication apprehension, but the scores also served as a baseline comparison. Ayres et al. were able to precisely determine just how high the subjects' levels of communication apprehension were prior to any exposure to

treatment, and then they compared these scores with posttreatment levels of communication apprehension when the same participants filled out the same scale again following treatment.

Pretests can also help to assure that all comparison groups are equivalent before treatment exposure. If all treatment groups, the placebo group, and the control group in the Ayres, Heuett, and Sonandre study have approximately the same high levels of communication apprehension before any treatment is received, then the pretest is an additional way of demonstrating that no group was significantly different from any other at the onset of the study. In the study by McDevitt and Chaffee (2000) described earlier, using a pretest was especially important because individual students could not be assigned to treatment conditions. The researchers were interested in testing the effects of the *Kids Voting* civics curriculum on a number of voting behaviors and attitudes, media use, and discussion with parents. By providing students with a pretest of these variables along with an analysis of other factors, the investigators could make a strong case that the school groups were equivalent before half of them were exposed to the *Kids Voting* curriculum.

As we mentioned earlier, *controlling* the manipulation of the independent variable is central to the causal argument made by experimental researchers. Implementing the elements of comparison groups, random assignment, and pretests-posttests along with the independent variable manipulation enables researchers to strengthen their claims that the independent variable is the source of the effects observed in the dependent variable. The absence or presence of these three elements changes the research design. Designs in which some or all of the elements are lacking result in weaker support for causal arguments; these are called **preexperimental** and **quasi-experimental designs.** Designs that make use of all three elements *and* employ random sampling methods provide the strongest evidence for causal arguments, and are called **true experimental designs** (Campbell & Stanley, 1963, p. 8). We shall examine these more closely in the next section.

Types of designs
Preexperimental designs Three preexperimental designs are presented in order of the weakest to the strongest within this design type: one-shot case study (or ex post facto design), one-group pretest-posttest

EXHIBIT 6.2	Types of Preexperimental Designs		
One-shot case study		X	O_1
One-group pretest-posttest design	O_1	X	O_2
Static-group comparison		X	O_1
			O_2

where

    O = observation or measurement of dependent variable

    X = manipulation of independent variable

(Based on Campbell & Stanley, 1963, p. 8.)

EXHIBIT 6.3	Quasi-Experimental Designs
Time series	O_1 O_2 O_3 X O_4 O_5 O_6
Nonequivalent control group	O_1 X O_2
	O_3 O_4

where

    O = observation or measurement of dependent variable

    X = manipulation of independent variable

(Based on Campbell & Stanley, 1963, p. 40.)

design, and the static-group comparison design. All of them lack at least one element described in the previous section (random assignment). The designs are depicted in Exhibit 6.2.

One-shot case studies are studies designed so that some manipulation of the independent variable occurs with an attempt to measure its effect on the dependent variable. For example, suppose you wished to assess the effects of a presidential candidate debate on voting behavior. The last debate is scheduled three weeks prior to the general election. After the debate, the majority of people vote for candidate B instead of candidate A. The researcher concludes that candidate B must have won the presidential debate. This type of design is also called the **ex post facto design** because the studies must argue the cause *after the fact* of observing the effects. The one-shot case study gives the weakest support for a causal argument, as you will see in the warrants section of this chapter.

The next two designs, the one-group pretest-posttest design and the static-group comparison design, add an element that strengthens the investigator's causal argument. Using the example above and the first design, the **one-group pretest-posttest design** would require that the researcher administer a pretest (or measurement of voter preference for the presidential candidates) prior to the participants viewing the debate. Then, after the debate, the researcher would use actual voting outcomes as evidence of the debate effects. By administering the pretest, the researcher has some baseline level of voter preference before exposure to the debate. The pretest enables the researcher to show a distinct change or no change between the pretest and the posttest measures. However, there are still many problems in assuming that the independent variable, *X*, is the source of those changes.

Likewise, the **static-group comparison design** adds an element of control by using a comparison group, but without a pretest or random assignment, you would not be able to confirm that the groups are initially equivalent. You would then find it difficult to rule out a variety of extraneous sources of influence. In this particular study example, you may not be able to find a group that hadn't seen the presidential debate, and who could therefore serve as a control group. In studies like these, researchers often use candidates from senate or representative races in other states where exposure to debates or any other form of media coverage is unlikely. For example, in Weaver Lariscy and Tinkham's (1999) study mentioned previously of the sleeper effect in political commercials, the researchers used fictitious Congressional candidates from the state of Kentucky, not from the residence state of the study participants, "to avoid potential context contamination from any known candidates in the ongoing campaign cycle" (p. 20).

Quasi-experimental designs This represents a step up in strength of evidence given to support a causal argument. This second group contains two designs: the time series design and the nonequivalent control group design. There are actually many variations on these two themes, but these designs provide the basic structures depicted in Exhibit 6.3. The **time series design** assesses levels of the dependent variable at several points in time prior to and following the manipulation of the independent variable. The rationale for this design is that if the dependent variable remains stable until the administration of the treatment and then changes, the researcher has greater evidence for attributing these effects to the independent variable and not some other competing factor. Such a design is particularly useful if the researcher suspects that some developmental factor, a competing factor that incrementally changes over time, might interfere with the treatment.

For example, let's say you want to test the effects of media on children's remembering program material. A group of children are exposed to a visually rich curricular program (computer-based) in the middle of the semester. If you have been measuring recall and retention abilities generally at several points in time before the children are exposed to the program and found that their ability levels are relatively stable, you are in a much stronger position to identify the probable source of these effects as the independent variable, the new program, especially if you find a significant change following exposure that again stabilizes at the new level. The time series design permits you to demonstrate that gains in retention are not simply due to internal development in this age group of children. Even if the children's retention abilities are improving naturally over time, you will be able to estimate how much of the change in the dependent variable scores is due to the curricular program, and how much is due to normal maturation, or age-related development. The time series design is still vulnerable to other problems, but the way in which the design elements are implemented make it a design that is generally stronger than any of the preexperimental designs.

The second type of quasi-experimental design is called the **nonequivalent control group design.** In this case, you would use a comparison group, a control that is not exposed to the treatment. In the example we have already used several times, McDevitt and Chaffee (2000) were unable to randomly assign children to the treatment group (those who were exposed to the *Kids Voting* curriculum) and the control group (those who were not). The researchers were very sensitive to the possibility that the two groups would not be equivalent and hence biased in some way. They had to conduct several analyses of both groups' characteristics before they could claim that these two groups did not differ in any way sig-

---

EXHIBIT 6.4 True Experimental Designs

Pretest-posttest control group design	R	O_1 X O_2
	R	O_3 O_4
Posttest-only control group design	R	X O_1
	R	O_2
Solomon four-group design	R	O_1 X O_2
	R	O_3 O_4
	R	X O_5
	R	O_6

where

R = random assignment to treatment and control conditions

O = observation or measurement of dependent variable

X = manipulation of independent variable

---

nificant to their study. Fortunately, exposure to the curriculum was not dependent upon any student's personal choice. Additionally, data was obtained on a variety of student and family characteristics such as their socioeconomic status, school grades, gender, ethnicity, and year in school. A statistical test showed that student participation in the curriculum was not related to any of these, and that all of these characteristics were equally represented in each group. Without taking these additional measures, the investigators would not have been able to establish any good reason for comparing the treatment group to the control group. When you are unable to use the three design elements for maximizing control, comparison groups, random assignment, and pretests-posttests, your research design will be vulnerable to numerous problems that threaten the validity of the study. The specific threats will be examined in the warrants section.

True experimental designs These designs make the greatest use of the elements (at least two and sometimes all three of the elements) and also provide the strongest evidence for causality. True experimental designs include the pretest-posttest control group design, the posttest-only control group design, and the Solomon four-group design (see Exhibit 6.4).

The **pretest-posttest control group design** uses comparison groups, random assignment to place participants into the treatment and control groups, and the pretest-posttest procedure. Random assignment and pretesting help to establish equivalence of groups;

pretests also provide baseline levels for precise comparisons; and comparison groups permit you to isolate the effects of the independent variable from other potential sources or causes. A variation of this type of design was employed by Ayres et al. (1998), who randomly assigned research subjects to five experimental conditions: three treatment conditions where exposure to the type of therapy for communication apprehension was varied, a placebo condition, and a control condition. This design has only one identifiable weakness: there is no way of assessing whether the pretest can interact with the effects of the independent variable through test sensitization in generalizing the findings to any other group beyond the study's sample. Test sensitization is controlled for in the study's current sample. The problem occurs only when you try to generalize findings to people outside of the current study.

To avoid this potential interaction, the second design, the **posttest-only control group,** eliminates the pretest. Random assignment helps to assure equivalence between groups; however, without a pretest, you have no baseline from which to calculate precise estimates of change in the independent variable.

In order to combine the strengths of both designs, the **Solomon four-group design** includes two groups that use the pretest-posttest control group design, and two groups that use the posttest-only control group design. With this design, you can assess the specific effects of taking the pretest as a potential weakness of the design and eliminate it without sacrificing the information the pretest provides.

The greatest drawback to this design is the demands it makes in terms of time and effort. You must coordinate two test periods for two groups and one test period for two additional groups in a relatively comparable time frame. The number of subjects for each group must be fairly large so that the sample will reflect an adequate level of variation to establish confidence in your results. You will explore these issues further as problems with validity and reliability in the warrants section of this chapter. In this next section, we will describe the particular ways in which experimental data are collected and analyzed.

Data Collection and Analysis

Data collection strategies As we pointed out earlier, most experimental research involves the manipulation of the independent variable as a causal test of its effects on the dependent variable. Recall that the independent variable constructed by the researcher is called the *stimulus* variable. Or it can naturally occur as an assumed cause, in which case it is called an *organismic* variable. In experimental research when there is more than one presumed cause, the independent variables are called **factors,** and the designs we discussed in the previous section are all types of **factorial designs** (Smith, 1988, p. 208).

The visual representation of variables in those designs depicted in Exhibits 6.2 through 6.4 makes it appear as if there is only one independent variable, X. However, experiments frequently assess the effects of more than one factor. Look again at Exhibit 6.1. Hypotheses 1, 2, and 5 all predict effects for more than one independent variable. In H_1, Gorham, Cohen, and Morris (1999) wanted to test the effects of instructor immediacy and instructor attire on student learning variables. Both the independent variables of instructor immediacy and attire are factors that are expected to have an influence on student learning. In H_5, van der Molen and van der Voort (2000) investigated the effects of media format (television vs. print), news format (children's vs. adults' news), and age groups (adults vs. children) on recall of news information. There are three independent variables or factors tested in this fifth hypothesis.

Stimulus variables are traditionally categorical in nature. The experimenter constructs the treatment and control conditions. These are measured with a nominal scale, one of the measurement scales described in Chapter 5. Each condition represents a separate category. In the experiment by Ayres, Heuett, and Sonandre (1998) described earlier, there were five experimental conditions: three treatment conditions, a placebo condition, and a control condition. Each of these represents one category of one independent variable measured at the nominal level. The researchers were also interested in testing the influence of another independent variable: three types of participant characteristics that distinguished their preferences for processing perceptual information (verbalizers, verbalizers/visualizers, and visualizers). This variable was organismic. By combining an organismic variable with a stimulus variable, Ayres et al. used a *mixed model* to explore the potential effects on several different measures of communication apprehension.

Independent variables in experimental research can also be measured with an ordinal scale. For example, in a study by Le Poire and Yoshimura (1999), trained coders rated confederate participants as displaying either high or low levels of involvement with various nonverbal behaviors. In this particular case, the level of involvement was artificially constructed as a stimulus variable (rather than an organismic variable) because the confederate participants intentionally changed their nonverbal behavior to reflect either high or low involvement with the other conversational partner. High and low levels of this variable reflect an ordinal scale.

To clearly display the number of independent variables tested by their specific number of categories per variable, researchers typically use a **research design statement,** usually expressed in numbers. In the Ayres et al. (1998) study, the design statement was 5×3. This meant that there were two independent variables: the first had five categories (three experimental conditions, one placebo condition, and one control condition) and the second had three categories (one group of participant verbalizers, one group of participant verbalizers/visualizers, and one group of participant visualizers). The study of media effects on recall by van der Molen and van der Voort (2000) used a 2 (television vs. print) $\times$ 2 (adults' news vs. children's news) $\times$ 2 (adult vs. children age groups) design statement.

In a similar study, Valkenburg and Semetko (1999) conducted an experiment to test the effects of the type of news story content (crime vs. the status of the U.S. economy) and framing condition (four types of frames plus a control group) on participants' thoughts about each story. News framing occurs when a reporter composes or structures the story in order to "simplify and give meaning to events, and to maintain audience interest"; they do it by providing a context for interpreting the story's meaning (p. 551). In this particular case, stories were "framed" with four contexts (conflict, human interest, responsibility issues, or economic consequences), or they received no frame at all (control group). This experiment used a 2 (types of content) $\times$ 5 (types of frame) design statement. Virtually every experiment has a research design statement that explains how many independent variables will be tested, and how many categories each independent variable will have. This statement is, in effect, a way of seeing how the dependent variable will be divided up or partitioned in the analysis of the data—a topic to which we now turn our attention.

Analysis of variable effects The traditional test of the effects of the independent variables on the de-

Table 6.2.   A 2 $\times$ 2 Research Design

	Female instructors	Male instructors
Small classes	$\bar{X}_1$	$\bar{X}_2$
Large classes	$\bar{X}_3$	$\bar{X}_4$

pendent variable is called the *analysis of variance,* a test we will explore at length in Chapter 9, "Testing Differences and Relationships." In this section, you will learn how the results from this type of test are typically interpreted. When just one independent variable is manipulated and tested for effects, the analysis is called a *one-way analysis of variance.* Defined in detail in Chapter 9, we will say briefly here that "one-way" refers to one factor or independent variable. If there are two independent variables, then the test is called a two-way analysis. If there are three independent variables, then the test is called a three-way, and so forth. Whenever there are more independent variables than just one, there are two types of effects that researchers explore: main effects and interaction effects.

Main effects are the effects of each separate independent variable on the dependent variable. Suppose, for instance, you wanted to test the effects of instructor sex (female, male) and classroom size (small, large) on communication apprehension. This experiment has a 2 $\times$ 2 design statement. There are two factors, instructor sex and classroom size. You would therefore expect at the most two main effects, one for each factor. If you obtained a main effect for instructor sex, you would be saying that students' communication apprehension scores with female instructors would be significantly different than those students' communication apprehension scores with male instructors. The sex of the instructor would have a significant main effect on communication apprehension levels. On the other hand, if you obtained a main effect for classroom size, you would be saying that students in small classes would have significantly different communication apprehension scores than students in large classes. The size of the classroom would have a significant main effect on communication apprehension levels.

This 2 $\times$ 2 design results in four cells of data, as depicted in Table 6.2. The mean, $\bar{X}$, in each cell of data is the average for all the scores represented by that cell. So $\bar{X}_1$ stands for the average communication apprehension score for the small class with the female

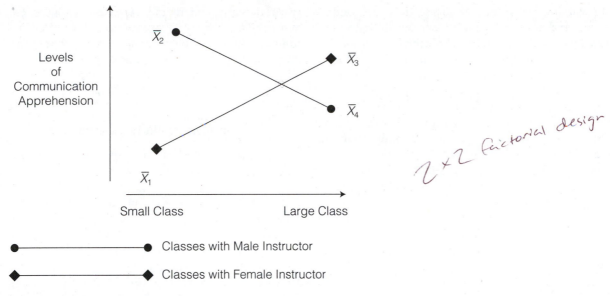

FIGURE 6.2 Interaction effect for instructor sex and class size on levels of communication apprehension.

instructor, and $\bar{X}_2$ stands for the average communication apprehension score for the small class with the male instructor. In the third and fourth cells, $\bar{X}_3$ and $\bar{X}_4$ stand for the average communication apprehension scores for the large classes with female and male instructors, respectively.

The second type of effect tested is an **interaction,** a combined effect of two or more independent variables on the dependent variable. There are a variety of different types of interactions. One possibility in the above example is that students in small classes with female instructors express the lowest levels of communication apprehension, but students with male instructors in small classes express just the opposite, the highest level of communication apprehension. This interaction effect is depicted in Figure 6.2.

Occasionally, factorial designs make use of **repeated measures.** In this type of design, the researcher exposes the same group of participants to several treatments, events, or time periods. The repeated measure becomes one of the independent factors. For example, a study described earlier by Afifi and Burgoon (2000) tested the effects of viewing videotaped conversation segments on perceived uncertainty and attractiveness. All participants were shown four segments of a couple's conversation: In the first segment, they were primed by being shown

a positive or negative exchange by level of expressed involvement/interest (that is, the more involved/interested was considered a positive exchange, and so forth). Then participants saw three additional interaction segments. In the control condition, the level of involvement was held constant; all other participants saw one of four possible violations (treatment conditions) of expected behavior in the last interaction segment.

The number of conversational segments was the repeated measure because each participant saw all four interaction segments. This measure is called the **within-subjects factor.** The second independent variable was comprised of the four treatment/one control conditions; because participants were separately assigned to each of the five conditions, it is called the **between-subjects factor.** When researchers use both types of factors as they did in our example, the study is called a **mixed independent groups/repeated measures design** (Smith, 1988, p. 209).

There are three basic advantages in choosing a repeated measures design over other design types (Smith, 1988, pp. 209–210). First, researchers do not have to worry about whether the groups are comparable. Since they are the same people across at least one set of differences, they are clearly comparable. Other potential problems may threaten the accuracy of the measures, as you will discover in the warrants section. A second advantage is that repeated measures may also require fewer subjects. If the researchers show three videotaped political advertisements to the same group of subjects, they will use fewer subjects than if they showed the advertisements to three separate groups.

Finally, the researcher may be interested in a variable that is, by its nature, best captured with a repeated measure. For example, in the study of the effects of teacher immediacy and attire on student perceptions, Gorham, Cohen, and Morris (1999) asked students to rate their teachers both at the initial meeting and at midterm. They reasoned that factors like attire and immediacy will have more of an effect on first impressions, but with time students attenuate their judgments based on a much broader basis of knowledge about the instructor. Using two different time periods as a repeated measure was the optimal design choice based directly on the nature of the variables they were interested in examining.

Research design and analysis should be constructed carefully to provide the most accurate and reliable test of hypotheses possible in each experiment. As you learned earlier in this chapter, the purpose of experimental research is to provide strong evidence for causal arguments. By selecting design elements such as random assignment, comparison groups, and pretests, you will be attempting to isolate the effects of the independent variables while controlling for rival factors or causes. Establishing grounds for causality reflect the essential values of precision, power, and parsimony, which are assured using the standards of validity and reliability. It is to these warrants that our attention now must turn.

EXPERIMENTAL RESEARCH WARRANTS

Because controlling rival explanations is central to any causal argument, experimental researchers are especially concerned with a study's validity and reliability, introduced initially in Chapter 4, "Warrants for Research Arguments." *Validity* refers to the accuracy or truthfulness of the tests for claims; *reliability* refers to the consistency of those tests. As you learned in Chapter 4, there are several different types of validity. *Internal validity* generally refers to the ability of a study to accurately assess the hypothesized relationship be-

tween the independent and dependent variables. *External validity* refers to how accurately the findings from one study can be generalized to a different setting or to the population at large. Generally, any study with strong internal and external validity is also considered a reliable test of the hypotheses.

Internal Validity Threats

In experimental research, your manipulation of the independent variable as a test of your causal claim is considered successful to the degree that you have established strong internal validity by controlling rival causes. In Chapter 4, you learned that measurement validity refers to the accuracy of measurement used in one study. When measurement validity is assessed, you are concerned with the presence or lack of bias, a threat to the internal validity of a study. You will learn a great deal about bias in Chapter 8, "Descriptive Statistics and Hypothesis Testing." For now, we will say that when a study's measures are biased, you are unable to rule out factors that potentially rival your independent variable as the cause of the observed pattern of effects. These factors are called **confounding variables** because they confound or interfere in the relationship between the independent and dependent variables.

In this chapter, we indicated numerous times that understanding why experimenters choose certain design elements is dependent upon understanding how these help establish valid and reliable tests of claims. In this section, you will begin to see how this occurs. If the study is an experiment, the validity issues are directly related to design elements, and the potential threats are from biases specific to those design elements. There are essentially two types of bias that are related to the internal construction of experimental designs: threats related to time progression and threats called reactivity effects. They can affect both internal and external validity. There is also a third set of effects that specifically threatens the external validity of the study's claims.

Time progression effects   Time progression effects refer to those factors that rival the independent variable as sources or causes of effects because the experiment takes place over a period of time. Preexperimental and quasi-experimental designs that make use of a pretest and posttest or a repeated measures design are vulnerable to six of these time progression effects, as are other designs where there is a time lapse between the manipulation of the independent variable and measuring the dependent variable. The six time progression effects as threats to internal validity include history, maturation, mortality, statistical regression, testing, and instrumentation (Cook & Campbell, 1979).

History The effect of **history** refers to the occurrence of an event that happens during the course of the study that is external to the study, but that affects the outcome in such a way that the event rivals or threatens the independent variable as the source of influence on the dependent variable. Recall our example of assessing the effects of a presidential debate on voter preference used to illustrate preexperimental and quasi-experimental designs. If any other event can rival the debate as a cause of voter behavior, such as a breaking news story that implicates one of the candidates in a scandal of some sort, or a dip in the economy, then the study's design is vulnerable to the history effect. One way to control for the effect of history is to use a control group that is exposed to all of the same events as the treatment group. You can then compare variable scores after those events have had their effect; presumably, dependent variable scores in a treatment group (the group that viewed the debate) will change more than scores in a control group (the group that didn't), despite any history effect.

Maturation The effect of **maturation** is obtained because of some naturally occurring developmental change that coincides with the administration of the independent variable and the test of its effects. The developmental change can be short term and temporary, or long term and permanent. In the short term, participants who become fatigued because the experimental situation requires lengthy or complex testing are experiencing maturational changes. Sometimes, these rival the effects of the independent variable. For example, let's say you argued that teachers who were distant and unapproachable (nonimmediacy) adversely affect student performance, but then you gave students learning tasks that were too long or complex to comfortably complete. As a result, you could not tell whether the adverse effects were due to teacher style or task complexity. If the design included a control group who received the same test of student performance without exposure to the teacher, then we would be able to discern the portion of the effects that were due only to teacher style.

You might run into a maturation threat over a longer period if you were assessing younger student performance over the course of a year; an improvement in scores could be explained simply by the students growing older and more competent generally. In illustrating the rationale for using a time series design, we explained that some studies are susceptible to developmental changes. If you wanted to test the effects of a certain type of curricular program over a long period (the school year), you would need to design your experiment in a way that would allow you to track changes due to the differences in curricular programs versus natural developmental changes in children's competence. If you did not collect repeated measures and had no control group for comparison, your study results would be confounded by a maturation effect.

Mortality **Mortality** is an effect where subjects disproportionately drop out of an experiment. Suppose you wished to test the effects of teaching interpersonal negotiating strategies to romantic couples on the perceived satisfaction with their partners. First, you required participants to undergo three one-hour training sessions, and over that period of time, a number of participants dropped out. As a rule in this type of study, those that drop out are also most likely to be those who are having relational problems or have broken up with their partners. The resulting scores of the remaining participants show increased levels of perceived satisfaction. Was this increase due to the effectiveness of the negotiating strategies or because those who were having the most relational difficulties dropped out? When the low scorers dropped out, it artificially inflated the average score for those who remained. The use of control groups and random assignment would help to separate time progression effects due to mortality from those due to manipulating the independent variable.

Statistical regression The effect of **statistical regression** occurs when participants have been selected who represent the extremes on the dependent variable scale. Participants who receive extremely low scores on any measure are more likely to get higher scores the second time around just by chance. If you get a zero, the only direction you can go is up. Likewise, participants who score very high on some measure will most likely do worse on a subsequent measure. Statistical regression can sometimes rival the independent variable as an explanation for the observed effects.

For example, in a study we have used frequently for illustration, Ayres et al. (1998) tested the effectiveness of various therapies on communication apprehension. They also used a true experimental design so that they could rule out rival effects like statistical regression because they were interested in observing effects on participants who were extreme scorers on the communication apprehension scale. But suppose a researcher interested in the same relationship had not used random assignment and control groups, and had selected a group of communicators who had scored extremely high on communication apprehension. Chances are without any therapy at all the scores would naturally regress toward the middle or average score; that is, the scores would appear to show less communication apprehension when no actual reduction has occurred simply because the initial scores were so high.

Testing   **Testing** effects can happen any time the research design calls for a pretest. This effect occurs when participants become sensitized to the content of the test. In one type of testing effect, participants can improve their scores just from the *practice effect* of taking the test or measure more than one time. This is the rationale that underlies taking the PSAT during the third year of high school. Practice usually helps to improve performance.

In another type of testing threat, the test actually acts as a cueing device to sensitize participants to the goals of the study so that they respond to the manipulation of the independent variable in some way they would not have if they had not taken a pretest. Suppose you wanted to find out about cheating behavior by placing participants in a situation where they were given the opportunity to observe a confederate cheating. Before they witness any cheating, the participants take a pretest that measures their attitudes toward cheating. The test serves as a cue to be wary of cheating situations. When they are then confronted with a cheating confederate, they may be more likely, because of the pretest, to express harsher judgments toward the cheating they observed than they initially would have. You can minimize this testing effect by using random assignment and a control group, and by using designs that do not rely just on the pretest-posttest design element.

Instrumentation   The **instrumentation** effect happens when the researcher changes the instruments used to measure the dependent variables between the pretest and the posttest. The instrument itself should remain constant across the duration of the study. If, for example, you evaluated communication competence with one scale in the pretest, the posttest should include the same measure of competence; otherwise, changes in the dependent variable could be attributed to scale content and construction characteristics rather than changes produced by manipulating the independent variable.

The instrumentation effect is of central importance when considering the stability or reliability of measurements as test–retest assessments. It is sometimes tempting to revise an instrument when you discover problems with its construction following a pretest. Rather than using the pretest to evaluate the scale's validity and reliability, you should use a pilot study or manipulation check with a separate group of participants as we have indicated earlier. In the last chapter, you learned in detail how the structure of an interview or questionnaire could adversely affect the validity and reliability of these measures.

Reactivity effects   Reactivity effects are a set of effects or threats due to participants' responses to some design feature of the experimental situation. Participants may react differently than they would in everyday life because they have been targeted for a study. In this section, we outline six reactivity effects: the threats of selection, treatment diffusion, compensatory behavior, researcher attributes, demand characteristics, and evaluation apprehension (Cook & Campbell, 1979; Smith, 1988).

Selection   The effect of **selection** occurs when the researcher is unable to randomly assign subjects to treatment and control conditions. As you learned earlier in the chapter, random assignment helps to establish equivalent groups at the beginning of a study. Without this procedure, groups can differ in ways that systematically interfere with the effects of the independent variable. McDevitt and Chaffee's (2000) study of the effects of the *Kids Voting* curricular program with two different groups of high school students was vulnerable to a selection effect. That is why McDevitt and Chaffee went to such great lengths to assure that intact classrooms of students who could not be randomly assigned to groups did not possess any distinguishing characteristics. Potentially, any difference in the groups could have rivaled the independent variable in explaining the results they obtained.

Treatment diffusion The **treatment diffusion** effect, sometimes called *contamination,* occurs when participants in the treatment group tell participants in the control group about the treatment, thereby "contaminating" the control group. Let's say you were interested in studying the effects of deception on suspicion. The participants in the treatment group were exposed to a confederate who fabricated a story to elicit suspicious responses. In the control condition, the confederate did not tell any lies. However, participants in the treatment condition told participants in the control condition about the lying confederate because both groups of participants shared a class together. After the treatment group contaminated the control group, participants in the control group showed greater suspicion of the confederate than they would have normally because they suspected deception based on what they had been told.

It is difficult to control this effect unless you can guarantee participants from both groups will remain separated during the duration of the study. Sometimes, this arrangement just isn't feasible; studies of married or cohabitating persons are especially vulnerable to this effect. In a study of fright reactions to films, Sparks, Pellechia, and Irvine (1999) attempted to control this effect by asking participants to refrain from discussing the experiment until they were informed in class that the experiment was over. These researchers were dependent upon the good will of their study participants to follow their instructions.

Compensatory behavior The **compensatory behavior** threat is actually a cluster of effects that can happen when the control group becomes aware that the experimental group is being treated differently. If the treatment seems to be a positive gain, then control groups can try to outperform the experimental group to receive the same treatment, or they can become frustrated and upset at the unequal treatment and withhold normal behaviors as a result. In either case, the unaffected behavior of the control group becomes decidedly influenced by the absence of the treatment. For example, let's say you wished to test the effects of using computer games to help students learn a series of math functions. Students in the control group are required to learn the same math functions without the benefit of the computer games. Suppose the control group discovered the treatment group was allowed to play computer games during the testing session; the control group participants might try harder at the learning tasks in order to be allowed to play the same games. Or they may become discouraged at the lack of an opportunity to play the games and may make less of an effort than they would have in the absence of the experiment. Again, the most effective way to eliminate this threat is to ensure that both groups have no contact while the study is ongoing.

Researcher attributes Researchers can possess physical or psychological characteristics as **researcher attributes** that may influence the way participants respond, thus affecting the outcome of the experiment. For example, Lucchetti (1999) asked personal questions about participants' sexual history as it related to knowledge about safe sex practices. Sometimes male participants are reluctant to discuss very detailed sexual behavior with female researchers (and vice versa). In such cases, the study would benefit from a research team so that attribute effects could be distributed across the gender of the researchers, males and females. In this particular case, it would also be wise to assure participants of complete confidentiality as a means of gaining trust and establishing rapport.

Demand characteristics In some cases, participants become aware of the goals of a particular study because the research team, the testing materials, the experimental design, or some combination of these factors inadvertently provides them with cues. If participants think that they know what the investigators are looking for, they can try to cooperate and give the researchers what they want, or they can resist complying to obstruct the research process, or the participants can simply try to forget what the goals are and act as they normally would. Obviously, researchers hope participants will choose the last option. Any time subjects vary their behavior because they are aware of the research goals, the effect is called **demand characteristics.** In a much-cited case, a study of workers at the Hawthorne Electrical Plant, demand characteristics were produced when employees became aware of the researchers' presence. Simple awareness of being targeted for research increased the employees' levels of productivity regardless of how environmental conditions were varied. The observed outcome of this study was called the **Hawthorne effect** (Frey, Botan, & Kreps, 2000, p. 121).

Frequently, demand characteristics can be controlled by using research assistants who are blind to or unaware of the goals of a particular experiment so that they cannot cue subjects on how to respond. For example, in a study of fright reactions to film segments cited earlier (Sparks, Pellechia, & Irvine, 1999), the experimenter did not know the study's hypothesis and which participants had various coping styles. Participants were classified as having a repressor or nonrepressor coping style because of the tendency to repress or not repress emotion. Sparks et al. expected that repressors would experience greater levels of physiological arousal after exposure to frightening films than nonrepressors. By keeping the experimenter who collected the data unaware of the research goals, she could not cue participants to act in ways that would confirm researcher expectations. Sparks et al. confirmed no demand characteristics were present by using a manipulation check to see if participants had guessed what the study was about.

Another way to control this effect is to introduce a bogus treatment or observe participants unobtrusively so that they will not learn the nature of the study. For example, in a study of compliance seeking and resisting behaviors in student drinking contexts, Wright and O'Hair (1999) disguised the purpose of the study by asking students unrelated questions about smoking and high-calorie food consumption in addition to questions about their alcohol use. They felt that if student participants were aware the researchers were interested solely in drinking behavior, the participants might be more likely to alter their normal responses.

Evaluation apprehension When researchers ask for information that is potentially embarrassing or negative in some way, then respondents often change their answers to give a more positive personal impression of themselves. This effect is called **evaluation apprehension.** In Chapter 5, you learned about the importance of gaining participants' trust, especially when asking for sensitive information. Experimenters who examine socially negative behavior, like cheating and deception, may find participants' responses inhibited by apprehension about the impressions they are giving. Likewise, measuring socially positive behavior, like comforting or altruistic behavior, may result in equally biased positive responses as participants try to strategically influence impressions about their personal integrity. If, for example, you wanted to find out about communication problems in newlywed couples, you would need to be sensitive to the fact that most newlyweds in our society want to be seen as having few problems.

In this section, you have explored six time progression effects and six reactivity effects as threats to the internal validity of an experimental design. Aside from the research progression and reactivity effects identified here, there are more complex effects due to the interaction of two or more of these. However, it is comforting to note that using the control elements of true experimental designs, such as comparison groups, random assignment, and pretests, greatly reduces the potential threat to the internal validity of the study.

External Validity Threats

Reactivity effects along with sampling deficiencies can also affect the external validity of the study's claims. As you learned in Chapter 4, *external validity* refers to generalizing the results of a study to a larger population or across settings.

Sample representativeness Recall our discussion of representativeness from Chapter 3. If a sample represents the parent population well, then the results obtained from a sample should also be representative of those you would find conducting the same test in the population. The best way to ensure representativeness is to use some form of random sampling. You learned about four random sampling methods used by communication researchers in Chapter 3. When nonrandom methods are selected for experimental research, the samples are much more likely to be biased; that is, they are likely to vary in systematic ways that do not accurately represent the characteristics of the population from which they were drawn. This is called a **sampling effect.**

Many experiments in communication research are limited by the difficulties imposed on the researcher for obtaining random samples. It may be prohibitively costly in terms of time, effort, and money to obtain random samples. As a result, experimental researchers may depend on alternative means, such as statistically assessing the amount of bias or noise present in a particular sample and using it to indicate whether results are generalizable.

Setting appropriateness Reactivity effects make it very clear that participants may be affected by the situational features of the experimental setting. Repeating a study's design in a different setting strengthens the claim that the study's results can be generalized across settings. When the same pattern of results is assured across settings, we say the study has strong *ecological validity,* a concept you learned about in Chapter

4. Many researchers have identified various strategies to help participants experience the laboratory settings as more natural environments to avoid artificial setting effects. For example, a study cited earlier by Wright and O'Hair (1999) investigated student compliance gaining and resisting strategies in drinking situations. They constructed the laboratory to resemble a "small living room environment" with snacks and drinks on the coffee table and a bar containing a variety of alcoholic beverages. All lab sessions were conducted in the evening when drinking alcohol would seem more likely and appropriate under normal circumstances.

Replicating studies also helps to ensure ecological validity, and it is also a means of assuring reliability of research design and measurement, as you may recall from Chapter 4. For example, in the study of the influence of teacher immediacy and attire on student learning cited earlier, Gorham et al. (1999) actually reported on three experiments: Study 1 tested the effects of instructor attire on student perceptions. Study 2 was designed as replication of Study 1 but added an additional independent variable, teacher immediacy. And Study 3 expanded the setting generalizability by replicating the investigation of teacher attire and immediacy with a broader range of instructors and across a longer time period to more closely capture an actual classroom environment.

In experimental research, the necessity of building a strong case for causality requires careful consideration of the design and measurements used to test claims. Through warranting these claims by demonstrating strong internal and external validity and reliability through experimental control, the researcher has developed a sound argument that the pattern of observed effects is best attributed to the experimenter's manipulation of the independent variable.

Before we end this chapter, it is important to consider the ways in which technology has influenced the process of experimental research.

TECHNOLOGY AND EXPERIMENTAL RESEARCH

There are two ways in which technology has influenced experimental research. First, some experiments focus on the cause-and-effect relationship between the uses of various technologies and their effects as *content* issues. A second way technology impacts experimental research is through the *processes* of data collection and analysis.

Technology as Experimental Research Content

Certainly, there have always been many communication research articles that analyze some form of mediated communication, whether in the form of print or visual media like film or television. Many of the most recent experiments have selected some of the newer technologies as their investigatory focus. For example, Buzzanell, Burrell, Stafford, and Berkowitz (1996) examined how accommodation theory might be applied to telephone answering machine messages. An increasingly popular form of technology content we have used for illustrations in this and other chapters is computer-mediated communication (CMC).

In a recent study of photographic images in CMC, Walther, Slovacek, and Tidwell (2001) examined the effects of providing members of task groups with pictures of each other. They conducted an interesting experiment, in which they tested whether online task groups used to working with each other (long-term) vs. groups newly formed (short-term) would experience increases or decreases in feelings of affection and attraction when supplied photographs of each other.

In this study, the authors found that generally short-term groups reported positive gains in their feelings when they were supplied with the pictures. However, having a photograph actually hurt assessments of each other in the long-term groups. Walther et al. proposed a "hyperpersonal theory" of relationships based on CMC in which "users sometimes experience intimacy, affection, and interpersonal assessments of their partner that exceed those occurring in parallel FTF [face-to-face] activities or alternative CMC contexts" (p. 109). In other words, having a picture meant that long-term members had to revise idealized impressions of each other, and that accepting a more realistic view of the other person led to disappointment in future interactions.

There are an increasing number of studies in and out of communication research on the effects of learning from the Web versus conventional forms of print media. Eveland and Dunwoody (2001) conducted an experiment to test four different treatment conditions and a control condition for effects on learning. Participants were randomly assigned to one of the five conditions: three Web versions of a news story on the flu, a print version of the same story, and unrelated printed material in the control group. The print version was constructed to appear as a magazine article with the same content. The three Web versions, called linear, nonlinear, and advisement, varied in terms of "the availability of navigation options between pages of the text, but the content remained the same" (p. 58).

Eveland and Dunwoody found some surprising results: hypermedia presentations reduced information recalled by participants compared to traditional forms of print. They suggested this set of effects could have been due to factors like "cognitive overload" and "disorientation" in participants who were more distracted by extraneous features in Web learning than they were by traditional print media forms. They also found that people with some Web expertise, unlike Web novices, were able to learn equally well across mediated contexts. The researchers suggested the Web experts might have learned to selectively scan Web images for relevant information. Technological advances have not only impacted what is studied in terms of content, but the way data is collected and analyzed.

Technology in the Experimental Research Process

The process of collecting and analyzing data in experimental research has involved the use of technology for some time. Certainly many studies use various media to record and collect observational data as well as self-report and other-report measures. As we noted in Chapter 5, some participants can even complete questionnaires and interviews online. Devices like remote microphones and Palm Pilots assist in data collection and field notes. More complex apparatuses have been designed to collect physiological data in experiments tracking arousal states. This data can now be automatically transformed into digital data directly without the researcher as a necessary interface. As our capacity to convert real spaces into virtual ones expands, we will undoubtedly be able to examine those conceptual territories with increasingly sophisticated technological tools.

In Chapter 5, you learned about a variety of statistical software packages used for data analysis. Packages like SAS, SPSS, and Microsoft Office Excel are the same software programs that are used for experimental data analysis. Just as survey research has relied on correlational analysis and frequency counts in the past, experimental research has traditionally relied upon various tests of group differences, most notably several different forms of analyses of variance. You will learn about these in much more detail in Chapter 9, "Testing Differences and Relationships." In this chapter, you will briefly explore four different types of analysis that are available (for the most part) in the three statistical packages identified earlier, SAS, SPSS, and Excel.

An analysis of variance tests differences among various groups or categories of the independent variable or variables for their effects on the dependent variable. As we explained in an earlier section of this chapter, a one-way analysis of variance (ANOVA) is used when there is just one independent variable with more than two categories, groups, or levels. For example, in the Eveland and Dunwoody (2001) study of Web- and print-mediated messages on learning, one independent variable consisted of five different conditions or groups: groups who were exposed to one of three Web-based news stories, one traditional print-mediated news story, or were in the control group not exposed to any of the experimental treatments. If this had been the only independent variable, the authors would have used a one-way ANOVA in the analysis of their results. This is one of the easier types of analyses to use in any of the statistical programs.

The assumption underlying the use of ANOVAs is that the independent variable is categorical, measured at the nominal or ordinal levels. When there are two or more categorical independent variables tested for their effects on the dependent variable, the analyses of variance software programs are set up to statistically check for sets of main effects and complex interactions. Software programs can also be used to conduct an *analysis of covariance* (ANCOVA), a test that permits portioning out the effects of one or more independent variables to examine separately the effects of the remaining independent variables.

When you want to test more complex relationships of multiple continuous and categorical independent variables on a dependent variable, you might use a *multivariate analysis of variance* (MANOVA) in any of the software packages mentioned previously. This last test, however, is more sophisticated and usually requires more software support to manage large and complex data files. You learn more about these tests in Chapter 9.

Beyond statistical tests of hypotheses, laboratory environments can now be equipped with continuous video recording equipment that sends data directly to a preprogrammed statistical package. This new capacity really streamlines the data collection and analysis process and drastically increases the amount of data that can be incorporated. The newest version of SPSS is one example of software that can now handle downloaded video information directly into data sets to be used in analysis. As you can see, technological advances in software programs for statistical analysis have greatly expanded the possibilities for creating very complex experimental research designs, not only in terms of how the data is analyzed but how it is collected as well.

SUMMARY

In this chapter, you learned about communication experimental research in terms of the research-as-argument model. Our discussion of experimental research began with constructing causal explanatory claims that predict changes in communication attitudes and behaviors. We examined the sources and settings of experimental data and explored data collection strategies by identifying the elements of research designs, defining three design types, and specifying traditional forms of experimental data analysis. We discussed warrants for experimental research as controlling rival explanations for the observed effects on a dependent variable, by establishing validity and reliability. Two sets of threats were examined: time progression effects and reactivity effects. The chapter concluded by considering how technology has impacted experimental research in communication. The preceding chapter on survey research, this chapter on experimental research, and the next chapter on content analysis provide the conceptual framework and its application for understanding the forms of statistical analysis that will appear in Chapters 8 and 9.

KEY TERMS

Between-subjects factor

Comparison groups

Compensatory behavior

Confederates

Confounding variables

Control group

Cover story

Demand characteristics

Evaluation apprehension

Experimental control

Experimental groups

Ex post facto design

Factorial designs

Factors

Hawthorne effect

History

Instrumentation

Interaction effects

Intervening variables

Main effects

Manipulation checks

Maturation

Mixed independent groups/
   repeated measures design

Mixed model paradigm

Mortality

Nonequivalent control group design

One-group pretest-posttest design

One-shot case study

Organismic variable

Placebo

Posttest

Posttest-only control group design

Preexperimental designs

Pretest

Pretest-posttest control group
   design

Quasi-experimental designs

Random assignment

Reactivity effects

Repeated measures

Research design statement

Researcher attributes

Sampling effect

Selection

Solomon four-group design

Static-group comparison design

Statistical regression

Stimulus variable

Target participants

Testing

Time progression effects

Time series design

Treatment diffusion

Treatment groups

True experimental designs

Within-subjects factor

DISCUSSION QUESTIONS

1. Explain the three criteria for establishing causality described in this chapter. What makes an experiment a causal argument?

2. What do claims typically look like in experimental research? Why do experimental researchers construct claims in this way?

3. In constructing experimental data settings, identify some of the concerns a researcher might have. For example, why would you try to make a laboratory setting look more like a typical living room?

4. Random assignment is an important consideration in making treatment groups equivalent and compa-rable. But random assignment is not always practical. Suppose, for instance, you wanted to test the effects of mediated messages in children's television programs on two separate day care groups, using one of the groups as a control group. What kinds of problems might intervene in this type of situation?

5. Why are some experimental research designs considered better or stronger than others?

6. What is the difference between time progression effects and reactivity effects as threats to the validity of your research design? Is every design equally vulnerable to both types of effects?

"TRY IT!" ACTIVITIES

1. A researcher wishes to assess the effects of biological sex and news stories with three types of endings on participants' level of recall. Identify the independent and dependent variables. Identify the factors, the design statement, the number of data cells, and possible main effects and interaction effects.

2. Suppose you want to study comforting strategy selection in interaction. You assess the baseline level of comforting strategies in your participants by using a pretest, but you worry participants may not be truthful in their responses if they guess what behavior you are investigating. Many participants appear to be more comforting in the research context than they would actually be in a natural setting. Explain the type of research progression effect you are concerned about. Construct a plausible research design that would minimize this time progression effect.

3. Decide whether you think cover stories pose ethical problems in the practice of research. What problems are cover stories expected to solve? Could these problems be solved in any other way?

4. Look up the study by Ayres and Heuett (2000). On p. 233 of this article, the authors identify their research design as "a pretest/post-test control group design." Explain this type of design and how it was applied to this study. Your explanation should include design elements (comparison groups, random assignment, and pretests) that were used. Identify the type of experimental design it is (pre-, quasi-, or true), and explain the strengths and weaknesses of this particular design.

7

Content and Interaction Analyses

ABSTRACT

In this chapter, you will learn how to conduct content and interaction analyses, beginning with forming research claims about the structure, function, and effects of communication in particular contexts. Next, we will consider the appropriate data sources for content and interaction analyses. Each method begins with the selection of a representative sample (of either messages or communicators). Both methods rely primarily on quantitative data analysis. However, the data are treated differently in each method: In content analysis, we proceed by dividing messages into units of analysis and categorizing these units; interaction analysis proceeds by rating verbal and nonverbal communicator behaviors or characteristics, which have been manipulated in experimental conditions. In the last section of this chapter, we will consider three warrants for content and interaction analyses: the reliability and validity of coding and rating schemes, and the external validity of the data.

OUTLINE

Imagine that you are interested in analyzing the cause or effect of some particular message characteristic, such as the sex roles of women in 1980s television situation comedies. Imagine further that you want to use quantitative methods. You probably will want to learn either content or interaction analysis, or both. **Content analysis** is a primarily quantitative method of categorizing and describing communication messages in specific contexts (Bereleson, 1952; Krippendorf, 1980). **Interaction analysis** is also a quantitative method, used to make inferences about the effects of manipulating verbal and nonverbal communication behaviors in dyadic and group interactions. Interaction analysis "attempts to unitize, categorize, and analyze the communication behaviors in a manner which maintains their sequential ordering" (Courtright, 1984, p. 197).

The methods of content analysis and interaction analysis have been most closely associated with the discovery paradigm and were less likely to be used to support interpretive or critical claims; Carpenter's (1999) content analysis of Flemish newspaper articles on prostitution illustrates one exception and shows how critical theorists can use content analysis to support claims of evaluation and reform. Both content analysis and interaction analysis are considered scientific methods since the researchers who use these methods aim to produce generalizable conclusions about discourse (i.e., they strive for conclusions that can be replicated or confirmed by other similar studies). Therefore, both content and interaction analyses fit the epistemological assumptions of the discovery paradigm. But before we look at the type of claims that each of these methods can be used to support, a brief description of the history of each method is in order.

In 18th-century Sweden, a group of scholars and clergy first used content analysis to examine a collection of 90 hymns called the *Songs of Zion*. Since the *Songs* were not found in the established hymnbook of the Swedish church, their religious symbols were analyzed to see if they were blaspheming state doctrine. Finding no significant differences between the 90 hymns and those that were sanctioned by the church, researchers concluded that the *Songs of Zion* were acceptable alternatives to the established church music (Krippendorf, 1980, p. 13). Krippendorf (1980) defined content analysis as "a research technique for making replicable and valid inferences" from "data to

their context" (as cited by Smith, 1988, p. 263). Similarly, Bereleson (1952) defined content analysis as "a research technique for the objective, systematic, and quantitative description of . . . communication" (p. 18).

"Modern content analysis can be traced back to World War II, when allied intelligence units painstakingly monitored the number and types of songs played on European radio stations" (Wimmer & Dominick, 1991, p. 157). By comparing the music played on different stations, the allies were able to gauge degrees of change in the troops amassed on the continent. In addition, "communications between Japan and various island bases were carefully tabulated; an increase in message volume usually meant that some new operation involving that particular base was planned" (p. 157). In the later 19th century, content analysis was used to analyze newspaper articles and make quantitative judgments about trends in coverage (e.g., Keshishian, 1997; McComas & Shanahan, 1999; Ramsey, 1999). All of these examples, from song lyrics, to radio communications between troop bases, to trends in newspaper coverage, involve analyzing the content of communication **artifacts,** or texts. All of these examples concern the study of cultural patterns of meaning. Thomas (1994) asserted that "the main function of artifact analysis is to explicate this cultural meaning" (p. 685). Content analysis is one way to "study the artifact" (Thomas, 1994, p. 685).

Content analysis still is used primarily to investigate claims about mass communication, perhaps because the *content* of mediated messages is so readily available for this type of analysis. A search of the Communication Institute for Online Scholarship (CIOS) conducted in June 2003, using the keywords *content analysis* to scan all the available journal titles, located 402 abstracts, 46 of which were published in 2002–03. Many of those studies were published in journals that focus primarily on mediated communication, such as the *Journal of Broadcasting and Electronic Media, Public Opinion Quarterly,* and *Journalism and Mass Communication Quarterly.*

By contrast, interaction analysis involves the discovery of generalizable and replicable patterns in interactive discourse (e.g., Bavelas, Black, Chovil, Lemery, & Mullett, 1988; Burgoon, Buller, Guerrero, & Feldman, 1994; DeStephen, 1983; Le Poire, Shepard, & Duggan, 1999; Trees & Manusov, 1998; Waldron, 1990). In **interactive discourse,** all interactants share

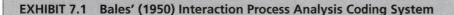

> **EXHIBIT 7.1   Bales' (1950) Interaction Process Analysis Coding System**
>
> 1. Shows friendliness————————————|
> 2. Dramatizes by telling a story—————— | |
> 3. Shows agreement————————| | |
> 4. Gives a suggestion—————— | | | |
> 5. Gives an opinion————| | | | |
> 6. Gives information —— | | | | | |
>   a   b   c   d   e   f
> 7. Asks for information — | | | | | |
> 8. Asks for an opinion———— | | | | |
> 9. Asks for a suggestion———— | | | |
> 10. Shows disagreement—————— | | |
> 11. Shows tension————————————| |
> 12. Shows unfriendliness————————————|
>
> a. problems of communication
> b. problems of evaluation
> c. problems of control
> d. problems of decision
> e. problems of tension reduction
> f. problems of reintegration

responsibility for speaking and listening, whereas in **narrative discourse,** the kind most often analyzed in content analysis, one participant has greater responsibility for speaking than do other participants (Smith, 1988).

Bales (1950) first conceptualized interaction analysis. Bale's Interaction Process Analysis (IPA) scheme was designed to link communicative behaviors of group members to group productivity. Researchers used the IPA to code conversational turns-at-talk in terms of participants' specific behaviors (see Exhibit 7.1). The IPA also allowed researchers to index three general directions, or values, in a group's interaction. First, the up versus down direction dealt with a participant's move to dominate the other or submit to the other interactants. Second, the positive versus negative direction dealt with moves that were more friendly or unfriendly. Third, the forward versus backward direction dealt with moves that were oriented more toward task or socioemotional relationships (Stiles, 1980). As a case in point, Hiltz, Johnson, and Turoff (1986) used the IPA to compare interaction processes and outcomes in face-to-face versus computerized conferences.

Interaction analysis has grown broader than Bales's IPA scheme during the past 50 years, and the term *interaction analysis* now refers by and large to scholarship practiced by relational communication research-

ers (Courtright, 1984). In some interaction analyses, the researchers ask subjects to rate the behaviors of confederate communicators (e.g., Burgoon & Le Poire, 1999; Le Poire & Yoshimura, 1999); in other cases, researchers rate communicator behaviors (e.g., DeStephen, 1983; Trees & Manusov, 1998).

As in content analysis, the epistemology of interaction analysis is still one of discovering generalizable, replicable patterns in talk. As in content analysis, the researcher, not the participants, determines what participants' communicative behaviors mean, whether the ratings come from researchers or from research subjects. However, in interaction analysis, either researchers or subjects typically rate behaviors in the context of interactive discourse, whereas content analysis is more likely to involve categorizing or coding narrative discourse. In Chapter 10, "Conversation and Discourse Analysis," you will learn about a more interpretive method for analyzing interactive discourse, called conversation analysis. In Chapter 12, "Traditional and Interpretive Methods of Rhetorical Criticism," you will learn some more interpretive and critical methods for examining narrative discourse.

Next, let's look at how you can use content and interaction analytic methods to support your claims of description, explanation and prediction, and evaluation and reform of communicative practices.

CLAIMS OF CONTENT AND INTERACTION ANALYSES

Three sets of claims are common to content and interaction analyses: description, explanation and prediction, and evaluation and reform. We will outline each of these types of claim and illustrate them with examples. As you read each section, think about the kinds of claims you might want to investigate using content and/or interaction analyses.

Descriptive Claims

Perhaps the most basic claim of content or interaction analysis is the attempt to *describe* communication messages or interaction characteristics in particular contexts. "Although the content of human interaction is infinitely variable, people's perceptions of interpersonal roles and relationships may be described by a small number of underlying dimensions" (Stiles, 1980, p. 359). Interaction analysts seek to describe these dimensions, as well as their causes and effects in interactive discourse.

Description is also a primary claim of content analytic communication research. This is a good point at which to reemphasize that content analysis is different than conversation analysis. The content analyst aims to discover, for example, what topics are included in a conversation, perhaps with respect to frequency of inclusion. The conversation analyst, however, is more likely to interpret what participants' talk about particular topics is accomplishing in a conversation (Sigman, Sullivan, & Wendell, 1988).

Conversely, content analysis is used to describe messages that occur in particular contexts. Some of the contexts that have been described using content analysis include computer-mediated communication (e.g., Bordia & Rosnow, 1998; Stewart, Shields, & Sen, 1998); health care (e.g., Andsager & Smiley, 1998; Barker, 1998; Cegala, McGee, & McNeilis, 1996); intercultural communication (e.g., Anderson, Martin, & Zhong, 1998; Chen, 1997); interpersonal relationships (e.g., Dainton, 1998); television talk shows (e.g., Johnson, Smith, Mitchell, Orrego, & Yun, 1999); and political communication (e.g., Barnhurst, 2003; Benoit & Currie, 2001; Lasswell, 1927; Schenck-Hamlin, Procter, & Rumsey, 2000).

Interaction analysis is used to describe verbal and nonverbal communication *behaviors,* rather than textual *messages.* A typical context for interaction analysis is a dyadic or group exchange, usually in a tightly controlled, laboratory setting (e.g., Guerrerro, Jones, & Burgoon, 2000; Hollingshead, 1996; Trees & Manusov, 1998; Wilson, Aleman, & Leatham, 1998). However, some interaction analyses have been conducted in field settings, where the dyadic or group interactions would occur naturally (e.g., Adelman, Greene, Charon, & Friedmann, 1992; DeStephen, 1983).

Describing communication characteristics in context is helpful for several reasons. Johnson et al. (1999) pointed out some of these reasons in their descriptive content analytic study of television talk show experts:

> These findings are designed to inform better those who create the shows, those who watch the shows, and those who critique the shows, the content and composition of the show. It also provides evidence for or against many claims made about experts and talk shows. . . . this descriptive study illustrates how talk shows operated in a typical month during this time frame (p. 94).

Thus, the general claim of Johnson et al.'s (1999) content analytic study can be stated as "The content of televised talk shows is . . .". However, Johnson and her colleagues examined several specific research questions, so their descriptive claims can be further specified:

1. The *issues* covered by television talk show experts are . . . (e.g., family relationships, self-improvement, crime/safety).

2. The *qualifications* of television talk show experts are . . . (e.g., Ph.D., health official, self-proclaimed).

3. The *nature of advice* given by television talk show experts is . . . (e.g., specific or nonspecific).

Consider a second example of a descriptive claim that can be supported using content analysis. Anderson et al. (1998) examined the content of written questionnaires from students, faculty, and staff in a Beijing university in order to describe Chinese persons' motivations for communicating with family and friends. The authors asked questions about "communication behavior in general and interpersonally" (p. 113), and they found that the university students and staff in their sample communicated with parents for relaxation, inclusion, pleasure, and control, but their primary motive for communicating with friends was inclusion. Notice that these authors analyzed the *con-*

tent of the survey questionnaire data, which is quite different than, for example, videotaping interactions between these Chinese participants (or between these participants and their families and friends).

The content analytic approach provides an ideal basis for comparative scholarship. You could compare Anderson et al.'s (1998) findings on the reasons for communicating in certain relationship types with findings from other culture-specific descriptions of communication. Or you could conduct a study of reasons for communicating in another context. The purpose of such a comparison might be to *describe* culturally specific (versus potentially generalizable) patterns of relational communication.

DeStephen's (1983) field study of decision-making groups' interactions illustrates this use of comparative studies. DeStephen sought to describe and compare the interactions of high- and low-consensus groups, both at their initial meetings and their final meetings. DeStephen argued that most studies of group decision making "reveal very little about the nature of ongoing interaction in groups with varying levels of consensus" (p. 340), even though consensus is a central topic in the study of group decision making. Her comparative descriptions of how high- and low-consensus groups interact, both initially and after regular meetings over time, aimed to contribute empirical support to theories of groups as developing over time, *from the interactions of members,* rather than being simple aggregates of individual members' expertise, talkativeness, trust levels, and so on. Hirokawa's (1980) study of effective and ineffective decision-making groups followed a similar logic. Such comparative descriptions can be used to inform explanations and predictions of the outcomes of group behaviors. Explanatory and predictive claims can also be tested using content and/or interaction analyses.

Explanatory and Predictive Claims

Content analysts usually seek "to infer the effects of the messages that they have analyzed, although actual data about such communication effects are seldom available" (Rogers, 1994, p. 215). For example, comparative scholarship based on the descriptive studies outlined above could be used to *explain* how intercultural misunderstandings are based on value differences. Both content and interaction analyses can be used to support predictive claims as well. For instance, predictions about media usage, voting behavior, and

the like are often inferred from content analysis of narrative discourse. In many cases, content and interaction analyses are used to support two types of claims simultaneously, either description and explanation, or explanation and prediction. We will outline three such cases below.

In the first example, Bordia and Rosnow (1998) conducted a content analytic study of rumormongering in computer-mediated communication. The authors *described* the content and participation levels of individuals as they contributed to a collective problem-solving process (i.e., dealing with rumors). But Bordia and Rosnow also *explained* that the process of dealing with rumors was similar in computer-mediated and face-to-face interaction settings.

In a second example, Evans (1996) advanced claims of prediction and explanation, comparing the astrological advice given in magazines that targeted working- versus middle-class women. Evans *predicted* that the content of the horoscopes depended more on social class than on zodiac sign: Middle-class horoscopes were more likely than working-class horoscopes to encourage women to travel and spend money. Both classes of horoscope advised women to nurture, be patient and cooperative, and avoid confrontations, which, Evans *explained*, are all stereotypically feminine communication prescriptions.

In a much larger attempt to *explain* and *predict* the effects of media messages, Emmers-Sommer and Allen (1999) conducted a meta-analysis of media effects studies that were published in *Human Communication Research* over 25 years. **Meta-analysis** literally means that the researchers conduct an analysis of many prior analyses. "Meta-analysis is a systematic quantitative technique used to ascertain relationships among variables" (Emmers-Sommer & Allen, 1999, p. 486). By comparing the results of many single-case studies, the researchers can synthesize useful conclusions. For example, Emmers-Sommer and Allen concluded that (1) age is related to the ability to process and understand media messages; (2) the mass media is a significant source of learning; and (3) the media can influence attitudes, which in turn may shape our behaviors.

Interaction analysis also can be conducted to test explanatory and predictive research claims (Courtright, 1984). Waldron (1990) conducted an interaction analytic experiment designed to *explain* how conversational planning behavior should vary as a function of planning constraints. Framing his study as contributing to the broad understanding of message production processes by linking cognition to action, Waldron hypothesized that two potential constraints on interaction planning, goal priority and goal complexity, should reduce creative planning and lead to direct information acquisition tactics. Thus, within his theoretic *explanation* (i.e., that interactional planning is reduced or made less effective in the face of situational and cognitive constraints), Waldron posed several specific hypotheses, or *predictions.* Three of his predictions are cited here for illustrative purposes:

H_1: As instrumental goal priority increases, planning becomes less creative and complex, with interactants reporting increased use of direct instrumental plans.

H_2: As instrumental goal priority increases, planning becomes less creative and complex, with interactants reporting decreased use of indirect instrumental plans.

H_3: As instrumental goal priority increases, planning becomes less creative and complex, with interactants reporting decreased use of plans designed to achieve strictly interpersonal goals (Waldron, 1990, p. 159).

In the laboratory experiment that Waldron conducted with students from an introductory college-level communication theory course, all three of these predictions were supported by empirical data.

Imagine that you want to request extra time to turn in a homework assignment without incurring a grade penalty, relative to your instructor's announced deadline for the assignment and/or late work policy. You may plan for the interaction in which you request this privilege. You have an instrumental goal that carries for you a certain priority and complexity, depending on your previous experience with similar situations, persuasive abilities, grade motivation, and so on. If you are very grade motivated and your instructor has a strict rule about enforcing late penalties on graded homework, the interaction will require from you a high workload (i.e., heavy thought). Waldron predicted that increasing cognitive workload would reduce interactants' use of creative planning and reduce the overall quality of the conversational planning in which interactants did engage. If, on the other hand, you care little for grades, or if your instructor rarely enforces a late-paper penalty, the planning workload for this interaction will be less. In those cases, you will more likely engage in creative

planning and/or attend to other types of goals in addition to your instrumental goal, like maintaining your identity as a good student and maintaining a positive relationship with your instructor.

We hope this example helps you, not to turn in late papers, but to see how interaction analysts view conversation as structured patterns of behaviors that meet goals or serve functions for interactants. The interaction analyst views conversational behavior, its causes and its effects, as describable, explainable, and predictable.

Evaluation and Reform Claims

As you know from Chapter 2, claims of evaluation are made when we use some form of data, usually textual evidence, to assess the worth of communication, the effects of particular messages, and so on. Both content and interaction analyses can be used to make such assessments. For example, Grabe (1999) performed a content analysis of crime stories published in television news magazine programs during 1994–95, in order to determine whether these stories upheld Durkheim's theoretic notion that social morals are constructed through public sanctions for criminal behavior (Douglas, 1967). In other words, if the crime stories we read in the newspaper, or that we see portrayed on television, actually help to construct social norms for moral behavior, then analysis of these stories' narrative content can help public policy makers, for example, create a moral society. Let's look at three examples in which content analysis is used to advance claims of evaluation and reform.

In the first case, Gow (1996) analyzed the content of 1990s MTV music videos in order to evaluate whether executive changes regulating the content and music format improved gender representation for women. Gow concluded that portrayals of women still focused on physical appearance, instead of musical ability. Gow's claim is evaluative; his research assessed whether an intended social change is indeed coming about. Claims of reform go beyond evaluating whether a change is happening and extend to actual efforts to induce change in the society (e.g., by changing the language used in a particular discourse context).

To this end, Andsager and Smiley (1998) evaluated the effectiveness of public information officers during a 1991–92 controversy about silicone breast implants. After content analyzing news stories, these authors concluded that media information officers relied too heavily on the medical community's framing of the controversy and suggested that the officers should find alternate ways to shape and transmit stories in order to increase the public's understanding of this health issue.

Clarke (1999) advanced an even stronger claim of evaluation and reform, regarding the content of printed mass media from 1974 to 1995. Clarke analyzed the qualitative meanings of these media's manifest and latent content. **Manifest meanings** are "those that are evident on the surface" (Clarke, 1999, p. 63). **Latent meanings** are "below the threshold of superficial observation" (Merton, 1968, p. 105).

Clarke's comparative analysis revealed a manifest emphasis on early detection of prostate cancer in these print media sources, but a latent gendering of prostate cancer as inherently masculine. She pointed out that a gendered portrayal of prostate cancer "may have implications for the potential willingness of men to engage in early detection" (p. 59). She *indicted* the media with the responsibility of framing meanings in ways that contribute to men's willingness to visit their doctor and to know the risk factors for this disease. If media messages avoid portraying maleness as unemotional and individualist, and instead portray masculinity as including emotional expression and collectivist values, then perhaps men will be more likely to be diagnosed and treated earlier.

The issue of manifest versus latent meanings has long been a central concern for content analysts. We can deal with both types of meaning in content analysis. For example, Thomas (1994) reported that she asked her undergraduate students to code the results of motor vehicle accidents in fiction television programs: "Upon completing the assignment, many observed how they had never noticed how relatively unhazardous TV accidents were" (p. 691). The students' conclusion, that TV portrayals depict such accidents as relatively harmless, is an analysis of latent message content.

DATA FOR CONTENT AND INTERACTION ANALYSES

Because both content and interaction analyses aim to produce replicable descriptions and evaluations of communication, both types of research study usually employ random selection methods and quantitative data analytic strategies. (Refer back to Chapter 3 for details of random selection methods and their value in discovery research.) Yet, even though both content and interaction analyses are discovery research methodologies, two key differences separate these methods: the type of data used and the way the data are treated by the researcher.

In content analysis, textual messages are first unitized, and then categorized, before the researcher can interpret the frequency with which the units being analyzed have occurred in each category. Narrative discourse, that is, messages that are "characterized by relatively fixed source–receiver roles," is the most common type of data used for content analysis, where narrative data are "physical traces or actuarial records of messages" (Smith, 1988, p. 351). Political speeches are characterized by fixed roles because the speechmaker does all the talking, and the audience typically just listens, until the speech is over. Audio- or videotaped political speeches are physical traces, records of messages spoken or written. Political speeches are narrative texts, as are television commercials, newspaper editorials, Web sites, classroom lectures, or Shakespearean soliloquies.

However, interactive discourse is "a communication form characterized by alternating source–receiver roles" (Smith, 1988, p. 349). As you might infer from the name, interactive discourse provides the data for interaction analysis. In interaction analysis, interval-level measurement scales are used by both participants and observers to rate communicator characteristics like dominance, involvement, or politeness. Dyadic conversations and group discussions are examples of interactive discourse suitable for interaction analysis. Just as with content analysis, interaction analysis requires the physical trace of discourse, whether those traces are audiotapes, videotapes, or written transcripts.

Therefore, the content analyst categorizes message content, whereas the interaction analyst rates verbal and nonverbal communicator behaviors. The sequence of operations for each method is outlined in Exhibit 7.2.

In this section, you will learn how to define a sampling population and select representative samples of messages (for content analysis) or conversational participants (for interaction analysis). You will also learn how to use coding and rating schemes, and how to make quantitative sense of your findings, by using descriptive frequencies and percentages, and in

---

EXHIBIT 7.2   Steps for Conducting Content and Interaction Analyses

Content analysis

1. Select representative sample of messages.
2. Divide messages into units of analysis.
3. Assign each unit to one category of a coding scheme.
4. Summarize the frequency of units in each category, and compare frequencies to infer relationships among or differences among categories.

Interaction analysis

1. Select representative sample of conversational participants.
2. Manipulate hypothesized causal variable(s), usually by selection or using confederate participants.
3. Have observers and/or naïve participants apply rating scales to interaction.
4. Interpret change in outcome variables for each experimental condition (see Step 2, above).

---

some cases, inferential statistical tests of relationships and differences among variables. The statistical aspects of data analysis you will need to conduct both content and interaction analyses will be fully elaborated in the next two chapters. However, the final issue of how to assess the consistency of your coding and rating judgments will be covered in the warrants section of this chapter.

Selecting Representative Sample Data

Both content and interaction analyses begin with the selection of a representative sample because both methods aim to produce generalizable and replicable results (i.e., results that can be applied to messages and interactions other than those observed in one study). Let's begin by reviewing the concept of random selection methods.

Sampling messages from populations As you know from Chapter 3, a population is a "comprehensive and well-defined group (a universal set) of the elements pertinent to a given research question or hypothesis" (Smith, 1988, p. 77). A **message population** is a well-defined set of messages pertinent to a given research question or hypothesis. Just as the U.S. population is defined by the Census Bureau's data, the population of particular kinds of messages can be defined in order to conduct communication research. For instance, Niquette and Buxton (1997) chose to examine the messages conveyed in cartoons that depicted 19th-century world's fair visitors. They collected 533 cartoons from 26 issues of the humor magazine *Puck*. Because *Puck* was published on the

site of the 1893 Chicago Columbian Exposition for that entire year, Niquette and Buxton argued that the cartoons they examined constituted a distinct message population.

A representative sample is a subset of population elements that has been "selected in such a way that it reflects well the characteristics of its parent population" (Smith, 1988, p. 78). The best way to ensure that a data sample represents the population from which it is selected is to use some form of chance when picking the elements to be included in a sample. If you use one of the random selection methods outlined in Chapter 3, you will be more likely to select elements that represent the population, and you will decrease the chance of selecting biased elements (i.e., elements that represent some, but not all, of the relevant population characteristics).

As you can imagine, a vast array of message populations may be defined, based on the research questions or hypotheses posed by communication researchers. Because mediated messages are such a prevalent source of data for content analysis, these message populations are often defined by the type of media outlet, such as newspaper, television, radio, film, and the like. The population of messages within a particular media outlet may be refined further by considering the genre, or type of content. For example, within a newspaper are articles, editorials, advertisements, and cartoons. On television, we see programs of news, drama, and comedy, as well as commercials. The topic of study may further delineate a message population, as when the researcher is particularly interested in mediated portrayals of gender, ethnicity, culture, and so on (e.g., Beasley & Standley, 2002; Billings, Halone, & Denham, 2002).

EXHIBIT 7.3   Some Message Samples Used for Content Analysis

Media sources
- Newspaper stories (e.g., Keshishian, 1997; McComas & Shanahan, 1999; Ramsey, 1999; Zoch & Turk, 1998)
- Mass print media depictions of prostate cancer (e.g., Clarke, 1999)
- Print cartoons of 19th-century world's fair visitors (e.g., Niquette & Buxton, 1997)
- Magazine astrology/horoscope columns (e.g., Evans, 1996)
- Personal ads (e.g., Hatala, Baack, & Parmenter, 1998)
- Scholarly journal articles (e.g., Fink & Gantz, 1996)
- Magazine advertisements of Latinos (e.g., Taylor & Bang, 1997)
- Slasher horror movies (e.g., Weaver, 1991)
- MTV music videos (e.g., Gow, 1996; McKee & Pardun, 1996)
- Television commercials (e.g., Cheng, 1997; Larson, 2001; Lin, 1997; Roy & Harwood, 1997)
- Television talk shows (e.g., Grabe, 2002; Johnson, Smith, Mitchell, Orrego, & Yun, 1999)
- Television news magazine crime stories (e.g., Grabe, 1999)
- Television characters (e.g., Lichter, Lichter, & Amundson, 1997; Matabane & Merritt, 1996; Scharrer, 2001)
- Appearance of politicians on commercial vs. public television (e.g., Brants & Neijens, 1998)

- Political advertisements (e.g., Schenck-Hamlin, Procter, & Rumsey, 2000)

Surveys filled out by communicators
- Open-ended questionnaires (e.g., Anderson, Martin, & Zhong, 1998; Cegala, McGee, & McNeilis, 1996; Fiebig & Kramer, 1998; Hess, 2000)
- Health care patients' critical incident descriptions (e.g., Anderson, 2001; Ruben, 1993)
- Interaction diaries (e.g., Dainton, 1998)

Computerized messages
- Individual messages from a CMC discussion group (e.g., Bordia & Rosnow, 1998; Honeycutt, 2001; Stewart, Shields, & Sen, 1998)
- Email messages (e.g., Pragg, Wiseman, Cody, & Wendt, 1999)
- Web sites (Chan-Olmstead & Park, 2000)
- Video games (Beasley & Standley, 2002)

Other sources
- Jury deliberations (e.g., Sunwolf & Seibold, 1998)
- Audiotaped group discussions of HIV/AIDS (e.g., Pittman & Gallois, 1997)
- Semistructured, open-ended interviews (e.g., Graham, 1997)

Another way to select messages from a population is to distribute survey questionnaires or communication diaries and to ask people to describe their own communication. For example, Fiebig and Kramer (1998) conducted a content analysis of emotional expression in organizational settings by asking employees to describe their decisions to reveal or camouflage feelings when their expectations were either met or violated. Dainton (1998) asked 55 married couples to keep a log of every dyadic interaction they had for one week and used those data to describe the type and duration of everyday interaction in marital relationships. Both of these examples illustrate a message population that is based on a communication setting or context (i.e., expression of emotions in organizations and marital interactions).

The past decade has seen an explosion of research concerning the process of computer–mediated communication (CMC). We will consider research claims about CMC in a special section on technology in content and interaction analyses, later in this chapter. But

whether you are most interested in traditional media outlets, communication surveys, diaries, or CMC messages, there are many sources from which to sample message populations. Exhibit 7.3 lists a number of message samples used in published content analytic studies over the past decade. These samples are grouped according to their source in media outlets, communicator surveys or diaries, CMC, and other sources.

Sampling verbal and nonverbal interactions

Just as you will want to select a representative sample of messages from a population for content analysis, you will want to select a representative sample of verbal and nonverbal interactions from its parent population for interaction analysis. Remember that you need interactive discourse for interaction analysis. You may analyze just two people, alternating between acting as source and receiver in a dyadic interaction. Of course, it is also possible that a number of people may take turns in these roles, as happens during a group discussion.

EXHIBIT 7.4   Some Communicator Samples Used for Interaction Analysis

- Individual subjects' messages constructed in laboratory settings (e.g., Hummert, Shaner, Garstka, & Henry, 1998; Trees & Manusov, 1998; Wilson, Aleman, & Leatham, 1998)
- Dyadic (or triadic) interactions in laboratory settings (e.g., Burgoon, Buller, Guerrero, & Feldman, 1994; Burgoon, Parrott, Le Poire, Kelley, Walther, & Perry, 1989; Chen, 1997)

- Dyadic interactions in natural settings (e.g., physician/patient interactions, Adelman, Greene, Charon, & Friedmann, 1992)
- Group discussions in laboratory settings (e.g., Hiltz, Johnson, & Turoff, 1986; Hollingshead, 1996; Meyers & Brashers, 1998)
- Group discussions in natural settings (e.g., DeStephen, 1983)

If you intend to observe naturally occurring interactions, then the question of *when* to observe depends greatly on your research question, as well as the specific type of observational method you will employ and whether you intend to take notes or record the interactions on audio- or videotape. If you want to select interaction samples from their naturally occurring contexts, you will have to think carefully about exactly when, and for how long, you wish to observe, as well as considering these various methods of capturing your observations. Contextual factors are often relevant for deciding when to observe. You may want to observe interaction in different settings, or at different times of the day, week, or season, if these are relevant to your research question. In addition, equipment and facility reservations often influence decisions about when and how long you will observe interactions. Review Chapter 6 on the issue of timing pre- and posttests. If your claim concerns the way that interactions change over time, then you will want your initial and subsequent observations to be spaced far enough apart for the predicted change to have occurred. On the other hand, you don't want to wait so long that other factors are likely to influence the interactions you sample in your second set of observations.

Whether the data you select for interaction analysis consists of face-to-face or mediated communications, interactions can be captured in the setting where they would naturally occur (i.e., the field), or they can be induced solely for the purpose of your study in a setting you control (i.e., the lab).

Since quite a large amount of laboratory interaction analysis has been done using message construction tasks, let's consider that aspect of data selection next. **Message construction tasks** require experi-

mental subjects to respond to communicative scenarios developed by a researcher. Usually, the subjects are asked to write down exactly what they would say to a target person if they were one of the interactants in that scenario (e.g., Hummert, Shaner, Garstka, & Henry, 1998; Wilson, Aleman, & Leatham, 1998). Then the researcher codes the participants' constructed messages according to some theoretic category scheme. Accordingly, Wilson et al. (1998) asked undergraduate students to respond to several compliance-gaining scenarios that involved being asked for favors, giving advice, and enforcing obligations with same-sex friends. Coders who were blinded to the purposes or hypotheses of Wilson et al.'s study counted the number of reasons that subjects gave for complying or refusing to comply with the scenario request. The coders also rated the level of approval or disapproval of each request that was expressed in the written responses.

Message construction tasks represent a compromise between naturally occurring interactions collected in the field, and hypothetical, recalled, or elicited interactions involving zero–history dyads (or perhaps a subject and a confederate) in the laboratory setting. Exhibit 7.4 lists some interaction samples used in published interaction analysis research over the past two decades.

Encoding texts Once a population of messages or interactions has been specified and a data sample selected, you can begin the process of encoding texts. Simply put, encoding text involves translating the selected messages or interaction behaviors into a form from which they can be analyzed. If the data are collected in written form (e.g., newspaper editorials, subway graffiti, personal letters), you can convert those written messages into digital form for analysis, either by typing or scanning the discourse into a computer. If the messages were gathered from verbal interactions (e.g., videotaped conversations or interviews), you will need to transcribe the data into written form (e.g., Graham, 1997). **Transcriptions** are verbatim records of the content of narrative or interactive discourse. Transcriptions contain the exact words of the messages or interactions, and they may also contain information about pause length, intonation, or other paraverbal cues. (In Chapter 10, "Conversation and Discourse Analysis," you will learn to do transcription.)

Data Treatment for Content Analysis

Once you have selected a data sample and encoded text if need be, your content analysis will proceed in two phases: unitizing and categorizing. In the first phase, **unitizing,** you will divide your text into **units of analysis,** such as words, sentences, paragraphs, or thematically coherent phrases or passages. In the second phase, **categorizing,** you will group those units into different categories. You will need to work with another person in this phase, since two or more coders usually work together to make judgments about which category each message fits into. This way, you will be able to assess the percentage of agreement across coder decisions, or intercoder reliability. We will talk more about intercoder reliability in the warrants section of this chapter. Wimmer and Dominick (1991) called coding data "the most time-consuming and least glamorous part of a content analysis" (p. 168). Let's consider each step in chronological order.

Unitizing messages When narrative discourse is available in written or digital form, the actual analysis of content begins by dividing messages into smaller, comparable units of analysis. Krippendorf (1980) identified five possible types of message units, which have become the standard for content analyses. We will define each of these units briefly. *Physical units* are identified by the amount of space or time used in the talk, such as one line of a transcript. *Syntactical units* are discrete bits of language, such as a word, sentence, or paragraph. *Referential units* are identified by their reference to a person, event, or issue, such as references to a candidate in an upcoming election. *Propositional units* are identified by the structures into which they place message content, such as anecdotes,

stories, and the like. Finally, *thematic units* are topics contained within messages of a certain structure, such as gender portrayals of women in music videos.

Krippendorf (1980) noted that these five possible message units grow subsequently more complex: Physical units are "obvious," and syntactical units, likewise, "do not require judgments on meaning" (p. 61). But propositional units better "approach the complexities of natural language" (p. 62) than do referential units, and "thematic units require a deep understanding of the source language with all its shades and nuances of meaning and content" (p. 63). Thus, the easiest units to code reliably (i.e., physical units) might be of least interest if you want to explain or evaluate the meaning of words as they are used in context. At the same time, it is quite difficult to achieve stability or equivalence of either unitizing or categorizing decisions when your unit of analysis is thematic.

Once you have divided your messages into units of analysis, you are ready to begin categorizing those units.

Categorizing messages In content analysis, you will probably be most interested in the frequency with which message units fall into particular categories. Content analysts sometimes use a set of theoretic categories as a prearranged **coding scheme,** categories that may come from their own or another researcher's published work. Alternatively, your coding scheme may emerge from the data you collect, or a coding scheme may combine categories suggested by past research with those you found in your data. For example, Ruben (1993) collected written critical incidents from patients in health care settings and categorized their most memorable positive and negative experiences, using categories that were partially derived from existing theoretic literature, even though no formal coding scheme was previously published.

Typically, a pilot study is done on a small portion of the data in order either to test the workability of a prearranged coding scheme, or to develop new coding categories. The coders are also trained prior to analyzing pilot data. In fact, a key purpose of the pilot study is to make initial assessments of unitizing and coding reliabilities, and if necessary, offer further training to ensure acceptably consistent coding decisions. Whether the categories are developed by you or come from prior research, you will want to make a standardized coding sheet for use by coders as they process the raw data. An example of a standardized coding sheet is provided in Exhibit 7.5.

EXHIBIT 7.5 A Standardized Coding Sheet

Program Title: _____

Host Name: _____

Date Program Aired: _____

Name of Expert: _____

VARIABLE	UNIT OF ANALYSIS	CATEGORIES
Issues addressed	Thematic	___ Abuse
		___ Safety/crime
		___ Family relationships
		___ Romantic relationships
		___ Drugs
		___ Self-improvement
Expert qualifications	Referential	___ PhD or formally trained
		___ Justice or health official
		___ Author/editor/teacher
		___ Self-proclaimed/media/other
Nature of advice given	Thematic	___ Specific
		___ Nonspecific
Number of turns	Physical	___ Turns in this show
		___ Turns by this expert

Note. Constructed by Merrigan and Huston based on Johnson, Smith, Mitchell, Orrego, & Yun (1999)

A sample coding scheme Johnson et al.'s (1999) study of television talk show experts provided a reasonably clear illustration of a coding scheme. Johnson et al. measured three variables. First, the *issues* addressed on each talk show were coded into six categories (i.e., abuse, safety/crime, family relationships, romantic relationships, drugs, and self- or material improvement). Second, the *qualifications* of the talk show experts were coded into four categories (PhD or formally trained; justice or health official; au-

thor/editor/teacher; and self-proclaimed/media/other). Finally, the *nature of advice* was categorized as either specific or nonspecific. Johnson et al. also counted the number of turns in each show and the number of expert turns. "A 'turn' was defined as the number of words spoken by an individual without being interrupted by someone else who then assumes the floor" (p. 95). Exhibit 7.5 shows what a standardized coding sheet for the Johnson et al. study might have looked like.

Data Treatment for Interaction Analysis

Whereas content analysts unitize and categorize narrative discourse, interaction analysts categorize and rate the verbal and nonverbal behaviors present in interactive discourse. To do this, you will either apply rating schemes to existing interactions, such as audio- or videotaped group meetings, or you might bring interactants into a laboratory setting and create hypothetical interactions. In this section, we will outline the procedures that you can use to manipulate hypothesized causal variables and rate interaction characteristics, whether you are studying naturally occurring interactions or those induced in a laboratory setting. We will also familiarize you with some sample rating schemes that have been used in published interaction analytic research.

Manipulating hypothesized causal variables A laboratory experiment allows you to control the interaction setting, as well as the type of interactants and topics discussed. With such control, you can make more precise comparisons about other conditions, such as micro-level interaction characteristics like eye gaze or friendliness cues. For example, Burgoon and Le Poire (1999) conducted an experiment in which they asked undergraduate students to discuss three moral-social dilemmas (e.g., plagiarism) and arrive at a consensus of what they would do in each case. In each videotaped interaction, three people were present, including the participant student, the observer student, and a confederate actor. The confederate played the role of someone with either a highly involved nonverbal style, or a detached and unpleasant nonverbal style. Burgoon and Le Poire hypothesized that the students *participating* in these triads would perceive the confederate's behavior in the same ways that the students *observing* the interactions would perceive those behaviors. Thus, Burgoon and Le Poire manipulated their hypothesized cause (i.e., nonverbal involvement style) and observed the effect of that manipulation on interaction outcomes (i.e., participant and observer ratings of intimacy, dominance, composure, and formality).

Waldron's (1990) experimental lab study of conversational planning processes illustrates another way to manipulate hypothesized causes (independent variables). Waldron gave 174 research subjects conversational tasks of varying goal priorities. They completed their conversational task with a partner, and that interaction was videotaped. Next, Waldron and the subjects participated together in a **cued recall technique**—asking subjects to describe what they were thinking as they watch a videotape of their own interaction behaviors. So the subjects discussed their conversational planning process as they watched their videotaped interactions with Waldron. Both strategies, using confederates and using the cued recall technique, are useful ways of inducing discourse for interaction analysis.

Rating interaction behaviors or characteristics

Whereas the second step in data treatment for content analysis is *categorizing* messages according to the particular units of analysis of interest to the researcher, the second step in treating data for interaction analysis is to *rate* interaction behaviors or characteristics. A **rating scheme** is used to assign numerical values to interaction features. You could rate the amount of eye contact your conversational partner is giving you, from "1 = Too little" to "3 = Too much." The subjects in Burgoon and Le Poire's (1999) study filled out a number of Likert-type scales in which they rated the confederate speaker's relational communication characteristics (e.g., intimacy, composure). In addition, pairs of raters who were trained by Burgoon and Le Poire rated these students' nonverbal behaviors, for their degree of immediacy, expressiveness, and relaxation.

Numerical ratings like these are used in quantitative data analysis, which is the focus of the next two chapters. Numerical data can be employed to describe interaction (e.g., the average amount of eye contact) or to determine relationships among interaction behaviors (e.g., as anxiety levels increase, eye gaze may decrease). Numerical data also can be used to determine areas of significant differences in interaction behaviors or characteristics (e.g., males use more direct eye gaze than females). You will learn about numerical data analysis in the next two chapters.

Sample interaction rating schemes As we mentioned earlier in this chapter, Robert Bales (1950) developed the IPA scheme (outlined in Exhibit 7.1) to analyze small group interactions in the settings where they occur naturally. Since then, a number of rating schemes have been developed to analyze interactions in natural settings and draw conclusions about the characteristics of relationships, outcomes of interaction, and so on. All of these rating schemes are used in similar ways. First, they all impose category schemes onto interaction data in order to describe interaction patterns. Second, all these rating schemes are used to explain why certain interaction patterns occur as they do (or why particular patterns are associated with particular outcomes). And third, all these schemes are used to support explanatory and predictive claims about patterned interactive discourse.

In this section, we will briefly review two research studies that employed interaction rating schemes. Like Bales's (1950) IPA, Ellis's (1976) Relational Communication coding system, RELCOM, was designed to analyze group *process* by examining relational control attempts used by interactants. Instead of process, Fisher's (1970) Interaction Analysis System (IAS) was developed to analyze the *content* of messages during group interactions. The two studies we present here used interaction rating schemes intended to analyze both message *content* and interaction *process* (Adelman et al., 1992; DeStephen, 1983).

As a case in point, DeStephen (1983) employed two interaction rating schemes to discover differences between high- and low-consensus groups. She compared the interactions among 19 groups of students in a group communication course at their first and final meetings of the term. DeStephen first used Fisher's (1970) IAS, which deals with the *content* of group discussion. Its dimensions measure the levels of agreement and disagreement with decision proposals made by group members. Seven categories of talk are coded in the IAS: (1) interpretations, (2) substantiations, (3) clarifications, (4) modifications, (5) agreement, (6) disagreement, and (7) procedural issues. Next, DeStephen employed Ellis's (1976) RELCOM. Whereas the IAS helped DeStephen explore consensus levels in her decision-making groups, RELCOM helped her examine relational control attempts by group members during their decision-making interactions. RELCOM consists of five categories: (1) domineering, (2) structuring, (3) equivalence, (4) deferring, and (5) submitting.

DeStephen trained three people to reliably rate both the relational and content behaviors from these 38 group discussions (i.e., 19 initial meetings and 19 final meetings). Then, she submitted the resulting data to statistical procedures that allowed her to compare the first meetings of high- and low-consensus groups, and to compare the final meetings. Recall DeStephen's descriptive claim, that some interaction pattern characterizes groups who achieve high-consensus decision making.

In a more recent interaction analytic study, Adelman et al. (1992) developed the Multi-Dimensional Interaction Analysis (MDIA) system to analyze audiotaped interactions between physicians and elderly patients in regular office visits in a primary care setting. The MDIA enabled Adelman et al. to assess the message content and process of routine, follow-up visits by elderly patients to their physicians. A team of physician and social science researchers looked at three variables in this study: First, the *content* discussed in these visits was coded into 36 topics, across five categories: medical, personal habits, psychosocial, doctor-patient relationship, and other. The second variable was a *process* variable, consisting of who initiated the discussion of each topic, the doctor or the patient. Finally, the team categorized the physician's *behavioral responsiveness* to each topic as fitting into one of three possible themes: asking questions, giving information, and being supportive. Each of these behaviors was then rated, from 1 = least or worst, to 4 = most or best.

In both of these studies (Adelman et al., 1992; DeStephen, 1983), the researchers used a combination of categorizing and rating interaction content and process variables. Both studies focused primarily on verbal interactions. However, nonverbal behaviors may also be observed and analyzed, although coding nonverbal behaviors is challenging because they are less discrete, more ambiguous, and occur on several channels simultaneously. Nonetheless, you may want to use videotaped observations of nonverbal interactions just as these researchers used audiotaped interactions. You can code nonverbal behaviors into particular categories and make comparisons across categories using frequency counts (i.e., how often certain categories of behavior occur in particular interactions). In some cases, you may think that the frequency with which a category of verbal or nonverbal behavior occurs is associated with a particular cause or outcome. Whether your claim is one of association or cause-and-effect, you will treat your interaction data by categorizing (or rating) behaviors, and then submitting the resulting frequencies to quantitative data analysis.

Quantitative Data Analysis

After you have unitized and categorized messages (in the case of content analysis) or categorized and rated communication characteristics (in the case of interaction analysis), you can test your research questions and hypotheses using statistics. These days, nearly all statistical analyses in communication research are completed by executing computer programs like the Statistical Package for the Social Sciences (SPSS), Excel, or other programs. Although SPSS is a frequent choice for communication researchers, Excel is sometimes used for small data sets and classroom projects, and it is often used in business environments for statistical analysis of data.

Two basic types of analyses are most relevant to content and interaction analytic research. First, you will want to use **descriptive statistics** to summarize the characteristics of your sample data, namely, the central tendencies and variations in your data set. Second, you will very likely use **inferential statistics** to estimate population characteristics, based on the characteristics of your sample data. Each of these data analytic moves is described below in relationship to content and interaction analysis. You will learn how to calculate measures of central tendency and dispersion in Chapter 8, "Descriptive Statistics and Hypothesis Testing," and you will learn how to conduct and interpret inferential statistical analyses in Chapter 9, "Testing Differences and Relationships."

Statistics for content analysis Descriptive statistics are always employed in content analysis, where they are used to summarize the frequency with which message units occurred in particular categories. As a content analytic researcher, you will probably be interested in the percentage of units that fit particular categories of your analytic scheme, as well as the raw frequency data (i.e., the number of units placed into each category of the coding scheme).

"Even the most simple content analyses generally proceed to examine the relationships between the unit categories" (Thomas, 1994, p. 692). When statistical analysis of significant relationships among, or differences between, content categories is undertaken, you will need to use inferential statistics. Specifically, the **chi-square statistic** will help you compare the actual distribution of your sample data (i.e., observed units per category) to the predicted distribution (i.e., expected units per category). The predicted distribution of messages may be based on a theoretic model or on a prediction of no significant differences, the expectation that all categories will occur with equal frequency. For example, if all persuasive strategies are equally effective in a given speech context, then no one type of strategy should occur more frequently than another, outside the limits of random variation. The chi-square statistic tests whether differences between the observed category frequencies and the predicted category frequencies are greater than those that may be attributed to random error. Notice that the chi-square statistic still provides *descriptive,* rather than *explanatory,* evidence, which is consistent with most content analytic claims. Next let's look at the way numerical evidence is analyzed for explanatory and predictive claims.

Statistics for interaction analysis Although you will use descriptive statistics in interaction analysis, descriptive statistics usually won't be adequate to test the predictions inherent in research hypotheses. Instead, you will use descriptive statistics to test your initial assumptions about your sample data, such as whether the interaction ratings you have collected represent the full range of variation theoretically possible for those variables.

To illustrate the importance of testing such assumptions, let's consider a hypothetical example. Say you believe that some individual characteristic of interactants is related to their conversational behavior. You might predict that increased argumentativeness, a trait of some communicators, is associated with more frequent interruption behavior. So you collect self-report measures of argumentativeness from a group of subjects and then videotape their dyadic interactions. You will need to compute descriptive statistics in order to summarize the argumentativeness levels of your subjects (i.e., individual scores and an average score for your data sample). You will also summarize the number of interruption behaviors per

subject and the average number of interruption behaviors per conversation in your data sample. You may even want to look at some visual descriptions of your data, such as bar graphs, as well. All of these data analytic procedures are covered in Chapter 8.

If none of your subjects is very argumentative, or if all of your subjects are highly argumentative, then it is unlikely that the effects you predicted will be seen in *your* sample data. The effect may exist in the population of communicators, but be invisible in your data because the full range of argumentativeness, or interruption levels, is not represented in your sample data.

Thus, one of the assumptions of inferential statistics is normal variation, which simply means that the sample data should represent the full range of possible theoretic values. If your data are sufficiently varied, you will be able to see the effects of different argumentativeness levels on interruption behavior, provided that such effects exist. Therefore, descriptive statistics will help you gauge the appropriateness of your sample data for testing your hypotheses.

Once you have checked to ensure that your interaction analysis data meet the assumptions upon which inferential statistics are based, you can use inferential statistics to test your predictions. In our example, you can ascertain whether argumentativeness and the number of interruptions in your data sample suggest a significant relationship between this individual trait and interaction behaviors for the population of all communicators. The statistical procedures you will use to analyze relationships among such variables (or differences between groups of different types of speakers) are outlined in detail in Chapter 9. For now, let's turn to the ways content and interaction analysts evaluate the worth of their research, the warrants.

WARRANTS FOR CONTENT AND INTERACTION ANALYSES

The ability to make generalizable inferences from any content analysis depends not only on the consistency or reliability of the category judgments made by coders, but also on the internal and external validity of the categories themselves. Since you already know about these concepts (from Chapter 4), let's consider how each of these issues is applied in content and interaction analyses.

Reliability of Coding and Rating

The results of both content and interaction analyses depend heavily on measurement reliability. For content analysis, we are concerned about the consistency with which messages have been unitized and categorized. For interaction analysis, communication characteristics must be categorized and rated consistently. The test of this consistency is called intercoder reliability for content analysis and interrater reliability for interaction analysis. In its simplest form, interrater reliability is calculated as the percentage of coding decisions on which all coders agree (e.g., Johnson et al., 1999). Sometimes, other, more complicated formulas are used, such as when McKee and Pardun (1996) used Scott's pi to assess intercoder reliability. Pittman and Gallois (1997) and Hess (2000) used Cohen's kappa, another test statistic, to assess the reliability of coding decisions. All of these tests are different ways of calculating agreement among coders, and estimating the degree to which coders' level of agreement differs from the level of agreement likely to occur by chance alone (Krippendorf, 1980). Lombard, Snyder-Duch, and Bracken (2002) argued that mass communication researchers too "often rely on percent agreement, an overly liberal index" (p. 587).

One way to accomplish a high degree of agreement among coders is to train the people who will code message content into categories or who will rate interaction characteristics. For example, in Anderson et al.'s (1998) content analysis of Chinese people's motivations for communicating with family and friends, the authors trained three graduate students to recognize the different motives, such as sharing ideas and interests, sharing feelings, and so on. As they read the subjects' written reasons for why they talked to a best friend, the coders were able to agree which motive was represented in a response about 78% of the time. This constituted an acceptable level of reliability for placing message content units into categories.

The researchers or research assistants who rate verbal and nonverbal behaviors in interaction analysis are also usually trained experts. For example, Burgoon and Le Poire (1999) employed "advanced undergraduates in a nonverbal communication course who underwent eight hours of individual and group training prior to coding the experimental tapes. Training consisted of reviewing definitions, viewing or listening to sample videotapes, and practicing actual coding on the pilot tapes" (pp. 111–112). During and after the practice coding, the authors computed preliminary reliability estimates to assure equivalence, before the raters analyzed the actual interactions to be included in their study. This is routine procedure for both content and interaction analyses, to first ensure reliable measurement of variables before testing research predictions.

Validity of Coding or Rating Schemes

Two kinds of accuracy are important when conducting content and interaction analyses. The first issue, *construct validity,* is whether the coding or rating scheme adequately addresses the concepts under investigation. The second issue concerns the size of the coding scheme or rating scale, including the size and contents of any "other" category in the coding scheme. We will use the term *parsimony* to refer to this issue. Since both of these ideas were introduced in Chapter 4, here we will elaborate on how to apply them to your content and interaction analytic studies.

Construct validity Construct validity directly confronts the question "Does my chosen measuring instrument accurately and completely measure the specific theoretical construct I seek to study?" Construct validity emphasizes the goodness of fit between a measuring instrument and the concept it is intended to measure. For content analysis, your coding scheme has construct validity to the extent that the categories in that scheme accurately address the content in question, and no other content. Imagine that you want to categorize persuasive messages. You could use just three categories and restrict your coding scheme to threats, promises, and "other" messages. But that scheme is too simple to accurately and completely measure all persuasive strategies. Thus, there is a poor fit between your coding scheme and the concept of persuasive strategies because your coding scheme is too simple to represent the complexity of all persuasive strategies.

Just as the validity of a content analytic study rests on the accuracy of the coding categories, interaction analytic studies that require subjects to complete message construction tasks also depend on the validity of those tasks. For example, if you are asking subjects to respond to persuasive scenarios (e.g., Wilson et al., 1998) or to contextual situations (e.g., Hummert et al., 1998), the message construction task you use will need to be realistic. If your task does not accurately reflect the way such messages are constructed by communicators outside research projects, then you are likely to elicit messages from subjects unlike the messages they would actually construct in such a situation if they encountered it outside the laboratory setting. Using message construction tasks is one way that you introduce a variable that you predict will cause particular interaction outcomes. This technique is called *manipulating* the independent variable. We will elaborate on some other ways to make sure your manipulation of variables is accurate later in this section.

Whether you are evaluating the construct validity of your coding categories or the validity of your message construction task, you are trying to represent the complexity of the phenomena you are studying. Yet, in a discovery research project, you have to balance the complexity of the phenomena you are studying against the value of parsimony, the preference for a simple, elegant explanation of social phenomena. Therefore, in the next section we will discuss how you can assess the parsimony of your content analytic coding scheme.

Parsimony Another way to assess the worth of a coding scheme is to look at the presence or absence of the "other" category. If too much of the data fits into the "other" category, the coding scheme may not be adequate to describe this message population. Indeed, the "other" category may be a sort of conceptual wastebasket, containing rich information that was not sorted out by this particular study. Always watch out for the "other" category in a coding scheme. Analyze the messages that are placed there, to see if there are commonalities that would point to a category you have overlooked and that should be added to your coding scheme.

External Validity

Remember from Chapter 4 that external validity refers to the accuracy of applying the findings from one study to another setting, or group of subjects. The results of a study can be internally valid, but still not be accurately applied in other settings or with other groups of people. In this section, we'll look at three factors you should consider to assess the external validity of a content or interaction analytic study. These include the degree of coder/rater training required for a research project, the accurate manipula-

tion of independent variables (if applicable), and the representativeness of the data sample.

Coder/rater training Content analyses are often premised on the notion that ordinary communicators interpret discourse categories in the ways that trained coders interpret those categories. The same assumption is sometimes made when researchers or participants categorize or rate communicator behaviors in interaction analysis. If the researcher makes this assumption, but requires intensive coder or rater training to achieve an acceptable level of reliability, the study can become suspect in terms of external validity. If coders need extensive training to recognize a message as fitting into a particular category or to rate a behavior reliably, then it is unlikely that communicators who are outside the study's context will recognize those messages in the same way. Therefore, the conclusions of a study in which coders are very extensively trained may be valid, in and of themselves, but they may not be externally generalizable because expert coders' or raters' interpretations will not match the judgments made by ordinary people interacting in nonresearch contexts.

The opening statement of Le Poire and Yoshimura's (1999) test of interaction adaptation theory well illustrates this assumption. The authors wrote: "In everyday interactions, individuals commonly react to both cognitive and behavioral influences. One influence ... is the set of expectations that individuals hold about other people and their behaviors" (p. 1). Le Poire and Yoshimura did not describe what amount and type of training their pairs of trained raters received prior to rating interaction data. So, it is impossible to assess the likelihood that people who were not trained for this study (especially people who are not students of communication) would reliably detect the same nonverbal behaviors that these pairs of trained raters detected.

Manipulation checks If you hypothesize a cause-and-effect relationship and use a message construction task to manipulate the causal variable, you will want to conduct a *manipulation check* to ensure that your constructed messages have external validity. Recall from Chapter 6 that a manipulation check ensures that the researcher's way of inducing or controlling the independent variable worked as it was expected to work. For instance, Trees and Manusov (1998) conducted a manipulation check to ensure that the behaviors they presented in videotapes, intended to represent more and less politeness, were actually perceived that way by the 286 undergraduate students who participated in their study of nonverbal politeness behaviors between female friends.

If, on the other hand, you are using self-report data to simply measure the causal variable, a manipulation check will help to ensure that the reports given by your subjects accurately match your conceptual definition of the independent variable. For instance, Hess (2000) asked undergraduate students to consider a nonvoluntary relationship with a disliked partner. In order to check whether the people selected by each subject were comparably "disliked," Hess included a measure of liking (1 = strong disliking to 9 = strong liking). The average score was 3.19 for the disliked, and 6.79 for the liked partners, which suggested that his measure of the independent variable (liked or disliked obligatory relationship) was valid.

Sample representativeness In order to achieve a high degree of external validity, you will need to select a representative sample of messages or communicators that adequately represent the population about which you wish to make inferences. As you know from Chapter 3, the surest way to garner a representative sample of a large population of elements is to introduce some element of chance, or randomization, into the sample selection process. But sample selection need not be purely random in order to be reasonably representative. For example, Sunwolf and Seibold (1998) used a convenience sampling procedure to select citizens for participation in a study about jury deliberation rules. The authors recruited participants for their study by requesting volunteers who had been summoned for jury duty and asking those who agreed to participate to complete an oral survey while they were waiting in the jury assembly room at the courthouse. It is highly likely that the volunteers in Sunwolf and Seibold's study represented the population of jurors in regular courtroom cases, the population the authors sought to represent.

Sample size also has something to do with the likelihood of representation, and thus with external validity. Usually, the larger the sample, the better. Cheng (1997) analyzed the content of 483 Chinese television commercials. Cheng concluded that a new advertising law that took effect on February 1, 1995, "did not reduce Western values depicted in Chinese commercials"—but this seems likely to be an impov-

erished conclusion, based on Cheng's sample of commercials aired in 1995. It's likely that all those commercials were produced before the new law took effect, and it may be that if commercials aired in 1996 were analyzed, some effects of the new law could be seen that were not seen in Cheng's data.

To summarize, you will need to pay attention to three things in order to achieve externally valid conclusions in your content or interaction analysis: First, you will need to ensure that your coders or raters reasonably approximate the abilities of people interacting in natural contexts, if you want to generalize those judgments from researchers to nonresearchers. Second, you will need to check to see that any manipulation of your independent variable worked the way you planned it would work. Finally, you need to select messages (or interactions) that well represent the population of messages (or communicators) to which you seek to generalize, and you will need to collect a large enough number of these messages (or interactions) to be reasonably sure you have given the possibility of random error an opportunity to work. "With small samples, the probability of selecting deviant samples is greater than with large samples" (Kerlinger, 1986, p. 119).

TECHNOLOGY AND CONTENT AND INTERACTION ANALYSES

As we've already said in other chapters, digital technology is influencing communication research methods in two sizeable ways. First, communication studies are contributing to our understanding of the nature of computer-mediated communication (CMC) and its likely impacts on individuals, relationships, work, politics, and community (e.g., Honeycutt, 2001; Rossler, 2001). Many of the claimed costs and benefits of our technological age can and are being investigated with communication research, including content and interaction analyses. Second, communication technology is influencing the methods by which we examine a host of other communicative claims because computers are now an inherent part of data collection and analysis for both content and interaction analyses. In this section, we will look at some of the CMC claims that content and interaction analysts have investigated, and we will consider the growing role of computer technology in conducting content and interaction analyses.

Claims About CMC Content or Interactions

In the past 10 years, CMC has been considered a new population of messages suitable for content analysis (e.g., Bordia & Rosnow, 1998; Pragg, Wiseman, Cody, & Wendt, 1999; Stewart, Shields, and Sen, 1998). Like other media sources, the population of CMC messages can be further defined by type of content and subject matter, such as email, listservs, discussion groups, chat rooms, and Web sites, among other types of content. The topics for any of these types of CMC are virtually limitless.

Furthermore, comparative studies of CMC versus face-to-face (FTF) communication are important in order to assess the relative strengths and limitations of this new medium for communication (e.g., Althaus, 1997; Chadwick, 1999; Flaherty, Pearce, & Rubin, 1998; Honeycutt, 2001; Scott & Fontenot, 1999). Comparing the different computer channels of communication available now is also important. Honeycutt (2001) compared email and synchronous online conferencing as vehicles for peer response using content analysis of online transcripts to sort out the relative advantages and disadvantages of these two modalities for helping students improve their writing. Bordia and Rosnow's (1998) study is another example of research made possible by and concerning communication technology. Those authors looked at rumor transmission via CMC by analyzing patterns of participation and message content over a six-day period; they found that the group development patterns of rumormongering in a computer-mediated setting were similar to those expected in a face-to-face setting.

CMC as a Source of Data

Survey questionnaires can now be distributed via the World Wide Web, and in some cases, those surveys provide data from which content analyses can be performed. For instance, customer perceptions of new products can be gathered through Internet or email surveys, and the results can be categorized in terms of product features like price, availability, and so on. A hosted service provider such as Zoomerang (www.zoomerang.com), based in Sausalito, California, can be contracted to either develop a survey on the Internet, or to assist customers in creating their own online, email, or Web site surveys. When the tar-geted number of respondents has filled out the survey, results are automatically tabulated for each question, as frequencies and percentages, and emailed to the designated recipient at the company. In some cases, the results from such surveys can even be downloaded into Excel, SAS, SPSS-PC+, or another statistical program, in order to test hypothesized relationships and differences, or to produce visual data descriptions like pie charts, bar graphs, and the like.

Computer Software for Categorizing Content

In addition to online surveys used to collect data for content analysis, computer software programs also can be used to analyze the content of messages that are available in digital form, like newspaper articles, Web sites, political speeches, television programs, and so on. "Computers will perform with unerring accuracy any coding task in which the classification rules are unambiguous" (Wimmer & Dominick, 1991, p. 168). Among the units of analysis Krippendorf (1980) identified, computers can reliably code physical and syntactical units of analysis. Referential, propositional, and thematic units are much more invested with subjective meanings and, therefore, much more difficult to articulate in terms of unambiguous classification rules.

Tesch (1990, 1991) reviewed a number of computer programs specifically designed to facilitate content analysis. As a case in point, Stephen (1999) conducted a computer-assisted concept analysis of articles published in *Human Communication Research* between 1974 and 1999 to show how those studies could be grouped into five large clusters, which essentially provided a bridge between the mass and interpersonal communication literatures. In fact, the fourth issue of *Human Communication Research* for 1999 was devoted to content analytic studies aimed at analyzing and celebrating that journal's history and contributions to the communication discipline.

In another example of computer-facilitated content analysis, Andsager and Smiley (1998) used a computer content analysis program called VBPro to calculate the most frequently occurring words in press releases published by three groups (i.e., medical groups, Dow Corning, and citizens' groups). All the press releases concerned the silicone breast implant controversy of 1991–92. Andsager and Smiley wanted to *evaluate* the relationship between policy actors and media frames, rather than merely counting occurrences of key terms. In order to do this, they first determined policy frames from the press releases, and then assessed which group's frame was most frequently and centrally featured in coverage by six major newspapers.

SUMMARY

Both content and interaction analyses are research methods used to support claims of description, explanation and prediction, and evaluation. Both rely on quantitative data collection and analytic strategies. For these reasons, both content and interaction analyses fit well within the paradigm of knowing by discovery. Although we combined these two methods in the same chapter because they are similar ways of knowing they also differ from one another in two important ways. First, content analysis uses narrative data (i.e., textual data), whereas interaction analysis uses interactive data, typically videotaped conversations between research participants, or between participants and research confederates. A second important difference between content and interaction analysis is the way the data are treated by the researcher: In content analysis, messages are unitized and categorized using a coding scheme that the researchers either develop themselves or borrow from existing scholarship on the topic. In interaction analysis, the behaviors of participants are rated in terms of the degree to which they fit the characteristics of some predetermined rating scheme, such as showing friendliness, giving eye contact, and the like.

We hope that by reading this chapter, you have learned to develop claims that are suitable for testing by content analysis and interaction analysis. You also should be able to articulate appropriate ways of selecting representative sample data, collecting the messages or interactions you wish to study, treating the data, and summarizing numerical data to either compare the frequency of messages in different categories, or to test predictions about outcome variables. You should be ready now for more detailed instruction about analyzing quantitative data, which we will provide in the next two chapters.

KEY TERMS

Artifacts

Categorizing

Chi-square statistic

Coding scheme

Content analysis

Cued recall technique

Descriptive statistics

Inferential statistics

Interaction analysis

Interactive discourse

Latent meanings

Manifest meanings

Message construction tasks

Message population

Meta-analysis

Narrative discourse

Rating scheme

Transcriptions

Unitizing

Units of analysis

DISCUSSION QUESTIONS

1. Why is it important that you know at the outset what type of claim you will be making in a content analytic or interaction analysis study?

2. How could you use content analysis to assist you at school? At work? In your personal goals?

3. Read Bordia and Rosnow (1998) or Honeycutt (2001). Based on these two articles, would it be fair to say that "comparative studies" typically stake out claims of description and explanation? Why or why not?

"TRY IT!" ACTIVITIES

1. *Interaction analysis.* Look back at Bales's IPA in Exhibit 7.1. Have your instructor videotape your research methods class during a small group discussion one day in class. Using the taped interaction, categorize each turn at talk into one of the twelve interaction behaviors identified in the IPA. Keep a sequential list of these turns and behaviors. Then look over the list to see if you can identify the up-down, positive-negative, and forward-backward dimensions of your group's interactions. Consider two questions about the behaviors and directions you identified: (a) How reliable are your coding/rating decisions? Do others in your group or class agree that a particular turn counts as giving a suggestion, for example? (b) How do these behaviors and value directions relate to your group's productivity, or ability to accomplish the task you were working on? How do they affect your group's satisfaction with the class?

2. *Content analysis.* Review the message samples listed in Exhibit 7.2. For each sample, see if you can define that message population in one phrase or sentence. Then check your population definitions this way: Can you specify another subset of this message population from which you could sample messages in order to replicate the study's findings?

3. *Designing studies.* Follow these steps to design a basic content analysis study of your own. Work with a partner for the best results:

   a. First, use the following suggested *message populations* to brainstorm your own, more specific, list of 20 different message populations: interactions in contexts, such as interpersonal, organizational, instructional; interactions via channels like FTF, CMC, telephone, and so on; mediated narratives in genres such as newspaper, radio, television, or Internet (and by type, such as news story, editorial, infotainment, commercial, etc.). *Note: These are some ideas to get you started. Add others!*

   b. Join another pair of students, and review your combined lists of 40 message populations. Identify which, if any, of the suggestions on your combined list actually represent the *same population.* Which are *different populations?* Define the population characteristics that make this so.

   c. Work with your original partner to select one message population from all those you've identified. Develop three Research Questions (RQs) about that message population. Be creative! What would you like to know about messages of that sort? Clue: Make sure your RQs concern issues of frequency, degree, magnitude, and so on, since these issues are appropriate for quantitative data analysis. If you can't make your RQ suitable for quantitative analysis, save it for another chapter.

   d. Review Krippendorf's (1980) five units of analysis (i.e., physical, syntactic, referential, propositional, and thematic), defined earlier in this chapter. For each RQ you wrote, identify the unit(s) of analysis needed to answer that question.

   e. Spend 1–2 hours with your partner at the library. Look for any previous existing research about the message population and unit(s) of analysis you want to study. Your goal is to determine whether any potential coding scheme for this message population already exists or can be identified from the literature.

   f. Try to make up your own "standardized coding sheet" for your message population, using the categories you identified in your library search. If you didn't identify any existing coding scheme (or even categories), give a rough sketch of what categories you might look for in a small sample of pilot data.

   g. Lastly, write a paragraph that describes, in detail, your plan for acquiring a representative sample of the population of messages and, if needed, what additional steps you would take to prepare those messages for analysis (e.g., transcription).

8

Descriptive Statistics and Hypothesis Testing

ABSTRACT

In this chapter, we will focus on the statistical analyses of data, in survey and experimental research and in content and interaction analyses. We will start by acquainting you with several visual representations of data. Next, you will learn to calculate descriptive statistics, including measures of a distribution's central tendencies, dispersion, and shape. Then, we will briefly identify three types of distributions: samples, populations, and sampling distributions. This chapter will conclude by introducing you to the logic and steps involved in testing hypotheses, and the way technology is used to generate descriptive statistics.

OUTLINE

Descriptive Statistical Analyses

Visual Representations of Variables

Sample Distribution Characteristics

Inferential Statistics

Three Types of Distributions

Estimation and Inference

The Logic of Hypothesis Testing

Technology and Descriptive Statistics

Summary

Key Terms

Discussion Questions

"Try It!" Activities

Communication research studies from the discovery paradigm that make use of some form of **statistical analysis** include the methodologies examined in the last three chapters: survey research, experimental research, and content and interaction analyses. Statistical analysis is defined as "the science of describing and reasoning from numerical data" (Smith, 1988, p. 93). Studies that use statistical analyses share many assumptions about the types of claims you can make, the nature of the data, and how that data can be warranted. Statistical analyses primarily serve two types of functions: description and inference. You will explore these two functions in detail in this chapter.

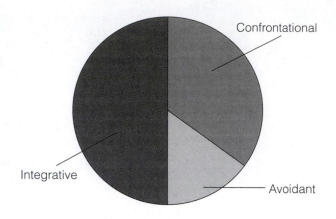

FIGURE 8.1 Pie chart display of conflict strategies.

DESCRIPTIVE STATISTICAL ANALYSES

The function of **descriptive statistics** is to describe how the collected sample data appears, both visually and in numerical terms. Thus, the statistics are defined as sample characteristics because they characterize some specific feature of a data sample. Recall that you were first introduced to the concepts of *sample* and *population* in Chapter 3. These terms were applied across various methodologies in Chapters 5 through 7, where you learned the importance of obtaining representative samples. You will now explore how they can be statistically described and tested. Before examining how samples are described, let's return to the concept of measurement from Chapter 3 and review the measurement scales for data.

In Chapter 5, you learned that data become variables when converted from concepts to numbers by using one of four measurement scales: nominal, ordinal, interval, and ratio. Nominal and ordinal scales generate categorical variables; in other words, data measured with nominal or ordinal scales will result in groupings of the variables by discrete categories or ranked preferences. Simple examples of categorical variables include sex (male/female), dichotomous responses (yes/no), experimental conditions (treatment vs. control groups), channel categories (face-to-face, phone, email, written memo), and ranked frequencies (greater than or less than). You can review more categorical variables measured by nominal and ordinal scales by reviewing Exhibits 5.7 and 5.8.

It is assumed that these categories or ranks are not mathematically related. That means that samples of nominal or ordinal data are not distributed along some measurement continuum but grouped for comparison. To represent this data numerically, you can calculate the frequencies of (or how many) members of your sample can be placed into the various categories. Let's say we have a sample of 50 people, where 35 of them are female and 15 are male. The frequency of 35 can also be expressed as a certain proportion or percent of the sample. In this case, 70% are female and 30% are male. The frequencies or proportions of various categories using nominal and ordinal data can be visually represented as well. Typically, these are depicted with pie charts and bar charts.

Visual Representations of Variables

Categorical Variables
Pie Charts Suppose you wanted to depict the relative frequencies with which people in your sample chose three types of strategies to deal with a conflict: confrontational, avoidant, and integrative (Sillars, 1980). **Pie charts** make very good graphic representations of the frequencies or proportions of data.

Figure 8.1 is based on the following sample data: 8 of 24 people chose confrontational strategies, 4 out of 24 chose avoidant strategies, and 12 out of 24 chose integrative strategies (Exhibit 8.1). The pie chart graph visually shows what proportion of the total circle is represented by each type of strategy. You can quickly see that integrative strategies make up half. Pie charts are often used to represent numerical data in textbooks, popular magazines, and newspapers. They are used less frequently in research journal articles.

EXHIBIT 8.1   Frequency Table for Conflict Strategies

TYPE OF STRATEGY	FREQUENCY OF OCCURRENCE	PERCENTAGE OF SAMPLE
Confrontational	8	33.33
Males	6	25.00
Females	2	8.33
Avoidant	4	16.67
Males	1	4.17
Females	3	12.50
Integrative	12	50.00
Males	6	25.00
Females	6	25.00
Totals	24	100.00

Bar Charts By using vertical bars along the *x*-axis, the **bar chart** in Figure 8.2 depicts the frequencies of strategy types. The ***x*-axis** (or **abscissa**) is the horizontal axis, the ***y*-axis** (or **ordinate**) is the vertical axis, and in the case of 3-D representations, the ***z*-axis** is the depth axis. Notice that the vertical bars are not connected along the *x*-axis. The separation between the bars denotes discrete groupings or categories of strategy types. The categories have no real mathematical relationship to each other on the *x*-axis. You could assign a "1" to integrative strategies, a "2" to confrontational strategies, and a "3" to avoidant strategies, but these would function purely as numerical "names" for each of the categories. The only real numbers (numbers with real values) on the graph are along the *y*-axis, which shows the frequency count for each type of strategy.

Bar charts can also be used to show how two or more groups compare across several categories. For example, suppose we found that 2 of the 8 people who used confrontational strategies were female, 3 out of 4 females used avoidant strategies, and 6 of the 12 used integrative strategies. The comparison of males and females across strategy types is shown in Figure 8.3.

You will often find **frequency tables** that summarize the frequencies and percentages of data that are visually displayed in pie chart or bar chart graphs. The tables are useful quick references for what you are seeing visually represented in the graphs. For example, Exhibit 8.1 is a frequency table that reflects the data used in Figures 8.1 through 8.3.

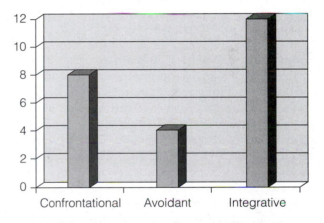

FIGURE 8.2 Bar chart display of conflict strategy categories.

In communication research, it is likely that you will come across the use of frequency tables but less likely that you will find pie or bar charts. For example, Bethea (2001) used this type of table to show frequencies and percentages of various demographic characteristics in her sample of older adults (p. 52). Recall from Chapter 5, that demographics are personal characteristics of sample participants. Bethea reported gender, marital status, education, and ethnic groups as demographic characteristics or variables of her older adult sample.

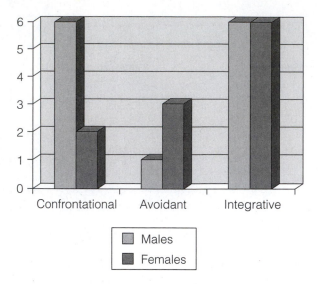

FIGURE 8.3 Comparison of males and females by strategy type.

Continuous Variables When data are measured with interval and ratio scales, the descriptive and visual representations of continuous variables become more complex. Each piece of data receives a scale score, and these are distributed along the x-axis. When testing for differences among various continuous distributions, the y-axis represents the frequency of those scores. You will learn more about these tests in the next chapter.

The way the scores are distributed along the x-axis is called a **frequency distribution.** For example, let's say you wished to examine the number of email contacts managers made with their employees over a one-week period. At the end of this period, each manager would receive a "contact score" that would represent the number of times the manager had interacted with any employees. At the end of the week, one manager had made contact with employees by email zero times, two managers had made contact one time, three managers had made contact two times, and so forth. See Exhibit 8.2 for the full display of this data example. Frequency distributions can be visually represented in histograms and frequency polygons.

Histograms Continuous data in a frequency distribution can be represented by a **histogram,** which is like a bar chart for data measured with interval or ratio scales. Note the bars are connected along the x-axis. This is a visual illustration that there is a math-

ematical relationship between the intervals along the x-axis, unlike the bars in a bar chart for data measured with nominal or ordinal scales. Because intervals are equidistant, the numbers stand for precise values. In the example illustrated in Figure 8.4, a manager who contacted employees by email four times in one week made twice as many contacts as the manager who made only two email contacts. The fact that the intervals along the x-axis are mathematically precise makes many types of numerical tests possible, as you will see in the next chapter.

Frequency Polygons Occasionally, researchers use frequency polygons to illustrate continuous data. Instead of using vertical bars, the **frequency polygon** is formed by connecting the pairs of points or graph coordinate points for the x- and y-axes. The first coordinates are 0, 1, the second coordinates are 1, 2, and the third set are 2, 3 (see Exhibit 8.2). These are obtained by taking pairs of x and y values. A frequency polygon for our example data set appears in Figure 8.5.

You will not commonly see data reported in communication research journals as histograms or frequency polygons. Usually these graphs are tools that you can use in your preliminary data analysis to estimate the likelihood of error, a process you will explore later in this chapter. However, there are occasional reports of graphs in the research literature. For example, Crowell and Emmers-Sommer (2001) used histograms to visually represent heterosexual participants' scores on a number of variables including perceived risk of getting HIV, level of trust in partner prior to getting HIV, and perceived safety of their partners. The histograms helped to illustrate quickly that there was a relatively low level of perceived risk in getting HIV, a moderate level of perceived trust in their partners, and a relatively high level of perceived safety in their partners.

Data measured at interval and ratio levels can also be visually represented in another way. In the next chapter, you will learn about tests for the relationships between two or more continuous variables. The relationships between these variables can be described as linear or curvilinear—terms that refer to complex patterns of variable change. Instead of exploring their shapes and what these represent in this chapter, you will see how they are used to interpret the results of statistical tests in the next chapter. In this chapter, you will be looking at distributions for just *one* variable.

EXHIBIT 8.2	Frequency Table of Manager Contacts
NUMBER OF CONTACTS IN A ONE-WEEK PERIOD (x-axis)	FREQUENCY OF CONTACT SCORES (y-axis)
0	1
1	2
1	
2	3
2	
2	
3	4
3	
3	
3	
4	4
4	
4	
4	
5	3
5	
5	
6	2
6	
7	1

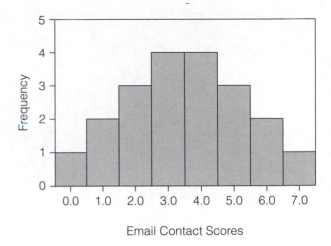

FIGURE 8.4 Histogram of data in Table 8.2 (manager contacts).

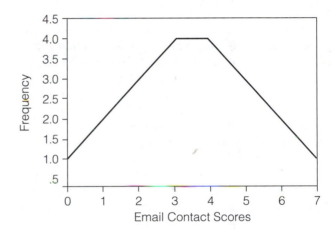

FIGURE 8.5 Frequency polygon of manager email contacts.

Indications of Error As mentioned earlier, you can check the shape of a graph to see if error is present when you visually represent a continuous variable. Recall from Chapter 4 that there are basically two types of error that can enter the measurements of a variable: *bias* (or constant error) and *noise* (or random error). Bias occurs whenever the internal validity of the research design is threatened in some way; noise occurs whenever reliability is threatened. A frequency distribution that has relatively little error is said to be **normally distributed;** its curve is **bell-shaped.** In Figure 8.6, the histogram from Figure 8.4 has been re-drawn with a normal curve superimposed upon it. Distributions with constant or random error present will be shaped differently than the normal curve. Shapes that indicate the presence of error can be described in terms of two dimensions: skew and kurtosis.

Skew Frequency distributions that are **skewed** display a horizontal shift in the majority of scores either to the right or left of the distribution's center with a

longer tail trailing away toward the opposite end of the distribution. **Positively skewed** data will have the majority of scores shifted to the left with the tail pointing in the direction of positive numbers, as shown in Figure 8.7. For example, in Chapter 6, you learned what would happen if research participants became afraid of being evaluated poorly by the researcher (evaluation apprehension). If the majority of participants experienced this apprehension in answering questions about personally undesirable behaviors, it would most probably result in an abnormal distribution of low scores with very few middle or

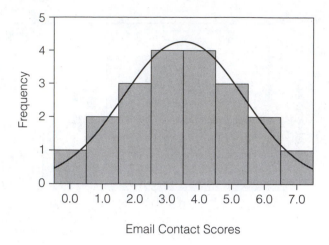

FIGURE 8.6 Histogram with normal curve for manager email contacts.

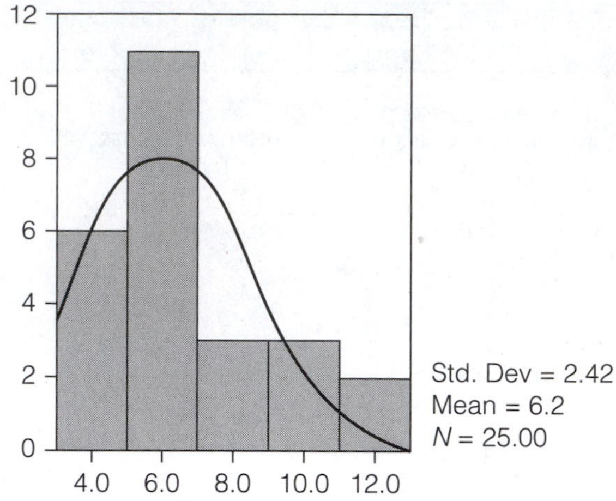

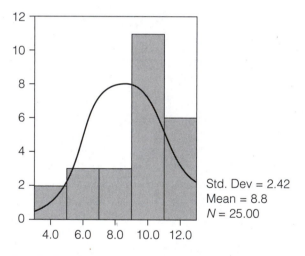

FIGURE 8.7 Histogram of positively skewed data.

high scores represented (a positive skew). In other words, most people experiencing evaluation apprehension would underreport their undesirable behaviors (e.g., cheating, criminal history, child abuse, etc.).

Negatively skewed data will have the majority of scores shifted to the right with the tail pointing in the direction of negative numbers, as shown in Figure 8.8. A negative distribution skew would occur if scores were abnormally inflated because of a validity threat. For example, if you asked people to report their pro-social behaviors, such as helping or comforting someone else, or other "nice" behaviors, they could easily overreport their occurrence. In either case, whether it is positive or negative, a skew in the data distribution is an indication of bias in which some measurement resulted in a constant error. As you will see later in this chapter, the numeric value of the skew measure is negative for a negative skew, is positive for a positive skew, and equals zero when the shape of the distribution is normal or bell-shaped.

Kurtosis Just as distribution skew represents abnormal shapes on the horizontal plane, **kurtosis** refers to abnormalities in the vertical dimension. Frequency distributions can be **leptokurtic,** or too peaked, resembling the shape of the data distribution in Figure 8.9. Leptokurtic distributions tell you that there is not much score variation happening in your data distribution. The tendency for members of the same culture to interpret "beauty" or "intelligence" in very

FIGURE 8.8 Histogram of negatively skewed data.

similar ways is like the tendency you are seeing in leptokurtic distributions. When distributions are too peaked, the majority of scores fall on one or two points or values, another indication of bias.

Frequency distributions can also be **platykurtic** (pronounced "plat" to rhyme with "flat"), or flat with "thick tails," like the one shown in Figure 8.10. Dis-

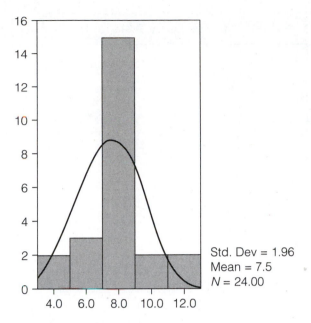

Std. Dev = 1.96
Mean = 7.5
N = 24.00

FIGURE 8.9 Leptokurtic or peaked distribution.

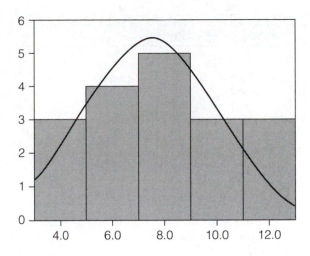

FIGURE 8.10 Platykurtic or flat distribution.

tributions that are too flat can indicate noise or random error. A frequent source of random error is an instrument that is unreliable in its measurement because, for example, the questions asked are ambiguous and several meanings can be imputed to the same question. The platykurtic shape indicates that each score is occurring with about equal frequency all along the x-axis. For example, if a scale designed to measure your level of communication competence had many ambiguous items included, you would not know how to answer the questions. You might be as likely to score low on this scale (on the left end of the x-axis), as you would be to score high on this scale (on the right end). In either case, your score would have little to do with your actual competence level. It would most likely be the result of too much random error present in the measure.

Sample Distribution Characteristics

Sample distributions can be visually represented, as we have seen in this section. They can also be characterized by using descriptive indices or measures. There are three types of descriptive measures: measures of central tendency, measures of dispersion, and measures of shape.

Measures of Central Tendency When we use variables as data, we work with them as sets of numbers. **Measures of central tendency** are descriptive statistics that reduce the data set to one number that best characterizes the entire sample. There are three measures of centrality: the mode, the median, and the mean. Consider the data in the frequency table shown in Exhibit 8.3. Numbers along the x-axis represent the number of friends in their social network as identified by the participants in the sample. Numbers along the y-axis are the frequency of participants' "scores" of the numbers of friends they report. So, for example, one person reported having one friend, three people reported having four friends, and six people reported having five friends.

Mode The **mode,** or Mo, is the most frequently occurring score in one data sample. For example, using the data from Exhibit 8.3, the most frequently occurring score (occurring 6 times, seen in the y-axis column) is 5 (the corresponding score in the x-axis column). In other words, six people reported five friends, a score that occurred more frequently than any other score in the x-axis column (see Exhibit 8.4). Some samples contain more than one mode. Sample distributions with two modes are called **bimodal,** and those with three modes are called **trimodal.** Distributions that have four or more modes are not desirable, indicating a flat or platykurtic curve.

EXHIBIT 8.3 Frequency Table for Measures of Central Tendency	
NUMBER OF FRIENDS (x-axis)	FREQUENCY OF TOTAL FRIENDS (y-axis)
1	1
2	2
3	3
4	3
5	6
6	5
7	3
8	1
9	0
10	1
$\Sigma X = 125$	$n = 25$

EXHIBIT 8.4 Frequency Table for Mode	
NUMBER OF FRIENDS (x-axis)	FREQUENCY OF TOTAL FRIENDS (y-axis)
1	1
2	2
3	3
4	3
5 (Mo)	6
6	5
7	3
8	1
9	0
10	1
$\Sigma X = 125$	$n = 25$

When a distribution has two score values for the mode but they are contiguous points along the x-axis, the distribution is still considered to be **unimodal,** or having just one mode (Smith, 1988). For example, the distribution in Figure 8.4 has two mode values; the numbers 3 and 4 occur equally as frequently. Even though we would still report more than one value for the mode (Mo = 3,4), this distribution is still called unimodal because the values 3 and 4 are contiguous points on the x-axis.

It is useful to know what the mode is for a distribution of categorical data. For example, as an illustration of a pie chart (Figure 8.1), we asked you to imagine that it visually represented the frequencies of three different types of conflict strategies used. The most frequently occurring strategy type was the integrative strategies, which occurred 12 out of 24 times. Suppose you had arbitrarily assigned a "1" to denote the category of integrative strategies, a "2" to confrontational strategies, and a "3" to avoidant strategies. The mode in this example is "1" because it occurs 12 times out of 24, rather than 8 times (confrontational strategies) or 4 times (avoidant strategies). Modes are not reported often for distributions of continuous variables because they are not generally meaningful. An exception occurs whenever you wish to show that there are two or more peaks in the data that occur across different points in time.

Median The second measure of central tendency is called the **median,** abbreviated as Mdn. The median is

defined as the midpoint score: 50 percent of the scores in the sample distribution occur above the median and 50 percent appear below. To return to the example data from Exhibit 8.3, the total number of scores, *n,* is 25, which is obtained by adding all of the frequencies in the y-axis column. This sum is an odd number, and so we know that the midpoint score must occur at the 13th position in the frequency column. The score value in the x-axis column that corresponds to this position is 5, and so the median for this sample is 5, as represented in Exhibit 8.5. Interpreting this measure, you know that 50 percent of the participants in this study reported having fewer than five friends, and 50 percent reported having more than five friends. The median and the mode are equal in this example.

The median is more difficult to calculate when the sample contains an even number of scores. For a data set with 10 scores (e.g., 1, 2, 2, 3, 3, 3, 4, 4, 4, 5), we must look at two central points, the 5th and the 6th positions. In this case, they both correspond to the score value 3, and so the median is 3 in this example. But suppose the data set were 1, 2, 2, 3, 3, 4, 4, 4, 5, 5. The score value in the 5th position is a 3, and the score value in the 6th position is a 4. The median in this case is obtained by adding the two score values, 3 + 4, and dividing by the number of scores, 2. The result is a median of 3.5.

Median scores are reported in interval and ratio level measurements of data but not for categorical variables. Typically, median scores are reported along with means or averages to show that distributions do

EXHIBIT 8.5 Frequency Table for Median	
NUMBER OF FRIENDS (x-axis)	FREQUENCY OF TOTAL FRIENDS (y-axis)
1	1
2	2
3	3
4	3
5 (Mdn)	6 (13th)
6	5
7	3
8	1
9	0
10	1
$\Sigma X = 125$	$n = 25$

EXHIBIT 8.6 Frequency Table for Mean	
NUMBER OF FRIENDS (x-axis)	FREQUENCY OF TOTAL FRIENDS (y-axis)
1	1
2	2
3	3
4	3
5 ($\bar{X}$)	6
6	5
7	3
8	1
9	0
10	1
$\Sigma X = 125$	$n = 25$

Mean:

$$\frac{\Sigma X}{n} = \bar{X}$$

$$\bar{X} = \frac{125}{25} = 5.00$$

not contain extreme or outlying scores. For example, Hoffman and Heald (2000) used both mean and median score values for the frequencies of tobacco advertisements, the frequencies of alcohol advertisements, and the frequencies of both types of ads per magazine issue targeted at Blacks. The authors showed that the data was distributed normally in each of the magazines examined because the mean and median values were close together.

Mean The final and most sensitive measure of central tendency for data distributions is the **mean,** or the arithmetic average, a term that we introduced in the previous example. The mean can be written as M or $\bar{X}$. In this text, we will use the latter symbol to denote the mean. The mean is considered the most sensitive measure of central tendency in the data distribution of a continuous variable because the equation for the mean includes all values from the data set.

You calculate the mean by summing all the scores in the x column, ΣX, and dividing by the total number of scores, n, as shown in Equation 8.1:

$$\bar{X}_1 = \frac{\Sigma x_1}{n_1} \qquad (8.1)$$

In the example of data from Exhibit 8.3, $\Sigma X = 125.00$, and $n = 25.00$. The mean is calculated by

$$\bar{X} = \frac{125.00}{25.00} = 5.00$$

Along with the mode and the median, the mean for this data sample is also 5 (see Exhibit 8.6). On average, participants reported having about five friends.

When the measures of central tendency are equal or nearly so for continuous variables, as they are in our sample data illustration from Exhibit 8.3, it is a general indication that the curve is fairly normal. When all three measures are different values, it indicates that skew is present. In skewed distributions, the mode and the median will be closer to the majority of scores (the highest part of the curve), while the mean will be pulled in the direction of the tail. In positive skews, the mean will fall to the right of the median and the mode; in negative skews, the mean will occur to the left of the median and the mode. Thus, when you calculate all three measures for your data, you receive an indication of what you should also be able to tell by looking at your graphs: whether the distribution is normal, or whether it is skewed positively or negatively.

To summarize, then, the measures of central tendency are used to characterize an entire sample with one best number or score value. Assessing these characteristics and applying them help us to ascertain whether error is present, and serve as checks when we visually graph the data. The mean, as the most sensitive measure of central tendency, is used frequently both in describing data and, as we shall see later on, in tests of inference. Just as the measures of central tendency describe the data by using just one score, the measures of dispersion explain how the scores are dispersed or scattered along the *x*-axis of the sample distribution.

Measures of Dispersion The measures of dispersion are assessments of how much variation in scores is present in the sample distribution. These measures include: the range, the variance, and the standard deviation.

Range The most general way of assessing the amount of variation in a sample is to calculate the **range,** which is obtained by subtracting the lowest score from the highest score. In our example from Exhibit 8.3, the range is equal to $10 - 1 = 9$. This means that the smallest number of friends reported by participants was 1 and the largest number of friends reported was 10. The range is a weak estimate of the total amount of variation present in any data sample. It does not consider the frequency of scores in its calculation. It is simply a calculation of the distance between the extreme data points along the *x*-axis.

Variance The sample **variance** is denoted by s^2, and has a more complex calculation, as denoted in Equation 8.2:

$$s^2 = \frac{\Sigma d^2}{n - 1} \qquad (8.2)$$

To obtain the variance of a set of scores, we must first calculate the deviation scores, *d*. The deviation scores are obtained by subtracting every x score from the mean, as shown in Equation 8.3:

$$d = X - \bar{X} \qquad (8.3)$$

These deviation scores are then squared and summed, Σd^2, and this term is called the sum of the deviation scores squared.

The data from our original example in Exhibit 8.3 is reformulated for calculating the variance in Exhibit 8.7. From Equation 8.2, the variance for our sample is

$$s^2 = \frac{\Sigma d^2}{n - 1} = \frac{100}{25 - 1} = 4.1\overline{6}$$

Variance scores are general indicators of how dispersed the scores are around the mean. However, in calculating the variance, deviation scores are squared so that they will not cancel each other out when added together. Squaring the values changes how the variable was originally measured. Thus, to find an average distance measure, we must take the square root of the variance. This measure is called the standard deviation.

Standard Deviation Once we have calculated the variance, the standard deviation is considerably easier to obtain. As we just explained, the standard deviation, *s,* is the square root of the variance. In Exhibit 8.7, this value is $s = \sqrt{4.1\overline{6}} = 2.04$. The **standard deviation** is the best indicator of the total amount of variation within a given sample. It is used instead of the variance because it converts deviation units to standard distance measures from the mean, and does so with the original units of measurement. So, for example, if you had a distribution of communication apprehension scores, the standard deviation would estimate distance intervals based on communication apprehension scores.

Consider the example of data you have been using in Exhibit 8.7. If you had a distribution of the number of friends reported by participants, the standard deviation would estimate standard distances away from the mean in intervals based on the numbers of friends. Using the mean, you can say that the first standard deviation is about ±2 friends away from the mean ($1s = 1 \times 2.04$), the second standard deviation is about ±4 friends away from the mean ($2s = 2 \times 2.04$), and the third standard deviation is about ±6 friends away from the mean ($3s = 3 \times 2.04$).

Means and standard deviations are the most commonly reported descriptive statistics in communication research. In a recent article, for example, Golish and Caughlin (2002) examined the topics that stepfamilies avoided discussing. They reported means and standard deviations for every topic teens and young adults avoided talking about with their parents and stepparents. By looking at these, it was clear that participants reported avoiding discussing sexual issues, relationship issues, and negative experiences with their stepparents more frequently than any other topic, and avoided these topics more frequently with their stepparents compared to their parents (see their table on p. 86).

By converting the variance to the standard deviation, you can estimate score distances away from the mean in the same units with which you originally began. Why you would want to travel standard distances above and below the mean will remain a mys-

EXHIBIT 8.7 Frequency Table for Variance and Standard Deviation

X	Frequency	$d = x - \bar{x}$	d^2
1	1 = total # of 1s	$-4 = (1 - 5)$	$(-4)^2 = 16$
2	2 = total # of 2s	$-3 = (2 - 5)$	$(-3)^2 = 9$
2			9
3	3 = total # of 3s	$-2 = (3 - 5)$	$(-2)^2 = 4$
3			4
3			4
4	3 = total # of 4s	$-1 = (4 - 5)$	$(-1)^2 = 1$
4			1
4			1
5	6 = total # of 5s	$0 = (5 - 5)$	$(0)^2 = 0$
5			0
5			0
5			0
5			0
5			0
6	5 = total # of 6s	$1 = (6 - 5)$	$(1)^2 = 1$
6			1
6			1
6			1
6			1
7	3 = total # of 7s	$2 = (7 - 5)$	$(2)^2 = 4$
7			4
7			4
8	1 = total # of 8s	$3 = (8 - 5)$	$(3)^2 = 9$
	0 = total # of 9s		0
10	1 = total # of 10s	$5 = (10 - 5)$	$(5)^2 = 25$
$\sum X = 125$	$n = 25$		$\sum d^2 = 100$

Variance:

$$s^2 = \frac{\sum d^2}{n - 1} = \frac{100}{25 - 1} = 4.1\overline{6}$$

Standard deviation:

$$s = \sqrt{s^2} = \sqrt{\frac{\sum d^2}{n - 1}} = \sqrt{4.1\overline{6}} \approx 2.04$$

tery for the time being. We will have more to say about this statistic in the section on various types of distributions. But before you learn about these, we will return to the concepts of skew and kurtosis briefly as descriptive statistics rather than visual anomalies.

Measures of Shape The last set of measures indicates the shape abnormalities we identified earlier when error is present. Normal distributions will have bell-shaped curves with no skew or kurtosis.

Skew In this section, you will see the equation terms for skew and kurtosis, and learn how to interpret the numeric value for these terms of shape. When skew and kurtosis were visually represented in the last section, we explained that both shapes indicate the presence of error and deviations from the normal curve. Skew indicates the presence of constant error or bias, and it is typically calculated using Equation 8.4:

$$g_1 = \frac{m_3}{m_2 \sqrt{m_2}} \qquad (8.4)$$

where g_1 is the value of the skew, which indicates whether it is positive or negative, and m_2 and m_3 are called **moments,** calculations closely related to the mean and standard deviation (Ferguson, 1981). This value is close to or equals zero when the shape of the distribution is normal or bell-shaped. You have already seen the visual graphs of positively and negatively skewed data samples in Figures 8.7 and 8.8.

Kurtosis An abnormality in the vertical dimension of a sample distribution is called kurtosis. It is an indication of bias when the curve is leptokurtic (peaked), and of random error, or noise, when the curve is platykurtic (flat). Kurtosis is calculated using Equation 8.5:

$$g_2 = \frac{m_4}{m_2^2} - 3 \qquad (8.5)$$

When g_2 is a positive number, the curve is leptokurtic or peaked. When g_2 is a negative number, the curve is platykurtic; it is relatively flat with thick tails at either end of the distribution curve. When the value is close or equal to zero, the vertical dimension of the curve is normal or bell-shaped (Ferguson, 1981).

Many of the statistical software packages currently used, like SPSS (Statistical Package for the Social Sciences), report all three types of measures: central tendency, dispersion, and shape. The great advantage of knowing how to interpret these values is that you will know if the distribution is normal without having to graph the data. The visual representation will be further corroboration for you that the curve is normal, or that it instead shows the presence of error. The assumption of normalcy in the way the data is distributed underlies the logic of hypothesis testing, the main process you will learn about in the second half of this chapter.

INFERENTIAL STATISTICS

The second main function of statistics is estimating characteristics of the larger group (population) from the characteristics of a smaller group (sample). Before we can examine this process, it will be necessary for you to learn about three types of data distributions: sample, population, and sampling.

Three Types of Distributions

Sample Distributions To this point in our discussion, the distributions of data we have been talking about are sample distributions. Simply defined, a *sample* is a subset or smaller grouping of members from a pop-

ulation. The **sample distribution** is the actual data set the researcher obtains when conducting the study. It contains the values or scores of a variable measure as they are distributed along the *x*- and *y*-axes. **Statistics** are the characteristics of a sample distribution expressed in numbers. The measures of central tendency, dispersion, and shape that we discussed in the last few sections constitute a sample's descriptive statistics.

Population Distributions In Chapter 4, you learned about the importance of obtaining a **representative sample**—a sample whose characteristics are good estimates (valid and reliable) of the population characteristics. The *population* refers to the entire set of data from which a sample is drawn. Whenever you select a sample for studying some communication phenomenon, two different conceptions of a population come into play: target populations and survey populations.

A **target population** is "an idealized group representing the totality of target elements that interest a researcher"; a **survey population** is "an aggregation of all the elements from which a researcher's sample will actually be taken" (Smith, 1988, p. 77). Practically speaking, if you wanted to test gender differences in using persuasive strategies, it isn't possible to sample males and females from the target population of women and men. You are usually satisfied to obtain a random sample of available participants with as much variation as possible drawn from the survey population. For example, you might select women and men from the local telephone directory as a survey population. Because you can rarely sample all of the members of the target population or even the survey population, you will have to make inferences about their characteristics based on the data you have obtained in your sample.

When samples are representative, their distributions should closely approximate the **population distribution,** or the way the same elements or data would be distributed in the population. Ideally, the statistics, or sample characteristics, should be close estimates of the population characteristics; these are called **parameters.** The mean of the sample, $\bar{X}$, should reflect the mean of the population, μ_X, denoted by the Greek letter *mu*. The variance and standard deviation of the sample, s^2 and s, should be good estimates of the population's variance and standard deviation, σ_X^2 and σ_X, denoted by the Greek letter *sigma*. Using the various symbols for sample and population characteristics helps clarify when and how sample statistics are used as estimates of population parameters. This process of estimation is based on the third type of distribution, the sampling distribution.

Sampling Distributions Sampling distributions provide us with the ability to make inferences about population parameters from sample statistics. This is the core concept of inferential statistics and hypothesis testing. Based on probability theory and sampling techniques, you can actually estimate how far your sample statistics are likely to deviate from the population parameters; this general estimation rule is called **sampling error** (Babbie, 1995, p. 195). The term is derived from a **sampling distribution,** which is a theoretic distribution of all possible values of any sample statistic from any given population; it specifies the probabilities associated with each of the values.

Probability theory makes it possible to hypothetically construct a sampling distribution of sample means, sample variances, sample standard deviations, or any other sample statistic. By theoretically assuming that an infinite number of these statistics from samples is drawn from the same population, a sampling distribution can be constructed for any of these statistics. For example, in this way, we can construct a sampling distribution of means. Virtually any statistic that is obtainable at the sample level can provide the basis for a hypothetical sampling distribution of that statistic.

When we have obtained a sampling distribution of a statistic, we can "use the sampling distributions to calculate the probability that sample statistics could be due to chance and thus to decide whether something that is true of a sample statistic is also likely to be true of a population parameter" (McNeill, 2001, p. 8). This decision is an essential part of the statistical inference process that eventually leads to hypothesis testing.

Estimation and Inference

As we stated at the beginning of this chapter, statistics serve two functions. They can be used to describe data distributions as we have seen in the last section. They also permit the researcher to make inferences about the population parameters in order to test a research hypothesis. Smith (1988) identified four assumptions governing sample distributions that will be used as a basis for inferential statistics:

(1) All sample data are to be selected randomly, insofar as possible, from some well-defined population; (2) the characteristics of each random sample drawn from a population are related to the true population parameters; (3) multiple random samples drawn from the same population yield statistics that cluster around the population parameters in predictable ways; and (4) we can calculate the sampling error associated with a sample statistic, estimating how far a population parameter is likely to deviate from a given sample statistic (p. 106).

Sampling errors are derived from sampling distributions based on the way multiple samples "cluster around the population parameters in predictable ways"; they are used to estimate the likelihood that certain statistics come from populations. As McNeill (2001) noted, "It is hard to overestimate the importance of sampling distributions of statistics. The entire process of inferential statistics (by which we move from known information about samples to inferences about populations) depends on sampling distributions" (p. 8).

Central Limits Theorem In addition to these assumptions, inferential statistics includes the **central limits theorem,** which states that larger samples have a greater chance of approximating the true population distribution (Kerlinger, 1973). It also states that random selection of samples is the chief way of obtaining true statistical estimates of population parameters. Thus, when you cannot obtain either large or random samples, it is especially important to determine whether the sample under investigation is normally distributed before you can begin hypothesis testing.

The Normal Curve Recall from the last section on descriptive statistics that normal distributions indicate little error in the data; this means that normally distributed data will yield statistics that are good estimates of the population parameters. Many continuous variables are assumed to have normal distributions. For example, communication apprehension, verbal aggressiveness, and relational satisfaction are variables that you can assume are distributed normally. Most people fall in the midsection of the bell-shaped curve for these communication variables; just a few are assumed to represent the extremes.

Areas Under the Normal Curve Normal curves are so regular that the areas under the curve can be predicted at regular intervals. The distance measure used to evaluate

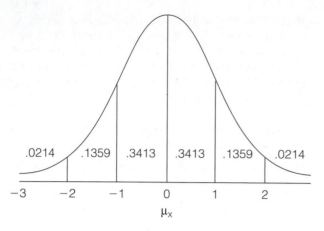

FIGURE 8.11 Areas under the normal curve.

these areas is the standard deviation of the sample. It allows you to estimate what proportion of scores will fall along various intervals of the distribution's measurement scale (x-axis).

As you can see in Figure 8.11, approximately 68% of the sample's distribution of scores will fall between plus or minus (±) 1 standard deviation of the sample's mean, about 95% fall within ±2 standard deviations, and more than 99% fall between ±3 standard deviations. This is called the **empirical rule** of normal distributions (Holmes, 2001). These estimates enable you to determine those scores that are likely to be part of the sample distribution and those that are not—an important part of hypothesis testing.

How does this inference process work? Sampling distributions can be calculated to estimate the likelihood sample statistics come from a particular population. Let's suppose you have hypothetically drawn 100 sample means from a population for your sampling distribution of means. Only one mean value will actually correspond to the population mean. The rest will cluster around this value in predictable ways (Smith, 1988). This sampling distribution of means is also normally distributed, and so the sample means should conform to the empirical rule of normal distributions.

Standard Error The empirical rule of normal distributions enables us to predict how far a sample mean, $\overline{X}$, is likely to be from the population mean, μ_X (see Figure 8.11). With the sampling distribution of means, we can use the standard error to estimate the interval

of distance between the sample mean and the population mean. The standard error is the standard deviation of the sampling distribution of means.

Confidence Interval and Level To use a textbook case example, imagine that the standard error is calculated to be 0.5, and the sample mean is 3.0. By applying the empirical rule, we can estimate that 68.26% of the sample means will fall between $\pm 1 s_{\overline{X}}$ (standard error), or between the values 2.5 and 3.5. This interval of means is called the **confidence interval,** and the percentage of means expected to fall within this interval (68%) is called the **confidence level** (Smith, 1988, pp. 106–109).

In analyzing the data, you will typically be interested in the intervals that have confidence levels of 95.44% and 99.72%, those levels that are associated with standard error estimates that are about ±2 and ±3 standard deviations away from the sample mean. For our previous example, these levels correspond to regions between the values 2.0 and 4.0, or $\overline{X} \pm 2(s)$, and between the values 1.5 and 4.5, or $\overline{X} \pm 3(s)$, respectively. At these levels, we can say that we are 95.44% and 99.72% confident that the true population mean will fall within these intervals.

To summarize, the standard error is the standard deviation for sampling distributions. In a sampling distribution of sample means, the standard error estimates how far the sample mean is likely to deviate from the true population mean. As such, the standard error is an estimate of the sampling error associated with the distribution. The smaller the standard error, the closer the sample mean is to the population mean.

Reducing sampling errors depends upon two factors: the homogeneity of the population (and, hence, the sample) and the sample size. As homogeneity and the sample size increase, the sampling error is decreased. There are standard formulas that permit researchers to determine the effects of increasing the level of homogeneity (see Smith, 1988, p.111), and what sample size is optimal based on projected population size (see, for example, Frey, Botan, & Kreps, 2000, p. 322).

When you minimize sampling error, you are making the inferential process more accurate. You will be using what you know about sample statistics to estimate the characteristics or parameters of the population. You can also use inferential statistics to test your predictions, or hypotheses, about relationships between communication variables. It is the inverse process of estimation: there you start with what is known (sample statistics) and predict what is unknown (population parameters). In hypothesis testing, you begin with a prediction and "then generate sample data to confirm or disconfirm our a priori assumptions" (Smith, 1988, p. 111).

The Logic of Hypothesis Testing

In order to test hypotheses, you will complete five steps: (1) formulating hypotheses, (2) estimating the probability of error, (3) developing a decision rule as a basis for comparing obtained and critical values of test statistics, (4) calculating the test statistic, and (5) deciding whether hypotheses can be accepted or rejected (Smith, 1988).

Formulating Hypotheses There are two basic types of hypotheses in formulating predictions about relationships between communication variables: the research hypothesis and the null hypothesis.

The Research Hypothesis The **research hypothesis** is the prediction you are trying to test, often predicting "two or more populations are different in one or more respects" (Smith, 1988, p. 111). For example, Afifi and Burgoon (2000) hypothesized that the type of interaction, positive or negative, would have an effect on a partner's perceived attractiveness. Participants who experienced a positive interaction ($\bar{X}_1$) would be more attracted to their partners than those who experienced a negative interaction ($\bar{X}_2$). This research hypothesis can be expressed as $H_1 : \bar{X}_1 > \bar{X}_2$. This is an example of a **directional hypothesis**—one mean is projected to be greater (or less) than the other mean.

A **nondirectional hypothesis** predicts an inequality or difference, but does not specify how that difference will occur: $H_1 : \bar{X}_1 \neq \bar{X}_2$. In Afifi and Burgoon's experiment, a nondirectional hypothesis would be expressed by stating that the effects of a positive interaction would be significantly different than the effects of a negative interaction on perceived attractiveness, but the projected difference would not indicate which mean would be greater (or less) than the other. We will have more to say about testing directional research hypotheses in the next chapter.

The Null Hypothesis The **null hypothesis,** usually expressed as H_0, is "the antithesis of the research hypothesis," predicting no effects of one variable on another or no relationship between the variables (Smith, 1988, p. 112). You should assume the null hypothesis is true until enough evidence is accumulated to reject it. As

Smith noted, the null hypothesis is analogous to a criminal court proceeding, where the accused is presumed innocent and the burden of proof is on the prosecutor to establish enough evidence to finally reject that conclusion. This concept is sometimes referred to as the **falsification principle** (Popper, 1962).

Estimating Error Probabilities The second step of hypothesis testing is to establish the probability of error associated with accepting or rejecting the null hypothesis. In the last section, you were shown how to calculate the sampling error associated with estimation. Using sampling distributions for testing the relationship between the variables, you can project a confidence level with its corresponding interval that will be associated with accepting or rejecting the null hypothesis. Depending on the actual statistics you obtain for your sample data, you can determine the probabilities that certain statistics like the mean are drawn from same or different populations.

Developing a Decision Rule As the third step in hypothesis testing, by custom, researchers have agreed that the probability of error in supporting the research hypothesis should be less than 5%. Another way of stating this rule is that we can say we are 95.44% confident that we can reject the null hypothesis. When we make this decision, the probability level (called p or *alpha* level) associated with this decision is less than .05 based on the areas under the normal curve (refer to Figure 8.11). This probability level is usually expressed with the test statistic as $p < .05$ (or some value smaller than .05).

Calculating the Test Statistic The fourth step of hypothesis testing requires that you calculate the actual test statistic. There are two basic types of relationships between variables: tests of difference and tests of relationship. In Chapter 6, you learned about the first type of relationship as a causal prediction about the effects of an experimentally manipulated independent variable on a dependent variable. This type of claim requires a test of significant differences. You can also test the significance of the degree of association or relatedness between two or more variables. We will explain these statistical tests in detail in the next chapter. Each test yields an obtained value that is compared to critical values needed to reject the null hypothesis. Critical values are associated with the probability levels explained in the third step.

Making the Decision The fifth and final step in the hypothesis-testing process is to make a decision to accept or reject the null hypothesis. Statistical tests of hypotheses depend on sample data, but in most cases, these are used as evidence to support (or falsify) a generalizable claim about significant findings at the population level. You can accept the research hypothesis (and reject the null hypothesis); this decision is either correct or incorrect. Or you can fail to reject the null hypothesis (and not support the research hypothesis); similarly, this decision will either be correct or incorrect. Table 8.1 illustrates the decision possibilities.

Incorrect decisions result in two types of errors: *Type I and Type II* errors. A **Type I error** occurs when we decide to reject the null hypothesis but we shouldn't have; in truth, our research hypothesis cannot be supported. This type of error is sometimes called an *alpha error* because alpha corresponds to the *p* level, or probability level (Smith, 1988, p. 115). If you have established a probability level of significance at $p < .05$, the chance of making an error is less than 5%. However, when the error does occur, it is a *Type I* error. When tests of significance are conducted with software like SPSS, then the reported *p* level is as low as it can be for the obtained calculation. Sometimes, the *p* level is $<.0001$, which means that you have a chance of less than one in ten thousand of committing a *Type I* error!

The second type of error, a **Type II error,** occurs when we decide not to reject the null hypothesis but we should have; failure to reject the null hypothesis results in making an error in this case. Type II errors are also called *beta errors* (Smith, 1988, p. 116). When variable instruments have strong measurement validity and reliability, the chance of committing a *Type II* error decreases. The probability associated with not making a *Type II* error is called the **statistical power** of a variable. From the central limits theorem, we know that the more we increase the sample size, the closer the sample statistics approximate the true population parameters. One good way to minimize the chance of a *Type II* error occurring is to use larger samples. By doing so, a researcher actually decreases the chances that either type of error will occur. Larger samples make statistics more stable generally and the decisions we make about them more accurate (Smith, 1988, p. 117).

The five steps of hypothesis testing will appear throughout the next chapter as the "steps to determine the significance" of the test statistics you will obtain. These steps complete the inferential process of estimation in helping you determine, in very precise and systematic ways, whether your data can statistically support your claims. You will learn how to complete each of these steps for two types of tests in the next chapter: tests of difference and tests of relationship. Before we leave this chapter, however, it is important to note how technology has impacted the process of obtaining descriptive statistics.

Table 8.1 Decision Matrix for Type I and Type II Errors

Sample statistics	Population parameters	Outcome
No significance	No significance	Correct decision
Significance	No significance	Type I error
Significance	Significance	Correct decision
No significance	Significance	Type II error

TECHNOLOGY AND DESCRIPTIVE STATISTICS

Many computer programs enable you to calculate whole summary tables of frequencies and descriptive statistics for any type of data measured categorically or continuously. Several times in this chapter we have alluded to output on descriptive statistics generated by SPSS. SAS, another statistical analysis software program for social scientists, and Microsoft Excel just as easily generate the same type of statistics. If you use Excel, you will typically have to add the Analysis ToolPak, an add-in feature that you have to choose to install from Microsoft Office 97 or 2000. Your computer won't automatically install it for you unless you select that option. Along with measures of central tendency, dispersion, and shape, SPSS, SAS, and Excel will permit you to generate a series of graphs, like bar charts, histograms, and others you have learned about in this chapter. You can even generate a chart in Word using the "Insert" command, but the charts are rudimentary and generally more difficult to construct and manipulate. We encourage you to try using the data in the activities at the end of the chapter to experiment with the various statistical programs you may have readily available.

SUMMARY

We began this chapter by explaining the two basic functions of statistical analysis: description and inference. You learned how categorical and continuous data distributions can be visually described with different types of graphs. We introduced you to sample distribution characteristics in terms of three sets of measures: central tendency, dispersion, and shape.

In the second part of the chapter, you learned about the process of making statistical inferences by estimation and by testing hypotheses. The relationship between estimation and inference was explored using the three types of distributions: sample, population, and sampling distributions. In estimating population parameters, we explained the importance of establishing a normal curve. You learned how sampling distributions are used to estimate the standard error and to establish confidence intervals and confidence levels.

The last section of the chapter reviewed the process of hypothesis testing. Testing a hypothesis requires a sequence of five steps: (1) formulating hypotheses, (2) estimating probabilities, (3) developing a decision rule, (4) calculating the test statistic, and (5) making a decision. We also introduced you to a few software programs that make calculating descriptive statistics for any set of data an easy task. Now that we have explored the general steps necessary to conduct statistical analyses, we can give you a detailed explanation of the various tests for difference and relationship, the subject of the next chapter.

KEY TERMS

Abscissa	Measures of central tendency	Sampling distribution
Bar chart	Median	Sampling error
Bell-shaped curve	Mode	Skew
Bimodal distribution	Moments	Standard deviation
Central limits theorem	Negative skew	Statistical analysis
Confidence interval	Nondirectional hypothesis	Statistical power
Confidence level	Normal curve	Statistics
Descriptive statistics	Null hypothesis	Survey population
Directional hypothesis	Ordinate	Target population
Empirical rule	Parameters	Trimodal distribution
Falsification principle	Pie chart	Type I error
Frequency distribution	Platykurtic distribution	Type II error
Frequency polygon	Population distribution	Unimodal distribution
Frequency table	Positive skew	Variance
Histogram	Range	x-axis
Kurtosis	Representative sample	y-axis
Leptokurtic distribution	Research hypothesis	z-axis
Mean	Sample distribution	

DISCUSSION QUESTIONS

1. In what ways are the visual descriptions (graphs) of categorical variables different than the visual descriptions of continuous variables?

2. Why is the mean considered the most sensitive measure of central tendency in a sample distribution?

3. Why is the range considered the weakest measure of dispersion? Why is the standard deviation used more frequently as a distance measure than the variance?

4. How is the sample distribution different from a population distribution and a sampling distribution? Try to come up with examples for each.

5. In the term *statistical inference,* what is the word "inference" referring to?

6. How is a Type I error different than a Type II error? What tells you what chance you have of committing a Type I error? What is one way you can minimize both types of error?

"TRY IT!" ACTIVITIES

1. What is the median score for the following data distribution: 13, 14, 15, 15, 16, 16, 17, 17, 17, 18, 18, 19?

2. A researcher studying phone conversations between students and teachers determines the average length of the conversations to be 7.3 minutes with a standard deviation of 1.20 minutes. What is the confidence interval for about 99% percent of the sample? What percentage of the sample (confidence level) is characterized by the score range 6.1 minutes and 8.5 minutes (confidence interval)?

3. Try your Internet skills for obtaining a data set that you can use for calculating descriptive statistics. Go to http://www.math.yorku.ca/SCS/StatResource.html. At that URL, you will find a listing of many different types of statistical resources. Go to the subheading "Data." Click on the link to "The Data and Story Library." This is an online library of data files and stories that you may use for calculating any statistics. Under the "Datafile Subjects," click on "Consumer." Then select "Magazine Ads Readability." Calculate the measures of central tendency, dispersion, and shape of the number of sentences in advertisement copy for each of the three groups of educational levels (highest, medium, and lowest). You may calculate the three sets of measures by hand or by using a statistical software program like Excel, SPSS, or SAS. Explain which group has the greatest number of sentences based on the measures of central tendency. Explain which group has the most score variation based on measures of dispersion. Explain which group has the most error based on measures of shape.

4. A researcher has selected two groups of dating couples to test the effects of training in interpersonal conflict skills. One of the groups of couples was exposed to a four-week conflict skills training workshop. During the workshop, the researcher stressed the importance of increasing communication with one's partner. The other group received no instruction on improving skills, nor were they exposed to any part of the four-week training session. Following the workshop, the researcher was interested in discovering how many contacts between dating partners were made by both groups over a five-day period. The researcher was attempting to determine whether the workshop had an effect on the number of contacts between dating partners. The independent variable is skills training workshop with two categories (exposure/no exposure). The dependent variable is the number of contacts in a five-day period. The data for the two groups is

Group #1: Control (no training)				Group #2: Treatment (training)			
0	3	5	7	3	7	6	7
2	3	4	6	8	6	7	7
1	3	4	6	3	6	7	7
1	2	2	4	4	6	5	8
3	4	5	5	6	7	7	3

Using this data distribution as your basis, find the measures of central tendency and dispersion for each group. Then draw and label histograms for each group's data on graph paper; each graph axis should also have a label. Finally, type a summary paragraph or two using the descriptive measures that you calculate to verbally describe the distributions. You should use the indices of central tendency and dispersion as ways of contrasting the differences between the two groups. Use them also in the discussion of the shape of the groups' distributions. Remember: The shape of the distribution will indicate presence or lack of error. Statistics that describe that shape will *not* let you make any claims about supporting or rejecting the research hypothesis.

9

Testing Differences
and Relationships

ABSTRACT

In this chapter, you will review the five basic steps of testing hypotheses, and apply these steps to analyzing group differences and linear relationships. You will learn how to calculate and interpret both nonparametric and parametric tests for analyzing group differences, including chi-square, z-test, t-test, and analysis of variance. You will also learn how to calculate and interpret the basic statistical test for associative relationships, the correlation. You will learn to recognize regression as a more complex causal test of linear relationships for multiple variables. Finally, we will introduce the difference between bivariate and multivariate analyses and will conclude with a discussion of the role technology has played in generating analytic software. Once you have completed this chapter, you will be able to appreciate the purposes of these tests when you read about them in original research reports.

OUTLINE

In the last chapter, you explored how statistics are used to describe samples and infer population characteristics through estimation. Estimation is generally a process that begins with what you know (sample statistics) to infer about what you don't know (population parameters). Hypothesis testing is the opposite procedure: making predictions about what you don't know, to be tested against what you do know, or your observations (Smith, 1988, p. 111).

You will begin this chapter where you ended the last, by identifying the five steps necessary for testing research hypotheses: (1) formulating hypotheses, (2) estimating the probability of error, (3) developing a decision rule as a basis of comparing obtained and critical values of test statistics, (4) calculating the test statistic, and (5) deciding whether hypotheses can be accepted or rejected.

As stated in this sequence of steps, empirical research associated with the discovery paradigm begins with advancing one or more claims that are statistically tested to see whether there is sufficient evidence to support them. There are generally two types of predictions that can be made: claims of difference and claims of relationships. In this chapter, you will explore both of these types of claims and the statistical analyses used to test them.

TESTS OF DIFFERENCES

All statistical tests of difference are variations on basically the same proportion or ratio. The ratio is of observed differences between sample or group means to an estimate of the difference that is due to chance variation. The ratio is expressed as

$$\frac{\text{Observed group mean differences}}{\text{Chance mean differences}}$$

The observed group mean differences are usually referred to as the **between-groups variance,** and the chance mean differences, or sampling error, is called **within-groups variance.**

In certain types of tests, calculation of this ratio enables you to estimate whether the samples you are comparing are likely to be drawn from the same or different populations. Recall from the last chapter that sampling distributions allow you to estimate the probability that any sample statistic came from a given population. Sampling distributions also permit

you to compare two statistics, like sample means, to decide whether they are likely to have been drawn from the same or different populations. Statisticians use sample distributions to establish "critical rejection regions," or areas under the normal curve that are associated with probability estimates that indicate the two statistics are not from the same population. The greater the ratio of observed sample mean differences to chance mean differences, the greater the likelihood that the means are significantly different. A **significant difference** between sample means, $\overline{X}_1 - \overline{X}_2$, would establish the likelihood that the sample means are not drawn from the same population.

When deciding how to statistically analyze your data, you must think about the way the data was originally conceptualized and measured. Ideally, this decision naturally develops out of the research design you construct to test your claims. Once you have reached the point of operationalizing your variables, you will assume certain statistical tests will follow. Nominal and ordinal scales will yield categorical variables; interval and ratio scales will yield continuous variables. When independent and dependent variables are categorical, they are analyzed using tests of differences between the frequencies of the various categories. Many of these are classified as nonparametric tests. When independent variables are categorical and/or continuous and the dependent variables are continuous, you will use distributions that test a more complex type of difference. These tests are referred to as parametric tests. In the next two sections of this chapter, you will learn some of the basic differences between nonparametric and parametric tests.

Nonparametric Tests

Nature of Data and Assumptions From many of the research examples in Chapters 5 through 7, you learned that there are many ways that variables can be measured with nominal scales. Dichotomous variables on surveys are measured by two response categories (e.g., yes/no or true/false). Some organismic or naturally occurring variables like biological sex (male and female) are categorical variables.

Various content categories used in content analysis and interaction analysis are also usually measured with nominal or ordinal scales. For example, Signorelli (2000) conducted a content analysis of prime-time programs with sexual content in the 1990s. She used a series of nominal scales for measuring her content categories. She rated programming content for

---

EXHIBIT 9.1   Data for Single-Sample Chi-Square with Calculation

	TYPES OF CONFLICT STRATEGIES		
	Avoidant	*Confrontational*	*Negotiating*
Observed frequencies			
(*O*)	4	19	7
Expected frequencies			
(*E*)	10	10	10

Single-sample chi-square calculation

$$\chi^2 = \Sigma \left[\frac{(O-E)^2}{E}\right] = \frac{(4-10)^2}{10} + \frac{(19-10)^2}{10} + \frac{(7-10)^2}{10}$$

$$= \frac{(-6)^2}{10} + \frac{(9)^2}{10} + \frac{(3)^2}{10}$$

$$= 3.6 + 8.1 + 0.9$$

$$\chi^2 = 12.60$$

---

relevance to the plot as either (1) no sex, (2) significant sex, or (3) gratuitous or incidental sex. She also rated the program context in which sexual content occurred as either (1) serious, (2) humorous, (3) both or ambiguous, or (4) no sexual context. She further rated the type of program genre as (1) sitcom, (2) action adventures, (3) drama, and (4) reality-based programs. She was interested in finding out how frequently each of these categories occurred. To analyze the data, she selected a test of difference that matched the way her data was measured.

If the variables are categorical, then there are several tests of difference you can select. A common and versatile one is the **chi-square,** χ^2, a nonparametric test. **Nonparametric tests** are used when you are able to make few assumptions about the way the parent populations are distributed. In the last chapter, you learned that normal distributions are assumed to reflect distributions of continuous variables measured at interval and ratio levels (Ferguson, 1981). But nonparametric tests are used when the data is not distributed in the same way as these continuous variables.

Chi-Square   The chi-square test can be used with a single sample or multiple samples. Because it is a nonparametric test, the chi-square is expressed as a ratio of the observed frequencies within variable categories over expected frequencies within variable categories.

That means that we test the actual frequencies we have for each category and compare them to frequencies expected by chance alone to see if there are significant differences between the two. The formula for chi-square is expressed in Equation 9.1:

$$\chi^2 = \Sigma \left[\frac{(O-E)^2}{E}\right] \qquad (9.1)$$

where *O* stands for the observed frequencies of the variable, and *E* stands for the expected frequencies by chance.

Single-Sample Chi-Square   **Single-sample chi-square** analyses are relatively easy to calculate. For example, let's say that you have a sample or group of 30 people, and you want to know which of three conflict strategies these 30 people will choose in dealing with a fictitious conflict scenario you created for this study. If you used Sillars's (1980) typology of conflict strategies (a very common one in communication research), the three conflict strategies would include a distributive/confrontational type of strategy, an avoidant/withdrawing type of strategy, and an integrative/negotiating type of strategy.

The three types of strategies represent three mutually exclusive categories. The participants' responses can be placed in one, and only one, category. Exhibit 9.1 shows that 4 of the 30 participants chose avoidant strategies, 19 chose confrontational strategies, and 7 chose negotiating strategies. Just by looking at these values, you can tell that these observed frequencies are different than the expected frequencies. But are they significantly different?

The expected frequencies are those due to chance variation among the three types of strategies. The null hypothesis (H_0) for this example is that all three strategy choices will occur equally frequently, and none will occur with any greater or lesser frequency than we can predict by chance. The expected frequencies for each choice, then, are the total number of participants (N) divided by the number of strategy types or categories (k):

$$E = \frac{N}{k} = \frac{30}{3} = 10 \qquad (9.2)$$

In a group of 30 people, the laws of chance predict that each strategy will have 10 chances in 30 (or 1 in 3 chances) of being selected by the participants. Both the observed and expected frequencies appear in Exhibit 9.1 and are used to complete the chi-square calculation.

The research hypothesis (H_1) states that the pattern of strategy selection will be significantly different than predicted by chance. The greater the value of the obtained chi-square, the less likely the differences are due to random or chance variation. In your single-sample chi-square problem, the chi-square value you calculate is 12.60. Once you have obtained this value, you will compare your value with the values in the chi-square distribution located in Appendix C.

The chi-square distribution contains critical values of the statistic that occur proportionately with random variation. Obtained values must exceed critical values as the test of significance. To find the appropriate critical chi-square, you will determine the **degrees of freedom** (df), or the number of frequency categories that are free to vary. In a single-sample chi-square, the number of degrees of freedom is equal to the number of variable categories minus one: $df = (k - 1)$. In our example, the $df = 3 - 1 = 2.00$. The values of df correspond to the far left column of the table in Appendix C.

As one of the steps in determining the significance of the differences measured by a single-sample chi-square, we are required to apply a decision rule that will estimate the probability of error in comparing the critical and obtained values. Remember that in the last chapter, you learned that researchers by agreement have standardized the acceptable level of error at no greater than .05, or 5% chance of a Type I error. When applied to a chi-square analysis, this rule

---

EXHIBIT 9.2 Steps to Determine the Significance of χ^2

1. Find the value of the obtained chi-square:
   $\chi^2_{obt} = 12.60$
2. Determine the degrees of freedom: $df =$ (# of categories – 1)
   $df = (3 - 1) = 2$
3. Choose lowest possible probability level, $p < .05$ or smaller.
4. Find the critical chi-square from chi-square distribution table:
   $\chi^2_{crit} = 5.991, p < .05$
   $\chi^2_{crit} = 9.210, p < .01$

---

means that the researcher is wrong about 5% of the time in claiming that the observed frequencies are significantly different than those predicted by chance variation. The level of error associated with each tabled value of chi-square corresponds to the top row of probabilities in Appendix C.

If we go down to 2 in the left-hand column for df and over to the probability level of .05 for the top row of the table in Appendix C, we will find that the corresponding tabled or critical chi-square value for 5% (.05) with 2 df is equal to 5.991. This means that our obtained value must exceed 5.991 to claim that the differences in strategy selection are significant—and it is! Remember that our calculated or obtained chi-square was equal to 12.60. In this example, our test for significance was confirmed and the research hypothesis was supported. Another way of saying the same thing is that we can reject the null hypothesis. Again, the null hypothesis (H_0) for this example is that all three strategy choices will occur equally frequently in our sample of people. The steps to determine the significance of our obtained chi-square are summarized in Exhibit 9.2. The same general procedure is used to test multiple samples with chi-square.

Multiple-Sample Chi-Square When you wish to test the relationship between the frequencies of one categorical variable that is independent from another, you can choose the **multiple-sample chi-square,** also called a **contingency table analysis** (Ferguson, 1981), as the statistical test. There are other tests of frequencies, such as z-tests for frequency of proportions (Smith, 1988), but they do not generally have

---

EXHIBIT 9.3   Data for Two-Sample Chi-Square with Expected Frequency Calculation

TYPES OF CONFLICT STRATEGIES

	Avoidant	Confrontational	Negotiating	Row sums
Males				
Observed frequency (O)	5	20	5	30
Expected frequency (E)	$E_1 = 6$	$E_2 = 15$	$E_3 = 9$	
Females				
Observed frequency (O)	5	5	10	20
Expected frequency (E)	$E_4 = 4$	$E_5 = 10$	$E_6 = 6$	
				Grand sum
Column sums	10	25	15	50

Calculation for expected frequency

$$E = \frac{\text{row sum} \times \text{column sum}}{\text{grand sum}}$$

$$E_1 = \frac{30(10)}{50} = \frac{300}{50} = 6 \qquad E_4 = \frac{20(10)}{50} = \frac{200}{50} = 4$$

$$E_2 = \frac{30(25)}{50} = \frac{750}{50} = 15 \qquad E_5 = \frac{20(25)}{50} = \frac{500}{50} = 10$$

$$E_3 = \frac{30(15)}{50} = \frac{450}{50} = 9 \qquad E_6 = \frac{20(15)}{50} = \frac{300}{50} = 6$$

---

the degree of flexibility demonstrated in the multiple-sample chi-square.

In order to demonstrate how the frequencies of multiple samples are compared using chi-square analysis, return to the example of conflict strategy selection. Suppose this time our research hypothesis states that women and men will make significantly different choices in the types of conflict strategies they select in resolving a conflict scenario, and let's add that the size of the two groups is different. The flexibility of chi-square permits it to handle different sizes of groups easily. Our new set of figures appears in Exhibit 9.3.

There are several notable differences in a two-sample chi-square with unequal groups. We cannot determine the expected frequencies as easily as we could in the single-sample example. We must now use the expected frequency formula that appears below the rows and columns of data in Exhibit 9.3. It is found by multiplying the row sum by the column sum, and dividing that total by the grand sum. The grand sum is equal to adding across the column

sums $(10 + 25 + 15)$ *or* down the row sums $(30 + 20)$; the grand sum is equal to 50 in this example.

Once the expected frequency values have been calculated for each of observed frequencies, we are ready to calculate the chi-square. The equation for a two-sample chi-square is identical to the one we used for the single-sample test. The steps for determining its significance are almost the same as well. The one distinction is in the formula for degrees of freedom, which is the number of rows minus one (# of rows − 1) multiplied by the number of columns minus one (# of columns − 1). The example of a two-sample chi-square calculation we have been using is presented in Exhibit 9.4.

It is important that we select the smallest probability level (p) for a Type I error in determining the significance of chi-square. The tabled values of the chi-square distribution in Appendix C have probability levels as low as $p < .001$. If you use a statistical software program, such as SPSS (Statistical Package for Social Scientists), the computer will calculate and report the lowest p level associated with a significant obtained value.

EXHIBIT 9.4   Calculation of a Two-Sample Chi-Square with Steps to Determine Significance

$$\chi^2 = \sum \left[\frac{(O-E)^2}{E} \right]$$

$$\chi^2 = \frac{(5-6)^2}{6} + \frac{(20-15)^2}{15} + \frac{(5-9)^2}{9} + \frac{(5-4)^2}{4} + \frac{(5-10)^2}{10} + \frac{(10-6)^2}{6}$$

$$\chi^2 = \frac{1}{6} + \frac{25}{15} + \frac{16}{9} + \frac{1}{4} + \frac{25}{10} + \frac{16}{6}$$

$$\chi^2 = 0.1\bar{6} + 1.6\bar{6} + 1.7\bar{7} + 0.25 + 2.50 + 2.6\bar{6}$$

$$\chi_{obt} = 9.03$$

Steps to determine the significance of χ^2

1. Find the value of the obtained chi-square: $\chi^2_{obt} = 9.03$
2. Determine the degrees of freedom: df = (# of rows − 1)(# of columns − 1)
$$df = (2-1)(3-1) = 2$$
3. Choose lowest possible probability level, $p < .05$ or smaller.
4. Find the critical chi-square from chi-square distribution table:
$\chi^2_{crit} = 5.991$, $p < .05$
$\chi^2_{crit} = 7.824$, $p < .02$

Both single-sample and multiple-sample chi-squares are used to compare the observed frequencies of various categories relative to the expected frequencies. As we have already pointed out, chi-square analysis is fairly frequent in content analyses where variables are typically coded by categories using nominal scales. For example, Tamborini, Mastro, Chory-Assad, and Huang (2000) calculated chi-squares for a series of content categories depicting ethnicity and character roles in court settings. Signorelli (1996) also used chi-square analysis to determine how frequently certain types of sexual content were occurring by program genre.

Survey and experimental research also makes use of nominal scale measures. On a questionnaire in one survey study, Lucchetti (1999) asked college students to respond to dichotomous questions (yes/no and true/false) regarding their sexual experiences, disclosure of their sexual histories, and safe-sex practices. For example, she asked them to answer the following question with "yes" or "no": "Before engaging in sexual activity, have you ever told your partner about your past sexual history (i.e., the number of previous

sexual partners you have had)?" Affirmative responses were coded as one category, and negative responses were coded as a second category.

Determining the relative frequency of response categories for this sample of college students is an example of using single-sample chi-square. But Lucchetti (1999) was also interested in testing the effects of gender and awareness of safe-sex practices on disclosure and deception about personal sexual histories. To explore relationships between independent and dependent variables, you must use multiple-sample chi-squares. Among numerous reported results, she found that significantly more women than men incorrectly identified using oral contraceptives as a safe-sex practice; she also found that significantly more women than men were correct in believing "that disclosing one's number of previous sexual partners is required before becoming sexually intimate" (p. 306).

As we said at the beginning of this section, nonparametric tests do not make many assumptions about the distributions of the parent populations from which samples are drawn. Tests of nominal or ordinal level data are usually nonparametric because the researcher does not know much about the parent population, or because it is known that the variable distributions under investigation deviate substantially from the shape of normal distributions we described in the last chapter (Ferguson, 1981). Tests of interval and ratio level data are more clearly articulated and are called parametric tests.

Parametric Tests

Nature of Data and Assumptions In testing the null and research hypotheses, nonparametric tests are used to test the claim that frequency distributions are either equal (H_0) or they are not (H_1). They do not permit the researcher to assume any shape whatsoever about the parent population distribution, nor can sample statistics be used to estimate population parameters (e.g., μ_x or σ_x) as we discussed in the last chapter.

By contrast, **parametric tests** assume population distributions are shaped in a specific way; they have normal distributions. Moreover, because population distributions are assumed to be normal, their associated sampling distributions are also assumed to be normal. This means that you can estimate the population parameters from sample statistics and calculate the sampling error associated with each characteristic. This ability makes parametric tests more powerful.

We shall consider five parametric tests: three that test differences between variances (z-test, t-test, and the analysis of variance) and two that test degrees of association between variables (correlation and regression).

z-test The z-test has many variations. They are often referred to as standardizing tests because you will always assume that the mean is 0.0 and the standard deviation is equal to 1.0 before beginning this test. Because of these assigned values, the variance and standard deviation are more easily calculated (Ferguson, 1981, p. 71). The z-test is based on the assumption that the distribution of data scores is normal, and it can be used to plot any area of the data distribution under the normal curve by converting any set of numbers to standard scores.

The z-test is used when you have to convert two different sets of scores to a common base so that they can be compared. For example, Hoffman and Heald (2000) wanted to determine whether the frequency of tobacco advertisements in magazines targeted at African-American audiences was significantly different than the frequency of these advertisements in

"general audience magazines" (p. 417). Because the number of pages for each magazine varied so widely, the researchers had to convert page length proportions to represent the number of ads per 100 pages for every magazine. To illustrate briefly, a 50-page magazine with 3 tobacco ads has twice as many tobacco ads as a 100-page magazine with 3 tobacco ads.

When a z-test is used as a test of difference, it is called a **z-test for mean differences,** defined as assessing "differences between two population means based on data derived from large independent random samples, typically groups containing at least 30 scores each" (Smith, 1988, p. 129). The independent variable is categorical, creating two groups, and the dependent group is continuous. The z statistic is expressed by the formula in Equation 9.3:

$$z = \frac{\bar{x}_1 - \bar{x}_2}{s_{\bar{x} - \bar{x}_2}} \qquad (9.3)$$

The numerator represents the difference between two sample means, and the denominator is the calculation for estimating the amount of error due to random or chance variation. The expression $s_{\bar{x} - \bar{x}_2}$ is referred to as the **standard error of difference between means** and is calculated using Equation 9.4:

$$s_{\bar{x} - \bar{x}_2} = \sqrt{\left(\frac{s_1^2}{n_1}\right) + \left(\frac{s_2^2}{n_2}\right)} \qquad (9.4)$$

To illustrate a z-test for significant differences of means, let's consider an example. In a study of teacher immediacy behavior, Frymier and Houser (1998) defined immediacy as "the perception of physical and psychological closeness between people" (p. 122). Suppose you wish to discover whether students exposed to a teacher with a high frequency of immediacy behaviors learned more than students who were exposed to teachers with low frequencies of immediacy behaviors. The *independent variable* contains two categories or groups: teachers who express high levels of immediacy behaviors and teachers with low levels of immediacy behaviors. Teachers who express high immediacy nonverbally smile and nod more in response to their students, have higher levels of eye contact, and move or stand closer to their students than teachers who express low immediacy nonverbally. The *dependent variable* is the level of learning measured as a continuous variable. To construct this example as an illustration, we have visually displayed the sample statistics, formulas, and steps required to compute the z-statistic in Exhibit 9.5.

The null hypothesis in the z-test is that any variation we observe between the sample means is random or due to chance. Another way of saying this is that the samples are both drawn from the same population, $H_0 : \mu_1 = \mu_2$. Applying this to the example, the null hypothesis predicts that students with

---

EXHIBIT 9.5   Calculating a z-Test for Mean Differences

SUMMARY DATA FOR TWO LARGE GROUPS

Group 1 (exposed to teacher with high immediacy)   Group 2 (exposed to teacher with low immediacy)

Means: $\bar{X}_1 = 6.2$ $\bar{X}_2 = 4.0$
Sample sizes: $n_1 = 50$ $n_2 = 50$
Sums of squared
mean deviations: $\sum d_1^2 = 110$ $\sum d_2^2 = 75$

Formulas required for computing z

$$z = \frac{\bar{x}_1 - \bar{x}_2}{s_{\bar{x} - \bar{x}_2}}$$

$$s_{\bar{x} - \bar{x}_2} = \sqrt{\left(\frac{s_1^2}{n_1}\right) + \left(\frac{s_2^2}{n_2}\right)}$$

$$s^2 = \frac{\sum d^2}{n - 1}$$

Steps required to compute z

1. Compute the variance (s^2) associated with each sample.

$$s_1^2 = \frac{\sum d_1^2}{(n_1 - 1)} = \frac{110}{49} = 2.25$$

$$s_2^2 = \frac{\sum d_2^2}{(n_2 - 1)} = \frac{75}{49} = 1.53$$

2. Compute the standard error of the difference between the sample means ($s_{\bar{x}_1 - \bar{x}_2}$).

$$s_{\bar{x}_1 - \bar{x}_2} = \sqrt{\left(\frac{s_1^2}{n_1}\right) + \left(\frac{s_2^2}{n_2}\right)} = \sqrt{\frac{2.25}{50} + \frac{1.53}{50}} = .275$$

3. Compute the z score.

$$z = \frac{\bar{X}_1 - \bar{X}_2}{s_{\bar{x}_1 - \bar{x}_2}} = \frac{6.2 - 4.0}{.275} = 8.00$$

---

high-immediacy teachers will learn the same amount as students with low-immediacy teachers. By calculating the z-test statistic, we will be able to determine whether we can reject the null hypothesis and support the research hypothesis, $H_0 : \mu_1 \neq \mu_2$. The research hypothesis in this illustration predicts that students with high-immediacy teachers will learn significantly different amounts of material than students

with low-immediacy teachers. Once we calculate the z statistic, we can compare our obtained value to the tabled or critical value of z required to reject the null hypothesis.

In the last chapter, you learned that research hypotheses can be directional or nondirectional for tests of difference. The example of teacher differences assumes that students who are exposed to teachers with high levels of immediacy will learn *more than* students exposed to teachers with low levels of immediacy, or $H_1 : \overline{X}_1 > \overline{X}_2$. The research hypothesis (H_1) is directional in this case.

Directional tests of difference are called one-tailed tests; when the tests are nondirectional, they are called two-tailed tests. A **one-tailed test** is a "statistical test that takes the probability level required to reject the null hypothesis (typically 5%) from the area under only one tail of the sampling distribution" while **two-tailed tests** use critical rejection regions under both tails of the normal curve distribution (Smith, 1988, p. 115). What this means is that it is actually more difficult to find support for your research hypothesis with a two-tailed test.

In our example, we have a one-tailed test since we are assuming that one group mean will be greater than the other. The observed z value, 8.00, is compared to the critical z value. Because z distributions are standard normal curves, the value of z that must be exceeded for a one-tailed test at $p < .05$ is equal to 1.65, and at $p < .01$ is equal to 2.32. Because the z distribution is the normal curve, the test is not dependent on the size of the samples; it is therefore not necessary to calculate the degrees of freedom. Our obtained z of 8.00 is greater than the critical value of z at $p < .01$, so in this example we have supported our research hypothesis that students who are exposed to teachers with high levels of immediacy learn more than those exposed to teachers with low levels.

Because the z-test does not take the size of the sample into account, it is best used in larger samples (greater than 30) where the standard error is unlikely to fluctuate by much. When studies have samples smaller than 30 subjects, then the preferred test of difference is the t-test.

t-test Like the z-test, the **t-test** is used when the independent variable is categorical with two groups or categories, and the dependent variable is continuous. The t-test can be used with samples that are not related, like males and females. This type of t-test is called an **independent-samples t-test.** The samples can be related or matched, which occurs when the same sample is exposed to two different treatments. For example, we could match the scores of communication apprehension for a group of people before they gave public speeches and after their presentations. This type of t-test is called a **paired t-test.** The t-test is also used when at least one of the groups

is smaller than 30. Like the z-test, it can be expressed by the same ratio of observed mean differences as the numerator and chance differences or variation as the denominator. Chance variation is the estimate of the sampling error because the t distribution is also assumed to be normal.

Many communication studies use t-tests to determine the significance of differences observed between two groups. In a recent study, Weber, Martin, and Patterson (2001) used a paired t-test to assess whether students enrolled in a special program made significant gains in learning between their entry-point scores and their scores at the end of the year. In this part of the study, Time 1 and Time 2 serve as the two "categories" of the independent variable; learning level was the continuous dependent variable. They used another paired t-test to compare the frequencies of response strategies used by their teachers from the special program with the frequencies of response strategies used by their teachers from the previous year. Current teachers comprised the first group of the independent variable, and teachers from the previous year made up the second group of the independent variable. Level of prosocial strategy use was the dependent variable. They found that current teachers used significantly more prosocial strategies than their previous teachers.

Independent-samples t-tests are often used in conjunction with other more complex statistics. They are used to test the comparison between two groups of the independent variable that are assumed not to be related in any way to see if they exert independent and significantly different influences on the dependent variable. For example, Neuliep, Chaudoir, and McCroskey (2001) compared Japanese and American students (both men and women) on measures of ethnocentrism (i.e., the tendency to favor one's own cultural values and norms over others). Among the Japanese students, independent t-tests indicated that Japanese men scored significantly higher on ethnocentrism than did Japanese women. The same pattern of results was found for American students: American males scored significantly higher on ethnocentrism than American females. In both comparisons, gender was treated as the independent categorical variable (males, females), and the level of ethnocentrism was the continuous dependent variable.

The calculation of the independent-samples t statistic is an estimate of the probability that two means are from the same population. This is presented as the

---

EXHIBIT 9.6   Calculation of t-Test with Data Samples

PLATONIC FRIENDS   **ROMANTIC PARTNERS**

X_1	f_1	$d_1 = X_1 - \bar{X}_1$	d_1^2		X_2	f_2	$d_2 = X_2 - \bar{X}_2$	d_2^2
0	1	−3.5	12.25		3	1	−2.5	6.25
1	1	−2.5	6.25		4	1	−1.5	2.25
3		−.5	.25		5		−.5	.25
3	3	−.5	.25		5	4	−.5	.25
3		−.5	.25		5		−.5	.25
4	2	.5	.25		5		−.5	.25
4		.5	.25		6	2	.5	.25
5	1	1.5	2.25		6		.5	.25
6	2	2.5	6.25		7	1	1.5	2.25
6		2.5	6.25		9	1	3.5	12.25
35	10	0	34.5		55	10	0	24.50
ΣX_1	$\Sigma f_1 = n_1$	Σd_1	Σd_1^2		ΣX_2	$\Sigma f_2 = n_2$	Σd_2	Σd_2^2

Calculation of t

$$t = \frac{\bar{X}_1 - \bar{X}_2}{\sqrt{\left(\dfrac{\Sigma d_1^2 + \Sigma d_1^2}{n_1 + n_2 - 2}\right)\left(\dfrac{n_1 + n_2}{n_1 n_2}\right)}}$$

$$t = \frac{3.5 - 5.5}{\sqrt{\left(\dfrac{34.5 + 24.5}{10 + 10 - 2}\right)\left(\dfrac{10 + 10}{10(10)}\right)}}$$

$$t = \frac{-2}{\sqrt{\left(\dfrac{59}{18}\right)\left(\dfrac{20}{100}\right)}}$$

$$t = \frac{2.00}{1.81\,(0.20)}$$

$$t_{obt} = 5.5249$$

---

null hypothesis, $H_0 : \mu_1 = \mu_2$. When the means are derived from random samples that are normally distributed with approximately equal variances, the formula for the t-test is expressed in Equation 9.5:

$$t = \frac{\bar{X}_1 - \bar{X}_2}{\sqrt{\left(\dfrac{\Sigma d_1^2 + \Sigma d_2^2}{n_1 + n_2 - 2}\right)\left(\dfrac{n_1 + n_2}{n_1 n_2}\right)}} \quad (9.5)$$

where $|\bar{X}_1 - \bar{X}_2|$ is the absolute value (the positive value) of the difference between the means of the independent samples (or groups), Σd_1^2 and Σd_2^2 are the sums of the deviation scores from their means squared, and n_1 and n_2 are the sizes of each sample (Smith, 1988, p. 127).

As an illustration of this test, suppose we wish to test the frequency of contacts between platonic friends ($\bar{X}_1$) and romantic couples ($\bar{X}_2$) over the period of one week. The data are expressed in Exhibit 9.6. We expect that the mean for the romantic couples group will be higher than the mean for the platonic friends, or $H_1 : \bar{X}_2 > \bar{X}_1$, and so we will be conducting a one-tailed test. The calculation of the t-test also appears in Exhibit 9.6.

Once we have calculated a t statistic, we will compare our obtained value and the tabled critical value for the t distribution. This distribution appears in Appendix D. Just as in other tests of significance you have already learned, the obtained value of t must exceed or be equal to the critical value in order to reject the null hypothesis, $t_{obt} \geq t_{crit}$. In order to find the critical value of t, we will complete the steps listed in Exhibit 9.7. The degrees of freedom for a t–test are

---

EXHIBIT 9.7   Steps Required to Determine the Significance of t_{obt}

1. Calculate the t statistic, $t_{obt} = 5.5249$.
2. Find the degrees of freedom, $n_1 + n_2 - 2 = 18$ df.
3. Determine whether the test is one-tailed or two-tailed. In the illustration, the test is one-tailed, $\bar{X}_2 > \bar{X}_1$.
4. Estimate the probability at $p < .05$ or smaller.
5. Find the tabled t value, $t_{crit} = 1.7341$, $p < .05$;
   $t_{crit} = 2.8784$, $p < .005$.

---

determined by calculating $n_1 + n_2 - 2$; in this example, there are 18 df.

As you can see from the table, our obtained value of t is greater than the critical t value, $5.5249 > 2.8784$, at $p < .005$. That means that we have reduced the chance of a Type I error to one-half of one percent ($p < .005$) in obtaining such a high t value. According to our hypothesis, we have supported the prediction that romantic partners make more frequent contact with their significant others than do friends. If our research hypothesis was nondirectional, or $H_1 : \bar{X}_1 \neq \bar{X}_2$, then we would conduct a two-tailed test, which corresponds to the second row of probability estimates, or significance levels, of the t distribution. We would only be able to reduce the error term to $p < .01$, the lowest reported level of significance for critical or tabled t values with a two-tailed test. If we were using SPSS, or other statistical software, the computer would automatically calculate the lowest p level associated with our t value for one- or two-tailed tests—a definite advantage of using computed probability levels instead of relying on tabled critical values.

In the last chapter, you were introduced to the term *statistical power* to refer to the probability of not making a Type II error. One way to increase the statistical power of the t-test is to increase the sample size; this effect also minimizes the chance of committing a Type II error. The t formula is dependent on sample size. Reading critical values on the table, the size of the sample will affect the degrees of freedom. Note what happens to the tabled t values as we increase the degrees of freedom. The critical values become smaller, making it easier to find significance at the .05 level. You will be less likely to make a Type II error as a result. The table of the t distribution is one

way that we can illustrate how the concept of statistical power works.

But what happens when we wish to test an independent variable with more than two categories or samples, or if we want to determine the effects of more than one independent variable on the dependent variable? In order to address either of these possibilities, you will need to learn about the last test of group differences presented in this chapter, the analysis of variance.

Analysis of Variance The **analysis of variance** tests are also called ANOVAs and F-tests. They share some of the same assumptions of t-tests and z-tests: (1) the distributions of the dependent variables are assumed to be normal, (2) the F statistic expresses the same ratio of group mean differences divided by chance differences, and (3) the greater the proportion of differences expressed by the F ratio, the greater the likelihood that the groups were not drawn from the same population. The numerator of the ratio is called the between-groups variance, and the denominator is called the within-groups variance. F-tests can be calculated for independent samples or as repeated measures with the same sample.

There are basically two types of analyses of variance you will learn about in this chapter: single-factor analysis of variance and multiple-factors analysis of variance. A **single-factor analysis of variance** is the statistic chosen to test the effects of one independent variable with more than two categories on one dependent continuous variable. The test is also called a **one-way analysis of variance.** The term **factor** refers to the independent variable (recall our discussion of factors from Chapter 6).

In a study of employee dissent, Kassing and Avtgis (2001) tested three different types of employee groups to see if they were significantly different in the degree of dissent they expressed. The independent variable was comprised of the three types of employee groups: internals, moderates, and externals. This variable is categorical; it is sometimes referred to as the "grouping" variable. "Internal" employees believe they are in control of what happens to them; "external" employees, on the other hand, assume "that luck, chance, fate, or powerful others are responsible for outcomes in life" (p. 119). Moderates were people who neither scored high nor low on the perceived control measure. Kassing and Avtgis found that internals expressed significantly more dissent than either moderates or externals.

EXHIBIT 9.8   Data Set for One-Way Analysis of Variance

GROUP 1 (stories with neutral endings)			GROUP 2 (stories with positive endings)			GROUP 3 (stories with negative endings)		
X_1	d_1	d_1^2	X_2	d_2	d_2^2	X_3	d_3	d_3^2
6	−3.2	10.24	8	−2.7	7.29	12	−2.2	4.84
7	−2.2	4.84	9	−1.7	2.89	12	−2.2	4.84
8	−1.2	1.44	10	−0.7	0.49	13	−1.2	1.44
8	−1.2	1.44	10	−0.7	0.49	13	−1.2	1.44
9	−0.2	0.04	10	−0.7	0.49	14	−0.2	0.04
9	−0.2	0.04	10	−0.7	0.49	15	0.8	0.64
10	0.8	0.64	12	1.3	1.69	15	0.8	0.64
10	0.8	0.64	12	1.3	1.69	16	1.8	3.24
12	2.8	7.84	13	2.3	5.29	16	1.8	3.24
13	3.8	14.44	13	2.3	5.29	16	1.8	3.24

$\Sigma X_1 = 92$

$n_1 = 10$ $\Sigma d_1^2 = 41.60$

$\bar{X}_1 = 9.2$

$\Sigma X_2 = 107$

$n_2 = 10$ $\Sigma d_2^2 = 26.1$

$\bar{X}_2 = 10.7$

$\Sigma X_3 = 142$

$n_3 = 10$ $\Sigma d_3^2 = 23.6$

$\bar{X}_3 = 14.2$

To illustrate more precisely how a one-way analysis of variance works, suppose you wish to test the effects of news stories with three types of endings on listeners' recall levels. The data for this example appears in Exhibit 9.8. Groups 1, 2, and 3 correspond to the treatment groups where each group was exposed to a videotaped news story with a varying type of ending: Group 1 saw the story version with the neutral ending, Group 2 saw the story with the positive ending, and Group 3 saw the version with the negative ending. Following the tape, all three groups were given a test to see how many items they recalled from the content of the news story. The numbers of recalled items are represented by the X scores for each of the groups (X_1, X_2, X_3).

The null hypothesis is that the means of the three groups are equal and the groups appear to be drawn from the same population, $H_0 : \mu_1 = \mu_2 = \mu_3$. If the obtained F statistic exceeds or is equal to the critical tabled value, then at least two group means are significantly different and are assumed to represent different populations. Notice that the research hypothesis stipulates that just one contrast between two group means must be significantly different in order for H_1 to be supported regardless of how many categories or groups the independent variable has. In other words, the F statistic will tell us that one of the

contrasts is significant, but it will not identify which one, or how many of the contrasts are different.

To obtain the F statistic, the means and deviation scores squared are calculated for each group. These are used to find the SS_b, or the **sums of squares for between groups** (as the numerator portion of the test ratio), and the SS_w, or the **sums of squares for within groups** (as the denominator portion of the test ratio). Another way of expressing this ratio is to say that the SS_b is an estimate of the difference between group means, and the SS_w is an estimate of chance variation, or the sampling error. The calculation of the sums of squares for both between and within groups of the example data appears in Exhibit 9.9.

The sums of squares for between and within groups are divided by the number of degrees of freedom associated with each estimate to find the mean squares. The df for between groups is called the numerator df and is calculated by *k−1* , or the number of groups minus one. The df for within groups is called the denominator df and is found by *N−k* , or the total number of scores across groups minus the number of groups. The mean squares are used to determine the final F ratio as expressed in Equation 9.6:

$$F = \frac{MS_b}{MS_w} \quad (9.6)$$

EXHIBIT 9.9   Calculation for Between-Groups and Within-Groups Sums of Squares

Between-groups, SS_b:

$SS_b = \Sigma n\,(D^2)$

$SS_b = 10(9.2 - 11.3\bar{6})^2 + 10(10.7 - 11.3\bar{6})^2 + 10(14.2 - 11.3\bar{6})^2$

$SS_b = 10(-2.1\bar{6})^2 + 10(-0.6\bar{6})^2 + 10(2.8\bar{3})^2$

$SS_b = 46.9\bar{4} + 4.4\bar{4} + 80.28$

$SS_b = 131.66$

where n = number of scores per group,

$D = (\bar{X}_j - \bar{X}_g)$, $\bar{X}_j$ = every group mean,

and $\bar{X}_g$ = grand mean

Grand mean calculation:

$\bar{X}_g = \dfrac{\bar{X}_1 + \bar{X}_2 + \bar{X}_3}{n_{\bar{x}}}$

$\bar{X}_g = \dfrac{9.2 + 10.7 + 14.2}{3}$

$\bar{X}_g = 11.3\bar{6}$

Within-groups, SS_w:

$SS_w = \Sigma[\Sigma(d_j)]^2$

$SS_w = \Sigma d_1^2 + \Sigma d_2^2 + \Sigma d_3^2$

$SS_w = 41.60 + 26.1 + 23.6$

$SS_w = 91.30$

where Σd_j^2 = the sum of the deviation scores squared for every group

---

To help clarify your findings, we may report our results for a one-way analysis of variance by using a summary table. An example of a summary table appears in Exhibit 9.10.

The F value obtained for our data in the example was 19.48 at 2 and 27 *df*. To determine the significance of our F_{obt}, we would follow the steps that appear below the summary table. When we consult the F distribution in Appendix E, the obtained *F* value exceeded the critical value of *F* at the .01 level (19.48 > 5.4881 at $p < .01$); the data supports the research hypothesis. In other words, for the example we are using, there are significant differences among the three news story types and their effects on listeners' recall.

To find out whether all of the group means are significantly different or only certain pairs, we would conduct tests of individual contrasts between pairs of groups. These tests are called **post hoc comparisons** or **follow-up tests** because they are calculated following the calculation of the F statistic. They are similar to t-tests while attempting to control the amount of error in the calculations. The Scheffe test is the most conservative test of contrasts, which means that its criteria make significance harder to achieve; Tukey's or the least significant difference tests, however, have more liberal criteria for estimating significant differences.

In the data example, contrast tests show that two of the three possible comparisons are significantly different: $\bar{X}_1 \neq \bar{X}_3$ and $\bar{X}_2 \neq \bar{X}_3$, but $\bar{X}_1 = \bar{X}_2$. The contrast tests help us interpret the data; in this case, that means that news stories with neutral endings and news stories with positive endings produce significantly lower recall rates than news stories with negative endings. But news stories with neutral endings were not significantly different than news stories with positive endings for their effects on listeners' recall.

Single-factor analyses are less common than the second type of analysis of variance, called the **multiple-factors analysis of variance.** It is considerably more complex than the single-factor, or one-way, analysis of variance. Multiple-factors ANOVAs are computed for the effects of more than one independent categorical variable on a continuous dependent variable. The simplest of these designs can be illustrated by using a 2 × 2 research design matrix. (Recall from Chapter 6 that a 2 × 2 research design refers to two independent variables with two categories each.)

Earlier in the chapter, we referred to an experiment conducted by Frymier and Houser (1998) to test the effects of immediacy on students' levels of cognitive learning. These researchers also wished to test the effects of topical relevance on cognitive learning as well. They chose a 2 × 2 design in which high

---

EXHIBIT 9.10 Summary Table and Steps to Determine Significance of F Statistic

SOURCE OF VARIANCE	SS	df	MS	F_{obt}
Between	$\sum_n(D^2)$	$k-1$	$\dfrac{SS_b}{k-1}$	
	$= 131.66$	$3-1=2$	$\dfrac{131.66}{2} = 65.83$	$F_{obt} = \dfrac{MS_b}{MS_w}$
				$F_{obt} = \dfrac{65.83}{3.38}$
				$F_{obt} = 19.48$
Within	$\sum[\sum d_j]^2$	$N-k$	$\dfrac{SS_w}{N-k} =$	
	$= 91.30$	$30-3=27$	$\dfrac{91.30}{27} = 3.38$	

STEPS TO DETERMINE THE SIGNIFICANCE OF F_{OBT}

1. Calculate the F statistic, $F_{obt} = 19.48$.
2. Determine the *df* for between and within groups:

   $df_b = k-1 = 3-1 = 2$ (numerator *df*)

   $df_w = N-k = 30-3 = 27$ (denominator *df*)
3. Estimate the probability level at .05 and .01.
4. Find tabled *F* values:

   $F_{crit} = 3.3541, p < .05$

   $F_{crit} = 5.4881, p < .01$

EXHIBIT 9.11 Design Matrix for a 2 × 2 Multiple-Factors ANOVA

	HIGH IMMEDIACY	**LOW IMMEDIACY**	
High relevance	$n = 5$	$n = 5$	$\bar{X}_{HR} = 3.5$
	$\bar{X}_2 = 4.0$	$\bar{X}_4 = 3.0$	
Low relevance	$n = 5$	$n = 5$	$\bar{X}_{LR} = 4.0$
	$\bar{X}_1 = 4.6$	$\bar{X}_3 = 3.4$	
	$\bar{X}_{HI} = 4.3$	$\bar{X}_{LI} = 3.2$	

---

and low levels of immediacy represented the two categories of the first factor, and high and low levels of relevance represented the two categories of the second factor. The design matrix for this study is presented in Exhibit 9.11. We are using means that are approximate (not exact) values of those reported in the original study. We take this liberty for illustration purposes only. The means within the cells correspond to the sample mean for each cell. The means outside of the matrix are combined averages for each category of the separate factors, or independent variables.

The calculation of the means needed for this 2 × 2 factorial design appears in Exhibit 9.12. Cell means are calculated for each experimental condition: exposure to (1) a teacher with high level of immediacy and high level of relevance, (2) a teacher with high

---

EXHIBIT 9.12   Computation of Means for 2 x 2 ANOVA

GROUP 1 (HI/LR)	GROUP 2 (HI/HR)	GROUP 3 (LI/LR)	GROUP 4 (LI/HR)
4	3	2	2
4	4	3	2
5	4	3	3
5	4	4	4
5	5	5	4
$\Sigma X_1 = 23$	$\Sigma X_2 = 20$	$\Sigma X_3 = 17$	$\Sigma X_4 = 17$
$\bar{X}_1 = 4.6$	$\bar{X}_2 = 4.0$	$\bar{X}_3 = 3.4$	$\bar{X}_4 = 3.0$

Mean for high immediacy: $\bar{X}_{HI} = \dfrac{23 + 20}{10} = 4.3$

Mean for low immediacy: $\bar{X}_{LI} = \dfrac{17 + 15}{10} = 3.2$

Mean for high relevance: $\bar{X}_{HR} = \dfrac{20 + 15}{10} = 3.5$

Mean for low relevance: $\bar{X}_{LR} = \dfrac{23 + 17}{10} = 4.0$

Grand mean: $\bar{X}_g = \dfrac{\Sigma \bar{X}}{n_{\bar{x}}} = \dfrac{4.3 + 3.2 + 3.5 + 4.0}{4} = \dfrac{15}{4} = 3.75$

---

level of immediacy and low level of relevance, (3) a teacher with low level of immediacy and low relevance, and (4) a teacher with low level of immediacy and high level of relevance. Outside of the matrix, we have calculated the mean for high immediacy across both relevance conditions, the mean for low immediacy across both relevance conditions, the mean for low relevance across both immediacy conditions, and the mean for high relevance across both immediacy conditions (see Exhibit 9.12).

The next step in the calculation of F is to find the between-groups sums of squares for each main effect. Recall from Chapter 6 that a **main effect** is the change in the dependent variable that is directly attributable to each separate factor.

For this particular study, Frymier and Houser expected to find two main effects, one for immediacy and one for relevance, as predicted in the research hypotheses:

H_1: Students who are exposed to teachers with higher levels of immediacy will experience significantly greater increases in their cognitive learning than students exposed to teachers with lower levels of immediacy.

H_2: Students who are exposed to teachers expressing higher levels of topical relevance will experience significantly greater increases in their cognitive learning than students exposed to teachers expressing lower levels of topical relevance.

Using the computed means from Exhibit 9.12, we can calculate the sums of squares for immediacy and the sums of squares for relevance, as illustrated in Exhibit 9.13. Then, in order to find the F statistic associated with each main effect, the within-groups sums of squares are found by calculating the sum of the deviation scores squared for each of the four groups. The results are reported in Exhibit 9.14.

The data in Exhibits 9.13 and 9.14 provide the information necessary to determine the F statistic for the main effects of immediacy and relevance on cognitive learning, but not the interaction effect. Recall from Chapter 6 that the **interaction effect** is the combined influence of two or more independent variables on the dependent variable. The information in Exhibit 9.15 is needed to find the F statistic associated with testing the interaction effect:

EXHIBIT 9.13   Between-Groups Sums of Squares (SS_{bI} and SS_{bR})

	IMMEDIACY MAIN EFFECT			RELEVANCE MAIN EFFECT	
	High	Low		High	Low
n	10	10	n	10	10
$\bar{X}$	4.3	3.2	$\bar{X}$	3.5	4.0
D	0.55	−0.55	D	−0.25	0.25
D^2	0.3025	0.3025	D^2	0.0625	0.0625
nD^2	3.025	3.025	nD^2	0.625	0.625

Immediacy: $SS_{bI} = \Sigma nD^2 = (3.025 + 3.025) = 6.05$

Relevance: $SS_{bR} = \Sigma nD^2 = (0.625 + 0.625) = 1.25$

where D = the deviation of each group mean from the grand mean.

$$D = \bar{X} - \bar{X}_g = \bar{X} - 3.75$$

EXHIBIT 9.14   Within-Groups Sums of Squares (SS_w)

GROUP 1 (HI/LR) $\bar{X}_1 = 4.6$			GROUP 2 (HI/HR) $\bar{X}_2 = 4.0$		
X_1	d_1	d_1^2	X_2	d_2	d_2^2
4	−0.6	0.36	3	−1	1
4	−0.6	0.36	4	0	0
5	+0.4	0.16	4	0	0
5	+0.4	0.16	4	0	0
5	+0.4	0.16	5	+1	1
		$\Sigma d_1^2 = 1.2$			$\Sigma d_2^2 = 2.0$

GROUP 3 (LI/LR) $\bar{X}_3 = 3.4$			GROUP 4 (LI/HR) $\bar{X}_4 = 3.0$		
X_3	d_3	d_3^2	X_4	d_4	d_4^2
2	−1.4	1.96	2	−1	1
3	−0.4	0.16	2	−1	1
3	−0.4	0.16	3	0	0
4	+0.6	0.36	4	+1	1
5	+1.6	2.56	4	+1	1
		$\Sigma d_3^2 = 5.2$			$\Sigma d_4^2 = 4.0$

$$SS_w = \Sigma \left[\Sigma d_j\right]^2 = (1.2 + 2.0 + 5.2 + 4.0) = 12.4$$
where d_j are the deviation scores for each group

H_3: Students who are exposed to teachers expressing higher levels of both immediacy and topical relevance will experience significantly greater increases in their cognitive learning than students exposed to teachers expressing lower levels of immediacy and topical relevance.

Now that we have determined the sums of squares associated with each between-groups main effect, the interaction effect, and the within-groups variance, we are ready to calculate the F statistic for each relationship. The summary table of the results appears in Exhibit 9.16.

EXHIBIT 9.15   Interaction Sums of Squares (SS_{bIR})

	GROUP 1 (HI/LR)	GROUP 2 (HI/HR)	GROUP 3 (LI/LR)	GROUP 4 (LI/HR)
Group means	$\bar{X}_1 = 4.6$	$\bar{X}_2 = 4.0$	$\bar{X}_3 = 3.4$	$\bar{X}_4 = 3.0$
Immediacy effect removed (D)	−0.55	−0.55	+0.55	+0.55
Relevance effect removed (D)	−0.25	+0.25	−0.25	+0.25
Group means minus effects	3.8	3.7	3.7	3.8
D from grand mean ($\bar{X}_g = 3.75$)	+0.05	−0.05	−0.05	+0.05
D^2	0.0025	0.0025	0.0025	0.0025
nD^2 ($n = 5$)	0.0125	0.0125	0.0125	0.0125

$$SS_{bIR} = \Sigma nD^2 = (0.0125 + 0.0125 + 0.0125 + 0.0125) = 0.05$$

where D = deviation of group means when main effects are removed from the grand mean
$(\bar{X}_g = 3.75)$

$$SS_t = (SS_{bI} + SS_{bR} + SS_{bIR}) + SS_w$$
$$SS_t = (6.05 + 1.25 + 0.05) + 12.4 = 19.75$$

EXHIBIT 9.16   Summary Table: Calculating F for a 2 × 2 ANOVA

SOURCE OF VARIANCE	SS	df	MS (variance)	F
Immediacy	6.05	$\dfrac{(k-1)}{1}$	6.05	$\dfrac{6.05}{0.775} = 7.81*$
Relevance	1.25	$\dfrac{(k-1)}{1}$	1.25	$\dfrac{1.25}{0.775} = 1.61$
Immediacy x relevance (interaction)	0.05	$\dfrac{(k-1)}{1}$	0.05	$\dfrac{0.05}{0.775} = 0.06$
Error	12.4	$(N-k)$ 20 − 4 = 16	0.775	

$$df_n = 1 \text{ and } df_d = 16$$

$*p < .05$

From the summary table, you can draw the following conclusions:

1. H_1, predicting a main effect for immediacy, was supported. Students who were exposed to teachers expressing higher levels of immediacy experienced significantly greater increases in their cognitive learning than students exposed to teachers expressing lower levels of immediacy.

2. H_2, predicting a main effect for relevance, was *not* supported. Students who were exposed to teachers expressing higher levels of topical relevance did not experience significantly greater increases in their cognitive learning than students exposed to teachers expressing lower levels of topical relevance.

3. H_3, predicting an interaction effect for immediacy and relevance, was *not* supported. There were

no significantly different combined effects of both immediacy and topical relevance on cognitive learning.

To interpret these findings, observe the F values in the last column of the summary table. The F_{obt} value associated with the immediacy main effect is 7.81. If we consult the F distribution in Appendix E, the critical value of F at $df_n = 1$ and $df_d = 16$ is 4.4940, $p < .05$. We cannot reduce the probability level to .01 because at that level the critical F value is greater than our obtained F value. None of the other obtained F values are large enough to exceed the critical F values. We do not know which pairs of groups represent significantly different comparisons for the main effect of immediacy. In order to assess group contrasts, we would conduct a post hoc comparison test as we described previously for single-factor analyses of variance.

More complex tests of difference are applied with different research designs. For example, an **analysis of covariance** (ANCOVA) is used to "'control' or 'adjust for' the effects of one or more uncontrolled variables" that might intervene between the independent variable and the dependent variable in explaining the observed effects (Ferguson, 1981, p. 358). In Chapter 6, you learned various ways researchers could control rival explanations by study designs. An analysis of covariance allows you to apply a statistical control for such moderator variables.

Researchers investigating the relationships between independent variables as factors on multiple dependent continuous variables will use a **multivariate analysis of variance** (MANOVA). Calculation of these tests is beyond the scope of this textbook, but you will undoubtedly encounter them if you continue on in statistical methods, or you can read about them now in more advanced discussions (see, for example, Pedhazur, 1982). At this point, we will consider the second general type of claim made, the claims of relatedness or association, and the tests of relationships used to assess their significance.

TESTS OF RELATIONSHIPS

The tests of relationships assess how changes in one continuous variable are associated with or predict changes in one or more continuous variables. Rather than use measures of central tendency, such as the mean, to examine differences between groups, tests

of relationships make greater use of the entire amount of information about each variable that is available to you. You will begin this section by learning about the general concept of **correlation,** also called **covariance.** Then you will explore ways of interpreting correlations, and the types of possible relationships between variables. You will also examine tests of correlation or covariance, and a brief identification of more advanced methods.

Correlation

Nature of Data and Assumptions When variables are correlated, it is assumed they co-vary, or have variance in common; that means that change in one of the variables is systematically shared by the other variable. The statistics that estimate the degree of association are not direct tests of causality. In Chapter 6, you learned that causal claims require correlation as one condition of causality, but it is an insufficient condition by itself.

Many critics of social science underscore the importance of not assuming causality in correlations. For example, Ferguson (1981) noted that intelligence and motor abilities may be correlated because of the presence of some third and unacknowledged factor like age. Remove the factor of age and the association disappears. Because of the complexity of human relationships, there are probably multiple causes for any event, and this event itself is probably composed of many variables. Assuming causality can lead to a **spurious correlation,** or two variables that appear to be associated when they are not causally related. Ferguson noted that both the birth rate and alcohol consumption rose after World War II, although establishing a causal link between the two leads to humorous if not dangerous conclusions (p. 138).

Associations of variance between just two continuous variables are called **bivariate relationships;** between more than two, the associations are called **multivariate relationships.** In this section, you will explore calculations and interpretations for statistics based on bivariate relationships.

For many bivariate relationships, the strength of this association is estimated with a statistic called a **correlation coefficient.** One of the most frequent tests of correlation begins with calculating a statistic, a coefficient that is represented by an r for samples, and by ρ (Greek letter rho) at the population level. The formal name of the test statistic is the *Pearson's*

EXHIBIT 9.17   Data for Correlation Coefficient (R) Calculation

X (CA)	d_x $(X - \bar{X})$	d_x^2	Y (Pro)	d_y $(Y - \bar{Y})$	d_y^2
60	−10	100	15	−1.5	2.25
65	−5	25	15	−1.5	2.25
65	−5	25	16	−0.5	0.25
70	0	0	16	−0.5	0.25
70	0	0	16	−0.5	0.25
70	0	0	17	+0.5	0.25
70	0	0	17	+0.5	0.25
75	+5	25	17	+0.5	0.25
75	+5	25	18	+1.5	2.25
80	+10	100	18	+1.5	2.25
$\Sigma X = 700$			$\Sigma Y = 165$		
$n_x = 10$		$\Sigma d_x^2 = 300$	$n_y = 10$		$\Sigma d_y^2 = 10.5$
$\bar{X} = 70.0$			$\bar{Y} = 16.5$		

product-moment coefficient of correlation, or Pearson's *r*. This test assumed the variables are normally distributed, the null hypothesis is written as $H_0 : \rho = 0.0$, and the research hypothesis is written as $H_1 : \rho \neq 0.0$.

Pearson's *r* To illustrate the calculation of *r*, let's say that you wish to measure the strength or magnitude of the association between two continuous variables, communication apprehension and level of procrastination in speech preparation, an example based on a study by Behnke and Sawyer (1999). Consider the data in Exhibit 9.17. The variable X represents communication apprehension scores; procrastination scores are designated as the values of the Y variable.

In tests of difference, you observed how two or more samples were different on their dependent variable scores. For Pearson's *r*, you will examine how the *same sample* varies on two separate measures, communication apprehension and procrastination. To calculate the *r* coefficient, we must find the deviation scores for both X and Y. The equation for r_{xy} requires that we also determine a new sum, the sum of the cross products, illustrated in Exhibit 9.18. We obtain this column by multiplying every d_x score by every d_y score, and then we sum down this column of cross products.

It is very important to notice that the deviation scores used to calculate the sum of the cross products are not squared. Using this column permits us to determine the sign of the correlation coefficient. When

EXHIBIT 9.18   Sum of Cross Products for r_{xy}

d_x $(X - \bar{X})$	d_y $(Y - \bar{Y})$	$d_x d_y$
−10	−1.5	−10(−1.5) = 15
−5	−1.5	−5(−1.5) = 7.5
−5	−0.5	−5(−0.5) = 2.5
0	−0.5	0(−0.5) = 0.0
0	−0.5	0(−0.5) = 0.0
0	+0.5	0(+0.5) = 0.0
0	+0.5	0(+0.5) = 0.0
+5	+0.5	+5(+0.5) = 2.5
+5	+1.5	+5(+1.5) = 7.5
+10	+1.5	+10(+1.5) = 15
		$\Sigma d_x d_y = 50.0$

X and Y scores either increase or decrease together, the sum of the cross products will be a positive number. If X scores increase as Y scores decrease, or vice versa, the sum of the cross products will be a negative number. We will have more to say about the sign of a correlation coefficient shortly.

Once we have finished calculating the cross products sum, we are now able to calculate r_{xy}. This calculation is shown in Exhibit 9.19. We obtained an r_{xy} of +.89. To test the hypotheses, we compare our obtained value to the critical value of correlation coefficients at

---

EXHIBIT 9.19   Calculation of the Correlation Coefficient, r_{xy}

Calculate r_{xy}:

$$r_{xy} = \frac{\Sigma(d_x d_y)}{\sqrt{(\Sigma d_x^2)\,(\Sigma d_y^2)}}$$

$$r_{xy} = \frac{50.0}{\sqrt{300(\,10.5)}}$$

$$r_{xy} = \frac{50}{56.1249}$$

$$r_{xy} = +.89$$

Steps to determine the significance of r_{xy}:

1. Calculate correlation coefficient, $r_{xy} = +.89$.
2. Identify *n* where *n* is the total number of study participants, *n* = 10.
3. Select probability level for a two-tailed test starting at $p < .05$.
4. Find tabled correlation coefficient, $r_{crit} = .7079$, $p < .01$.

EXHIBIT 9.20   Guidelines for Interpreting Correlation Magnitudes

0.0: No relationship
±.01–.25: A weak relationship
±.26–.55: A moderate relationship
±.56–.75: A strong relationship
±.76–.99: A very strong relationship
±1.00: A perfect relationship

Note. From Smith (1988), p. 152.

$p < .01$ found in Appendix F. The steps are listed following the calculation for r_{xy} in Exhibit 9.19. The value of r_{xy} we obtained exceeds the critical value of *r*, and so the research hypothesis is supported. In the example, this means that procrastination levels and communication apprehension levels vary together significantly more of the time than predicted by chance variation or error variance. In order to interpret this correlation value further, you will need to examine three of its characteristics: magnitude, sign, and coefficient of determination.

Magnitude   The correlation coefficient, *r*, is expressed as a value between +1.00 and −1.00; the value of *r* is its **magnitude** or strength. The polar inverses of +1.00 and -1.00 represent perfect correlations, an ideal that does not occur in practice. Perfect correlations happen when the changes in value that happen in one variable are exactly the same as those that happen in another variable. As such, they represent ideal endpoints rather than actual values. The value of 0.0 midway between the two endpoints means that the variables are not related in any way. They are independent of each other.

As we said in determining the significance of the correlation coefficient, the null hypothesis assumes the relationship is equal to zero at the population level, H_0: $\rho = 0.0$. Another way of saying this is that there is no association between the two variables; they do not change together. The research hypothesis is expressed as H_1: $\rho \neq 0.0$. For example, it is fairly logical to assume that competence is not related to physical attractiveness in any systematic way. Persons may be considered attractive but not competent, or vice versa; they may possess both characteristics, or neither. On the other hand, we might predict that the general trait of anxiety is strongly associated with communication apprehension, and we might test this relationship by calculating a correlation coefficient.

Many variables in communication research are believed to be correlated. To list just a few examples, Chesebro (1999) explored the relationship between listening styles and conversational sensitivity, two variables measured with interval scales. Based on past research, Chesebro suspected that some styles would naturally be associated with conversational sensitivity but others would not be. He found that conversationally sensitive people were most likely to use the "People listening style" while there was no relationship between the "Time listening style" and conversational sensitivity (p. 237).

In other studies of correlational hypotheses, Bachman and Zakahi (2000) found moderate to weak relationships between attachment love schemas and affinity-seeking communication strategies. Behnke and Sawyer (1999) found strong to moderate relationships among procrastination, communication apprehension, and perceived public speaking competence. Interpreting magnitude values is done using some established guidelines. Exhibit 9.20 provides a typical set of ranges. The magnitude of the correlation obtained in the example was .89; there is a very strong relationship between communication apprehension and procrastination.

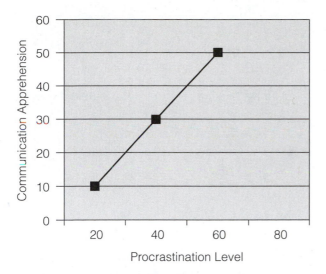

FIGURE 9.1 Positive correction.

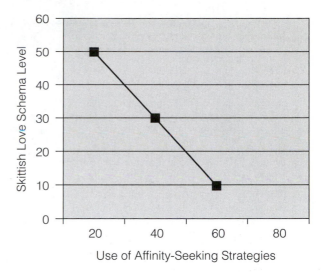

FIGURE 9.2 Negative correlation.

Sign In addition to the magnitude or strength of the correlation, you also use the sign of the correlation to determine the type of relationship that exists between the variables. As we noted earlier, a **positive correlation** describes the relationship between variables that are changing in the same way; they are either increasing or decreasing together. In the example, you calculated a very strong positive correlation between public speaking procrastination and communication apprehension. This is similar to the value reported in the original study, $r = +.70$ (Behnke and Sawyer, 1999). The higher the students' levels of communication apprehension, the more likely they were to procrastinate in preparing their speeches. A positive correlation is graphically represented in Figure 9.1.

When the relationship between the variables is a **negative correlation,** it is called an inverse relationship, where variables are changing in opposite directions. As one increases, the other decreases, or vice versa. For example, Bachman and Zakahi (2000) found a moderate negative correlation between the "skittish love schema" (uncomfortable with closeness) and use of affinity-seeking strategies ($r = -.35$). People who scored higher on the skittish love schema scale (say that 10 times fast!) were more likely to score lower on the affinity-seeking measure. The more skittish you are about love, the less likely you are to use strategies designed to express affection. A negative correlation is graphically represented in Figure 9.2.

Positive and negative correlations express **linear relationships.** Occasionally associations between

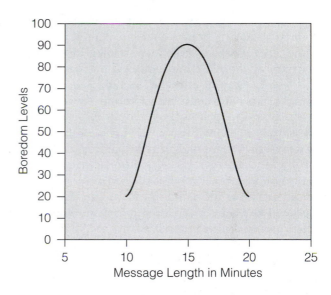

FIGURE 9.3 Inverted U-shaped relationship.

variables are more complex, expressing **curvilinear relationships.** The most common forms are the U-shape curve and the inverted U-shape curve. The **inverted U-shaped correlation** occurs when both variables initially increase together as a positive relationship, and then one variable declines over time and the correlation becomes negative. A graph of this type of curvilinear relationship appears in Figure 9.3. Smith (1988) identified the association between message length and boredom levels as demonstrating this

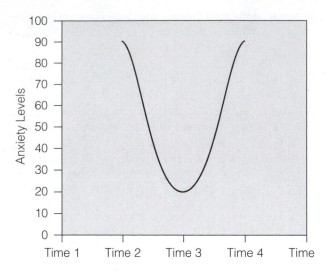

FIGURE 9.4 U-shaped relationship.

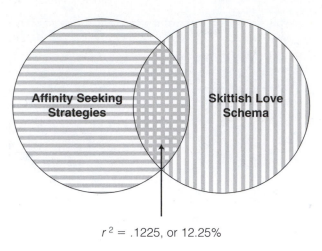

$r^2 = .1225$, or 12.25%

FIGURE 9.5 Venn diagram of shared variance estimate in the Bachman and Zakahi study.

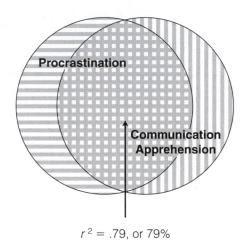

$r^2 = .79$, or 79%

FIGURE 9.6 Venn diagram of shared variance estimate in the Behnke and Sawyer study.

type of relationship (p. 153). Initially, people are interested and boredom is low, but it increases over time. Then, people usually increase their interest levels once again toward the end of the message.

The **U-shaped correlation** reflects an association like the one found by Behnke and Sawyer (2000) between milestone speech preparation periods and anticipatory anxiety patterns in public speakers. Levels of anxiety were high after initially receiving the speech assignment, but dropped off during speech preparation laboratory sessions. Anxiety then increases again significantly just before delivering the speech (see Figure 9.4). Curvilinear relationships express patterns between variables that shift in direction at several points across time.

Estimate of shared variance The final way correlation coefficients are interpreted is by estimating the actual amount or proportion of variance that two (or more) continuous variables have in common. The statistic used for this estimate is called the **coefficient of determination** and is found by squaring r_{xy}. In Bachman and Zakahi's study of the relationship between the skittish love schema and the use of affinity-seeking strategies, the coefficient of determination $(r_{xy})^2$ was equal to $(-.35)^2 = .1225$

You can multiply the coefficient of determination by 100 and obtain a percentage: the estimate of shared variance between the two variables in the Bachman and Zakahi study was 12.25%. This percentage of shared variance can be graphically de-

picted by Venn diagrams (see Figure 9.5). In the example based on the Behnke and Sawyer study, the percentage of shared variance between procrastination and communication apprehension was $(.89)^2 \times 100 = 79.21\%$, as depicted in Figure 9.6.

Bivariate and Multivariate Statistical Analysis

The Venn diagrams of the correlations in these figures illustrate bivariate relationships. As we explained earlier, these are defined as correlations between just two variables. There are many tests of bivariate linear and curvilinear relationships for continuous and categorical variables including Pearson's correlation (r), the eta coefficient (η), chi-square methods (χ^2), Pearson's phi coefficient (ϕ), and Cramer's V coefficient. Though none of these is discussed in this text, you are very likely to see these methods used in more advanced treatments of quantitative analyses.

Nature of Data and Assumptions Often, correlations in communication research entail investigating the relationships among whole sets of variables. Researchers use tests of multivariate relationships that permit the researcher to explore how several variables are interrelated through tests of multiple correlations. For example, Chesebro (1999) examined the relationships among four listening styles and conversational sensitivity. He first calculated a multiple correlation coefficient among the variables to explore how each of the styles might be related to each other as well as to conversational sensitivity.

The **coefficient of multiple correlation** statistic, designated with the symbol R, represents the combined degree of association between the independent variables and the dependent variable. In Chesebro's (1999) study, R refers to the multiple associations among all four listening styles and conversational sensitivity. Just as r^2, the coefficient of determination, is an estimate of the amount of shared variance for r, R^2 is the **coefficient of multiple determination** and estimates how much of the variance in the dependent variable (conversational sensitivity) is shared, or *explained,* by the independent variables (four listening styles).

In the above example, Chesebro determined the multiple correlation coefficient between listening styles and conversational sensitivity. To find out how each style was separately related to conversational sensitivity, Chesebro conducted a **partial correlation analysis** and removed (partialed out) the contributions made by the other three styles to the correlation. By exploring each of the styles separately, he was able to determine their unique contributions. He found three styles were positively related (although two were fairly weak) and one style was negatively related to conversational sensitivity.

Partialing out the effects of variables except for two helps the researcher to begin to construct a complex picture of multiple variables as independent variables, and their effects on dependent variables. In tests of association, sometimes independent variables are termed the **predictor variables,** and dependent variables are called **criterion variables.** You are likely to see these terms in studies where these tests are used.

The more elaborate tests of multivariate relationships that include multiple correlations also include regression analysis, canonical correlation, path analysis, and log linear analysis. You are very likely to find these in articles reporting statistical analyses in communication research. In this text, we will confine our discussion to one test of a multivariate relationship, regression analysis. You will have to take a more advanced class in statistical analysis to learn how to use the others.

Regression Analysis Regression analysis is a common test statistic in communication research. In bivariate and multiple correlation tests, the researcher is interested in assessing the magnitude of the relationship between several continuous variables. With regression analysis, the researcher can actually predict unknown values of the dependent variables from the obtained values of one or more of its predictors. The variables are expected to co-vary, or share some proportion of variance. The estimate of the variance they have in common is the amount of the criterion variable's variance that is *explained* by the variance in the predictor variable.

As an illustration of regression analysis, Messman and Mikesell (2000) explored the relationship between competition and conflict messages in romantic couples. Rather than use nominal scales to identify categories of competition and conflict strategies, they used interval scale measures of these variables. To preserve the information inherent in continuous variables, they used regression analysis to assess the areas of competition that were the best predictors of using integrative (negotiating) and distributive (confrontational) conflict strategies.

Like the correlation coefficient, regression analysis can be calculated for the relationship between one predictor and one criterion variable. This form is called linear or simple regression. It is expressed by Equation 9.7:

$$Y = a + bX \qquad (9.7)$$

where Y is the criterion variable along the vertical axis, X is the predictor variable along the horizontal axis, and a and b are **regression weights** or **beta coefficients.** This formula is actually an equation for a line: a is the *intercept* (where the line intersects the

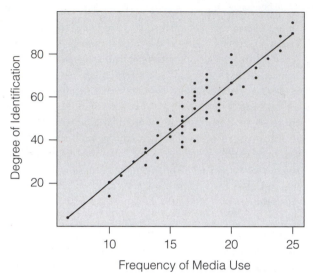

Degree of Identification = −25.06 + 4.38 × Media Use

FIGURE 9.7 Scatter plot of two continuous variables: media use and identification.

vertical *y*-axis) and *b* is the *slope* of the line estimating how much change should occur in *Y* based on a unit of change in *X*. The line itself is the best estimate of the relationship between *Y* and *X*.

To illustrate this linear regression, suppose a researcher wished to predict the relationship between the frequency of participants' media use and their sense of identification with a particular social group. A study like this was conducted by Morton and Duck (2000), examining how gay media use influenced personal identification with the gay community. In a much-simplified version of their study, we will focus on the relationship between just two variables: the frequency of gay media use as the predictor variable and degree of identification as the criterion variable. As frequency of media use increases, participants reported greater personal identification with the gay community. The scatter plot in Figure 9.7 is a visual representation of the relationship between the two variables.

The regression equation allows researchers to predict unknown values of the criterion variable (in this case, identification) from the known values of the predictor variable (media use). Just from eyeballing the graph, you could predict, for instance, that a person who scores a 40 on media use (*x*-axis) will score

about a 15 on the identification measure (*y*-axis) even though these point coordinates are not among the actual data.

As you can see from the graph, the two variables, *X* and *Y*, are not perfectly correlated. They are scattered about the regression line. It is a line that "best fits" the data. Because the variables are assumed to be normally distributed and the relationship between them is assumed to be linear, a standard error can be calculated for *X* and *Y* values that estimates the accuracy of the predictions made by the regression line. From the standard error, we can predict a range of values where *X* is most likely to be located.

In regression analysis, there are also bivariate relationships and multivariate relationships. We have been considering just a bivariate relationship up to this point because we have considered only two variables. But many studies in communication research are investigations of multivariate relationships. In these studies, the researcher uses some form of **multiple regression analysis** to explore the relationship between a set of predictor variables and the criterion variable.

Multiple regression analysis is an extension of multiple correlation analysis. It calculates a coefficient of multiple correlation (R) that estimates whether the predictor and criterion variables are significantly associated. It also calculates a coefficient of multiple determination (R^2) as an estimate of the variance explained in the criterion variable by the combined predictors. It derives regression weights (also called beta coefficients) from the linear equation so that we can assess how much of the total variance of the criterion variable can be explained by each individual predictor.

Two of the more common forms of multiple regression analysis are stepwise regressions and hierarchical regressions. Researchers using **stepwise regression** instruct the computer to try various combinations of predictors until it finds the "best fit" equation. In Figure 9.7, the scatter plot of data also shows a best fit line superimposed on the points of data. Messman and Mikesell (2000) used stepwise regression in their study of the relationship between areas of competition and conflict strategies. They reported that the "best prediction was a model that included the competition factors of Controversy, Altruism, and Play" for integrative strategy usage. These factors explained about 9% of its total variance.

In a study of parental mediation and children's aggression, Nathanson (2001) used **hierarchical regression,** a form of multiple regression in which the researcher stipulates the order of variables entered into the linear equation based on theory and past research. To isolate the effects of parental mediation and coviewing (parents watching television with their children), Nathanson first entered control or intervening variables (like violent TV watching, children's gender and age, and parental education) that she suspected would explain some of the variance in the children's aggressive tendencies. Past research has shown that each of these variables tends to influence children's expressed aggression.

After removing the control variable effects, Nathanson found that two types of mediation still explained a significant amount of the variance in children's aggressive tendencies but coviewing did not make a significant contribution. Because she could construct an equation for each predictor, Nathanson found some evidence that the relationship between parental restrictive mediation (strict enforcement of viewing rules) and children's expressed aggressive behavior was curvilinear; that is, high and low levels of restrictive mediation in the parents were better predictors of aggression in their children than moderate levels of parental restrictive mediation.

Linear bivariate and multiple regression analyses—not to mention the many more complex multivariate analyses available—make the use of computer programs essential. If you decide to continue your training in research methods, you will undoubtedly come across the more advanced tests in that level of course. At this point, we would like to briefly explain how the tests we have described in this chapter can be analyzed by statistical software instead of calculating them by hand.

TECHNOLOGY AND STATISTICAL ANALYSES

In the past few years, resources available to students in research have mushroomed along with other avenues of information on the World Wide Web. In this section, you will learn about two areas of this technology that have directly contributed to statistical research: analytic software tools and data sets.

Analytic Software Tools

There are a variety of computer software programs available to conduct the tests we have been discussing in this chapter. A common program is SPSS, the Statistical Package for Social Sciences. It can analyze data using every test we have identified in this chapter plus many more. The latest version, SPSS 10.0, is very user-friendly and has menu-driven programs at each step of analysis. Even knowing little about "fields" or cell properties, the novice at computer-based statistical analysis can learn to input information for descriptive and inferential statistics. In addition to the basic programs, the SPSS Web site has links to data sets, discussions, and additional resources.

Another statistical package frequently used in the social sciences is SAS, Statistical Analysis System software. To find out just how extensive their offerings are, we encourage you to visit the SAS Institute Inc. Web site and browse for yourself. Like SPSS, you can find tutorials and information guides as well links to data sources on the Web. Both SPSS and SAS support offshoot software programs that perform a variety of more sophisticated functions depending on how advanced you want your analysis to get.

Students can also use Microsoft Office Excel for the same analyses. The later versions permit the user to customize the "Tools" menu with the Analysis ToolPak add-in from the original compact disk used for installing the Microsoft Office Suite. The data analysis option offers an array of statistics including descriptive statistics, t-tests, z-tests, analysis of variance, correlation, and regression. Students sometimes find Excel commands and requirements for entering the data more difficult than the SPSS programs. The advantage of Excel is that most students have the program readily available to them through Microsoft.

For the activity suggestions at the end of this chapter, some members of your class may complete a task using SPSS, others may use Excel, and still others may complete the calculations by hand. The calculation of an analysis of variance without a computer may seem a bit daunting, but we have heard students say that figuring out how to plug the data into the equations gave them a much better sense of what the analysis was actually accomplishing than feeding data into the computer and trying to make sense out of an output file after the analysis was completed. We encourage you at some point to give all three methods a try to decide for yourself which one you most prefer. And we think you will be surprised at the number of connections you begin to see between the data and the analysis with every new trial.

Data Sets

Another way that the Internet has contributed to statistical data analysis is to provide access to many different resources of information that serve as data warehouses. Large, general data sets can be retrieved from the WWW Virtual Library, and the Web site StatLib has archived data sets from many sources, including from many statistical texts. Another interesting site is one maintained by DASL ("dazzle") that

provides both data files and problem descriptions as "stories" in a variety of subjects, including some for social scientists. There is also the ICPSR homepage (the Inter-university Consortium for Political and Social Research), which boasts the "world's largest archive of computerized social science data." It includes some very interesting data sets like those compiled by researchers for *ABC News* and *Washington Post* poll series. You will find references to, and applications for, many of these in some of the problems and activities from the last chapter as well as those in this chapter. And undoubtedly as you browse the Web, you will find a number of new sites that have emerged since we wrote this textbook.

SUMMARY

You began this chapter with a review of the five steps for testing research hypotheses. Following this initial introduction, you learned about two basic types of hypothesis testing: tests of difference and tests of relationships. For the first test of difference, you examined the nonparametric tests of a one-sample chi-square and a multiple-sample chi-square by discussing the nature of the data and underlying assumptions of the analysis. The second type of tests of difference were the parametric analyses of the z-test for the difference between sample means, the t-test, and the analysis of variance. We contrasted the one-way, or single-factor, ANOVA with a two-way, or multiple-factor, ANOVA. As part of this discussion, you were shown how the data requirements dictate the choice of statistic and the nature of the assumptions made about parametric tests in general.

As tests of relationship, you explored the tests of correlation and regression. We contrasted bivariate relationships (and their appropriate tests) and multivariate relationships (and their appropriate tests). The concept of correlation was examined in relation to the concept of causality. For each analysis, you were introduced to the data requirements and assumptions made about the analyses.

The chapter alluded to more complex analyses that are common to communication research but beyond the scope of this text. Finally, you were given information about some very broad features of employing computer software designed for the types of analyses explained in this chapter.

KEY TERMS

Analysis of covariance (ANCOVA)

Analysis of variance (ANOVA)

Beta coefficients

Between-groups variance

Bivariate relationships

Chi-square

Coefficient of determination

Coefficient of multiple correlation

Coefficient of multiple determination

Contingency table analysis

Correlation coefficient

Covariance

Criterion variable

Curvilinear relationships

Degrees of freedom

Factor

Follow-up tests

Hierarchical regression

Independent-samples t-test

Interaction effect

Inverted U-shaped correlation

Linear relationships

Magnitude

Main effect

Multiple-factors analysis of variance

Multiple regression analysis

Multiple-sample chi-square

Multivariate analysis of variance (MANOVA)

Multivariate relationships

Negative correlation

Nonparametric tests

One-tailed test

One-way analysis of variance

Paired t-test

Parametric tests

Partial correlation analysis

Positive correlation

Post hoc comparisons

Predictor variable

Regression analysis

Regression weights

Significant difference

Single-factor analysis of variance

Single-sample chi-square

Spurious correlation

Standard error of difference between means

Stepwise regression

Sums of squares between groups

Sums of squares within groups

t-test

Two-tailed test

U-shaped correlation

Within-groups variance

z-test for mean differences

DISCUSSION QUESTIONS

1. Explain the main difference between parametric and nonparametric tests.

2. For tests of difference, explain the main distinctions among the following: z-tests, t-tests, and F-tests. In what ways are these tests similar?

3. What is the essential difference between tests of difference and tests of relationship? How do the data requirements change for each?

4. Review the underlying assumptions of the discovery paradigm from Chapter 1. See if you can explain why statistical analysis is used in many methodologies associated with this paradigm.

"TRY IT!" ACTIVITIES

1. A researcher recently asked 100 Republicans and 75 Democrats if they were "for" or "against" (two categories) the President's domestic policy. Among Republicans, 35 were "against" and 65 were "for." Among Democrats, 50 were "against" and 25 were "for." (Hint: These are the observed frequencies.) Solve for the expected frequencies for Republicans and Democrats for and against the President's domestic policy (see Exhibit 9.3). Once you have calculated the expected frequencies for each cell, calculate the chi-square statistic. This calculation is relatively easy and can be computed by hand (with the aid of a calculator). Using the steps to determine significance from Exhibit 9.4 and the statistical table of chi-square values (Appendix C), explain whether you have obtained an acceptable level of significance, and what significance means in this

test. In what ways are the observed frequencies different than you would expect by chance?

2. A researcher is interested in finding out whether there are significant differences between romantic partners ($\overline{X}_2$) and close friends ($\overline{X}_1$) in terms of communication frequency. The research hypothesis is $H_1 : \overline{X}_2 > \overline{X}_1$ Exhibit 9.21 shows the data obtained. Calculate the t-test statistic (this can be done by hand). Using the steps to determine significance in Exhibit 9.7, and the tabled t values in Appendix D, explain whether your obtained value is greater than the critical value and what this means in terms of significance. Have you supported (failed to support) the research hypothesis, and what does this mean?

3. A researcher wishes to measure the degree of association between two variables. One is measured by a

EXHIBIT 9.21	Communication Frequency for Romantic Partners and Close Friends	
ROMANTIC PARTNERS		CLOSE FRIENDS
5		2
6		2
7		3
8		3
9		5

EXHIBIT 9.22	Scores for Uncertainty and Liking From a Sample of 10 People	
UNCERTAINTY		LIKING
5		1
4		1
5		1
4		2
3		3
3		4
2		4
1		5
1		4
2		5

scale to assess relational uncertainty; the other is a scale that measures degree of liking. Both of these are Likert-type scales (interval level measurement scales). It is predicted that as relational uncertainty decreases, the level of liking will increase. Exhibit 9.22 shows the set of scores that was obtained from a sample of 10 people. Calculate the correlation coefficient (this can be completed by hand). Once you have obtained the correlation coefficient, interpret it in terms of magnitude, sign, and coefficient of determination.

Using the steps to determine significance from Exhibit 9.19 and the tabled r values from Appendix F, explain whether your correlation coefficient is significant, and what these results mean.

10

Conversation and Discourse Analysis

ABSTRACT

In this chapter, you will learn how to analyze conversational texts closely in order to support claims of description, explanation and prediction, and interpretation. We begin with an historical overview of the ways that conversation and discourse analytic methods emerged from ethnomethodology. Knowing the history of these methods will help you appreciate the ways you can develop descriptive, explanatory and predictive, and interpretive claims about conversation and discourse structures and functions. Next, you will learn some ways of collecting, transcribing, and analyzing interaction data. Finally, you will learn to apply the standards by which you can evaluate the effectiveness of conversation and discourse analyses, including assessing transcription veracity, detail level, interaction naturalness, and using additional data sources to build a case for the plausibility of your arguments.

OUTLINE

The methods of conversation and discourse analysis arose over the past 30 years from the historical precedent of ethnomethodology. Conversation analysis (CA) and discourse analysis (DA) are both ways of studying ordinary communicative interactions between people, but these methods differ from one another in important ways. In this chapter, we will first describe the connections and differences among these three methods. Once we have done that, we will focus on the practice of conversation and discourse analysis in communication research.

In Chapter 7, we used two similar and related terms to refer to research that employed quantitative data analysis to support causal arguments about communicative interactions. Now let's clarify the difference between discourse analysis and interaction analysis: Interaction analysis uses experimental design and survey data collection to advance arguments about the relationships between observable communication behaviors and subjects' internal responses, or attributions about such behaviors. By contrast, discourse analysis uses thematic categories developed from talk, or textual data, as well as the researcher's cultural knowledge of the situation to inform those categorizing decisions, in order to advance explanations of macro-level social order (e.g., ideological structures evidenced in the way people talk about things).

Before studies were ever published in which the authors called their methods *conversation analysis* or *discourse analysis,* there was **ethnomethodology** (Bode, 1990). Ethnomethodological research focuses on broadly conceived social situations, not specifically on communicative interactions. Rather, "it is important to keep in mind that *talk as an aspect of social activity* is the concern of the ethnomethodological approach to conversation" (Sigman, Sullivan, & Wendell, 1988, p. 165). But, to the conversation or discourse analyst, communicative interactions are worthy of study in their own right, not as indicators of some other variables of interest (Hutchby & Wooffitt, 1998; ten Have, 1999; Zimmerman, 1988). "The conflict over 'conversation(al) analysis' and 'discourse analysis' as appropriate labels for the enterprise is further evidence of the infancy of the field" (Sigman et al., 1988, p. 164).

Indeed, some communication researchers have tried to distinguish conversation from discourse analysis

by the kinds of claims each is used to support, or the types of data employed (e.g., Potter & Wetherall, 1987; Schiffrin, 1997). In this case, conversation analysis is distinguished by its micro-level view of closely transcribed conversational data, emphasizing the rules, structure, or patterns that interactants display in their talk (e.g., Atkinson & Heritage, 1984; Beach, 1989a; McLaughlin, 1984). Discourse analysis is more likely to be concerned with the macro-level view of social order, albeit order that is achieved by enacting micro-level social practices or routines.

Just so, some researchers have resisted differentiating conversation from discourse analysis (e.g., Frey, Botan, & Kreps, 2000; Potter & Wetherall, 1987; Sigman, et al., 1988). Potter and Wetherall (1987) wrote that "the term 'discourse analysis' has been used as a generic term for virtually all research concerned with language in its social and cognitive context" (p. 6). Potter and Wetherall (1987) used the term *discourse* "to cover all forms of spoken interaction, formal and informal, and written texts of all kinds," and they noted that "all in all, there is great potential for confusion" (p. 7).

Despite these conflicts about naming their enterprise, all conversation and discourse analysts seek to describe, explain and predict, or interpret message structures and functions. Whereas conversation analysts work from the epistemological assumptions of the discovery paradigm, discourse analysis is more likely to fit the assumptions of the interpretive paradigm. To review these assumptions briefly, conversation analysts attempt to draw conclusions about their observations using careful, systematic, and repetitive procedures. They use the processes of generalization and discrimination as the means for exploring what can be known about conversational order. They believe that "social order exists independently of social scientific inquiry" (Beach, 1989a). Remember the discovery paradigm assumption that any researcher who uses the same definitions and same procedures will observe the same pattern of results in the tests of the research claims. By contrast, discourse analysts are more likely to embrace subjective knowledge, and to assume that there are multiple plausible interpretations of textual data. Nonetheless, both conversation and discourse analysts emphasize the ways in which meanings are constructed and interpreted by conversational participants in their talk.

THE ROOTS OF CONVERSATION AND DISCOURSE ANALYSES IN ETHNOMETHODOLOGY

Ethnomethodology literally means "the people's practices" (Garfinkel, 1967). Ethnomethodologists concern themselves with the ways people make sense of their everyday lives and institutions (Hutchby & Wooffitt, 1998; O'Keefe, 1980). "As its name suggests, the subdiscipline of ethnomethodology is concerned with the study of (ology) ordinary people's (ethno) methods" (Potter & Wetherall, 1987, p. 18). Ethnomethodologists assume that people are constantly trying to make sense of a situation in order to produce appropriate behavior of their own. Garfinkel's early research was based on working with juries, but since then, ethnomethodology is used more broadly to focus on "how language is used in everyday situations" (Potter & Wetherall, 1987, p. 19).

Ethnomethodology is based on three principles: (1) People assume things are as they appear to be unless there is a reason to believe otherwise; (2) the knowledge held by people is typically incomplete; and (3) when people engage in coordinated actions with others, they usually assume that others see things as they do (Schutz, 1967). Deviating from these principles, or **breaching,** disturbs everyday life, even when the deviation is interpreted as meaningful. Ethnomethodologists believe that social situations are constrained by rules systems, even though rules are often unspoken. Rules are general prescriptions for behavior that have to be elaborated in context in order to be applied. Garfinkel (1967) called this the **et cetera clause.** Because we sometimes deviate from the rules, the reasons we give for such deviations, our **accounts,** also are important topics of study in ethnomethodological research (e.g., Buttny, 1987).

In any situation, we have to sort out who we are being, to whom we are speaking, and the topic, in order to produce seamless interactions (Potter & Wetherall, 1987). Ethnomethodologists believe that people actively make sense in this way in order to "go on," or to coordinate our everyday actions. You might begin by looking for routine situations in which people have trouble going on, or situations in which people do manage to go on, despite factors that would seem to an outside observer to be problematic. For instance, imagine that you enter an elevator and find that the other three people already on board are facing the back of the elevator and are staring at the floor. If you see that there is an interesting bug on the floor at the back of the elevator, you will be able to account for their behavior and go on as though nothing out of the ordinary has occurred. But until you find some sensible explanation for their disturbing behavior, you probably will feel that you cannot just proceed as usual. You may feel that you are in a different culture or that they are from somewhere else. If you have lived in more than one culture or in a multicultural setting, you have no doubt experienced this process of making sense in order to go on with mundane, everyday life experiences.

A major premise of ethnomethodology is that interactants work together to accomplish sense making. Discovering exactly how participants display whatever sense they are making of the situation, in their interactions, is the more specific focus of conversation analysis. For example, Watson and Goulet's (1998) ethnomethodological study compared two speakers' discourse about power, a Dene Tha man who was a native of northern Alberta, Canada, and a well-respected social scientist. Watson and Goulet concluded that in both cases, the men interpreted their *visible and tangible power* as being based on *invisible and nontangible forces.*

Think for a minute about your own situation as a college student. Your teacher has visible and tangible power because of his or her advanced degree, formal authority, positioning in the classroom, and so on. You and your fellow students, on the other hand, have visible and tangible power as members of a collective group. Both your teacher's power and your power are based on invisible and intangible forces that have to do with cultural knowledge of the role of teachers and students, relationship histories in your department, and so on. "If only (but not only) because these forces are invisible and intangible, work has to be performed to make them stick" (Watson & Goulet, 1998, p. 96). Consider: what work must your research methods teacher perform on a daily basis in order to make his or her formal power *stick* in your classroom?

A second major premise of ethnomethodology is the assumption of **contextuality**—the focus on everyday life interactions in their natural contexts. "Naturally occurring interaction is the foundation of all understanding of society" (Adler, Adler, & Fontana, 1987, p. 219). Describing the perceptions, feelings, and meanings that people experience, and the structures they create in interactions with one another, is the focus of ethnomethodological research, whether the interactions under consideration are institutionalized (e.g., courtroom, classroom, medical examining room) or not. Adler et al. (1987) noted that although conversation analysis diverged from ethnomethodology because of the more micro-level focus of conversation analysis, the two approaches complement one another and can be used together to good effect. Likewise, discourse analysis also differs from ethnomethodology in that DA makes central the analysis of linguistic data (i.e., talk is *the* aspect of interest to the researcher, not just *one* aspect of the social situation). But discourse analysis retains the ethnomethodologist's focus on culture as a context for sense making.

CONVERSATION AND DISCOURSE ANALYTIC CLAIMS

Whether you are doing conversation or discourse analysis, you will be concerned with how people competently communicate and with the structures that undergird ordinary daily interactions (Adler et al., 1987; Beach, 1989a; Heritage, 1985; ten Have, 1999). In conversation analysis, you will try to determine what one utterance *does,* or accomplishes, in relation to the utterances that precede it. Each speaker's next turn at talk will be taken as evidence that that speaker is oriented to the previous speaker's turn, and so on (Hutchby & Wooffitt, 1998). In this way, you can focus on the participants' own understandings as those understandings are revealed during interaction. This is why conversation analysts prefer to study the production of everyday language in naturally occurring situations (Schenkein, 1978). "They focus on tape recording minute, detailed 'instances,' the raw, primary data of actual conversation" (Adler et al., 1987, p. 226). This emphasis on one observable reality is also why conversation analysis is more closely aligned with the discovery paradigm, rather than the interpretive or critical paradigms.

Conversation analysis begins with this focus on a sequence of talk: "Students of conversation consider talk to be an organized or rule-governed activity whose patterns can be discerned" (Sigman et al., 1988, p. 164). In addition to analyzing the units that

make up a conversational sequence, conversation analysts also consider other aspects of interaction management, such as the integration of vocal and nonvocal interaction behaviors, or institutionalized contexts for interaction, like medical interviews or classroom situations. Notice that the research questions that address relational functions, and the work that is being accomplished *between* interactants, represent both discovery and interpretive claims. This is why we have placed this chapter as a bridge from the discovery to the interpretive paradigm methods in this book. Exhibit 10.1 shows some research questions that have been addressed in published conversation and discourse analytic research.

Descriptive Claims

The purposes of ethnomethodology and conversation and discourse analyses are "to explicate the methods that members of a culture use in accomplishing everyday activities" (Pomerantz, 1990, p. 231). Many conversation analytic scholars *describe* the characteristics of conversation, such as its inherent structure and organization (e.g., Beach, 1989b; Buttny, 1987; Zimmerman, 1988):

> Since conversation proceeds as speakers arrange their participation through delicately orchestrated sequences of utterances, our studies are necessarily preoccupied with the sequential emergence of conversation: the orderliness of conversational sequences is quite spectacular, and these studies exhibit that orderliness in unprecedented detail (Schenkein, 1978, p. 3).

Pomerantz (1990) specified three types of claims that are routinely made by conversation analysts, the first of which is "to assert that interactants are 'doing' particular social actions, identities, or roles" (p. 231). When you offer a compliment, show your feminist leanings, act like a student, and so on, you are performing particular social actions, identities, and roles. When you want to make this kind of claim about conversational interactions, you need to describe and explain how interactants perform such actions, identities, or roles. Pomerantz (1990) called this a **claim of characterization.**

You might start your conversation analysis project by *describing* some conversational **units of analysis,** whether those units are utterances, sentences, or larger

---

EXHIBIT 10.1   Sample Conversation and Discourse Analytic Research Questions

I. Describing interaction structures

    A. Adjacency pairs in ordinary talk

        1. Compliment-response (Pomerantz, 1978; Valdes & Pino, 1981)

        2. Question-answer

        3. Greeting-return greeting

        4. Complaint/apology-justification

    B. Other sequential structures (action chains) in ordinary talk

        1. How do interactants accomplish turn taking? (Sacks, Schegloff, & Jefferson, 1974; West & Zimmerman, 1983)

        2. How are conversations sequenced? (Beach, 1989b; Schlegoff, 1968)

        3. How are phone calls begun in France versus U.S.? (Godard, 1977)

        4. How do conversations end? (Grant & Starks, 2001)

    C. Sequential structures in institutionalized interaction contexts

        1. What is the ordinary structure of a medical intake interview? (Robinson, 1998)

        2. How do physicians and patients achieve the transition from medical history to physical examination? (Robinson & Stivers, 2001)

        3. What is the ordinary structure of a courtroom interaction? (Atkinson & Drew, 1979)

        4. How are calls for help sequenced? (Whalen & Zimmerman, 1987)

II. Explaining and predicting communicative functions (in order to . . .)

    A. Referential function

        1. How do speakers use quasi-lexical objects to manage interaction? (Heritage, 1984, on "oh")

        2. How do speakers integrate vocal and nonvocal activities? (Goodwin, 1980, on achieving mutual eye gaze in turn beginnings)

    B. Relational function

        1. How do speakers negotiate power relations between speakers using interruptions, leading questions, and challenges? (West, 1982; West & Zimmerman, 1983)

        2. How do speakers display their social identities and membership in various speech communities by code switching? (Scotton, 1985; Valdes & Pino, 1981)

        3. How do nonnative speakers of English use "yeah" to manage their images during disfluent interactions? (Wong, 2000)

        4. How do speakers manage heterosexist talk in interactions? (Speer & Potter, 2000)

III. Interpreting the work that is being accomplished within rules systems

    A. How do speakers negotiate conflicting rules systems? (Braithwaite, 1997a)

    B. How do speakers negotiate gendered rules systems? (Leidner, 1991)

    C. How do speakers negotiate politeness norms? (Beck, 1996)

Note. Adapted from Adler, Adler, & Fontana (1987) and used by permission.

---

sequences (Sigman et al., 1988). A sizeable body of research about conversational sequences exists on one particular type of sequence called the adjacency pair.

Adjacency Pairs Adjacency pairs are two-part conversational structures in which the **first pair part** calls for or invites the **second pair part.** Such well-known conversational sequences as the question-answer, compliment–response, greeting-return greeting, complaint-apology/justification, or invitation-accept/decline are all adjacency pairs. Questions call for or invite answers, compliments call for or invite responses, and so on.

Research on adjacency pairs answers descriptive questions like "How do speakers construct the parts of the adjacency pair?" or "What is the preferred second pair part for a particular first pair part?" In addition to these purely structural research questions, you may also want to *describe* contextual influences on the performance of adjacency pairs, asking, for example, "How do speakers enact a compliment within a particular culture or group?"

Let's consider an example in more detail to show how you might develop descriptive claims about adjacency pairs. Perhaps the most researched adjacency pair is the compliment-response sequence. The way we respond to compliments from others, our rules for constructing and interpreting this second pair part, is examined by conversation analysts in part because compliments represent a situation in which there is a contextual standard for behavior—modestly accept the compliment. Yet, we often deviate from such standards, such as when we reject the compliment, downplay it, or accept it quite proudly. "To examine compliment behavior is to examine behavior where actual performances are often discrepant from ideal or preferred performances, and where actual performances are reported as at least somewhat problematic" (Pomerantz, 1978, p. 80). These situations make an ideal research problem for conversation analysis. Of course, the standard for preferred performances is always particular to a specific context and situation, which is what makes ethnomethodology and conversation/discourse analysis such closely related and compatible research methods. In the next chapter, you will also learn how ethnographic methods can contribute to understanding participants' interpretations of such problematic situations.

Compliments and responses to compliments are part of what Pomerantz (1978) called **action chains,** "a type of organization in which two ordered actions . . . are linked such that the performing of Action$_1$ provides the possibility of performance of Action$_2$ as an appropriate next action" (p. 82). Acceptance is one potentially appropriate response when a compliment is proffered. But Pomerantz noted that compliment acceptance was often expressed by way of giving *appreciation tokens* (e.g., "thank you"). Appreciation tokens recognize a compliment without necessarily accepting its content.

In some cases, acceptance of a compliment may be followed by *agreement components* (e.g., from Pomerantz, 1978, "Isn't he cute?" "Oh, he's adorable."). Alternatively, appreciation tokens may be paired with *disagreement components,* also known as negations (e.g., "You look nice in that dress." "It's just a rag my sister gave me."). This last example is taken from a husband's letter to Dear Abby. Ostensibly, the preferred response to a compliment in U. S. American culture is appreciation and acceptance. But Pomerantz noted that whenever appreciation was paired with acceptance, appreciation was placed first (p. 88). This last observation *describes* another bit of communicative structure.

We mentioned earlier that the standard for performing adjacency pairs is always specific to a context, situation, or a culture. So a natural research question for conversation analysis is "How does this performance vary in another context or cultural setting?" Valdes and Pino (1981) extended Pomerantz's analysis of compliment-responses in American

English-only speakers by examining the same situations among bilingual Mexican-American speakers. They compared the strategies Pomerantz identified with the strategies used by Mexican-American bilingual speakers and by monolingual Spanish-speaking Latin Americans. Their findings showed use of all the structural patterns identified by Pomerantz, as well as some additional conversational strategies, including a greater variety of acceptance patterns, and the use of two languages to both give and respond to compliments. Valdes and Pino (1981) noted that **codeswitching,** mixing the rules of one speech community with the rules of another, gave bilingual speakers more options for dealing with situational constraints—options that monolingual speakers do not enjoy. Scotton (1985) also asserted that speakers strategically employ their options to codeswitch, when they are able to do so, sometimes in order to assert identities that "other participants cannot claim" (p. 113). If your research question begins with the phenomenon of codeswitching and aims to explain why participants codeswitch and the effects of such behavior on larger interaction sequences, you probably need to take a discourse analytic (rather than conversation analytic) approach to collecting and analyzing interaction data.

Other Sequential Structures Although adjacency pairs are the unit of analysis of interest to many conversation analysts (Sigman et al., 1988), other sequential units have been studied, such as conversational openings and closings (Godard, 1977; Grant & Starks, 2001; Schlegoff, 1968; Schlegoff & Sacks, 1973) and medical intake interviews (Robinson, 1998). If your research question requires natural, unplanned talk across several different speakers' turns, you are likely to prefer the sequential unit of conversation for your analysis. But if you only focus on natural spontaneous talk without the requirement of different speakers' turns, you may also be interested in nonsequential units. Goffman's (1971) concept of **embeddedness** described one conversational structure nested within a larger, similar structure. Embeddedness has been used in narrative communication research to analyze anecdotes within larger stories (see Chapter 12 for more coverage of narrative research). So, depending on your research question, you may be interested in a structural aspect of talk contained entirely within one individual's speaking turn (e.g., an anecdote, account, or joke).

Furthermore, your claim of characterization can be based on nonverbal as well as verbal conversational behaviors. Robinson (1998) analyzed 86 audio- and videotaped doctor-patient consultations in a British health clinic. Robinson focused on the openings of these visits and analyzed how "doctors used eye gaze and body orientation to communicate that they are preparing but are not yet ready to deal with" patient complaints (p. 97). Robinson characterized these openings as being marked by *interactional asymmetry:* doctors, and not patients, routinely opened the conversations. It is possible that doctors nonverbally controlled the opening of these interactions because they were reproducing social power relationships, in which "doctors are powerful and patients subordinate" (p. 115). Alternatively, the interactions may have been asymmetrical because "patients are unlikely to know exactly when doctors are ready to deal with the chief complaint and thus wait for and allow doctors to solicit the chief complaint" (p. 115). Such explanations of interaction processes typically are made in order to test predictions about what interaction behaviors are likely to occur under particular circumstances. This leads us to the second type of discovery-oriented claim that can be supported by conversation and discourse analyses, explaining and predicting interaction processes.

Explanatory and Predictive Claims

Conversation analysis and ethnomethodology can go well beyond description to explain and predict what interactants are accomplishing as they talk (e.g., Craig, Tracy, & Spisak, 1986; Tracy & Tracy, 1998). If you make this kind of claim, you will attempt to explain and predict conversational structures and functions (Schiffrin, 1997). **Structure** is a recognizable pattern or way of organizing talk in which utterances are somehow interrelated (Smith, 1988). Of course, recognizing conversational structures is one important precursor for being a competent conversationalist.

But what if you want your talk to serve a particular purpose? Let's say that you want to offer a compliment, but you don't know how to do so competently in a particular context or social situation. Conversation analysis can explain why the act of complimenting must be accomplished in a particular way (e.g., *X* happens because *Y* culture prefers that behavior). Thus, explanatory and predictive claims in conversation analysis address the functions of ordinary conversation, as well as its structure.

Functional analyses of conversations ascertain what we do with or to others when we talk, what is being accomplished in our interactions (Smith, 1988). In this section, we will consider three kinds of conversational accomplishments: facework (i.e., politeness behavior), role/identity performances, and style shifting.

Facework How do you show that you are being polite, respecting others, or trying not to intrude on another's personal space? These are conversational accomplishments of politeness behavior (Brown & Levinson, 1987). Conversation and discourse analyses are good ways to study **facework,** the use of politeness behaviors to show respect for and avoid offending other people. As a case in point, Tracy and Tracy (1998) analyzed two telephone calls by citizens in a large city to a 911 emergency call center. By comparing the discourse in these two calls with the existing published literature on facework, Tracy and Tracy showed "the subtle and blatant ways in which vocal delivery, substance and type of selected speech acts, second pair parts, and selected stance indicators do face attack" (p. 225). Tracy and Tracy's (1998) study of how face attacks, the opposite of facework, are accomplished in 911 calls fits with what Pomerantz (1990) called the **claim of proposed methods**—*explaining* what is accomplished by a particular sequence of talk. A claim of proposed methods can also be used to explain or predict the outcomes of such sequences of talk.

Harvey Sacks (1972, 1984), the sociologist credited with inventing conversation analysis, began by studying problems of conversational function. He worked in a suicide prevention center in Los Angeles, where he recorded a number of telephone calls and tried to figure out how workers at the center could politely secure their caller's name without directly asking for it. In analyzing the taped telephone conversations, Sacks noticed that if workers gave their names first, the callers would reply predictably by giving their names. Knowing this, we might train hotline call-takers to give their names as one way of enacting their role as a supportive person. Explaining how to perform a role or identity is another claim of proposed methods (Pomerantz, 1990).

Role/Identity Performances Explanatory and predictive claims are made whenever conversation analysts "offer methods that interactants use in accomplishing particular actions, roles, or identities" (Pomerantz, 1990, p. 231). Explanatory conversation analytic claims are based on the work that is being performed by participants at a micro-level, *during* their ongoing interaction, rather than being based on preexisting factors like cultural rules, social roles, or random individual differences:

> Within the conversation analysis framework, one goal of research is to consider the interaction role(s) constructed by participants when producing and/or eliciting particular behavior units, rather than the predictive value of previously abstracted social roles, for producing behavior (Sigman et al., 1988, p. 167).

For example, a group of people working together on a task may or may not have a designated leader. Even if there is a designated task leader, another group member may lead at a particular conversational moment by producing certain behavioral units. Similarly, a formally designated task leader may adopt the interactional role of a group member for moments within an egalitarian group. In other words, the leader of a group interaction may be identified by his or her actions, rather than by the roles designated to group members before the interaction began. In conversation analysis, we view interaction as having its own organization, apart from the speakers' roles, personalities, or other individual characteristics. We can discover that organization *in the talk itself,* by considering the ways in which rules for turn taking, vocal intonation, negotiation of power relations, and so on are enacted by those present (Sigman et al., 1988; Zimmerman, 1988).

Style Shifting   Let's consider another type of explanatory claim about conversational functions. How and why do speakers switch their style of talking during a conversation? **Style shifting** is "a change from one style of language to another within the same conversational turn" (Scotton, 1985, p. 106). Language, dialect, and style are useful labels that connote increasingly specific social groups: Language is the broadest category; dialects represent subgroups within a language, and styles are merely rule variations within dialects (Scotton, 1985). So, style shifting is a form of codeswitching.

Scotton's (1985) study of style shifting *explained* that speakers switch styles not only due to the characteristics of the speech situation (i.e., the topic, medium, and participants), but also due to their personal goals and motivations. "A pattern of switching asserts that the speaker has at least two salient identi-

ties in the current exchange, those associated as unmarked choices with two different rights and obligations balances" (p. 113). In this way, "the speaker is boasting symbolically of the *range* of his/her identities" (p. 113; emphasis in original).

After all, language has both referential and relational functions (Scotton, 1985). The **referential function** of language is to convey information, but the **relational functions** of language are to encode a speaker's relationship to the topic being spoken about, the person(s) spoken to, and the situation. "Social meaning may be carried by the presence, absence, or varying frequency of single phonological, syntactic, or lexical choices" (Scotton, 1985, pp. 103–104).

Asking a classmate, "J'eet?" rather than "Did you eat?" carries at least two possible relational messages, if only one referential message. The relational messages carried by such an informal style may be that you and your classmate are involved in a close relationship, one in which informal slang is appropriate, and that you somehow care about your classmate's nutritional status or activities. The referential message is about eating behavior (recent presence or absence of it), whether your speaking style is informal or formal. Each style casts you and your classmate into a slightly different relationship.

As teachers, we sometimes switch from an informal to a formal style (or from a nontechnical to a technical style) of speech in order to take charge of a situation. Another functional reason for style switching might be to express solidarity with another speaker; downshifting from formal to casual style "may encode a desire for more engagement between participants and less social distance" (Scotton, 1985, p. 111). We do this in hallway interactions with our students.

Scotton (1985) *described* style shifting as a phenomenon and *explained* the reasons why speakers shift styles and who initiated the shift. She hypothesized that the attempt to shift styles in interaction functions as a nonverbal assertion that the shifter has the power to define the tenor of the discourse. If other participants accept this nonverbal assertion and also shift their speaking style, they have accepted the first speaker's definition of their relationship. This shift could happen seamlessly (i.e., without any apparent verbal or nonverbal evaluation of the shift by either participant).

All of these are examples of relational functions of language. However, conversation and discourse analytic research also may be used to advance claims that predict, as well as explain, conversational functions. Thimm, Rademacher, and Kruse (1998) predicted that the communication of technical instructions for how to use a clock radio alarm would be adapted for the age of the message target. Specifically, they hypothesized that instructions "addressed to an imagined 82-year-old partner should show different communicative patterns than instructions to an imagined 32-year-old partner" (p. 70). They further predicted that when an elderly person was described in negative terms, such as being forgetful or frequently ill, the speaker who was giving the instructions would communicate in more patronizing ways than when the elder was described only by age or was described in more positive terms, like being eager to start new things. The features of patronizing talk that were coded in Thimm et al.'s transcripts included such variables as the total number of words used, number and length of pauses, and volume. Both of these authors' predictions were supported in their experiment.

A third type of claim you can make using conversation analysis is to propose how some interaction sequence or feature works *for participants*. Pomerantz (1990) called this the **claim of proposed sequence or interactional features,** and it is a claim of interpretation. Interpretive claims are the focus of our next section.

Interpretive Claims

Conversation analysts readily acknowledge the role of their own interpretations in making sense of the talk they study, so conversation analytic claims are interpretive as well as descriptive, explanatory, and predictive (Heritage, 1985). Discourse analysts, in particular, try to understand the interpretative work being accomplished by participants in interactions (Gumperz & Field, 1995; Lemke, 1999; Watson & Goulet, 1998). One way of understanding the interpretative work that interactants are doing is to analyze their rules for constructing and interpreting messages.

Bilmes (1976) distinguished two approaches to studying communication rules: normative and interpretive. In the normative approach, people internalize standards for behavior through enculturation, and internalized norms "automatically channel behavior in such a way as to maintain social order" (p. 44). Bilmes pointed out that the normative approach depended on the assumption that "actors are able to

recognize in unison when normative rules have been breached" (p. 44). "In the interpretive approach . . . such recognition–in–unison is made problematic" (Bilmes, 1976, p. 45). The interpretive approach also depends on the presence of more or less clear rules, but in this approach, the nature of the situation and action being performed are always open to the participants' interpretation.

At times, there is no agreed–upon rule for how to act in a certain situation. Or, even though a situation has many rules, there may be no rule for dealing with one particular aspect of a situation. Sometimes, conflicting rules exist. In these cases, participants have to *work* to determine the appropriate or next action, an assertion that echoes the first major premise of ethnomethodology. Bilmes (1976) argued that such interactions involve not only interpretation by the participants, but negotiation. The work that is accomplished by interactants is not the sole property of any one individual, nor is it the mere sum of more than one person's contributions. It happens in the interaction between the parties. In this respect, the interpretive approach is consistent with a view of communication as interactional, a process by which reality is socially constructed between people, rather than a transactional exchange of meanings, or even an action-reaction sequence.

You have probably heard the saying "Rules are made to be broken." In the interpretive view of communication rules, "ideals are there to be used, not followed" (Bilmes, 1976, p. 54). Norms, rules, or values about which participants share knowledge serve as communicative resources in interaction (e.g., Miller, 2000). Thus, interpretive claims of conversation and discourse analyses frame talk as rule related, but not rule governed. This is an important distinction, whether we have rules systems that can be used to interpret behaviors, or whether rules *determine* behavior. We do not always behave according to rules, even rules we believe in and endorse as appropriate. Hence, we choose our conversational actions "on a moment-by-moment basis" (Sigman et al., 1988, p. 168). If a rule exists about how to respond to compliments appropriately, that rule constrains what we may do when we receive a compliment, and what consequences are likely to accrue for each option. Rather than try to predict what outcomes will result from particular conversational actions, interpretative conversation analysts try to uncover what options are available to a speaker, given the constraints of a particular unfolding situation and existing rules systems. We can then consider a

> range of permissible (and non-permissible) alternative behaviors, any limitations placed on participants' selections from these alternatives, given the structure and content of the earlier turn(s), and the consequences of the 'responding' speaker's selection for subsequent turns at talk (Sigman et al., 1988, p. 168).

Now that you have some idea of the range of claims you can support with conversation and discourse analysis, let's consider the evidence you will need to support those claims.

CONVERSATION AND DISCOURSE ANALYTIC DATA

Conversation and discourse analyses involve the collection, transcription, and analysis of naturally occurring communication interactions, or discourse. Usually, the interactions are captured as they occur in natural settings, either by audio- or videotaping, and they are transcribed to written or digital form by the researcher prior to beginning data analysis. Because conversation and discourse analysts "ground their analytic concerns in detailed observations instead of preformed models" (Schenkein, 1978, p. 6), the methods of collecting and transcribing interaction data in natural contexts are of great importance. These methods are the focus of our next section.

Collecting Interaction Data in Natural Contexts

Conversation analytic data are "not elicited, remembered, or invented to provide illustrations for some analytic design." Rather, they are "drawn from actual interactions occurring in their natural environments" (Schenkein, 1978, p. 2). Much of the interaction analyzed in studies published in the United States consists of conversations conducted in English by white, middle-class speakers "for whom interactional competency is not obscured by accent, impediment, or other speech distortions" (Schenkein, 1978, p. 2). Even so, a wide range of conversational circumstances have been studied, including home and work settings, situations varying from meals, to arrests, to sales, to

therapy and health care. The data for these studies has been collected over the telephone and intercom, in hidden and open microphones, on the Internet, via participant observation and field notes, and so on.

Verbatim Conversations in Natural Settings
The focus on natural settings and interactions is a key aspect of data collection for conversation and discourse analysis. "It would seem to follow that the logical place to observe . . . is an occasion where talk and conduct are not contrived, channeled, or constrained for research purposes" (Zimmerman, 1988, p. 420). If you are new to conversation analysis, you will be amazed at the lengths to which researchers go to document how talk is organized.

For instance, Goodwin (1979) analyzed over 50 hours of "videotapes of actual conversations recorded in a range of natural settings" (p. 113). His essay showed how one sentence "can be shaped and reformed in the process of its utterance" (p. 97). For Goodwin, a sentence was much more than a mere linguistic unit of analysis (those words that appeared between a capital letter at the beginning and a period or similar punctuation mark at the end). Instead, he showed how a sentence must be interpreted in the context of its situated production. To put it differently, the length and meaning of a sentence emerge as products of a dynamic process, the interaction between speaker and hearer.

Goodwin's (1979) essay focused on a sentence taken from a videotaped conversation that happened during "dinner in the home of John and Beth, attended by their friends Ann and Don" (p. 98). John stated that he gave up smoking cigarettes a week earlier. Goodwin showed how John used eye gaze to accomplish the function of "who is being addressed?" John oriented to the relationship between himself and the hearers by adding, "A week ago today, actually," as he looked at his wife, Beth. Since the dinner guests, Ann and Don, had only learned of John's decision to quit smoking when he announced it that night, John did not need to add the words "A week ago today, actually," until his gaze moved to his wife, Beth. Beth was a hearer who knew the precise timing of John's decision to give up cigarettes. In other words, John's turn at talk was mutually constructed between himself and his hearers. We hope that this example helps to show you how important the use of verbatim conversations from natural settings is to the conduct of conversation analysis. Without the videotaped dinner table talk, Goodwin may never have been able to show how sentences are constructed and understood as a joint production of situation, speaker, and hearer(s).

So verbatim conversations are crucial for conversational analysis. Of course, some conversational analysts use a combination of verbatim recordings and transcripts, along with other sources of data. Shimanoff (1985) used couples' self-report surveys in combination with transcripts of their naturally occurring talk to study emotional expressiveness in everyday marital interactions. She requested that the couples in her study tape-record "all conversations between each other for one complete day. If that equaled less than 1 hour, they were to continue to tape on subsequent days until they had recorded at least 1 hour of conversation" (p. 152).

After each couple had recorded their conversations, Shimanoff (1985) returned to their homes to administer several questionnaires. Husbands and wives each filled out questionnaires that measured the frequency with which they felt certain emotions, the frequency with which they disclosed the emotions they felt, and their perceptions of the appropriateness of such disclosures. Shimanoff compared the emotions disclosed in the couples' tape-recorded conversations with their self-reported accounts of disclosure. Her survey data provided a triangulated basis for comparing the couples' attitudes about emotional expression with their expressive behaviors. Expanding the collection of data beyond the interaction transcripts themselves is the focus of our next section.

(Con)text Sources on a Social Situation Some scholars working from the ethnomethodological tradition, particularly discourse analysts, have argued that other sources of data inform their interpretations of conversational structure and function (e.g., Buttny, 1987; Leidner, 1991; Sachweh, 1998; Sigman et al., 1988; Stokoe & Smithson, 2001; Tracy & Tracy, 1998). This is another point of overlap between ethnography, ethnomethodology, and discourse analysis (see also Chapter 11). Tracy and Tracy wrote:

> In putting these two calls in a category by themselves, we used our everyday knowledge about rudeness. . . . In analyzing the calls, we used action-implicative discourse analysis (K. Tracy, 1995), a type of discourse analysis that uses ethnographic background knowledge to aid interpretation (p. 230).

Thus, one form of additional evidence you use to warrant your inferences about a conversational transcript may be your own prior cultural knowledge of, or experience with, the kinds of conversations you are analyzing (Stokoe & Smithson, 2001). Alternatively, you may collect some additional evidence from ethnographic observations, informant interviews, surveys, and so on.

In addition to cultural knowledge gained as a member, discourse analysts also engage in participant observations prior to audio- or videotaping conversations in a given setting. Accordingly, you may want to conduct interviews with participants before or after making conversational recordings (Sigman et al., 1988). Sachweh's (1998) study of secondary baby talk in German nursing homes for the aged was based on a two-week phase of participant observation prior to beginning recording 40 hours of morning care interactions between nursing staff and residents. The purpose of the participant observation phase was to "gain insights into institutional routines and to familiarize participants with the researcher's presence" (p. 52), thus improving the researcher's chance of capturing naturally occurring, rather than contrived, interactions.

Whether your additional (con)text data come from your own cultural membership in the setting or from ethnographic research methods, those data are "always defined in relation to something else that is the primary focus of attention" (Schiffrin, 1997, p. 76). Perhaps the broadest view of context is that offered by ethnographers of communication (see Chapter 11 for more on this view). The strict **empirical language requirement** observed by some conversational scholars, that is, reliance on transcripts alone as evidence for a claim, represents the most contracted view of context for examining a social situation (ten Have, 1999). If you observe the strict empirical requirement for conversation analysis, you will not ignore context; instead you will focus on how speakers orient to and create the context in the talk itself (i.e., the evidence will be found in the transcript).

In fact, Heritage (1984) observed both that talk is a reflection of prior context as framed by each speaker and that talk creates a new context. Schiffrin (1997) called this a "dynamic and emergent view of context" (p. 79). Conversations have some features that can be generalized across situations (e.g., recognizable opening and closing behaviors), but at the same time, those features can be adapted to the constraints of particular situations. Time is one example of a situational exigency to which speakers constantly adapt. We have preferred ways of opening and closing conversations, but these may be adapted when more or less time is available for their performance. An extended appreciation and agreement sequence may be reduced to "Bye!" or a wave of the hand, to save time.

Case Studies of Communication in Everyday Social Situations   Tracy and Tracy's (1998) study of face attacks in 911 telephone calls constituted one example in which the authors used a **case study** of communicative behavior in a routine social situation. In another case study of communicative behavior, this time in a work-related context, Leidner (1991) examined flexible interpretations of gender-appropriate work in the United States. She selected two routinized interactive service jobs, for which "interactions are directly controlled by employers" through scripting, uniforms, rules about proper demeanor and appearance, and so on (p. 156). She used participant observations and interviews to study the workers on the window crew at McDonald's and life insurance agents at Combined Insurance. She noted that these jobs "are neither gender neutral nor entirely saturated with assumptions about gender" (p. 158). Perhaps because of this fact, "workers in both jobs tried to make sense of de facto job segregation by gender, interpreting their jobs as congruent with proper gender enactment" (p. 158). In other words, the workers in both jobs tried to make enough sense of the situation to *go on,* in spite of what might otherwise have been remarkable circumstances (e.g., noticing that all the window crew at a fast-food hamburger chain were females, but all the grill workers were males).

Leidner (1991) collected data by combining participant observations and interviews, which we will discuss more extensively in the next chapter. She attended training classes both for McDonald's and Combined Insurance employees. She worked in the drive-through window at McDonalds. She interviewed trainers and employees in both companies. The workers in both companies were aware that Leidner was there as a researcher.

Within her research report, Leidner presented an abbreviated case study for each organization. The two case studies contained descriptions of the social situations at these two companies, focusing in each case on the standardized roles (i.e., scripts, uniforms, rules) proscribed for workers. The McDonald's window crew were all women, who "took the division of labor

by gender for granted and did not seem to feel any need to account for it" (p. 163). The life insurance agents were men, and even though some aspects of their jobs called for feminine qualities, they reinterpreted or deemphasized those feminine aspects of the job. For example, the men were expected to behave as though congenial and eager to please, which might contradict the unemotional demeanor expected of males in many settings. Normally, ingratiating behavior would likely be associated with a feminine interaction style or low-power behavior. However,

> Combined Insurance's trainers and agents interpreted the agent's job as demanding manly attributes. They assigned a heroic character to the job, framing interactions with customers as contests of will. To succeed, they emphasized, required determination, aggressiveness, persistence, and stoicism. These claims were accurate, but qualities in which women excel, including sensitivity to nuance and verbal dexterity, were also important for success (Leidner, 1991, p. 166).

After comparing these two case studies of gender role construction in interactive service jobs, Leidner drew three conclusions: First, work seen in one setting as *natural* and *appropriate* for women (McDonald's window crew) was seen in another setting as improbable or even impossible for women (Combined Insurance's sales agents). Second, Leidner noted that the actual features of the job did not themselves determine whether the work would be defined as more appropriate for men or women: "Rather, these features are communicative resources for interpretation that can be drawn on by workers, their superiors, and other audiences" (Leidner, 1991, p. 174). Finally, the interpretation of gender appropriateness in both these organizations was "made to seem natural—an expression of the essential natures of women and men" (p. 174). The employees took the presence of *all women* or *all men* in their jobs as *evidence* of the gender appropriateness of the job. They worked to find reasons why that interpretation made sense. A critical interpretation of these data might be to teach the workers to recognize the ways that such sense-making efforts helped them endorse and participate in their own oppression (see Chapter 13, "Critical Studies," for more on such evaluative and reformist research claims, and Baxter, 2002, for a sample critical DA study).

Leidner's (1991) case study of gender roles in these two industries showed the difficulty of categorizing some research studies as clearly fitting one research methodology. Her study best fits our description of ethnomethodology, how employees make enough sense of the gender segregation in their jobs to keep going on, to "interpret their jobs as congruent with proper gender enactment" (p. 159). Leidner's study does not fit the strict empirical language requirement for conversation analysis, however. Although her participant observations did capture spontaneous talk among the workers, she did not analyze turn-by-turn talk using transcripts. Rather, she used field notes and interview data to draw her macro-level conclusions about gender role constructions in the two case studies.

As a footnote to this section on collecting conversational data, we acknowledge that some discourse analysts analyze communicative interactions that do not come from naturally occurring conversations. Specifically, **constructed conversation samples,** fictional interactions written by the researcher (or taken from a film, novel, etc.), and **laboratory conversation samples,** interactions induced for the purpose of conducting research, in a setting controlled by the researcher, have been the source of some discourse analytic research (McLaughlin, 1984). If the focus of analysis is across multiple speakers' turns at talk, then the work still fits our definition of conversation analysis. But, ultimately, inferences about the structure and function of conversational interactions must be supported by rigorous analysis of ordinary talk, or data that is "drawn from the domain of naturally occurring talk and action" (Zimmerman, 1988, p. 420).

Transcribing Interaction Data

In order to perform the close, systematic analysis of talk required for conversation analysis, you will have to convert tape-recorded conversations into digital or print representations. The process of converting audio- or videotaped interactions into digital or print form is called **transcription.** "Transcript preparation requires extraordinarily close attention to the production details of the talk under study" (Schenkein, 1978, p. 3). Sigman et al. (1988) divided the process of collecting and transcribing interactions into four discrete tasks: source selection, recording techniques, notation, and formatting.

Source Selection Although conversation research has been performed on various types of interaction data, the clear preference for most conversation analysts is to use spontaneously generated talk from everyday settings (Sigman et al., 1988). Of course, conversational studies are not limited to face-to-face conversations; spontaneously generated talk in chat rooms, over the telephone, and other mediated channels also provide a ready source for conversation analysis. Hopper (1992) published an entire book entitled *Telephone Conversation.* The conversational source you select will greatly influence your means of capturing those data on audio- or videotape, or in digital form.

Recording Techniques Traditionally, audiotaping has been used to capture conversations for analysis. This is probably still the easiest and most practical method of recording natural, offline conversations. However, McLaughlin (1984) and others have noted that nonverbal behaviors are important in conversational structure and function, along with verbal and paraverbal behaviors. Videotaping can capture the nonverbal aspects of conversation and may be preferable, depending on your research question (Manusov & Trees, 2002).

Despite these advantages, videotaping is complicated by intricacies of lighting, camera angles, and so on. It is also more expensive, less readily accessible to most researchers, and in most settings, it is more intrusive than audiotape recording. It is very likely that videotaping will compromise the naturalness of the conversational data you collect, unless the setting is one in which videotaping is already routine prior to your study. Otherwise, the nature of video cameras and recording equipment can be very intrusive (Wiemann, 1981).

Audio tape recorders typically are smaller and less intrusive, yet still produce excellent sound quality, which enhances their fit with the requirement of naturalness in conversational data acquisition. Of course, recent increases in video surveillance in public locations in the United States—along with many people's increasing familiarity and ease with video cameras, and innovations in ever-smaller and more powerful video cameras—are rapidly changing the potential of videotaped interaction observations in social settings.

Conventions for Notating Transcripts Transcripts are the translated spoken words and sounds in written form, although nowadays, written form typically means digital form. "Transcription is observation: the

Table 10.1   Standard Notation Conventions for Conversational Transcription

Symbol	Name	Function
[ ]	Brackets	Beginning or ending of overlapping utterances
=	Equal sign	Join together continuous utterances without overlap
(1.3)	Timed pause	Intervals within or between speaker's utterances, in tenths of seconds
(.)	Micropause	Brief pause of less than .2 second
:::	Colon(s)	Prior sound, syllable, or word is prolonged or stretched; more colons indicate longer stretching
.	Period	Falling vocal pitch or intonation. Punctuation marks in a transcript *do not* indicate the usual grammatical functions (e.g., end of sentence).
?	Question mark	Rising intonation or inflection
-	Hyphen	Halting, abrupt cutoff of sound, syllable, or word
cold	Italics	Vocal stress or emphasis (underlining may be used)
OKAY	CAPS	Extreme loudness compared with surrounding talk
hhh	H's	Audible outbreaths, possible laughter. More h's mean a longer aspiration.
((noise))	Scene details	Transcriber's comments (e.g., gestures, coughing)
( )	Parentheses	Empty parentheses indicate indecipherable message. Words in parentheses are those the transcriber isn't sure of.
pt	Lip smack	Often preceding an inbreath
hah heh	Laugh	Laughter is noted as open (hah) or closed (heh or hoh).
//	Double slash	Beginning of overlapping talk

Note. Selected from Jefferson's conventions as published by Atkinson & Heritage (1984). Reprinted with the permission of Cambridge University Press.

noticing and recording of events of talk that might otherwise elude analytic attention" (Zimmerman, 1988, p. 413). Table 10.1 shows some of the standard conventions for notating conversational features developed by speech act theorist Gail Jefferson. Of course, these conventions are for audiotaped conversations. You will need additional conventions for transcribing the nonverbal aspects of videotaped interactions (for help, see Goodwin, 1981; Gumperz & Field, 1995; Manusov & Trees, 2002; and Wiemann, 1981).

One big issue for the conversation analyst is time. It takes forever to transcribe tape-recorded conversations. In fact, most introductory students of conversation analysis are shocked at how slow and tedious the work of transcribing conversation is. Hiring someone more experienced than you to transcribe your taped conversations may be tempting. However, West and Zimmerman (1983) estimated that it takes an experienced transcriber 8 to 10 hours to transcribe 1 hour of audiotape, so the required time would be even more for videotape. Another study estimated a 30:1 ratio for transcription to tape time (Patterson, Neupauer, Burant, Koehn, & Reed, 1996). Given either of these estimates, paid transcription for a 10-minute conversation, at a rate of about $25 per hour, will be expensive!

Perhaps more importantly, many of your initial ideas about what is going on in a segment of interaction will probably occur during transcription (Sigman et al., 1988). As you listen to the tape repeatedly, and type out the words and paraverbal behaviors of the speakers, you will begin to make some sense of the data. In the course of conducting a conversation analytic study, you will read your transcripts and listen to the tapes many, many times (Patterson et al., 1996; Sigman et al., 1988). Staying close to your data is advisable no matter what paradigm your research fits into and no matter what methodological choices you have made about collecting and analyzing communicative data.

The detail level you elect to include in your conversation transcript will depend on two issues: your research question and your anticipated uses of the data. First, consider your research question. What level of detail will you need to answer your question satisfactorily? Will the words by themselves be enough, or will you need to include paraverbal details like pause length, interruptions, or overlapping segments of talk (i.e., talk-overs)? Second, consider the uses to which you anticipate putting your data. If you are the only person who will ever use these data, and only for this one study, you can transcribe just as much detail as your current research question demands.

But if you think you will be conducting future conversation analytic studies someday, or if you would like to share your conversational data with other researchers, then you may want to anticipate those needs in your current transcription. For example, you may transcribe paraverbal details, even though they are not the focus of your current research question, so that your transcripts can be used to answer other research questions in the future. Another option is to keep your tapes and enter your discourse into a computer software program, so that you can revise your transcripts later according to your needs. You probably will not know in advance just how much transcription detail you are going to need, so it's a good idea to get advice from a more experienced colleague on this issue, at least for your first conversational study.

The standard notation conventions for transcribing natural conversations aim to provide vocalic details of emphasis, intonation, and so on, in addition to the exact words of the speakers (see Table 10.1). Never attempt to fix participants' speech, "the practice of rendering what was said into 'proper' language" (Sigman et al., 1988, p. 175). Whether you consider yourself to be discovering naturally existing conversational structure or function, or an interpretive researcher who wants to privilege participants' views, you need to protect the integrity of the text precisely as it was spoken by the interactants. Patterson et al. (1996) found that reliable transcription of verbal content was easier to achieve than paraverbal content (except pause length). To transcribe pause length, try using a stopwatch to time the pause at least three times, then record the average time on your transcript.

Formatting Transcripts The page layout you use in transcription should ease the tasks of reading your transcript and locating information within the transcript. The way you visually represent verbal and nonverbal interactions on a page or screen is important to consider because "transcription is a selective process reflecting theoretical goals and definitions" (Ochs, 1979, p. 44). One artifact of page layout is that how you format your transcript will influence what your readers notice and interpret about an interaction.

If you place Speaker C's turn at talk just below Speaker G's turn at talk, readers are likely to view those two utterances as contingent upon one another, or at least sequential, which may not have been the case. Ochs pointed out that certain formats encourage

readers to link adjacent utterances, and she argued that such a move would likely be more appropriate when transcribing adult western speech than when transcribing the speech of language-acquiring children.

So as transcript readers analyzing interactions, we are likely see adjacent utterances as related to one another. We also make meaning of the way pages are spatially organized. "As members of a culture, we bring into the transcription process a biased spatial organization" (Ochs, 1979, p. 45). In the English language, we bring a top-to-bottom bias and a left-to-right bias, so that things at the top left are attended to first.

Given these cautions about formatting pages and cultural biases, it is nonetheless common practice in this country to format transcripts so that turns at talk follow one another in sequence, with notation for overlaps, interruptions, and the like. It is also standard practice to number each line of a transcript (i.e., each line on a page), so that the location of an utterance in the total transcript can be shown. A brief sample of transcribed talk is shown in Exhibit 10.2.

Determining the Unit of Analysis

The first and perhaps most difficult step in analyzing conversational data, once you have a transcript of conversation with which to work, is determining the unit of analysis. For conversation analysts, units of analysis are the "behavioral building blocks of talk" (Sigman et al., 1988, p. 165). Many different units of talk have been identified and studied, including utterances, turns, acts, moves, stories, lists, descriptions, and so on. Some contexts, like interviews or conversations, can themselves be considered units of analysis (Schiffrin, 1997). For example, Mandelbaum (1987) published a conversation analytic study of couple's shared stories, a relatively large unit of analysis compared to Sacks et al.'s (1974) study of turn taking in conversations. Of course, your unit of analysis will depend on your research question.

Until you know your exact research question, though, one good place to begin determining your unit of analysis is to decide whether the units you wish to study are larger or smaller than one sentence. The units typically studied in conversation analysis vary from a single lexical unit (e.g., laughter), to a sentence, a single speaker's turn at talk, or sequential chains across two or more speakers' turns (Sigman et al., 1988).

The function and/or structure of talk you want to know about will also help you decide what unit of

---

EXHIBIT 10.2 Transcription Sample

The following transcription represents 56 seconds of talk, taken from an interview Merrigan conducted with three first-year college students in 1989. The two students represented here were first introduced to each other in a similar interview, two weeks earlier.

I = Interviewer   M = Male   F = Female

01 **I:** (softly) hh okay (.) were there OTHER things that you expected that werrrepretty

02 much the way (softly) you thought they would be?

03 **M:** No cheating (sound of 7-8 soft taps)

04 **I:** // (on 6th tap) hmm mmm] (laughing)

05 **M:** // I mean]uh in HIGHschool I-ya-know-I I indulged in a little (.) trade paper paper

06 trade. Sometimes (softly) ya know and uh (small click) mean it wasn't just because in

07 highschool you almost got into (.) set of uh ((trailing off)) mindset that-tuh ((I)) mean

08 you cheat so you make it easier. Not because you don't know it (.4) you just cheat so

09 you can

10 **I:** //-hhh] (interrupting over "can") whatEVER would be // handy]

11 **M:** //get it done.] Yeah //I mean-]

12 **F:** //Ittt's] alright // (laughter)]

13 **M:** //I mean]

14 **F:** that (still laughing) was, that was my (no longer laughing) whole senior year //

15 (inaudible)]

16 **M:** //and] you just cheat so you can get it over with quickly (softly) end the test. You

17 just get it over with quickly because you //don't really feel like doing] it.

18 **F:** //that's okay (inaudible)]

19 **I:** yeah

20 **M:** And uh (.) pt here=

21 **F:** =I thought I was the only // (laughter) one so I forgot or something

22 **I:** (laughter)

23 **F:** Gee

24 **M:** Here, uh

25 **F:** (laughter bubbling in over M, above)

26 **M:** Here it's, you know it's different. To mean you don't (.2) you wanna do ((th))is

27 yourself and uh

28 **I:** (very softly) yeah

29 **M:** And also nobody else wants to give you their answers.

Note. The number of zeroes anticipates the number of lines in a transcript. This numbering will accommodate up to 99 lines of talk. From a study conducted by Staton, Johnson, & Jorgensen-Earp (1995). Printed here for the first time, and used by permission.

---

analysis to examine in your transcripts. Consistent with the interpretive paradigm, discourse analysts who view rules about appropriate behavior in particular contexts or cultures as *constraining,* rather than *determining,* behavior may be unable to specify their units prior to analysis. Rather, you must study the tapes and transcripts and examine "the sequential placement and consequences of each utterance in its turn and across turns" (Sigman et al., 1988, p. 172). A single utterance may serve more than one function, too. Because interpretive analyses are almost always performed in iterations (i.e., repeated sequences or cycles of action), it is okay to make an initial decision, and then revise your unit of analysis as you work through the transcription and analytic processes.

Once you know what your unit of analysis is, you may find that you want to examine particular types of utterances across many conversations or transcripts. If you are interested in the apology-accept/decline adja-

cency pair, for example, you may have some instances of apologies on tape or in transcript form. You may want to broaden your database by examining conversational materials available from another source, such as transcripts you collected in a previous study, or transcripts collected by another researcher working on apologies. The University of Texas at Austin has a library of conversational tapes and transcripts (visit www.utexas.edu/depts/specom/). Once you have accrued an adequate sample of your selected conversational units, you are ready to interpret their structure and/or function(s).

Discovering the Structure and Function of Conversational Units

Claims about the functional relationships among units of analysis in conversation are interpretive claims because each speaker's next turn at talk is used as an analytic resource for making sense of the prior turn (ten

Have, 1999). It is impossible for you to describe the nature of conversational units (i.e., utterances, sentences, action chains), or to explain the relationships among those units, without making interpretations about what sense your participants are making and how they display that sense in their ongoing interactions.

In doing conversation analysis, we not only claim that some aspect of conversation might be viewed in a certain way, but that it actually is so interpreted by the interactants who construct and make sense of the talk (Sigman et al., 1988; Lawrence, 1999). For most conversational researchers, such a claim is substantiated in the transcript alone, à la the strict empirical language requirement (Sigman et al., 1988; ten Have, 1999).

The placement of talk in a sequence of interaction is one example of the type of evidence that might be selected from a transcript to support an interpretation of function. For instance, saying, "Well, I need to go now," signals the imminent "Buh-bye," that ends a telephone conversation. But placement of talk is not the only type of evidence that may be used to support a claim of interpretive function. Empirical conversation analyses may also use nonspoken actions that are available in the audio- or videotapes and transcripts to resolve a problem of hearing and interpretation in the interaction. For example, in response to one interactant's words, "This dish needs more salt," another interactant passes the salt shaker. The second interactant's nonspoken action, passing the salt, is interpreted as a response to the first speaker's functional request.

Another way to interpret the function of a conversational unit is to consider the consequences of an utterance in an ongoing interaction. When a mother clears her throat during her teenager's account of why he arrived home after curfew, followed by the son's words, "No! Really!" then the throat clearing may be interpreted as an expression of doubt on the mother's part. The son's response provides a clue as to the meaning of the throat clearing, at least from the son's perspective.

The son's "No! Really!" utterance in this hypothetical example may be regarded as repair work. Goffman (1971) used the term **repair work** for actions that interlocutors take to fix disruptions in interaction, either because a speaker feels he or she has violated a norm, or is being accused of such a violation by someone else in the conversation. The mother's throat clearing might be seen by the son as a signal that he has violated a norm (e.g., being truthful), which prompts the son to engage in repair work. Just as we are doing in this example, conversational scholars use their "knowledge of

the social situation, the participants' history of shared experiences, and manifest goals of the interaction in order to arrive at the conversational uses of particular linguistic forms" (Sigman et al., 1988, p. 178).

Shared subtopics of conversation may indicate that one conversational partner comprehends what the other is saying, just as a lack of shared subtopics may indicate lack of comprehension, cooperation, or both. Overt statements of difficulty (e.g., "I don't get that"), requests for repair ("Could you repeat that?"), and overt requests for verification ("Did you say you caught *ten* fish?") provide even stronger evidence of failed comprehension. Back-channeled responses (e.g., "uhm-hmm") provide very weak evidence of comprehension.

Of course, consistent with the philosophy of the interpretive paradigm that you read about in Part I, discourse analysts value subjectivity and believe there are multiple plausible interpretations for any one utterance, whereas a conversation analyst will usually try to demonstrate the most plausible order that can be supported by the transcript itself, which might include talk that serves more than one purpose simultaneously. "Thus, conversation analysts consider that numerous functions can be served by interactants' behavior and multiple interpretations by participants of the same behavior are possible" (Sigman et al., 1988, p. 168). In terms of interaction sequences, one speaker cannot control a sequence. We can initiate what we think is the first part of a sequence, but our interactional partner's response will have as much to do with the organization of subsequent talk as will our original utterance. Geri may want to compliment Carole on her new haircut:

> Geri: "Hey, Carole. Did you get your hair cut? It looks terrific!"
>
> Carole: "Are you saying my hair looked terrible before?"

Geri may think she is giving Carole a compliment, but the interaction can take the direction of a face-threatening incident or even an argument. It is likely that some sort of repair sequence needs to ensue with Geri's next turn at talk.

Analytic Induction

One important way that conversation and discourse analysts support their claims is to argue from example. Jackson's (1986) description of analytic induction, which we presented in Chapter 4, showed how conversational researchers sometimes proceed to analyze messages in order to support claims of description, explanation and prediction, and interpretation. Arguing from examples should be systematic and careful work (Cappella, 1990; Heritage, 1984; ten Have, 1999). To help make it so, conversation analysts sometimes work cooperatively in data sessions, where they listen to audiotapes or watch videotapes together (e.g., scholars at the University of Texas, Austin, hold these sessions weekly). They act as a team to elaborate patterns they see in the data, brainstorm potential interpretations, and sometimes perform the conversations as a resource for understanding what participants are doing in their talk (Jarmon, 1996). Data sessions are terrific training grounds for conversation analysts (ten Have, 1999). The National Communication Association's annual meeting usually includes at least one such session.

In data sessions or working alone, you not only find and present examples from the data that support your claims, but you also learn to actively seek out counterexamples. Counterexamples are instances of data that do not fit your claim and that might support different, even competing claims (see Chapter 11 for more discussion of negative case analysis). It follows that using counterexamples helps to assure that your examples really do support your claim. So let's now consider the warrants for conversation and discourse analysis.

CONVERSATION AND DISCOURSE ANALYTIC WARRANTS

In conversation analysis, we assume that every speaker's turn at talk represents an orderly response to prior turns (ten Have, 1999). So we use the next-turn process to demonstrate that a specific interpretation of one speaker's turn at talk makes sense, given what happened in the next speaker's turn. Ideally, of course, you will present a number of cases that reveal a regular pattern of conversational structure or function. In this way, the worth of your interpretations will be empirically demonstrated in the recorded interactions and their transcriptions (Sigman et al., 1988; ten Have, 1999).

Conversation and discourse analyses and ethnomethodological research are evaluated using war-

rants from both the discovery and interpretive paradigms, as outlined in Chapter 4. The first two warrants we develop in this section, transcription veracity and detail level, clearly reflect discovery paradigm assumptions and values, especially the value of precision. The latter two warrants for conversation and discourse analyses, sample naturalness and additional (con)text sources of data, rely more on the assumptions and values of the interpretive paradigm. Thus, as we have said before, these methods serve as a bridge from discovery to interpretive communication research.

Given the interpretive values of subjectivity and rich description, and the processes of triangulation, conversational researchers have various ways of demonstrating their credibility as researchers, the plausibility of their interpretations, and the transferability of their findings. Conversational researchers, like ethnographers, must hone their skills at observing details very closely, describing what they observe, and systematically making sense of a myriad of detailed observations (Hutchby & Wooffitt, 1998). So you may want to read the next chapter in conjunction with the rest of this chapter because we will build on the concepts introduced here in the warrants section of that chapter.

But for now, we will begin with warranting strategies that are more particular to conversation and discourse analysis, including the means of demonstrating transcription veracity and detail level, the degree to which interactions being studied are naturally occurring, and the use of additional data sources to ensure plausible interpretations.

Transcription Veracity

Transcription veracity refers to the degree of correspondence between the words typed on a page (or in a computer file) and those recorded on a segment of audio- or videotape. Veracity is typically judged as a matter of agreement. If two people write down the same words after listening to one bit of taped interaction, the transcript is considered to have high veracity.

In fact, Patterson and colleagues (1996) conducted an experiment designed to measure **intertranscriber reliability**. Recall that reliability means consistency in measurement; so, intertranscriber reliability means that two or more people accomplish consistent transcription of conversation into a written record. Patterson et al. (1996) wondered whether written transcripts could be reliably produced by college students, who had only about one-half hour's training, and who used their own familiar recording and word-processing equipment. Based on their results, Patterson et al. (1996) concluded that "with a minimum of training, multiple independent transcribers are capable of producing similar transcripts from the same source tape" (p. 87). And even though notation *agreement* does not guarantee the *accuracy* of transcription, Patterson et al. wrote, "It does provide corroboration and a greater likelihood of accuracy" (p. 81).

Of course, the agreement rates achieved in Patterson et al.'s study differed depending on the type of communication being notated. The highest level of agreement among the college student transcribers (94%) was for verbal content. Agreement rates were slightly lower for notating speakers' areas of overlapping talk (86%), and for either rising or falling intonations (82%). The lowest agreement rate (49%) was when the students attempted to transcribe pauses in interaction. Interestingly, most of the disagreements Patterson et al. (1996) discovered occurred because one transcriber failed to notate something that other transcribers did notate (i.e., error by omission, rather than by misinterpretation).

Most of the published conversation analytic studies you read will not use multiple people to transcribe a tape. Typically, conversation analysts either transcribe their own tapes or hire a person to transcribe their tapes. So most published conversation analytic studies do not assess or report intertranscriber reliability. Nonetheless, based on Patterson et al.'s (1996) results, it may be a good idea to use more than one transcriber and check the rate of agreement between two or more notations of a tape, especially when your research question implicates paraverbal interaction features, like pause length.

Detail Level

For conversation and discourse analysis, both the tape-recorded interactions and the written transcripts constitute data sources (Patterson et al., 1996; Sigman et al., 1988). "It is, after all, because we can review the recordings and study the transcripts endlessly that we come to see the details of conversational organization hidden by real time and ordinary sensibilities" (Schenkein, 1978, p. 3). One warrant for the worth of a researcher's argument is demonstrating that you have recorded and transcribed the appropriate level of detail

to fit your research question. If your claim is an explanation of interruption behavior in a cross-cultural context, you will need to demonstrate that your transcription of the presence of and length of pauses is sufficiently detailed and accurate before you start interpreting the function of particular instances of overlapping talk in the transcript. You may also want to ensure that those who produce the written transcripts from audio- or videotapes are members of the culture being studied. (See our discussion of degree of membership in Chapters 4 and 11 for more on this issue.)

Sample Naturalness

When considering any given study, nearly endless philosophical arguments may be raised about whether a particular interaction was natural, or about how natural was a certain sample of conversational behavior. We do not want to raise such philosophical abstractions here. Instead, we hope to point out a basic, albeit nonspecific, principle. The samples you select for conversation and discourse analyses should, insofar as possible, represent talk *as it would have occurred* if no research project were being conducted. To the extent that talk is contrived or influenced by your presence as a researcher, sample naturalness will be threatened. Without sample naturalness, all claims of describing, explaining and predicting, or interpreting ordinary conversational behavior and sense making will be suspect.

Additional (Con)text Sources

As we have stressed repeatedly, the empirical language requirement for conversation analysis dictates reliance only on the information available in a transcript and a recording of talk to make interpretations about the data (Sigman et al., 1988; ten Have, 1999). But even before inspecting a transcript for the first time, perhaps while transcribing interaction from audio- or videotape to digital form, you may have a hunch about what is noteworthy in the interaction (Hutchby & Wooffitt, 1998). For example, you may suspect that a particular structural sequence or function of interest to you is displayed in the talk:

> For those following within the ethnomethodological tradition, the researcher's background knowledge regarding talk cannot be eliminated; it constitutes an indispensable methodological tool. . . . Conversation researchers should be asked to

defend the applicability of their cultural understandings to the particular transcripts and recorded events under study. If the analyst advances a member-of-the-culture warrant for his/her ability to do conversation analysis—i.e., to provide meaningful organization for the verbal data—then he/she should also demonstrate that the talk being investigated was in fact produced by members of the same culture for which the analyst claims membership and cultural awareness (Sigman et al., 1988, p. 183).

If you want to analyze the discourse of fraternity and sorority members from a cultural insider's perspective, you should be prepared to demonstrate both that you are a member of that culture yourself, and that the talk you analyze was produced by members of that culture. If you hope to interpret the structure or function of these members' turns at talk, you will need to be able to recognize what activities they are engaging in when they interact (Hutchby & Wooffitt, 1998).

Some conversation and discourse analysts do not restrict themselves to the transcript and recording evidence in order to warrant their claims, however. Instead, these researchers collect additional sources of data, beyond the interaction itself. Sigman et al. (1988) listed three additional sources of data for conversation and discourse analyses: (1) background knowledge of the event from prior observations of events similar to the one now under analysis; (2) informant interviews that address the goals and organization of particular conversation events; and (3) subjects' reactions to and interpretations of the tape-recorded and transcribed interactions. These data sources are likely to be used in conjunction with your own analysis of the transcripts and recordings, not to confirm, but rather to "provide weight in favor or against particular interpretations" (Sigman et al., 1988, p. 184). Interpretive researchers call this work *building a case* for a particular interpretation (Jackson, 1986; Sigman et al., 1988).

As a case in point, Bastien and Hostager (1992) used a combination of participant observations, interviews, and transcript analysis to examine how jazz musicians cooperatively accomplished the organization of an improvisational concert performance. Their claim was one of communicative function. How is the structure of an improvised jazz performance organized by the performers' verbal and nonverbal discourse?

Briefly, Bastien and Hostager (1992) first observed and videotaped a performance. Then they analyzed the videotape and transcribed the spoken and nonspoken actions of all the participants. They interviewed one participant while watching the videotape and elicited a blow-by-blow description of all the turns in the interaction. Using their observations, the videotape, the transcript of the concert, and the transcript of the interview, they interpreted how these jazz musicians accomplished organizing. Bastien and Hostager's (1992) study was similar to Eisenberg's (1990) examination of how basketball players organize improvisational "pick-up" games. In both studies, the research question might be phrased this way: "How do strangers, who know the rules for a social situation, but do not know each other, or have assigned roles in their performance of the situation, structure their interactions in ways that accomplish sense making?"

You may use informant data for more than one specific purpose in doing discourse or conversation analysis. You might ask your participants to (1) assist in the segmentation of discourse into appropriate units of analysis; (2) provide explanations and interpretations of their behavior; (3) augment the number and type of cases recorded by the investigator; and (4) validate, qualify, or refute the researcher's own interpretations (Sigman, 1985, p. 120).

However, you will need to be cautious about some potential problems with informant data (Sigman et al., 1988; Stokoe & Smithson, 2001). The perspective offered in an interview may not be exactly the perspective participants actually employ when they are engaged in interaction, since interviews often allow more time for reflection, or encourage face-saving interpretations of the interviewee's interactional competence. It is also likely that your interview questions will structure what the participant reveals to you about a situation's organization or an utterance's function (i.e., demand characteristics). Questions invite answers, and interview data are always subject to the limitations of questions asked and unasked by the researcher.

TECHNOLOGY AND CONVERSATION/DISCOURSE ANALYSIS

In Chapters 5 through 9, we outlined how technological changes are impacting each research method, both the claims that are being made about communication as it is impacted by technology, and the role of digital technology in conducting research. However, it is more challenging to find published conversation analyses of digitally mediated conversations, although Lemke (1999) examined discourse *about* Web site development.

Stewart, Shields, and Sen (1998) used a combination of content and discourse analysis with the transcripts of listserv interactions among 22 college students as their data. Their critical finding was that, despite claims of gender and cultural equality in online discussions, this group reproduced the existing social structure in their online discourse: Men sent longer and more messages then women, Whites were more willing to adopt the technology than other group members, and so on.

It may be that the preference for "naturally occurring conversations" has so far meant primarily face-to-face interactions to conversation analysts. However, few would deny that chat rooms, discussion groups, and instant messaging provide ready instances of conversations occurring online all the time, without researcher intervention (Mabrito, 1995). "Naturally occurring" means the talk is not induced for research purposes, so online talk certainly is natural, in that sense. Online interactions also provide conveniently available data sources in already-digitized form; of course, there are some serious ethical implications regarding informed consent (Lindlof & Schatzer, 1998).

Perhaps the more relevant impact of computer technology for conversation analysts relates to the archiving and sharing of conversational databases, and the innovations in equipment for capturing and transcribing data. For example, digital video cameras provide split-second time records of interactional features such as pause length, and some computerized cameras will even produce transcripts of the verbal interaction content. This greatly reduces the time required for transcription, if you are willing to live with the detail level that machine produces.

One more example here will show the combined value of videotape technology and conversation analysis: Couchman (1995) used videotaped interactions and conversational analysis to train nurses who were working with people with learning disabilities. The combination of videotaped interactions with a micro-level focus on interaction features helped nurses learn to provide appropriate nonverbal support to people with learning disabilities and to distinguish between communication behaviors that were discriminatory, rather than accommodating.

SUMMARY

In this chapter, we discussed the descriptive, explanatory and predictive, and interpretive claims that typically are supported by the methods of conversation and discourse analyses. We began the chapter by outlining how these methods emerged from ethnomethodology, a method of studying ordinary people's day-to-day ways of making sense of situations. Even though some ethnomethodologists, conversation analysts, and discourse analysts would differentiate these methods on the basis of the claims each can support, the preferred data sources, or the strict empiricist language requirement, we argue that these methods complement one another and can be used together to good effect.

After reading this chapter, you should have a good understanding of how to collect interaction data in natural contexts, transcribe that data, determine the unit you wish to analyze, and interpret the structure and/or function of those conversational units. Finally, you should be able to apply the warrants discussed in this chapter, including transcription veracity and detail level, sample naturalness, and con(text) sources used to build a case for plausible interpretations, either to insure the worth of your own conversation or discourse analysis, or to evaluate the worth of published studies using these methods.

KEY TERMS

Accounts	Case studies	Codeswitching
Action chains	Claim of characterization	Contextuality
Adjacency pairs	Claim of proposed methods	Constructed conversation samples
Breaching	Claim of proposed sequence	Embeddedness

Empirical language requirement	Laboratory conversation samples	Style shifting
Et cetera clause	Referential function of language	Transcription
Ethnomethodology	Relational functions of language	Transcription veracity
Facework	Repair work	Transcripts
First pair part	Second pair part	Units of analysis
Intertranscriber reliability	Structure	

DISCUSSION QUESTIONS

1. How important is it to use "naturally occurring" conversation in conducting conversation analysis (i.e., as opposed to constructed conversation samples and/or laboratory conversation samples)? What potential benefits can you identify of using naturally occurring conversations and avoiding the use of other sources of interactive data? What limitations?

2. Do you agree or disagree with the *empirical language requirement* of conversation analysis (i.e., the idea that claims can be supported by the text alone, without relying on the researcher's cultural knowl-edge of the situation, observations, interviews with the interactants, or other context sources of data)? What are some of the pros and cons of permitting additional context sources of data in discourse analysis?

3. What are the ethical implications of studying people's ordinary, natural conversations? Identify at least two ethical dilemmas that might arise if you were conducting a conversation or discourse analytic study, and identify what you might do to resolve those dilemmas. Be sure to consider how your resolution would affect the warrants for your study.

"TRY IT!" ACTIVITIES

1. Tape-record a brief conversation (i.e., 5 minutes or less) from your daily interactions. Be sure you get permission from everyone involved in the interaction, either before or after the recording takes place. Transcribe your conversation using the conventions developed by Jefferson and outlined in Table 10.1. You might work with a small group of students from your research methods class so that each person transcribes 1 minute of the interaction. What did you learn from this activity?

2. Have another student in your class transcribe the same conversation (or portion of a conversation) that you transcribed in the previous activity. Compare your written transcripts. What differences and similarities do you notice? How would you evaluate your own transcription veracity?

3. Using the transcripts you and your classmates developed in Activity 1, determine one unit of analysis that could be applied to your conversational database (i.e., all your transcribed conversations). Code all the transcripts for that unit of analysis. Based on your work so far, what tentative hypotheses can you develop about the structure and function of those conversational units in your database?

11

Ethnographic Research

ABSTRACT

In this chapter, you will learn how to do ethnographic studies of communication, beginning with research claims of description, interpretation, evaluation, and reform. We will consider the sources of ethnographic data, procedures for field data collection, and strategies for data analysis. Finally, we will develop further the warrants of the interpretive paradigm, as those are applied in ethnographic research arguments, including the values of subjectivity and rich description, issues of researcher credibility, plausible interpretations, and transferability of findings.

OUTLINE

Ethnography does not have one universal definition, perhaps because there are many forms of ethnographic research (Stewart, 1998). In general, ethnography is a method for grasping "the native's point of view" (Malinowski, 1922, p. 25); "it is the trademark of cultural anthropology" (Schwartzman, 1993). **Ethnography of speaking** is a specific method for describing and explaining culturally distinct communicative patterns and practices using Dell Hymes's (1962) SPEAKING acronym (described later in this chapter) as a theoretic framework. In practice, ethnography of speaking is often associated with Philipsen (1975, 1976, 1989, 1992) and his colleagues from the University of Washington. Ethnography, ethnography of speaking, and **ethnography of communication,** the focus on speech communities, are similar to, but not exactly the same as, grounded theory (Glaser & Strauss, 1967; Strauss & Corbin, 1998) and naturalistic inquiry (Frey, 1994b; Frey, Botan, & Kreps, 2000; Lincoln & Guba, 1985). Let's first distinguish each of those terms and see how they relate to ethnography.

Grounded theory is a methodology that is intended to be used to develop theories by systematically gathering and analyzing field data. Rather than a theorist imagining how a communicative process *might* work in practice, grounded theory "evolves during actual research, and it does this through continuous interplay between analysis and data collection" (Strauss & Corbin, 1998, p. 158). For example, Stamp (1999) examined 288 interpersonal communication research studies published in *Human Communication Research* between 1974 and 1999 and used constant comparison to place these articles into a 17-part category system (e.g., cognition, nonverbal communication, compliance gaining, etc.). By examining the categories in relationship to one another, Stamp developed an overall theory, or model, of interpersonal communication. Thus, grounded theory begins with observed evidence, whereas many other theories begin with researchers' ideas about how communication happens, ideas that are then tested in subsequent data collection and analysis, or in logical argument and reasoning. Stamp's (1999) study shows us that grounded theory can be used in ways that are quite distinct from the goals of ethnography (i.e., grasping the natives' point of view); yet ethnographic research shares with grounded theory the preference for starting with data: "The analysis must be made on the ground. We must know what patterns are available in what contexts, and how, where, and when they come into play" (Hymes, 1962, p. 105).

In the same way, naturalistic inquiry complements, but is different from, ethnography, ethnographies of speaking, or ethnographies of communication. **Naturalistic inquiry** is "the study of how people behave when they are absorbed in genuine life experiences in natural settings" (Frey et al., 2000, p. 427). Both grounded theory and naturalistic inquiry are inductive methods that are more local than general. Naturalistic inquiry may be used to test communication theory, but it is not necessarily meant for developing theory, as is grounded theory methodology (e.g., Browning & Beyer, 1998). Ethnographers of communication often combine grounded theory and naturalistic inquiry, and they usually view these methods as complementary, rather than competitive (Strauss & Corbin, 1998).

Ethnographers of communication assume that "the effective communicative resources for creating shared meaning and coordinating action vary across social groups" (Philipsen, 1989, p. 258). Unlike the discovery paradigm, this interpretive approach does not assume that there is one most effective way to communicate in any social group. Rather, "there are moments of communicative effectiveness" in which participants "act as if they express a common sense" (Philipsen, 1989, p. 258). For the interpretive researcher, these moments of acting as if meaning is truly shared suggest ways that participants are able to coordinate actions and share some of the meanings in their everyday lives. Interpretive researchers believe that truth is subjective and take participants' coordinated actions as evidence of their common sense of a situation. Participants coordinate actions in this same way, by interpreting actions that initially appear to be divergent *in ways that can be perceived to be harmonious patterns* (Philipsen, 1989, p. 259). But the coordination of actions, the creation of these harmonious patterns in the collective perception process, is particular to a culture and/or group: There is a "community-specific system of resources for making shared sense and for organizing action" (p. 260).

As we mentioned in the first paragraph of this chapter, there is no universal definition of ethnography. However, in addition to differentiating ethnography in its general sense from ethnography of communication or ethnography of speaking, it is also helpful to consider Spradley's (1980) distinction between macro- and micro-ethnography. Macro-ethnography involves years of research and numerous ethnographers, whereas micro-ethnographies address the study of a single social situation, perhaps by one researcher. In the past few years, there has been a growing use of **autoethnography,** an ethnographic study of a social setting or situation for which the key informant is the researcher himself or herself (e.g., Crawford, 1996; Miller, 2002). Spradley argued that a project that focuses on one social situation (versus a macro-ethnography) is "no less sophisticated, but only more limited in scope" (p. 47). The general goals are the same, to "discover the cultural knowledge people are using to organize their behavior and interpret their experience" (Spradley, 1980, p. 31). Thus, ethnographic research is another bridge from communication research as discovery, to interpretation, and even reform. Now that you have some sense of the potential scope of ethnographic research, let's look at the communication claims you can examine with these methods.

ETHNOGRAPHIC CLAIMS

Ethnographers use an inductive approach to framing research questions. Consistent with the interpretive paradigm values for subjectivity and privileging of participant views, ethnographers often proceed to collect initial data without first specifying research questions. They need to know something about the nature and quality of the relationships in that social situation in order to know what questions can be effectively pursued there.

As a novice ethnographer, it is first important that you select a research topic you sincerely care about. After all, you will be immersed in collecting and analyzing ethnographic data about that topic for an extended period of time. Start where you are now; survey your personal situation, both in terms of your current involvements and activities, and those situations to which you are remotely related because of your personal history (Lofland & Lofland, 1984; Morse, 1998). As a student, perhaps working full- or part-time to pay your way through college, perhaps you are a waitperson in the food service industry, or a sales representative, or a customer service representative in a retail environment. Ethnographers often "'make problematic' that which is problematic in our lives" (Lofland & Lofland, 1984, p. 8). What situation in your purview most stands out as you consider moments of communicative effectiveness (Philipsen, 1989) or the cultural knowledge used to organize experience (Spradley, 1980)?

Once you have selected a topic area, you can begin thinking more specifically about potential research questions. This can happen in one of two ways, inductively or deductively. An inductive approach will mean that you allow your research questions to emerge during fieldwork; a deductive approach will suggest that you deduce the type of fieldwork you need to conduct largely from your research questions. It's best to begin with some general research questions as early as possible in your ethnographic research project, even if you "are in a highly inductive mode" (Miles & Huberman, 1994, p. 25). As you write all your research questions down and review them, you will be making your theoretical assumptions more clear and helping to channel subsequent data collection and analysis in the right directions.

Once you have a list of potential research questions about the situation or setting you intend to examine, try writing the questions on note cards and sorting them in different ways to see, for example, how a structured set of interview questions might emerge. Of course you could easily do this sorting exercise on your computer, too. Either way, as you consider the questions you've developed so far, you may be able to see what framework (i.e., what conceptual or theoretical perspective) might join these questions coherently. If you have more than four or five questions, try grouping them into major questions and subquestions. Miles and Huberman (1994) suggested that researchers formulate questions three times during a research project. Spend the most time on your first formulation, after you have some initial exposure to the topic area and after you have conducted an initial literature review. "Drafting and iterating a set of six or seven general research questions should take at least 2 or 3 hours" (Miles & Huberman, 1994, p. 25). Your questions will likely improve if you do this work in more than one sitting.

After you have selected a topic and formed your research questions (and perhaps made some initial observations in the field), keeping a written list of your questions nearby and reviewing them regularly during your fieldwork will help you take better field notes. The simplest observations and field notes are answers to ethnographic questions, even if the questions remain unstated (Spradley, 1980). If you are a member of the culture or group you study, you probably already have great insights to bring to your analysis. Keeping research questions close at hand will help you articulate those insights and apply them during observations and interviews.

Ethnographers of communication most often stake claims of description, interpretation, and evaluation. Recently, critical ethnographers have taken actions with and on behalf of their participants that push their arguments beyond evaluation, into claims of reform (e.g., Conquergood, 1991, 1995; Gordon, 2002). We will illustrate each of these types of ethnographic claim with examples from published communication research.

Descriptive Claims

Ethnographic research conducted via participant observation and interviewing is likely to put emphasis on "*description* and *explanation* more than on measurement and prediction" (Fitch, 1994, p. 32). In doing ethnography, you will very likely claim to *describe* the norms and practices used by people in a particular group or culture (Philipsen, 1989; Spradley, 1980). A group is a set of "3–12 people who interact regularly over a period of time and conceive of themselves as a social entity" (Lofland & Lofland, 1984, p. 85). By contrast, a **culture** is defined as a system of shared meanings (webs of significance) that are held in common by group members (Geertz, 1973).

Philipsen (1989) suggested two kinds of descriptive claims you might pursue by conducting ethnography of a culture or group. First, you may want to describe distinctive **communication resources**—the knowledge shared by members of a culture or group, used to interpret and organize action (for example, rules). Second, you might want to delineate the nature and scope of cultural variation in communicative conduct. Before we consider some examples of each of these kinds of descriptive claim, we need to elaborate the relationship between theory and research methods for ethnographers.

Although ethnographic claims have been advanced in support of various theories, the research conducted by Philipsen and colleagues, called ethnography of speaking, inherently and necessarily links theory and method (Philipsen, 1975, 1976, 1977, 1989, 1992, 1997). Ethnographers of speaking focus on describing the way members of a culture name their speech events, the components of those speech events (e.g., senders, receivers, message forms, channels, etc.), and the functions of speech events (i.e., what is being accomplished by that speech event?). A descriptive framework called SPEAKING, developed by sociolinguist Dell Hymes (1962), is preferred by ethnographers of speaking. Here is what SPEAKING stands for:

Scene and setting (from the perspective of members)

Participants (age, role, gender, ethnicity, etc.)

Ends (goals of the participants and actual outcomes of the event)

Act sequence (structure and topic of the messages)

Key (tone or manner of the communication)

Instrumentalities (channels of communication, jargon, dialects, etc.)

Norms of interaction and interpretation (how to make sense of messages)

Genre (categories like poetry, myth, joke, etc.)

The elements of the SPEAKING framework are used to *describe*

> what a child internalizes about speaking, beyond rules of grammar and a dictionary, while becoming a full-fledged member of its speech community. Or, it is a question of what a foreigner must learn about a group's verbal behavior in order to participate appropriately and effectively in its activities. The ethnography of speaking is concerned with the situations and uses, the patterns and functions, of speaking as an activity in its own right (Hymes, 1962, p. 101).

A **speech community** is a group of people who share rules for using and interpreting speech (Romaine, 1982). Dollar and Merrigan (2002) listed examples of speech communities that have been represented in published ethnographies of speaking, including street youth (Dollar & Zimmers, 1998), a charismatic church (Sequeira, 1993), a regional symphony (Ruud, 1995), organizational groups in a television station (Carbaugh, 1988), and a group of Vietnam veterans (Braithwaite, 1997c). Each of these studies advanced the first sort of descriptive claim Philipsen outlined in 1989; each described culturally distinct knowledge used by members of a social group to organize and interpret speaking.

Within a particular speech community, the set of rules for speaking and interpreting others' speech is the **communication code** (Carbaugh, 1993; Dollar, 1999; Philipsen, 1992, 1997). As we mentioned in the previous chapter, codeswitching occurs any time that people mix the rules of one speech community with the rules of another, so it is a natural ethnographic focus for the student of intercultural communication. A number of ethnographic studies have advanced *descriptive* and *explanatory* claims about the practice of codeswitching. Chien's (1996) ethnographic study of codeswitching among Chinese college teachers in Taiwan is one example: First, Chien described the verbal strategies (communicative resources) used within a speech community of bilingual teachers in Taiwan. She then defined codeswitching more specifically as "embedding English words, sentences, or constituents in a Chinese-based interaction" (p. 267). She explained how codeswitching helps these teachers either to show group solidarity (i.e., "We all speak English and Chinese here") or to establish social distance (i.e., "I am different than you, because I can speak in both of these codes"). However, Chien (1996) did not use the SPEAKING framework (Hymes, 1962) to describe communication strategies and their functions among the Chinese college teachers.

If you want to describe communication messages or explain their functions in a context, without observing interactions among people in that context, then your work is probably better described simply as naturalistic inquiry (or perhaps grounded theory) rather than ethnography. As we mentioned earlier, ethnography and naturalistic inquiry are compatible, closely related research methods, which have been used to advance claims in support of various theories, not just the ethnography of speaking.

For example, Stringer Cawyer and Smith-Dupre' (1995) observed weekly meetings of an HIV/AIDS support group over a 3-month period. They *described* how group members used feedback and self-disclosure to prepare themselves to live with AIDS, to express emotions, and to change the societal context in which HIV/AIDS is viewed. Instead of the ethnography of speaking framework, Stringer Cawyer and Smith-Dupre' used prior social support research as their theoretic base, and constant comparison of their observations and the support strategies described in the literature as their data analytic strategy. Constant comparison is a data analytic strategy from grounded theory that we will talk more about later in this chapter. Here, our point is just that ethnographers sometimes marry theory and method, and sometimes use ethnographic methods in support of a variety of

other theories, including communication theories (Dollar & Merrigan, 2002).

Interpretive Claims

A third element of the research agenda for ethnographers of communication is to ascertain the relationships between culture and communication (Philipsen, 1989). This is a claim of interpretation. One such relationship is the **communal function** of communication—the ways that communication is used to create and affirm shared identities (Philipsen, 1992). Philipsen's (1975) "Speaking 'Like a Man' in Teamsterville . . ." illustrated the communal function by offering one interpretation of how cultural roles were enacted by men in a Chicago blue-collar community.

On the other hand, Murillo's (1996) ethnography of a Latin American *mojado* festival illustrated an interpretive claim that was not about the way cultural messages function *within* the group. Rather, Murillo's study was about how the *mojado* frames and produces Latin American culture and communicative practices for others. Murillo called this process pedagogical and expressive, where the function of the communication was to teach nonmembers about La Raza culture.

Of course, some ethnographic studies make both kinds of interpretive claims (i.e., how members of a group construct interpretations of their own culture based on shared knowledge and practices and how those interpretations can mean different things to people inside and outside the group or culture). Trujillo's (1992) ethnography of the communication among employees at a major league baseball stadium advanced both of these kinds of interpretive claims. In the first case, Trujillo showed how employees at the ballpark created and maintained three different interpretations of their work through their communicative actions and interactions: (1) baseball is a business; (2) the ballpark is a social community for family members; and (3) baseball is a dramatic, theatrical experience. In the latter case, Trujillo explained how three world views affected the connotative meanings of these employees' interpretations of baseball:

> *Romantics* interpret baseball in an ideal, even idyllic way. Not surprisingly, they ignore the *business* of baseball. . . . Romantics celebrate the *community* interpretation of the game. . . . *Functionalists,* on the other hand, use sport to teach us about the realities of mainstream American culture and to demonstrate how

sport helps us adapt to those realities. . . .
Functionalists use the *community* interpretation to demonstrate how sport integrates us
into society. . . . And functionalists use the
drama interpretation to reveal how our cultural and political values are enacted. . . . *Critics* argue that the *business* of sport reaffirms
the ideology of American capitalism. . . .
Critics write that this "commoditas" of sport
has led to the decline (and commodification)
of the ballpark *community* because it has
transformed fans from active enlightened
participants in the ritual contest into passive
pleasure-seeking consumers at an amusement
park (1992, p. 365).

Trujillo (1992) offered these three interpretations of
baseball (romantic, functionalist, and critical); he did
not judge the interpretations in terms of their beauty,
utility, or other criteria. Although interpretive ethnographers actively avoid making such evaluations,
some researchers do use ethnographic methods in
order to evaluate communication. Let's consider
ethnographic claims of evaluation next.

Evaluative Claims

The claim of evaluation is advanced when ethnographers judge the worth or value of the communicative practices or messages that they are studying. We
consider two such studies here.

Imagine that you were asked to develop an orientation program for high school students who
would attend your college or university next year, or
that you were asked to evaluate the orientation program already in place on your campus. How would
you begin? You might use ethnographic methods to
stake a claim of evaluation. Searle's (1991) study of
supermarket checkout operators in Australia was designed to *evaluate* the training programs that employees attended on the job and to develop programs that
better met their communication training needs.
Searle recommended teachers use participant observation as she did, to assess their students' learning and
to evaluate the effectiveness of their own teaching
practices. Two kinds of evaluation may be conducted
using ethnographic methods: formative and summative. **Formative evaluation** is used during a communication process, so that the evaluation data can
form the process as it unfolds. For example, midterm
feedback can help your teacher adjust the learning to

better meet your needs. **Summative evaluation** occurs after a communication process is completed.
End-of-term teaching evaluations are summative assessments of your teachers' effectiveness, just as letter
grades are summative assessments of your classroom
performance.

Dorazio and Stovall (1997) advised that market
researchers conduct formative evaluations of product usability in the field, the cultural context in
which products will be purchased and used. Traditionally, product usability studies have been conducted in laboratory settings. But Dorazio and
Stovall advocated that formative evaluations, decisions about the product's value that can be used to
change the product before it is marketed to a larger
audience, incorporate ethnographic as well as laboratory methods. Specifically, the ethnographic researcher can learn who the product users are, how
and when they will use the product, what their environments are like, and how the technical information given to support product use (i.e., user manual)
is working. Thus, ethnographic methods can reveal
strengths and weaknesses of a product before it hits
the marketplace.

Ethnographic methods could also be used in service of summative evaluation; that is, efforts to assess
whether a product or program is effective can be
made after the product or program has been used by
its intended audience. For example, Weitzel and Geist
(1998) used ethnographic observations and interviews with members of a community decision-making
group to evaluate how parliamentary procedure was
practiced in that community. Much of the existing
research about decision-making groups has relied on
laboratory studies of relationships between decision-
making processes and group outcomes. So one purpose
of the study was to "determine the generalizability
of process-outcome relationships identified in laboratory investigations" of decision-making groups
(Weitzel & Geist, 1998, p. 247).

As you can see from the above examples, evaluative claims are quickly put to use in support of changing, perhaps improving, communication practices in
a particular group or context. It may be that you, the
researcher, will decide what changes are needed, or
you may give the results of your analysis to another
person or group who will then decide what changes
to attempt. Either way, it is a short step from evaluating communicative practices to reforming them, and
the next section deals specifically with reform claims.

Critical Ethnography as a Bridge to Reform Claims

Around 1990, critical ethnographies began to emerge that focused on showing how norms of power usage privilege some group members and oppress others (Ang, 1990; Conquergood, 1992, 1994; Crawford, 1996; Gordon, 2002; Trujillo, 1993; Witmer, 1997). Critical ethnographers go beyond describing and evaluating cultural variations in speech codes and "attempt to take action against the social inequalities exposed in their research, action aimed at challenging the status quo and calling for a rebalancing of power" (Dollar & Merrigan, 2002, p. 6).

Perhaps the earliest and most well known proponent of critical ethnography in communication is Conquergood (1991, 1992, 1994, 1995). His participatory research with a Chicago Latino gang included actions aimed at helping gang members stay out of jail, learn to read and write, and gain a more empathic voice in the media (Conquergood & Seigel, 1990). Conquergood's attempts to understand this cultural group moved well beyond description and interpretation for its own (or theory's) sake. An equally important goal of his research was his attempt to redress power imbalances experienced by members of the cultures:

> The difference between critical and conventional ethnographic topic choice begins with a passion to investigate an injustice (e.g., racism); social control (language, norms, or cultural rules); power; stratification; or allocation of cultural rewards and resources to illustrate how cultural meanings constrain existence (Thomas, 1993, p. 36).

Another example of actions taken by a critical ethnographer to restructure power balance in a cultural group is Adelman's documentary film making of the lives of HIV/AIDS patients (Adelman & Frey, 1994). The films were passed on to family members as memoirs for patients who did not have access to the financial and technical resources required for such an endeavor.

As you read critical ethnographic studies and conduct those studies yourself, you may notice a blurry line between making claims with ethnography, and writing about or performing a culture. Goodall (2000) argued that critical ethnographers approach *writing as inquiry*. In critiquing power relations within a culture,

or between cultural groups, writing is not merely something you do after the research is conducted. Instead, writing is the manner of interrogating and exposing power relations within the social situation. It may be even be a way of interrogating your own beliefs and participation in an oppressive social system by using autoethnographic writing or by participating in collaborative writing (Trujillo, 1999).

Furthermore, performance studies scholars sometimes use ethnographic observations and interviews to create their performances. For example, Jenkins's (2000) play, *A Credit to Her Country,* is about gays and lesbians who served in the U.S. military. Jenkins wrote the play based on her ethnographic oral history interviews with men and women who were discharged from military service because of their sexual orientation. For another example of Jenkins's combination of ethnographic research with performance studies, see her (1999) autoethnographic poem entitled "What to Do If You Find Out You Have Breast Cancer."

Ethnographic research can move beyond evaluation, to reform claims about changes that *should* be made in a particular group or setting, as Markham's (1996) account of ambiguous communication at a small environmental design firm showed. When Markham began her case study of Far End Design (FED), her goal was to *describe* the metaphors that eight members of this firm used to frame their work at FED. But over the two years in which she observed interactions at FED, interviewed members, and studied her field notes, Markham began to notice that official accounts of life at FED rarely matched members' accounts. She observed that "all the designers associated their experiences at FED with physically and psychologically damaging problems outside of work" (p. 397), such as insomnia, colitis, alcohol and drug abuse, and divorce. Markham decided to read her field notes more critically, and to look for relationships among the ambiguous and paradoxical communication practices and the environment of power and tension at FED. She concluded:

> As critical researchers we need to acknowledge and more fully address the complex and often surprising workings of power in organizations. This is not only crucial for our own edification, but for the critical goal of providing organizational actors with alternatives (p. 417).

Markham (1996) concluded that reform claims pose ethical dilemmas for the ethnographic researcher; namely, the researcher's presence affects the lives of research participants, for better or worse. "Just as there are many political ideals which can claim the allegiance of persons of good will, so ethnography leads its practitioners to the careful study and appreciation of many discourses, including, on occasions, discourses of power" (Philipsen, 1992, p. 329). With these sobering thoughts in mind, let's turn our attention to the sources and strategies for ethnographic data collection and analysis.

ETHNOGRAPHIC DATA

In this section, we will discuss four major sources for ethnographic data collection, ranging from participant observations and interviews to analysis of archival documents and cultural artifacts. Next, we will consider the procedures you can use to collect these data, from gaining access to selecting key informants, taking field notes, and exiting the field. Finally, we'll discuss four basic strategies for analyzing ethnographic research data: transcribing interviews, coding and reducing data, applying descriptive frameworks to analyze communication norms and rules of interaction, and writing case studies. All of these ideas will build on the concepts you learned in Chapter 3, "What Counts as Communication Data?"

Sources for Data Collection

Two of the defining characteristics of ethnographic research are that "the investigator goes into the field, instead of bringing the field to the investigator" (Schwartzman, 1993, p. 3), and that data are represented from the view of the participants (Stablein, 1996). The data you encounter in ethnographic fieldwork can take many forms, including participant observations, interviews with key informants, archival documents, and artifacts (i.e., texts). **Participant observation** is the process of watching and learning about the setting and participants, while you are participating in the daily realities you are studying (Lofland & Lofland, 1984; Spradley, 1980). Interviews with **key informants** are the interactions between you, the researcher, and informed, articulate members of the culture or group you want to understand. Key informants usually are not researchers (Lofland

& Lofland, 1984). **Archival documents** are written or symbolic records of the cultural communication, such as letters, newspapers, Web sites, billboards, or memos. **Artifacts** are objects used by group or cultural members, such as clothing, jewelry, buildings, tools, or toys.

In doing ethnography, you will typically rely on two or more data sources either simultaneously or in iterative sequences. For example, you may follow a period of document analysis and participant observation with some interviews, then do some more observations. Your ethnographic data collection will likely proceed from making broad descriptive observations to making increasingly more selective and focused observations (Spradley, 1980). In this section, we will outline how you can proceed to collect each of these four sources of ethnographic data.

Participant Observation   Your level of participation in an ethnographic setting can range from nonparticipant (i.e., observer only) to complete participation (Smith, 1988; Spradley, 1980), depending on your research question and the access you have to that setting, which we will discuss later in this chapter. For example, Braithwaite's (1997b) ethnography of Navajo educational communication practices was based on 8 months of participant observation, during which Braithwaite lived in a dormitory at Navajo Community College in Tsaile, Arizona. As he observed over 100 hours of classroom interactions, Braithwaite collected more than 300 pages of field notes, including descriptions of class content and specific verbal and nonverbal speech events. In this setting, he was a participant in the sense that he resided in the dormitory with the Navajo students, but he was a faculty member rather than a student, and he was not of Navajo descent.

In his ethnographic study of baseball, Trujillo (1992) used participant observation and interview methods to gather data over 2 years at a major league baseball stadium, including over 500 hours of fieldwork. His participant observations included a variety of roles and settings. He began the process of data collection by observing numerous off-season "luncheons, banquets, autograph appearances, and speaking engagements" (p. 353). Then, during the two seasons under study, Trujillo "attended a total of 67 home games" (p. 353), where he participated as a *fan, invited observer,* and *ballpark wanderer,* observing and conducting brief interviews in many locales. During these interviews and observations, Trujillo took extensive field notes to reconstruct the communicative actions of workers. We will discuss procedures for taking field notes in more detail later in this chapter.

Whatever your degree of participation during observations, it is important that you develop and maintain trusting relationships with the group members you study. Your access to participants' knowledge is relative to the kinds of relationships you establish with group members and, in particular, with which group members you establish relationships. The roles that these members play in their local network and their goals in relating to you also influence your degree of participation and the observations you are able to collect. For example, Schely-Newman (1997) observed instances of codeswitching as she interviewed members of her family and friends who all lived in an Israeli *moshav* or cooperative community:

> Members of the older generation speak Arabic, French, and Hebrew with varying degrees of fluency, and codeswitching is an unmarked choice within the community. Nevertheless, because each language has different connotations and prestige, the choice of a dominant language may result from the immediate context (participants), the subject discussed (Israeli politics are discussed in Hebrew; the concerns of women and children, in Arabic), or the image being presented by the narrator (sophistication is marked by French) (p. 405).

Schely-Newman observed that "as the formality of the event and the heterogeneity of the participants increases, the mixing of languages occurs less often" (p. 405). Such an observation could be made only if she selected informants capable of performing multiple language codes, and if her relationship to the informants allowed them to share stories with her during which codeswitching occurred naturally because she was a family member.

As these examples suggest, you will need to possess or develop certain skills and attitudes in order to be an effective participant-observer. The skills you will need involve recognizing and performing communication that is the normal standard in the social group you are studying (Dollar, 1995; Lindlof, 1995). You will also need to be good at "creating sharp, detailed, and theoretically informed descriptions" (Lindlof, 1995, p. 135). That is, you must be skilled in

writing, organizing, filing, and synthesizing field notes. These skills can be learned if you do not already possess them.

In order to be an effective participant-observer, though, you will also need certain attitudes or sensitivities. You will need to be capable of and comfortable with fading into the background of a social situation—what Lindlof (1995) called a tolerance for marginality. You will also need to be sensitive to all the verbal and nonverbal communication cues that are available in a social setting, not just visual and auditory cues. Instead, we can "open up our sensing to the tastes, smells, tempers, touches, colors, lights, shapes, and textures of the cultures we study" (Lindlof, 1995, p. 138). Finally, to be an effective participant observer, you will need to be good at "giving people the benefit of the doubt, getting along by going along, and not being overly querulous or contentious" (Fine, 1993, as cited by Lindlof, 1995, p. 139).

Participant observation will allow you to see what the members do and say in their setting; interviews with key informants, on the other hand, will help you to describe what members *report* that they do and say, and what sense members make of those actions and interactions. For example, you may observe the stories participants tell, to whom those stories are told, where, with what structures, forms of elaboration, and so on. The stories participants tell one another in their natural settings may be quite different than the stories they relate to you, the researcher in the context of an interview. Thus, observations provide a different window into the participants' worlds than does participants' talk about their world. Interviews with key informants are one of the ethnographer's methods for uncovering participants' talk about their world.

Interviews with Key Informants The **ethnographic interview** is "the most informal, conversational, and spontaneous form of interview" (Lindlof, 1995, p. 170). Ethnographic interviews take the forms of conversations and storytelling between participants and researchers. The interview is a way to find out things that you cannot directly observe (Newman & Benz, 1998; Patton, 1990).

Just as selecting participants to interview is critical to your participation in and observation of a setting, establishing rapport with informants is essential if you are to gain useful interview data. Your demeanor and appearance, listening skills, and nonverbal style all contribute to your effectiveness as a human research instrument in the interview process. In a collaborative ethnography, you may want to use **interviewer training** to ensure that interviews are conducted consistently (i.e., interactions with one informant are comparable to interactions with another informant and interviews conducted by one researcher are comparable to interviews conducted by another researcher working on the same research project). You may want to review the information in Chapter 5, "Survey Research," on interviewer training as well.

Interviews can be structured or unstructured, standardized or nonstandardized (Spradley, 1980). If structured, check your interview schedule to ensure that your questions and organizational pattern are consistent with your study's purpose. Typically, ethnographic interviews are unstructured or minimally structured. You may not have any questions written out before beginning to observe the setting and participants because the participants' actions will indicate to you what questions are important to ask (Spradley, 1980; Schwartzman, 1993). Indeed, participant observations will almost certainly be needed to determine whom you will want to interview.

If you are adopting the interpretive or critical paradigm perspectives, you will likely use unstructured, face-to-face interviews. As interview formats become less structured and more personal, your role will be more interactive. Whatever degree of structure you plan to incorporate, use these guidelines for a successful ethnographic interview: (1) Respondents must feel that their interactions with you will be pleasant and satisfying; (2) they need to see your study as being worthwhile; and (3) barriers to the interview in their minds need to be overcome (Frankfort-Nachmias & Nachmias, 1996).

Before you conduct your first interview with an informant, develop face sheets and postinterview comment sheets. Both of these items will help you develop an audit trail, a record of all the data you are about to collect (Lofland & Lofland, 1984). **Face sheets** include details about the interviews, such as a code or name for the participant; the date, place, and time of the interviews; and any relevant demographic information about the interviewees. **Comment sheets** are for you to jot down notes after your interviews, perhaps concerning the emotional tone of the interview, your insights and reflections about any difficulties you encountered during the interview, and so on.

In addition to creating face sheets and comment sheets, you will need to develop an introduction to the interview. What will you say to a participant before you begin the interview? You will probably want to tape-record interviews, so you can think and talk, and not be occupied with field notes, during the interview (Lofland & Lofland, 1984). But you should take a few notes while the tape is running, just to help you pay attention.

As a novice ethnographer, never enter the interview scene without some interview guide. Your guide might be a page of one-word notes about themes, symbols, and patterns observed in artifacts or other data, but it would never be a strict schedule of questions. If you are doing ethnography of speaking, you may want to have a copy of Hymes's SPEAKING mnemonic with you during observations or interviews. Give yourself enough of a guide to focus your interviews, but not so much as to override the direction your key informant suggests for your conversation.

In some cases, you may want to combine participant observations and/or interviewing key informants with analysis of archival documents or cultural artifacts (i.e., texts). Let's consider each of these sources of ethnographic evidence next.

Archival Documents Archival documents are written texts that an ethnographer encounters in the field. Archival documents are sometimes implicated in the talk or actions of participants whom you are observing. Alternatively, archival texts may help you gain background knowledge needed to reconstruct past events or processes that are not available for you to observe. Finally, library research about a setting or situation, including conducting a literature review on the topic area you are studying, also makes use of archival documents, although in this section, we will refer more to those documents encountered in the field data collection itself. Participant diaries, memos, newsletters, email messages, and newspaper clippings are all examples of such archival documents. For instance, in her ethnography of Far End Design, Markham (1996) analyzed official company literature and diaries kept by employees, along with her field notes from observations and interview transcripts. By considering not only the content of those documents, but also their format characteristics, origins, uses, circulation, and so on, in conjunction with her other evidence, she identified some of the ambiguities and contradictions experienced by those employees. In the same way, archival documents can supplement your ethnographic evidence and help you understand how participants are making sense of their situations.

You may also want to incorporate visual media, such as film, video, or still photography, in your ethnographic project, which are also considered *texts* for analysis, in conjunction with participation observations or interview data. In Chapter 13, "Critical Studies," we will consider some examples of entire research projects based on textual interpretation and evaluation of media sources. But for interpretive ethnography, those texts are usually used to triangulate evidence gained from self-report interviews or observations with participants.

Artifacts Finally, you may want to examine actual objects used by participants in the setting you study in order to understand the participants' communication rules, meanings, or behaviors. Such artifacts could include the participants' costumes and dress, items used in routine activities like eating, cooking, bathing, meeting or interacting with other participants, and so on. As we just mentioned, artifacts typically support other kinds of ethnographic evidence, but artifactual analysis plays a more central role in rhetorical criticism and critical studies (see Chapters 12 and 13 for examples from published communication research).

Strategies for Data Collection

Now you know something about the sources of data for ethnographic communication research. But before you can conduct ethnographic research, you will need to know some procedures for collecting these data. In the following sections, we will briefly describe these procedures. Their sequence can vary across different ethnographic research projects, depending on the participants and the kinds of claims you are attempting to support (Philipsen, 1982).

You will need to think about the issue of time management at the beginning of your ethnographic project. Allow extra time to develop skills you do not already have, since things go more slowly the first few times, whether it's interviewing, taking field notes, coding data, writing reports, or whatever. As you think about the amount of time needed for your project, consider some of the tasks you will need to accomplish. You will be entering a site of data collection; conducting a literature review; spending days, weeks, or months at the site; writing up and coding interview transcripts; analyzing data within and across cases; writing up notes from site visits; holding weekly meetings with other researchers, if applicable; and writing interim and final reports. Miles and Huberman (1994) estimated 185 days for such a task list, which is probably a conservative estimate. Trujillo's 2-year study of baseball culture involved over 500 hours, or over 60 workdays, 8 hours a day, in just the fieldwork tasks! "Time plans usually suffer from excessive optimism. Get a cynical skeptic to critique them" (Miles & Huberman, 1994, p. 47). One issue in planning your timeline is gaining access to the field.

Gaining Access to the Setting "Stepping into a setting for the first time is probably the most significant phase of the entire ethnographic process" (Schwartzman, 1993, p. 49). "Everything counts" (Goodall, 1989, p. xv, as cited by Schwartzman). Ethnographers call the process of getting permission and approvals for doing research in a particular setting **gaining access,** or entry (Lindlof, 1995; Spradley, 1980). It is at this stage that you will have the opportunity to make the strange familiar and make the familiar strange (Frey et al., 2000). You can elect different roles at this point, depending on the degree of participation you desire in the setting, ranging from pure or even covert observer, to full, overt participant, or somewhere in between these two.

Ethnographers sometimes refer to the period prior to gaining access as "casing the scene" (Lindlof, 1995). Your initial entry into the setting may be "simply a matter of walking through the door" (Witmer, 1997, p. 329). While casing the scene, you can collect some initial impressions of the setting and participants, and consider, "Is *this* the right project *now, for me?*" (Lindlof, 1995, p. 82). Go into these places, "looking, listening, touching, and smelling—*hanging out*" (Lindlof, 1995, p. 82). Of course, you will already have some idea that this setting and your timing are appropriate, but your initial observations may change your idea of whether your study is actually feasible. For example, can you devote the amount of time needed to adequately study communication in this setting? What expenses will you incur for traveling to and/or participating as a group member in this setting? Finally, consider whether you are competent in the cultural communication code(s) needed to function effectively as a research instrument and participant in this setting (Lindlof, 1995; Philipsen, 1997; Spradley, 1980).

One hotly debated topic among ethnographers of communication over the past 10 years has been the issue of the researcher's membership in the culture being studied. Some ethnographers feel it is essential that you be a full member of the culture; others acknowledge that degrees of membership are possible and helpful in data collection and interpretation, especially in gaining access to the setting (Lindsley, 1999). Your degree of cultural membership impacts your ability to enter the setting, to choose which concepts to attend to, and the interpretations you are able to make about the data (Dollar, 1995; Dollar & Merrigan, 2002; Spradley, 1980).

Not only can you gain access to the setting more easily as a cultural insider, but membership also allows you to recognize features of meaning that would be unrecognized by a nonmember. For example, Dollar and Zimmers's (1998) use of the term *houseless,* rather than homeless, youth stemmed from Zimmers's 5-year participation as a job placement coordinator in that community. Zimmers recognized that the youth in this study intentionally used the term *houseless* to mean something different than homeless. They constructed themselves as being without a house (i.e., the building), but as having homes in the places they hung out, ate, and slept. Your degree of membership and the roles you can enact in a setting will also influence your selection of key informants for ethnographic interviews.

Selecting Key Informants Your ethnographic observations will rely upon and be influenced by identifying key informants, members of the group under study whom you can interview. Key informants are either highly articulate, or especially helpful and wise, relative to other participants in that setting (Lofland & Lofland, 1984). Key informants provide information about the relationships, groups, and cultures you seek to describe. One good way to identify key informants in your setting is to look for **gatekeepers,** the participants who have power to grant or deny your access to the setting. In addition, you might want to identify sponsors. A **sponsor** is a participant who "takes an active interest in the project, vouches for its goals, and sometimes helps the researcher locate informants or move into participation roles" (Lindlof, 1995, p. 109). In short, you will want to select key informants because you are "already aware that they know something, or have had some experience, that is important for the project" (Lindlof, 1995, p. 125).

You can select informants who will provide a wide range of qualities that are present in the scene to be studied by using maximum variation sampling (Lincoln & Guba, 1985). Or, you can ask key informants to suggest other people from whom data can be gathered, thus using the snowball selection method (Lindlof, 1995). Recall from Chapter 3 that the snowball selection method takes its name from the way a sample of informants accumulates, like a snowball rolling downhill, as one informant nominates others, who nominate still others (e.g., Lindsley, 1999). Of course, you can also use less formal means of selecting informants, such as convenience sampling. Finally, if you are conducting grounded theory, you may want to use **theoretical sampling,** a process of collecting the additional data specifically needed to fill out one part of the emerging theory (Glaser & Strauss, 1967; Janesick, 1998). Such additional data will give you a way to check the adequacy of emerging categories, and the relationships you are theorizing among those categories. In addition, deviant case sampling may be used to sort out contradictions or inconsistencies in the observations you have already collected (Janesick, 1998; May & Pattillo-McCoy, 2000).

Once you have some sense of who the key informants from a scene will be, a key consideration for you and your participants is how many contacts, or interview opportunities, will be needed, and what will be the duration of those contacts? The next step in preparing for participant observations or interviews is to think about how you will record and organize your field notes.

Taking Field Notes Since ethnography depends greatly on your prolonged immersion in and observations of the field setting and its participants, keeping field notes is a crucial aspect of ethnographic data collection. It is a good idea for you to keep an informal log of problems or questions you encounter as you plan your study and collect and analyze the data. Such a log will be immensely useful when you are writing up your study (Miles & Huberman, 1994; Lofland & Lofland, 1984). Your field journal can be used for recording your "experiences, ideas, fears, mistakes, confusions, breakthroughs, and problems that arise during fieldwork" (Spradley, 1980, p. 71). Journal entries should be dated, as your entries will be "an important source of data" when you start writing up the study (Spradley, 1980, p. 71).

It is sometimes feasible to make notes quite openly during participant observations. Sometimes, you can incorporate note taking into the roles you are already playing in the field, by disguising note taking as some other situationally appropriate behavior, like doing homework in an educational setting, or working on a report in an organizational context (Lindlof, 1995). Trujillo (1992) sometimes posed as a "reporter" while taking notes in the pregame dugout and in the baseball locker rooms. As a "fan," Trujillo carried his notebook inside a game program, where he made brief notes as he observed ballpark employees; he elaborated these notes during lulls in ballpark action and dictated additional ideas into a tape recorder as he drove home from the games.

When there is no situationally appropriate ploy for taking notes, you can withdraw or be shielded for moments in order to record notes. You might retreat to a bathroom, your car, or just around the corner (Lofland & Lofland, 1984). Tardy and Hale's (1998) participant observations of mother-toddler playgroup meetings were essentially collected when "the attending researcher sat as unobtrusively as possible near sites of conversations, and essentially, 'eavesdropped'" (p. 342).

Data logging is an ethnographic term for carefully recording various forms of data, including field notes from participant observations, write-ups from interviews, maps, photography, sound recordings, document collections, and so on (Lofland & Lofland, 1984, p. 46). The researcher who boasts, "I didn't take notes because nothing important happened" is either being arrogant or naïve, or perhaps both. Your ability and motivation to record detailed notes during or shortly after interactions with participants, and to organize these notes effectively in order to later make sense of them, is vital to doing good ethnographic research.

Exiting the Field As you can see by now, ethnographers may be involved with members of a group or culture over months or even years. You are likely to develop a variety of relationships with group members, if you did not already have those relationships prior to beginning your study. So the idea of *exiting the field,* as it has been traditionally called in anthropological research, is more complicated than just closing your notebook after writing your last field note and then not returning for additional observations or interviews.

Of course, you could just leave the field of data collection, but more likely, you will have some process of disengagement over time. For example,

your official observations may cease by agreement between you and your key informants, but unofficial reflections may come to you in the setting long afterward. Perhaps you will continue to interact with participants on topics not related to the research project per se. Or you may invite group members to read and respond to your interview transcripts or to a report of your interpretations of the group's communication practices. In any case, exiting the field of human communication relationships is as delicate and important an issue as entering that field, and for ethnographic researchers, both access and exit require serious attention and care. Morse (1998) advised that it is time to exit the field when you recognize that you are putting other goals ahead of the research:

> For instance, the researcher may suddenly realize that he or she did not record an event, because it may reflect poorly on the participants, or because it was 'everyday' and not special or interesting enough. . . . If the researcher is not learning anything new, he or she may be reasonably sure that the data are saturated (pp. 78–79).

Of course, you will need to be continually analyzing your data in order to know when you've reached this saturation point. So let's now consider some strategies for analyzing ethnographic data.

Strategies for Data Analysis

For the ethnographer of communication, "The analysis of data begins shortly after the data collection commences and continues during data collection and beyond" (Morse, 1998, p. 75). You will amass field notes from observations, interviews, and archival and artifactual texts, and at some point, you will have to face the daunting task of somehow reducing and interpreting these large amounts of data, and reporting the whole process, from conceptualization through data collection and analysis, to interpretations and conclusions. "Transcripts and notes must be easily retrieved, easily cross-referenced, and easily separated from and linked with their original sources" (Morse, 1998, p. 75).

Strategies for data analysis in ethnographic research typically begin with transcription, that is, translating audio- or videotaped records of interview conversations with key informants into written form. You will be trying to integrate the transcripts with your field notes, including observations of and reflections about the participants, the setting, relevant artifacts, and so on. One way to integrate multiple sources of data and multiple types of inferences is by reducing many specific observations into themes or categories. This process is called **coding** the data. At some point, you may apply a descriptive framework that consists of predetermined categories, such as the SPEAKING mnemonic used by ethnographers of speaking, presented earlier in this chapter. Finally, you might write a case study, a narrative account of the communication practices in a particular setting and among specific participants (Philipsen, 1982). Each of these data analytic processes is outlined in more detail below.

Transcribing Interviews At some point during or after field observations, you will need to produce written transcriptions of your interviews with key informants. At the very least, your transcripts will reproduce the verbatim verbal interaction between you and the informant(s), although your transcripts may also contain paraverbal indicators such as pause length, word stress, interruptions, and so on. Plan, at a minimum, to spend "at least as much time immediately studying and analyzing the interview material as you spent in the interview itself" (Lofland & Lofland, 1984, p. 61). This means studying transcripts *as you go along,* so that you will *know* when you need to collect more data; where to classify and file observations, notes, or transcripts; and so on. Doing your own transcription is a chore, but one of enormous value since it keeps you close to your data. You will be making interpretations as you listen to the tapes many times.

Ethnographers' transcripts range from verbatim texts of verbal and nonverbal interactions to summaries of what was said at what point, combined with your own tentative ideas, early bits of analysis, as well as notes on methodological difficulties and your personal or emotional experiences from an interview or observation session. You already know some elements to consider in formatting transcripts and some of the conventions for notating paraverbal interaction cues from the last chapter. Next, let's look at the steps you might take to make sense of your collected field notes.

Coding and Reducing Field Notes Feldman (1995) described the problem of working through massive quantities of field data that included audiotapes, floppy disks, documents, field notes, and thousands of pieces of electronic and hard mail. She noted that the complexity and ambiguity was at times overwhelming: "The task at hand is to create an interpretation of the setting or some feature of it that will allow people who have not directly observed the phenomena to have a deeper understanding of them" (p. 2). Ethnographers create interpretations based on participants' meanings. In order to do so, you have to somehow get away from two kinds of prepackaged interpretation. First, you must avoid creating interpretations that are based only on what you knew about the setting before you began collecting data. Second, you must avoid creating interpretations that are based only on what you know about other similar settings. In other words, your interpretations need to come from your field notes.

Accordingly, then, as an ethnographer you will necessarily be involved in reducing and coding data as you form interpretations and develop theoretic propositions about relationships between concepts in the setting you study. You may impose coding categories onto your data from the outset, as is the case when ethnographers of speaking apply the SPEAKING framework. Alternatively, you could induce categories for coding data after considerable immersion in the setting, as is the case when you use constant comparisons to develop a grounded theory (Glaser & Strauss, 1967) or when you use analytic induction (Goetz & LeCompte, 1984). For example, Lindsley (1999) used inductive reasoning to categorize different types of misunderstandings and conflicts encountered by U.S. American and Mexican employees at a *maquiladora* (i.e., a U.S.-owned assembly plant located in Mexico). Based on data collected in interviews, nonparticipant observations, and written periodicals on the *maquiladora* industry, Lindsley used constant comparison to group problematic interactions into three categories (e.g., negatively stereotyped identities).

Another way that you can begin to analyze a culture or group is to identify and describe the participants' rules for interaction. Rules are prescriptions for who can speak, on what topics, in what settings, and how speaking by others is to be interpreted. One form that a communication rule can take is "Do *X* in order to be seen as *Y*." College students know many such rules, such as "Show up for class on time in order to be seen as a serious, motivated student." Rules are followable, prescribed, and contextual (Shimanoff, 1980). Therefore, rule-governed behavior is controllable, criticizable, and contextual (Dollar &

Beck, 1997). All of these characteristics suggest strategies you can use to describe and evaluate the rules for conduct within a culture or group. For example, you can look for *breaches*—instances when members violate rules and are called to account for their behavior; you can try to analyze what rule has been violated in that case.

Applying Descriptive Frameworks Frameworks are favored by some ethnographers who believe that it is impossible to enter a social scene completely free of any interpretive categories (Philipsen, 1992), and a variety of descriptive frameworks may be used to analyze communication within a group or culture. As we have already mentioned, Hymes's (1962) SPEAKING framework is used by ethnographers of speaking to analyze a variety of cultural groups (e.g., Dollar, 1999; Philipsen, 1975, 1992; Ruud, 1995; Sequeira, 1993). One of the benefits of using the same descriptive framework across many groups is the ability to compare interpretations across more than group or culture. If your interest is in comparing groups or cultures, you will probably tend to see a description of any one social setting as a case study.

Writing Case Studies At a time when quantitative research predominated the social sciences, entailing issues like sample size in critiques of research, Mitchell (1983) and Philipsen (1982) both argued that theoretically plausible interpretations could be made from one good case (e.g., Braithwaite, 1997a; Eisenberg, Murphy, & Andrews, 1998; Hall & Noguchi, 1993). A typical case is one instance of communicative behavior or practice that "is similar in *relevant* characteristics to other cases of the same type" (Mitchell, 1983, p. 189). Philipsen (1977, 1982) advocated that researchers scan a number of cases for familiar concepts that can be analyzed, and in order to hypothesize links between those cases and particular theories. The data for comparing cases can be gained from participant observations, interviews, archival documents, artifacts, or some combination of these data sources.

Braithwaite's (1997a) ethnography of interaction management rules in naturally occurring conversations at a blood plasma donation center well illustrates the value of a case study. Braithwaite donated plasma 16 times over a 2-month period in order to observe conversations between other donors and the technicians who worked at the center. He discovered that conversational rules that are *normal* in other settings were consistently violated at the plasma donor center. His analysis showed how task requirements in that setting took precedence over the usual rules for interaction management. But he also showed how the normal rules for conversation management applied in this setting, even though they were routinely violated whenever "successfully accomplishing a task takes precedence over a 'normal' conversation" (p. 70). Braithwaite (1997a) gave several examples from other settings in which participants prioritize task requirements over following normal conversational rules, such as parents conversing together while watching their children play in a park, or professors trying to get to their next class while engaging in a hallway conversation with a student. Consistent with the interpretive paradigm's view of truth as subjective and comprised of multiple realities, incongruencies among cases will likely be seen as illustrative, rather than problematic, by the interpretive researcher. The idea of how such contradictions are framed leads us to consider the warrants for ethnographic research.

ETHNOGRAPHIC WARRANTS

In this section we will reiterate some of the ideas that we first presented in Chapter 4, "Warrants for Research Arguments"—ideas about how interpretive researchers demonstrate multiple realities by valuing subjectivity and rich description, and how they connect claims to data or evidence:

> Ethnographers have long been concerned with the problem of the adequacy of their evidence. By "evidence," I mean the proper mixture of data and reasoning so that a skeptical outsider might evaluate the understanding offered of the life of some group (Agar, 1983, p. 32).

In Chapter 4 we introduced the form of argument, values, and warrants for the interpretive research paradigm, but here we will focus more specifically on *how* ethnographers demonstrate the adequacy of their evidence, including data collection sources and strategies, data analytic moves, and conclusions. We will begin by considering how the interpretive values of subjectivity and rich description are enacted in ethnographic research.

Valuing Subjectivity and
Rich Description

Subjectivity refers to our ability to know using our own minds, our thoughts, feelings, and reasoning processes. Your perceptions of the social situation you study, and your ability to represent participants' perceptions of communication in that situation, are as important in interpretive ethnography as any objective reality that exists independent of your perceptions or the perceptions of participants.

Interpretive researchers stand for the value of subjective knowledge. Ethnographers act on this value by privileging participant views and field settings for data collection. The kinds of ethnographic data you collect, the time you spend immersed in the group or culture, and the detail level of your interviews and field notes will allow you to richly describe that situation, its participants, their actions, and relationships. Ultimately, you will be presenting a subjective understanding of those participants' meanings.

May and Pattillo-McCoy (2000) argued that "collaborative ethnography can be useful for providing a richer description, highlighting perceptual inconsistencies, and recognizing the influence of the ethnographers' personal and intellectual backgrounds on the collection and recording of data" (p. 65). As you know from Chapter 3, collaborative ethnography happens whenever "two or more ethnographers coordinate their fieldwork efforts to gather data from a single setting" (May & Pattillo-McCoy, 2000, p. 66). Remember that May and Pattillo-McCoy together observed a neighborhood recreation center in Chicago, but they recorded their observations separately. They then photocopied their field notes and examined points of similarity and difference in their written observations. They found that their combined field notes contained more details than either researcher's notes alone. Their combined notes also brought out points of inconsistency in their recorded observations, which they resolved by discussing during team meetings or in informal conversations. Accordingly, they advocated that collaborative ethnographers write their field notes separately in order to "minimize the extra contamination that exists when the ethnography team members talk about their joint field experiences" (p. 85).

Alternatively, several researchers may gather data on the same social phenomenon but in different social settings (e.g., Communication Studies 298, 1999;

Trujillo, 1999). Although both of these procedures for using collaborative ethnography will complicate your data collection by adding an extra layer of coordinating activities with other researchers, either procedure will help you to enact the values of subjectivity and rich description. Collaborative ethnography

> allows for more complete coverage of the setting and a more rapid period of data collection. . . . the insights of one person trigger new perspectives or insights in other team members. Thus leads may be confirmed or refuted more quickly. However, the team must have several characteristics: Team members must be able to brainstorm together frequently, preferably every day; members must have respect for the contributions of others; and relationships among team members must be excellent and egalitarian (Morse, 1998, p. 75).

Whether you are conducting ethnography alone or in collaboration with other researchers, you will need to establish your credibility as an interpreter of the group or culture. Your credibility as an ethnographer comes from a combination of your training and experiences; your degree of membership in the situation you are studying; and your faithfulness in collecting, analyzing, and reporting evidence.

Researcher Credibility

We will use the term **researcher credibility** to cover a number of concerns that have been referred to by many names. including authenticity, veracity, training and experience, and others (LeCompte & Goetz, 1982; Lincoln & Guba, 1985). In all likelihood, you are reading this book as part of your initial training as a communication researcher, and although you may have little or no experience conducting ethnography, you have some experience with the group or culture you intend to study. So in this section, we will consider two specific credibility issues: The first issue is your degree of membership in the group or culture; here, we will also address your key informants' degree of membership in the culture or group, as indicated by their recognition and performance competencies (Dollar, 1995). The second is the issue of **faithfulness,** the steadfastness with which you engage in ethnographic data collection, analysis, and reporting.

Degree of Membership The issue of your credibility as a human measuring instrument in the field is closely related to your degree of membership in the culture or group you seek to understand (Fitch, 1994). First, the researcher should be "deeply involved and closely connected to the scene, activity, or group being studied" (p. 36). Second, the researcher "should achieve enough distance from the phenomenon to allow for recording of action and interactions relatively uncolored by what she or he might have had at stake" (p. 36).

You may recognize these two requirements as a sort of dialectic tension. Your ability to become deeply involved in a social situation is enhanced by membership, whereas your ability to distance yourself from interactions you observe, or in which you participate, may be inhibited by being a member. Remember the Martian and the Convert roles we described in Chapter 4 (Davis, 1973)? The Convert makes unfamiliar actions and situations familiar by becoming deeply involved; the Martian tries to make everything strange, or unfamiliar, so as not to impose his or her own cultural knowledge on the situation. You will want to be "both or either," not just one of these roles (Lofland & Lofland, 1984, p. 16).

For many ethnographers, the researcher who is more of a cultural insider is a more credible instrument. Regardless of your degree of membership in the group or culture, you will need to evaluate credibility of your key informants. Both you and your informants enact your degree of membership when you competently recognize and perform culturally appropriate communication (Dollar, 1995, 1999). Your abilities to recognize and perform a range of communicative practices, to avoid making blunders or mistakes in communication and to recognize violations when they occur, and to play with cultural language (e.g., jokes, teasing) all demonstrate your degree of membership (Dollar, 1995, 1999). Of course, recognizing these communicative patterns is different from being able to *perform* culturally competent communication, such as interacting competently with members you do not already know, or making a joke that others in the culture will recognize and appreciate. Dollar (1999) argued that recognition and performance competencies might indicate differences in degree of membership.

The insider status, helpfulness, and articulateness of your key informants are especially important when your degree of membership in the group or culture is limited (Lofland & Lofland, 1984). The people with whom you interact, those you observe and interview, must be *good* representatives of their group or culture. They should represent different types of participants in that setting (i.e., different roles) if you are to capture the full range of subjective meanings available to members. For example, Dollar (1999) distinguished between *hotel* and *parking lot* Deadheads, according to where they slept and ate while they were following the band's performances in different cities. If all of her interviews and observations were conducted with hotel Deadheads, typically those with full-time jobs that afforded them the resources to rent hotel rooms and eat in restaurants, her view of the Deadhead culture would have been unduly limited. Being honest about your own degree of membership and working to locate and build relationships with credible key informants are both related to faithfulness, a second warrant for ethnographic evidence. Let's take a look at what else you can do to be a faithful ethnographer.

Faithfulness No matter how much training and experience you have as a researcher, no matter what your degree of cultural membership, inevitably there will be limits to your credibility. As the measuring instrument during field data collection, your memory, hearing, and recognition skills will all influence the credibility of the data you collect and the interpretations you make of those data. Even though some of these limits on your credibility are physical or biological (such as memory or hearing), some are limits of faithfulness, your steadfast commitment to represent the participants' meanings fully and fairly. Recognizing and acknowledging these sorts of limitations is part of operating faithfully as an ethnographer.

Faithfulness is further achieved by spending enough time in the field, going over field notes many (rather than a few) times, maintaining close and trusting relationships with key informants, and searching for additional sources of data to corroborate those already considered (Miles & Huberman, 1994; Lofland & Lofland, 1984; Spradley, 1980). Your faithfulness paves the way for you to make plausible interpretations.

Plausible Interpretations

In conducting ethnography, you will typically triangulate data to ensure plausible interpretations. As you know, this means using a combination of participant observations or interviews, archival documents, and artifact analyses. By using some form of triangulation, you have opportunities to compare interpretations of what things mean across more than one data source (e.g., self-reports, observations of behavior) or data collection strategy (i.e., sight, sound, sight-and-sound records).

Accordingly, interviews with key informants and participant observations will provide you with instances of verbal and nonverbal communication as practiced in the speech community; archival documents may also provide such instances, but in ways that are more public and verifiable. Artifacts provide additional sources from which to triangulate interpretations about participant meanings and suggest concepts you should analyze because they seem important to participants.

Smart (1998) triangulated participant observations with interviews and document analysis at a Canadian bank to argue that "professional communities create, through their discursive practices, the specific forms of knowledge they need for carrying out their work" (p. 111). Yet Smart acknowledged that this interpretation was "one of many possible renderings of the economists' professional activity" (p. 124). Ethnographers typically feel comfortable with there being more than one reasonable, possible account of a situation: "The ultimate goal of this interpretive study—like all ethnographic research—is to reveal multiple plausible interpretations which can enrich our understanding of our organizations, our cultures, and ourselves" (Trujillo, 1992, p. 365).

Let's consider a more detailed illustration of triangulation from published communication research. Kim, Lujan, and Dixon (1998) integrated the emic and etic perspectives in their study of American Indian identity integration. They began with broad categories of identity that came from two guiding theories (i.e., Berry's identity modes and Kim's cultural-intercultural identity continuum). The overall study and those initial categories were molded by the authors' emic perspective. The six-member research team conducted individual interviews with 182 American Indians in Oklahoma, talked with 17 community informants who were American Indian residents of various Oklahoma communities, and conducted observations at six research sites in Oklahoma. Kim et al. (1998) conceptualized this triangulated approach as strengthening their research, since the strengths of one approach compensated for the weaknesses of another, and vice versa.

If you are going to embrace the idea of multiple subjective realities in your research, then you have to consider whether the interpretations you are making are believable or can be supported with arguments and reasoning (Dollar, 1995; Fitch, 1994). Several types of arguments are presented in this section to address plausibility, including adequate quantity and coherence of supporting examples, and giving attention to alternative interpretations, also known as addressing counterclaims.

Adequacy of Evidence Evidence given in support of an ethnographic research claim should be based on an adequate selection of the total corpus of data (Fitch, 1994). Having some part of your ethnographic data come from publicly accessible observation records will help you bolster the plausibility of your interpretations because it will allow people other than you (the researcher) to check your subjective interpretations of the data. In addition, your ethnographic data collection and analysis will need to include your consideration of "inferences and interpretations as well as concrete phenomena" (Fitch, 1994, p. 36). For example, your presentation of examples from transcripts should allow the reader of your research report to see the communicative phenomenon of interest, how that event was represented in the data set, and your analytical inferences. This is more powerful than simply extracting examples of particular phenomena as the only source of evidence (Fitch, 1994). This way, "readers can decide for themselves whether or not to believe the ethnographer's account of what it is that a particular group of people are doing at any given time" (McDermott, Gospodinoff, & Aron, 1978, p. 245).

In fact, Trujillo (1992) contended that all ethnographic field notes are **inscriptions**—first-level interpretations of events. The ethnographer's inscriptions create texts through which other people (e.g., readers of research reports) can interpret the understandings of members. Selecting evidence that represents more of the data set, rather than less, and presenting that evidence coherently will help you to ensure plausible interpretations. Furthermore, Philipsen (1977) suggested three questions that you could ask yourself to test "the adequacy of statements which purport to represent the native's view" (p. 49):

First, does the report use the native's own terms or verbatim description? Second, and failing the first test, do the ethnographer's terms or descriptions refer to something that the native agrees is a recognizable feature of his social world, and if so, can the native person give it a name? Third, does the native person agree that the ethnographer's insight enables him (the native) to better understand his own social world? (p. 49)

Philipsen concluded that the last two of these three tests provided evidence of the *validity* of an ethnographic researcher's observations. Although a discovery researcher is likely to frame validity as accuracy, per se, ethnographers see room for more than one accurate, plausible interpretation of a situation or phenomenon. Paying attention to other possibly valid interpretations is the next warrant for ethnographic research.

Attention to Alternative Interpretations A second way to ensure plausible interpretations in ethnographic research is to attend to **counterclaims**—other interpretations that could be potentially supported by a data set. Consider what other possible claims your data could support. One way you might do this is relevant when you are coding or reducing data into categories or themes. As you organize instances of talk into categories, consider all the instances of talk that don't fit into any one of your categories. If there are too many of those instances, then perhaps your overall data set does not support that interpretation adequately. Perhaps another interpretation will make better use of the data (Agar, 1983).

You should also search for disconfirming observations, if they do not readily appear in your analysis of the data, in order to ensure that your interpretations are plausible. Refer back to our discussion of negative case analysis in Chapter 4. Consider whether you need to collect more observations using deviant case sampling (Patton, 1990), that is, returning to the field and trying to find instances of data that do not fit the interpretation you have tentatively identified. To the degree that no such instances of communicative data can be located, your interpretations are warranted as plausible.

Transferable Findings

Interpretive researchers have as a goal "producing meaning-centered investigations of social life that can be coherently tied to other such investigations" (Fitch, 1994, p. 36). Your attempt to tie your ethnographic study to other similar studies can be thought of as an issue of **transferability.** Will your interpretations transfer, or be applicable, to another group or culture? In this section we will introduce three criteria that ethnographers use to ensure transferability: confirmability, relevance, and generality.

Confirmability means that the findings you posit, based on your analysis of data, can be confirmed, or echoed, by another person who had similar access to those same data sources. This is akin to *agreement among judges,* a form of validity in discovery research. This is, in part, why Fitch (1994) argued that researchers ought to try to make claims for which at least part of the data come from publicly accessible observation records. She also urged ethnographers to be "deeply involved and closely connected to the scene, activity, or group studied" (p. 36), which should help you ensure transferable findings that are relevant to that group and others like it.

Relevance means that your interpretations are germane, or salient to the people in the group or culture that you are studying. An interpretation or conclusion is only relevant if it matters to the participants. You should be able to show how participants orient to and signal others about the communication practices that you are describing, interpreting, or evaluating (McDermott et al., 1978). Perhaps members reference the context for their own behaviors; they may hold one another accountable to proceed in contextually appropriate ways, or their collective positioning (actions) may indicate what they are trying to accomplish together. Your ability to represent these matters will make your interpretations relevant, and more likely transferable as a result.

Finally, to establish **generality** means that you try to make interpretations and inferences that apply to more than one participant or moment in the communicative group or culture you study. One way that you can do this is by faithfully basing your claims on the total corpus of data, rather than one or two isolated observations within a data set. Another way is to use the same descriptive framework in more than one study, so that the findings from multiple studies can be compared with one another, as the ethnographers of speaking do with Hymes's (1962, 1974) SPEAKING mnemonic. In this way, general interpretations about communication in more than one group may be discerned, either by you or by other researchers using the same framework you used in your study.

TECHNOLOGY AND ETHNOGRAPHIC RESEARCH

Given the emphasis on face-to-face, naturally occurring interactions in ethnography, there have been relatively few published ethnographic studies of computer-mediated communication. Lindlof and Schatzer (1998) outlined four ways that such ethnographic studies differ from traditional ethnography. First, the nature and boundaries of a virtual community differ from those of communities that are embodied within shared geographic places. Second, physical presence in a traditional community differs from social presence in a virtual community. Third, the strategies for entering and becoming a member are different in virtual communities. Fourth, and finally, the procedures and ethical issues related to data collection are quite different in the case of a virtual community.

However, despite these important differences, virtual digital communities are ripe for ethnographic analysis because of their cultural nature (i.e., shared values and knowledge form the basis of membership) and because of the relevance of the communication code to demonstrating membership in a virtual environment. Unlike a face-to-face community, membership in a virtual community is not enacted by one's visual, nonverbal presentation; rather, more depends on the demonstration of competence in the interaction itself (Lindlof & Schatzer, 1998). Furthermore, research questions about virtual communities, such as "What do these interactions mean to participants?" and "What is being accomplished in their talk?," are still well answered by ethnographic methods. For example, Bakardjieva and Smith (2001) examined how lay users of the Internet in Vancouver, British Columbia, creatively appropriated the technology in their everyday lives.

Yet, ethnography based solely on CMC data brings with it particular ethical issues, whether the data come from a chat room, email messages, or a listserv group. CMC interactions are more readily observed in a covert fashion, and there are still vast "unsettled distinctions between 'public' and 'private' behavior across a range of cyberspace contexts" (Lindlof & Schatzer, 1998, p. 186). The processes of gaining participants' informed consent, disclosing research procedures and making agreements with participants, negotiating access, and so on are all impacted by differences between virtual and embodied communities. Finally, because the data for such research

projects already exists in digital form, production of these studies would be

> fully compatible with the World Wide Web's system architecture. . . . Similarly, ethnographies of CMC culture can be envisioned which would provide the discursive threads that underpin an analysis, along with field notes, full-text interviews, generations of Web page design, graphic materials, and URLs to the ethnographic sites themselves and related research projects (Lindlof & Schatzer, 1998, p. 187).

But technology impacts the conduct of ethnographic communication research well beyond the study of virtual communities online. Miles and Huberman (1994) gave an overview of some of the computer software programs that can be used in ethnographic data analysis, including word processors, word retrievers, text-base managers, code-and-retrieve programs, theory builders, and conceptual network builders (see also Witmer, 1997). They reviewed several types of software and concluded that "on the order of two dozen programs well suited to the needs of qualitative researchers are now available" (p. 43). According to their survey, three out of four qualitative researchers reported using computer software "for entering data, coding, search and retrieval, making displays, or building concepts" (p. 43).

Quite a few tasks involved in ethnographic research can be done with a basic word processor—entering and editing field notes, coding data into categories, or using key words for subsequent search-and-retrieval procedures. In addition, most ethno-graphers use the word processor to enter their progressive notes as they analyze the data from field notes and interview transcripts, and to prepare their final reports. Some tasks require special computer software programs, like doing content analysis, storing a database, or displaying data via graphic maps. NUD-IST is a computer software program, for example, that has been associated with grounded theory methodology (Strauss & Corbin, 1998). Finally, some ethnographic data collection is now occurring over the Internet (some examples from published communication research include Bakardjieva & Smith, 2001; Cezec-Kecmanovic, Treleaven, & Moodie, 2000; LaRose & Whitten, 2000). It is very likely that ethnographers' reliance on computer software for data collection and analysis, as well as hypermedia programming tools (Singer, 1995) will continue.

Of course, the prevalence and ease of email and other interactive digital communication media is also changing the conduct of ethnography, especially for collaborative ethnographers. Trujillo (1999) has conducted a number of collaborative ethnographies with his students at Sacramento State University, as well as other researchers in the United States. He listed at least three benefits of the team's use of communication technology in those studies: (1) The team's "email discussions helped to maintain the dialogue needed to develop a stronger sense of teamwork" (p. 715); (2) the importance of the research topic was "validated by others across the country" (p. 716); and (3) the researchers could share their field notes on a World Wide Web site.

SUMMARY

We began this chapter by distinguishing ethnographic research methods from two related research methodologies, grounded theory and naturalistic inquiry. We then discussed some procedures you can use to develop research questions that can be investigated with ethnographic research methods, and we outlined the sorts of descriptive, interpretative, and evaluative claims that typify ethnographic studies of communication in context. We also talked about critical ethnography, the use of ethnographic data collection and analytic strategies to support claims about how communication should be reformed in a certain context, as a bridge from the interpretive to the critical research paradigm.

The next section of the chapter focused on ethnographic data collection sources, including participant observation and interviews with key informants, as well as the analysis of archival documents and artifacts. We presented strategies you can use to collect ethnographic data, including ways you can gain access to a particular setting, select key informants, take field notes, and exit the field. We then discussed a key difference in ethnographic data analysis, relative to data analysis in survey and experimental research methods: Ethnographic data analysis begins almost as soon as data collection commences, and continues during and after data collection, whereas survey data analysis commences only after data collection is completed. We presented some ways of transcribing interview data, coding and reducing field notes, applying descriptive frameworks to ethnographic data, and writing case study reports of communication in context.

In the warrants segment, we reviewed some of the interpretive paradigm values and standards for evaluating research that you read about in Chapter 4. But here, we tried to show you more specifically how ethnographers enact those warrants. For example, we included a discussion of collaborative ethnography as a triangulation strategy that enacts the values of subjectivity and rich description. We developed examples of how you can demonstrate your credibility as a human research instrument, show the plausibility of your interpretations, and demonstrate the transferability of your findings. Finally, we mentioned two ways that CMC and ethnographic research methods overlap; first, we are beginning to see ethnographies published of virtual communities, and second, ethnographers, like all researchers, are making use of innovative technologies in their data collecting, analysis, and reporting their findings.

KEY TERMS

Archival documents	Communicative resources	Ethnography of speaking
Artifacts	Confirmability	Face sheets
Autoethnography	Counterclaims	Faithfulness
Case study	Culture	Formative evaluation
Coding	Data logging	Gaining access (or entry)
Comment sheets	Ethnographic interviews	Gatekeepers
Communal function	Ethnography	Generality
Communication code	Ethnography of communication	Grounded theory

Inscriptions   Participant observation   Sponsors

Interviewer training   Relevance   Summative evaluation

Key informants   Researcher credibility   Transferability

Naturalistic inquiry   Speech community

DISCUSSION QUESTIONS

1. Think about the cultures to which you belong. What interpretations are "common sense" for members of those cultures?

2. What do you think it means to "make the familiar strange"? What are some of your familiar messages or ways of interacting that might be "made strange" for ethnographic analysis?

3. Make a list of the speech communities to which you belong. What are some of the rules for speaking, and interpreting the speech of others, in one of these communities? Compare your list with those of your classmates. Do you see any commonalities?

4. Think about the groups in which you participate and communicate. Does codeswitching occur in those groups? How frequently? When do members switch from one way of speaking to another "code" and why?

5. Write a short essay describing the communication practices in your family of origin. Use the warrants described in this chapter (i.e., credibility, plausibility, and transferability) to evaluate your description. Is it adequate?

"TRY IT!" ACTIVITIES

1. Participate in and/or observe a group or cultural scene for about 30 minutes.

    a. Write down three research questions that you think might be investigated about the communication in this social situation (Spradley, 1980).

    b. If you are a member of this group or culture, note what patterns or processes are likely to be misunderstood by an outsider in this situation.

    c. If you are an outsider to this group or culture, try to notice what you do *not* understand in this setting.

2. Spend 2 or 3 hours visiting one of the social situations that you are considering for your ethnographic research (Spradley, 1980).

    a. Try to identify 1 or 2 people that you suspect might be *key informants* in that setting and describe what led you to identify these people.

    b. What initial topics or questions might you want to talk about with these key informants?

    c. What artifacts or archival documents might you be able to use to triangulate your interviews with key informants?

    d. What would you need to do in order to gain access to this setting?

12

Traditional and Interpretive Methods of Rhetorical Criticism

ABSTRACT

In this chapter, you will learn about methods of rhetorical criticism from the discovery paradigm (neo-Aristotelian, historical, and genre criticism) and the interpretive paradigm (metaphoric analysis, dramatism, fantasy theme analysis, and narrative criticism). Several studies will serve as examples of bridges to the critical paradigm methods. As part of an historical overview of these methods, we will discuss the types of claims you would be likely to assert with each method and the different sorts of texts that provide the data or evidentiary sources for these analyses. For each method, you will learn to apply the warrants of traditional and interpretive approaches to rhetorical criticism, including validity and reliability, adequacy of evidence, triangulation, and plausibility of interpretations through coherence and fidelity. We conclude the chapter by considering the contributions of technology to the content and process of rhetorical criticism.

OUTLINE

In the last two chapters, you have learned about interpretive methods of analyzing communication that occurs between two people or among members of a group or culture. In this chapter, we will focus on methods of rhetorical criticism, methods that analyze communication as text. The methods of rhetorical criticism in general reflect a very close connection between the claim the researcher advances and the text chosen for analysis. As a result, we have chosen to present claims and data together throughout this chapter.

As you will see, claims can be made about many different types of texts: a speech, a film, this textbook that you are reading. Barry Brummett (1994), a noted rhetorical theorist and critic, defined text as "a set of signs related to each other insofar as their meanings all contribute to the same set of effects or functions" (p. 27), and so the concept of texts has been expanded to include many different types of verbal and nonverbal signs. A television advertisement, a collection of songs, and styles of dress can all be considered texts. You will explore the many forms that communication data as texts can take in each of the methods presented in this chapter. The first three methods we situate in the discovery paradigm: neo-Aristotelian, historical, and genre criticism. The last four approaches are methods from the interpretive paradigm: metaphoric analysis, dramatism, fantasy theme analysis, and narrative analysis.

TRADITIONAL RHETORICAL CRITICISM

The first three methods, neo-Aristotelian, historical, and genre criticism, are considered the traditional methods of rhetorical criticism. They are situated in the discovery paradigm because of a number of characteristics they have in common. As described by Brock, Scott, and Chesebro (1990), traditional methods share this set of assumptions:

1. Society is stable: people, circumstances, and rhetorical principles are fundamentally the same throughout history.

2. Rhetoricians have discovered the essential principles of public discourse.

3. Rhetorical concepts are reasonably discrete and can be studied apart from one another in the process of analyzing rhetorical discourse.

4. A reasonably close word-thought-thing relationship exists. Rhetorical concepts accurately reflect and describe an assumed reality (p. 28).

The emphasis on a common and universal set of principles to be applied in the analysis of rhetorical discourse, and the belief that these principles can accurately reflect and describe an assumed reality, is at the core of the discovery paradigm. We call these methods "traditional" because they were the earliest of the more contemporary approaches and because, as noted by Brock et al. (1990), it was the accepted approach "for at least thirty years" (p. 25). We will begin by exploring neo-Aristotelian approaches to rhetorical criticism.

Neo-Aristotelian Criticism

All methods with this type of approach obviously have their root in Aristotle's conception of rhetoric. It is important to note, however, that classical and neo-classical methods are not equivalent terms. The approaches described in this section have less to do with how Aristotle and other classical philosophers originally conceived of rhetoric than how their methods were later interpreted and applied. This distinction has sometimes been at the core of heated debate in our field (see, for example, the series of essays in Gross & Keith, 1997).

Neo-Aristotelian criticism is a term that loosely binds together various forms of rhetorical criticism applied to the analysis of speech texts from the early part of the 20th century through the 1960s. Its methods included the interpretation and application of the classical philosophers toward the goal of creating effective speakers (Lucaites, Condit, & Caudill, 1999, p. 8). Its approach was exemplified in Herbert Wichelns's (1925) essay, "The Literary Criticism of Oratory," in which he identified rhetorical criticism's central purpose as "concerned with effect. It regards a speech as a communication to a specific audience, and holds its business to be the analysis and appreciation of the orator's method of imparting his ideas to his hearers" (p. 209).

Wichelns went on to outline in some detail the methodological approach the critic should use. It was based on Aristotle's ideas as later codified in the canons of rhetoric. Other scholars in the field, such as Hochmuth Nichols (1955) and Thonssen & Baird (1948), elaborated on his general approach. During this period, neo-Aristotelian criticism was greatly influenced by *modernism*. Recall from Chapter 1 in the discussion of philosophical perspectives that modernism is a reliance on objectivism and the pursuit of universal truths. Situated squarely in the discovery paradigm, modernism has been described as

> a commitment to scientism, and objective, morally neutral, universal knowledge. In the modern worldview, the universe is a relatively simple, stable, highly ordered place, describable in and reducible to absolute formulas that hold across contexts. Disagreement, in such a worldview, is treated as an unnecessary pathology that arises primarily from ignorance and irrationality. The solution or cure for social discord is therefore greater research, less passion, more rationality, and more education (Lucaites, Condit, & Caudill, 1999, p. 11).

Traditional neo-Aristotelian criticism was the epitome of the modernist perspective, stressing the goals of objectivity and an amoral detachment. It assessed whether a speech was effective by how well it conformed to Aristotelian means of persuasion. "To the degree that a speech employed all of the means available to it, it was judged to be a good speech," and the critic was expected to "maintain objective distance from the critical object" (Lucaites et al., p. 11).

As you will learn in the next section, the neo-Aristotelian critic analyzes the argument of a text by evaluating how well the speaker used various persuasive devices and how effective the argument appeared to be based on the observed reactions of the targeted audiences. Rather than focus on elements like the hidden motivations of the speaker or the rhetorical situation, this type of criticism focuses on the features of the text and the intended effects on the audience (Leff, 1999).

Claims and Data: Emphasis on the Text and the Audience The claims in neo-Aristotelian approaches are descriptive and explanatory. As a much-cited example, Hill's (1972) analysis of Nixon's Vietnam speech text in 1969 required describing the situation and characteristics of Nixon's audience. He then explained the effectiveness of Nixon's argument in terms of the evidence he used for persuasion, and finally he explained the effects of the speech on the targeted audience.

One or more rhetorical artifacts comprise the data of neo-Aristotelian critics. Foss (1996) used the term **rhetorical artifact** to refer to the speeches or other rhetorical texts selected for analysis. Artifacts are the "text, trace, or tangible evidence" of a rhetorical act; for example, a rhetorical act might be a speech made by President Bush to a target audience, and the rhetorical artifact of that speech would be a written transcript of that speech (p. 7). Critics typically use transcripts and audio and video recordings of the text as well as any artifactual documentation or evidence that would help the critic identify any critical elements, such as historical records, letters, or other accounts from eyewitnesses.

Foss (1996) listed three basic steps in conducting neo-Aristotelian analyses: reconstructing the context, analyzing the rhetorical artifact, and assessing its effects (pp. 27–31). The critic usually begins by situating the artifact in time and place, identifying as part of the context any notable characteristics of the intended audience. For example, Hill (1972) began his analysis with a brief description of the situation and Nixon's targeted audience. In effect, Hill set the stage for the next step, a lengthier analysis of the speech itself.

During the second phase, the speech text is examined in terms of invention, organization, style, and delivery. These are derived from the **canons of rhetoric.** We have omitted memory, a canon that originally helped speakers learn more effective ways of memorizing their speeches. We do not address it here because most speakers today do not memorize their texts, and because it is absent from most neo-Aristotelian critical analyses. The remaining four canons are explained in some detail.

Invention As a neo-Aristotelian critic, you might focus most of your attention on this canon. **Invention** has been defined as "the speaker's major ideas, lines of argument, or content" (Foss, 1996, p. 29). An argument can be supported by two types of evidence or proofs: inartistic and artistic. **Inartistic proofs** are external forms such as testimony from witnesses or key documents. **Artistic proofs** are internal constructions of the speaker and include *logos, ethos,* and *pathos* (Foss, p. 29).

The term *logos* refers to the logical or rational appeals a speaker makes by identifying the central claims made and the evidence used to support them. Aristotle listed several major logical devices or strategies applied through inductive and deductive reasoning. We consider just one of them in detail here: the enthymeme.

The **enthymeme,** a form of deductive reasoning, is a device used strategically to engage an audience. It is based on a syllogism consisting of three parts: an observation, a generalization, and an inference (Harper, 1973, p. 306). At least one of these parts is omitted so that the audience must participate by filling in the blanks (Aden, 1994; Bitzer, 1959). The rhetor or speaker relies on the existing ideas, beliefs, and attitudes of an audience to complete the enthymeme.

For example, Hill (1972) argued that Nixon used several enthymemes to establish his basic premises. When Nixon stated that immediate withdrawal from Vietnam would result in the punishment and murder of innocent people, he used the general predictive rule that "the future will resemble the past" in the implicit comparison of North Vietnam to South Vietnam (Foss, 1996, p. 40). He also implied that good Americans ought to feel loyalty toward their allies just as individuals should feel personal loyalty toward their friends in identifying the consequences for South Vietnam in the event of an immediate departure of American soldiers.

As a contemporary study of this Aristotelian device, Aden (1994) extended the application of the enthymeme to a televised talk show to explore David Duke's argument. David Duke was an avowed white supremacist and former Ku Klux Klan member prior to his bid for a congressional seat. During his campaign, however, he dismissed these associations as earlier "youthful indiscretions." After the election, he returned to criticize the Louisiana State Assembly. Aden argued that Duke's antigovernment attacks made use of subjects so "deeply ingrained in the American psyche—ethnic origin, work ethic, government's role in society, etc." that his use of the enthymeme omitted "both a generalization and an inference" (p. 6):

Observation: Government actions, especially welfare and affirmative action, hurt whites economically and socially.

Generalization (implied): Minorities are the recipients of these government programs.

Inference (implied): Minorities are the cause of the social and economic problems suffered by whites (p. 6).

By relying on the power of the enthymeme, Aden contended that Duke was able to voice prejudicial views without stating them explicitly.

The second form of artistic proof, ***ethos,*** refers to the character or credibility of the rhetor. As the critic,

you would specifically examine how the speaker's character influences the audience to accept or reject the argument's claims (Foss, 1996, pp. 29–30). *Ethos* is defined by three basic components: moral character, intelligence, and goodwill. Moral character refers to the speaker's perceived integrity or honesty; the intelligence of the speaker "has more to do with practical wisdom and shared values" than it does with intellectual training or knowledge. The speaker's goodwill rests in the perception that the speaker regards the audience positively and will act in their best interests (Griffin, 2000, p. 279).

In your role as a neo-Aristotelian critic, you would present evidence that the speaker has demonstrated the correct *ethos.* For example, you could show that the speaker's moral character was connected to the audience's moral values. You might argue that a speaker's intelligence was displayed by "common sense, good taste, and familiarity with current topics and interests." A speaker's sense of goodwill might be demonstrated by showing how the speech itself conveyed honesty, identification with, and praise for the audience (Foss, 1996, p. 30). Rather than argue that a speaker's actions were morally reprehensible, your role as a neo-Aristotelian rhetorical critic is to offer tangible evidence that the speaker demonstrated *ethos.*

In two interesting contemporary studies of *ethos,* J. L. Pauley (1998) and McGee (1998) analyzed public transformations of character. According to Pauley, Louis Farrakhan, an African-American political leader, adopted the persona of the *prophet.* By identifying himself as a modern-day prophet, Farrakhan cast himself as "a voice of both hope and warning," declaring "impending doom if God's people do not repent 'today'" (p. 518). As Pauley pointed out, prophets have a history of saying unpopular things and of being persecuted by the established ruling class, and yet they are compelled to go forward, to "speak God's message" (p. 518). By adopting this persona, Farrakhan not only avoided damage to his *ethos,* but the "prophet" characterization actually enhanced it, helping his Christian and Muslim audiences accept his harsh judgments about the injustices of racial prejudice.

On the opposite end of the spectrum, McGee (1998) analyzed the transformation of *ethos* in David Duke, described in an earlier example as a one-time leader of the KKK and self-proclaimed white supremacist. McGee analyzed Duke's half-hour gubernatorial campaign film for Christian references. He found that Duke made frequent use of "witnessing" and powerful conversion rhetoric from a "born-again" Christian. These strategies made renunciation of his former affiliations and reconstruction of his *ethos* seem plausible and acceptable to his voter audiences. While he did not win the gubernatorial race, Duke was enormously popular among white Evangelical voters and won a congressional seat in a district that was 99% white. Based primarily on the effect of his argument, McGee concluded Duke was moderately successful in changing his *ethos.*

The third and final form of artistic proof is **pathos,** or emotional appeal. More specifically, your task as the critic would be to discover what emotions were aroused by the speaker and how effective they were in facilitating the audience's acceptance of the speaker's claims (Foss, 1996, p. 30). To return to an earlier study, Aden (1994) demonstrated how David Duke strategically used various devices to evoke racist and antigovernment sentiments in his audience. Using the same speaker, McGee (1998) showed how effectively Duke's use of conversion rhetoric directly appealed to the strong values and emotions of his Christian audiences.

Organization The second canon of rhetoric is called **organization** (Foss, 1996, p. 30) or sometimes arrangement (Brock et al., 1990). It refers to the structure or general pattern of the various components in a rhetorical text. Your role as critic would be to try to determine whether the order or placement of the main claim, as well as the major evidence and warrants used to support them, change the effectiveness of the rhetor's argument. As an example, Rybacki and Rybacki (1991) pointed to Theodore Roosevelt's "Man with the Muckrake" speech to illustrate that the order of points will affect the impact on the audience. The speech contained three main claims, but, as the authors indicated, only "his discussion of the evils of muckraking received more attention than his other points" (p. 61).

Style The neo-Aristotelian critic should also consider **style,** the third canon of rhetoric. Style is often equated with the language the rhetor uses. The task of the critic is to discover "whether the language style contributes to the accomplishment of the rhetor's goal—assists in the development of the thesis, facilitates the communication of ideas, and thus helps to create the intended response" (Foss, 1996, p. 30, pp. 77–78). Hill's (1972) analysis investigated how Nixon's style was designed to convey "clarity and forthrightness," which shifted about two-thirds of the way through his speech to emphasize a new sense of "gravity and impressiveness" (p. 104). In another analysis of presidential rhetoric, G. E. Pauley (1998) explored the way in which President Lyndon Johnson used religious terminology to bring "the sacred into the present" (p. 40). Speaking of historical events regarding the civil rights movement, the religious style of words he chose underscored his exhortation, "If America fails to fulfill its promise and do God's will, the nation will have faltered" (p. 41).

Delivery The final canon of rhetoric we will consider is **delivery**—the rhetor's presentation. It includes the mode of presentation, that is, whether the rhetor presents an impromptu speech, speaks extemporaneously from an outline, or orally presents a manuscript of a speech. It also refers to the medium of transmission, such as radio or television, that the speaker may use. The term *delivery* also encompasses a speaker's nonverbal and vocal behaviors, such as gestures, appearance, and vocal resonance. G. E. Pauley's (1998) analysis of President Johnson used a taped presentation of the speech. He focused on not only President Johnson's style in choice of words and timing, but also his delivery: "The tone of his voice, his speaking rate, and his vocal emphasis give him the persona of a preacher" (p. 43). By considering style and delivery in President Johnson's rhetoric, Pauley provided a dimension of analysis often overlooked in studies that emphasize the inventions and organization of the rhetor's argument.

Once you have completed the first two steps of neo-Aristotelian analysis by reconstructing the context and analyzing the rhetorical artifact using one or more of the canons, the last step is the assessment of the effects of the rhetorical act on the audience (Foss, 1996). As the critic, you would assume the rhetor had a purpose in speaking to the audience. Your task is to determine whether the rhetor achieved that purpose. To evaluate the outcome of the speech, you would look for evidence that the outcome had or had not been successful; then you would apply several standards of evaluation in determining the strength or worth of the evidence as warrants.

Warrants: standards of evaluation Before you explore the effects of a text on an audience, it is important to consider how the basic assumptions from this discovery paradigm perspective can be applied to the two standard warrants of validity and reliability. The underlying assumptions of neo-Aristotelian methodology include assuming rhetorical principles used in a classical analysis will remain the same throughout history. This set of principles is universal in substance and in application. The canons of rhetoric can be applied rationally and objectively to assess whatever is there in the text, and also to explain its effects on an audience. Your goal as the critic is to first reconstruct the text so that it is an accurate representation of the original text. Your second goal is to accurately apply one or more of the rhetorical canons to demonstrate the strengths (or weaknesses) of the rhetor's skillfulness. The concern for accuracy and truthfulness of representation underscores the importance of *validity* as a standard evaluation, as we have noted in previous chapters.

As a neo-Aristotelian critic, you will also assess the level of logical consistency in the argument presented by the rhetor. The evidence presented should not be contradictory in any way, but should be "sufficient, representative, relevant, and clear" (Rybacki & Rybacki, 1991, p. 58). Consistency is also frequently extended to mean that the argument used was appropriately situated in its historical context to withstand the temporal test of *reliability* (Rybacki & Rybacki, 1991), a warrant we have described in earlier chapters. As the critic, you should evaluate whether the rhetor has made consistent and valid choices in the application of the evidence in support of the text's central claim.

The standards of *validity* (accuracy and probable truth in representation) and *reliability* (internal consistency and consistency across time) are the means of explaining any short- and long-term effects. One common way the neo-Aristotelian critic has attempted to assess the immediate reactions of the audience to the rhetorical act is by examining historical documentation of those effects. Looking at newspaper accounts of crowds listening to a speech is one of the ways critics might use this documentation. Assessing the long-term effects depends on the temporal distance between the rhetorical act and the critic. Most critics apply this perspective retrospectively instead of forecasting future effects. In this regard, neo-Aristotelian criticism coincides with historical criticism.

Historical Criticism

Historical criticism shares many characteristics with the neo-Aristotelian approach to criticism. Both are oriented toward the speaker's rhetorical response to the problems presented in a historically situated context. Both share the four assumptions identified earlier as the grounding beliefs of the traditional perspective. And finally, both approaches claim "Aristotle identified the fundamental rhetorical process" (Brock et al., 1990, p. 28).

The differences between these two critical approaches lie more in emphasis and degree rather than fundamental distinctions. As a neo-Aristotelian critic, you would tend to concentrate on the message characteristics and their effects on the audience. As an historical critic, your analysis would focus on the "historical elements" of the rhetor and the situation. These emphases may take form in biographical studies (i.e., studies of the rhetor) or in case studies (i.e., studies of the situation).

Claims and Data: Emphasis on the Rhetor and the Situation Claims in biographical analyses are descriptive and explanatory. By careful and systematic description of the context, your role as a rhetorical critic would entail historically situating the rhetoric of a particular speaker across several rhetorical acts within one particular time period or throughout a speaker's life span. In biographical studies, you will find that presidents are often popular targets. For example, Johnstone (1995) analyzed Ronald Reagan's rhetoric during the 1984 presidential campaign. In this case, the critic examined the unique characterization of the rhetoric because it came from the same source, the same person. As a biographical rhetorical critic, you would obviously have to keep the emphasis on the rhetor.

If you took a case study approach to rhetorical criticism, your approach would differ from biographical analyses in focusing on the rhetorical situation rather than the rhetor. In some studies, for example, one particular rhetorical act is explored as an historical event. For example, Black's (1994) study of Lincoln's Gettysburg Address showed the significance of the geographical references made in the historical context of his audience. Weitzel (1994) analyzed Martin Luther King's "I Have a Dream" speech, claiming that the fact that the text was spoken to a live audience was a significant factor in King's apparently spontaneous addition of the "dream" section. McClure's (2000) recent study demonstrated how Frederick Douglass's Fourth of July oration was a "defining rhetorical moment" marking the speaker's shift in opinion of the Constitution as a proslavery document to an antislavery document. Each of these cases represents a rhetorical event that responded to the specific dictates of each situation.

Occasionally, you might combine biographical and case study approaches. For example, Casey (2001) showed how the rhetoric of Alexander Campbell, a well-known preacher and reformer during the 19th century in America, marked a general shift in sermons as rhetorical texts. In other case studies, the emphasis is on the argument or rhetoric surrounding a specific historical event. As an illustration, Scott's (2001) recent analysis was a case study of the debate surrounding public policy on routine testing of pregnant women and newborn infants for HIV. Regardless of whether you emphasize the rhetor or the rhetorical situation as critic, you will still be concerned with warranting the claims you make with the evidence you have provided.

Warrants: Standards of Evaluation Because historical and neo-Aristotelian approaches share a similar foundation, warranting historical criticism is nearly the same process as warranting neo-Aristotelian approaches. The emphasis is on accuracy or *validity* in the description and representation of the rhetor and the rhetorical situation, based on the assumption that there is "a causal relation between events in history and public address" (Brock et al., 1990, p. 26). As noted by Brock et al. (1990), "If critics strive for objectivity and believe that rhetorical principles reflect a relatively stable reality, it follows that an accurate reconstruction of history is their goal" (p. 28). Obviously, the emphasis is also on the consistency or *reliability* of the analysis over time, a function made more possible by situating rhetorical texts in their historical contexts. Now that you have seen how claims and data are constructed in neo-Aristotelian and historical criticism, and the warrants used to evaluate them, you are ready to examine the last of the traditional methods, genre criticism.

Genre Criticism

The rationale for placing genre criticism in the traditional perspective is that it represents one of the earlier approaches to rhetorical criticism in our field, and it has classical origins shared with the other traditional approaches. Generally, generic criticism is the attempt to find a **genre**—a common pattern in rhetorical texts across similar types of contexts. Foss (1996) identified the central assumption of generic criticism as the belief that "certain types of situations provoke similar needs and expectations among audiences and thus call for particular kinds of rhetoric"

(p. 225). In classical times and early on in our contemporary methods, the role of the generic critic was to classify or categorize specific types of rhetoric. This is one of the hallmark features of the discovery paradigm we described in Chapter 1. Recently, the concept of genre has become a more complex conception leading to new treatments. You will learn about these in the sections that follow.

Traditional Forms Early studies made use of Aristotle's identification of three types of oratory: deliberative, forensic, and epideictic. **Deliberative rhetoric** was political discourse, speeches given on the floor of the legislative assembly for the purpose of establishing or changing a law. Because it was rhetoric directed toward the making of policy, it was described as future-oriented (Gill, 1994). The goal of this type of oratory was identifying the expedience (advantage) or nonexpedience (injury) in accepting a policy, achieved through the strategies of exhortation and dissuasion, or identifying the benefits and drawbacks of adopting a particular policy (Foss, 1996; Hauser, 1991).

The second type of rhetoric, termed **forensic,** was characterized by the legal discourse of courtroom proceedings. The people of Athens in ancient Greece did not have professional lawyers to defend them. Aristotle was classifying the type of speeches made by ordinary citizens seeking justice in the courtroom, employing strategies of accusation and defense (Foss, 1996; Hauser, 1991). Because of the nature of the context, this type of speech is oriented in the past; that is, it concerns the accounts of actions already committed (Gill, 1994).

A study by Johnson and Sellnow (1995) may help to distinguish between deliberative and forensic rhetoric. They investigated the rhetoric surrounding the Exxon tanker *Valdez* and the 1989 oil spill into Alaska's Prince William Sound. In the first phase of such a crisis, much of the rhetoric was devoted to discovering who was at fault and how blame should be assigned. In this phase of accusation and defense, the rhetoric was decidedly forensic; it was focused on past events. During the second phase of the crisis, the rhetoric shifted to establishing policies to prevent the problems and ensuing crisis in the future. The rhetoric of this phase was then classified as deliberative because of its forward emphasis on creating policy.

Aristotle listed a third type of rhetoric as **epideictic.** This genre refers to ceremonial speeches given on special occasions to praise or blame another's actions, to uphold an individual as virtuous, or condemn an individual as corrupt. This type of rhetoric is considered oriented to the present (Gill, 1994). As Johnson and Sellnow pointed out in the example above, there are elements of the epideictic genre in both phases since the castigation of Exxon and the organization's responses involved blaming and defending the integrity or character of the organizational leadership.

Claims and Data The claims of generic criticism are primarily descriptive in the classification process and explanatory in the use of inductive or deductive reasoning to explain the significance of the classification. If you are conducting generic criticism, you will choose one of several options. In establishing a new genre, you would first analyze several rhetorical texts to determine inductively whether a genre exists (Campbell & Jamieson, 1978; Foss, 1996). Foss termed this approach **generic description.** The second option is called **generic participation,** a deductive process of comparison where you would compare the characteristics of several genres with the characteristics of several rhetorical artifacts for the purpose of classifying the artifacts by genres. The final option, **generic application,** occurs when you deductively explain how the characteristics of genre should be applied to a specific rhetorical text to assess whether it is a good or poor fit (Foss, 1996, pp. 229–234). Confusion about what constitutes a good fit as well as the recognition that Aristotle's classifications were incomplete has led to reconceptualizing this methodological approach and the emergence of new genres (Campbell & Jamieson, 1978; Jamieson & Campbell, 1982).

New Approaches to Genre Studies Generic critics have been quick to point out that the process of identifying a genre and/or applying it to a rhetorical artifact is not a clean and easy set of classifying procedures. One of the difficulties is in deciding what constitutes a genre. The genres that Aristotle identified were those most common to his experience, confined specifically to oratory. Contemporary studies have considerably expanded the list. Among the first in our field, genre studies included diatribes (Windt, 1972), papal encyclicals (Jamieson, 1973), doctrinal rhetoric (Hart, 1971), women's rights rhetoric (Campbell, 1973), eulogies (Jamieson & Campbell, 1982), jeremiads (Ritter, 1980), and apologias (Ware & Linkugel, 1973). This list is certainly not exhaustive but provides a sample of early genre criticism.

After investigating a number of genre studies, Jamieson and Campbell (1982; Campbell & Jamieson, 1978) argued that generic criticism could not be considered a simple classification procedure. For example, they pointed out that there were elements from several genres in one rhetorical artifact. By analyzing eulogies for Senator Robert Kennedy, they showed that eulogies are a distinct genre by themselves, and yet they may contain deliberative elements as well. Further investigation led them to define genres as "dynamic fusions of substantive, stylistic, and situational elements and as constellations that are strategic responses to the demands of the situation and the rhetor" (Jamieson & Campbell, p. 146). They noted that this definition preserves Aristotle's conception of genre while adding Burke's perspective of "rhetorical acts as strategies to encompass situations" (p. 146). This represents a shift from a classical, discovery paradigm perspective to a more interpretive framework.

Foss (1996) described the three elements present in the Campbell and Jamieson definition: (1) *situational requirements,* or recognition that certain situations evoke certain rhetorical responses, (2) *substantive and stylistic characteristics,* or content and form characteristics that comprise the features of the genre, and (3) *organizing principle,* or "the root term or the notion that serves as an umbrella term for the various characteristic features of the rhetoric" (pp. 226–227). Conceptualizing genre in this more complex way has helped to resolve some of the problems critics experienced after their initial attempts at generic criticism. Originally, generic critics tended to emphasize substantive and stylistic characteristics to the exclusion of the other two elements of genre. More contemporary studies have emphasized the situation or a general organizing principle as *interpretive guides* rather than searching for characteristics that are tied to specific features of the text.

One of the current studies includes Stoda's (2000) investigation of the **jeremiad,** the organizing term of this genre. Stoda argued that Solzhenitsyn's commencement address at Harvard conformed to the four-part sequence earlier authors had identified as essential substantive and stylistic characteristics of the genre. The jeremiad was defined as the prophet's voice, one that castigated a group of people by announcing their violation, reviewing their punishment, detailing the violation, and urging them to repent. Solzhenitsyn was a well-known Russian novelist who made world headlines in his repeated efforts to immigrate to the United States. Stoda concluded that his speech was heavily criticized in part because it "contained little that could be even loosely considered praise" and was instead "a moral indictment of the West." Solzhenitsyn had ignored the situational requirements, giving what was "hardly a typical commencement speech" and "not even the type of address many had expected to hear" from this particular person (pp. 28–29).

Benoit's (1995) work on image restoration represents the development of a theory based in part on the genre of **apologia,** speeches made in self-defense. Combining the rhetorical approaches to genre criticism and Burkean dramatism (a method we discuss later in this chapter) with social science research on accounts, Benoit developed an extensive typology of image restoration strategies. Some of his applications include investigations of President Nixon's Cambodia Address, Union Carbide and the Bhopal tragedy, Exxon and the *Valdez* oil spill, and the advertising campaign launched by Coke and Pepsi as attack and defense strategies. Benoit's main assertions is that his image restoration theory expands and redefines all three elements of the genre definition: its organizing principle is image restoration covering a more expansive ground than apologias or Burke's conceptions; it identifies a greater number, and with greater depth, of the substantive and stylistic features of this type of genre; and finally, it provides a broadened and clarified description of the situational requirements in which image restoration attempts will be made.

Reconceptualizing generic criticism has helped critics to gain greater understanding of this methodological approach. How it is defined and applied impacts the warrants, or the standards used to evaluate its claims in light of the evidence offered to support them. Along with the standard warrants of validity and reliability, the newer studies and criticisms of the methodology itself suggest that a more interpretive perspective may be ultimately more useful.

Warrants: Standards of Evaluation The earlier studies in generic criticism share a concern for the accuracy of describing the characteristics of a genre along with its situational constraints. They also emphasize consistency in deciding how specific rhetorical artifacts should be placed within a genre. Accuracy (or *validity*) and consistency (or *reliability*) are warrants of the discovery paradigm. As part of the process of argument, the overall approach to generic criticism relies primar-

ily on the deductive and inductive processes of generalization and discrimination described as central to the discovery paradigm in Chapter 1.

To illustrate, you may choose the process of generic description, a process described by Foss (1996) as the inductive form of analysis. The claim is descriptive, using inductive reasoning to examine rhetorical artifacts as the data as proof of whether a genre exists. In contrast, you may choose generic application as the primary deductive form (Foss, 1996). In this case, the claim is descriptive and explanatory, using deductive reasoning as predictive of the types of characteristics and situational constraints that should apply in a particular genre.

The evaluation of generic criticism has recently added a new standard of evaluation to accuracy and consistency. Miller (1998) claimed that failure to establish a genre or how it is applied might happen in three ways. The first failure may result from the critic's inability to determine any recurring significant substantive or stylistic similarities across several rhetorical texts from similar situations. This is still largely a problem of accuracy and consistency in the inductive process. She also noted, however, that generic claims without this level of evidence are rarely made.

The second type of failure is that all of the elements in a particular genre are not clearly identified and/or applied. Stoda's (2000) analysis of Solzhenitsyn's address illustrated the difficulties of accurate application. The address had features of both jeremiads and commencement speeches. Do these represent particular instances of epideictic oratory? Or are they distinctive hybrids, each with their own mutually exclusive set of characteristics? Miller (1998) argued that Aristotle's classification was too broad for contemporary rhetorical situations, and that has led to finding elements of two or all three genres in the same text, as we noted in earlier studies. Again, this problem seems primarily related to accuracy and consistency and the definition of genre.

A third failure posited by Miller (1998) has taken generic criticism in a very different direction, one that points the way to alternative paradigms. She argued that a generic claim must also be a pragmatic one, that a genre should be considered a form of social action. A critic must be able to find a "rational fusion of elements" across similar types of rhetorical texts to consider these a genre. Miller's analysis of environmental impact statements led her to conclude that the documents were similar in substantive and stylistic elements and as situational or episodic responses. But one of the reasons they did not form a coherent genre is because "the cultural forms in which they were embedded provided conflicting interpretive contexts" (p. 137). With this criticism, Miller challenged the assumptions and warrants that underlie genre criticism as a discovery paradigm perspective. Because the primary function of genres is to provide a classification system, they cannot be vulnerable to multiple interpretations, or consistency and accuracy in applying that classification system is destroyed. As you have learned in earlier chapters, accepting multiple interpretations of a text is one of the assumptions of the interpretive paradigm. Moreover, emphasizing coherence (instead of validity and reliability) is one warrant you use to evaluate interpretive claims. Other methods of rhetorical criticism from the interpretive paradigm share these same distinctions. You will examine four main approaches from the interpretive paradigm in the next section.

INTERPRETIVE RHETORICAL CRITICISM

The methods of rhetorical criticism examined in this section have unique elements and procedures for applying them. Because of these distinctions, each method will be explored separately. Be mindful, however, that at the broadest level, they also share many of the same assumptions about what constitutes a claim, how it can be made and supported with data, and evaluated. From this paradigm perspective, interpretive methods begin with the assumption that reality is socially constructed out of many possible interpretations, and understanding rhetorical texts from these interpretive stances is the overarching goal.

Your task as critic will include making a claim that a rhetorical text or texts will be better understood by the application of the interpretive framework or method you have chosen as the first step. Your next step will be to describe the relevant portions of this method relevant to your study. The third step is the actual application of the method to your selected texts as data analysis. Your fourth and final step is to establish warrants for your claims based on the strengths of your evidence. The four interpretive frameworks or methods described in this section are metaphoric criticism, dramatism, narrative analysis, and fantasy theme analysis. Once again, we have combined claims and data into one section for each method, followed by how to apply the warrants for that method.

Metaphoric Criticism

The use of the **metaphor** as a rhetorical form comes to us originally from Greece. Originally, it was conceived of as a **trope,** or an ornamental literary device. Aristotle distinguished between a word with its "proper" meaning and a metaphor that creates an association to an unusual meaning for the purposes of adding a more vivid and colorful dimension to the description of a term. To say that registering for classes is a zoo is an example of a metaphor. It creates an analogy between class registration and the zoo. The poet Pablo Neruda (1972) constructed a metaphor in which the idea of unity was paired with one leaf, one flower, one fruit, one tree (pp. 90–91). The ability to see analogies between words that would otherwise not be connected was considered a sign of mastery in literary style, a talent not all people possessed (Kennedy, 1963).

Viewing metaphor as anything more than a stylistic decoration is only a comparatively recent change. According to Gill (1994), contemporary theories of metaphor have shifted its definition from a trope to a much broader meaning and significance. Cassirer, a philosopher, believed all language was metaphorical because language was, by its nature, symbolic and therefore representational. Later theorists, like Burke and Grassi, attributed creating meaning to metaphors used by everyone in common, ordinary language. If you start listening for metaphors in your conversations, you will probably be surprised to hear how many there are. Metaphors work very well to vividly portray our experiences.

One of the most influential philosophers on the subject of metaphor was I. A. Richards, who developed a model of metaphor, claiming that all thought was metaphoric or representational in some way. At the very beginning of a person's life, perceptions of reality are built from metaphors, constructing associations between different contexts of meaning. In effect, every meaning for every word has come from past metaphoric associations. In time, the new association is blended with the old so that you stop experiencing it as a metaphor; referring to the leg of a table and using terms of battle to describe fighting a disease are two common examples (Gill, 1994). The table actually has "legs," and the healing process is no longer interpreted as anything but a battle or a fight.

The linguists Lakoff and Johnson (1980) extended the idea of metaphor to understanding culture as well as the way you define your personal reality. Gill (1994) has described this process as constructing our cultural coherence:

> Metaphor constitutes a primordial activity that reveals or unconceals the deep structures of reality as experienced by humans. These deep structures do not exist in nature but in humans. Each of us, as makers of metaphor, whether intentional or unwitting, thereby participates in the societal creation of meaning (p. 71).

Metaphor serves a rhetorical function that is fundamental to the way you define and experience reality personally and socially. When you become a metaphoric critic, you develop a sense of how to apply metaphors at deeper levels of meaning.

Claims and Data Your stance in metaphor criticism becomes a means of exploring metaphors in the data Your claims will be interpretive and your data may refer to any type of rhetorical texts, including speeches, books, films, paintings, modes of attire, and songs; your goal will be to illustrate how the metaphors you have identified contribute to understanding. For example, Hardy-Short and Short (1995) analyzed metaphors in media texts. They claimed that two competing metaphors were used in the public debate surrounding the 1988 Yellowstone forest fires. The fires had been allowed to burn as part of a natural land management and reforestation policy. Politicians, journalists, and landowners banded together to attack the government "let burn" policy by pairing the images of fires voluntarily set with the metaphor of *death as destruction*. The U.S. Forest Service and park officials, proponents of the policy, were eventually able to convince most of the public that the death metaphor should be refined, and the fires should be viewed as part of the natural *rebirth* process.

Because of the major shift in metaphors, events were given new social interpretations: the fires were redefined as positive events, government and park officials were not forced to resign, and the "let burn" policy continued to be part of public policy. In this metaphoric analysis, the claim was interpretive. The goal of the criticism was to show how multiple interpretations of the same events were possible from different perspectives. The data consisted of multiple visual and verbal texts constructed by media and park representatives.

To examine widespread social acceptance of metaphors, Ausmus (1998) investigated the development of the metaphor *nuclear winter* by the noted scientist Carl Sagan and his colleague R. Turco. In this study, Ausmus claimed that the nuclear winter metaphor was significantly influential because it echoed the images of archetypal or root metaphors of the apocalyptic predictions of the world's ending from various cultural and religious perspectives. It was also evaluated in terms of its conventionalized use; that is, until the term was created, there was no unified understanding for the likely outcome of a nuclear holocaust.

As you have learned previously, how you evaluate the claims of research depends upon the paradigmatic view you have. The claims of metaphoric criticism demand different standards of evaluation than those applied from the discovery paradigm.

Warrants: Standards of Evaluation In Chapter 4, "Warrants for Research Arguments," we identified various standards for judging the plausibility of interpretations. Two standards will be examined here: adequacy of evidence and coherence. *Adequacy of evidence* refers to evaluating whether the critics reviewed enough relevant material so that a sufficient or a legitimate judgment could be made. For example, in a metaphoric study of the speeches made by President George H. W. Bush, Staton and Peeples (2000) made clear attempts to analyze a sufficiently large database. They identified all speeches made by President Bush about America 2000, using a procedure that is considered "the most complete full-text index for Presidential documents that is available with a search mechanism" (p. 308).

How much evidence was collected by Hardy-Short and Short (1995) was not discussed, but these authors didn't have to rely on the *quantity* of evidence as ground for adequacy. They identified the two metaphors of death and rebirth as archetypal metaphors. Ausmus (1998) was also interested in archetypal or root metaphors, using the apocalypse to establish a connection with the new metaphor of a nuclear winter. An **archetypal** or **root metaphor** is assumed to be so primal any individual in any context could understand its meaning (Osborn, 1967). If the appeal to understanding is made on the basis of their archetypal nature, then *quantity* of evidence is not as important as identifying the occurrence of these central metaphors across the debate of two opposing camps. Certainly, the investigators provided ample evidence that the metaphors they described were clearly present in the relevant rhetorical texts they examined.

The second standard or warrant relevant in metaphoric criticism is *coherence*. Coherence refers to whether our interpretations cohere or make sense. As noted in Chapter 4, one of the ways to establish coherence is by noting recurring patterns or themes. Analyzing metaphors helps us achieve this goal. In fact, Miles and Huberman (1994) specifically stated that metaphors are "pattern-making devices" and that their investigation can help us determine the significance of our interpretations (p. 252). Uses of the metaphors of rebirth in one study and nuclear winter in another helped us make more sense out of the experiences they represented, whereas America 2000 was critiqued precisely because it did not cohere. That particular metaphor actually interfered with people's ability to develop a unified understanding of the term.

In this section, you have seen how the metaphor is used as a rhetorical form of criticism; the next methodology from the interpretive paradigm is Kenneth Burke's dramatism.

Dramatism

There are several theories of criticism that use "drama" as a centralizing theme of rhetorical criticism but none so robust and frequent as Kenneth Burke's dramatism. Burke was a prolific writer and critic. He developed an extensive theory of motive based on his conception of dramatistic form (1969a, 1969b), but he wrote on language and symbolic form, religion, social structure, and many other subjects as well. In order to provide an adequate understanding of the claims and data of dramatism, you will learn about Burke's concepts of identification and redemption, cluster analysis, and the pentad (Brock, 1990; Brummett, 1994; Foss, 1996).

Claims and Data   The claims of dramatism are interpretive. The critic asserts that by applying Burke's dramatistic concepts, we will gain a better understanding of the texts under analysis. To understand these concepts, you will need to learn about several of Burke's beliefs. Burke described our society as dramatistic. He believed the essential drama of our society was its hierarchy. According to Burke, as the hierarchical structure is stabilized over time, its members associate the structure with order, and power with position. Individuals can either accept or reject their relative positions. Acceptance of the hierarchy leads to identification and order; rejection leads to alienation and disorder (Brock, 1990). The nature of hierarchy at any level of society is simultaneously the source of identification and pollution, two terms that are explained here in more detail.

According to Burke, any organization or institution has an established set of rules or principles, and by following these rules, individuals can find common ground and a means to act in concert with others. Finding common ground is the essence of Burke's concept of **identification.** We all belong to multiple organizations, each with a different hierarchy, each establishing a different kind of common ground and a different set of rules.

People do not follow the rules all of the time for a variety of reasons. Several hierarchical rule sets may be in conflict; that is, the rules established by your church may conflict with requirements imposed at your workplace. When people reject any hierarchical order, they "fall" metaphorically; that is, they have socially sinned and, as a consequence, become **polluted.** Any violation of the rules is also accompanied by feelings of guilt because, through the violation, people are no longer unified through identification. The only means of rectifying this condition is through purification.

Purification can be accomplished in one of three ways. By **mortification,** the person's act of self-sacrifice expiates the guilt and is redeeming. Relief from guilt can also be accomplished by **victimage,** which happens when a scapegoat suffers so that society can be redeemed. Once society is redeemed, order is restored. The third way that purification is accomplished is through transcendence. In **transcendence,** rule violation is mandated by moral necessity (a higher order). Thus, order, pollution, guilt, purification, and redemption are the necessary stages of Burke's **redemptive cycle.** The redemptive cycle is at the heart of the literary genres tragedy and comedy, and as a theoretic explanation of how we manage guilt (Brummett, 1994).

In a study using dramatism, Messner (1996) used Burke's redemptive cycle to explain the social significance and effectiveness of the 12-step codependency program as a therapy intervention for alcoholics and drug addicts. Messner contended that the program introduces codependency and the recovery process as closely aligned with Burke's key terms—pollution, purification, and redemption. She identified the codependency process as a two-act drama. In the first act, codependent persons are encouraged to admit their "polluted" actions of addiction. The second act is marked by two stages: purification and redemption. Codependents purify themselves by mortification (admitting that they are powerless) and are redeemed (turning their lives over to God). The data, or rhetorical artifacts, in this analysis were four key books produced from 1987 to 1990, three of which made the *New York Times Best Seller List.* Considering the widespread popularity of the 12-step recovery programs, Messner concluded that "it is rhetorically compelling and highly successful" (p. 20).

Burke identified two specific forms of data analysis: cluster analysis and pentadic analysis. As a means of exploring the concepts of identification and redemption, Burke introduced the method of **cluster analysis.** Burke believed that the language that speakers use reveals the speakers' meanings, attitudes, and motives. As a critic using cluster analysis, your goal would be to find these sources of identification by examining key terms used by the rhetor, then groupings or categories of strategies linked to those key terms, and finally whole patterns reflecting the rhetor's meanings, motives, and attitudes (Foss, 1996, p.65). Accordingly, the patterns you uncover should reflect the speakers' attempts to identify with or alienate their audiences (Brock, 1990).

As a form of cluster analysis, Kenny (2000) identified central themes in the vocabulary used by Dr. Jack Kevorkian, also known as "Dr. Death," a medical pathologist who assisted several people in committing suicide. Kenny's main claim was that Kevorkian's rhetorical intent or motive was distinctly different from the rhetorical situation or scene to which he was often assigned, that is, the moral dilemma of physician-assisted suicide. Kenny based his claim on the analysis of texts either written by or spoken by Kevorkian throughout the course of his career as a pathologist. Kenny showed that Kevorkian's vocabulary revealed an "occupational psychosis," another of Burke's concepts that explained what happened when the vocabulary associated with one's profession became so dominant that it obscured an individual's identification with any other social aspect of life. Kevorkian's motive was revealed as a preoccupation with death for the purposes of "experimentation, organ harvesting, and termination" where "the focus is not the person, but the experimental research" (pp. 390–391). His motive then, as revealed by Kenny's analysis, placed him squarely outside of the humanitarian debate regarding central "quality of life" issues.

Just as cluster analysis is a method Burke described in analyzing the grounds for identification, Burke's pentad was a method for exploring motivation. In conducting a **pentadic criticism,** you would apply the elements of drama to any symbolic act or text to understand its underlying motivation. The elements of the pentad include act, scene, agent, agency, and purpose. The relationships among these various elements reveal these various philosophies of life.

Act The **act** names or identifies in symbolic form the thought or behavior around which the drama occurs. To name an act gives it a particular identity. For example, if certain information is omitted in recounting past actions, the omission can be identified either as a deceptive strategy or as protecting a secret, depending on the person who commits the act, the context, and a variety of other factors we interpret as we identify the act. A famous example is President Clinton's trial deposition regarding Monica Lewinsky. Initially, he claimed the he "did not have sexual relations with that woman." In his later appearance before a federal grand jury investigating his conduct, President Clinton was forced to admit that he defined the term "sexual relations" as sexual intercourse, and in that narrow sense of the term, he had omitted crucial information. President Clinton then redefined the act as "wrongful and inappropriate conduct." The symbolic significance of this act that we are referring to here is his *testimony* rather than the actual relationship he had established with Ms. Lewinsky.

Scene The **scene** is the setting or situation in which the act occurred. In the previous example, the scene is the White House, where significantly President Clinton videotaped his testimony to the federal grand jury rather than appear before them in person.

Agent   The **agent** is the person or persons who commit the act. The agent must have the power or will to commit the act. In our example, President Clinton is identified as the sole agent of his action, testifying about his behavior to the federal grand jury.

Agency   The **agency** is the means by which the act is carried out. Again, in our example, it is significant that President Clinton used videotaping as the means of providing information to the federal grand jury. Independent Counsel Kenneth Starr had hoped to force the President to appear in court, but a judiciary committee permitted President Clinton to submit videotaped testimony.

Purpose   The **purpose** is not to be confused with the underlying motive, a complex construct that can only be understood by examination of all pentadic elements. The purpose is the reason for the action that the agent can readily provide for the act. The purpose that President Clinton gave for providing the grand jury with his testimony was to clarify his relationship with Ms. Lewinsky. Of course, his comments did not achieve that stated purpose.

Your task as pentadic critic is to complete three main steps: to identify and examine the five elements of the pentad; to apply the ratios, or the relationships among the elements; and to identify the motive based on examination of the ratios (Foss, 1996). The ratios are possible pairs of elements, like act–agent and act–scene, which are isolated to determine the effect each element has on every other element. By this process, the critic can discover which of the elements appears to be more important or significant than any other. In the previous example, you might argue that the act-agent and the act-agency were the ratios with the greatest significance. The act-agent ratio would explain how President Clinton's character enabled him to particularly define the words he chose in understanding his overall motivation. The act-agency ratio would help to explain the significance of videotaped testimony.

In reading articles that use dramatistic criticism, you may find any number of central concepts described in this section using Burke's theoretical approach. Keep in mind, however, that Burke was such a prolific author we have only been able to provide a thumbnail sketch of his writing. You are very likely to come across other concepts that Burke developed as you look for articles that use dramatism as the interpretive framework. For

example, Lindsay (1999) used a variety of Burkean forms including cluster analysis to explore the motives of David Koresh, the leader of the doomed Branch Davidian cult who led many of his followers to a disastrous confrontation with the FBI in 1993. As the data, Lindsay examined Koresh's unfinished manuscript of a reinterpretation of the Book of Revelation and a letter written to one of the federal negotiators. Cluster analysis was applied to the texts to reveal various themes of Koresh's identification with Christ, a type of identification Burke termed **entelechy.** Entelechy was defined as the perfection of being, or becoming entirely what one is supposed to become, and madness as "meaning carried to the extreme."

Lindsay called the combination of madness and entelechy "psychotic entelechy," saying that while Burke did not coin the term, he very well could have. Lindsay defined the term as "the tendency of some individuals to be so desirous of fulfilling or bringing to perfection the implications of their terminologies that they engage in very hazardous or damaging actions" (p. 272). He showed how Koresh had made extreme claims, ones that fit his interpretations. He also indicated that biblical scholars would have been successful negotiators if they had been permitted to "enter Koresh's entelechy." They could have attempted a "partial conversion" by considering possible alternative meanings to biblical passage interpretations rather than to disregard Koresh's interpretations, which is what those principally involved with Koresh ultimately did.

There are many examples of Burkean analyses in the critical analyses of our field. For example, Kuypers (2000) applied Burke's redemptive cycle and concept of "moral poetics" to an analysis of a letter written by Dr. Dobson *(Focus on the Family)* to his constituents. Snyder (2000) used cluster analysis to show how the Book of Revelation was an invitation to transcendence as a means of overcoming guilt. Appel (1997) used Burke's pentad, plus consideration of the redemptive cycle in comedies and tragedies, to show how Dr. Martin Luther King's rhetoric changed over the course of his life.

As you can see just from the very few studies we have reviewed here, Burke addressed many issues and developed numerous conceptual theories that can be applied to the analysis of rhetorical texts. Undoubtedly, you will find other concepts from Burke not specifically mentioned in this section since he remains one of the richest sources of knowledge and interpretation applied in rhetorical criticism. In order to understand the worth of dramatistic criticism, we must consider the warrants most appropriate for this methodology.

Warrants: Standards of Evaluation Because Burke's dramatism involves many interrelated complex conceptualizations, warrants for this type of research seem to rest in the *plausibility of various interpretations.* To establish the reasonableness of a claim, your role as critic would entail presenting Burke's concept as it is defined and explained by Burke with numerous references to original works Burke produced. You may also choose to cite accepted scholars, such as Rueckert (1982), who are recognized interpreters of Burke's books and essays, as a way of establishing the credibility of your interpretation. Additionally, the application of each Burkean concept or method requires a great deal of substantiation from the existing texts you wish to analyze. When Kenny (2000) advanced a claim about Kevorkian's character, he used most of the texts Kevorkian had produced up to that point as a way of building a case for the adequacy of his evidence. Lindsay (1999) had to rely on the only texts created by David Koresh to explore the Burkean concepts he claimed would clarify the motives of the Branch Davidian leader. Because there were few surviving documents, Lindsay's analysis is vulnerable to greater criticism when interpreting Koresh's actions, motives, means, and situation within the dramatistic framework.

Sometimes, you would not be interested in making broad claims about rhetorical texts. As mentioned earlier, Kuypers (2000) claimed the effectiveness of just one letter written by Dr. James Dobson, a minister associated with *Focus on the Family,* was due in part to its implicit appeal to Burke's redemptive cycle. In this case, the plausibility of interpretations was not based on the quantity of evidence but on demonstrated *coherence.* Your explanation must fit the actual features of the text, and add clarity and understanding.

In this section, you have read about dramatism as a common methodology found in rhetorical criticism. The examples of the Burkean analyses provided illustrate that Burke's concepts have just begun to be applied. No doubt you will continue to see a variety of concepts emerge from Burke's writings in new applications of dramatistic rhetorical criticism. In the next section, we will examine another rhetorical critical method based on communication as drama, fantasy theme analysis.

Fantasy Theme Analysis

Fantasy theme analysis is the work of Ernest Bormann, a communication scholar originally interested in explaining the communication behavior of small groups. Like Burke, Bormann was interested in communication as drama. Using Bales's interaction typology for group behaviors, Bormann (1972) became intrigued with the group's "dramatizing." (See Chapter 7, "Content and Interaction Analyses," for a description of these behaviors.) He called the set of behaviors "fantasy chaining" where members would describe "characters, real or fictitious, playing out a dramatic situation in a setting removed in time and space from the here-and-now transactions of the group" (p. 397). **Fantasies,** then, are not just imagined events but recollections of past events in the group or predictions about future events.

Fantasies function in different ways. Often, the overt or manifest content of the fantasy is symbolic of a hidden agenda. For example, one member might tell a humorous joke about a domineering wife and a passive husband that symbolically characterizes a current conflict between a group member and the leader. Fantasies also help groups establish a common culture as a way of making sense out of their experiences and developing a shared history. They can also be a powerful force for change as members publicly commit themselves to various attitudes as the dramas play out. Finally, fantasies provide the means for testing and legitimizing values and attitudes. Bormann described an example in which a group member told a story about embarrassing a politician. When it fell flat, the political attitude had been tested but not legitimatized.

Fantasies convey various themes that can be centralized in the setting, the characters, or the central actions. Whenever a fantasy becomes a "stock scenario" repeatedly told to the group, it becomes a fantasy type. It may be a fantasy about heroism, or loyalty, or tragedy. Whatever its content, it holds a particular significance for the group. When **fantasy themes** of one group become public and accepted by a much larger audience, they form a **rhetorical vision.** Shared rhetorical visions become the basis for entire social movements. Identifying fantasy themes as they contribute to a larger rhetorical vision is the task of the critic—a task made clearer as you explore the claims and data of fantasy theme analyses.

Claims and Data   Conducting a fantasy theme analysis was more common in the 1970s and 1980s than it is today; however, fantasy theme analysis has played a central role in the history of rhetorical criticism. Using this methodology, your claims would be interpretive, and your data analysis should include three steps: identifying the evidence of shared fantasy themes, coding fantasy themes apparent in the text, and demonstrating how rhetorical visions are constructed out of the fantasy themes (Foss, 1996, p. 127). The methodology is illustrated in Hubbard's (1985) fantasy theme analysis of male and female character portrayals and relationship styles in romance novels from 1950 to 1983. Hubbard described a fantasy theme as consisting of the characters, the plot, the scene, and the sanctioning agent. One fantasy theme or several could be combined to create one rhetorical vision.

Hubbard claimed that each decade of romance novels was characterized by a distinct rhetorical vision of relationships between women and men. The rhetorical vision for the 1950s was entitled "Cinderella as Virgin Earth Mother and the Prince as Benign Dictator." In this view of relationships, the man "has a monopoly on formal, overt power, and he assumes his right to rule. She gladly gives obedience in exchange for upward mobility, protection, and enduring love" (p. 116). Vision II of the 1960s was identified as "Cinderella as the Feisty Female and Prince as Subduer." From this view, "the hero finds that her spirit excites him and once he has learned to control that spirit, he offers her a lifetime of passionate love, marriage, safety and security" (p. 118).

The 1970s was characterized by Vision III, "Cinderella as Virgin Temptress and the Prince as Warrior." According to this view, there are fantasy themes of female sexuality and power; however, these are combined in the larger rhetorical vision that portrays her demands as threats to their happiness and security, which she realizes when "she is confronted and humbled repeatedly until she sees the error of her ways and embraces traditional male/female complementarity as a relationship style" (p. 119). The final rhetorical vision of the 1980s is called "The Liberated Heroine with Her Man as Equal Partner." This new vision has a set of new fantasy themes based on female power and male acceptance of equality.

Another exemplary study using fantasy theme analysis was conducted by Foss and Littlejohn (1986). The study investigated the fantasy themes embedded in the rhetorical vision of nuclear war. In this study, the authors compared two forms of data for fantasy themes: personal statements from a sample of 79 individuals and the made-for-television film *The Day After.* Generally, the authors found that the themes based on characters, settings, and plot that emerged in the personal statements were reiterated in the film. Characters were generally portrayed as victims with little or no choice left but to fight for survival or attempt to band together to restore a sense of order. The plot themes of death and destruction appear in both types of texts, while the scenic elements tended to reinforce the character and plot themes.

Foss and Littlejohn concluded that the overarching vision was one characterized by irony: one that demanded both involvement and detachment. The threat of nuclear war is a vision that involves everyone on the planet, but most people will be unable to exert any form of control over its occurrence. The authors' conclusion explained the tremendous impact the film had on American audiences because it successfully conveyed the rhetorical vision of nuclear war we all share.

Fantasy theme analysis has also been applied to other types of texts by critics of organizational discourse. For example, Jackson (2000) identified the fantasy themes and rhetorical vision created by Peter Senge, an organizational guru of the "learning organization." By analyzing a considerable database (three videoconferences, two books, 17 articles, and one audiocassette) created by Senge, Jackson conducted an impressive investigation of themes, vision, sanctioning agent, rhetorical community, and master analogue. Additionally, he examined 65 articles written about Senge to clarify and substantiate the rhetorical vision Senge had constructed.

The rhetorical vision was identified as the *learning organization,* supported by the setting themes of "living in an unsustainable world" and "working it out within the micro world," the character theme of the "manager's new work," and the plot or action theme of "getting control but not controlling" (pp. 196–201). The sanctioning agent was Peter Senge, who encapsulated his program into the slogan "The Fifth Discipline" (later supported by a book with the same title), targeting "senior executives, human resource developers and trainers, and educational administrators" as his rhetorical community (people who share a rhetorical vision). Peter Senge's program has been enormously successful because, according to Jackson, he understood what vision to create to meet the fantasy themes emerging from organizational members.

Fantasy theme analysis is a methodology that shares a Burkean focus on drama. It also contains many of the same elements we will find in the next methodology, narrative criticism. Before considering that approach, we will discuss the standards of evaluation that seem most appropriate for fantasy theme analysis.

Warrants: Standards of Evaluation In reviewing the four studies described in the previous section, the critics primarily emphasized evaluating rhetorical texts in terms of their effectiveness by solidifying or reiterating the rhetorical vision of the audiences for whom the texts were created. Effectiveness appears to be judged on the basis of *coherence* across themes, and relevance (*fidelity*) of themes and vision from the audiences' perspectives. One interesting addition to this form of research is the combination of qualitative and quantitative approaches as demonstrated by the Foss and Littlejohn study. The use of multiple methods suggests an appreciation for multiple perspectives of the same target of study. We have discussed this approach as *triangulation* in Chapter 4. It is a primary means of establishing researcher credibility and the adequacy of the evidence. Fantasy theme analysis has been a productive methodology in the analysis of rhetorical texts. Its focus on characters, plot, and setting establish a connection with the fourth type of methodology we will consider, narrative analysis.

Narrative Analysis

Contemporary studies of narratives represent widely varying theoretic bases and specific methodologies. Narratives are explored as myths, nonrational rhetorical artifacts, folklore, and social constructions of reality. Foss (1996) stated that the steps for conducting narrative analysis are the same as those for metaphoric analysis, dramatism, and fantasy theme analysis: (1) formulating a research question and selecting an artifact, (2) selecting a unit of analysis, (3) analyzing the artifact with the appropriate interpretive framework, and (4) writing the critical essay (pp. 401–406). Additionally, narrative criticism should include "(1) a comprehensive examination of the narrative; and (2) selection of the elements on which to focus" (p. 402).

Claims and Data As a narrative critic, formulating the research question is the process you would undergo in making an interpretive claim. The data you would collect and analyze are narrative texts that may be the traditional rhetorical artifacts, speech and written texts, but they are also frequently the transcripts of conversations, songs, or even the visual narrative represented in film, television, and print images. Rybacki and Rybacki (1991) defined **narratives** as "rhetorical acts conceptualized in story form, that is, symbolic action in the words and deeds of characters that provide order and meaning for the audience, who then create, interpret, and live that action" (p. 108).

The interpretive framework you would use for analyzing narratives would depend in part on your understanding of the concept of narrative and your training as a methodologist. One of the first rhetorical critics to write about narrative analysis in our field was Walter Fisher (1978, 1987), who began his work on narratives by investigating the "American Dream." Fisher identified several assumptions about narratives including the central belief that humans are storytellers, that life is a continual process of recreating our own stories, that values change by context (Fisher, 1989), and that ultimately our social realities construct and are constructed out of the narratives we tell. Fisher's initial contribution to narrative analysis has been complemented by the influences of Burke's dramatism and Bormann's fantasy theme analysis (discussed in the previous section) and theory of symbolic convergence, and the cultural or ethnographic approach to narratives and narratives as performance (discussed in Chapter 11, "Ethnographic Research").

Claims in narrative analysis begin as interpretive assertions. For example, Lee (1995) claimed that applying the "small town myth" as a narrative theme to former President Jimmy Carter's rhetoric would illuminate our understanding of several texts. In the application of this narrative theme to the texts as data, Lee contrasted Carter's campaign biography and several speeches at the end of his term as part of his campaign for reelection. In his first campaign, Carter stressed symbols of democratic equality, labor and the soil, and community life. By the end of his term, Carter's rhetoric emphasized the big city themes of competence and the public good as well as attempts to invoke small town values. It was this contradiction that Lee claimed was his downfall. By contrast, Dorsey (1995) showed how President Theodore Roosevelt successfully transformed the American frontier myth to support his policy of conservation. By application of various narrative themes, Dorsey argued that Roosevelt's effectiveness was derived from transforming three elements: the hero, the nature of the frontier, and the definition of progress.

Narrative analysis has also been applied to organizational communication research. For example, Meyer (1997) explored humorous narratives and how they functioned to unite or divide organizational members. The data in this study consisted of 19 interviews transcribed and analyzed for narratives. In another study, Stutts and Barker (1999) showed how Fisher's concepts of narrative coherence and fidelity were incorporated into questionnaires evaluating the advertisement campaign by Exxon.

One of the newer trends in narrative research is to explore contemporary narratives as the "current socio-economic, political, cultural, aesthetic, and spiritual situation of the people central to the historical narrative and their relative position to the dominant society/ies that currently surround them" (Clair, 1997, p. 8). For example, Lessl's (1999) analysis of the scientific narratives explaining Galileo's persecution by the Catholic Church showed that across many narratives, various themes emerge. Lessl claimed that the themes that emerged reflected "the master narrative of 'warfare between science and religion' that has been such a prominent feature of scientific rhetoric during the past century" (p. 163). This trend in narrative criticism to show how narratives are reconstructions of history, or serve as "collective memories," or explain the dominant themes of oppression or the marginalized themes of voice and liberation place these studies clearly in the critical paradigm, and these we will discuss fully in the next chapter. Before leaving narrative criticism, we will consider the warrants typically used to evaluate the effectiveness of narrative criticism.

Warrants: Standards of Evaluation   The warrants or standards of evaluation have actually received more direct treatment by Fisher and his associates than the theoretical components of narrative methodology. Fisher (1987) identified two standards to be applied to the evaluation of narratives: coherence and fidelity.

From Fisher's perspective, *coherence* refers to a consistency or rationality that can be applied to various aspects of the narrative. The narrative is judged for its ability to present a coherent "whole" as well as consistencies related to settings, characters, and temporal development of the plot. *Fidelity* refers to a narrative's ability to help readers make sense of their experiences. If a narrative demonstrates both coherence and fidelity, it is judged to be an effective and satisfactory text. In reviewing narrative analysis, Foss (1996) identified an additional way to establish warrants. The narrative critic constructs a central research question or claim for each analysis. To the degree that the critic focuses on the elements of the narrative that "provide the clearest, most coherent, and most insightful answer to the research question," the narrative analysis may be judged effective (p. 404).

In the narrative studies described in the previous section, the authors were concerned with establishing coherence and fidelity in answering their central claims. Lee's study of Jimmy Carter illustrated how the lack of coherence and fidelity in narrative themes interfered with the effectiveness of his presidential rhetoric. Dorsey's study of Theodore Roosevelt demonstrated just the opposite; Roosevelt was masterful in reconstructing themes that were coherent and faithful representations of the experiences common to his audiences. Meyer's study of humorous narratives was a coherent argument for using narratives strategically to achieve specific outcomes. As with other methodologies in this chapter, narrative analyses have unique features that must be considered when the critic uses them in the examination of a rhetorical text to ensure the most effective application.

The narrative analyses that signal trends toward incorporating the assumptions of the critical paradigm also are less concerned with using the warrants of coherence and fidelity (see Warnick, 1987, and Rowland, 1987, for criticisms of Fisher's concepts). As we will see in the next chapter, this research uses different warrants. For example, they are frequently evaluated in terms of how well they can reveal the hidden agendas of the dominant social, economic, and political institutions that form the structure of any society. For example, Lessl's study of scientific narratives about Galileo and the Catholic Church emphasized the dominance of the scientific explanations as the only legitimate sources. Studies from the critical paradigm may also directly argue for and be evaluated by their demonstration of the need for ideological reform. Warranting a research argument changes as a function not only of the type of methodology used but as a function of the underlying paradigmatic assumptions, as you will see in the next chapter.

As a final consideration of this chapter, we will explore how the interpretive methodologies of rhetorical criticism have been influenced by technological innovation.

TECHNOLOGY AND RHETORICAL CRITICISM

Recent advances in technology have influenced both the content and the process of interpretive rhetorical critical methods. The content is impacted by essays about understanding the nature of a technologically grounded society. The process of rhetorical criticism has been influenced by a number of new technological tools for analysis.

Technology as Content of Rhetorical Criticism

There is little doubt in perusing rhetorical analyses that relatively few focus on technological dimensions of communication as the central topic. In an essay, Jones (1998b) used metaphoric rhetorical criticism to identify the metaphors that best characterized the emergence of the new technologies as social movements. Concentrating on uses of the Internet and email, Jones argued that the new technologies were not best understood by either a transportation metaphor (i.e., "the information highway") or by the ritual metaphor (i.e., "community through storytelling and gossip"). Instead, the technologies would be better understood by adopting the language of boating or electromagnetism in describing the Internet or email messages as wakes or fields of influence.

Jones underscored the importance of constructing new meanings in metaphoric criticism also by introducing two new terms, *compunity* and *micropolis,* to underscore the need for a new vocabulary as technology has changed our experiences. **Compunity** refers to the combination of computers and community, while **micropolis** refers to a fragmented, smaller grouping of people, as an analog of *metropolis* (1998b, pp. 2–3). He also identified at least four themes in the "narrative pattern illustrating where social concerns lie: privacy, property, protection, and privilege" (p. 3). These have already become the subjects of legislative, judicial, and moral debate. Jones also listed potential gains from the new technologies, including increasing educational opportunities and greater participation in the democratic process as well as several others (p. 7).

Not everyone has painted such a glowing picture of the new technologies, however. In their rhetorical critique, Kolko and Reid (1998) analyzed a case study of what they considered identity and community failures in online communication. They stated, "From the perspective of a rhetorician, this ultimate breakdown seemed to be a quite clear lesson that virtual communities are not the *agora,* that they are not a place of open and free public discourse," arguing that the new language and position titles have once again established a social hierarchy "that can be every bit as restrictive and oppressive as some real life ones" (p. 217). They also claimed that the creation of multiple virtual characters in online chat rooms has led to fragmentation at both levels of the individual and the community.

The themes of alienation and fragmentation also appeared in Stroud's (2001) analysis of the film *The Matrix.* Using narrative form, Stroud identified themes of isolation and "solitary enlightenment" that separate the hero of the film from any community. In this analysis, the content of Stroud's rhetorical criticism deals with the significance of technology in our social narratives, but it also deals with a new text form, a film. As our appreciation of what constitutes a rhetorical text develops, the uses of the various technologies will increase as well. With both trends, we will undoubtedly see more rhetorical criticism of technology-based texts. At this point, you are more likely to encounter technological advances in the process, rather than the content, of rhetorical criticism.

Technology in the Process of Rhetorical Criticism

In the past, most studies in rhetorical criticism concentrated their analyses on printed texts of speeches. This emphasis was based on two obvious reasons: no other types of records existed for many texts, and our conception of "text" was limited. As we have acknowledged earlier, texts can take on many forms, including films, videos of television programs, CDs of popular musicians, nonverbal texts, online chat room conversations, and private email messages. Technological advances on many fronts have greatly expanded our repertoire of potential texts for analysis. Rhetorical critics have just begun to consider the implications of the form of the message as part of the critical process. For example, Mitchell's (2000) article on the rhetoric surrounding using Patriot missiles in Operation Desert Storm not only described the new virtual "Nintendo" warfare "with strategy and tactics plotted on computer screens and executed on remote video displays" (p. 125) but included photographs of video sequences that were used with American television audiences (pp. 131–132). One of Mitchell's criticisms is that close scrutiny of these virtual presentations actually showed high levels of misses in hitting intended targets, but audiences were mesmerized by the "high tech" presentation and overlooked that critical outcome. Mitchell's article is remarkable as a critique of the way in which technology has been used and also because it included actual photographs of video clips.

In another study, Miller (1999) analyzed the rhetoric involved in the legislation and construction of social policy regarding midwives in Florida. Miller analyzed about 100 articles as a body of discourse reflecting the debate of this topic. The articles appeared in popular magazines. She compared these to a random selection of television news or feature broadcasts as a means of triangulating her findings across two media. She also examined audiotapes of the legislative debates and committee proceedings in the Florida House and Senate during three sessions, and used various artifacts such as committee notes and staff analyses to complement the tapes. Finally, she used Newsbank and Nexus, two electronic databases, to obtain full text articles about the midwifery debate in Florida newspapers. In all, she used at least four different forms of text as a basis for analysis. Interestingly, she noted that in the future, researchers should consider using televisual texts of legislative proceedings, "particularly if they feature charismatic rhetors, as well as electronic texts from online arguments in chat rooms, lists and popular websites" (p. 363).

In a study described earlier in this chapter, Jackson (2000) collected texts authored by Peter Senge that included three videoconferences, two books, 17 articles, and one audiocassette, plus 65 articles written about Senge to clarify and substantiate the rhetorical vision Senge had constructed. In contrast, Goldzwig & Sullivan (1995) chose to investigate only postassassination eulogies that appeared in print, stating that eulogies in the televisual, electronic medium were limited because they were often "comprised of short, disconnected, decontextualized stories that are visually interesting and trade on novelty and revelation for its own sake instead of on the functionality of information presented for audiences" (p. 130). Undoubtedly, as more studies appear across the array of potential technologies and media, you will probably see more concern for the ways in which technology has influenced the significance of the text for its intended audience as well as the rhetorical critic.

Very infrequently, rhetorical critics employ some form of technology in the actual method of analyzing texts. In one notable exception, Staton and Peeples (2000) investigated President George H. W. Bush's discourse for metaphors used to represent the President's policy on education. The data included 38 speeches the President made regarding three educational reform documents entitled "America 2000." Through a qualitative procedure called Non-numerical Unstructured Data Indexing Searching and Theorizing (NUD★IST 4), a computer software program, the researchers concluded the main conceptual metaphor was confused with numerous other associations, including terms that were practical and concrete with terms that were more abstract and ambiguous. They argued that the confusion led to a negative audience evaluation of the America 2000 metaphor.

As you can see, rhetorical critics have just begun to consider the implications of new texts, new media, and new technologies for expanding the applications of the methodologies discussed in this chapter. In the next chapter, you will see how various technologies and their uses can provide bases for general social critiques.

SUMMARY

In this chapter, we have examined a number of methods of rhetorical criticism from the discovery paradigm (neo-Aristotelian criticism, historical criticism, and genre criticism) and the interpretive paradigm (metaphoric analysis, dramatism, fantasy theme analysis, and narrative criticism). We introduced you to the main conceptual components of each theoretical approach. You learned about the types of claims found associated with each method and the different types of texts as data sources for these methods. In exploring the warrants for the discovery paradigm approaches, we discussed validity and reliability as well as rational forms of logic, inductive and deductive reasoning. In discussing the warrants of the methods from the interpretive paradigm, we identified the tests of the adequacy of evidence, triangulation, and the plausibility of interpretations through coherence and fidelity. Additionally, we considered how trends in at least one type of method from this chapter have led to applications situated more appropriately in the critical paradigm, the subject of the next chapter. We ended the chapter with a discussion of the contributions that technology has made to the content and the process of rhetorical criticism.

KEY TERMS

Act	Generic participation	Pentadic criticism
Compunity	Genre	Pollution
Deliberative rhetoric	Identification	Purification
Delivery	Inartistic proofs	Purpose
Entelechy	Invention	Redemptive cycle
Enthymeme	Jeremiads	Rhetorical artifact
Epideictic rhetoric	*Logos*	Rhetorical vision
Ethos	Metaphor	Root metaphor
Fantasies	Micropolis	Scene
Fantasy themes	Mortification	Style
Forensic rhetoric	Narrative	Transcendence
Generic application	Organization	Trope
Generic description	*Pathos*	Victimage

DISCUSSION QUESTIONS

1. According to neo-Aristotelian methodology, attention to the artistic forms of proof as support for the speaker's argument is vitally important. Why are moral or emotional appeals considered along with logical appeals? Aren't rational appeals grounded in evidence always going to be superior to emotional appeals?

2. When conducting historical analyses, are the analysts representing factual events more or less accurately, or are they interpreting historical events from their subjective points of view?

3. Think of some common metaphors we use in language all of the time. We gave the example of a leg of a table in the chapter. What others can you think of? Are there any that specifically relate to being female or male? How do the metaphors we use help us construct meanings or interpretations of our experiences?

4. Think about your family get-togethers. What stories does your family tell about you? What do the stories say about your character, your aspirations, your humor? Explain how the stories your family tells are like the fantasies Bormann is describing in fantasy theme analysis. How do the stories of a family help constitute its culture?

"TRY IT!" ACTIVITIES

1. Find an article from a communication journal that uses neo–Aristotelian criticism. You may use any of the studies mentioned in this chapter. Identify the concepts the critic makes use of from this methodology. Does the critic complete all three steps of the analytical process (reconstructing the context, analyzing the rhetorical artifact, and assessing its effects)? Does one of the canons (invention, organization, style, delivery) receive more emphasis than the others? Does the critic concentrate on one of the artistic proofs *(logos, ethos, pathos)* more heavily than the other two?

2. Choose any article mentioned in this chapter in the section on metaphoric criticism, or find an article from a communication journal that uses metaphoric criticism. Try to answer two or three of the following questions: What does the choice of metaphors tell you about the rhetor? What values or attitudes might be implicit in using specific metaphors? What do they tell you about the audience? Do the metaphors clarify or confuse the claim or thesis of the rhetor? Are there any visual or nonverbal metaphors? (Some of these questions have been adapted from Foss, 1996, p. 364.)

13

Critical Studies

ABSTRACT

In this chapter, we will introduce you to critical studies in communication. You will learn how to analyze mediated and nonmediated texts, including actions, events, and your own experiences, in order to make claims of description, evaluation, and reform. We first distinguish structural from poststructural critical studies. We then describe the sources of data or evidence for critical studies, including historical and present day events, actions and texts (whether print, electronic, or spoken), and your experiences and beliefs. Finally, we show you how to warrant the worth of your critical studies project.

As we discussed in Chapter 2, "Making Claims," the epistemology of knowing by criticism is associated with the most recent changes in communication studies. Criticism can be defined as "the application of values for the purpose of making judgments" (Littlejohn, 2002, p. 226). "Critical scholars conduct their examinations by analyzing values and judging, or criticizing them" (Fink & Gantz, 1996, p. 115). As Littlejohn (2000) pointed out, critical scholarship is often focused on political and economic social structures as the forces that oppress people, and communication is always implicated. "In practice, critical theorists are usually reluctant to separate communication from other factors in the overall system of oppressive forces" (Littlejohn, 2002, p. 208). Perhaps, disciplinary turf boundaries are part of the oppressive social system these researchers seek to change. Therefore, we have chosen to use the term *critical studies*, rather than *critical communication studies,* in this chapter.

When you operate in the critical paradigm, you make claims to describe, evaluate, and reform societal communication processes. In the first section of this chapter, we will explain how to make each of these types of critical claims. Note that the claims are ordered according to the historical emergence of each type of criticism in our field.

In the second section of this chapter, we will describe three primary sources of data or evidence for critical studies: action and events, texts, and the researcher's own experiences and beliefs. Notice that our use of the word *data* is broader here than the traditional use of the word. In discovery and interpretive research, the term *data* is associated with the characteristics of empiricism (i.e., data must be systematic and observable). So adherents to these paradigms demand intersubjective agreement about observed events and situations. That agreement can be achieved by seeking consensus among researchers (e.g., interrater reliability) or among research participants (e.g., internal consistency estimates for Likert scales, or member checks in ethnographic research). But critical researchers embrace writing as inquiry. So their positions in society, race, class, gender, lived experiences, and ideological beliefs become the systematic, observable evidence against which they assess the need for social change. For this reason, critical researchers are more likely to refer to the *evidence* upon which their claims are based, rather than *data*.

In the third section of this chapter, we will show you how to make four data analytic moves that you can use in critical studies: deconstruction, narrative analyses, dialectical analyses, and speech act analyses. Although some of these procedures are also common to interpretive communication research, in this chapter we will focus on how they can help you act on the values of voice and liberation, and establish the need for ideological change in societal communication processes.

Finally, in the warrant section of this chapter, we will show you how to apply the values and standards of the critical paradigm. We will outline ways of establishing coherence, acknowledging subjectivity and freedom of choice, and evaluating the access to and emancipatory potential of public discourse. We conclude the chapter with a note about how technology is being critiqued using these standards.

One of the things that made this chapter difficult for us to write, and may make it hard for you to read as well, is the fact that there are so many forms of critical theory and research (Littlejohn, 2002). Furthermore, many of the data analytic moves employed by interpretive scholars also are used by critical scholars but for somewhat different purposes. Whereas the interpretive scholar analyzes discourse and semiotic texts for the purpose of unpacking meanings, critical scholars use **textual analysis** to reveal power-dominance relationships, describe consciousness (or lack of it), and depict hegemonic processes at work. **Hegemony** is the "process of domination, in which one set of ideas subverts or co-opts another" (Littlejohn, 2002, p. 211). Hegemony "constitutes a sense of reality for most people most of the time" (Conrad, 1988, p. 180).

"The goal of critical theory is emancipation and change" (Fink & Gantz, 1996, p. 117). Therefore, the key purpose of critical communication studies is to identify the historical, economic, and political sources of power that are based in ideology. An **ideology** is "a set of ideas that structure a group's reality, a system of representations or a code of meanings governing how individuals and groups see the world" (Littlejohn, 2000, p. 228). In conducting critical communication studies, you will be trying to identify the sources of ideological domination, so that some means of equalizing power for all members of a society can be found. "This suggests an underlying research question for this tradition: What creates hegemony in the subjects of study (e.g., people, events, phenomena, artifacts, etc.); should the values of that hegemony be changed; if so, how?" (Fink & Gantz, 1996, p. 116).

In this chapter, you will learn about two basic factions in critical scholarship, structuralists and poststructuralists. Marxist critical researchers believe that social structures are the root causes of unequal power distribution for individuals and groups. Some feminist and cultural criticism follows from similar views (e.g., Dow, 1990; McLaughlin, 1991). But poststructural and postmodern critics believe that "there is no objectively real structure or central meaning and that oppressive 'structures' are ephemeral" (Littlejohn, 2002, p. 209). Researchers engaged in postcolonial criticism also follow this line of thinking. As Littlejohn stated, "There is a struggle, but it is not a struggle between monolithic ideologies. It is a struggle between fluid interests and ideas" (p. 209).

CLAIMS FOR CRITICAL STUDIES

Critical scholars embrace subjectivity (Peshkin, 1988). They believe that their subjective views are impossible to avoid in doing research. Furthermore, they see their subjectivity as a desirable asset in describing, evaluating, and reforming social oppression. Littlejohn (2002) identified three essential features of critical social science: (1) emphasis on "the lived experiences of real people in context," (2) attempts to "uncover oppressive arrangements," and (3) "a conscious attempt to fuse theory and action" (p. 207). Whether the oppression you want to study stems from social structures like the institutions of class, race, or the media, or from ideological beliefs such as those associated with culture or gender, your critical study will aim to liberate oppressed people or groups by making them aware of their oppression. Once aware of hidden oppression, individuals have the opportunity to choose other ways of speaking, acting, and interpreting the messages and events in their lives.

Of course, social structures and ideologies are not easily separated. Furthermore, our opportunities to choose other ways of participating are limited by our different positions in our social and economic structures. In fact, "critical scholars have emphasized the importance of identifying and investigating the role of context—the microcontexts of place and situation as well as the macrocontexts of historical, economic, and political structures" (Martin & Flores, 1998, citing Katriel, 1995, p. 295).

As we pointed out in Chapter 2, it is difficult, and in some ways silly, to classify some studies as exclusively interpretive or critical (Swanson, 1993). The same thing is true for dividing critical studies into those that are clearly structuralist or poststructuralist. In the subsections below, we have selected research examples that we feel most clearly illustrate the claims of these two camps. We are making this categorizing move, even though we feel it is futile in some ways, because we want to make things as clear as possible for you while you are being first introduced to this type of communication research. Rest assured, we expect to complexify, or muddy, these categories even as you read the rest of this chapter. As Thomas Merton (1962) wrote:

> When I said I was fed up with answers, I mean square answers, ready-made answers, answers that ignore the question. All clear answers tend to be of this nature today, because we are so deep in confusion and grab desperately at five thousand seeming glimmers of clarity. It is better to start with a good acceptance of the dark.

Describing, Evaluating, and Reforming Social Structures

Models of Marxist, feminist, and cultural criticism try to show how privileged groups oppress marginalized groups, like economic, cultural, and political minority groups in a society. At present in the United States of America, such groups might include people of color, females, and members of the most recent groups to immigrate to this country. If you use these forms of structural criticism, you will try to identify the social structures most responsible for unequal power distributions, so that those structures can be changed or adapted, primarily by reforming economic, political, and cultural means of power distribution. Let's consider each of these structural criticism models in turn.

Marxist Criticism The writings of Karl Marx that were published in the late 1800s and early 1900s have been used widely by scholars in many disciplines to critique the dominant existing social structures. Those criticisms especially focus on the economic basis of social structures:

> Traditional Marxism separated 'society', the material features of a socioeconomic system, and 'culture', the sense-making processes

members of a social collective employ to create meaning of their experiences and context (Conrad, 1988, p. 180).

For Marx, cultural forms and artifacts reproduced the material or economic base of the social structure. The influence of social structures on individuals was static, overt, deterministic, and unidirectional. Working class groups are inherently oppressed in capitalist societies. In order for that power imbalance to be reformed, the social structure itself had to be changed from capitalism to socialism. Individual people were viewed by Marx as "passive victims of social forces" (Conrad, 1988, p. 180). But if they were able to unite and clash with the ruling class, a higher social good could result (Littlejohn, 2002).

However, for Marxist critics, domination by a ruling class is usually thought to be unrealized by the general population, and impossible to eliminate, even if one is made aware of it. Those at the margins of society are thought not to realize just how they are being dominated. To be sure, prior to the 1960s in the United States, phrases like "the system" or "the man" were not common terms in the lexicon of ordinary citizens. The adoption of phrases like that (following the activism of the Black Panthers and other groups) speaks to the growing awareness in this country of the social system's domination of most of our lives. However, for Marxists, awareness makes liberation possible, not assured.

Yet once aware, those in oppressed positions in society can at least withdraw their participation from the oppressive structures of the dominant order. The host of the public television show *Tony Brown's Journal* has long urged African Americans to save and spend their money in banks and businesses owned by other African Americans, in order to further their economic power and avoid furthering the power of white Americans. You can probably think of other examples in which members of a group have been guided to preserve their collective social power.

But participating in or withdrawing from oppressive social structures is more complicated than merely collaborating for collective social power. Let's illustrate with a local example. Imagine that you prefer to support a small, independently owned coffee shop instead of a large national chain. Perhaps you are trying to withdraw your participation from a structure of economic oppression. But we sometimes benefit from the structures that, at other times, limit or even

harm us. Maybe the national coffee chain has several stores near where you live and work; perhaps their coffee is cheaper, they may offer a wider selection of flavors and products, or let you purchase their beans at the grocery store where you already shop. These access issues benefit you as you budget both time and money, and those benefits exist in tension with your belief that big national chain stores unfairly oppress small, independently owned local businesses.

One way we participate in our social structures is our use of language. Language is a key means through which the dominant ideology affects our individual notions of reality. The dominant language "defines and perpetuates the oppression of marginalized groups" (Littlejohn, 2000, p. 228). When you speak the language of the dominant class, you understand social situations in ways that help you to benefit from them. You can probably identify with this notion in terms of your role as a student. If you are the first person in your family to ever go to college, you may find a great deal of the language here foreign or unfamiliar. But if you speak the language of academia (maybe your mother is a professor), you benefit. You will probably know how best to participate in (or subvert) the existing power structure in college. For example, if you speak the language of academia, you know what reasons to offer that will get you enrolled in a class that has been closed, or how to arrange to turn in a late paper without incurring a grade penalty.

Even though speaking the language of the dominant group can empower lower-power members of society, you can also be co-opted, or inadvertently induced to participate in your own oppression, when you "talk the talk" of the dominant group (Townsley & Geist, 2000). McMillan and Cheney's (1996) essay on the implications and limitations of the *student as consumer* metaphor showed how widespread application of that metaphor has helped to produce some negative educational consequences for students, such as increased distance between students and teachers, or reinforcing individualism at the expense of community in academia.

Feminist Criticism As we mentioned in the introduction to this chapter, some published feminist criticism follows the Marxist idea of social structure as the controlling source of all potential life experiences for people (e.g., Ferguson, 1990; Hanmer, 1990; Stoller, 1993). In this case, the lived experiences of women in a patriarchal society are seen as dictated by the privileged position of males over females in education, medicine, religion, work, and all aspects of daily life. This kind of feminist criticism emphasizes the "gendered nature of institutional structures and practices" and the impact of "exclusionary norms" (Ashcraft & Pacanowsky, 1996, p. 217).

In addition to Marxist-feminist scholarship, current feminist criticism incorporates an immense variety of theoretical explanations, including liberal, radical, psychoanalytic, socialist, poststructuralist, and postcolonial approaches (Calas & Smircich, 1996). These diverse approaches to feminist critical studies vary in their intellectual roots, epistemological positions, and favored methodologies.

A Marxist feminist critic might rely on **econometrics,** the historical analysis of macro-level social data, such as that provided by the U.S. Department of Labor or the Census Bureau, whereas a postmodern feminist critic is more likely to use textual analysis, especially a strategy of discourse analysis called deconstruction. We will discuss textual analysis and deconstruction in more detail later in this chapter, but to illustrate, Dow (1990) used these data analytic strategies to show how the *Mary Tyler Moore* show televised in the 1970s maintained patriarchal relationships and male hegemony. Dow's study confronted the ironic contradiction between Mary Tyler Moore as a liberated career woman and male dominance in the work world.

Whether your feminist research follows structuralist or poststructuralist assumptions, all feminist scholarship critiques the status quo. So it is "always political" (Calas & Smircich, 1996, p. 219). Let's consider an example in more depth.

Ropers-Huilman (1996) explored the uses of silence and language in feminist teaching, and she focused on "how silence communicates meaning and indications of engagement" (p. 3). Ropers-Huilman interviewed 22 teachers who identified themselves, or were identified by their peers, as practicing feminist teaching. She also observed one of those teachers for an entire semester. In her analysis, she showed how those feminist teachers have framed participating in classroom interactions as an important part of learning; yet, in some situations, they prescribed silence on certain issues or topics. For instance, they told their students not to talk when the teacher was lecturing, or not to make racist or homophobic comments, in order to make the classroom a safe space for women and people of color.

Ironically, the teachers felt that limiting certain types of speech in their classrooms was "not only acceptable but desirable and perhaps necessary to foster the most productive learning and growth of all" (p. 4). Silence, then, is a **paradox;** it has inherently contradictory qualities. It can create space for some speakers but oppress others. Furthermore, for some more vocal speakers, learning when to be silent and listen is part of gaining an additional source of power. A woman may learn when "*not* to say" all that she is thinking (p. 5, quoting Eileen, a teacher that Ropers-Huilman interviewed; emphasis in original). Ropers-Huilman (1996) shared her own experience as a student in women's studies classes and reflected, "Was my silence an act of resistance, oppression, or something else?" (p. 4).

In fact, the concepts of *silence* and *voice* are central to critical studies, since language is the means to representation, and representations are the means to domination (and to emancipation). The *Western Journal of Communication* published a series of a dozen or so essays on "voice" in volume 61 (1997), essays that "grapple[d] with the theoretical, personal, social, and political issues related to the voices in which we write and the voices of those we study and about whom we write" (Vande Berg, 1997, p. 87).

Another variation of feminist criticism that has emerged recently is **womanist criticism** (e.g., Davis, 1999; Sheared, 1994). Womanist criticism focuses on the domination of women on the basis of structural and cultural categories like gender, race, class, nationality, and sexuality, and the ways that these arrangements intersect within a patriarchal society (e.g., Anzaldua, 1987; hooks, 1990; Lee, 1998b; Moraga & Anzaldua, 1983). Feminist and womanist criticism also is complemented by cultural studies of masculinity and hegemony (e.g., Collinson & Hearn, 1994; Hanke, 1998; Trujillo, 1991; Wood & Inman, 1993). Hanke's (1998) analysis of the *mock-macho* situation comedy *Tool Time* with actor Tim Allen is one example of cultural criticism aimed at describing how a text can work to reiterate hegemonic masculinity. Hanke argued that the show "induces pleasure in the realization of masculinity as a gender performance" (p. 74). Similarly, Trujillo (1991) described five ways that baseball pitcher Nolan Ryan was portrayed and commodified in print and television sports media. Namely, Ryan was portrayed as (1) an embodiment of male power, (2) an ideal image of the capitalist worker, (3) a family patriarch, (4) a white rural cowboy, and

(5) a phallic symbol. In each of these ways, media portrayals of Ryan's celebrity status reproduced hegemonic masculinity. Both Hanke (1998) and Trujillo (1991) suggested how patriarchal ideology can oppress males, as well as females, within a society.

However, some critical scholarship that co-exists with feminist, womanist, and masculinist criticism argues that gender and sexuality are fluid, performative constructs, rather than binary categories dictated by cultural ideology (e.g., Butler, 1990, 1993; Speer & Potter, 2000). Sloop's (2000) essay on the Brandon Teena story (of the movie *Boys Don't Cry*) is one example of critical rhetorical scholarship that showed how "the dominant rhetoric/discourse of gender continues to ideologically restrain," rather than to disrupt, a gender binary system (pp. 167–168). Cooper (2002) read the same narrative as liberatory because *Boys Don't Cry* privileged female masculinity and celebrated its difference from heterosexual norms. Queer and transgender criticism also work to show how gender representations and significations are power-laden, rather than neutral, cultural artifacts (e.g., Yep, Lovaas, & Ho, 2001; Yep, Lovaas, & Pagonis, 2002). As a case in point, Battles and Hilton-Morrow used feminist and queer theory to show how the popular television situation comedy *Will & Grace* "can be read as reinforcing heterosexism and, thus, can be seen as heteronormative" (2002, p. 87). The authors argued that "*Will & Grace* makes the topic of homosexuality more palatable to a large, mainstream television audience by situating it within safe and familiar popular culture conventions, particularly those of the situation comedy genre" (p. 89).

Cultural Criticism Cultural criticism is the investigation of the ways that culture is produced by struggle among dominant ideologies (Hall, 1986). Unlike interpretive cultural analyses, which focus on descriptions of cultures as systems of shared meanings, cultural criticism explicitly aims to reform cultural meanings and practices (Littlejohn, 2002). Cultural critics try to change Western society by identifying internal contradictions and by providing descriptions that will help people see that change is needed (Littlejohn, 2002, p. 217). The struggles among competing ideologies are always happening and are always changing.

Cultural critics often point to education, medicine, religion, and government—and media, to the extent that media sources are often controlled by those institutions—as the social structures that work to preserve the dominant ideology. However, unlike Marxists, cultural critics see the relationships among social structures and individual actions as dynamic, bidirectional, and interdependent. The chief claims of cultural studies are attempts to expose ways in which the ideologies of powerful groups are unwittingly perpetuated, and to make people aware of ways to disrupt the power held by members of the dominant coalitions. High school and college courses in media literacy are an outgrowth of cultural criticism; those courses try to make learners aware of how television, advertising, and other media sources frame what is good, bad, and who is central to the society versus who is a fringe element of the society.

Research conducted from the critical-cultural perspective is extremely diverse. Some shared interests can be identified, such as the concepts of consciousness, alienation, ideology, power, emancipation, and domination. For example, Scheibel's (1994) empirical study of graffiti written by film school students on the walls of their editing rooms extended the interpretive approach to organizational culture to include cultural criticism. "The critical-cultural perspective views organizations as constructions that are interrelated with encompassing historical, social, and economic contexts" (Scheibel, 1994, p. 4). Recently, work on the social and linguistic construction of democracy in corporate organizations has been done that reflects the intersection of these economic, historical, and social contexts (Cheney, 1995; Cheney & Carroll, 1997; Deetz, 1992a, 1992b). Organizations are the focus of much cultural criticism because they play such central roles in the lives of individuals and because they are the "site of hegemonic struggles" (Mumby, 1988, 1993, 1997b).

Evaluating and Reinventing Discourse Processes

Unlike structural critical studies, deconstructionist, poststructuralist, postmodernist, and postcolonialist models of criticism identify value and belief systems, ideology, as the source of unequal power relations, rather than existing economic, political, or social structures. These scholars aim to reform the very ideas that structure a group's reality, and the language or code of meanings through which all ideas, values, and beliefs are filtered. Accordingly, poststructuralist feminist deconstruction aims to expose ways that the language of society privileges males and introduces new vocabulary designed to eliminate such privilege (e.g., Ferguson, 1990; Kendig, 1997; Martin, 1990).

Poststructural criticism frames social structure and individual participation as influencing one another. Thus, reconstituting language forms is one way that individuals can change the social structures in which they participate (Ely, 1995; Foucault, 1983; Gramsci, 1971; Mumby, 1997b). "It is Gramsci's contribution to have emphasized hegemony as complex, fluid patterns of consciousness that must continually be renewed, recreated, and defended through symbolic acts of members of society" (Conrad, 1988, p. 180). The link between mental life (thought) and material life (experience) is "not linear causality but circular interaction within an organic whole" (Lears, 1985, as cited by Conrad, 1988, p. 181).

Notice that the claims of poststructuralist critics go beyond merely evaluating and changing to actually reinventing the ideas and language of a society. Because those scholars believe that adapting oppressive ideology and language will be forever inadequate, they feel that in order for change to occur, a new ideology and language must be invented. Judith Butler's (1990, 1993) work has shown how gender norms are at once highly proscribed by cultural logic and open to subversion through individual performances. Wittig (1990) and Speer and Potter (2000) made similar claims regarding heterosexist talk.

Postmodern Criticism Lyotard (1984) and Foucault (1980, 1983) are the theorists most closely associated with the movement known as postmodern criticism. Lyotard (1984) first coined the term, the **postmodern turn,** to refer to a general movement away from social structure as the explanatory means of domination, toward ideology, representation, and discourse as the sites of struggle for social power (e.g., Clair & Kunkel, 1998; Hallstein, 1999; Parker, 1992). For the postmodern critic, there is no one rational or correct view of the world. Rather, postmodernists view "all rationality as relative, or as a product of a given set of historically situated institutional practices" (Mumby & Putnam, 1992, p. 467). Postmodern critics have condemned traditional social science as reductionist because of the tendency of social scientists to collapse complex, abstract phenomena into neater, simpler categories; they feel such categories obscure important differences and layers of meaning.

Nonetheless, despite a tendency to eschew social structures like the economy or educational and religious organizations, postmodern critics who follow Foucault are concerned with the structure and func-

tion of discourse within specific historical periods of time (Jones, 1992). As Foucault pointed out, it is "impossible for people in one period to think like those of another" (Littlejohn, 2002, p. 220). It is also impossible to separate what we know from the language forms we use to think about and express that knowledge. Foucault called such ways of knowing **discursive formations,** and he argued that power was an inherent part of all discourse.

In order to illustrate how the struggle for power is materially constituted in practice, or in the lived experiences of people, consider Herman and Sloop's (1998) case study of a legal and popular controversy over the song "The Letter 'U' and the Number '2'." The song was produced by a Los Angeles rock band, Negativland. Herman and Sloop used the song, and the lawsuit that arose from it, to explore the postmodern question of authenticity. Specifically, they examined, "copyright and trademark infringement in the age of sampling and digital reproduction" (p. 4).

Negativland's song was a parody of the U2 single "I Still Haven't Found What I'm Looking For." First, Negativland sampled sounds from the U2 song, quotations from broadcast interviews with members of U2, and clips from popular radio shows on which the U2 song was featured; then, Negativland added their own vocal and instrumental parody of the U2 song to that montage. After some U2 fans purchased the single, thinking it was a U2 production, Negativland was sued by U2's record label and music publisher and "compelled to pay over $90,000 in legal fees and damages, and attempt to remove all copies of the single from circulation" (Herman & Sloop, 1998, p. 4).

In the ensuing court case, Negativland advanced the notion of creative theft as a historical practice. They argued that their appropriation of U2's sounds and ideas was authentic and therefore appropriate. But U2, and their legal surrogates as represented by music and recording industry lawyers, won out with a more traditional definition of authenticity as "the artist as free-standing author of his/her own ideas, created solely by him/her" (p. 5). Herman and Sloop inferred from their case study that a postmodern view of authenticity and judgment, for example, in relation to electronic media and hypertext, does not "lead to an erasure of such concepts as authenticity and ownership, so much as their transformation" (p. 14).

In another postmodern study of how power struggles are constituted in people's material and discursive practices, Trujillo (1993) attempted to uncover the power relations that influenced how visitors to Dealey Plaza, the site where President John F. Kennedy was assassinated in 1963, reproduced or resisted interpretations of cultural ideology. Trujillo used ethnographic methods of participant observation and interviews at the site, on the date of the 25th anniversary of Kennedy's death. But his purpose in analyzing the field notes was to "reveal how Dealey Plaza stands as a fragmented site of ideological struggle and accommodation in American culture" (p. 450). Trujillo noted that critical ethnography such as his study of Dealey Plaza "encourages us to enter a field and study *performances*" (p. 463). It is in the field, he argued, "that the paradoxes of post-modernism may best be understood and experienced" (p. 464).

One such paradox is the competing interests at work in many ideological situations. Consider three short examples: First, Tretheway's (1997) analysis of a social welfare agency that was designed to foster independence for women welfare recipients showed how the agency actually encouraged dependence through a variety of discursive practices. The self-perpetuating interest of the workers in that system contradicted the interest in liberating the women they were mandated to serve; if women no longer needed those services, then the workers would need new jobs.

McNeil (1986) demonstrated a similar tension in school teachers' control of knowledge with their students. At the same time that teachers seek to share knowledge with students, we also sometimes mystify and omit information in order to maintain our position as above students in the knowledge hierarchy.

In a third example of paradox, Mattson and Brann (2002) argued that patient confidentiality is both privileged and threatened within a managed care environment. Each of these examples represents a site of competing interests ripe for postmodern critical analysis.

Poststructural Criticism Poststructuralism is a general reaction against structural theories of language and discourse, such as the rules approach to communication, speech act theory, and conversation analysis (Littlejohn, 2000). Unlike the approaches we discussed in Chapter 10, "Conversation and Discourse Analysis," poststructuralist critics do not view discourse as primarily spoken words, through which meaning can be conveyed and functions fulfilled. Poststructuralists view discourse as much broader than speech, instead relying on written texts for their

analyses (e.g., Capper, 1992; Foucault, 1983; Fischer & Bristor, 1994; Littlejohn, 2002). They reject the idea that language has any definite meaning.

To illustrate, although the impetus for Ropers-Huilman's (1996) study of silence in feminist classrooms began with feminist criticism, her interpretations of the text of her interview data came largely from poststructuralism. One idea central to her analysis was that "power is not stable or consistent, but flows through all of us, given certain contexts or positions" (p. 6). Power also can be expressed in numerous ways, including voice and silence, as well as who speaks and who listens. Another notion that was important in her analysis was the shared responsibility for learning between teachers and students. Both notions, fluid power and shared responsibility, blur the clear, distinct features of structural categories, and in this way, both ideas move Ropers-Huilman away from structural criticism and toward poststructural criticism.

Postcolonial Criticism Slemon (1995) located postcolonial criticism as a subset of postmodern and poststructural criticisms. Literally, colonial societies are those geographic, historical locales in which existing political, economic, and cultural milieu has been colonized by others, as the United States of America was once the 13 colonies of Great Britain. Taken less literally, the power of the societal system over individual members may also be seen as colonial (Bhaba, 1990; Said, 1984).

By either the metaphorical or literal sense of the term, the basic project of colonial studies is to define colonialism as "both a set of political relations and as a signifying system, one with ambivalent structural relations" (Slemon, 1995, p. 49). A growing body of work published in cultural studies, and more recently, in communication journals, has focused on voices of the other (e.g., Conquergood, 1983; Tanno & Jandt, 1994; Yep, 2000). Such research fits Slemon's (1995) articulation of the goals of postcolonial criticism (e.g., Bhabha, 1990, 1995; Bowers, 1996; Collier, 1998; Delgado, 1998a, 1998b; McPhail, 1998; Noelle Ignacis, 2000; Schönfeldt-Aultman & Yep, 2002; Varallo, Ray, & Ellis, 1998; Yep, 2000). Let's consider a more detailed example.

Delgado (1998b) examined Latina/o expressions of ethnic identity by analyzing reader letters to *Low Rider Magazine,* and he described the complicated categories that letter writers used to refer to themselves. He urged communication scholars to be cautious in exploring the "content, meanings, and uses of ethnic identifiers" (p. 420). Consider the terms you may use to refer to persons of Latin American descent such as *Latina/o, Chicana/o, Hispanic, Mexican American,* and so on. How we name ourselves and others is a research question in postcolonial studies because it represents the ideologic struggle for power: Who can name a group, and whose name is to be preferred? In California, where the Latina/o population and associated political and economic power is large and growing, the terms *Latina/Latino* are used more often than the term *Hispanic. Hispanic* was the term given by white power holders to describe Mexican Americans as *Other* (Alcoff, 1995), whereas *Latina/o* is the term people from Central and South America have adopted to describe themselves. *Latina/o* also particularize gender identity, which is obscured by the term *Hispanic* (Fairchild & Cozens, 1981).

To wit, colonialist theorizing "refuses to articulate a simplistic structure of social causality in the relation between colonialist institutions and the field of representations" (Slemon, 1995, p. 48). The oppression of colonialist power intersects with other types of oppressive power uses, and these intersections are "always complex and multivalent" (Slemon, p. 52). In fact, Slemon pointed out a danger of postcolonial theorizing within Western academic institutions, whose very structures colonial discourse critiques. Namely, colonial discourse theory may be appropriated, repackaged, and in effect colonized, in "terms of reference that are entirely European in origin" (p. 51).

Clair's (1997) observations about herself in relation to the Treaty of New Echota also are relevant here. The focus of Clair's essay was the life of Kilakeena (a.k.a. Elias Boudinot), a member of the Cherokee Nation. Kilakeena lived through the removal of the Cherokee tribe from Turtle Island, Georgia, to reservation land in Oklahoma and Arkansas in 1838–39. The evaluative claim Clair made in her essay was that this historical situation illustrated two ways by which oppressed peoples are silenced: naming and fractionating. Clair is of mixed ancestry, partly Cherokee, French, and Irish-Catholic.

> Being of mixed ancestry which crosses cultural and racial boundaries, and which includes traces of both the oppressor and the marginalized, speaks to the incredible complexity of naming a fractionated identity. I am the colonized. I am the colonizer. . . . I am a

reminder that life is not black and white (or red and white) (Clair, 1997, p. 329).

Clair's words remind us that group memberships are fluid, historic, and partial; even so, postcolonial studies often focus on the relations of oppressor and oppressed, mainstream and marginal. Categorical opposites are rarely so clear or binary in practice as they are made to appear in language. So postcolonial scholars also focus on blurred categories, such as hybridity, or mixed category memberships (e.g., Anzaldua, 1987; Bhaba, 1995; Kraidy, 1999, 2002; Shome, 1998; Yep, Lovaas, & Ho, 2001).

Both Clair (1997) and Delgado (1998a, 1998b) staked claims of *description* and *evaluation.* The urge of postcolonial criticism is toward *reform.* Communication scholars' calls for research that makes a difference in the world outside the academy bear witness to this reformative impulse. Delgado urged communication researchers to begin to see "from the margins in and not simply from the center out" (p. 430). He noted that "producing research and knowledge is, in the end, an effort to push boundaries and break down barriers. It seems only right that we should begin with our own" (p. 435). Similarly, Slemon (1995) acknowledged: "If we overlook the local and the political applications of the research we produce, we risk . . . at best a description of global relations, and not a script for their change" (p. 52). Indeed, as other scholars have argued, academic researchers already are implicated in the knowledge production process of the center because we are members of hierarchical and political systems that privilege certain forms of knowing and marginalize other forms. We define what counts as legitimate and good research and what does not (Alcoff, 1995; Yep, 2000). With this in mind, let's turn to consider what counts as data, or evidence, in critical studies.

DATA/EVIDENCE IN CRITICAL STUDIES

The very term *data* has quite a different cast in critical studies than it does in discovery or interpretive research. Critical and postmodern theorists object to "any totalizing narrative" (Stablein, 1996, p. 509), in part because these researchers believe strongly that some voice or view will be oppressed in any such narrative (Varallo et al., 1998). Additionally, issues of power and domination determine whose voices are represented and whose are not in any attempt to select and interpret data, so all representations are political.

The basic method for critical scholarship is to apply "an ideological perspective to some phenomenon in order to generate a value-based critique" (Fink & Gantz, 1996, p. 118). In the section below, we will describe some of the phenomena toward which you might turn your attention, including actions and events, texts, and your own beliefs and experiences.

Actions and Events

One way to focus on the lived experience of real people, in context, is to conduct a case study. As you know from Chapter 11, "Ethnographic Research," case studies highlight the actions of individuals and groups, and the events of which their actions are a part. Whether you consider actions and events that occurred in the past or in the present, their historical context will be an important feature of your critical analysis. Ashcraft and Pacanowsky (1996) observed formal company meetings, informal work interactions, and a social function at a small business organization they called Office Inc. These actions and events formed the basis for their feminist critique of how present-day women participate in their own devaluation in the work setting. Some of the actions and events that they observed during six months of participant observations at Office Inc. included the president's beginning a maternity leave and the termination of a lawsuit in an "agreeable settlement" (p. 224). Tretheway's (1997) analysis of the intake interview at a women's social service organization is another example of an action, or discursive practice, that helped to oppress women, ironically in the process of trying to empower them. Both of these case studies applied the ideology of feminism in order to generate value-based critiques of present-day organizational actions and events.

Of course, you might select an action *or* event from the past for your analysis. Lee (1998b) advanced a postcolonial feminist analysis of discourse against a longtime cultural practice in China, footbinding. It was a "gendered practice that physically mutilated the feet of Chinese women in the Han ethnicity from middle- and upper-class families" for over 800 years (p. 11). "It was a bone-crushing experience in a *literal* sense" (p. 14, emphasis in original). For centuries, opposition to the practice of footbinding was silenced, but in the late 19th century, a collective movement to speak up brought an end to footbinding for many Chinese girls and women. Lee's (1998b) analysis showed how the well-meaning antifootbinding discourse was at once emancipatory and oppressive, a site of identity struggle that implicated the race, class, and nationality of the dissenters as much as it did the women of the class and ethnicity whose feet were bound. Lee used the case of footbinding to explore a paradoxical research question, "How is it possible to foster oppression in the midst of an emancipatory movement?" (p. 16).

Texts

Critical-interpretive scholars use the term *text* in a much broader sense than just written words, whether the words are written in a book or magazine, a letter, an email message, on a billboard, or in some other mode (Bowman & Kistenberg, 1992; Gray, 1996). Texts are discursive representations of the world, and as such, a text may refer to spoken language (e.g., in a telephone interaction, a film, a television commercial, a musical performance) or to a symbolic representation (e.g., a gesture, a dance movement, architecture). As you can see from these examples, texts can be mediated or nonmediated, and the variety of texts available for analysis is theoretically endless. The stories we tell to represent ourselves and our experiences of the world are also texts that can be appropriated for critical analysis (e.g., Clair, 1993, 1994, 1997; Clair & Kunkel, 1998; Tretheway, 1997; Yep, Lovaas, & Pagonis, 2002).

Semioticians, on the other hand, are likely to analyze symbolic representations that are entirely nonlinguistic. For example, Drzewiecka and Nakayama (1998) argued that urban geographical spaces could be distinguished as modern or postmodern. San Francisco is a city with a "stronger modernist influence with their more traditional neighborhoods that are divided by social divisions" (p. 23). San Francisco has neighborhoods that are characterized by ethnicity and culture, like Chinatown, Japantown, North Beach (Italian), the Castro (gay), Hunter's Point (African American), and the Mission (Latino/a). During the year 2000, a number of high technology firms rented spaces in the Mission that were once more affordable to the existing Latino/a population, which created a sort of cultural turf war (Glionna, 2000; Nieves, 2000). Such category battles further underscore the modernist interpretation of these neighborhood spaces. By contrast, the complexity and postmodernity of Los Angeles, and of Phoenix, was reflected in the blurring and fragmenting of traditional structural neighborhoods, as well as the presence of multiplicitous, hybrid areas formed by highly mobile, multicultural groups of people (Drzewiecka & Nakayama, 1998). In this study, the organization of neighborhood spaces in each city was the *text* to which the authors applied their ideological framework.

Of course, more traditional means of collecting texts are also useful in critical communication studies. Participant observation and interviews are key routes by which you can access participants' lived experiences. The field notes and interview transcripts that you create in these ways also constitute texts for analysis. Papa, Auwal, and Singhal (1995, 1997) used a triangulation strategy, combining participant observations with personal and focus group interviews, analysis of existing documents, and a field survey of bank employees, in order to study the ways in which social change is organized. Specifically, they examined a bank's funding of grassroots micro-enterprises in Bangladesh. Watts and Orbe (2002) combined focus group interviews with college students enrolled in a media criticism course and textual analysis of television commercials and their associated media coverage to answer their research question, "'Whassup' with the Budweiser Guys?"

Finally, you can collect existing texts in less intrusive ways, as is the case whenever newspapers, films, photographs, television shows, song lyrics, and such are used (e.g., Carpenter, 1999; Conrad, 1988; Lewis, 1997; McLaughlin, 1991; Shugart, 1997; Tavener, 2000). Let's look at two brief examples to see how texts are used as evidence for evaluation and reform claims.

When we **appropriate** something, we make it our own, or set it aside for a specific use. A number of critical studies have focused on how texts have been appropriated by specific people for their own uses (e.g., Herman & Sloop, 1998; Shugart, 1999). Delgado (1998a) argued that a variety of Chicano artists have appropriated the rap music genre in order to articulate elements of Chicano ideology and help Mexican Americans see themselves as a unified, politically engaged group. In doing so, these artists promote Chicano political ideology and open a space in the mass media for that traditional, nationalist agenda to be heard and absorbed by contemporary Chicano audiences. Delgado showed that rap music, which has "always had a political bent" (p. 95, citing Cleary, 1993), may be used in two ways. First, rap can serve as a vehicle for promoting the dominant Chicano ideology; second, it can be part of a more critical discourse aimed at resisting the mainstream ideology and providing a "voice from the margins" (Delgado, p. 95). Delgado (1998a) also commented on the mix of poetic and political in Chicano rap music, both in terms of the structural similarities of rap music to poetry and the political content of its lyrics. Mumby (1993) and other critical scholars have also noted the blend of poetic and political in critical studies, more generally.

Scheibel (1994) argued that the students in a Los Angeles film school used graffiti to create and reflect their sectional interests. He analyzed the graffiti students had written on the walls of their editing rooms, and he showed how they depicted the interests of the dominant power-holders in that setting (i.e., the faculty and those who control the film and movie industries). In Scheibel's study, graffiti was the text used to represent tensions between student alienation and domination. Scheibel took photographs and copied down the contents of about 900 pieces of graffiti. He also examined the editing rooms and conducted interviews with film students at three other schools in Southern California, the heart of the film/movie industry on the West Coast of the United States.

Researchers' Experiences and Beliefs

A debate waged among interpretive and critical scholars over the past decade or so centers on the question of who has a right to assign meaning to actions, events, texts, or experiences? In critical studies, we refer to this issue as the **politics of representation.** All representations of actions, events, and texts are political because all those representations broach the same questions: Whose voice should be heard? Whose interpretation is correct? Who says what reforms are needed in a society? At the crux of the debate are the issues of membership in and naming of a social category or group. Mumby (1993) asked, "How can researchers claim to speak for (i.e., construct representations of) social groups to which they do not belong?" (p. 18). Even if you are a member of the group you want to represent, how legitimate is it for you to represent the voices of research participants, the people whose stories you collect and in whose events you participate?

We raise this question because your own experiences and beliefs are an important source of evidence in critical studies (Foss & Foss, 1994). Your beliefs and experiences are not thought of as biases to be ignored or controlled, as might be the case in discovery research. Your experiences are not just acknowledged as they affect your interpretations, as would be the case in the interpretive paradigm (Peshkin, 1988). Rather, in critical studies, your experiences and beliefs are the basis for your analysis of power, dominance, and the argued need for reforming ideology (Lannamann, 1991; Foss & Foss, 1994).

ANALYTIC MOVES IN CRITICAL STUDIES

Consistent with the critical paradigm values of voice and liberation, there is no one method or procedure for conducting critical communication studies (Sprague, 1992). There are various ways to proceed in selecting textual evidence for analysis, just as there are a series of moves one can make in analyzing those texts. We will describe four such analytic moves in this section: (1) deconstruction, (2) narrative analyses, (3) dialectical analyses, and (4) speech act analyses. Each of these forms of analysis has a rich (and in some cases, lengthy) history of its own, to which we cannot do justice in this short space. Rather, we will try to show you what the basic move is in each case and suggest some initial places to look if you want to try making these moves yourself!

Deconstruction

Deconstruction is the critical studies term associated with unpacking, or taking apart, the meaning of a text (Derrida, 1976, 1978, 1981). However, Gunkel (2000) pointed out that any attempt to merely break apart the two halves of a binary opposite constitutes *analysis,* which is part of, but insufficient for, deconstruction. Deconstructionists aim to show how texts have hidden dualisms and inner contradictions, or repressed meanings.

> Meanings are not embedded within a text, but rather they are constructed through dichotomies or binary opposites that are constantly shifting. Derrida reasoned that textual meaning is only apparently stable because it

"privileges" (makes present) one term over the other (Mumby & Putnam, 1992, p. 468).

Deconstruction goes beyond taking apart two "opposite values," and it "always proceeds in an irreducible double gesture" (Gunkel, p. 52). The first part of deconstruction is **inversion**; since two opposite terms are rarely equally valued, inversion is the attempt to "bring low what was high" (Derrida, 1981, p. 42, as cited by Gunkel). In an old Phil Donahue episode, the talk show host assumed the body posture and facial expression of a centerfold model, while fully clothed, onstage. It was a way of showing how that physical posture and facial expression functioned to present a nude female model as subservient. The image of an adult white male in that posture, showing that facial expression, fully clothed, made the function of the pose and expression apparent to the audience, and resulted in laughter. "This inversion, however, like all revolutionary operations, does little or nothing to challenge the system that is overturned" (Gunkel, 2000, p. 52).

In the second phase of deconstruction, a new concept emerges that could never have been included in the previous dualism (i.e., the binary opposite terms that were unpacked during inversion). For example, Gunkel's (2000) essay showed how virtual reality is neither *real* nor *simulation,* but something those two terms cannot fully encompass. Instead, virtual reality displaces the very metaphysical foundation it is based on, the hierarchical and causal relationship between real and represented.

Deconstruction is used as a general strategy for critical textual analysis. We interpret texts to show their multiple possible meanings, but "deconstruction shows that whatever meaning is derived is wrong" (Littlejohn, 2002, p. 205). Thus, analysis and deconstruction are used to critique dominant meanings and sometimes to propose alternative interpretations that will better serve the interests of formerly marginalized groups. If you only go as far as inverting the traditional relationship between two binary opposites (e.g., mind/body, male/female, self/other), then the point may simply be "to reject one ideology and embrace another" (Parks, 1997, p. 483).

But, in the case of feminist deconstruction, "the point of such work is not simply to introduce women into the equation . . . but rather it is to rewrite the equation itself" (Mumby, 1993, p. 23). If the equation is not reinvented by feminist research, perhaps at least such studies function to "introduce radical doubt into segmented modes of thought" (Mumby, p. 24). Awareness of a need for change is, after all, the starting point for all reform (Mies, 1991; Ramazanoglu, 1992).

In some cases, the specific goal of deconstruction is to reveal how individuals and groups participate in their own domination by the meanings they privilege in certain texts. Clair's (1993, 1994) studies of sexual harassment stories in organizations evaluated the ways in which these gendered discourse practices about sexuality in organizations contributed to and perpetuated hegemony, and how that discourse could be used to resist domination.

Like many critical scholars, Clair deconstructed a paradox. Women in organizations face a double bind when they are sexually harassed: In order to stop the harassment, they need to tell someone about it, but, as lower-power members, their stories are likely to threaten the interests of the dominant members of the organization. Most organizations discourage open discussion of sexual harassment incidents and call for confidentiality when dealing with those complaints. Following the poststructuralist view of ideology (rather than social structure) as oppressive, Clair pointed out that sexual harassment is not something that exists *within* the organization. Rather, "sexual harassment is discursive action that hegemonically reproduces an oppressive organizational society" (p. 115).

Your critical deconstruction may focus on the lived realities of the participants in your research, or it may focus on you, yourself. This concept is called **self-reflexivity.** Allen (1996) concluded her essay by considering some implications of her experiences for the theory and practice of organizational socialization. One implication she drew from her analysis was that researchers should consider their motives for studying organizational communication: "If they investigate it to understand and to effect change, rather than to predict and control, their research methods and outcomes will look different" (p. 267). Allen also urged organizational socialization researchers to obtain input from "a variety of persons, particularly the traditionally disenfranchised" (p. 267). She acknowledged that her own research had already begun to emancipate her. "My sense of myself and my worth as a scholar have increased tremendously since I began this project. Just as [feminist standpoint theory] was designed to do, it has helped me to elicit knowledge that empowers me" (p. 268). She concluded, "I plan to learn as I go, and I welcome suggestions about how to proceed" (p. 268). We hope that this example helps you to see how one critical scholar deconstructed her experiences in order to offer a value-based critique of one communicative process, organizational socialization.

Narrative Analyses

We presented some interpretive uses of narrative analysis in Chapter 12. Interpretive narrative analysis focuses on the meanings people make through the stories they tell, whereas critical narrative analyses push these meanings one step farther. Critical narrative analyses seek to expose hegemony (Littlejohn, 2002). Mumby's (1988, 1993) work on the political nature of storytelling in organizations has done much to elaborate this perspective. He showed how stories told over and over in organizations create and maintain power relations, and usually perpetuate the interests of the dominant group, management. Analyzing members' stories is one way that you can access the "lived experiences of real people in context" for critical scholarship (Littlejohn, 2002, p. 207). Of course, critical narrative analyses can extend well beyond the organizational communication context.

Yep et al. (2001) analyzed narratives in which queer Asian Americans constructed and dealt with their relationships with their family members. The authors asserted that personal narratives "allow us to understand personal experiences and challenges from the perspective of the individual, first, to minimize the dangers of 'speaking for' (Alcoff, 1995)" (p. 6). They attempted to create a polyphony of voices by selecting stories of Americans from various Asian cultures such as Chinese, Filipino, Hawaiian, Japanese, Korean, and Vietnamese, and by including gay, lesbian, bisexual, and transgendered speakers from a variety of social classes and political ideologies. Depending on your epistemology, the analysis of such narratives can either raise awareness of the intersections of race, class, gender, and sexuality, or it can obscure knowledge that could and should be gained through systematic observation of categorical relationships and differences (Parks, 1997).

The content of the stories we tell is just one feature of narrative analysis. Your critical narrative analysis might also address the situated features of storytelling, such as, Who can tell this story? When can this story be told? Where must this story be told? What is being accomplished in the telling of this story? To illustrate this in a simple way, think of one joke that you find very funny. To whom, and in what times and places, would you tell this joke? In what situations would you avoid telling this joke, or mask your true feelings if someone else shared the joke? The different answers you have for these questions may help you see some of the situated features of narratives in a more critical light.

Dialectic Analyses

A **relational dialectic** is a simultaneous push–pull, a tension between two competing and perhaps contradictory goals in a relationship (Baxter & Montgomery, 1998). Yep et al. (2001) explored three relational dialectics in the narratives of queer Asian Americans: (1) autonomy from versus connectedness with family, (2) openness versus secrecy, and (3) certainty versus unpredictability. In each case, the participants had to negotiate these competing goals in their relationships with their families.

Clair's (1997) essay on the Treaty of New Echota also used dialectic analysis. This time, the competing tensions were between silence as voice and voice as silence. She wrote that her essay's title, "'Organizing Silence,' can be interpreted in at least two ways: "It simultaneously refers to the ways in which interests, issues, and identities of marginalized people are silenced and to how those silenced voices can be organized in ways to be heard" (p. 323). Clair chose the paradoxical title in order to call attention to the dialectic aspects of silence and voice.

As in narrative critical analyses, the shift from interpretive to critical epistemology in dialectic criticism is subtle, but distinct. In critical studies, we begin with the assumptions of discursive and/or material domination, which Mumby called the hermeneutic of suspicion. We begin with an assumption of domination and analyze the struggle among fluid, competing interests in terms of their various ways of representing actions and events (e.g., Mumby & Stohl, 1991; Papa, Auwal, & Singhal, 1997).

In dialectical analyses, we believe we can discern a structure or meaning that is typically hidden or obscured from the consciousness of individuals participating in everyday life (Lannamann, 1991). Through careful tacking, back and forth, between the whole and the parts of the text, action, or event, we proceed to uncover this meaning. The movement back and forth, between the general and specific meanings of texts, is called the **hermeneutic circle.**

Speech Act Analyses

The Frankfurt scholar Juergen Habermas contributed a fourth data analytic move to critical studies in communication. Habermas's (1979) model of communicative competence was based on the critical analysis of linguistic acts. He described society as a mix of interests, including work (technical), interaction (practical), and power (emancipatory). Critical scholarship aims to empower people by making them aware of hidden, oppressive social structures. For Habermas and his followers, language is the primary means to emancipation, and communicative competence is needed to participate in social discourse and help make group decisions (Blyler, 1994; Felts, 1992).

Habermas's theory, called *universal pragmatics,* outlined three types of speech acts: (1) **Constatives** are assertions, such as "*X* is true," (2) **regulatives** are influence attempts, such as a command or promise, and (3) **avowals** describe the speaker's internal state, such as "I feel happy." Habermas proposed three different types of discourse, three kinds of communication required when a speaker's statements are challenged. **Theoretic discourse** is needed to argue the *truth* of a constative statement. **Practical discourse** is used to argue the *appropriateness* of a regulative statement. Finally, **metatheoretical discourse** is required to argue the *sincerity* of an avowal.

Thus, a fourth move for critical analysis is to isolate the three speech acts that Habermas identified, as well as the presence or absence of their accompanying forms of discourse. In this way, a critical scholar can assess whether a speaker's statements are being challenged, whose statements are challenged (or not challenged), and with what effects. Habermas described the **ideal speech situation** as one that included free, accessible public discourse and equal distribution of power to all parts of society. If events, actions, texts, and experiences suggest that these conditions are not being fulfilled in a situation, it is unlikely that any discourse can take place that would help to emancipate the oppressed members of that society. If such discourse does take place, the critical researcher can evaluate its direction and likelihood of equalizing power relations. Because the goal of critical scholarship is to unite theory and action, to actually change existing power relations, criticism of these three linguistic acts and their accompanying forms of discourse can help critical researchers evaluate social changes already in progress.

Cezec-Kecmanovic, Treleaven, and Moodie (2000) used this move to explore how CMC both enabled and inhibited knowledge sharing during a university restructuring process. They applied Habermas's framework of linguistic acts and implied validity claims (the kinds of discourse needed when each act is challenged) to a set of email messages exchanged during the university's change process.

WARRANTS FOR CRITICAL STUDIES

There are still relatively fewer critical studies published in communication journals, compared to discovery and interpretive research, and the standards for evaluating this type of research are less clear than for the other two paradigms. In part this is because the paradigm is still emerging in practice; however, it is also because these theories resist categorization and standardization, except for their "unabashedly value laden" stance (Littlejohn, 2002, p. 229). Although some published critical essays are purely theoretic in nature, more and more critical studies are appearing in print that use actions and events, texts, and researcher experiences and beliefs as evidentiary sources to demonstrate the need for ideological change. As you learned in Chapter 4, critical scholars especially focus on the voices of people who are underrepresented in the current societal discourse, with the hope of liberating them from the bonds of ideological oppression (i.e., liberation through awareness).

Several warrants are used as standards by which you can evaluate your own or another person's critical study. Among these are the coherence of interpretation of the text, and the degree to which subjectivity of interpretations is acknowledged. In relation to these, the writer's positionality on the topic and the readers' freedom of choice with respect to their own interpretations should be acknowledged. Finally, the presence of free, accessible public discourse may be explored as evidence for claims about reforming power imbalances. Each of these warrants is considered in turn in the subsections below.

Establishing Coherence

Deetz (1982) first pointed out that coherence, rather than accuracy, is the most appropriate warrant for critical studies. **Coherence** means that the author's interpretations are logical, consistent, and intelligible. In

critical studies, "understanding which makes the text maximally reasonable and coherent should be sought" (Deetz, 1982, p. 144). Of course, this raises a question: "*To whom* does this understanding of the text appear 'maximally reasonable and coherent'?" Deetz concluded that the "most complete interpretation demonstrating maximum rationality should be preferred even when there are competing ones" (1982, p. 144).

Fink and Gantz (1996) stated that "those who share the critical perspective of the researcher are free to accept or reject the argument" (p. 119). Those who disagree with the researcher's ideology, in all likelihood, will not see the researcher's interpretations as coherent. Bochner (1985) called this *free consensus,* which suggests that "verification can only be left to those who agree with that perspective" (as cited in Fink & Gantz, 1996, p. 129).

Critical analyses typically include attention to the broader social system of which the text is a part, including social structures like class, race, education, and so on, as well as the historical positioning of the act or event, as one way of achieving coherence. Even actions that appear unreasonable may be shown to be rational or necessary when their broader historical and social contexts are examined (Ramazanoglu, 1992). Some actions that appear irrational actually are reasonable responses to unreasonable situations (Clair, 1993; 1994; Yep, Lovaas, & Pagonis, 2002). So, "one should not pass judgment on an individual without understanding the inherent logic which makes his or her actions meaningful" (Deetz, 1982, p. 144). Conquergood's (1991) critical cultural ethnography of Latino gang members in Chicago showed how young men participated in gangs in order to fulfill their social needs for inclusion, affection, and control; this was one early example of research that made coherent the seemingly incoherent, even life-threatening behavior of joining a street gang.

Another way you can achieve coherence in your critical study is to become intimately familiar with the texts you analyze. For this reason, membership in the social group under study is just as important an issue for critical studies as it is in interpretive research. Even as a member of one of the social groups under study, you will need to stay aware of multiple possible interpretations of the text. You must "search for the texts which best represent what is thinkable and doable" in that social situation (Deetz, 1982, p. 144). Only when you are intimately familiar with the situation, when you know "how to get things done . . . how to avoid unpleasant outcomes, how to recognize critical features," as well as "with whom to talk, what counts as adequate information," and so on (pp. 140–141), can you achieve a coherent interpretation. Without a coherent interpretation, you cannot possibly evaluate power imbalances or oppression, or suggest what actions should be taken to reform those conditions.

Acknowledging Subjectivity

The idea of subjective interpretation is familiar and common sense to interpretive and critical researchers. It is one of the points on which these researchers typically disagree with social scientists from the discovery paradigm. Traditional social scientists typically try to control for their subjective biases, as well as those of their research subjects. By contrast, when you do interpretive and critical research, you acknowledge your subjectivity and include it in your analysis. Critical researchers believe it is neither possible nor desirable to eliminate subjectivity or to work around it in doing research. So acknowledging subjectivity becomes one of the ways that you warrant the worth of your critical inquiry.

As a researcher, how can you know when your subjectivity is engaged? Peshkin (1988) recalled noticing "the emergence of positive and negative feelings, the experiences I wanted more of or wanted to avoid, and when I felt moved to act in roles that reached beyond those necessary to fulfill my research needs" (p. 18). When that happened, Peshkin would write himself a field note; later, he categorized those notes into groups, according to which *"I"* seemed to be manifest on each occasion (e.g., the Justice-Seeking *"I"*). Peshkin advocated this sort of disciplined, systematic self-monitoring of subjectivity as a kind of workout "so that I may avoid the trap of perceiving just that which my own untamed sentiments have sought out and served up as data" (p. 20).

Allen (1996) spoke "from her vantage point as an African-American faculty member at a predominantly White, research university" and "recounts her lived experiences to demonstrate the value of eliciting insight from an 'outsider within'" (p. 257). Allen was overtly subjective in her essay; she used the personal pronoun *I* repeatedly and used "self-interview data" (p. 258) to depict her experience of anticipating and being assimilated as a faculty member in a predominantly white research university. She wrote,

"I speak from a perspective that 'I own and am rigorously reflective about'" (on p. 261, citing Marshall, 1993, p. 123). And she further acknowledged, "My experiences do not necessarily represent those of other women of color, of other women, or of other persons of color" (p. 261). Allen's comments demonstrated her recognition that her social location is distinct from another person's location and experience (see also Yep, 2000; Tanno & Jandt, 1994). As you read critical studies, you will notice that questioning the correctness of an interpretation receives far less attention than acknowledging multiple, plausible interpretations. This leads us to the next warrant, acknowledging freedom of choice for the writer and readers of a critical essay.

Acknowledging Freedom of Choice

"Conducting research in the right manner has often been confused with being right" (Deetz, 1982, p. 143). In critical scholarship, subjective experiences and beliefs are embraced as legitimate, so various approaches to studying and interpreting actions and events are seen as natural and valuable (Sprague, 1992). "The appeal for the appropriateness of the method needs to be made to the object of analysis, not the existing standards of a research community" (Deetz, 1982, p. 143).

In conducting critical studies, try to view different texts (i.e., different representations of the same action, event, or thing) as having their own integrity. Texts have their own meanings as representations of things; they are not merely (or even) true maps of the thing itself. For example, Watts and Orbe (2002) acknowledged that the students in their focus groups had different views of the marketing strategy behind Budweiser's "Whassup" ad campaign. "Most participants felt that the advertising campaign was highly effective, with African Americans focusing on the inclusion of the black community, and non-African Americans applauding the use of humor [that could be] enjoyed across racial barriers" (p. 15). Neither of those interpretations were central to the authors' analysis, that Budweiser's attempts to reproduce "authentic" blackness reproduce a basic tension between the depiction of black Americans as simultaneously same and other.

As a critical scholar, you are free to choose different actions, events, and texts as data for analysis, and to support the worth of your analysis with different warrants. Only you must acknowledge the choices you have made and try to avoid presenting those choices as correct, or as any guarantor of truth (Deetz, 1982). Fink and Gantz (1996) noted that "scholars in this tradition accept nonscientific generalizations. . . . [They] also accept critical research that does not support a broader, ideologic perspective, but criticizes only a single text or context" (p. 129). In short, the warrants for critical studies in communication largely still rest on Deetz's (1982) observation that "rigor is possible in the maintenance of these principles rather than the following of a prescribed method or procedure" (Deetz, 1982, p. 143).

Critical studies essays often contain explicit admonishments to readers that they are free to choose another interpretation or to deconstruct the author's interpretation of the actions and events. For instance, in Shugart's (1999) analysis of Susan Dorothea White's painting *The First Supper,* the author analyzed that painting as a "subversive, postmodern ironic reading of Leonardo da Vinci's famed work *The Last Supper*" (p. 433). In the first paragraph of her essay, she declared that

> irony invites multiple readings on multiple levels, thereby creating multiple audiences. Significantly, although the subversive function of irony is this instance may be apparent to a post-modern audience, the text may be just as likely to function hegemonically for other audiences (Shugart, 1999, p. 433).

Similarly, Battles and Hilton-Morrow (2002) argued that *Will & Grace* is a "potentially subversive program that portrays male homosexuality in a way that many different audiences can identify with, appreciate, and enjoy" (p. 101). The show preserves viewers' freedom of choice about homosexuality, at once presenting positive images of gays and lesbians, and conforming to dominant cultural discourses about heterosexual romance as the norm against which all interpersonal relationships are measured.

Evaluating Public Discourse

As we discussed earlier in this chapter, Habermas (1979) identified the presence of a free, accessible public discourse about issues that are being challenged in a society as one guarantee of the validity of reform claims. If oppressed people are being liberated, then their concerns should be openly discussable. In fact, as researchers, we ourselves must have free, accessible discourse about our own statements as they are being challenged and defended. In particular, it is important that a community of scholars engage in public discourse about what should be studied and how best to conduct research.

Without this free, accessible discourse, which Habermas called the ideal speech situation, it is unlikely that any interactions will occur that can challenge the statements coming from one dominant group (see Burgoon & Bailey, 1992; Parks, 1997). Just to continue our example for a moment, in academic research, there are scholarly gatekeepers, such as the journal editors, admission committees for doctoral programs, and tenure evaluation committees at universities; these gatekeepers influence what research gets conducted, published, and disseminated. If there is insufficient or closed discourse about research topics or methods, then those who at present dominate in those endeavors will likely continue to do so, and the interests of other persons or groups will likely remain marginalized.

One way to promote public discourse that might lead to emancipation comes from the work of Augusto Boal (1998). Boal's Forum Theatre and Legislative Theatre are performance workshops used in conference and educational settings to promote interaction, reflection, and discussion from the conference attendees.

In one such workshop for students, faculty, and regional social service personnel in Omaha, Nebraska, in 1995, this forum was used to develop potential laws that should be enacted to address the problems identified by members of that community. Kendig (1997) examined how Boal's Forum Theatre could provide a framework within which dominant gender scripts could be critiqued, disrupted, and at times transformed. In the process, Kendig argued, participants develop self-reflexivity and learn from the insights and experiences of other group members.

Conquergood (1983) also has argued that performances of the *other* can give insight into and intensify the dialectical tensions between openhearted participation and detached observation. It is possible that performance of discourse (in a theatric venue) can pave the way for free, accessible public discourse in other venues about issues of oppression, domination, and liberation (e.g., Gilbert, 1997).

TECHNOLOGY AND CRITICAL STUDIES

The relevance of technological changes to critical studies rests primarily with the contributions of structural and poststructural criticisms of technology. Whether the author's theoretic stance comes from Marxist, feminist, cultural, postmodern, poststructural, or postcolonial thinking, critical studies address questions of access, power-dominance relations, and consciousness about technological changes as they affect communication. In this section, we will review a few such studies briefly, to show how you might analyze the text of technological actions, events, or your own experiences using deconstruction, narrative analysis, dialectical analysis, or even speech act analysis.

First, as several scholars have observed, the hegemonic power structures at work in our dominant social institutions (i.e., government, education, religion) are being reproduced and reified on the Internet, since the geography of cyberspace mirrors colonial and European cultural structures (Gunkel & Gunkel, 1997; Steinberg & MacDowell, 2003). Gunkel (2000) examined the technology of virtual reality and deconstructed the concept of representation itself. He pointed out that the term *simulation* has always been associated with *imitation*. But virtual reality cannot be critiqued for its *realism,* Gunkel argued. Further, as Derrida (1981) specified about deconstruction, virtual reality cannot be understood simply as "the mere substitution of images for reality" (Gunkel, p. 55). "Artificial reality is neither image nor reality, but something other, something that is neither/nor and either/or" (p. 57). In the end, Gunkel concluded, "virtual reality is fundamentally a political matter" (p. 59).

Other scholars have observed that the same cultural values marginalized in face-to-face and mediated interaction offline are also marginalized in digital communication forms. Brookey and Westerfelhaus (2002) argued that *The Fight Club* DVD's extra text, the interviews, commentaries, and behind-the-scenes clips that were "not included in the film's theatrical release or video version" (p. 22) worked as a sort of "digital closet" (p. 21). "We argue that the supplemental material included on the DVD is used to make the product more marketable to mainstream audiences by framing the homoerotic elements of the film as homosocial behavior" (p. 22). Brookey and Westerfelhaus contended that DVD extra text does more than just offer additional material to DVD viewers; it "directs the viewers' experiences of the film" (p. 25).

Stewart, Shields, and Sen (1998) conducted a critical discourse analysis of cultural and gender differences in listserv interactions in order to see whether college students would discursively reproduce the norms of face-to-face interactions online. After all, proponents of the Internet have lauded its anonymity as potentially leveling power relationships, by masking social group memberships, for example. Stewart et al. examined transcripts collected from students' online interactions over one semester. They looked at relative message frequency and length, willingness to adopt technology, and dominating behaviors in online interactions, comparing men and women, Whites and "other cultural groups." Men sent longer, more frequent messages and Whites sent more messages than other cultural groups. Men were more willing to adopt the technology than women, and Whites were more willing to adopt than other cultural groups. Men presented more dominating behavior online. In short, these college students' interactions reproduced the dominant social structure, even in online interactions over a few months.

We hope that these three examples suggest some of the ways that critical studies methodologies can be used to address claims of description, explanation, evaluation, and reform about technology.

SUMMARY

In this chapter, we have presented our version of the most recent paradigm in communication research, critical studies. We have outlined some of the many variations of critical communication scholarship. Although we appreciate the reasons that critical scholars resist categorization, we have, for pedagogical reasons, initially separated critical studies into two basic groups: those with structural (including Marxist, feminist, and cultural) assumptions versus those with poststructural (including postmodern and postcolonial) assumptions.

We have presented instances of the descriptive, evaluative, and reforming claims in these six subsets of critical studies. In addition, we have attempted to illustrate how you can employ actions and events, texts, and your own experiences as evidence, toward the end of evaluating and reforming social structures and discourse practices.

We also outlined four analytic moves you can use to conduct a critical study: deconstructing textual meanings, analyzing narratives, analyzing dialectic tensions, and analyzing speech acts. Although these sources of evidence and forms of analysis also are used in interpretive communication research, we noted that they are put to slightly different purposes in critical studies. Whereas interpretive researchers select and analyze data for the purpose of unpacking representative meanings, critical researchers make use of evidence to identify sources of ideological domination, equalize power relations, or show how oppressive structures are temporarily constituted in language.

Finally, we presented four warrants for critical studies, based on the values of voice and liberation that we identified in Chapter 4. You must first warrant the ideological need for change by demonstrating a coherent, reasonable argument that there exists a dominant ideology that perpetuates hegemony. Second, you may warrant a critical study by acknowledging your own subjective position and social location. The worth of your critical argument rests equally on the standpoint from which you speak and also on your critical reflexivity.

The third and fourth warrants are closely related to one another. The value of critical study is warranted by your acknowledgment of freedom of choice about what to study, how to study it, and which interpretations are being privileged. A free and accessible public discourse about these choices, and their merits, further warrants the value of critical studies (and of any research, in our opinion). Ultimately, critical studies may raise awareness of ideological influences on groups and individuals, including instances of domination and oppression. But it remains to be seen in the public discourse and actions whether such awareness actually results in structural and cultural change, or not.

KEY TERMS

Appropriate (verb)

Avowal speech acts

Coherence

Constative speech acts

Deconstruction

Discursive formation

Econometrics

Hegemony

Hermeneutic circle

Ideal speech situation

Ideology

Inversion

Metatheoretical discourse

Paradox

Politics of representation

Postmodern turn

Practical discourse

Regulative speech acts

Relational dialectic

Self-reflexivity

Textual analysis

Theoretic discourse

Universal pragmatics

Womanist criticism

DISCUSSION QUESTIONS

1. Write a brief description of yourself that you would be willing to share with your classmates and instructor. Would you share the same description with your parents? Your employer? Your significant other? What are the politics of representing yourself? How different do you think those politics are when trying to represent another person or event outside yourself?

2. Hanke (1998) and Trujillo (1991) conducted studies that described the hegemonic nature of masculinity as portrayed in a television sitcom and in media coverage of a baseball player. What other examples can you think of that show how masculine and feminine roles are portrayed, parodied, and critiqued in the media you encounter in your daily life?

3. Consider Brenda Allen's (1996) assertion, "I speak from a perspective that 'I own and am rigorously reflective about'" (on p. 261, citing Marshall, 1993, p. 123). What perspective do you own? What do you think it means to be rigorously reflective? How could we become more reflective about our own positions in our society?

4. An important question with respect to acknowledging subjectivity in critical studies concerns the practical problem of conflicting interpretations of the text. Should critical scholars check their interpretations with others (e.g., the participants in their studies)? If so, and participants disagree with the scholar, whose interpretation is correct? Whose ideas should be privileged in the written research report?

"TRY IT!" ACTIVITIES

1. Think of one story you have told recently about some aspect of your real, lived experience. Deconstruct this story in terms of these six *W*s: To whom did you tell the story? When? Where? Why? What was the story about? What do you think you accomplished in telling this story? Does your story illustrate some hegemonic process? If so, what?

2. In a small group of about five people, share the stories you analyzed in the previous activity. Rather than looking for commonalities (or generalizable features) in your group's stories, consider which stories provide the richest, most coherent and compelling interpretation of the social situation. How reflective are you and your group members about your own experiences and beliefs?

3. Select some text (e.g., a passage from a film, book, or television show containing dialogue or a segment of interaction from email, a telephone conversation, or face-to-face interaction). Analyze the text in order to isolate the three types of speech acts identified by Habermas: constatives, regulatives, and avowals. Is there any *discourse* in this text, as in "the special kind of communication required when a speaker's statements are challenged" (Littlejohn, 2002, p. 215)? Which types of discourse can you detect? Based on the speech acts, and any accompanying discourse you have identified, answer the following questions: (a) Who has more power in this situation? Who is being oppressed? (b) Is the discourse present in this situation likely to rectify any power imbalance between/among these participants? (c) Do the participants seem to be aware of this power imbalance, or is it hidden from their everyday lived experience?

4. Deconstruct the movie *Deconstructing Harry* (or the movie of your choice or your instructor's choice). What social structures, events, or actions is the movie describing? Do you think the writer is interested in evaluating and/or reforming these structures, events, or actions? What warrants are demonstrated for the worth or value of this author/producer's analysis?

5. Look at several issues of wedding magazines (e.g., *Bride*). What assumptions of race, class, sex, and gender are being reproduced in the articles and advertisements in a wedding magazine?

APPENDIX A

Writing Research Reports and Critical Essays

ABSTRACT

In this appendix, we will introduce you to the process of writing research for academic audiences such as professional associations, scholarly journals, trade journals, or popular press publications. Research writing by discovery, interpretive, and critical scholars varies somewhat in tone and format, but some features can be recognized across paradigms: the use of academic writing style and the (re)construction of the elements of the research-as-argument model can be found in all written research reports and essays. We present an overview of two basic forms, the research report and critical essay. Finally, we will describe some aspects of style and organization that are particular to writing in the discovery, interpretive, and critical research paradigms.

OUTLINE

How can you learn to write a research report? "As most professional writers will affirm, the only way to learn to write is *to write*" (Spradley, 1980, p. 160, emphasis in the original). You cannot learn to write a research report simply by reading published research, although that is very helpful. Learning to write is analogous to learning to swim (Spradley, 1980). We don't learn to swim by watching people swim, or even reading books about swimming, although instruction from a book or an experienced swimmer can be helpful. We learn to swim by combining all of these modalities: We watch it, we try it, and we have someone more expert than ourselves coach us as we do it! Learning to write research reports and critical essays is a lot like learning to swim. You may have trouble keeping your head above water when you are trying to write your first manuscript; but with practice, you will become much more competent and feel more at ease with the process.

"Unless you are emotionally engaged in your work, the inevitable boredom, confusion, and frustration of rigorous scholarship will make even the completion—much less the quality—of the project problematic" (Lofland & Lofland, 1984, p. 10). Whether you are involved in knowing by discovery, interpretation, or criticism and regardless of what methodology you are using to study communication, you will need to pursue a project that engages you intellectually and emotionally, or your motivation to work will suffer, along with the quality of your work.

It is also important to have strong relationships within the staff of a team research project, since those relationships will need to last over time and through adversity. Obviously, this will work best if you think about your team relationships and roles at the beginning of your project. If you are involved in a collaborative research team, group efforts may well extend beyond designing the project, collecting, and analyzing data, to a variety of tasks including writing up the manuscript.

If you are part of a collaborative interpretive research project, it is important that all team members participate in all phases of the project, up to and including the iterative writing of the research report or essay. Miles and Huberman (1994) advised avoiding "sharp senior-junior divisions of labor, such as having juniors do the fieldwork and the seniors do the analysis and writing" (p. 46). May and Pattillo-McCoy (2000) added that though collaborative approaches to ethnographic research have gained popularity, too

often "these studies are written by one voice (or perhaps two voices), who compiles the data collected by others" (p. 65). Therefore, one standard for evaluating the quality of an interpretive research report based on collaborative research "might be the extent that multiple perspectives find their way into the narrative" (Miller, Creswell, & Olander, 1998, p. 489).

Even as an individual working alone on a research project, you will need to allow time to develop skills you don't already have. Things go slower the first few times, whether it's interviewing, taking field notes, coding data, writing reports, and so on. "Time plans usually suffer from excessive optimism. Get a cynical skeptic to critique them" (Miles & Huberman, 1994, p. 47).

AUDIENCES FOR COMMUNICATION RESEARCH

"Research is complete only when the results are shared with the scientific community" (American Psychological Association, 2001, p. 3). The word *scientific* might be replaced by *interpretive* or *peer* community. The pursuit of knowledge is almost never wholly individual. Indeed, "all knowledge production is a social business. . . . Though we may toil individually, we always work on common problems" (Stablein, 1996, p. 510).

Whatever your research topic, you are probably trying to know about subjects for which interest is shared among one or more communities of people (Hickson, Stacks, & Bodon, 1999; Katzer, Cook, & Crouch, 1998). At minimum, those communities might consist of other researchers, the research participants themselves, and the practitioners who apply and use the knowledge the research produces. We need to write differently and target different publication outlets to reach these different audiences, since they don't all read the same publications, or even have the same criteria for effective writing (Childress, 1998).

Whether you are writing a research manuscript for a class assignment, for presentation at a professional association meeting, for publication, or for some other purpose, it is important to consider your readers. Stablein (1996) identified four possible audiences for research: (1) the researcher's peers, (2) those who teach courses in which research comprises some of the content to be learned, (3) students who read research summaries in textbooks, and (4) people who rely on and read research in the course of their work or personal experiences (Stablein, 1996).

The first audience, your research peers, is in most cases a small, rather homogenous group. It might be just the students in your research methods course. To consider a larger example, let's say that you are concerned with research in organizational communication studies, which was published in the English language in a scholarly journal. For this type of research, Stablein (1996) estimated that the peer audience "would not exceed a few thousand world-wide" (p. 510). Perhaps "tens of thousands" of people teach organizational studies, Stablein estimated, although many of those teachers "will publish infrequently over their career" (p. 510).

Strauss and Corbin (1998) addressed yet a fifth possible audience for communication research, the participants:

> We have obligations to the actors we have studied: obligations to "tell their stories" to them and to others—to give them voice— albeit in the context of their own inevitable interpretations. We owe it to our "subjects" to tell them verbally or in print what we have learned, and to give clear indications of why we have interpreted them as we have (p. 174).

In the subsections below, we will describe in more detail two types of outlets for written research, primary and secondary sources. **Primary sources** are original research reports or critical essays, written by the researcher, which describe the claims, data, warrants, and backing for a research study. Professional association meetings and scholarly journals are the most common distribution outlets for primary sources. **Secondary sources** are not original research summaries; they are another writer's summary and interpretations of an original research project. Trade journals, popular press publications, and textbooks are some common distribution outlets for secondary sources of communication research.

Professional Associations

The first audience for written research reports and critical essays is typically the researcher's peer community of scholars in a given discipline or topic area. Original research reports are presented at conferences, usually annual meetings sponsored by a **pro-**

fessional association, a dues-paying group of academics in a particular field of study. Some of the professional associations frequented by scholars of communication, and their respective Web site addresses, are listed in Exhibit A.1. In addition, we chose to also list some interdisciplinary professional associations that are frequented by communication scholars (e.g., those whose conference notices are printed in *Spectra,* a publication of the National Communication Association).

Professional association meetings help communication scholars stay abreast of the most recent developments in our field. In professional associations, we maintain ongoing dialogues about issues of interest, as well as relationships with peers who share these interests. But professional associations also allow us, as researchers, to gain important feedback from our primary audience, our peers. The feedback we get from peers after we present our research at a professional association meeting helps us to revise our written manuscripts to determine what other audiences, if any, should be pursued for a given research report. Feedback from peers, both formal and informal, also helps us determine which research ideas or topics to pursue and how to pursue them in the future.

Scholarly Journals

Scholarly journals are published under the sponsorship of professional associations in a given discipline. Their purpose is to convey the very best theoretic and research scholarship in that field to a community of scholarly peers. Only a very small percent of the research reports and critical essays presented at professional meetings are ever published in a scholarly journal. One reason is that some of the papers presented at professional association meetings are works in progress. Also, some of the research presented at conferences will never be submitted to scholarly journals. If a research report is submitted for publication at a peer-reviewed journal, then two or more scholars who share the researcher's areas of theoretical, methodological, or topical expertise will closely evaluate the manuscript. Based on feedback from these reviewers, the journal editor will decide whether or not to publish the research report, usually with revisions suggested by the peer reviewers (Katzer et al., 1998). The journals sponsored by the National Communication Association report over a 90% rejection rate. That means that less than 1 in 10

EXHIBIT A.1   Professional Association Meetings Attended by Communication Scholars

Communication Disciplinary Associations

American Communication Association
(www.americancomm.org)

American Forensics Association (AFA)
(www.americanforensics.org)

Communication Association of Japan
(www.japonet.com/caj/)

European Speech Communication Association
(wwwesca.ikp.uni-bonn.de/home.html)

International Association of Business Communicators
(www.iabc.com)

International Association for Intercultural Communication Studies (IAICS)(www.trinity.edu/org/ics/)

International Communication Association
(www.icahdq.org)

International Listening Association (ILA)
(www.listen.org)

International Network on Personal Relationships
(INPR) (www.inpr.org)

International Society for the Study of Personal Relationships (ISSPR) (www.uwinnipeg.ca/~isspr/)

Kenneth Burke Society
(www.home.duq.edu/~thames/kennethburke)

National Communication Association
(www.natcom.org)

Oral History Association (www.dickinson.edu/oha/)

Public Relations Society of America (www.prsa.org)

United States Regional Communication Associations

Central States Communication Association
(www.csca-net.org)

Eastern States Communication Association
(www.ecasite.org/)

Southern States Communication Association
(http://ssca.net)

Western States Communication Association
(www.csufresno.edu/speechcomm/wsca.htm)

Speech Communication Association of
Puerto Rico

World Communication Association (WCA)
(http://ilc2.doshisha.ac.jp/)

Interdisciplinary Associations Frequented by Communication Scholars

International Information Management Association
(mass communication) (http://64.177.207.251/)

International Society for General Semantics
(www.generalsemantics.org/about/ISGS_DIR.HTM)

Society for the Study of Symbolic Interaction
(http://sun.soci.niu.edu/~sssi/)

Note. In addition to the listings above, many state-level communication associations exist in the United States (e.g., California Speech Communication Association).

---

articles that are submitted for peer review are eventually accepted for publication.

Exhibit A.2 lists some of the scholarly journals that publish communication research. Notice that journals affiliated with professional associations in communication, as well as other relevant disciplines, are listed separately.

Trade Journals and Popular Press Publications

It is quite common to see summaries of communication research presented in trade journals and quoted in popular press publications. This makes sense because of the centrality of human communication to other aspects of our daily lives.

Trade journals are written publications aimed at practitioners in a particular business or industry. Just as scholarly journals are sponsored by the profes-

sional associations to which academics belong, trade journals are sponsored by the professional associations to which business and industry practitioners belong. And just as scholarly journals and professional associations function to maintain the community and interests of academic researchers and teachers, so do trade journals and associations work to preserve and carry out the interests of the business, educational, or other institutional community. Some examples of professional and trade journals that publish or refer to communication research include *Advertising Age, Harvard Business Review, Public Relations Strategist,* and *Training & Development.*

Popular press publications are those secondary sources that are aimed at the general public, largely without regard to their readers' fields of academic study or particular occupations. Think of the magazines or other print media that you subscribe to or that you might purchase at a newsstand. Chances are, these are

---

EXHIBIT A.2   Scholarly Journals That Publish Communication Research

Journals Affiliated With Communication Associations

- Canadian Journal of Communication
- Communication Education
- Communication and the Law
- Communication Monographs
- Communication Quarterly
- Communication Reports
- Communication Research
- Communication Research Reports
- Communication Studies
- Communication Teacher
- Communication Theory
- Communication Yearbook
- Critical Studies in Mass Communication
- Electronic Journal of Communication
- Gender & Communication
- Health Communication
- Howard Journal of Communication
- Human Communication Research
- Journalism Quarterly
- Journal of Applied Communication Research
- Journal of Communication
- Journal of Film and Television
- Journal of Health Communication
- Journal of Popular Culture
- Journal of Public Relations Research
- Journal of Social & Personal Relationships

- Journal of the Northwest Communication Association
- Mass Communication & Society
- National Forensic Journal
- Philosophy & Rhetoric
- Political Communication
- Public Relations Journal
- Quarterly Journal of Speech
- Southern Communication Journal
- Text & Performance Quarterly
- Western Journal of Communication
- Written Communication

Journals Affiliated With Other Professional Associations

- Discourse and Society
- Discourse Processes
- Group and Organization Management
- Journalism & Mass Communication Quarterly
- Journal of Business Communication
- Journal of Broadcasting & Electronic Media
- Journal of Contemporary Ethnography
- Journal of Social & Personal Relationships
- Language and Society
- Management Communication Quarterly
- Qualitative Inquiry
- Research on Language and Social Interaction
- Sex Roles
- Small Group Research

---

popular press publications. Both trade journals and popular press publications constitute secondary sources for published communication research. Web sites are among the fastest-growing types of secondary source for reporting research today.

Traditional academic views of research methodology privileged the writing of primary research reports for the audiences of a researcher's peers. For example, Schwartz (1987) described how organizational *scientists* and practitioners viewed one another:

> The practitioner's role is limited to supplying problems to the researcher and testing the theories that the scientist develops. Practi-

tioners thus stand in a subordinate position to scientists, and their problems come to seem like matters of detail and application, unworthy of serious intellectual consideration and unlikely to benefit from it in any case (p. 615).

Some of today's communication scientists, interpretive and critical scholars, privilege audiences other than (or in addition to) their research peers. In some cases, our peers are still the most desired audience to whom research findings are conveyed in written reports. But for interpretive scholars, the participants in the research project have also come to constitute a primary audience for research findings and interpretations (Brodkey, 1987). Critical scholars, whose claims often address the needed reforms of societal ideology, sometimes target as their audience the policy makers in social situations of their concern (e.g., the reports that are filed to funding agencies who sponsor research). In some situations, the best access to policy makers may be through a trade journal. Or, if the researcher's goal is liberation through awareness, then the most desirable source of publication may be the popular press periodical or book, where the greatest number and type of individuals will be exposed to the researcher's claims and conclusions.

RESEARCH REPORTS AND CRITICAL ESSAYS: TWO KINDS OF MANUSCRIPTS

Writing is a learned, albeit highly personal, skill. Therefore, writing research manuscripts is a sustained and skill-driven activity, one that will become easier with practice. Writing research is not something that happens one day when a researcher sits down and types, the way that some students still write term papers. Writing research is an **iterative process.** It involves a cycle of activities that are repeated over time. The cycle varies somewhat for each of the paradigms we've developed in this book, but the repetitious aspect is true of all academic writing (Booth, Colomb, & Williams, 1995).

The best research manuscripts emerge over time. Furthermore, the writing of a research manuscript is divided into a number of small tasks or steps. It follows that breaking the task of writing a research report into smaller, discrete steps "and placing these in sequence will simplify the work and improve one's performance" (Spradley, 1980, p. 168).

In the two sections below, we will compare and contrast two kinds of manuscripts, research reports and critical essays, because these are two fairly distinct types of writing you will encounter in studying communication. We will use the term **research reports** to refer to written summaries of research projects that include some form of data collection source taken from self-reports, other-reports, or observations, or from a combination of those sources, perhaps with textual data, as well. We will use the term **critical essays** to refer to manuscripts based primarily (or only)

on textual data sources, whether the text being analyzed is a speech, an artifact, or the researcher's experience as evidence given in support of a claim.

Writing Research Reports

As we just said, the term *research report* refers to a written summary of a research project that includes some form of data collection source taken from self-reports, other-reports, or observations. These data sources may be used in combination with textual data, as a form of triangulation (see Chapter 3 for more on triangulation). Whether you consider yourself to be involved in knowing by *discovery, interpretation,* or some combination of those two paradigmatic goals, your research report will have six identifiable elements in common: (1) reviewing the literature; (2) describing and warranting the data sources, settings, and collection strategies; (3) describing and warranting the data analytic procedures; (4) presenting key findings; (5) discussing interpretations, limitations, and suggested directions for future study; and (6) the abstract.

Even though we will you give advice about each element of the research report, as you write your own research report, you will need to read sample studies that employed the particular methodology that you are using. Sample studies will provide you with more specific details, models that will show you how your report should look and read. Reading exemplary studies is one of the best ways to get a sense of what constitutes an acceptable research report for a particular community of peers. Ask your research methods instructor to suggest some exemplary articles for the methodology that you are using, or select studies and methodology sources from the reference list in this textbook.

Review the Published Literature An introduction and review of literature provides the frame or context for academic research reports. "The purpose of an introduction . . . is to introduce the problem area, establish its significance, and indicate the author's perspectives on the problem" (Pyrczak & Bruce, 1992, p. 33). The introduction to a research report is usually organized deductively, beginning with the broadest relevant overview of the topic first, and leading to the specific claim(s) you intend to make in your study. Discovery and interpretive research claims usually are stated in the form of research questions or hypotheses, except for the claims in rhetorical criticism and textual analyses, which are more likely to be presented as purpose statements.

You should explicitly state the significance of the project in the introduction to your research report. Your research project may be of personal, social, or theoretical significance; it may be significant in all of these ways. To establish **personal significance,** state why the study is important to you as an individual. To establish **social significance,** state what problem the research is designed to address, and what harms will accrue, or are already accruing, if the research problem is not addressed. To establish **theoretical significance,** state precisely how you expect your study to contribute to communication theory (e.g., by developing a new theory, or by testing or extending an existing theory). Keep in mind the intended audience for your research report. You will need to adjust the amount of detail you include in your introduction and statements of significance to suit the audience's knowledge of and interest in your research topic.

The next section of your research report is very important. It is in this section that you will select and review the existing, published works that are most closely related to your research topic. This is called the **literature review.** "An effective review of the literature is an essay organized around a topic outline . . . and takes the reader from topic to topic" (Pyrczak & Bruce, p. 36).

Conducting and writing a literature review are two very different, although related, processes. In order to *conduct* a literature review, you will need to locate and read all that you can in a topic area (Helmericks, Nelsen, & Unnithan, 1991). Usually, the great bulk of this work will occur before you begin a research project. For academic researchers, who conduct and publish research over the course of their careers, locating and reading topic-relevant literature is an ongoing process. If it is your first research project, you will need to locate and read a large number of sources on the topic before you can fully conceptualize your research project (i.e., what claims you want to make, the appropriate types of data to collect and analyze, methods of analysis, etc.). Make every effort to find and read a representative range of essays and research studies on your research topic because a well-founded literature search will help you participate most effectively in the conversations already taking place among a community of scholars or practitioners most interested in your topic.

We will not provide instruction in library research strategies or sources in this book. Communication **research strategies** are techniques for searching the communication literature at the library, on the Inter-

net, and via electronic databases. Some of the **research sources** that you might find using those strategies include general sources, periodicals, and information compilations. If you need to learn more about research strategies and sources, check out Rubin, Rubin, and Piele's (2000) *Communication Research: Strategies and Sources.* Investigate your university's information competence or library requirement. The ability to find, read, grasp, and evaluate research reports, critical essays, and secondary source publications about a variety of topics is a vital skill for most people living in the United States today.

In any case, once you have located and read the relevant literature, it is a very good idea to begin writing your literature review by making an outline of the topics you want to cover. You probably will not need to include every study you have read or know of in your literature review. Instead, select and emphasize only the findings and significance of previous research that relate directly to your project. The literature review is an important part of your research argument, since it frames the context in which your claim(s) will be presented. Use your literature review to point out trends and themes in prior research on your topic, as well as gaps in the existing literature, and to establish the need for your project (Galvin, 1999; Pyrczak & Bruce, 1992). It is fine for you to express your own opinions in the course of reviewing the literature as long as you provide reasons for those opinions. To this end, you may want to comment on the quality of a particular study or on the importance of the research that you are citing.

In addition to describing the existing published literature on a topic and presenting your opinions about those works, you may want to use quotations from previous research or theoretic essays to build your argument in the literature review. "Use quotations only to emphasize an important point or as proof of your conclusions" (Dangle & Haussman, 1963, p. 10). We will discuss some issues related to formatting the literature review, including how to present quoted materials, in a later section of this appendix, "Academic Writing Style." And as we already suggested, reading published literature reviews on your topic should be of immense help to you, both in reviewing the content literature, and in developing the structure and format of your own literature review.

Present the Research Claim(s)   The literature review section of a research report typically includes the researcher's claim, which may be phrased in the form of a purpose statement, hypothesis, or research question. If you, as the researcher, cannot state what the aim of your project is in one or two sentences, then you probably have not achieved enough clarity to be writing a research report. For empirical research reports, you should be able to state your hypotheses or research questions, and their justification in the extant literature, before you begin collecting data. As you read in Chapter 2, hypotheses are declarative statements, predictions about the expected relationships or differences between two or more variables. "Hypotheses should be as simple as possible yet expressed in a single sentence" (Pyrczak & Bruce, 1992, p. 3). Empirical research reports typically also include explicit definitions of the variables for each hypothesis (refer to Chapter 5 for a discussion of conceptual and operational definitions).

However, as Philipsen (1977) stated, "naturalistic inquiry is characterized by a weak commitment to make such advance specifications, and having made them, to follow the plans as drawn" (p. 42). So in naturalistic inquiry, it is quite ordinary to have a different framing of your purpose, claim, or research problem after you've begun observing, participating with, and interviewing participants in the social setting (i.e., after you've begun collecting data). This does not make the naturalistic investigator "theoretically aimless and methodologically shifty" (Philipsen, 1977, p. 42). Moreover, this is another reason why we have stated that the order of the claim-data-warrant components for our research-as-argument model is arbitrary.

Once you have introduced your topic, reviewed the relevant literature, and specified your claim, you will be ready to write the methodology section of your research report. The first part of the methodology section usually consists of a description of the sources, settings, and strategies for data collection.

Describe and Warrant the Data Selection Sources, Settings, and Strategies   The amount of detail you provide about data collection depends entirely on the paradigm to which you adhere. Empirical research reports tend to contain the most detailed descriptions of data collection sources, settings, and selection strategies. Interpretive research reports vary immensely in their precision and detail levels when it comes to describing and warranting the data sources, settings, and collection strategies.

Your *empirical research report* should contain detailed and yet succinct descriptions of the texts or the sub-jects whose observed interactions, self-reports, or other-reports constituted the data source(s). You will also need to report the exact means by which your data were selected and, when your claim involves generalizing beyond the sample data, the population your selected messages or subjects were intended to represent. In addition, report the details of sample size such as response rate, dropout rate, and so on. Empirical research reports also describe the measurement instruments used in considerable detail, including their past uses, format, and range of potential scores (Pyrczak & Bruce, 1992). If you employed a coding or rating scheme to analyze textual data, describe the development of the categories or variables the scheme contained. Likewise, you will need to describe the research design you developed to provide causal evidence of time order, covariation, and control over standard rival hypotheses, at least in standard terminology (e.g., pretest-posttest design with control group).

Lofland and Lofland (1984) presented some practical advice for authors aiming to write an *interpretive research report*. Namely, the focus of and data for your study should reflect your intimate familiarity with the setting, address one or more units of social analysis, answer one or more questions about those units, and be interesting. First, you will need to describe the setting you studied, and the sources and strategies you used to become familiar with that setting, in enough detail to show your familiarity. For example, if you used participant observation, describe your role in the setting of study, as well as your key informants, how you gained access to the field, your procedures for making and retrieving field notes, and so on. If you conducted interviews, describe how they were scheduled and conducted, as well as any procedures you used to capture the interview data, such as recording and/or note taking, and transcription, if used. If you analyzed a rhetorical artifact or text, describe the details of its context, historical, social, or other significance.

The design and presentation of your interpretive research report should pose a general question at the opening, introduce the specific data you studied, review previous works on the topic, describe the actual data collection and analysis processes, then proceed to your analysis (Lofland & Lofland, 1984). Analysis should constitute the largest part of your report. But you need to balance data analysis with description. The best way to do this is to let your readers encounter some of the actual data (i.e., text, features of the text, etc.). Alternate between displaying textual data in your report and elaborating your analysis of that data through description. We will talk more about displaying data in the interpretive research report later in this appendix. Once you have presented your analysis, state your conclusions and their implications for future research or practice.

Scan a number of primary research reports in order to get a clearer sense of the standard conventions for describing data collection sources, settings, and strategies, given the particular methodology you are using. Specifically look at studies that report the methodology you are using, and try to familiarize yourself with the conventions accepted within that interpretive community. If you are writing for a particular publication, try to analyze the ways that standard conventions are enacted or ignored in that publication. Writing research is a cultural and normative activity, and one of the ways we learn to be competent in a culture is by observing others.

Describe and Warrant the Data Analytic Procedures In addition to your descriptions of data collection sources, settings, and strategies, your research report should also contain descriptions of the standards by which you can warrant your data analytic procedures. In *empirical research reports,* the data analytic section(s) will include attention to issues like coder/rater training, intercoder or interrater reliability estimates, and so on. You should also describe the statistics you calculated to test your hypotheses (e.g., percentages, chi-square, correlation, ANOVA) and the degree to which your data met or violated those statistics' assumptions (e.g., normal distribution).

The data analysis section for *interpretive research reports* typically contains some description of the researcher's interpretive schema, or categorization process. You may want to keep an informal log of problems or questions that you encounter while you are planning, collecting, and analyzing data and writing. If you are conducting ethnographic research, such a log will be useful when writing up a study (Miles & Huberman, 1994). If you are doing conversational analysis, you will revisit your transcripts and audio- or videotapes many, many times before you decide on a final version. In that case, a log can help you track your own different interpretations of the data, along with any evidence that guided you as you changed those interpretations. If you are conducting rhetorical criticism, we suggest that you use the log to track your interpretations of events, actions, or texts in this same way.

No matter what sort of interpretive methodology you are using, keeping good records is a part of making good sense when you try to describe and warrant your procedures for data analysis. In fact, Buchmann (1992) argued that "a measure of sound conclusions is their reasonableness . . . hence associated with circumspection, due caution and concern for others, skill and know-how, vision, rationality, effectiveness, responsibility, the exercise of will, common sense and good feeling, and the avoidance of harm and evil" (pp. 316–317). However, as she also noted, "available evidence often allows for more than one reasonable interpretation; thus, many conclusions will have competitors" (p. 317).

Present Key Observations and Interpretations In presenting and discussing analytic findings and interpretations, the research report typically specifies which hypotheses were supported and which were not supported, or the extent to which research questions were answered by a study. In quantitative research, you will use numeric statements to present your findings in the results section of the report, and then you will present your findings in linguistic terms in the discussion section (Pyrczak & Bruce, 1992). Whether your findings are numerical or qualitative in nature, elaborate their meanings in the discussion section, usually by returning to the theoretical or other basis for your study in prior research. Another way to elaborate the meaning of your findings is to state the implications of your results for those who will conduct future studies and for those who practice in your topic area.

You may also want to discuss some of the ways that your results relate to previously developed models or unsolved questions in the field. Compare your findings to some of the research you cited in your literature review: In what ways are your findings consistent, or inconsistent, with existing research on this topic? It is acceptable to speculate on the meaning of your results, or to invite your readers to think about your results in more than one way (Pyrczak & Bruce, 1992). Just be clear which of your statements are based on the data you analyzed and which of your ideas go beyond that data, and are therefore more speculative in nature.

Discuss Limitations and Suggest Directions for Future Research Most research reports include cautionary notes about the limitations of the researcher's data collection sources, settings, and selection strategies. In fact, a common direction for future study is the attempt to repair these limitations, for example, by including a larger or more diverse sample of messages or persons. Your research report should also include your suggestions for future research and practice in the topic area. It is important to consider both the strengths and weaknesses of your data collection and analytic strategies when you outline the implications of your analysis. If you call for more research on a topic, give the readers some guidelines about what sorts of research would be most helpful and desirable.

After you have finished writing the above five elements of the research report, you are ready to prepare front- and back-end materials for your report. The abstract appears at the front of your article; the reference list (and tables, if applicable) appear at the back of your article. Use the reference list at the end of this book as a model, or consult a style guide such as the *Publication Manual of the American Psychological Association* for assistance in formatting your reference list. We will address some additional points about front- and back-end materials in the "Academic Writing Style" section. For now, though, you are ready to summarize your study by writing an abstract.

Write the Abstract An **abstract** is a brief paragraph, usually 100–120 words, that provides your readers with an overview of the study, in much the same way that a speech introduction gives listeners an overview of the speaker's purpose, argument, and conclusions. According to the *Publication Manual of the American Psychological Association,* a style guide used by many authors of research reports, the abstract should be "dense with information but also readable, well-organized, brief, and self-contained" (p. 8). The abstract greatly influences whether, and how, a reader will consume the rest of your research report. State the problem your study investigated in one sentence, first. Then briefly describe your data collection sources, strategies, and data analytic strategies. Reference your key findings and limitations in the last sentences of the abstract. You will be using an abstract when you write critical essays, too. Let's turn to the elements of the critical studies essay next.

Writing Critical Essays

We hope that this appendix so far has helped you better understand how to write research reports. As we mentioned in the introduction to this appendix, research reports are quite different kinds of manuscripts than critical essays. A critical essay is a summary of

research in which the primary evidence given in support of a claim is textual evidence. In critical essays, the text being analyzed may be a speech, a cultural artifact, or the text of the researcher's experiences and beliefs. Whereas the research report writer typically prefers to speak of how *data* supports, or fails to support, a research claim, the critical essay writer is more likely to speak of how the text may be interpreted as *evidence* in support of a claim.

Because research reports and critical essays differ in this important way, the elements or parts of the critical essay manuscript also differ from those we just presented for the research report. In the sections below, we will describe five elements of the critical essay: (1) introducing your topic; (2) describing the text and contexts; (3) describing the unit of analysis; (4) reporting the findings and discussing the contribution that your analysis made to answering the research question; and (5) writing the abstract. "These components do not need to be presented in separate sections, or identified with headings, but in some way they should be included in the essay" (Foss, 1996, p. 16).

Introduce the Topic of Study Both the research report and the critical essay are organized deductively: Both start with a broad overview of the topic and proceed to the specific points their authors wish to present. The introduction to a rhetorical criticism essay generally functions to describe what rhetorical "artifact is being analyzed, the research question that is the impetus for analysis, and the contribution to rhetorical theory that will result from the analysis" (Foss, 1996, p. 16).

Critical essays often begin with reference to an artifact, experience, or organizing construct that the author intends to use in his or her analysis of the text. An **artifact** is any object made by human work: It could be a speech, a television commercial, or a personal letter. But artifacts are not limited to words; an artifact may also be a piece of jewelry, a painting, or even a building. As you read in Chapter 13, an immense variety of texts can be artifacts.

In some cases, the particular artifact a researcher has analyzed fits into a larger class of artifacts. For example, Martin Luther King's "I Have a Dream" speech fits into the general category of persuasive speeches by famous people. If you analyzed this speech, you might begin your essay by referring to the ways that famous speakers have changed our views on important topics and our ideas about how to speak effectively. The introduction to the topic of study should orient your readers to the artifact you have analyzed, at the broadest relevant level. For example, McMillan and Cheney's (1996) analysis of the implications of the student as consumer metaphor began this way:

> We rely so heavily on metaphor that we often overlook its practical and powerful role in our discourse. Euphemisms such as the currently popular organizational terms "downsizing" or "rightsizing" become so widely accepted that many users forget the old-fashioned and more brutally direct terms "firing" and "layoffs." . . . These and other metaphors can be compelling to users and hearers, not only in the sense of making conversation or written speech more lively, but also in winning an argument or altering a viewpoint (p. 1).

McMillan and Cheney's (1996) introduction was designed to draw readers' attention to the organizing construct for their essay, the metaphor. In particular, they analyzed the student-as-consumer metaphor as it has been used in North America and Western Europe. So their topic statement provided both an organizing construct (metaphor) and a particular artifact within that class of artifacts (student as consumer).

We will now turn to the second element of the critical essay, the description of the artifact being analyzed in a particular study.

Describe the Text and Context(s) Since readers of a critical essay do not necessarily have access to the artifact, text, or experience that you analyzed, it is important that you describe the evidence fully in the text of your manuscript. For instance, if the artifact is a film, you would describe its plot, as well as its characters and any significant technical features (Foss, 1996).

As a case in point, Scheibel's (1994) analysis of graffiti and film school culture opened with an anecdote about Nicole, a senior film student at Loyola Marymount University, sitting in a small editing room working on her final project for an Advanced Film Production class. Following that anecdote, Scheibel located graffiti (the class of artifact he intended to analyze) within the larger scheme of research conducted on written communication as a way of "getting the job done" (p. 2). Thus, Scheibel nested his organizing concepts deductively from the broadest relevant level, written communication, to

graffiti as a general class of artifact, and then moved specifically to the graffiti written on the walls of editing rooms by film students.

In writing a critical essay, you should describe the historical, social, and economic contexts for the texts you analyzed, to the extent that these contextual details are appropriate and relevant to your research claim or purpose. Your description of the text and its context(s) should justify why it was "a particularly appropriate or useful one to analyze in order to answer the research question" (Foss, 1996, p. 17). As Foss noted, it is impossible to separate purely *description* from *interpretation* in this part of the critical essay. To put it another way, some critical essays analyze texts and present evidence for their authenticity, validity, and relevance without ever referring to the term *data* in the manuscript.

Describe the Unit of Analysis As the writer of a critical essay, you will need to help your readers understand the unit of analysis you have used to analyze the text or artifact under consideration in your study. We discussed the term *unit of analysis* in at least two chapters. In Chapter 10, we said that conversation analysts view units of analysis as "the building blocks of talk" (Sigman, Sullivan, & Wendell, 1988, p. 165). In Chapter 5, we showed how survey researchers view units of analysis as the building blocks of *samples,* since survey units of analysis are either the people or messages that comprise data selected for a study. Just so, the units of analysis in a critical essay are blocks of textual evidence upon which you assemble your argument in support of a claim.

We have stressed that units of analysis are analyzed iteratively by interpretive methods like conversation analysis and ethnography. Once you have identified a unit of analysis, you apply that unit to the collected evidence, over and over again, until a rich understanding of the evidence emerges. Rhetorical scholars tend to privilege those understandings that best fit their subjective sense of the text's meanings, whereas the understandings privileged by ethnographers and ethnomethodologists are those that best fit the participants' sense of the text's meanings. Whether the researcher's interpretations or the participants' meanings are privileged, the same iterative process is used to examine your units of analysis (Booth et al., 1995).

Some units of analysis derive from a formal method of criticism, such as the fantasy themes and rhetorical visions used in fantasy theme analysis, or the five dimensions of the pentad used in Burkean dramatistic analysis (refer to Chapter 12 for more detail on these methods). For example, the findings of a pentadic analysis will typically reveal the critic's conclusion about which element(s) of the pentad are dominant in this artifact, and why (Foss, 1996, p. 462).

As we already mentioned above, in metaphoric criticism, the metaphor itself is the unit of analysis. In that case, your findings will include a description of the pattern with which that metaphor recurred in the text and the functions it served. In narrative criticism, the narrative dimensions become the units of analysis, such as the view of the narrator (e.g., first person, second person), the order of events in the story, the characters, and the segmentation of the narrative into parts, perhaps as simply as beginning, middle, and ending.

In some cases, however, your unit of analysis will not be clearly specified by a formal rhetorical or critical framework. For example, in feminist criticism, the unit of analysis may be the "construction of gender as revealed in rhetoric" (Foss, 1996, p. 173). In that case, findings may include features of the artifact that privilege male ways of knowing, being, and communicating, or features that perpetuate hegemonic masculinity.

Critical studies essays in which the analysis proceeded via deconstruction, narrative, dialectical, or speech act analyses often contain descriptions of and warrants for the appropriateness and value of these analytic moves (Kraidy, 2002; Park, 1998; Scheibel, 1996; Tavener, 2000). In the case of a dialectical criticism, for example, the unit of analysis is the "simultaneous unity and difference" that the researcher investigates, which is evidenced in the utterances of people, usually about their relationships to one another, to things, or to society (Baxter & Montgomery, 1998, p. 2).

Report the Findings of Your Analysis The bulk of the critical essay consists of the findings of analysis. A good way to do this is to present samples of the textual data or the artifact (Foss, 1996, p. 19). For example, you might include quotations from a speech, or describe scenes in a novel, film, or other text, in order to show how that evidence led you to your conclusions about the text.

> The critic's task, in reporting the findings, is not to provide the one correct interpretation of the artifact or to uncover the truth about it. . . . Objectivity and impartiality also are impossible in reporting the findings because the

critic can know the artifact only through a personal interpretation of it (Foss, 1996, p. 18).

Thus, the task for the critical essay is to substantiate the *reasons why* you are making a particular claim. In feminist criticism, this section of the critical essay will likely contain suggestions about how patriarchy is maintained by/with this artifact, or how it can be transformed (Foss, 1996, p. 173). In critical studies, this part of the essay would be more likely to include a description of "the dominant ideology manifest in the artifact, the interests and groups it serves, and the rhetorical strategies that promote it over other ideologies" (Foss, 1996, p. 298).

Conclude your critical essay by discussing the contribution you feel your analysis makes to answer your research question or purpose. You may want to mention the implications of your analysis or suggest why your conclusions are important for others interested in rhetorical or critical studies (Foss, 1996).

Write the Abstract The abstract for a critical essay should also contain the topic statement in one sentence. Your next sentences will describe your study's purpose, thesis, or organizing construct(s). Indicate to readers whether the scope of your essay will be more comprehensive or selective. Then describe the artifacts you analyzed, or the texts you used as evidence in support of your claims (e.g., personal observations, previously published studies, written texts, etc.). In the last sentences of your abstract, briefly state your key conclusions.

Just as many speech writers advocate that the introduction be written last, after the body of the speech has already been developed, we suggest that you write the abstract of your research report or critical essay after you have already drafted the other elements of your manuscript. At that point, you can address the elements of tone and organization that differentiate discovery, interpretive, and critical research manuscripts. But before we turn to those particular points on tone and organization, let's briefly consider the issue of academic writing style more generally.

Academic Writing Style

You probably recognize already that writing a research report or critical essay demands a somewhat different approach than creative writing. "In general, writers must use a clear, lucid style, adhere to the rules of grammar and spelling, and present the report in an accepted format" (Rubin et al., 2000, p. 218).

Communication scholars typically use one of three style manuals to guide their style choices, for example, about how to format source citations in the text and on the reference list, pagination, internal headings, and so on. The sources for these published guidelines are the *Publication Manual of the American Psychological Association* (2001), the *Chicago Manual of Style* (University of Chicago Press, 1993), and the *MLA Handbook for Writers of Research Papers* (Gibaldi, 1995). Most of the scholarly journals sponsored by professional associations in communication allow or require use of the guidelines published by the American Psychological Association (Rubin et al., 2000).

Both research reports and critical essays typically begin with title pages and abstracts. A **title page** includes the title of the paper, the writer's name and institutional affiliation, as well as contact information such as address, telephone number, and email address. As we have already explained, an abstract is a brief summary of the research in one paragraph (i.e., 100–120 words) that orients readers to the content and tone of the manuscript (Pyrczak & Bruce, 1992).

Critical essays conclude with reference lists. Research reports conclude with tables and appendices, after the reference list. A **reference list** appears at the end of written research reports and essays and contains the full citations for all the works cited in your manuscript.

Most of the citations in your reference list will be the published works you included in your literature review. Consult Rubin et al. (2000), one of the above style manuals, or look at the reference list for this text for guidance about how to format citations within a reference list. Since one purpose of a reference list is to allow readers of your research report to locate and read all of the materials on which you relied, a complete and accurate reference list is a must for both research reports and critical essays.

In some cases, you may want to quote from the sources you cite in your manuscript. Quotations from existing studies need to be formatted according to the guidelines of the style manual you select. For example, APA style indicates that a short quotation—one consisting of four or fewer lines—should be enclosed in quotation marks and combined smoothly as part of your own sentence. Quotations longer than four lines should be set apart from the text by single-spacing the quoted material and indenting the quote one-half inch from each side of the regular margin. Quotation marks are not used for quotations longer than four lines because the single-spacing and inden-

tation indicates that the material is a quoted passage. Whether you are quoting or paraphrasing another person's idea, you can preserve intellectual integrity by giving credit where credit is due:

> *Never plagiarize.* When you use sources closely in your writing, give credit to the original author. It is *never* acceptable to copy anything directly from another's materials without using quotation marks and citing the original source. As we have noted, even paraphrasing requires proper citation to that person's work (Rubin et al., 2000, p. 223).

In addition to format guidelines, the style manuals we have mentioned in this section also provide advice about the elements of writing, including verb tense, passive and active voice, using transitions, grammar, and syntax. Due to space limitations, we will not discuss those issues here. Refer to one of the style guidelines for assistance and proofread your research report or essay. In the worst-case scenario, one careless error can change the substance of your research report. At best, errors in spelling, grammar, syntax, or academic style distract readers from the content of your report, and decrease your credibility in the eyes of your audience (e.g., referring to a causal argument as a casual argument).

CHARACTERISTICS OF DISCOVERY RESEARCH REPORTS

Content and interaction analysis, survey and experimental research designs, and classical rhetorical criticism are the research methodologies that we have identified in this text as most closely fitting the discovery research paradigm. In this section, we will outline the standards by which empirical research reports are evaluated (i.e., precise, detailed, and objective reporting). We will then present some advice about organizing your discovery research report.

Precise, Detailed, Objective Reporting

Empirical research reports are written in "a formal and objective style" (Dangle & Haussman, 1963, p. 10). Empirical research reports generally employ a highly predictable outline sequence that includes an abstract, literature review with hypotheses or research questions embedded in it, methodology, results, discussion, and conclusions. For rhetorical criticism within the discovery paradigm, writing is also rational and formal, but the structured outline sequence is, of course, somewhat different.

Within the empirical research report, statistical symbols and text tables are used to summarize numerical data, giving well-informed readers the opportunity to interpret the data themselves, given particular criteria that the author has provided. Discovery researchers typically make no reference to themselves, although such references are sometimes made in the third person (e.g., "The first author coded the transcripts").

In rhetorical criticism, you will have selected a rhetorical artifact or textual evidence that represents some action or event, such as a speech or perhaps a Web site. So, in your research report, you will want to describe that artifact in some detail, since your reader may not have the same access to it that you had. Then, you should articulate the unit of analysis, or the structural components of interest in your essay, as we discussed above in the section on elements of the critical essay. Report the means by which you applied the unit of analysis, or the rhetorical framework, to the evidence you considered. Also report how you evaluated whether those components were or were not present in the text. You will be reporting, then, what you have *discovered* about the artifact or text, in terms of those structural components.

Organizing Empirical Research Reports

Whereas the elements of the critical essay that we described earlier in this appendix probably provide sufficient guidance for you to organize your rhetorical criticism essay, empirical research reports have a highly predictable internal structure and a more rigid organizational pattern. Pyrczak and Bruce (1992) is a very helpful resource for organizing your first empirical research report.

Empirical research reports typically begin with a one-paragraph abstract, which highlights the questions, methodology, and results of the study (Pyrczak & Bruce, 1992). Following the abstract, these reports turn to a logical, deductive literature review, which begins at the broadest level of abstraction relevant to the project, and ends with the hypotheses deduced

from that literature. Research questions also may be presented, usually when the existing literature on a topic is insufficient to justify a predictive hypothesis.

Once you have reviewed the existing literature and presented your hypotheses or research questions, you will need to describe the methodology you used for your study. Include descriptions of the sample (i.e., the messages, texts, or persons) that you included in the study, as well as the procedures you used to select the sample. Next, outline your procedures for data analysis and any steps that you took to warrant the effectiveness of those procedures.

Then present the results of your discovery or the findings from your analysis. In empirical research reports, results are presented in the most straightforward fashion possible, usually in direct response to the hypotheses or research questions posed at the beginning of the report (Pyrczak & Bruce, 1992). If your data are numerical, then the written results will likely include some descriptive and some inferential statistics, followed by a discussion of what those numbers mean. If you are reporting a rhetorical criticism, you will want to present examples that show how you developed your conclusions regarding the events or artifacts that you examined.

Ideally, a report based on qualitative data (e.g., interview transcripts) should address counterexamples from the data, that is, instances that do not fit with or support your conclusions. The writing of such argument-from-example research reports is one of the very points still hotly debated between adherents to the discovery and interpretive research paradigms. Read Cappella (1990) and Jacobs (1990) for opposing views on this issue, as well as Jackson (1986) for an early description of some of those same ideas, the ideas upon which our communication research-as-argument model is based.

After you have presented and discussed results of data analysis, you still need to construct two more standard segments of the empirical research report. You will need to acknowledge the known limitations of your research, and you probably will want to provide some suggestions for future research and practice in the topic area. You can acknowledge your study's limitations by referring back to some of the standard warrants for the methodology you used (refer to Chapter 4 or the appropriate methodology chapter in Part II of this book). For example, a survey instrument's limited reliability, or a bias in selecting research subjects, may dictate caution in believing the current findings or in generalizing them to other settings and people (Katzer et al., 1998).

Although classical rhetorical criticism methods fit within the discovery research paradigm as we have outlined it in this book, much rhetorical criticism scholarship is conducted and reported in distinctly more interpretive ways. Thus, we will deal specifically with the reporting of narrative and dramatistic criticism, along with reports of other interpretive research methods, which are our focus in the next segment of this chapter.

CHARACTERISTICS OF INTERPRETIVE RESEARCH REPORTS

In this section, we turn to some of the issues that are specific to the reports of ethnographic, ethnomethodological, and conversation analyses, as well as some forms of narrative and dramatistic criticism (i.e., the interpretive methods in this book). Discovery researchers typically treat writing the report as an activity to be completed after research has been conducted. By contrast, interpretive researchers are more likely to view writing as an emergent and iterative process, so they advocate writing before, during, and after their research. For example, writing tasks occur throughout the ethnographic cycle (Spradley, 1980). Ethnographic researchers don't proceed in sequential order to first collect data, then take field notes, and then analyze the data (Philipsen, 1977). If they did proceed in this linear way, Spradley advised, they would "confront unnecessary problems" (p. 35). Instead, ethnographers and most other interpretive researchers have to write as they go in order to determine what additional data is needed, when they have enough data, and when new questions are arising from the data they have already begun to analyze. Perhaps because of this different organization of time and writing tasks, relative to the discovery researcher, some interpretive researchers have articulated the role of their writing as a form of inquiry (Goodall, 2000).

Writing as a Form of Inquiry

One way to use writing as a form of inquiry is to explore, through writing, your identity as the author of an interpretive essay. Why do you see things as you do? This notion is called *self-reflexivity*. Accordingly,

May and Pattillo-McCoy (2000) wrote about a neighborhood community center from the perspective of two ethnographers who were quite similar to one another and to the people they studied. Both May and Pattillo-McCoy are African-American sociologists, and perhaps not surprisingly, their experience led them to suggest "more diversity among collaborating ethnographers" (p. 66).

Ellingson's (1998) autoethnographic account of an oncology clinic also explored the impact of self-reflexivity in ethnographic fieldwork. Herself a cancer survivor, Ellingson described her struggle to write about her research in a "new form" (p. 511):

> This piece integrates narrative and essay, embodying the dynamism of perspective within its structure. The narratives break into the essay in much the same way that they break into my train of thought as I write; my cancer experiences evoke narratives of patients and staff in the clinic, which evoke commentary from a researcher perspective, which evokes a personal illness narrative, and so forth (p. 511).

Ellingson (1998) noted that the use of experimental writing forms like hers "are becoming more common in academic journals, irreversibly contaminating the body of social science knowledge with the messiness of lived experience" (p. 511).

Despite Ellingson's confident assertion, above, Childress (1998) bemoaned the scarcity of "exemplary, compelling, whole ethnographies" in the published literature, "not because good ethnographic work doesn't exist, but because it doesn't easily get past editorial boards and journal reviewers and even library acquisition panels" (p. 249). One form of writing inquiry that has been published in scholarly journals is Van Maanen's (1988) concept of telling multiple ethnographic tales in research reports, thus representing field realities in multiple ways.

Telling Multiple Tales

In his book, *Tales of the Field: On Writing Ethnography,* Van Maanen (1988) outlined several possible ways of writing ethnography, each way resulting in a distinct type of story or narrative: (1) the realist tale, (2) the confessional tale, (3) the impressionist tale, and (4) the critical tale. The **realist tale** is a relatively straightforward recounting of the researcher's observations in the field: "Realist tales claim authenticity, are written in the third person voice, and follow the recipe, 'the x did this'" (Weick, 1989, p. 307). "Clear writing is not synonymous with realist tales, but it is easy to mistake one for the other" (Weick, 1989, p. 309).

A **confessional tale** focuses more on the fieldworker than on the culture or other social situation under study: "Confessional tales claim honesty, are written in the first-person, and follow the recipe, 'I saw the x do this'" (Weick, 1989, p. 307). By contrast, the **impressionist tale** represents "an explicit attempt to bring the knower (confessional tales) and the known (realist tales) together in a representational form" (Weick, 1989, p. 308). The value of impressionist tales is assessed by the criteria of narrative rationality, that is, whether they are interesting, coherent, and have fidelity for the reader. The **critical tale** shows "concern for representing social structures as seen through the eyes of disadvantaged groups" (Van Maanen, 1988, p. 128).

Each of these types of ethnographic tale (except perhaps the realist tale) constituted experimental forms of writing in 1988. Each provided a different voice with which to represent the social realities encountered by an interpretive researcher in the field. As such, these tales provided ethnographic instantiations of writing as inquiry. Since then, the various types of ethnographic tales have been adopted by interpretive and some critical researchers as means of inquiring by writing different forms (Trujillo, 1999). We will describe one such interpretive research report, a set of three tales about a soup kitchen for homeless people, next.

Miller, Creswell, and Olander (1998) narrated realist, confessional, and critical tales about a soup kitchen for homeless and near-homeless people. The three ethnographic tales were based on those authors' four months of participant observation in the soup kitchen. First, the authors wrote a *realist tale* in which they gave a concrete and specific account of the soup kitchen. They described its cultural setting in a predominately white, Midwest U. S. city of 200,000 people, the cultural themes present in that setting, and five rules they discerned in that setting (e.g., "Anyone is welcome at the soup kitchen—no judgments are made," p. 480).

The authors then reported that a *confessional tale* emerged from their retelling of the realist tale in writing and orally, at conferences, and as they taught their college research methods classes. The confessional tale

added to, rather than replaced, their realist tale. Its audience was primarily the authors' students of research methodology. Miller et al. told their students, for example, that their original purpose for conducting the study was "to learn how to write a 'good' ethnography" (p. 482). The confessional tale that emerged disclosed how they had gained access to the shelter setting through the shelter's director. They also disclosed their lack of prior experience with homelessness and homeless people. They revealed that the data that impacted and influenced them the most were the differences between the shelter guests' stories and their own stereotypes of homeless people. They also confessed their secret discomfort at doing covert research, since the guests who came to eat at the shelter thought the authors were merely volunteers and did not know about the research study.

Finally, Miller et al. reconstructed their realist and confessional tales as a *critical tale*. The critical tale Miller and colleagues constructed was written down shortly after they attended a social justice conference, at which they presented the realist tale of their soup kitchen ethnography. The critical tale told their positions on a series of issues, like the economic issues faced by homeless people, including underfunding of soup kitchens, as well as their responses to questions posed by their audience at the social justice conference. Two of the questions that they addressed in the critical tale were "How did you reciprocate with guests for their stories and the privilege to write about the soup kitchen and about them?" (p. 487) and "Did you serve to empower this population or further marginalize them?" (p. 488). The critical tale brought to the surface issues of equity, researcher positionality, and the role of accuracy and truth in ethnographic reporting.

Miller et al. (1998) concluded their report of all three tales by reflecting on the relationship between ethnographic writing and retelling:

> Our retelling represents further data analysis, completed after we left the field. . . . The retelling of an ethnography may be as important as the initial writing of it. . . . Although three tales provides a useful heuristic to see different perspectives about the soup kitchen, perhaps in the end they are all part of the same story, with multiple perspectives depending on the teller, the receiver, and the participants in the event (p. 489).

Organizing Interpretive Field Research Reports

A research report should be a convincing argument, in which you systematically present data to support your claim and to refute alternative or competing claims (Morse, 1998). In fact, "researchers often *write* as though order were implicit . . . and inhered in the data, when what they really meant was that order emerged from interaction between the researcher, his/her data, and some theoretical sensitivity suggested by the original research question" (Strauss & Corbin, 1998, p. 180). So, although there is no hard and fast rule about how to organize an interpretive research report, the general logic of your report should be clear to you and your readers.

"Two main approaches to designing an interpretive research essay are (a) to write the article as though the reader is solving the puzzle with the researcher, and (b) to present a summary of the major finding and then present the findings that supports the conclusion" (Morse, 1998, p. 79). Another way to organize your field research report is to divide your analysis of a social setting into two sections, one that analyzes the situation and one that reports strategies the participants have developed for dealing with the situation (Lofland & Lofland, 1984).

Your general design may be an outline or a set of topics arranged in the order in which you plan to cover them in the report. Your general design will need to be revised, refined, and perhaps even wholly redone as you write the report, in much the same way that interpretive data collection is revised, refined, and sometimes redesigned during fieldwork.

> The general design specifies an *interrelated* set of questions, topics, or areas. It makes it possible for someone reading your report for the first time to grasp the basic concepts you are dealing with, and to have a sense that the report is starting somewhere, proceeding through a logical sequence, and then arriving at a natural point of termination (Lofland & Lofland, 1984, p. 139).

Displaying Data in a Field Research Report

Although Bilmes (1976) used a transcription of a Thai village meeting to illustrate his claims about interactional interpretation of rules, he displayed very little of the raw data in his article. Such an approach is consistent with a discourse analysis or an ethnomethodological study of communication. But when you employ other interpretive methods, such as conversation analysis and ethnography, you will likely want to display more data in the written report of the study (Brodkey, 1987). Reports of conversation analysis often include micro-level details about the data being displayed, as well as the data itself, such as the line number from the transcript.

Ethnographers often "present field notes in their published texts, giving readers an opportunity to explore the discrepancies and consistencies within data collection" (May & Pattillo-McCoy, 2000, p. 83). Of course, you will select a very small portion of the transcript or field notes you have collected to present in your research report. "After eight or ten sessions of making observations, then expanding on notes taken in the field, beginning ethnographers sometimes have between seventy-five and a hundred pages of notes" (Spradley, 1980, p. 155). You have to choose how much raw data, field notes, and transcriptions you will present in the report. Often, deciding to include more data or field notes will mean electing for more abbreviated coverage of prior research and theory (i.e., the literature review). The other place to cut space is in discussion of your interpretations or conclusions about the findings.

In order to make good decisions about what to include and what to exclude from your interpretive research report, be sure you have kept an **audit trail.** The audit trail describes the development of your research, and it includes all of your field notes from participant-observation, plus expanded accounts, journal entries, or notes about analysis and interpretation. All these records need to be retrievable as you write up your research report.

One question that is frequently asked in interpretive writing concerns the amount of editing a researcher can appropriately make to a participant's quoted words. Morse (1998) argued that it is legitimate to remove "mmm's" and pauses "unless the intonation and expression are important for the meaning" (p. 79). Of course, if you follow the strict empiricist requirement for conversation analysis, you will present participants' words, precisely as spoken, with no attempt to edit or "fix" their speech.

If you have employed audio- or videotaping and transcription in your interpretive study, then you should also include in your report some information about the permissions used for the recording. For example, did you guarantee anonymity or merely confidentiality? What uses of the tapes were permitted by those who participated in your study? Furthermore, you should specify in your report the type of transcription conventions you used and your rationale for choosing those conventions (Sigman et al., 1988).

Your *interpretive research report* may need to show where in the transcript you were led to make a particular interpretation. If so, the usual way to do this is to include quotes from the actual transcript in your report. Whenever you place segments of talk into your report, you will also need to give some abbreviated information for the reader that suggests the location and original source of that talk within the overall transcript or data sample. Beware, though, to balance the information readers require with the privacy needs of your research participants: "Tagging quotations with participant numbers may also place participants at risk of being identified" (Morse, 1998, p. 80).

Following all the aforementioned procedures and advice will not guarantee that you produce an interpretive research report of any value or interest to anyone! It is easy to get bogged down in the details of data, or in anxieties about producing the right kind of research manuscript, and produce writing that is "unappealing—awkward, tedious, or very abstract" (Buchmann, 1992, pp. 320–321). Research communication that suffers from these problems will fail to attract and hold readers' attention and interest. That is why we began this appendix with a discussion of some of the potential audiences for research, because audience analysis is as important in writing research as it is in presentational speaking. You will need to consider what prior knowledge your intended audience has about your topic, as well as your own knowledge of writing styles and issues of credibility, in addition to the content you intend to report in your essay (i.e., the details of your claim-data-warrant backing).

Using the Personal in Name of the Political
Denzin (1999) called for a new "ethics of writing, asking that writers put their texts in forms that readers can use in their own lives" (p. 568). "The authors of autoethnographic dramas, ethnographic poetry and fiction, performance texts, and dramatic readings use personal experiences and memory as the point of departure for writing things that matter in everyday life" (p. 568). Jenkins's plays *A Credit to Her Country* and *She Rises . . .* illustrate this writing of things that matter to the author and others, as well as her (1999) poem, "What to Do If You're Told You Have Breast Cancer." Jenkins uses oral history interviews, participant observations, and textual analysis to inform her playwriting and producing.

"Writing culture in this way is more than using the personal in service of the therapeutic, although the therapeutic is not to be diminished" (Denzin, 1999, p. 571). Denzin asserted that such "new writing asks only that we each conduct our own ground-level guerrilla warfare against the repressive structures in our everyday lives" (p. 572).

Beware, however, the naivete of what Gouldner (1988) called the **ritual of frankness** because "it is difficult to be explicit and unreserved, not only due to the likely conflict of honesty with interests," but also because we only partially know what we value or where our own value conflicts and contradictions lie. A tone of smugness may be conveyed when we write as though "my values are good enough" (Buchmann, 1992, p. 320). Instead, if you want to write explicitly about your personal values and interests, it is important to go beyond simple frankness to "clarify how *having* particular values and interests 'affects the worth, the scope, the bite, and the objectivity' (Gouldner, 1988, p. 112) of a particular piece of . . . research" (Buchmann, 1992, p. 320).

CHARACTERISTICS OF CRITICAL STUDIES ESSAYS

As Sprague (1992) pointed out, "The practice of critical scholarship is not bound by a single method, but relies on several assumptions about inquiry" (p. 182). Among these assumptions are the focus on interaction among individuals, groups, and the social system; the focus on discursive practices as they are used to maintain and to resist domination; and the politics of representation, or the idea that "there is no such thing as neutral knowledge" (p. 182). Sprague began her essay by noting that the preparation of a literature review, for example, "used to be a straightforward task" (p. 181). But from a critical perspective, however, "even a simple literature review runs the risk of privileging existing patterns of thought" (p. 181). In other words, the critical essay is an act of representation in itself and, as such, must be approached with the hermeneutics of suspicion. As you read in Chapter 13, this means that you begin your critical essay with the assumption of discursive domination, and you proceed by analyzing the struggles among fluid, competing interests in terms of their various ways of representing actions and events (Mumby, 1997a).

To illustrate the characteristics and organization of a critical essay, let's examine Watts and Orbe's (2002) essay. The authors began by speculating how the inventor of Budweiser's most successful 60-second commercial ever, *Whassup?!,* must have felt:

> Charles Stone, III must have felt as though he had gone to sleep and awoken in Oz. It was three short years ago that he captured on film candid moments among three of his friends, and edited them into an engrossing and visually stunning short film called 'True,' and used it as a video resume. Stone was 'floored' when Anheuser-Busch asked him to translate his film into a 60-second commercial spot for Budweiser beer. . . . It must have seemed even more surreal to be in Cannes . . . and to hear his friends' greeting, now the world's most famous catchphrase, bouncing off café walls and rippling along the beaches—'Whassup?!" It must have been bizarre to witness the usually stodgy Cannes judges joyfully exchanging the greeting in international accents" (p. 1).

Watts and Orbe (2002) presented their view of how Charles Stone III *must have felt* as a way to introduce the organizing concept upon which their analysis was based, the concept of spectacular consumption.

Spectacular consumption treats "spectacle as a rhetorical construction" and "a mediated phenomenon that transforms persons' lived reality" (Watts & Orbe, 2002, p. 3). The *Whassup?!* Budweiser commercial, a simple "verbal high five" among friends, was at once "baffling" *and* the "Superbowl's most popular" ad (p. 2). These authors began their analysis with a suspicion that "references to the ads' 'universal' qualities obscure the way in which blackness can be made to behave in accordance with the American ideology of universalism. . . . We argue that the ad campaign constitutes and administers cultural 'authenticity' as a market value" (pp. 2–3).

The next section of the essay is a literature review. First, Watts and Orbe developed their definition of spectacular consumption based on previous theoretic works. Next, they examined and critiqued the "crossover appeal" (p. 5) of the Budweiser commercial, deconstructing the dialectic tension underneath white America's appropriation of black communication styles. Using cites from previously published primary and secondary sources, they argued that "white kids want to be as cool as black kids" (citing MTV's Chris Connelly, on p. 7), but "white folk do not want to *become* black" (citing bell hooks, 1992).

Next, Watts and Orbe conducted a textual analysis of the *Whassup?!* commercial itself for evidence of self-reflexivity. They wondered whether these three friends "recognize (that is, see) the ways that their 'play' is overvalued as an 'authentic' cultural performance" (p. 8). Finally they conducted focus groups with undergraduate communication students to see how the *Whassup?!* ads were consumed by different viewers. They presented quotes from those students in the essay itself to illustrate interpretive themes that were based on repetition, recurrence, and forcefulness of a topic in the focus group interactions. The essay concluded with the authors' reiteration of their claim and summary of the evidence used to support their interpretations.

In writing a critical studies essay, you are creating another layer of text, another multiplicity of meanings that may be associated with that which you study. "In this sense, providing accounts of . . . phenomena is both a poetic and a political process" (Mumby, 1993, p. 20). It is poetic in that it gains credibility by adhering to the conventions, or forms that are accepted by the researcher's **interpretive community** (i.e., an academic discipline, or perhaps several disciplines). It is political because it usually separates researchers as "other," or different from, research participants and because there is no neutral representation of knowledge (Sprague, 1992).

By being actively engaged with the phenomenon under study while writing the essay, you are helping to create the phenomenon you study. You are at least attempting to represent that phenomenon through language. Van Oosting (1996) argued that through writing, the writer comes to understand both performance and composition better, and differently, than is possible through performance alone. In your case, writing research can enhance your understanding of the phenomena you seek to study.

Writing Interesting Fiction

Critical scholars understand their essays to be fictions, that is, rich representations of the actions, events, and texts they studied, which are inherently biased by their own experiences, values, and purposes. This does not mean that your critical essay will lack rigor, or that you will intentionally abuse your power of representing actions and events through language. In fact, since critical scholarship is characterized by concerns about the *politics of representation,* every choice about what you say (and what you leave out) has ramifications that are linked to power and ideology. One way that you can deal with the politics of representation in your writing is by being self-reflexive (Pelias, in press).

The principle of rigorous self-reflection dictates that you examine your motives, word choices, and framing of an essay with immense care (Allen, 1996). Even then, you should not claim to have captured the true meaning of an act or event. Instead, approach your critical essay as interesting fiction, to be evaluated for its ability to "read texts in their full variety, rather than to get beneath or behind them" (Deetz, 1982, p. 137). Specify the criteria by which your research may be evaluated in the essay itself. Make your descriptions of the texts, actions, events, or experiences "rich and compelling" (Deetz, 1982, p. 147). "Objectivity is sustained in the inability of the [research] community to deny the results [of inquiry] through undistorted discussions of them" (Deetz, 1982, p. 147).

Organizing Critical Studies Essays

Critical essay writers tend to resist a standardizing form or structure, which is consistent with their philosophy that standardization always privileges some persons or values, and oppresses others. Thus, you will see considerable variety in the ways that critical studies essays are organized. But even though the procedure for organizing a critical essay varies, critical scholars do not abandon the tradition of a logical-deductive structure. This may be because essays written in other forms have not managed to break through the gatekeepers of traditional academic journals, which publish these works (Ellingson, 1998; Sprague, 1992).

Very often, the critical essay begins with a description of the broad social situation, which sets the stage for the evidence to be analyzed. For example, Clair's

(1997) essay on the Treaty of New Echota began with a description of the people of Turtle Island; next, she recounted the development and enforcement of a treaty that removed the Cherokee from the land they occupied in Georgia to new land west of the Mississippi. Finally, Clair articulated the discursive practices that effectively silenced Cherokee people's resistance to that move, and she closed the essay with a traditional summary and review of her main points. Although her essay was broadly organized from the general to the specific, there were many points at which she tacked back and forth between *whole* and *part,* in the practice of the hermeneutic circle.

Disclosing the Author's Standpoint

It is important in the critical essay to disclose your standpoint as the author. From what perspective do you view the text, and what is your motive for conducting the analysis? It is one thing to say that you are doing participant observation research, even to disclose your degree of participation in a group or event of which you are a part. It is another to disclose why you became interested in that text, what motivated you to carry out the research project and write the report, who will benefit from the work being done and precisely how. Even though the politics of representation beg this sort of full disclosure by researchers, even critical essays still lack many of the elements of such disclosure (see Allen, 1996; Nakayama, 1998; Ono, 1998; and Yep, 1997, for some notable exceptions).

In Chapter 4, we discussed the issues of group membership, subjectivity, and critical analyses. Critical scholars agree that it is important to disclose one's membership (or lack thereof) in the critical essay, but the guidelines for participant inclusion and discourse about interpretations are much less clear. If a group member and the research participant-observer disagree about an interpretation, should both interpretations go into the critical essay? How should such disagreements be "framed" in writing the research essay? What do you think?

KEY TERMS

Abstract	Confessional tale	Impressionist tale
Artifact	Critical essay	Interpretive community
Audit trail	Critical tale	Iterative process

Literature review

Personal significance

Popular press publications

Primary sources

Professional associations

Realist tale

Reference list

Research report

Research sources

Research strategies

Ritual of frankness

Scholarly journals

Secondary sources

Social significance

Theoretical significance

Title page

Trade journals

"TRY IT!" ACTIVITY

Read several different research reports, preferably from the different paradigms of discovery, interpretation, and criticism. If possible, use the reports prepared by yourself and your classmates for this activity. Discuss your reactions in a small group, or write your responses to the following questions in a short paper: (a) How easy or difficult was the report for you to read? What helped you read and grasp the report? What made it difficult? (b) How believable was the content of the report to you? Did your belief in the author's interpretations or conclusions change as you read the entire report? (c) How do you think reading this research report will impact you, if at all? Will you think, act, or communicate any differently as a result of having read this report? (Adapted from Buchmann, 1992.)

APPENDIX B

Table of Random Numbers

10480	15011	01536	02011	81647	91646	69179	14194	62590	36207	20969	99570	91291	90700
22368	46573	25595	85393	30995	89198	27982	53402	93965	34095	52666	19174	39615	99505
24130	48360	22527	97265	76393	64809	15179	24830	49340	32081	30680	19655	63348	58629
42167	93093	06243	61680	07856	16376	39440	53537	71341	57004	00849	74917	97758	16379
37570	39975	81837	16656	06121	91782	60468	81305	49684	60672	14110	06927	01263	54613
77921	06907	11008	42751	27756	53498	18602	70659	90655	15053	21916	81825	44394	42880
99562	72905	56420	69994	98872	31016	71194	18738	44013	48840	63213	21069	10634	12952
96301	91977	05463	07972	18876	20922	94595	56869	69014	60045	18425	84903	42508	32307
89579	14342	63661	10281	17453	18103	57740	84378	25331	12566	58678	44947	05585	56941
85475	36857	53342	53988	53060	59533	38867	62300	08158	17983	16439	11458	18593	64952
28918	69578	88231	33276	70997	79936	56865	05859	90106	31595	01547	85590	91610	78188
63553	40961	48235	03427	49626	69445	18663	72695	52180	20847	12234	90511	33703	90322
09429	93969	52636	92737	88974	33488	36320	17617	30015	08272	84115	27156	30613	74952
10365	61129	87529	85689	48237	52267	67689	93394	01511	26358	85104	20285	29975	89868
07119	97336	71048	08178	77233	13916	47564	81056	97735	85977	29372	74461	28551	90707
51085	12765	51821	51259	77452	16308	60756	92144	49442	53900	70960	63990	75601	40719
02368	21382	52404	60268	89368	19885	55322	44819	01188	65255	64835	44919	05944	55157
01011	54092	33362	94904	31273	04146	18594	29852	71585	85030	51132	01915	92747	64951
52162	53916	46369	58586	23216	14513	83149	98736	23495	64350	94738	17752	35156	35749
07056	97628	33787	09998	42698	06691	76988	13602	51851	46104	88916	19509	25625	58104
48663	91245	85828	14346	09172	30168	90229	04734	59193	22178	30421	61666	99904	32812
54164	58492	22421	74103	47070	25306	76468	26384	58151	06646	21524	15227	96909	44592
32639	32363	05597	24200	13363	38005	94342	28728	35806	06912	17012	64161	18296	22851
29334	27001	87637	87308	58731	00256	45834	15398	46557	41135	10367	07684	36188	18510
02488	33062	28834	07351	19731	92420	60952	61280	50001	67658	32586	86679	50720	94953
81525	72295	04839	96423	24878	82651	66566	14778	76797	14780	13300	87074	79666	95725
29676	20591	68086	26432	46901	20849	89768	81536	86645	12659	92259	57102	80428	25280
00742	57392	39064	66432	84673	40027	32832	61362	98947	96067	64760	64584	96096	98253
05366	04213	25669	26422	44407	44048	37397	63904	45766	66134	75470	66520	34693	90449
91921	26418	64117	94305	26766	25940	39972	22209	71500	64568	91402	42416	07844	69618
00582	04711	87917	77341	42206	35126	74087	99547	81817	42607	43808	76655	62028	76630
00725	69884	62797	56170	86324	88072	76222	36086	84637	93161	76038	65855	77919	88006
69011	65795	95876	55293	18988	27354	26575	08625	40801	59920	29841	80150	12777	48501
25976	57948	29888	88604	67917	48708	18912	82271	65424	69774	33611	54262	85963	03547
09763	83473	73577	12908	30883	18317	28290	35797	05998	41688	34952	37888	38917	88050
91567	42595	27958	30134	04024	86385	29880	99730	55536	84855	29080	09250	79656	73211
17955	56349	90999	49127	20044	59931	06115	20542	18059	02008	73708	83517	36103	42791
46503	18584	18845	49618	02304	51038	20655	58727	28168	15475	56942	53389	20562	87338
92157	89634	94824	78171	84610	82834	09922	25417	44137	48413	25555	21246	35509	20468
14577	62765	35605	81263	39667	47358	56873	56307	61607	49518	89656	20103	77490	18062
98427	07523	33362	64270	01638	92477	66969	98420	04880	45585	46565	04102	46880	45709
34914	63976	88720	82765	34476	17032	87589	40836	32427	70002	70663	88863	77775	69348
70060	28277	39475	46473	23219	53416	94970	25832	69975	94884	19661	72828	00102	66794
53976	54914	06990	67245	68350	82948	11398	42878	80287	88267	47363	46634	06541	97809
76072	29515	40980	07391	58745	25774	22987	80059	39911	96189	41151	14222	60697	59583
90725	52210	83974	29992	65831	38857	50490	83765	55657	14361	31720	57375	56228	41546
64364	67412	33339	31926	14883	24413	59744	92351	97473	89286	35931	04110	23726	51900
08962	00358	31662	25388	61642	34072	81249	35648	56891	69352	48373	45578	78547	81788
95012	68379	93526	70765	10592	04542	76463	54328	02349	17247	28865	14777	62730	92277
15664	10493	20492	38391	91132	21999	59516	81652	27195	48223	46751	22923	32261	85653

16408	81899	04153	53381	79401	21438	83035	92350	36693	31238	59649	91754	72772	02338
18629	81953	05520	91962	04739	13092	97662	24822	94730	06496	35090	04822	86774	98289
73115	35101	47498	87637	99016	71060	88824	71013	18735	20286	23153	72924	35165	43040
57491	16703	23167	49323	45021	33132	12544	41035	80780	45393	44812	12515	98931	91202
30405	83946	23792	14422	15059	45799	22716	19792	09983	74353	68668	30429	70735	25499
16631	35006	85900	98275	32388	52390	16815	69298	82732	38480	73817	32523	41961	44437
96773	20206	42559	78985	05300	22164	24369	54224	35083	19687	11052	91491	60383	19746
38935	64202	14349	82674	66523	44133	00697	35552	35970	19124	63318	29686	03387	59846
31624	76384	17403	53363	44167	64486	64758	75366	76554	31601	12614	33072	60332	92325
78919	19474	23632	27889	47914	02584	37680	20801	72152	39339	34806	08930	85001	87820
03931	33309	57047	74211	63445	17361	62825	39908	05607	91284	68833	25570	38818	46920
74426	33278	43972	10119	89917	15665	52872	73823	73144	88662	88970	74492	51805	99378
09066	00903	20795	95452	92648	45454	09552	88815	16553	51125	79375	97596	16296	66092
42238	12426	87025	14267	20979	04508	64535	31355	86064	29472	47689	05974	52468	16834
16153	08002	26504	41744	81959	65642	74240	56302	00033	67107	77510	70625	28725	34191
21457	40742	29820	96783	29400	21840	15035	34537	33310	06116	95240	15957	16572	06004
21581	57802	02050	89728	17937	37621	47075	42080	97403	48626	68995	43805	33386	21597
55612	78095	83197	33732	05810	24813	86902	60397	16489	03264	88525	42786	05269	92532
44657	66999	99324	51281	84463	60563	79312	93454	68876	25471	93911	25650	12682	73572
91340	84979	46949	81973	37949	61023	43997	15263	80644	43942	89203	71795	99533	50501
91227	21199	31935	27022	84067	05462	35216	14486	29891	68607	41867	14951	91696	85065
50001	38140	66321	19924	72163	09538	12151	06878	91903	18749	34405	56087	82790	70925
65390	05224	72958	28609	81406	39147	25549	48542	42627	45233	57202	94617	23772	07896
27504	96131	83944	41575	10573	08619	64482	73923	36152	05184	94142	25299	84387	34925
37169	94851	39117	89632	00959	16487	65536	49071	39782	17095	02330	74301	00275	48280
11508	70225	51111	38351	19444	66499	71945	05422	13442	78675	84081	66938	93654	59894
37449	30362	06694	54690	04052	53115	62757	95348	78662	11163	81651	50245	34971	52924
46515	70331	85922	38329	57015	15765	97161	17869	45349	61796	66345	81073	49106	79860
30986	81223	42416	58353	21532	30502	32305	86482	05174	07901	54339	58861	74818	46942
63798	64995	46583	09785	44160	78128	83991	42865	92520	83531	80377	35909	81250	54238
82486	84846	99254	67632	43218	50076	21361	64816	51202	88124	41870	52689	51275	83556
21885	32906	92431	09060	64297	51674	64126	62570	26123	05155	59194	52799	28225	85762
60336	98782	07408	53458	13564	59089	26445	29789	85205	41001	12535	12133	14645	23541
43937	46891	24010	25560	86355	33941	25786	54990	71899	15475	95434	98227	21824	19585
97656	63175	89303	16275	07100	92063	21942	18611	47348	20203	18534	03862	78095	50136
03299	01221	05418	38982	55758	92237	26759	86367	21216	98442	08303	56613	91511	75928
79626	06486	03574	17668	07785	76020	79924	25651	83325	88428	85076	72811	22717	50585
85636	68335	47539	03129	65651	11977	02510	26113	99447	68645	34327	15152	55230	93448
18039	14367	61337	06177	12143	46609	32989	74014	64708	00533	35398	58408	13261	47908
08362	15656	60627	36478	65648	16764	53412	09013	07832	41574	17639	82163	60859	75567
79556	29068	04142	16268	15387	12856	66227	38358	22478	73373	88732	09443	82558	05250
92608	82674	27072	32534	17075	27698	98204	63863	11951	34648	88022	56148	34925	57031
23982	25835	40055	67006	12293	02753	14827	23235	35071	99704	37543	11601	35503	85171
09915	96306	05908	97901	28395	14186	00821	80703	70426	75647	76310	88717	37890	40129
59037	33300	26695	62247	69927	76123	50842	43834	86654	70959	79725	93872	28117	19233
42488	78077	69882	61657	34136	79180	97526	43092	04098	73571	80799	76536	71255	64239
46764	86273	63003	93017	31204	36692	40202	35275	57306	55543	53203	18098	47625	88684
03237	45430	55417	63282	90816	17349	88298	90183	36600	78406	06216	95787	42579	90730
86591	81482	52667	61582	14972	90053	89534	76036	49199	43716	97548	04379	46370	28672
38534	01715	94964	87288	65680	43772	39560	12918	86537	62738	19636	51132	25739	56947

SOURCE: Abridged from *Handbook of Tables for Probability and Statistics,* 2nd ed., edited by William H. Beyer (Cleveland: The Chemical Rubber Company, 1968). Used by permission of The Chemical Rubber Company.

APPENDIX C

Chi-Square Distribution

df	.99	.98	.95	.90	.80	.70	.50	.30	.20	.10	.05	.02	.01	.001
1	.000157	.000628	.00393	.0158	.0642	.148	.455	1.074	1.642	2.706	3.841	5.412	6.635	10.827
2	.0201	.0404	.103	.211	.446	.713	1.386	2.408	3.219	4.605	5.991	7.824	9.210	13.815
3	.115	.185	.352	.584	1.005	1.424	2.366	3.665	4.642	6.251	7.815	9.837	11.345	16.266
4	.297	.429	.711	1.064	1.649	2.195	3.357	4.878	5.989	7.779	9.488	11.668	13.277	18.467
5	.554	.752	1.145	1.610	2.343	3.000	4.351	6.064	7.289	9.236	11.070	13.388	15.086	20.515
6	.872	1.134	1.635	2.204	3.070	3.828	5.348	7.231	8.558	10.645	12.592	15.033	16.812	22.457
7	1.239	1.564	2.167	2.833	3.822	4.671	6.346	8.383	9.803	12.017	14.067	16.622	18.475	24.322
8	1.646	2.032	2.733	3.490	4.594	5.527	7.344	9.524	11.030	13.362	15.507	18.168	20.090	26.125
9	2.088	2.532	3.325	4.168	5.380	6.393	8.343	10.656	12.242	14.684	16.919	19.679	21.666	27.877
10	2.558	3.059	3.940	4.865	6.179	7.267	9.342	11.781	13.442	15.987	18.307	21.161	23.209	29.588
11	3.053	3.609	4.575	5.578	6.989	8.148	10.341	12.899	14.631	17.275	19.675	22.618	24.725	31.264
12	3.571	4.178	5.226	6.304	7.807	9.034	11.340	14.011	15.812	18.549	21.026	24.054	26.217	32.909
13	4.107	4.765	5.892	7.042	8.634	9.926	12.340	15.119	16.985	19.812	22.362	25.472	27.688	34.528
14	4.660	5.368	6.571	7.790	9.467	10.821	13.339	16.222	18.151	21.064	23.685	26.873	29.141	36.123
15	5.229	5.985	7.261	8.547	10.307	11.721	14.339	17.322	19.311	22.307	24.996	28.259	30.578	37.697
16	5.812	6.614	7.962	9.312	11.152	12.624	15.338	18.418	20.465	23.542	26.296	29.633	32.000	39.252
17	6.408	7.255	8.672	10.085	12.002	13.531	16.338	19.511	21.615	24.769	27.587	30.995	33.409	40.790
18	7.015	7.906	9.390	10.865	12.857	14.440	17.338	20.601	22.760	25.989	28.869	32.346	34.805	42.312
19	7.633	8.567	10.117	11.651	13.716	15.352	18.338	21.689	23.900	27.204	30.144	33.687	36.191	43.820
20	8.260	9.237	10.851	12.443	14.578	16.266	19.337	22.775	25.038	28.412	31.410	35.020	37.566	45.315
21	8.897	9.915	11.591	13.240	15.445	17.182	20.337	23.858	26.171	29.615	32.671	36.343	38.932	46.797
22	9.542	10.600	12.338	14.041	16.314	18.101	21.337	24.939	27.301	30.813	33.924	37.659	40.289	48.268
23	10.196	11.293	13.091	14.848	17.187	19.021	22.337	26.018	28.429	32.007	35.172	38.968	41.638	49.728
24	10.856	11.992	13.848	15.659	18.062	19.943	23.337	27.096	29.553	33.196	36.415	40.270	42.980	51.179
25	11.524	12.697	14.611	16.473	18.940	20.867	24.337	28.172	30.675	34.382	37.652	41.566	44.314	52.620
26	12.198	13.409	15.379	17.292	19.820	21.792	25.336	29.246	31.795	35.563	38.885	42.856	45.642	54.052
27	12.879	14.125	16.151	18.114	20.703	22.719	26.336	30.319	32.912	36.741	40.113	44.140	46.963	55.476
28	13.565	14.847	16.928	18.939	21.588	23.647	27.336	31.391	34.027	37.916	41.337	45.419	43.278	56.893
29	14.256	15.574	17.708	19.768	22.475	24.577	28.336	32.461	35.139	39.087	42.557	46.693	49.588	58.302
30	14.953	16.306	18.493	20.599	23.364	25.508	29.336	33.530	36.250	40.256	43.773	47.962	50.892	59.703

SOURCE: Taken from Table IV of Fisher and Yates: *Statistical Tables for Biological, Agricultural and Medical Research,* published by Longman Group UK Ltd., 1974.

APPENDIX D

Critical Values for Student's t Distribution

	LEVEL OF SIGNIFICANCE FOR A DIRECTIONAL (ONE-TAILED) TEST					
	.10	.05	.025	.01	.005	.0005
	LEVEL OF SIGNIFICANCE FOR A NONDIRECTIONAL (TWO-TAILED) TEST					
df	.20	.10	.05	.02	.01	.001
1	3.078	6.314	12.706	31.821	63.657	636.619
2	1.638	2.353	3.182	4.541	5.841	12.941
4	1.533	2.132	2.776	3.747	4.604	8.610
5	1.476	2.015	2.571	3.365	4.032	6.859
6	1.440	1.943	2.447	3.143	3.707	5.959
7	1.415	1.895	2.365	2.998	3.499	5.405
8	1.397	1.860	2.306	2.896	3.355	5.041
9	1.383	1.833	2.262	2.821	3.250	4.781
10	1.372	1.812	2.228	2.764	3.169	4.587
11	1.363	1.796	2.201	2.718	3.106	4.437
12	1.356	1.782	2.179	2.681	3.055	4.318
13	1.350	1.771	2.160	2.650	3.012	4.221
14	1.345	1.761	2.145	2.624	2.977	4.140
15	1.341	1.753	2.131	2.602	2.947	4.073
16	1.337	1.746	2.120	2.583	2.921	4.015
17	1.333	1.740	2.110	2.567	2.898	3.965
18	1.330	1.734	2.101	2.552	2.878	3.922
19	1.328	1.729	2.093	2.539	2.861	3.883
20	1.325	1.725	2.086	2.528	2.845	3.850
21	1.323	1.721	2.080	2.518	2.831	3.819
22	1.321	1.717	2.074	2.508	2.819	3.792
23	1.319	1.714	2.069	2.500	2.807	3.767
24	1.318	1.711	2.064	2.492	2.797	3.745
25	1.316	1.708	2.060	2.485	2.787	3.725
26	1.315	1.706	2.056	2.479	2.779	3.707
27	1.314	1.703	2.052	2.473	2.771	3.690
28	1.313	1.701	2.048	2.467	2.763	3.674
29	1.311	1.699	2.045	2.462	2.756	3.659
30	1.310	1.697	2.042	2.457	2.750	3.646
40	1.303	1.684	2.021	2.423	2.704	3.551
60	1.296	1.671	2.000	2.390	2.660	3.460
120	1.289	1.658	1.980	2.358	2.617	3.373
∞	1.282	1.645	1.960	2.326	2.576	3.291

SOURCE: From Table III of Fisher and Yates, *Statistical Tables for Biological, Agricultural, and Medical Research*, published by Longman Group UK Ltd., 1974.

APPENDIX E

Critical Values for the F Distribution

Denominator n_1 Degrees of Freedom for Numerator

df = n_1	1	2	3	4	5	6	7	8	9	10	11	12	14	16	20	24	30	40	50	75	100	200	500	∞
1	161	200	216	225	230	234	237	239	241	242	243	244	245	246	248	249	250	251	252	253	253	254	254	254
	4,052	4,999	5,403	5,625	5,764	5,859	5,928	5,981	6,022	6,056	6,082	6,106	6,142	6,169	6,208	6,234	6,258	6,286	6,302	6,323	6,334	6,352	6,361	6,366
2	18.51	19.00	19.16	19.25	19.30	19.33	19.36	19.37	19.38	19.39	19.40	19.41	19.42	19.43	19.44	19.45	19.46	19.47	19.47	19.48	19.49	19.49	19.50	19.50
	98.49	99.00	99.17	99.25	99.30	99.33	99.34	99.36	99.38	99.40	99.41	99.42	99.43	99.44	99.45	99.46	99.47	99.48	99.48	99.49	99.49	99.49	99.50	99.50
3	10.13	9.55	9.28	9.12	9.01	8.94	8.88	8.84	8.81	8.78	8.76	8.74	8.71	8.69	8.66	8.64	8.62	8.60	8.58	8.57	8.56	8.54	8.54	8.53
	34.12	30.82	29.46	28.71	28.24	27.91	27.67	27.49	27.34	27.23	27.13	27.05	26.92	26.83	26.69	26.60	26.50	26.41	26.35	26.27	26.23	26.18	26.14	26.12
4	7.71	6.94	6.59	6.39	6.26	6.16	6.09	6.04	6.00	5.96	5.93	5.91	5.87	5.84	5.80	5.77	5.74	5.71	5.70	5.68	5.66	5.65	5.64	5.63
	21.20	18.00	16.69	15.98	15.52	15.21	14.98	14.80	14.66	14.54	14.45	14.37	14.24	14.15	14.02	13.93	13.83	13.74	13.69	13.61	13.57	13.52	13.48	13.46
5	6.61	5.79	5.41	5.19	5.05	4.95	4.88	4.82	4.78	4.74	4.70	4.68	4.64	4.60	4.56	4.53	4.50	4.46	4.44	4.42	4.40	4.38	4.37	4.36
	16.26	13.27	12.06	11.39	10.97	10.67	10.45	10.27	10.15	10.05	9.96	9.89	9.77	9.68	9.55	9.47	9.38	9.29	9.24	9.17	9.13	9.07	9.04	9.02
6	5.99	5.14	4.76	4.53	4.39	4.28	4.21	4.15	4.10	4.06	4.03	4.00	3.96	3.92	3.87	3.84	3.81	3.77	3.75	3.72	3.71	3.69	3.68	3.67
	13.74	10.92	9.78	9.15	8.75	8.47	8.26	8.10	7.98	7.87	7.79	7.72	7.60	7.52	7.39	7.31	7.23	7.14	7.09	7.02	6.99	6.94	6.90	6.88
7	5.59	4.74	4.35	4.12	3.97	3.87	3.79	3.73	3.68	3.63	3.60	3.57	3.52	3.49	3.44	3.41	3.38	3.34	3.32	3.29	3.28	3.25	3.24	3.23
	12.25	9.55	8.45	7.85	7.46	7.19	7.00	6.84	6.71	6.62	6.54	6.47	6.35	6.27	6.15	6.07	5.98	5.90	5.85	5.78	5.75	5.70	5.67	5.65
8	5.32	4.46	4.07	3.84	3.69	3.58	3.50	3.44	3.39	3.34	3.31	3.28	3.23	3.20	3.15	3.12	3.08	3.05	3.03	3.00	2.98	2.96	2.94	2.93
	11.26	8.65	7.59	7.01	6.63	6.37	6.19	6.03	5.91	5.82	5.74	5.67	5.56	5.48	5.36	5.28	5.20	5.11	5.06	5.00	4.96	4.91	4.88	4.86
9	5.12	4.26	3.86	3.63	3.48	3.37	3.29	3.23	3.18	3.13	3.10	3.07	3.02	2.98	2.93	2.90	2.86	2.82	2.80	2.77	2.76	2.73	2.72	2.71
	10.56	8.02	6.99	6.42	6.06	5.80	5.62	5.47	5.35	5.26	5.18	5.11	5.00	4.92	4.80	4.73	4.64	4.56	4.51	4.45	4.41	4.36	4.33	4.31
10	4.96	4.10	3.71	3.48	3.33	3.22	3.14	3.07	3.02	2.97	2.94	2.91	2.86	2.82	2.77	2.74	2.70	2.67	2.64	2.61	2.59	2.56	2.55	2.54
	10.04	7.56	6.55	5.99	5.64	5.39	5.21	5.06	4.95	4.85	4.78	4.71	4.60	4.52	4.41	4.33	4.25	4.17	4.12	4.05	4.01	3.96	3.93	3.91
11	4.84	3.98	3.59	3.36	3.20	3.09	3.01	2.95	2.90	2.86	2.82	2.79	2.74	2.70	2.65	2.61	2.57	2.53	2.50	2.47	2.45	2.42	2.41	2.40
	9.65	7.20	6.22	5.67	5.32	5.07	4.88	4.74	4.63	4.54	4.46	4.40	4.29	4.21	4.10	4.02	3.94	3.86	3.80	3.74	3.70	3.66	3.62	3.60
12	4.75	3.88	3.49	3.26	3.11	3.00	2.92	2.85	2.80	2.76	2.72	2.69	2.64	2.60	2.54	2.50	2.46	2.42	2.40	2.36	2.35	2.32	2.31	2.30
	9.33	6.93	5.95	5.41	5.06	4.82	4.65	4.50	4.39	4.30	4.22	4.16	4.05	3.98	3.86	3.78	3.70	3.61	3.56	3.49	3.46	3.41	3.38	3.36
13	4.67	3.80	3.41	3.18	3.02	2.92	2.84	2.77	2.72	2.67	2.63	2.60	2.55	2.51	2.46	2.42	2.38	2.34	2.32	2.28	2.26	2.24	2.22	2.21
	9.07	6.70	5.74	5.20	4.86	4.62	4.44	4.30	4.19	4.10	4.02	3.96	3.85	3.78	3.67	3.59	3.51	3.42	3.37	3.30	3.27	3.21	3.18	3.16
14	4.60	3.74	3.34	3.11	2.96	2.85	2.77	2.70	2.65	2.60	2.56	2.53	2.48	2.44	2.39	2.35	2.31	2.27	2.24	2.21	2.19	2.16	2.14	2.13
	8.86	6.51	5.56	5.03	4.69	4.46	4.28	4.14	4.03	3.94	3.86	3.80	3.70	3.62	3.51	3.43	3.34	3.26	3.21	3.14	3.11	3.06	3.02	3.00
15	4.54	3.68	3.29	3.06	2.90	2.79	2.70	2.64	2.59	2.55	2.51	2.48	2.43	2.39	2.33	2.29	2.25	2.21	2.18	2.15	2.12	2.10	2.08	2.07
	8.68	6.36	5.42	4.89	4.56	4.32	4.14	4.00	3.89	3.80	3.73	3.67	3.56	3.48	3.36	3.29	3.20	3.12	3.07	3.00	2.97	2.92	2.89	2.87
16	4.49	3.63	3.24	3.01	2.85	2.74	2.66	2.59	2.54	2.49	2.45	2.42	2.37	2.33	2.28	2.24	2.20	2.16	2.13	2.09	2.07	2.04	2.02	2.01
	8.53	6.23	5.29	4.77	4.44	4.20	4.03	3.89	3.78	3.69	3.61	3.55	3.45	3.37	3.25	3.18	3.10	3.01	2.96	2.89	2.86	2.80	2.77	2.75
17	4.45	3.59	3.20	2.96	2.81	2.70	2.62	2.55	2.50	2.45	2.41	2.38	2.33	2.29	2.23	2.19	2.15	2.11	2.08	2.04	2.02	1.99	1.97	1.96
	8.40	6.11	5.18	4.67	4.34	4.10	3.93	3.79	3.68	3.59	3.52	3.45	3.35	3.27	3.16	3.08	3.00	2.92	2.86	2.79	2.76	2.70	2.67	2.65
18	4.41	3.55	3.16	2.93	2.77	2.66	2.58	2.51	2.46	2.41	2.37	2.34	2.29	2.25	2.19	2.15	2.11	2.07	2.04	2.00	1.98	1.95	1.93	1.92
	8.28	6.01	5.09	4.58	4.25	4.01	3.85	3.71	3.60	3.51	3.44	3.37	3.27	3.19	3.07	3.00	2.91	2.83	2.78	2.71	2.68	2.62	2.59	2.57
19	4.38	3.52	3.13	2.90	2.74	2.63	2.55	2.48	2.43	2.38	2.34	2.31	2.26	2.21	2.15	2.11	2.07	2.02	2.00	1.96	1.94	1.91	1.90	1.88
	8.18	5.93	5.01	4.50	4.17	3.94	3.77	3.63	3.52	3.43	3.36	3.30	3.19	3.12	3.00	2.92	2.84	2.76	2.70	2.63	2.60	2.54	2.51	2.49
20	4.35	3.49	3.10	2.87	2.71	2.60	2.52	2.45	2.40	2.35	2.31	2.28	2.23	2.18	2.12	2.08	2.04	1.99	1.96	1.92	1.90	1.87	1.85	1.84
	8.10	5.85	4.94	4.43	4.10	3.87	3.71	3.56	3.45	3.37	3.30	3.23	3.13	3.05	2.94	2.86	2.77	2.69	2.63	2.56	2.53	2.47	2.44	2.42

Denominator

n_1 Degrees of Freedom for Numerator

df = n_1	1	2	3	4	5	6	7	8	9	10	11	12	14	16	20	24	30	40	50	75	100	200	500	∞
21	4.32	3.47	3.07	2.84	2.68	2.57	2.49	2.42	2.37	2.32	2.28	2.25	2.20	2.15	2.09	2.05	2.00	1.96	1.93	1.89	1.87	1.84	1.82	1.81
	8.02	5.78	4.87	4.37	4.04	3.81	3.65	3.51	3.40	3.31	3.24	3.17	3.07	2.99	2.88	2.80	2.72	2.63	2.58	2.51	2.47	2.42	2.38	2.36
22	4.30	3.44	3.05	2.82	2.66	2.55	2.47	2.40	2.35	2.30	2.26	2.23	2.18	2.13	2.07	2.03	1.98	1.93	1.91	1.87	1.84	1.81	1.80	1.78
	7.94	5.72	4.82	4.31	3.99	3.76	3.59	3.45	3.35	3.26	3.18	3.12	3.02	2.94	2.83	2.75	2.67	2.58	2.53	2.46	2.42	2.37	2.33	2.31
23	4.28	3.42	3.03	2.80	2.64	2.53	2.45	2.38	2.32	2.28	2.24	2.20	2.14	2.10	2.04	2.00	1.96	1.91	1.88	1.84	1.82	1.79	1.77	1.76
	7.88	5.66	4.76	4.26	3.94	3.71	3.54	3.41	3.30	3.21	3.14	3.07	2.97	2.89	2.78	2.70	2.62	2.53	2.48	2.41	2.37	2.32	2.28	2.26
24	4.26	3.40	3.01	2.78	2.62	2.51	2.43	2.36	2.30	2.26	2.22	2.18	2.13	2.09	2.02	1.98	1.94	1.89	1.86	1.82	1.80	1.76	1.74	1.73
	7.82	5.61	4.72	4.22	3.90	3.67	3.50	3.36	3.25	3.17	3.09	3.03	2.93	2.85	2.74	2.66	2.58	2.49	2.44	2.36	2.33	2.27	2.23	2.21
25	4.24	3.38	2.99	2.76	2.60	2.49	2.41	2.34	2.28	2.24	2.20	2.16	2.11	2.06	2.00	1.96	1.92	1.87	1.84	1.80	1.77	1.74	1.72	1.71
	7.77	5.57	4.68	4.18	3.86	3.63	3.46	3.32	3.21	3.13	3.05	2.99	2.89	2.81	2.70	2.62	2.54	2.45	2.40	2.32	2.29	2.23	2.19	2.17
26	4.22	3.37	2.98	2.74	2.59	2.47	2.39	2.32	2.27	2.22	2.18	2.15	2.10	2.05	1.99	1.95	1.90	1.85	1.82	1.78	1.76	1.72	1.70	1.69
	7.72	5.53	4.64	4.14	3.82	3.59	3.42	3.29	3.17	3.09	3.02	2.96	2.86	2.77	2.66	2.58	2.50	2.41	2.36	2.28	2.25	2.19	2.15	2.13
27	4.21	3.35	2.96	2.73	2.57	2.46	2.37	2.30	2.25	2.20	2.16	2.13	2.08	2.03	1.97	1.93	1.88	1.84	1.80	1.76	1.74	1.71	1.68	1.67
	7.68	5.49	4.60	4.11	3.79	3.56	3.39	3.26	3.14	3.06	2.98	2.93	2.83	2.74	2.63	2.55	2.47	2.38	2.33	2.25	2.21	2.16	2.12	2.10
28	4.20	3.34	2.95	2.71	2.56	2.44	2.36	2.29	2.24	2.19	2.15	2.12	2.06	2.02	1.96	1.91	1.87	1.81	1.78	1.75	1.72	1.69	1.67	1.65
	7.64	5.45	4.57	4.07	3.76	3.53	3.36	3.23	3.11	3.03	2.95	2.90	2.80	2.71	2.60	2.52	2.44	2.35	2.30	2.22	2.18	2.13	2.09	2.06
29	4.18	3.33	2.93	2.70	2.54	2.43	2.35	2.28	2.22	2.18	2.14	2.10	2.05	2.00	1.94	1.90	1.85	1.80	1.77	1.73	1.71	1.68	1.65	1.64
	7.60	5.42	4.54	4.04	3.73	3.50	3.33	3.20	3.08	3.00	2.92	2.87	2.77	2.68	2.57	2.49	2.41	2.32	2.27	2.19	2.15	2.10	2.06	2.03
30	4.17	3.32	2.92	2.69	2.53	2.42	2.34	2.27	2.21	2.16	2.12	2.09	2.04	1.99	1.93	1.89	1.84	1.79	1.76	1.72	1.69	1.66	1.64	1.62
	7.56	5.39	4.51	4.02	3.70	3.47	3.30	3.17	3.06	2.98	2.90	2.84	2.74	2.66	2.55	2.47	2.38	2.29	2.24	2.16	2.13	2.07	2.03	2.01
32	4.15	3.30	2.90	2.67	2.51	2.40	2.32	2.25	2.19	2.14	2.10	2.07	2.02	1.97	1.91	1.86	1.82	1.76	1.74	1.69	1.67	1.64	1.61	1.59
	7.50	5.34	4.46	3.97	3.66	3.42	3.25	3.12	3.01	2.94	2.86	2.80	2.70	2.62	2.51	2.42	2.34	2.25	2.20	2.12	2.08	2.02	1.98	1.96
34	4.13	3.28	2.88	2.65	2.49	2.38	2.30	2.23	2.17	2.12	2.08	2.05	2.00	1.95	1.89	1.84	1.80	1.74	1.71	1.67	1.64	1.61	1.59	1.57
	7.44	5.29	4.42	3.93	3.61	3.38	3.21	3.08	2.97	2.89	2.82	2.76	2.66	2.58	2.47	2.38	2.30	2.21	2.15	2.08	2.04	1.98	1.94	1.91
36	4.11	3.26	2.86	2.63	2.48	2.36	2.28	2.21	2.15	2.10	2.06	2.03	1.98	1.93	1.87	1.82	1.78	1.72	1.69	1.65	1.62	1.59	1.56	1.55
	7.39	5.25	4.38	3.89	3.58	3.35	3.18	3.04	2.94	2.86	2.78	2.72	2.62	2.54	2.43	2.35	2.26	2.17	2.12	2.04	2.00	1.94	1.90	1.87
38	4.10	3.25	2.85	2.62	2.46	2.35	2.26	2.19	2.14	2.09	2.05	2.02	1.96	1.92	1.85	1.80	1.76	1.71	1.67	1.63	1.60	1.57	1.54	1.53
	7.35	5.21	4.34	3.86	3.54	3.32	3.15	3.02	2.91	2.82	2.75	2.69	2.59	2.51	2.40	2.32	2.22	2.14	2.08	2.00	1.97	1.90	1.86	1.84
40	4.08	3.23	2.84	2.61	2.45	2.34	2.25	2.18	2.12	2.07	2.04	2.00	1.95	1.90	1.84	1.79	1.74	1.69	1.66	1.61	1.59	1.55	1.53	1.51
	7.31	5.18	4.31	3.83	3.51	3.29	3.12	2.99	2.88	2.80	2.73	2.66	2.56	2.49	2.37	2.29	2.20	2.11	2.05	1.97	1.94	1.88	1.84	1.81
42	4.07	3.22	2.83	2.59	2.44	2.32	2.24	2.17	2.11	2.06	2.02	1.99	1.94	1.89	1.82	1.78	1.73	1.68	1.64	1.60	1.57	1.54	1.51	1.49
	7.27	5.15	4.29	3.80	3.49	3.26	3.10	2.96	2.86	2.77	2.70	2.64	2.54	2.46	2.35	2.26	2.17	2.08	2.02	1.94	1.91	1.85	1.80	1.78
44	4.06	3.21	2.82	2.58	2.43	2.31	2.23	2.16	2.10	2.05	2.01	1.98	1.92	1.88	1.81	1.76	1.72	1.66	1.63	1.58	1.56	1.52	1.50	1.48
	7.24	5.12	4.26	3.78	3.46	3.24	3.07	2.94	2.84	2.75	2.68	2.62	2.52	2.44	2.32	2.24	2.15	2.06	2.00	1.92	1.88	1.82	1.78	1.75
46	4.05	3.20	2.81	2.57	2.42	2.30	2.22	2.14	2.09	2.04	2.00	1.97	1.91	1.87	1.80	1.75	1.71	1.65	1.62	1.57	1.54	1.51	1.48	1.46
	7.21	5.10	4.24	3.76	3.44	3.22	3.05	2.92	2.82	2.73	2.66	2.60	2.50	2.42	2.30	2.22	2.13	2.04	1.98	1.90	1.86	1.80	1.76	1.72
48	4.04	3.19	2.80	2.56	2.41	2.30	2.21	2.14	2.08	2.03	1.99	1.96	1.90	1.86	1.79	1.74	1.70	1.64	1.61	1.56	1.53	1.50	1.47	1.45
	7.19	5.08	4.22	3.74	3.42	3.20	3.04	2.90	2.80	2.71	2.64	2.58	2.48	2.40	2.28	2.20	2.11	2.02	1.96	1.88	1.84	1.78	1.73	1.70
50	4.03	3.18	2.79	2.56	2.40	2.29	2.20	2.13	2.07	2.02	1.98	1.95	1.90	1.85	1.78	1.74	1.69	1.63	1.60	1.55	1.52	1.48	1.46	1.44
	7.17	5.06	4.20	3.72	3.41	3.18	3.02	2.88	2.78	2.70	2.62	2.56	2.46	2.39	2.26	2.18	2.10	2.00	1.94	1.86	1.82	1.76	1.71	1.68
55	4.02	3.17	2.78	2.54	2.38	2.27	2.18	2.11	2.05	2.00	1.97	1.93	1.88	1.83	1.76	1.72	1.67	1.61	1.58	1.52	1.50	1.46	1.43	1.41
	7.12	5.01	4.16	3.68	3.37	3.15	2.98	2.85	2.75	2.66	2.59	2.53	2.43	2.35	2.23	2.15	2.06	1.96	1.90	1.82	1.78	1.71	1.66	1.64
60	4.00	3.15	2.76	2.52	2.37	2.25	2.17	2.10	2.04	1.99	1.95	1.92	1.86	1.81	1.75	1.70	1.65	1.59	1.56	1.50	1.48	1.44	1.41	1.39
	7.08	4.98	4.13	3.65	3.34	3.12	2.95	2.82	2.72	2.63	2.56	2.50	2.40	2.32	2.20	2.12	2.03	1.93	1.87	1.79	1.74	1.68	1.63	1.60
65	3.99	3.14	2.75	2.51	2.36	2.24	2.15	2.08	2.02	1.98	1.94	1.90	1.85	1.80	1.73	1.68	1.63	1.57	1.54	1.49	1.46	1.42	1.39	1.37
	7.04	4.95	4.10	3.62	3.31	3.09	2.93	2.79	2.70	2.61	2.54	2.47	2.37	2.30	2.18	2.09	2.00	1.90	1.84	1.76	1.71	1.64	1.60	1.56
70	3.98	3.13	2.74	2.50	2.35	2.23	2.14	2.07	2.01	1.97	1.93	1.89	1.84	1.79	1.72	1.67	1.62	1.56	1.53	1.47	1.45	1.40	1.37	1.35
	7.01	4.92	4.08	3.60	3.29	3.07	2.91	2.77	2.67	2.59	2.51	2.45	2.35	2.28	2.15	2.07	1.98	1.88	1.82	1.74	1.69	1.62	1.56	1.53
80	3.96	3.11	2.72	2.48	2.33	2.21	2.12	2.05	1.99	1.95	1.91	1.88	1.82	1.77	1.70	1.65	1.60	1.54	1.51	1.45	1.42	1.38	1.35	1.32
	6.96	4.88	4.04	3.56	3.25	3.04	2.87	2.74	2.64	2.55	2.48	2.41	2.32	2.24	2.11	2.03	1.94	1.84	1.78	1.70	1.65	1.57	1.52	1.49
100	3.94	3.09	2.70	2.46	2.30	2.19	2.10	2.03	1.97	1.92	1.88	1.85	1.79	1.75	1.68	1.63	1.57	1.51	1.48	1.42	1.39	1.34	1.30	1.28
	6.90	4.82	3.98	3.51	3.20	2.99	2.82	2.69	2.59	2.51	2.43	2.36	2.26	2.19	2.06	1.98	1.89	1.79	1.73	1.64	1.59	1.51	1.46	1.43
125	3.92	3.07	2.68	2.44	2.29	2.17	2.08	2.01	1.95	1.90	1.86	1.83	1.77	1.72	1.65	1.60	1.55	1.49	1.45	1.39	1.36	1.31	1.27	1.25
	6.84	4.78	3.94	3.47	3.17	2.95	2.79	2.65	2.56	2.47	2.40	2.33	2.23	2.15	2.03	1.94	1.85	1.75	1.68	1.59	1.54	1.46	1.40	1.37
150	3.91	3.06	2.67	2.43	2.27	2.16	2.07	2.00	1.94	1.89	1.85	1.82	1.76	1.71	1.64	1.59	1.54	1.47	1.44	1.37	1.34	1.29	1.25	1.22
	6.81	4.75	3.91	3.44	3.14	2.92	2.76	2.62	2.53	2.44	2.37	2.30	2.20	2.12	2.00	1.91	1.83	1.72	1.66	1.56	1.51	1.43	1.37	1.33

Denominator									n_1 Degrees of Freedom for Numerator																
df = n_1	1	2	3	4	5	6	7	8	9	10	11	12	14	16	20	24	30	40	50	75	100	200	500	∞
200	3.89	3.04	2.65	2.41	2.26	2.14	2.05	1.98	1.92	1.87	1.83	1.80	1.74	1.69	1.62	1.57	1.52	1.45	1.42	1.35	1.32	1.26	1.22	1.19
	6.76	**4.71**	**3.88**	**3.41**	**3.11**	**2.90**	**2.73**	**2.60**	**2.50**	**2.41**	**2.34**	**2.28**	**2.17**	**2.09**	**1.97**	**1.88**	**1.79**	**1.69**	**1.62**	**1.53**	**1.48**	**1.39**	**1.33**	**1.28**
400	3.86	3.02	2.62	2.39	2.23	2.12	2.03	1.96	1.90	1.85	1.81	1.78	1.72	1.67	1.60	1.54	1.49	1.42	1.38	1.32	1.28	1.22	1.16	1.13
	6.70	**4.66**	**3.83**	**3.36**	**3.06**	**2.85**	**2.69**	**2.55**	**2.46**	**2.37**	**2.29**	**2.23**	**2.12**	**2.04**	**1.92**	**1.84**	**1.74**	**1.64**	**1.57**	**1.47**	**1.42**	**1.32**	**1.24**	**1.19**
1000	3.85	3.00	2.61	2.38	2.22	2.10	2.02	1.95	1.89	1.84	1.80	1.76	1.70	1.65	1.58	1.53	1.47	1.41	1.36	1.30	1.26	1.19	1.13	1.08
	6.66	**4.62**	**3.80**	**3.34**	**3.04**	**2.82**	**2.66**	**2.53**	**2.43**	**2.34**	**2.26**	**2.20**	**2.09**	**2.01**	**1.89**	**1.81**	**1.71**	**1.61**	**1.54**	**1.44**	**1.38**	**1.28**	**1.19**	**1.11**
∞	3.84	2.99	2.60	2.37	2.21	2.09	2.01	1.94	1.88	1.83	1.79	1.75	1.69	1.64	1.57	1.52	1.46	1.40	1.35	1.28	1.24	1.17	1.11	1.00
	6.64	**4.60**	**3.78**	**3.32**	**3.02**	**2.80**	**2.64**	**2.51**	**2.41**	**2.32**	**2.24**	**2.18**	**2.07**	**1.99**	**1.87**	**1.79**	**1.69**	**1.59**	**1.52**	**1.41**	**1.36**	**1.25**	**1.15**	**1.00**

SOURCE: Reprinted by permission from *Statistical Methods,* 8th ed., by George W. Snedecor and William G. Cochran. Copyright © 1980 by Iowa State University Press, Ames, Iowa 50010.

APPENDIX F

Correlation Distribution Table

LEVELS OF SIGNIFICANCE

n	.1	.05	.02	.01	.001	n	.1	.05	.02	.01	.001
1	.98769	.99692	.999507	.999877	.9999988	16	.4000	.4683	.5425	.5897	.7084
2	.90000	.95000	.98000	.990000	.99900	17	.3887	.4555	.5285	.5751	.6932
3	.8054	.8783	.93433	.95873	.99116	18	.3783	.4438	.5155	.5614	.6787
4	.7293	.8114	.8822	.91720	.97406	19	.3687	.4329	.5034	.5487	.6652
5	.6694	.7545	.8329	.8745	.95074	20	.3598	.4227	.4921	.5368	.6524
6	.6215	.7067	.7887	.8343	.92493	25	.3233	.3809	.4451	.4869	.5974
7	.5822	.6664	.7498	.7977	.8982	30	.2960	.3494	.4093	.4487	.5541
8	.5494	.6319	.7155	.7646	.8721	35	.2746	.3246	.3810	.4182	.5189
9	.5214	.6021	.6851	.7348	.8471	40	.2573	.3044	.3578	.3932	.4896
10	.4973	.5760	.6581	.7079	.8233	45	.2428	.2875	.3384	.3721	.4648
11	.4762	.5529	.6339	.6835	.8010	50	.2306	.2732	.3218	.3541	.4433
12	.4575	.5324	.6120	.6614	.7800	60	.2108	.2500	.2948	.3248	.4078
13	.4409	.5139	.5923	.6411	.7603	70	.1954	.2319	.2737	.3017	.3799
14	.4259	.4973	.5742	.6226	.7420	80	.1829	.2172	.2565	.2830	.3568
15	.4124	.4821	.5577	.6055	.7246	90	.1726	.2050	.2422	.2673	.3375
						100	.1638	.1946	.2301	.2540	.3211

Probability values are for two-tailed tests.

SOURCE: We are grateful to the Literary Executor of the late Sir Ronald A. Fisher, F. R. S., to Dr. Frank Yates, F. R. S., and to Longman Group Ltd., London, for permission to reprint Table VII from their book *Statistical Tables for Biological, Agricultural, and Medical Research* (6th Edition, 1963).

APPENDIX G

"Try It!" Activities Answer Key
for Chapters 8 and 9

CHAPTER 8 ANSWERS TO "TRY IT!" ACTIVITIES, P. 172

1. The median for this data distribution is 16.5, calculated by $\frac{16 + 17}{2}$ because 16 and 17 are at the 6th and 7th positions.

2. The confidence interval for 99% is between 3.7 and 10.9 ($\overline{X} \pm 3s$). The percentage of the sample for the interval between 6.1 and 8.5 minutes is 68%.

3. This is an Internet activity.

4. For the control group, the measures of central tendency are as follows: $\overline{X} = 3.5$, Mdn = 3.5, and Mos = 3 and 4. The measures of dispersion are as follows: range = 7, $s^2 = 3.421$, $s = 1.850$. For the treatment group, the measures of central tendency are as follows: $\overline{X} = 6.0$, Mdn = 6.5, and Mo = 7.0. The measures of dispersion are as follows: range = 5, $s^2 = 2.526$, and $s = 1.589$. The graphs show the control group has a fairly normal distribution, also indicated because the measures of central tendency all aligned. The treatment group graph shows the distribution is negatively skewed, which is an indication of bias or constant error. This is corroborated by the measures of central tendency, which are not aligned.

CHAPTER 9 ANSWERS TO "TRY IT!" ACTIVITIES, PP. 199–200

1. The obtained chi-square is 17.19. With 1 *df* and $p < .001$, the tabled or critical value of chi-square is 10.827 (see Appendix C, p. 310). The obtained chi-square is significant; the observed frequencies are significantly different than the expected frequencies.

2. The obtained *t* statistic is 4.47. With 8 *df* and $p < .005$ for a one-tailed test, the critical *t* value is 3.355 (see Appendix D, p. 311). The researcher has supported the research hypothesis and rejected the null hypothesis because the obtained value is greater than the critical value.

3. The $r_{xy} = -.913$, a very strong negative (or inverse) correlation. For $n = 10$ at $p < .001$, $r_{crit} = .8233$ (see Appendix F, p. 315). There is a significant relationship between the two variables. The estimate of shared variance, $r^2 = .8335 \times 100$, or 83.35%.

Glossary

Abscissa: Horizontal axis of a graph.

Abstract: A brief paragraph, usually 100–120 words, that provides readers with an overview of the study, in much the same way that a speech introduction gives listeners an overview of the speaker's purpose, argument, and conclusions.

Accounts: The reasons communicators give for deviating from the rules.

Act: One of five key elements in the pentad of Burkean dramatism, it is the identification of the thought or behavior around which the drama occurs.

Action chains: A conversational sequence in which the first action performed makes possible or likely the next action, and so on.

Action research: Research that is conducted for the purpose of its more practical and applied outcomes rather than for the sole purposes of developing theory or increasing knowledge. An example of action research would include assessing the performance of individuals within various program, organizational, or institutional units.

Adequacy: Demonstrated when a researcher has collected enough evidence to account for and understand multiple plausible interpretations.

Adjacency pairs: Two-part conversational structures in which the first pair part calls for or invites the second pair part.

Agency: One of five key elements in the pentad of Burkean dramatism, it is the means by which an act is carried out.

Agent: One of five key elements in the pentad of Burkean dramatism, it is the person or persons who commit an act.

Agreement among judges: Equivalence of different people's interpretations.

Alternate forms method: Equivalence across different measures.

Analysis of covariance (ANCOVA): A statistical test used to control the effects of one or more variables that could intervene between the independent variable and the dependent variable in explaining the observed effects.

Analysis of variance (ANOVA): A statistical test of the effects of one or more categorical independent variables on a continuous dependent variable; also called an F test, expressed as the ratio of the differences in group means divided by chance differences.

Analytic induction: *See* Inductive reasoning.

Anonymity: Protecting human subjects' privacy by purposely not collecting any identifying information about individuals, or by collecting such information in a way that is it does not become known to the researcher.

Apologias: In genre criticism, speeches made in self-defense.

Applied research: Research that focuses on satisfying practical outcomes by solving specific problems in field settings.

Appropriate (verb): To make something your own, or set it aside for a specific use.

Archetypal metaphor: A metaphor assumed to be so primal any individual in any context could understand its meaning. Also called a root metaphor.

Archival documents: Written or symbolic records of communication, such as letters, newspapers, Web sites, billboards, or memos.

Archive: A preexisting collection of textual data or evidence.

Artifacts: Objects made by human work, and used by group or cultural members, such as clothing, jewelry, buildings, photographs, tools, or toys, which can be read as texts for the purpose of cultural analysis or criticism.

Artistic proofs: *Logos, ethos,* and *pathos* as internal constructions of the speaker in neo-Aristotelian criticism.

Associative claim: A claim that two communication phenomena are in some way related; a change in one phenomenon is accompanied by a change in the other phenomenon although one change does not cause the other.

Audit trail: Documents the development and progress of an interpretive research project, including the field notes from participant observation and/or interviews, classification schemes, drafts of data analysis at various stages, permissions/agreements with participants, and so on.

Autoethnography: An ethnographic study of a social setting or situation for which the key informant is the researcher himself or herself.

Avowal speech acts: Descriptions of the speaker's internal state, such as "I feel happy."

Background variables: Variables that represent characteristics of the participants that are already present before they take part in the study.

Bar chart: Visually depicts the frequencies of categories with bars along the horizontal axis for nominally and ordinally scaled variables.

Basic research: Research that emphasizes investigating theoretic relationships among variables where practical outcomes in specific contexts may be implicit or unknown.

Behaviorism: A school of psychology that emphasized observing, manipulating, and measuring human behavior as empirical tests of hypotheses.

Bell-shaped curve: The shape of a data distribution that is normally distributed along the horizontal axis.

Beta coefficients: In the formula $Y = a + bX$ for linear regression, the beta coefficients are a and b, where a is the *intercept* (the point at which the line intersects the vertical y-axis) and b is the *slope* of the line (estimation of how much change should occur in Y based on a unit of change in X); also called *regression weights.*

Between-groups variance: Observed differences between group means.

Between-subjects factor: An independent variable comprised of different treatment conditions in which groups of participants are separately assigned to each condition.

Bias: Systematic or constant error in the measurement of a variable; a threat to measurement validity.

Bimodal distribution: A sample distribution with two modes.

Bivariate relationships: Associations of variance between just two continuous variables.

Breaching: Deviating from the principles on which ethnomethodology is based.

Canons of rhetoric: Invention, organization, style, delivery, and memory.

Case study: A narrative account of the communication practices in a particular setting and among specific participants.

Categorical variables: Variables measured at the nominal and ordinal levels.

Categorizing: Grouping units into different categories.

Causal claim: A claim that predicts that a change in one communication phenomenon is preceded and influenced by a change in another.

Central limits theorem: Large and randomly selected samples have greater chances of approximating the true population distribution.

Chi-square statistic: A comparison of the actual distribution of the sample data (i.e., observed units per category) to the predicted distribution (i.e., expected units per category).

Claim: The central assertion or premise of an argument; in the research-as-argument model presented in this book, claim is a central assertion or premise that is argued in a research report or critical essay.

Claim of characterization: A claim that explains how conversational interactants are performing social actions, identities, or roles.

Claim of proposed methods: A claim that explains what is accomplished by a particular sequence of talk, or what are the outcomes of a particular sequence of talk.

Claim of proposed sequence: An interpretive claim about how some interaction sequence or feature works for participants.

Closed-format questions: Questions that provide specific response options to research participants; multiple-choice questions are examples of closed-format questions.

Cluster analysis: In Burkean dramatism, a form of analysis in which the rhetor examines key terms, groupings of those terms, and whole language patterns in one or several rhetorical texts, which are presumed to reflect the rhetor's meanings, motives, and attitudes.

Codeswitching: Mixing the rules of one speech community with the rules of another.

Coding: Reducing many specific observations into themes or categories.

Coding scheme: A set of categories into which message units are placed.

Coefficient of determination: In tests of correlation, an estimate of the actual proportion of variance that two continuous variables have in common, expressed as r^2.

Coefficient of multiple correlation: The combined degree of association between the predictor variables and the criterion variable, expressed as "R."

Coefficient of multiple determination: An estimate of how much of the variance in the criterion variable (dependent variable) is shared, or explained, by more than one predictor variables (independent variables), expressed as R^2.

Coherence: The degree to which a researcher's interpretations of actions, events, or texts are logical, consistent, and intelligible.

Cohort studies: Studies in which members of two or more groups are sampled at two or more points in time.

Collaborative ethnography: A form of team research where multiple researchers provide viewpoints on a setting, or similar settings.

Comment sheets: Records for the researcher to jot down notes after interviews, perhaps concerning the emotional tone of the interview, insights and reflections about any difficulties encountered during the interview, and so on.

Communal function: The ways that communication is used to create and affirm shared identities.

Communication code: The set of rules for speaking and interpreting others' speech within a particular speech community.

Communicative resources: The knowledge shared by members of a culture or group, used to interpret and organize action (for example, rules).

Comparison groups: Groups of study participants who are exposed to the manipulated levels of the independent variable.

Compensatory behavior effects: A cluster of confounding effects that can happen when the control group becomes aware that the experimental group is being treated differently. If the treatment seems to be a positive gain, then control groups can try to outperform the experimental group to receive the same treatment, or they can become frustrated and upset at the unequal treatment and withhold normal behaviors as a result.

Compunity: A newly coined term signifying the combination of computers and community.

Computer–assisted interviews: Programs that can provide greater consistency by prompting both interviewers and participants with the appropriate questions to ask at every phase of the interview.

Conceptual definition: A description of a construct that relates it to other abstract concepts.

Concurrent validity: Accuracy warranted by presenting an existing measuring instrument as validation of a newly created instrument, because the two instruments produce similar results.

Confederates: People who pose as naive study participants when, in fact, they have received special instructions to help the researchers manipulate the independent variable without the real or targeted study participants' knowledge; often used to create a plausible cover story.

Confessional tale: A recounting written in the first-person voice that focuses more on the field-worker than on the culture or other social situation under study.

Confidence interval: The interval of distance between various proportions of sample means and the population mean.

Confidence level: The percentage of sample means associated with each of the confidence intervals.

Confidentiality: Protecting research participants' privacy by withholding their identifying information from the transcripts, field notes, or written research reports.

Confirmability: The degree to which findings that a researcher posits, based on analysis of data, can be confirmed, or echoed, by another person who had similar access to those same data sources.

Confounding variables: Factors that interfere in the relationship between the independent and dependent variables as rival causes or sources of influence.

Constant error: Bias or systematic error in the measurement of a variable; a threat to measurement validity.

Constative speech acts: Assertions, such as "X is true."

Construct validity: Accuracy warranted by establishing that the results from an instrument's administration converge with, or diverge from, the results achieved by other instruments that measure different, but theoretically related, concepts.

Constructed conversation samples: Fictional interactions written by the researcher (or taken from a film, novel, etc.).

Constructivism: A philosophy whose central premise is that there are multiple realities that are socially constructed when people assign meanings to observations.

Constructs: Phenomena that can only be observed indirectly.

Consumer research: Research designed to assess consumer attitudes and preferences for various products or services.

Content analysis: A primarily quantitative method of categorizing and describing communication messages in specific contexts.

Content validity: *See* Face validity.

Contextuality: The focus on everyday life interactions in their natural contexts.

Contingency questions: Questions that depend upon responses to filter questions.

Contingency table analysis: Multiple-sample chi-square.

Continuous variables: Constructs measured with interval and ratio scales.

Control group: A comparison group that is not exposed to the manipulation of the independent variable but is in every other way the equivalent of the treatment group(s).

Convenience sampling: Selecting whatever data is easily accessible to the researcher.

Convergent validity: Accuracy established when the results of one instrument's administration are compared with the results of another measure of the same concept, provided that the second measuring instrument has already been shown to be accurate.

Correlation coefficient: An estimate of the strength of the association between two continuous variables, expressed as r_{xy}, showing the degree to which two variables are systematically related to one another, or co-vary.

Counterclaims: Other interpretations that could be potentially supported by a data set.

Covariance: *See* Correlation coefficient.

Cover story: A deceptive story designed to reduce participants' reactions to the experimental situation by obscuring the real testing situation so that the procedure will seem more natural to participants.

Criterion validity: Accuracy warranted by the measuring instrument's relationship to other instruments that have already been shown to be valid.

Criterion variable: In tests of association, the term for dependent variable.

Critical essays: Manuscripts based primarily (or only) on textual data sources, whether the text being analyzed is a speech, an artifact, or the researcher's experience as evidence given in support of a claim.

Critical tale: A narrative that represents a social situation as it might have been seen by the members of a disadvantaged group.

Cronbach's alpha: A coefficient that measures the internal consistency or homogeneity of an interval scale.

Cross-sectional research design: A research design where a sample of data collected at one point in time is used to draw inferences about the research question.

Cued recall technique: Asking subjects to describe what they were thinking as they watch a videotape of their own interaction behaviors.

Culture: A system of shared meanings (webs of significance) that are held in common by group members.

Curvilinear relationships: A complex relationship between two variables that changes directions at several points during their association.

Data: The evidence or grounds for a claim.

Data collection settings: The places where observation, self-report, and other-report data are gathered or found.

Data collection sources: The points from which the data originate.

Data collection strategies: How data for a study are gathered.

Data logging: Carefully recording various forms of data, including field notes from participant observations, write-ups from interviews, maps, photography, sound recordings, document collections, and so on.

Deconstruction: Unpacking, or taking apart, the meaning of a text. *See also* Inversion.

Deductive reasoning: Moves from broad and abstract toward specific and concrete.

Degree of membership: The extent to which one belongs to a social group.

Degrees of freedom: The number of frequency categories that are free to vary.

Deliberative rhetoric: Political discourse, a genre of speeches given on the floor of the legislative assembly for the purpose of establishing or changing a law.

Delivery: The rhetor's presentation, including presentation format and nonverbal cues, as one of the five canons of rhetoric.

Demand characteristics effects: Confounding effects where research participants vary their normal behavior because they think they have discovered the research goals.

Demographics: The general characteristics common to any group of people, such as age, biological sex, socioeconomic class, level of education, and ethnicity.

Dependent variable: A communication phenomenon that has been influenced by a change in another communication phenomenon; the "effect."

Derived terms: Concepts whose essential characteristics are not directly observable, and thus, which can only be defined by referring to previously agreed-upon concepts.

Descriptive claim: Assertions about how to characterize some particular communication phenomenon.

Descriptive statistics: A depiction of how the collected sample data appears, both visually and in numerical terms; the characteristics of sample data.

Deviant case sampling: Selecting people or messages (i.e., cases) that are extremely different from those already included in an existing data sample.

Dichotomous variables: Responses to survey questions based on two choices.

Directional hypothesis: A prediction that specifies the exact nature of the change between variables, either group differences or relationships.

Discrimination: Sorting objects by their differences.

Discursive formation: The language forms (specific to a historical time period) that allow people to think about and express their knowledge.

Divergent validity: Accuracy established when the results of one measuring instrument are shown to be unrelated to the results of another measuring instrument, provided that the concepts these two instruments purport to measure are theoretically unrelated.

Double-barreled questions: Questions that ask two things simultaneously.

Ecological validity: The relationship between the data in a research study and the larger setting, or environment, of which that data is a part.

Econometrics: The historical analysis of macro-level social data.

Ego-centered network analysis: A method that aims to describe a system of social relationships from one individual communicator's point of view.

Emancipate: Set free.

Embeddedness: One conversational structure nested within a larger, similar structure.

Emic view of culture: Ingroup members' understandings of a social situation are privileged over an outside observer's understandings of the same situation.

Empirical language requirement: Reliance on transcripts alone as evidence for a claim.

Empirical methods: Methods that rely on measuring observations systemically.

Empirical rule: The rule of distributions that approximately 68% of the sample's distribution of scores will fall within ±1 standard deviation of the sample's mean, about 95% fall within ±2 standard deviations, and more than 99% fall within ±3 standard deviations.

Empiricism: A philosophy whose central assumption emphasizes that objective reality is known through observing and explaining sensory information.

Entelechy: In Burkean dramatism, the perfection of being or becoming entirely what one is supposed to become.

Enthymeme: A form of deductive reasoning that is based on a syllogism in which at least one of three parts, observation, generalization, and inference, is omitted so that the audience must participate by filling in the blanks.

Epideictic rhetoric: Ceremonial speech genre given on special occasions to praise or blame another's actions, to uphold an individual as virtuous, or condemn an individual as corrupt.

Equivalence: Consistency across measures or across researchers.

Errors in data processing: Errors that occur when data are translated from one form to another.

Et cetera clause: Garfinkel's idea that all rules must be elaborated in context in order to be applied.

Ethnographic interviews: Informal conversations and storytelling between participants and researchers.

Ethnography: A way of studying social settings or situations that privileges the participants' meanings by using participant observations, perhaps along with interviews and/or textual analysis.

Ethnography of communication: A specific theoretic approach to ethnography that focuses on speech communities.

Ethnography of speaking: A specific theoretic approach to ethnography that uses Dell Hymes's S-P-E-A-K-I-N-G framework in data collection and analysis.

Ethnomethodology: A way of studying people's ordinary daily practices.

Ethos: One of the artistic proofs that refers to the character or credibility of the rhetor.

Etic view of culture: Outside observers' understandings of a social situation are privileged over ingroup members' understandings of the same situation.

Evaluation apprehension effect: As a confounding effect, the tendency for respondents, when asked for information that is potentially embarrassing or negative in some way, to change their answers to give a more positive personal impression of themselves.

Evaluative claims: Claims establishing a set of criteria or standards and rendering judgments about how well or how poorly a communication phenomenon meets those standards.

Exhaustive categories: All possible categories of the variable are listed, from which the research participant (or researcher/coder) will choose a response.

Experimental control: A research objective achieved by checking the manipulation of the independent variable for its effectiveness, and through controlling alternative rival explanations for the observed set of effects on the dependent variable.

Experimental groups: Groups that receive some exposure to the manipulation of the independent variable.

Explanatory claims: Claims explaining the relationships between various communication phenomena, often by identifying reasons or causes for communication phenomena.

Explicit cultural knowledge: Knowledge used to interpret experience, or to read cultural artifacts, physical environments, and behavior and events.

Ex post facto design: A type of preexperimental study, also called a one-shot case study, in which there is virtually no control over the manipulation of the independent variable or over the observation of the change in the dependent variable; one of the weakest causal arguments.

External validity: Accuracy of applying conclusions from one study to another setting or to other people.

Face sheets: Records containing details about the interviews, such as a code or name for the participants; the date, place, and time of the interviews; and any relevant demographic information about the interviewees.

Face-to-face interviews: Personal interviews between the interviewer and the participant.

Face validity: The degree to which a measuring instrument appears to be accurate, in the view of a trained expert (also known as content validity).

Facework: The use of politeness behaviors to show respect for and avoid offending other people.

Factorial designs: Experimental research designs that frequently contain multiple independent variables manipulated for their effects on one or more dependent variables.

Factors: The term used to refer to independent variables when there are two or more within the experimental design.

Faithfulness: The degree to which researchers remain steadfast in their commitment to conduct an important, believable study during ethnographic data collection, analysis, and reporting.

Falsification principle: The assumption that the null hypothesis is true until enough evidence is accumulated to reject it.

Fantasies: Recollections of past events in the group, predictions about future events, or fictitious constructions of imagined events.

Fantasy themes: Depiction of people, settings, and story lines reflected in the fantasies of a group.

Field settings: Sites for data collection in the places where communication occurs just as it would when research was not being conducted.

Filtered data collection procedures: Ways of collecting information from people or texts that involve the researcher imposing preordained categories onto the data.

Filter questions: Questions that direct people to respond to various portions of a questionnaire.

First pair part: The first half of an adjacency pair.

Focus group: A small group of respondents (4 to 10 participants) who are selected by convenience, purposive, or snowball sampling methods and interviewed, generally with a loose structure, so that a wide range of information may be collected about a particular subject.

Follow-up tests: *See* Post hoc comparisons.

Forensic rhetoric: The genre of legal discourse in courtroom proceedings.

Formative evaluation: Evaluation that is used during a communication process, so that the evaluation data can form the process as it unfolds.

Formulas: Mathematical principles used in physical and applied sciences.

Free-recall technique: A technique in which participants are asked to list all of the members of their social network, and then to answer a series of questions about each of those people.

Frequency distribution: The way that scores are distributed along the x-axis.

Frequency polygon: Visual representation of data distributions for continuous variables formed by connecting the pairs of data points or graph coordinate points on the x-and y-axes.

Frequency table: Useful quick references summarizing the frequencies and percentages of data that are visually displayed in pie chart or bar chart graphs.

Fronting: Participants' attempts to avoid telling the whole truth when being interviewed.

Gaining access (or entry): The process of getting permission and approvals for doing research in a particular setting.

Gatekeepers: The participants who have power to grant or deny access to a setting.

Generality: Applicability of interpretations and inferences to more than one participant or moment in the communicative group or culture studied.

Generalizability: Findings from one study may be applied to other similar messages or persons because the sample selected adequately represents the population of interest.

Generalization: Grouping or categorizing objects together by their similarities.

Generic application: Deductively explaining how the characteristics of genre should be applied to a specific rhetorical text to assess whether it is a good or poor fit.

Generic description: Analyzing several rhetorical texts to determine inductively whether a genre exists.

Generic participation: A deductive process of comparing the characteristics of several genres with the characteristics of several rhetorical artifacts or texts for the purpose of classifying the artifacts by genres.

Genre: A common pattern in rhetorical texts across similar types of contexts.

Grounded-theory approach: A research method in which the investigator builds theory by systematically and repeatedly gathering and analyzing field data during the data collection process; thus the theory is grounded inductively in the data.

Hawthorne effect: A specific example of a demand characteristic effect in which simple awareness of being targeted for research increased the employees' levels of productivity regardless of how environmental conditions were varied.

Hegemony: A (usually hidden) form of power that comes from privileging one ideology over another.

Hermeneutic circle: Movement back and forth, between the general and specific meanings of texts.

Hermeneutics: A way of understanding the full meanings of messages or texts by examining in detail the embedded historical and sociocultural contexts in which they were created.

Hierarchical regression: A form of multiple regression in which the researcher stipulates the order of variables entered into the linear equation based on theory and past research.

Histogram: Visual representation of variables measured with interval or ratio level scales where numbers along the x-axis are true values mathematically related to each other at equidistant intervals.

History effect: The occurrence of an event external to the study that affects the outcome in such a way that the event rivals or threatens the independent variable as the source of influence on the dependent variable.

Homogeneity: The degree to which each item in a measuring instrument consistently refers to the same underlying concept (also known as internal consistency).

Hypotheses: Statements that make specific predictions about relationships between communication variables.

Ideal speech situation: Free, accessible public discourse and equal distribution of power to all parts of society.

Identification: In Burkean dramatism, the process of finding common ground and acting in concert with other individuals by following an established set of rules or principles.

Ideology: A group's system of beliefs and values, the ideas upon which a social system is based.

Impressionist tale: An interesting and coherent narrative that represents both the researcher's and the participants' views of a social situation; a combination of realist and confessional tales.

Inartistic proofs: External forms such as testimony from witnesses or key documents.

Independent samples t-test: A test of difference between an independent variable with two samples, or groups of an independent variable that are unrelated, for their effects on a continuous dependent variable.

Independent variable: A communication phenomenon presumed to be the source or cause of change in another communication phenomenon.

Inductive reasoning: Generalizing from particular cases.

Inferential statistics: Numerical procedures for estimating population characteristics, based on the characteristics of sample data.

Inscriptions: First-level interpretations of events.

Institutional Review Boards (IRBs): Committees charged with the protection of human subjects in research (also known as research participants).

Instrumentation effect: A confounding effect that happens when the researcher changes the instruments used to measure the dependent variables between the pretest and the posttest.

Instrument clarity: The degree to which a measuring instrument is free from ambiguity.

Interaction analysis: A quantitative method used to make inferences about the effects of manipulating verbal and nonverbal communication behaviors in dyadic and group interactions.

Interaction effects: Two or more independent variables acting together to impact the dependent variable.

Interactive data collection procedures: Ways of collecting information from people or texts that make the researcher an active participant in the situation being studied, and that purposefully influence the data.

Interactive discourse: Discourse in which all interactants share responsibility for speaking and listening.

Intercoder reliability: The agreement among two or more researchers who are categorizing messages.

Internal consistency: *See* Homogeneity.

Internal validity: The ability of a study to accurately test its claim(s); including the validity of the research design, procedures, and measurement.

Interpretive claims: Claims about how communicators create and interpret meanings.

Interpretive community: A group of people who share rules for how to encode meanings or interpret meanings when decoding others' messages. *See also* Speech community.

Interrater reliability: The agreement among either research participants or researchers who rate communication characteristics of a single target. *See also* Intercoder reliability.

Intertranscriber reliability: Consistent transcription of video- or audiotaped conversation into a written record by two or more people.

Interval scales: Scales used to measure communication variables that express values of magnitude and have equal distances between each value.

Intervening variables: Other independent variables that produce effects in the dependent variable that are not controlled and so weaken the cause-and-effect relationship observed in the study.

Interviewer training: Information and activities carried out before data collection begins, to ensure that field interviews by different people are conducted consistently.

Interview formats: Different types of interview guides for asking questions ranging from structured to unstructured formats.

Invention: One of the canons of rhetoric that refers to the speaker's ideas or main points of an argument.

Inversion: The first move in performing deconstruction, in which researchers attempt to show how one half of a binary opposite has been privileged over the other half.

Inverted U-shaped correlation: Two variables initially increase together as a positive relationship, and then one variable declines over time and the correlation becomes negative.

Item response rate: The percentage of completed items on each individual survey.

Iterative process: A cycle of activities that are repeated over time.

Jeremiads: A speech genre consisting of castigating a group of people by announcing their violation of social norms, reviewing their punishment, detailing the violation, and urging them to repent.

Key informants: Informed, articulate members of the culture or group a researcher wants to understand.

Knowing by authority: Believing something is true because someone regarded as an expert thinks it is true.

Knowing by criticism: The method of knowing by increasing our awareness of the ways in which society or the dominant group constructs our realities, primarily through the processes of privilege and oppression.

Knowing by discovery: The method of knowing by discovering objective reality through precise, systematic, and repetitive observations of communication phenomena.

Knowing by interpretation: The method of knowing by understanding multiple interpretations people attach to their subjective experiences of the world.

Knowing by tenacity: Customary knowledge; knowing something is true because it is commonly held to be true.

Knowing by the method of science: Testing claims for reasonableness through logical consistency, observation, systematic analysis, and experience.

Knowing on a priori grounds: Testing claims against standards of reasonableness derived from logic, aesthetics, or moral codes.

Kurtosis: The vertical dimension of a sample distribution's shape that refers to how peaked or flat it is when error is present.

Laboratory conversation samples: Interactions induced for the purpose of conducting research, in a setting controlled by the researcher.

Laboratory settings: Sites for communication data collection that are selected and controlled by the researcher(s).

Latent meanings: The meanings that become apparent with careful analysis and synthesis of messages.

Laws: The immutable, physical laws of nature (gravity, for example).

Leading questions: Questions that direct respondents to answer in a specific way.

Leptokurtic distribution: A sample distribution that is peaked because the distribution is biased.

Liberation: Overcoming oppression, gaining equal rights.

Likert scales: A type of interval scale that asks the study participant to indicate varying levels of responses to questions. Typically, the scale asks for varying levels of agreement (i.e., Strongly Agree, Agree, Neutral, Disagree, Strongly Disagree) or frequency (i.e., Always, Sometimes, Never).

Linear relationships: A simple association between two continuous variables where they change together proportionately in the same or opposite directions.

Links: Connections or ties based on communication between two people within the same network.

Literature review: A review of the existing published works that are most closely related to a research topic.

Logical positivism: A philosophy that combines deductive logic with empirical observations in order to test causal predictions about phenomena.

Logos: One of the artistic proofs referring to the logical or rational appeals a speaker makes by identifying the central claims made and the evidence used to support them.

Longitudinal research design: A research design where data are collected at several points in time.

Magnitude: The size or strength of the correlation coefficient.

Main effect: The change in the dependent variable that is directly attributable to each separate factor or independent variable.

Mall intercept surveys: Surveys in which participants are found in shopping malls.

Manifest meanings: The overt, surface-level meanings of messages.

Manipulation checks: Procedures that directly test whether the independent variable was manipulated the way it was intended to be.

Maturation effect: A confounding effect that happens when a naturally occurring developmental change accounts for some, or all, of the observed effect on the independent variable.

Maximum variation sampling: Selecting people or messages that are as different from one another as possible for inclusion in a data sample.

Mean: Arithmetic average of variable values used as a measure of central tendency for a sample distribution.

Measurement reliability: Consistency in research observations over time, across settings, subjects, and instruments.

Measures of central tendency: Descriptive statistics that reduce the data set to one number that best characterizes the entire sample (i.e., mean, median, or mode).

Median: The midpoint score used as a measure of central tendency for a sample distribution.

Member checks: Allowing your research participants to review, and perhaps verify, some or all of the materials that you have prepared, such as field notes, interview transcripts, and narrative research reports.

Message construction tasks: Tasks that require experimental subjects to respond to communicative scenarios developed by a researcher.

Message population: A well-defined set of messages pertinent to a given research question or hypothesis.

Meta-analysis: A statistical analysis of many prior analyses.

Metaphor: An analogy created by linking two or more symbols through language to add meaning.

Metatheoretical discourse: Discourse that argues the sincerity of an avowal.

Methodological awareness: Experience with and knowledge of research methodologies.

Micropolis: A newly coined term in technology meaning a fragmented, smaller grouping of people through technology-based links, as an analog of *metropolis*.

Mixed independent groups/repeated measures design: A research design using both within-subjects and between-subjects factors.

Mixed model paradigm: A design mixing stimulus variables with organismic variables.

Mode: The most frequently occurring score used as a measure of central tendency for a sample distribution.

Modernism: A philosophy that stresses theoretical knowledge based on reasoned action and the technological means for achieving it.

Moments: Calculations that permit estimating how much the sample distribution's statistics deviate from those expected with a normal curve.

Mortality effect: A confounding effect where subjects disproportionately drop out of an experiment affecting the sum total of change measured in the dependent variable.

Mortification: In Burkean dramatism, a person's act of self-sacrifice to expiate guilt and find redemption.

Multidimensional variables: Variables with different subconstructs representing each of the different dimensions.

Multiple-factors analysis of variance: A test of group differences for the effects of more than one independent categorical variable on a dependent continuous variable.

Multiple regression analysis: A test of the relationship between a set of predictor (independent) continuous variables and the criterion (dependent) continuous variable.

Multiple-sample chi-square: A test of the relationship between the frequencies of two or more categorical variables that are independent from one another.

Multistage cluster sampling: A random selection method used when no population sampling frame is available, in which the researcher lists and then randomly samples from within progressively more specific clusters of elements.

Multivariate analysis of variance (MANOVA):   A test of the relationships between two or more independent variables as factors on multiple dependent continuous variables.

Multivariate relationships: Associations of variance between more than two continuous variables.

Mutually exclusive categories: Categorizing characteristics that require each data entry be placed in one and only one category.

Narrative: Symbolic acts told in story form.

Narrative discourse: Discourse in which one participant has greater responsibility for speaking than do other participants.

Naturalism: A professed adherence to studying people in their everyday lives as played out in their natural settings.

Naturalistic inquiry: Inductive method for studying human behavior in specific contexts.

Negative case analysis: A conscientious search for counterexamples.

Negative correlation: An association between two continuous variables where the change in one variable is accompanied by an inverse change in the other; for example, as one variable increases in frequency, the other variable decreases in frequency.

Negative skew: A shift in the majority of scores to the right with a tail pointing in the direction of negative numbers.

Network analytic research: An approach that aims to describe and explain communication processes and structures by collecting data about relationships among people, symbols, or groups.

Network sampling: Selecting people to participate in a study and asking each person to solicit additional participants (perhaps with similar characteristics); also called snowball sampling.

Noise: Measurement error derived from random sources; a threat to reliability.

Nominal scales: Scales that assign one value of the variable for one and only one category or subgroup of the variable.

Nondirectional hypothesis: A hypothesis that predicts an inequality or difference between two or more group means, but does not specify the direction of that difference.

Nonequivalent control group design: A type of quasi-experimental research design using a control group and a treatment group but whose participants were not randomly assigned to either group. The equivalence of groups is thus not assured.

Nonfiltered data collection procedures: Ways of collecting information directly from people, or texts, without imposing preordained categories on the data.

Noninteractive data collection procedures: Ways of collecting information from people, or texts, that minimize the researcher's role as an active participant in the situation being studied, and his or her influence on the data.

Nonparametric tests: Statistical tests where all of the variables are categorical (measured with nominal or ordinal scales) from which no assumptions about populations can be made.

Nonrandom selection methods: Ways of selecting people and texts that do not ensure that the resulting data sample represents some theoretically generalizable population.

Nonreciprocated links: Links between people within a network that are not confirmed by one member of the pair.

Normal curve: Presumed shape of many continuously measured variables when there is little error present and that therefore yield statistics that are accurate and reliable estimates of the population parameters.

Null hypothesis: A prediction that there is no relationship between two or more variables, no difference between groups, or the logical opposite of the research hypothesis.

Observed interactions: Researcher's representations of the characteristics of communicative messages, channels of communication, or communicators.

Obtrusive data collection procedures: Ways of collecting information that make the researcher's presence known to the research participants.

One-group pretest-posttest design: A type of preexperimental design in which administration of the pretest enables the researcher to discover a distinct change or no change between the pretest and the posttest measures. However, there are still many problems in assuming that the independent variable, X, is the source of those changes.

One-shot case study: A type of preexperimental study, also called an ex post facto design, in which there is virtually no control over the manipulation of the independent variable or over the observation of the change in the dependent variable; one of the weakest causal arguments.

One-tailed test: A test that uses critical rejection regions under only one tail of the normal curve distribution.

One-way analysis of variance: A test of group differences between one independent categorical variable, having three or more levels, and one continuous dependent variable.

Open-ended questions: Questions that ask respondents to provide unstructured or spontaneous answers or to discuss an identified topic.

Operational definition: A precise specification of every operation, procedure, and instrument needed to measure a construct.

Operationalization: The process of specifying the operations, procedures, or instruments used to measure communication phenomena as variables.

Order effects: The adverse effects of earlier questions on the way respondents answer later questions in a questionnaire.

Ordinal scales: Scales that measure rankings of various categories of variables.

Ordinate: Vertical axis.

Organismic variables: Variables that represent organic or natural differences in the participants' internal characteristics, or characteristics that the participants have chosen for themselves (such as marital status).

Organization: One of the five canons of rhetoric referring to the structure or general pattern of the various components in a rhetorical text.

Other-report: Perceptions about other people's behavior, beliefs, and/or characteristics.

Paired t-test: A test of group differences between an independent variable with two groups that are related or matched in some way and a continuous dependent variable; for example, between pretest and posttest scores for the same group of participants.

Panel of judges: A group of people selected to evaluate the content validity of a measuring instrument because they have particular knowledge or expertise on the topic being measured.

Panel studies: Studies that examine the same sample of individuals over time.

Paradigms: Different ways of knowing based on different sets of interrelated assumptions about theory and research.

Paradox: Something possessing inherently contradictory qualities.

Parameters: Characteristics of a population expressed in numbers.

Parametric tests: Statistical tests where at least one variable is continuous, allowing assumptions to be made about the way populations are distributed.

Parsimony: The combination of precision and power valued in discovery research.

Partial correlation analysis: A test of association between two continuous variables in which the effects of all other related variables are partialed out, or removed.

Participant observation: The process of watching and learning about the setting and participants, while the researcher is participating in the daily realities he or she is studying.

Pathos: One of the artistic proofs referring to the emotional appeal of a speaker.

Pentadic criticism: Applying the pentadic elements of drama to any symbolic act or text to understand the underlying motivation.

Performance tests: A form of member checking in which the researcher enacts specific behaviors in order to confirm his or her interpretations of how those behaviors will be received by members of the social situation.

Periodicity: A recurring pattern or arrangement that exists naturally in a sampling frame.

Personal significance: A researcher's unique, individual reasons for pursuing a topic of study.

Phenomenology: The study of, or understanding our subjective experiences through conscious attention as we live them.

Pie chart: Visually depicts the frequencies of categories with proportions of a circle for nominally and ordinally scaled variables.

Placebo: A false treatment given to one of the comparison groups for the purpose of fooling group members into thinking they have received a treatment when they have not.

Platykurtic distribution: A distribution that is flat, indicating the presence of noise or random error.

Political polling research: Research designed to assess political opinions and attitudes, often to predict voter preferences.

Politics of representation: The issue of who has a right to assign meaning to actions, events, texts, or experiences.

Pollution: In Burkean dramatism, the consequence of rejecting social hierarchical order, regarded as a social "fall from grace."

Popular press publications: Secondary sources that are aimed at the general public, largely without regard to their readers' fields of academic study or particular occupations.

Population: The entire set of cases or instances that the researcher is attempting to represent with a data sample. *See also* Survey population; Target population.

Positive correlation: An association between continuous variables that are changing proportionally in the same direction (increasing or decreasing together).

Positive skew: A shift in the majority of scores to the left with a tail pointing in the direction of positive numbers.

Post hoc comparisons: Tests of individual contrasts between pairs of groups following the calculation of the F statistic.

Postmodern turn: A general movement away from social structure as the explanatory means of domination, toward ideology, representation, and discourse as the sites of struggle for social power.

Posttest: An assessment of scores on the dependent variable after the independent variable has been manipulated.

Posttest-only control group design: A type of true experimental design in which participants are randomly assigned to comparison groups. The pretest is eliminated as an attempt to control for the test sensitization effect.

Power: The broad scope of a definition or measurement, which is most valued in discovery research.

Practical discourse: Discourse that argues the appropriateness of a regulative statement.

Precise observations: Observations made carefully for the sake of accuracy.

Precision: The detailed and accurate definitions and measurements of communication variables valued in discovery research.

Predictive claims: Claims that forecast expected outcomes or effects in the relationship between two or more communication phenomena or variables.

Predictive validity: Accuracy warranted by showing that the measure predicts scores on some other variable in the way that a theory predicts it should work.

Predictor variable: In tests of association, the term for the independent variable.

Preexperimental designs: Designs in which two or three of the elements of experimental control (comparison groups, pretest/posttest, random assignment) are missing, resulting in very weak support for causal arguments.

Pretest: An assessment of the baseline or naturally occurring levels of the dependent variable before the independent variable is manipulated.

Pretest-posttest control group design: A type of true experimental design that uses comparison groups, random assignment to place participants into the treatment and control groups, and the pretest-posttest procedure.

Primary sources: Original research reports or critical essays written by the researcher, which describe the claims, data, warrants, and backing for a research study.

Primitive terms: Concepts whose essential characteristics are directly observable.

Principles: Legal rules and statutes.

Professional associations: A dues-paying group of academic, business, or industry practitioners in a particular field of study.

Public scrutiny: Persons with considerable training and experience agree that a measure seems likely to yield accurate data; a test of face validity.

Purification: In Burkean dramatism, the absolution of guilt through mortification or victimage, and transcendence.

Purpose: One of five key elements in the pentad of Burkean dramatism, it is the reason for the action that the agent can readily provide for the act.

Purposive sampling: Selecting the particular people or messages needed to test a claim about communication within one specific context.

Quasi-experimental designs: Designs in which one or two of the elements of experimental control (comparison groups, pretest/posttest, random assignment) are missing, resulting in weaker support for causal arguments.

Questionnaire architecture: The general structure of a questionnaire: its length, comprehensibility, and question order.

Questionnaires: Written paper-and-pencil measures for data collection.

Quota sampling: A nonrandom sampling method for small, well-defined populations in which key population characteristics are proportionally represented in the data sample.

Random assignment: A procedure in which the researchers select subjects on a purely random basis to participate in either treatment or control conditions.

Random digit dialing: A procedure that first randomly identifies areas of a region to be sampled with their corresponding area codes and exchanges (first three numbers) and then randomly generates the last four digits of the telephone number.

Random error: Measurement error that constitutes noise or interference with the variable's true values; a threat to reliability.

Random individual or situational differences: Unique variations in individual persons or situations that threaten measurement reliability.

Random selection methods: Procedures that use some element of chance in order to select sample data that will represent a population.

Rating scheme: A way of assigning numerical values to interaction features or communication behaviors.

Ratio scales: Scales on which values represent points along a continuum separated by equal distances or intervals, with a true or absolute zero point.

Rationalism: A philosophy stressing reliance on the logical processes of the mind for discovery of an objective reality.

Reactivity effects: Effects or threats due to participants' responses to some design feature of the experimental situation.

Realism: A philosophy emphasizing the importance of accurately distinguishing objective reality from the subjective perspective of the perceiver.

Realist tale: A relatively straightforward recounting of the researcher's observations in the field, written in the third-person voice.

Reciprocated links: Network links that are confirmed by *both* network members. *See also* Nonreciprocated links.

Redemptive cycle: In Burkean dramatism, a repeating social drama characterized by the stages of order, pollution, guilt, purification, and redemption.

Reference list: A section appearing at the end of written research reports and critical essays and containing the full citations for all the works cited in the manuscript.

Referential function of language: To convey information.

Reflexivity: A process by which researchers recognize that they are inseparable from the settings, contexts, and cultures they are attempting to understand and represent.

Reformist claims: Evaluative claims that identify negative consequences of the existing social system as a way of instigating change.

Regression analysis: A statistical test of association between continuous variables, where one or more predictor variables (independent variables) are used to assess the values of the criterion variable (dependent variable).

Regression weights: *See* Beta coefficients.

Regulative speech acts: Influence attempts, such as a command or promise.

Relational dialectic: A simultaneous push-pull; a tension between two competing and perhaps contradictory goals in a relationship.

Relational functions of language: To encode a speaker's relationship to the topic being spoken about, the person(s) spoken to, and the situation.

Relevance: The degree to which ethnographic interpretations are germane, or salient to the people in the group or culture being studied.

Reliability: Consistency of measurement; a standard for evaluating discovery research.

Repair work: Actions that interlocutors take to fix disruptions in interaction, either because a speaker feels he or she has violated a norm, or is being accused of such a violation by someone else in the conversation.

Repeated measures: An experimental design in which the researcher exposes the same group of participants to several manipulations of the independent variable(s).

Repetitive observations: Observations that are repeated in various ways for the purpose of verification.

Representative sample: A sample whose characteristics are good estimates (valid and reliable) of the population characteristics.

Research design: The logical sequence used to connect a researcher's claim, data or evidence, warrants, and background reasoning.

Research design statement: A numerical statement of the number of independent variables by the specific number of categories per variable found in an experimental study; for example, a 2 × 3 research design statement refers to two independent variables, the first having 2 categories or levels and the second having 3 categories or levels.

Researcher attributes effect: A confounding effect that happens when researchers possess physical or psychological characteristics that influence the way participants respond, thus affecting the outcome of the experiment.

Researcher credibility: An umbrella term used in field research to cover a number of concerns, including authenticity, training and experience, and the like.

Researcher positionality: Both the researcher's standpoint and his or her reflexivity.

Research hypothesis: The predictive claim about the relationship between two or more variables to be tested with a statistical analysis.

Research questions: Questions that ask how a concept chosen for study can be classified or ask what relationship exists between various types of communication variables.

Research reports: Written summaries of research projects that include some form of data collection source taken from self-reports, other-reports, or observations, or from a combination of those sources, perhaps with textual data as well.

Research sources: Research reports and critical essays (primary sources), as well as encyclopedias, magazine and newspaper articles, Web sites, and so on (secondary sources), which can be examined in the process of conducting a literature review.

Research strategies: Techniques for searching the communication literature at the library, on the Internet, and via electronic databases.

Response bias: The tendency for respondents to get into the habit of responding in a particular way so that they cease being mindful of their responses.

Rhetorical artifact: Rhetorical texts such as speeches, personal correspondence, or films selected for analysis.

Rhetorical vision: In fantasy theme analysis, a collective social perspective formed when the fantasy themes of one group become public and accepted by a much larger audience.

Rich description: Using a broad range of data sources and settings to show how communication occurs, or how meaning is made in a particular context or social situation.

Ritual of frankness: The practice of candidly and directly presenting one's own view as a research finding, or as a way of warranting the worth of a particular conclusion.

Root metaphor: *See* Archetypal metaphor.

Roster method: A technique in which participants in the study are given a roster of all the members of their social system and are asked to respond to questions about all the other members with whom they regularly interact.

Rules: Reasons that any person living in our society would be likely to accept as a basis for some action.

Sample: A subset or smaller grouping of members from a population.

Sampling: Selecting a relatively smaller number of cases in order to represent some larger group of cases or instances of phenomena.

Sampling distribution: A theoretic distribution of all possible values of any sample statistic from any given population, specifying the probabilities associated with each of the values.

Sampling effect: A confounding effect that occurs when nonrandom methods are used to collect samples; these samples are much more likely to be biased, or they are likely to vary in systematic ways that do not accurately represent the characteristics of the population from which they were drawn.

Sampling error: Estimation of deviation between sample statistics and population parameters.

Sampling frame: A list of all members of the population.

Scene: One of five key elements in the pentad of Burkean dramatism referring to the setting or situation in which an act occurred.

Scholarly journals: Journals published under the sponsorship of professional associations in a given discipline, with the purpose of conveying the very best theoretic and research scholarship in that field to a community of scholarly peers.

Secondary sources: Another writer's summary and interpretations of an original research project.

Second pair part: The second half of an adjacency pair.

Selection: How researchers decide which people or messages to include in a research study.

Selection effect: A confounding effect when the researcher is unable to randomly assign subjects to treatment and control conditions. Without this procedure, groups can differ systematically in ways that interfere with the effects of the independent variable.

Self-report: Perceptions about one's own behaviors, beliefs, and/or characteristics.

Semantic differential scales: Scales consisting of a series of bipolar adjectives placed at either end of a continuum. The adjectives act as anchors for extremes; the respondents indicate where along the continuum between the extremes their perceptions lie.

Semantic network analysis: A method for studying relationships among the parts of a system based on the ways members of the system share symbolic meanings.

Semistructured interviews: Interviews that are guided by a format that calls for some general, open-ended questions combined with more specific and directive questioning.

Significant difference: The high probability that sample means are not drawn from the same population.

Simple random sampling: A random selection method in which each person (or text) in the population has an equal chance of being selected for inclusion in a study.

Single-factor analysis of variance: Test of the effects of one independent variable with more than two categories on one dependent continuous variable; also called a one-way analysis of variance.

Single-sample chi-square: A test of the difference between expected frequencies and obtained frequencies for one categorical variable.

Skew: A horizontal shift in the majority of scores either to the right or left of the distribution's center with a longer tail trailing away toward the opposite end of the distribution.

Snowball sampling: A nonrandom sampling method in which each subject selected to participate in a study also solicits additional subjects (perhaps with similar characteristics) to participate in the same study; also called network sampling.

Social significance: The reasons that a certain topic of study is important to a particular group of people, usually because of an existing problem or the harm caused by that problem.

Solomon four-group design: A type of true experimental design that includes two groups that use the pretest-posttest control group design, and two groups that use the posttest-only control group design.

Speech community: A group of people who share rules for using and interpreting speech.

Split-halves technique: A procedure to assess the internal homogeneity of a measurement scale where one half of the items are randomly chosen and correlated with responses from the other half.

Sponsors: A participant who actively helps the ethnographic researcher establish credibility with other participants, identify key informants, arrange interviews, and so on.

Spurious correlation: Two variables that appear to be associated when they are not actually related in any way.

Stability: Consistency of results obtained by one measuring instrument over time.

Standard error of difference between means: In z-tests, the estimation of the amount of error due to random or chance variation.

Static-group comparison design: A type of preexperimental design using a comparison group, but without a pretest or random assignment; the researcher is unable to confirm that the groups are initially equivalent.

Statistical analysis: Describing and inferring about data based on characterizing the data sample numerically.

Statistical power: The probability associated with not making a Type II error.

Statistical regression effect: This effect occurs when participants have been selected who represent the extremes (extreme high or extreme low) on the dependent variable scale during pretesting. Subsequent posttests are likely to show change in the direction of the mean; very high scores are likely to change to somewhat lower scores and very low scores are likely to change to somewhat higher scores simply because the pretest levels were so extreme.

Statistics: Characteristics of a sample expressed in numbers.

Status differential: A situation where one party to an agreement has more power resources than the other(s).

Stepwise regression: A common form of multiple regression analysis in which researchers instruct the computer to try various combinations of predictors until it finds the "best fit" equation.

Stimulus variable: A variable manipulated in order to provoke a targeted response.

Stratified sampling: A random selection method in which the population is first divided into relevant subgroups, so that each person or message within each subgroup has an equal chance of being selected for the data sample.

Structuralism: A philosophy whose goal was the discovery of embedded rules or laws grounded in observation and experience.

Structure: A recognizable pattern or way of organizing talk in which utterances are somehow interrelated.

Structured interviews: Interviews having protocols or schedules that dictate what questions to ask when.

Style: One of the canons of rhetoric referring to the language the rhetor uses.

Style shifting: A form of codeswitching in which a speaker changes from one socially recognized way of talking to another, within a single speaking turn.

Subjectivity: Our human ability to know using our minds, based on our thoughts and feelings.

Summative evaluation: Evaluation that occurs after a communication process is completed.

Sums of squares between groups: In tests of difference, an estimate of the difference between group means.

Sums of squares within groups: In tests of difference, an estimate of chance variation, or the sampling error.

Survey population: A large collection of population members from which the sample is actually drawn; it is usually a subset of the target population.

Symbolic interactionism: A school of sociology grounded in constructivism and naturalism emphasizing how people construct and interpret the meaning of their experiences in everyday interaction.

Systematic observations: Observations that are derived from clear, known procedures.

Systematic sampling with a random start: A random selection method in which the researcher selects the first element from a sampling frame by chance, and thereafter, selects each next element systematically (i.e., each "kth element").

Tacit cultural knowledge: Knowledge used to generate behavior in culturally intended ways including taking actions, feeling, and using cultural artifacts.

Target participants: Naive or true participants from whom researchers collect a sample of data to assess as the basis of the experiment.

Target population: The complete set of population members forming an "ideal" population.

Taxonomy: In the data collection process, a categorizing scheme for identifying communication phenomena (behaviors, roles, events, texts, dispositions, or messages) that are related theoretically or conceptually. *See also* Coding scheme.

Telephone surveys: Interviews conducted by telephone using random or nonrandom selection methods.

Testing effects: Two types of effects resulting from a pretest. In one type of testing effect, participants can improve their scores just from practicing taking the test or measure more than one time. The second type of testing effect occurs when the test actually acts as a cueing device to sensitize participants to the goals of the study so that they respond to the manipulation of the independent variable in some way they would not have if they had not taken a pretest, sometimes called sensitization.

Test–retest method: Equivalence across multiple administrations of the same measure in the same group of subjects.

Text: Written or spoken words, performances, and visual/pictorial symbols used as evidence to support communication research claims.

Textual analysis: Any of several methodologies, such as discourse analysis or rhetorical criticism, that systematically explores written or spoken words, performances, and visual/pictorial symbols to be used as evidence in support of research claims.

Theoretical sampling: A process of collecting the additional data specifically needed to fill out one part of an emerging theory.

Theoretical saturation: The point in data collection when any new data adds little that is new or useful to the explanation or categories that have already been generated.

Theoretical sensitivity: Experience with and knowledge of communication theories.

Theoretical significance: The reasons that a certain topic of study is important to a group of scholars, usually because the topic will develop a theory, or advance an existing theory by testing or refuting some of its premises.

Theoretic discourse: Discourse that argues the truth of a constative statement.

Time progression effects: Those factors that rival the independent variable as sources or causes of effects because the experiment takes place over a period of time.

Time series design: A research design that assesses levels of the dependent variable at several points in time prior to and following the manipulation of the independent variable.

Title page: A page including the title of the paper, the writer's name and institutional affiliation, as well as contact information such as address, telephone number, and email address.

Total response rate: The percentage of total surveys successfully completed and collected.

Trade journals: Written publications aimed at practitioners in a particular business or industry.

Transcendence: In Burkean dramatism, the state of transforming the social hierarchy into a higher moral order through the redemptive cycle.

Transcription: The process of converting audio- or videotaped interactions into verbatim digital or print form.

Transcription veracity: The degree of correspondence between the words typed on a page (or in a computer file) and those recorded on a segment of audio- or videotape.

Transcripts: The translated spoken words and sounds in written form.

Transferability: The ability to apply confirmable, relevant insights from one study to other settings, participants, or texts.

Treatment diffusion effect: This effect occurs when participants in the treatment group tell participants in the control group about the treatment, thereby "contaminating" the control group; also called contamination.

Treatment groups: Groups that receive some exposure to the manipulation of the independent variable.

Trend studies: Studies conducted by examining several different representative samples from the same population at different points in time.

Triangulation: The use of several different kinds of evidence to support a research claim.

Trimodal distribution: A sample distribution with three modes.

Trope: A metaphor used as an ornamental literary device.

True experimental designs: Research designs that make use of comparison groups, random assignment, and pretests-posttests and that employ random sampling methods.

t-test: A statistical test of the effects of one categorical independent variable with two groups or samples on a continuous dependent variable.

Two-tailed test: A test that uses critical rejection regions under both tails of the normal curve distribution.

Type I error: An incorrect decision to reject the null hypothesis; that is, identifying a significant difference or relationship in the sample data when no difference or relationship exists in the population.

Type II error: A failure to reject the null hypothesis when it should have been rejected; that is, overlooking a significant difference or relationship that probably does exist in the population.

Unidimensional variables: Variables that cannot be broken down into subconstructs or factors.

Unimodal distribution: A sample distribution with one mode.

Unitizing: Dividing texts into units of analysis.

Units of analysis: The basic element, or part of a thing, to be analyzed.

Unobtrusive data collection procedures: Ways of collecting information that do not make the researcher's presence known to research participants.

Unstructured interviews: Interviews with no prespecified questions, relying entirely on the participants to identify experiences and events that seem significant or meaningful.

U-shaped correlation: A curvilinear relationship expressing patterns between continuous variables that change in direction at several points across time, first by decreasing together, then flattening out, and finally by increasing together.

Validity: Accuracy of measurement, and/or accuracy of applying conclusions from one study to other settings, persons, or situations; a standard for evaluating discovery research.

Variable: A communication phenomenon with a set of characteristics or groupings or scores; a construct that can take on an array of numerical values.

Verstehen: In hermeneutics, the understanding that develops out of our conscious awareness and interpretation of our experiences.

Victimage: In Burkean dramatism, the suffering of a scapegoat so that society can be redeemed.

Voice: The right to express one's own view, choice, wish, or opinion.

Warrant: Standards for evaluating the worth of the data as evidence of the claim.

Within-groups variance: In tests of difference, random variation or chance mean differences in sample distributions, also known as sampling error.

Within-subjects factor: An independent variable comprised of different treatment conditions in which one group of participants is exposed to all conditions sequentially.

Womanist criticism: Criticism that focuses on the domination of women on the basis of structural and cultural categories like gender, race, class, nationality, and sexuality, and the ways that these arrangements intersect within a patriarchal society.

x-**axis:**   Horizontal axis.

y-**axis:**   Vertical axis.

z-**axis:**   Depth axis.

z-**test for mean differences:**   A statistical test of difference of the effects of an independent variable with two categories on a continuous dependent variable when it is necessary to convert the two categories to standard scores.

References

Abelman, R., & Atkin, D. (2000). What children watch when they watch TV: Putting theory into practice. *Journal of Broadcasting & Electronic Media, 44,* 143–154.

Abelson, R. P. (1995). *Statistics as principled argument.* Hillsdale, NJ: Lawrence Erlbaum.

Adelman, M. B., & Frey, L. R. (1994). The pilgrim must embark: Creating and sustaining community in a residential facility for people with AIDS. In L. R. Frey (Ed.), *Group communication in context: Studies of natural groups* (pp. 3–22). Hillsdale, NJ: Lawrence Erlbaum.

Adelman, R. D., Greene, M. G., Charon, R., & Friedmann, E. (1992). The content of physician and elderly patient interaction in the primary care encounter. *Communication Research, 19,* 370–380.

Aden, R. C. (1994). The enthymeme as postmodern argument form: Condensed, mediated argument then and now. *Argumentation & Advocacy, 31,* 54–64.

Adler, P. A., Adler, P., and Fontana, A. (1987). Everyday life sociology. *Annual Review of Sociology, 13,* 217–235.

Afifi, W. A., & Burgoon, J. K. (2000). The impact of violations on uncertainty and the consequences for attractiveness. *Human Communication Research, 26,* 203–233.

Agar, M. H. (1983). Ethnographic evidence. *Urban Life, 12,* 32–48.

Alcoff, L. M. (1995). The problem of speaking for others. In J. Roof and R. Weigman (Eds.), *Who can speak? Authority and critical identity* (pp. 97–119). Urbana, IL: University of Illinois Press.

Allen, B. J. (1996). Feminist standpoint theory: A black woman's (re)-view of organizational socialization. *Communication Studies, 47,* 257–271.

Althaus, S. L. (1997). Computer-mediated communication in the university classroom: An experiment with on-line discussions. *Communication Education, 46* (3), 158–174.

Altheide, D. L. (1985). *Media power.* Beverly Hills, CA: Sage.

Amason, P., Allen, M. W., & Holmes, S. A. (1999). Social support and acculturative stress in the multicultural workplace. *Journal of Applied Communication Research, 27,* 310–334.

American Psychological Association. (2001). *Publication manual of the American Psychological Association* (5th ed.). Washington, DC: American Psychological Association.

Amidon, P. (1971). Nonverbal interaction analysis coding system (Chapter 4). *Nonverbal interaction analysis.* Minneapolis, MN: Paul S. Amidon & Associates, Inc.

Anderson, C. M. (2001). Communication in the medical interview team: An analysis of patients' stories in the United States and Hong Kong. *The Howard Journal of Communications, 12,* 61–72.

Anderson, C. M., Martin, M. M., & Zhong, M. (1998). Motives for communicating with family and friends: A Chinese study. *The Howard Journal of Communications, 9,* 109–122.

Anderson, J. A. (1987). *Communication research: Issues and methods.* New York: McGraw-Hill.

Andrews, J. R., Leff, M., & Terrill, R. (1998). *Reading rhetorical texts: An introduction to criticism.* Boston: Houghton Mifflin.

Andsager, J., & Smiley, L. (1998). Evaluating the public information: Shaping news coverage of the silicone implant controversy. *Public Relations Review, 24,* 183–201.

Ang, I. (1990). Culture and communication: Towards an ethnographic critique of media consumption in the transnational media system. *European Journal of Communication, 5,* 239–260.

Anzaldua, G. (1987). *Borderlands/La frontera: The new mestiza.* San Francisco: Spinsters/Aunt Lute.

Appel, E. C. (1997). The rhetoric of Dr. Martin Luther King, Jr.: Comedy and context in tragic collision. *Western Journal of Communication, 61,* 376–403.

Armstrong, G. B., & Chung, L. (2000). Background television and reading memory in context: Assessing TV interference and facilitative context effects on encoding versus retrieval processes. *Communication Research, 27,* 327–353.

Ashcraft, K. L., & Pacanowsky, M. E. (1996). A woman's worst enemy: Reflections on a narrative of organizational life and female identity. *Journal of Applied Communication Research, 24,* 217–239.

Atkinson, J. M., & Drew, P. (1979). *Order in the court: The organization of verbal interaction in judicial settings.* London: Macmillan.

Atkinson, J. M., & Heritage, J. (Eds.). (1984). *Structures of social action: Studies in conversation analysis.* Cambridge: Cambridge University Press.

Ausmus, W. A. (1998). Pragmatic uses of metaphor: Models and metaphor in the nuclear winter scenario. *Communication Monographs, 65,* 67–82.

Ayres, J., & Heuett, B. L. (2000). An examination of the long term effect of performance visualization. *Communication Research Reports, 17,* 229–236.

Ayres, J., Heuett, B., & Sonandre, D. A. (1998). Testing a refinement in an intervention for communication apprehension. *Communication Reports, 11,* 73–86.

Babbie, E. (1995). *The practice of social research* (7th ed.). Belmont, CA: Wadsworth.

Babbie, E. (2001). *The practice of social research* (9th ed.). Belmont, CA: Wadsworth.

Bachman, G., & Zakahi, W. R. (2000). Adult attachment and strategic relational communication: Love schemas and affinity-seeking. *Communication Reports, 13,* 11–20.

Bakardjieva, M., & Smith, R. (2001). The Internet in everyday life: Computer networking from the standpoint of the domestic user. *New Media & Society, 3,* 67–83.

Bales, R. F. (1950*). Interaction process analysis: A method for the study of small groups.* Reading, MA: Addison-Wesley.

Barker, D. C. (1998). Political talk radio and health care (un)reform. *Political Communication, 15,* 83–97.

Barnes, J. A., & Hayes, A. F. (1995). Language arts practices in the instruction of oral communication in California high schools. *Communication Reports, 8,* 61–68.

Barnhurst, K. G. (2003). The makers of meaning: National Public Radio and the new long journalism, 1980–2000. *Political Communication. 20* (1), 1–22.

Bastien, D. T., & Hostager, T. J. (1992). Cooperation as a communicative accomplishment: A symbolic interaction analysis of an improvised jazz concert. *Communication Studies, 43* (2), 92–104.

Battles, K., & Hilton-Morrow, W. (2002). Gay characters in conventional spaces: *Will and Grace* and the situation comedy genre. *Critical Studies in Mass Communication, 19,* 87–105.

Bavelas, J. B., Black, A., Chovil, N., Lemery, C. R., & Mullett, J. (1988). Form and function in motor mimicry: Topographic evidence that the primary function is communicative. *Human Communication Research, 14,* 275–300.

Baxter, J. (2002). Competing discourses in the classroom: A post-structuralist discourse analysis of girls' and boys' speech in public contexts. *Discourse & Society, 13,* 827–842.

Baxter, L. A., & Goldsmith, D. (1990). Cultural terms for communication events among some American high school adolescents. *Western Journal of Speech Communication, 54,* 377–394.

Baxter, L. A., & Montgomery, B. M. (1998). A guide to dialectical approaches to studying personal relationships. In B. M. Montgomery & L. A. Baxter (Eds.), *Dialectical approaches to studying personal relationships* (pp. 1–15). Mahwah, NJ: Lawrence Erlbaum.

Beach, W. A. (1989a). Orienting to the phenomenon. In J. A. Anderson (Ed.), *Communication Yearbook, 13* (pp. 216–234). Newbury Park, CA: Sage.

Beach, W. A. (1989b). Sequential organization of conversational activities. *Western Journal of Speech Communication (special issue), 53,* 85–246.

Beasley, B., & Standley, T. C. (2002). Shirts vs. skins: Clothing as an indicator of gender role stereotyping in video games. *Mass Communication & Society, 5* (3), 279–293.

Beck, C. (1996). "I've got some points I'd like to make here": The achievement of social face through turn management during the 1992 vice presidential debate. *Political Communication, 13,* 165–180.

Behnke, R. R., & Sawyer, C. R. (1999). Public speaking procrastination as a correlate of public speaking communication apprehension and self-perceived public speaking competence. *Communication Research Reports, 16,* 40–47.

Behnke, R. R., & Sawyer, C. R. (2000). Anticipatory anxiety patterns for male and female public speakers. *Communication Education, 49,* 187–195.

Benoit, W. L. (1995). *Accounts, excuses, and apologies: A theory of image restoration strategies.* Albany: State University of New York Press.

Benoit, W. L., & Currie, H. (2001). Inaccuracies in media coverage of presidential debates. *Argumentation & Advocacy, 38,* 28–39.

Bereleson, B. (1952). *Content analysis in communication research.* New York: Hafner.

Berger, A. A. (1998). *Media research techniques* (2nd ed.). Thousand Oaks, CA: Sage.

Bernard, H., & Kilworth, P. (1977). Informant accuracy in social network data II. *Human Communication Research, 4,* 3–18.

Bernard, H., Kilworth, P., & Sailer, L. (1980). Informant accuracy in social network data IV: A comparison of clique-level structure in behavioral and cognitive network data. *Social Networks, 2,* 191–218.

Bernard, H., Kilworth, P., & Sailer, L. (1982). Informant accuracy in social network data V: An experimental attempt to predict actual communication from recall data. *Social Science Research, 11,* 30–66.

Berry, M., & Gray, T. (1999). Cutting film violence: Effects of perceptions, enjoyment, and arousal. *Journal of Social Psychology, 139,* 567–583.

Bethea, L. S. (2001). The function of humor within the lives of older adults. *Communication Quarterly, 2,* 49–56.

Bhabha, H. K. (1990). The Other question: Difference, discrimination, and the discourse of colonialism. In R. Ferguson, M. Gever, T. T. Minh-Ha, & C. West (Eds.), *Out there: Marginalization and contemporary culture* (pp. 71–88). Cambridge, MA: MIT Press.

Bhabha, H. K. (1995). Cultural diversity and cultural differences. In B. Ashcraft, G. Griffiths, & H. Tiffin (Eds.), *The post-colonial studies reader* (pp. 206–212). London: Routledge.

Billings, A. C., Halone, K. K., & Denham, B. E. (2002). "Man, that was a pretty shot": An analysis of gendered broadcast commentary surrounding the 2000 men's and women's NCAA Final Four Basketball Championships. *Mass Communication & Society, 5* (3), 295–315.

Bilmes, J. (1976). Rules and rhetoric: Negotiating the social order in a Thai village. *Journal of Anthropological Research, 32,* 44–57.

Bitzer, L. F. (1959). Aristotle's enthymeme revisited. *Quarterly Journal of Speech, 45,* 399–408.

Black, E. (1994). Gettysburg and silence. *Quarterly Journal of Speech, 80,* 21–36.

Blanchard, M. E. (1980). *Description: Sign, self, desire.* The Hague: Mouton.

Blyler, N. R. (1994). Habermas, empowerment, and professional discourse. *Technical Communication Quarterly, 3,* 125.

Boal, A. (1998). *Games for actors and non-actors* (A. Jackson, Trans.). London: Routledge.

Bochner, A. P. (1985). Perspectives on inquiry: Representation, conversation, and reflection. In M. L. Knapp & G. R. Miller (Eds.), *Handbook of interpersonal communication* (pp. 27–58). Beverly Hills, CA: Sage.

Bode, D. (1990). The world as it happens: Ethnomethodology and conversation analysis. In G. Ritzer (Ed.), *Frontiers of social theory: The new synthesis* (pp. 185–213). New York: Columbia University Press.

Bogdan, R. C., & Biklen, S. K. (1982). *Qualitative research for education: An introduction to theory and methods.* Boston: Allyn & Bacon.

Booth, W. C., Colomb, G. G., & Williams, J. M. (1995). *The craft of research.* Chicago: University of Chicago Press.

Bordia, P., & Rosnow, R. L. (1998). Rumor rest stops on the information highway: Transmission patterns in a computer-mediated rumor chain. *Human Communication Research, 25,* 163–179.

Bormann, E. G. (1972). Fantasy and rhetorical vision: The rhetorical criticism of social reality. *Quarterly Journal of Speech, 58,* 396–407.

Botan, C. (1996). Communication work and electronic surveillance: A model for predicting panoptic effects. *Communication Monographs, 63,* 293–313.

Bowers, D. L. (1996). When outsiders encounter insiders in speaking: Oppressed collectives on the defensive. *Journal of Black Studies, 26,* 490–503.

Bowman, M. S. (1996). Performing literature in the age of textuality. *Communication Education, 45,* 96–101.

Bowman, M. S., & Kistenberg, C. J. (1992). "Textual power" and the subject of oral interpretation: An alternate approach to performing literature. *Communication Education, 41,* 287–299.

Bradford, L., Meyers, R. A., & Kane, K. A. (1999). Latino expectations of communicative competence: A focus group interview study. *Communication Quarterly, 47,* 98–117.

Braithwaite, C. (1997a). Blood money: The routine violation of conversational rules. *Communication Reports, 10,* 63–73.

Braithwaite, C. (1997b). Sa'ah Naaghai Bik'eh Hozhoon: An ethnography of Navajo educational communication practices. *Communication Education, 46,* 1–15.

Braithwaite, C. (1997c). Were *you* there?: A ritual of legitimacy among Vietnam veterans. *Western Journal of Communication, 61,* 423–447.

Braithwaite, D. O., Dollar, N. J., Fitch, K. L., & Geist, P. (1996, Feb.). *Case studies for "ethics in qualitative research."* Panel presented at the annual meeting of the Western States Communication Association, Pasadena, CA.

Brants, K., & Neijens, P. (1998). The infotainment of politics. *Political Communication, 15* (2), 149–164.

Brock, B. L. (1990). Rhetorical criticism: A Burkeian approach revisited. In B. L. Brock, R. L. Scott, & J. W. Chesebro. *Methods of rhetorical criticism: A twentieth-century perspective* (3rd ed.), pp. 183–195. Detroit: Wayne State University Press.

Brock, B. L., Scott, R. L., & Chesebro, J. W. (1990). *Methods of rhetorical criticism: A twentieth-century perspective* (3rd ed.). Detroit: Wayne State University Press.

Brodkey, L. (1987). Writing ethnographic narratives. *Written Communication, 4,* 25–50.

Brookey, R. A., & Westerfelhaus, R. (2002). Hiding homoeroticism in plain view: The *Fight Club* DVD as digital closet. *Critical Studies in Mass Communication, 19,* 21–43.

Brown, P., & Levinson, S. C. (1987). *Politeness: Some universals in language usage.* Cambridge: Cambridge University Press.

Browning, L. D., & Beyer, J. M. (1998). The structuring of shared voluntary standards in the U. S. semiconductor industry: Communicating to reach agreement. *Communication Monographs, 65,* 220–243.

Bruess, C. J. S., & Pearson, J. C. (1997). Interpersonal rituals in marriage and adult friendship. *Communication Monographs, 64,* 25–46.

Brummett, B. (1994). *Rhetoric in popular culture.* New York: St. Martin's Press.

Buchmann, M., (1992). Observation: Dilemmas and virtues in research communication. *Curriculum Inquiry, 22,* 313–329.

Bulmer, M. (1979). Concepts in the analysis of qualitative data. *Sociological Review, 27,* 651–677.

Burgoon, J. K., Buller, D. B., Guerrero, L. K., & Feldman, C. M. (1994). Interpersonal deception VI: Effects of pre-interactional and interactional factors on deceiver and observer perceptions of deception success. *Communication Studies, 45,* 263–280.

Burgoon, J. K., Johnson, M. L., & Koch, P. T. (1998). The nature and measurement of interpersonal dominance. *Communication Monographs, 65* (4), 308–335.

Burgoon, J. K., & Le Poire, B. A. (1999). Nonverbal cues and interpersonal judgments: Participant and observer perceptions of intimacy, dominance, composure, and formality. *Communication Monographs, 66,* 105–124.

Burgoon, J. K., Parrott, R., Le Poire, B. A., Kelley, D. L., Walther, J. B., & Perry, D. (1989). Maintaining and restoring privacy through communication in different types of relationships. *Journal of Social and Personal Relationships, 6,* 131–158.

Burgoon, M. & Bailey, W. (1992). PC at last! PC at last! Thank God almighty, we are PC at last! *Journal of Communication, 42,* 95–104.

Burke, K. (1969a). *A grammar of motives.* Berkeley, CA: University of California Press.

Burke, K. (1969b). *A rhetoric of motives.* Berkeley, CA: University of California Press.

Burleson, B. R., & Samter, W. (1996). Similarity in the communication skills of young adults: Foundations of attraction, friendship, and relationship satisfaction. *Communication Reports, 9,* 127–140.

Butler, J. (1990). *Gender trouble: Feminism and the subversion of identity.* New York: Routledge.

Butler, J. (1993). *Bodies that matter: On the discursive limits of 'sex'.* New York: Routledge.

Buttny, R. (1987). Sequence and practical reasoning in account episodes. *Communication Quarterly, 35,* 67–83.

Buzzanell, P. M., Burrell, N. A., Stafford, S., & Berkowitz, S. (1996). When I call you up and you're not there: Application of communication accommodation theory to telephone answering machine messages. *Western Journal of Communication, 60,* 310–336.

Cai, X., & Gantz, W. (2000). Online privacy issues associated with Web sites for children. *Journal of Broadcasting & Electronic Media, 44,* 197–214.

Calas, M. B., & Smircich, L. (1996). From "the Woman's" point of view: Feminist approaches to organization studies. In S. Clegg, C. Hardy, and W. R. Nord (Eds.), *Handbook of organization studies* (pp. 218–257). London: Sage.

Campbell, D. T., & Stanley, J.C. (1963). *Experimental and quasi-experimental designs for research.* Chicago: Rand McNally.

Campbell, K. K. (1973). The rhetoric of women's liberation. *Quarterly Journal of Speech, 59,* 74–86.

Campbell, K. K. (1974). Criticism: Ephemeral and enduring. *Speech Teacher, 23,* 9–14.

Campbell, K. K., & Jamieson, K. H. (1978). Form and genre in rhetorical criticism: An introduction. In K. K. Campbell & K. H. Jamieson, (Eds.), *Form and genre: Shaping rhetorical action* (pp. 18–25). Falls Church, VA: Speech Communication Association.

Cappella, J. N. (1990). The method of proof by example in interaction analysis. *Communication Monographs, 57,* 236–242.

Capper, C. A. (1992). A feminist poststructural analysis of non-traditional approaches in education administration. *Educational Administration Quarterly, 28* (1), 103–124.

Carbaugh, D. (1988). Cultural terms and tensions in the speech at a television station. *Western Journal of Speech Communication, 52,* 216–237.

Carbaugh, D. (1993). "Soul" and "self": Soviet and American cultures in conversation. *Quarterly Journal of Speech, 79,* 182–200.

Carpenter, N. (1999). Pictures of prostitutes: The discursive battle of subject position. *Communicate, 28* (2), 21–44.

Casey, M. W. (2001). From British Ciceronianism to American Baconianism: Alexander Campbell as a case study of a shift in rhetorical theory. *Southern Communication Journal, 66,* 151–166.

Cegala, D. J., McGee, S., & McNeilis, K. S. (1996). Components of patient's and doctor's perceptions of communication competence during a primary medical care interview. *Health Communication, 8,* 1–27.

Cezec-Kecmanovic, D., Treleaven, L., & Moodie, D. (2000). Computer-mediated communication: Challenges of knowledge-sharing. *Australian Journal of Communication, 27,* 51–66.

Chadwick, S. A. (1999). Teaching virtually via the web: Comparing student performance and attitudes about communication in lecture, virtual web-based, and web-supplemented courses. *Electronic Journal of Communication, 9* (1).

Chang, H. J., & Johnson, J. D. (2001). Communication networks as predictors of organizational members' media choices. *Western Journal of Communication, 65,* 349–369.

Chan-Olmstead, S. M., & Park, J. S. (2000). From on-air to online world: Examining the content and structures of broadcast TV stations' web sites. *Journalism & Mass Communication Quarterly, 77,* 321–339.

Chen, L. (1997). Verbal adaptive strategies in U.S. American dyadic interactions with U.S. American or East-Asian partners. *Communication Monographs, 64,* 302–323.

Cheney, G. (1995). Democracy in the workplace: Theory and practice from the perspective of communication. *Journal of Applied Communication Research, 23,* 167–200.

Cheney, G., & Carroll, C. (1997). The person as object in discourses in and around organizations. *Communication Research, 24,* 593–630.

Cheng, H. (1997). Toward an understanding of cultural values manifest in advertising: A content analysis of Chinese television commercials in 1990 and 1995. *Journalism and Mass Communication Quarterly, 74,* 773–796.

Chesebro, J. L. (1999). The relationship between listening styles and conversational sensitivity. *Communication Research Reports, 16,* 233–238.

Chien, S. C. (1996). Code-switching as a verbal strategy among Chinese in a campus setting in Taiwan. *World Englishes, 15,* 267–280.

Childress, H. (1998). Kinder ethnographic writing. *Qualitative Inquiry, 4,* 249–264.

Chung, L.C., & Ting-Toomey, S. (1999). Ethnic identity and relational expectations among Asian-Americans. *Communication Research Reports, 16,* 157–166.

Clair, R. P. (1993). The use of framing devices to sequester organizational narratives: Hegemony and harassment. *Communication Monographs, 60,* 113–136.

Clair, R. P. (1994). Resistance and oppression as a self-contained opposite: An organizational communication analysis of one man's story of sexual harassment. *Western Journal of Communication, 58,* 235–262.

Clair, R. P. (1997). Organizing silence: Silence as voice and voice as silence in the narrative exploration of the Treaty of New Echota. *Western Journal of Communication, 61,* 315–337.

Clair, R. P., & Kunkel, A. W. (1998). "Unrealistic realities": Child abuse and the aesthetic resolution. *Communication Monographs, 65,* 24–46.

Clarke, J. N. (1999). Prostate cancer's hegemonic masculinity in select print mass media depictions (1974–1995). *Health Communication, 11 (1),* 59–74.

Cleary, R. M. (1993). Rap music and its political connections: An annotated bibliography. *RSR: Reference Service Review, 21* (2), 77–90.

Collier, M. J. (1996). Communication competence problematics in ethnic friendships. *Communication Monographs, 63,* 314–336.

Collier, M. J. (1998). Researching cultural identity: Reconciling interpretive and postcolonial perspectives. In D. V. Tanno & A. Gonzalez (Eds.), *Communication identity across cultures* (pp. 122–147). Thousand Oaks, CA: Sage.

Collinson, D., & Hearn, J. (1994). Naming men as men: Implications for work, organization, and management. *Gender, Work, and Organization, 1,* 2–22.

Communication Studies 298. (1999). Shopping for family. *Qualitative Inquiry, 5,* 147–180.

Conquergood, D. (1983). "A sense of the other": Interpretation and ethnographic research. In I. N. Grouch, & O. R. Gordon (Eds.), *Proceedings of the seminar/conference on oral traditions.* Las Cruces: New Mexico State University.

Conquergood, D. (1991). Rethinking ethnography: Towards a critical cultural politics. *Communication Monographs, 58,* 179–194.

Conquergood, D. (1992). Life in Big Red: Struggles and accommodations in a Chicago polyethnic tenement. In L. Lamphere (Ed.), *Structuring diversity: Ethnographic perspectives on the new immigration* (pp. 94–144). Chicago: University of Chicago Press.

Conquergood, D. (1994). Homeboys and hoods: Gang communication and cultural space. In L. R. Frey (Ed.), *Group communication in cultural context: Studies of natural groups* (pp. 23–55). Hillsdale, NJ: Lawrence Erlbaum.

Conquergood, D. (1995). Between rigor and relevance: Rethinking applied communication. In K. N. Cissna (Ed.), *Applied communication in the 21st century* (pp. 79–96). Mahwah, NJ: Lawrence Erlbaum.

Conquergood, D. (Producer), & Siegel, T. (Producer & Director). (1990). *The heart broken in half* [Videotape]. Chicago: Siegel Productions; New York: Filmmakers Library.

Conrad, C. (1988). Work songs, hegemony, and illusions of self. *Critical Studies in Mass Communication, 5,* 179–201.

Cook, T. D., & Campbell, D. T. (1979). *Quasi-experimentation: Design and analysis issues for field settings.* Chicago: Rand McNalley.

Cooper, B. (2002). *Boys Don't Cry* and female masculinity: Reclaiming a life & dismantling the politics of normative heterosexuality. *Critical Studies in Mass Communication, 19,* 44–63.

Cooper, B., & Descutner, D. (1997). Strategic silences and transgressive metaphors in "Out of Africa": Isak Dinesen's double-voiced rhetoric of complicity and subversion. *Southern Communication Journal, 62,* 333–343.

Couchman, W. (1995). Using video and conversational analysis to train staff working with people with learning disabilities. *Journal of Advanced Nursing, 22* (6), 1112–1120.

Courtright, J. A. (1984). Methods of integrating observational and traditional data analysis. *Communication Quarterly, 32,* 197–206.

Craig, R. T., Tracy, K., & Spisak, F. (1986). The discourse of requests: Assessment of a politeness approach. *Human Communication Research, 12,* 437–468.

Crawford, L. (1996). Personal ethnography. *Communication Monographs, 63,* 158–170.

Crowell, T. L., & Emmers-Sommer, T. M. (2001). "If I knew then what I know now": Seropositive individuals' perceptions of partner trust, safety and risk prior to HIV infection. *Communication Studies, 52,* 302–323.

Dahlberg, J. S. (2001). Message attributes of advertising found during daytime fringe talk show television: A descriptive analysis. *Communication Research Reports, 18,* 200–210.

Dainton, M. (1998). Everyday interaction in marital relationships: Variations in relative importance and event duration. *Communication Reports, 11,* 101–109.

Dangle, L. F., & Haussman, A. M., (1963). *Preparing the research paper* (3rd ed.). Fairfield, NJ: Cebco Standard Publishing.

Davis, F. (1973). The Martian and the Convert: Ontological polarities in social research. *Urban Life, 2,* 333–343.

Davis, O. I. (1999). In the kitchen: Transforming the academy through safe spaces of resistance. *Western Journal of Communication. 63,* 364–381.

Deetz, S. A. (1982). Critical interpretive research in organizational communication. *Western Journal of Speech Communication, 46,* 131–149.

Deetz, S. A. (1992a). *Democracy in an Age of Corporate Colonization.* Ithaca: State University of New York Press.

Deetz, S. A. (1992b). Disciplinary power in the modern corporation. In M. Alvesson & H. Willmott (Eds.), *Critical management studies* (pp. 21–45). Newbury Park, CA: Sage.

Delgado, F. P. (1998a). Chicano ideology revisited: Rap music and the (re)articulation of Chicanoism, *Western Journal of Communication, 62,* 95–113.

Delgado, F. P. (1998b). When the silenced speak: The textualization and complications of Latina/o identity. *Western Journal of Communication, 62,* 420–438.

Denzin, N. K. (1978). *The research act* (2nd ed.). New York: McGraw Hill.

Denzin, N. K. (1999). Two-stepping in the '90s. *Qualitative Inquiry, 5,* 568–572.

Denzin, N. K., & Lincoln, Y. S. (Eds.) (1998). *Strategies of qualitative inquiry.* Thousand Oaks, CA: Sage.

Derrida, J. (1976). *Of grammatology* (G. Spivak, Trans.). Baltimore: Johns Hopkins University Press. (Original work published in 1972.)

Derrida, J. (1978). *Writing and difference* (A. Bass, Trans.). Chicago: University of Chicago Press.

Derrida, J. (1981). *Positions* (A. Bass, Trans.). Chicago: University of Chicago Press.

DeStephen, R. S. (1983). Group interaction differences between high and low consensus groups. *Western Journal of Speech Communication, 47,* 340–363.

Dimmick, J., Kline, S., & Stafford, L. (2000). The gratification niches of personal e-mail and the telephone. *Communication Research, 27,* 227–249.

Doerfel, M. A., & Barnett, G. A. (1999). A semantic network analysis of the International Communication Association. *Human Communication Research, 25,* 589–603.

Dollar, N. J. (1995, Feb.). "What a long strange trip it's been": Understanding the expression of cultural identity. Paper presented at the annual meeting of the Western States Communication Association, Portland, OR.

Dollar, N. J. (1999). "Show talk" and communal identity: An analysis of Deadheads' ways of speaking. *Journal of the Northwestern Communication Association, 26,* 101–120.

Dollar, N. J., & Beck, C. (1997). *Advancing and supporting claims in ethnography of communication.* Workshop presented at the annual meeting of the Western States Communication Association, Monterey, CA.

Dollar, N. J., & Merrigan, G. (2002). Ethnographic practices in group communication research (pp. 59–78). In L. Frey (Ed.), *New directions in small group communication research.* Mahwah, NJ: Lawrence Erlbaum.

Dollar, N. J., & Zimmers, B. (1998). Social identity and communicative boundaries: An analysis of youth and young adult street speakers in a U.S. American community. *Communication Research, 25,* 596–617.

Dorazio, P., & Stovall, J. (1997). Research in context: Ethnographic usability. *Journal of Technical Writing and Communication, 27,* 57–67.

Dorsey, L. G. (1995). The frontier myth in presidential rhetoric: Theodore Roosevelt's campaign for conservation. *Western Journal of Communication, 59,* 1–20.

Douglas, J. (1967). *The social meanings of suicide.* Princeton, NJ: Princeton University Press.

Douglas, J. D. (1976). *Investigative social research: Individual and team field research.* Beverly Hills, CA: Sage.

Dow, B. J. (1990). Hegemony, feminist criticism, and "The Mary Tyler Moore Show." *Critical Studies in Mass Communication, 7,* 261–274.

Drzewiecka, J. A., & Nakayama, T. K. (1998). City sites: Politics of urban space and communication of identity. *Southern Journal of Communication, 64,* 20–31.

Eisenberg, E. (1990). Transcendence through organizing. *Communication Research, 17,* 139–164.

Eisenberg, E., Murphy, A., & Andrews, L. (1998). Openness and decision making in the search for a university provost. *Communication Monographs, 65,* 1–23.

Ellingson, L. L. (1998). "Then you know how I feel": Empathy, identification, and reflexivity in fieldwork. *Qualitative Inquiry, 4,* 492–514.

Ellis, D. G. (1976). *An analysis of relational communication in ongoing group systems.* Unpublished doctoral thesis, Department of Communication, University of Utah.

Ely, R. J. (1995). The power in demography: Women's social constructions of gender identity at work. *Academy of Management Journal, 38,* 589–634.

Emmers-Sommer, T. M. (1999). Negative relational events and event responses across relationship-type: Examining and comparing the impact of conflict strategy-use on intimacy in same-sex friendships, opposite-sex friendships and romantic relationships. *Communication Research Reports, 16,* 286–295.

Emmers-Sommer, T. M., & Allen, M. (1999). Surveying the effects of media effects: A meta-analytic summary of the media effects research. *Human Communication Research, 25,* 478–497.

Evans, W. (1996). Divining the social order: Class, gender, and magazine astrology columns. *Journalism and Mass Communication Quarterly, 73,* 389–400.

Eveland, W. P., Jr., & Dunwoody, S. (2001). User control and structural isomorphism or disorientation and cognitive load? Learning from the Web versus print. *Communication Research, 28,* 48–79.

Fairchild, H. H., & Cozens, J. A. (1981). Chicano, Hispanic, or Mexican American: What's in a name? *Hispanic Journal of Behavioral Sciences, 3,* 191–198.

Feeley, T. H. (2000). Testing a communication network model of employee turnover based on centrality. *Journal of Applied Communication Research, 28,* 262–277.

Feldman, M. S. (1995). *Strategies for interpreting qualitative data.* Thousand Oaks, CA: Sage University Paper (Qualitative Research Methods Series #33).

Felts, A. A. (1992). Organizational communication: A critical perspective. *Administration and Society, 23,* 495–513.

Ferguson, G. A. (1981). *Statistical analysis in psychology and education* (5th ed.). New York: McGraw-Hill.

Ferguson, M. (1990). Images of power and the feminist fallacy. *Critical Studies in Mass Communication, 7,* 215–230.

Fiebig, G. V., & Kramer, M. W. (1998). A framework for the study of emotions in organizational contexts. *Management Communication Quarterly, 11,* 536–572.

Fine, G. A. (1993). Ten lies of ethnography: Moral dilemmas of field research. *Journal of Contemporary Ethnography, 22,* 267–293.

Fink, E. J., & Gantz, W. (1996). A content analysis of three mass communication research traditions: Social science, interpretive studies, and critical analysis. *Journalism & Mass Communication Quarterly, 73,* 114–134.

Fischer, E., & Bristor, J. (1994). A feminist post-structural analysis of the rhetoric of marketing relationships. *International Journal of Research in Marketing, 11,* 317–331.

Fisher, B. A. (1970). The process of decision modification in small groups. *Journal of Communication, 20,* 51–64.

Fisher, W. R. (1978). Toward a logic of good reasons. *Quarterly Journal of Speech, 64,* 376–384.

Fisher. W. R. (1987). *Human communication as narration: Toward a philosophy of reason, value, and action.* Columbia: University of South Carolina Press.

Fisher, W. R. (1989). Clarifying the narrative paradigm. *Communication Monographs, 56,* 55–58.

Fisherkeller, J. (1999). Learning about power and success: Young urban adolescents interpret TV culture. *Communication Review, 3,* 187–213.

Fitch, K. L. (1994). Criteria for evidence in qualitative research. *Western Journal of Communication, 58,* 32–38.

Flaherty, L. M., Pearce, K. J., & Rubin, R. B. (1998). Internet and face-to-face communication: Not functional alternatives. *Communication Quarterly, 46* (3), 250–268.

Floyd, C., & Burgoon, J. K. (1999). Reacting to nonverbal expressions of liking: A test of interaction adaptation theory. *Communication Monographs, 66,* 219–239.

Foss, K. A., & Foss, S. K. (1988). Incorporating the feminist perspective in communication scholarship: A research commentary. In C. Spitzack and K. Carter (Eds.), *Doing research on women's communication: Alternative perspectives in theory and method.* Norwood, NJ: Ablex.

Foss, K. A., & Foss, S. K. (1994). Personal experience as evidence in feminist scholarship. *Western Journal of Communication, 58,* 39–43.

Foss, K. A., Foss, S. K., & Griffin, C. L. (1999). *Feminist rhetorical theories.* Thousand Oaks, CA: Sage.

Foss, K. A., & Littlejohn, S. W. (1986). *The Day After:* Rhetorical vision in an ironic frame. *Critical Studies in Mass Communication, 3,* 317–336.

Foss, S. K. (1988). *Rhetorical criticism: Exploration and practice.* Prospect Heights, IL: Waveland Press.

Foss, S. K. (1996). *Rhetorical criticism: Exploration and practice* (2nd ed.). Prospect Heights, IL: Waveland Press.

Foucault, M. (1980). *Power/knowledge: Selected interviews and other writings, 1927–1977* (C. Gordon and others, Trans.). C. Gordon (Ed.). New York: Pantheon.

Foucault, M. (1983). The subject and power. In H. Dreyfus & P. Rabinow. *Michel Foucault: Beyond structuralism and hermeneutics* (2nd ed., pp. 208–226). Chicago: University of Chicago Press.

Frankfort-Nachmias, C., & Nachmias, D. (1996). *Research methods in the social sciences* (5th ed.). New York: St. Martin's Press.

Frey, L. R. (1994a). The call of the field: Studying communication in natural groups. In L. R. Frey (Ed.), *Group communication in context: Studies of bona fide groups* (2nd ed., pp. ix–xiv). Mahwah, NJ: Lawrence Erlbaum.

Frey, L. R. (Ed.) (1994b). The naturalistic paradigm: Studying small groups in the postmodern era. *Small Group Research, 25* (4), 551–577.

Frey, L. R., Adelman, M. B., Flint, L. J., & Query, J. L., Jr. (2000). Weaving meanings together in an AIDS residence: Communicative practices, perceived health outcomes, and the symbolic construction of community. *Journal of Health Communication, 5,* 53–73.

Frey, L. R., Botan, C. H., & Kreps, G. L. (2000). *Investigating communication: An introduction to research methods* (2nd ed.). Boston: Allyn & Bacon.

Frymier, A. B., & Houser, M. L. (1998). Does making content relevant make a difference in learning? *Communication Research Reports, 15,* 121–129.

Furman, W., & Simon, V. A. (1998). Advice from youth: Some lessons from the study of adolescent relationships. *Journal of Social and Personal Relationships, 15,* 723–739.

Galvin, J. (1999). *Writing literature reviews: A guide for students of the social and behavioral sciences.* Los Angeles: Pyrczak Publishing.

Garfinkel, H. (1967). *Studies in ethnomethodology.* Englewood Cliffs, NJ: Prentice-Hall.

Geertz, C. (1973). *The interpretation of cultures: Selected essays.* New York: Basic Books.

Gerbner, G., Gross, L., Morgan, M., & Signorelli, N. (1986). Living with television: The dynamics of the cultivation process. In J. Bryant & D. Zillman (Eds.), *Perspectives on media effects.* Hillsdale, NJ: Lawrence Erlbaum.

Getis, A. (1995). *The tyranny of data.* San Diego, CA: San Diego State University Press.

Gibaldi, J. (1995). *MLA handbook for writers of research papers* (4th ed.). New York: Modern Language Association of America.

Gilbert, J. R. (1997). Performing marginality: Comedy, identity, and cultural critique. *Text and Performance Quarterly, 17,* 317–330.

Gill, A. (1994). *Rhetoric and human understanding.* Prospect Heights, IL: Waveland Press.

Gilligan, C. (1982). *In a different voice: Psychological theory and women's development.* Cambridge: Harvard University Press.

Glaser, B. G., & Strauss, A. L. (1967). *The discovery of grounded theory: Strategies for qualitative research.* Chicago: Aldine.

Glionna, J. M. (2000, Nov. 13)). Dot-com spurs angry protests: S.F. locals upset over rising land prices in city. *Los Angeles Times,* p. 02D.

Godard, D. (1977). Same setting, different norms: Phone call beginnings in France and the United States. *Language in Society, 6,* 209–219.

Goetz, J. P., & LeCompte, M. D. (1984). *Ethnography and qualitative design in educational research.* Orlando, FL: Academic Press.

Goffman, E. (1961). *Asylums.* Garden City, NY: Doubleday.

Goffman, E. (1971). *Relations in public.* New York: Harper and Row.

Goldzwig, S. R., & Sullivan, P. A. (1995). Post-assassination newspaper editorial eulogies: Analysis and assessment. *Western Journal of Communication, 59,* 125–151.

Goldzwig, S. R., & Sullivan, P. A. (2000). Narrative and counternarrative in print-mediated coverage of Milwaukee alderman Michael McGee. *Quarterly Journal of Speech, 86,* 215–231.

Golish, T. D., & Caughlin, J. P. (2002). "I'd rather not talk about it": Adolescents' and young adults' use of topic avoidance in stepfamilies. *Journal of Applied Communication Research, 30,* 78–106.

Goodall, H. L. (1989). On becoming an organizational detective: The role of context sensitivity and intuitive logics in communication consulting. *Southern Communication Journal, 55* (1), 42–54.

Goodall, H. L. (2000). *Writing the new ethnography.* Walnut Creek, CA: AltaMira Press.

Goodwin, C. (1979). The interactive construction of a sentence in natural conversation. In G. Psathas (Ed.), *Everyday language: Studies in ethnomethodology.* New York: Irvington Publishers.

Goodwin, C. (1980). Restarts, pauses, and the achievement of a state of mutual eye gaze at turn-beginning. *Sociological Inquiry, 50,* 277–302.

Goodwin, C. (1981). *Conversational organization: Interactions between speakers and hearers.* New York: Academic Press.

Gordon, J. (2002). From gangs to the academy: Scholars emerge by reaching back through critical ethnography. *Social Justice, 29,* 71–82.

Gorham, J., Cohen, S. H., & Morris, T. L. (1999). Fashion in the classroom III: Effects of instructor attire and immediacy in natural classroom interactions. *Communication Quarterly, 47,* 281–299.

Gouldner, A. W. (1988). The sociologist as partisan: Sociology and the welfare state. *American Sociologist, 3,* 103–116.

Gow, J. (1996). Reconsidering gender roles on MTV: Depictions in the most popular music videos of the early 1990s. *Communication Reports, 9,* 151–162.

Grabe, M. E. (1999). Television news magazine crime stories: A functionalist perspective. *Critical Studies in Mass Communication, 2,* 155–171.

Grabe, M. E. (2002). Maintaining the moral order: A functional analysis of "The Jerry Springer Show." *Critical Studies in Media Communication, 19* (3), 311–328.

Grabe, M. E., Lang, A., Shuhua, Z., & Bolls, P. D. (2000). Cognitive access to negatively arousing news. *Research, 27* (1), 3–27.

Graham, E. E. (1997). Turning points and commitment in post-divorce relationships. *Communication Monographs, 64,* 350–368.

Gramsci, A. (1971). *Selections from the prison notebooks* (Q. Hoare & G. Nowell Smith, Trans.). New York: International.

Grant, L., & Starks, D. (2001). Screening appropriate teaching materials: Closings from textbooks and television soap operas. *International Review of Applied Linguistics in Language Teaching, 39,* 39–51.

Gray, P. H. (1996). The thoroughbred and the four-wheeled cab: Performance beyond literature. *Communication Education, 45* (2), 102–107.

Griffin, E. (2000). *A first look at communication theory* (4th ed.). Boston: McGraw-Hill.

Gross, A. G., & Keith, W. M. (Eds.). (1997). *Rhetorical hermeneutics: Invention and interpretation in the age of science.* New York: SUNY Press.

Guerrero, L. K., Jones, S. M., & Burgoon, J. K. (2000). Responses to nonverbal intimacy change in romantic dyads: Effects of behavioral valence and degree of behavioral change on nonverbal and verbal reactions. *Communication Monographs, 67,* 325–346.

Gumperz, J. J., & Field, M. (1995). Children's discourse and inferential practices in cooperative learning. *Discourse Processes, 19* (1), 133–147.

Gunkel, D. J. (2000). Rethinking virtual reality: Simulation and the deconstruction of the image. *Critical Studies in Mass Communication, 17,* 45–62.

Gunkel, D. J., & Gunkel, A. H. (1997). Virtual geographies: The new worlds of cyberspace. *Critical Studies in Mass Communication, 14,* 123–137.

Guralnik, D. (Ed.) (1986). *Webster's new world dictionary* (2nd collegiate ed.). New York: Simon and Schuster.

Habermas, J. (1979). *Communication and the evolution of society.* Boston: Beacon.

Hacker, K. L., & Wignall, D. L. (1997). Issues in predicting user acceptance of computer-mediated communication (CMC) in inter-university classroom discussion as an alternative to face-to-face interaction. *Communication Reports, 10,* 107–114.

Hall, B. J., & Noguchi, M. (1993). Intercultural conflict: A case study. *International Journal of Intercultural Relations, 17,* 399–413.

Hall, S. (1986). *Cultural studies: Two paradigms.* London: Sage.

Hallmark, J. R., & Armstrong, R. N. (1999). Gender equity in televised sports: A comparative analysis of men's and women's NCAA Division I Basketball Championship broadcasts, 1991–1995. *Journal of Broadcasting and Electronic Media, 43,* 222–235.

Hallstein, L. (1999). A postmodern caring: Feminist standpoint theories, revisioned caring, and communication ethics. *Western Journal of Communication, 63,* 32–56.

Hammersley, M. (1992). Deconstructing the qualitative-quantitative divide. In J. Brannen (Ed.), *Mixing methods: Qualitative and quantitative research.* Aldershot: Avebury.

Hanke, R. (1998). The "mock-macho" situation comedy: Hegemonic masculinity and its reiteration. *Western Journal of Communication, 62,* 74–94.

Hanmer, J. (1990). Men, power, and the exploitation of women. *Women's Studies International Forum, 13,* 443–456.

Hardy-Short, D. C., & Short, C. B. (1995). Fire, death, and rebirth: A metaphoric analysis of the 1988 Yellowstone fire debate. *Western Journal of Communication, 59,* 103–126.

Harper, N. (1973). An analytical description of Aristotle's enthymeme. *Central States Speech Journal, 24,* 304–309.

Hart, R. P. (1971). The rhetoric of the true believer. *Speech Monographs, 38,* 249.

Hatala, M., Baack, D., & Parmenter, R. (1998). Dating with HIV: A content analysis of gay male HIV-positive and HIV-negative personal advertisements. *Journal of Social & Personal Relationships, 15,* 268–276.

Hauser, G. A. (1991). *Introduction to rhetorical theory.* Prospect Heights, IL: Waveland Press.

Helmericks, S. G., Nelsen, R. L., & Unnithan, N. P. (1991). The researcher, the topic, and the literature: A procedure for systematizing literature searches. *Journal of Applied Behavioral Sciences, 27,* 285–294.

Henningsen, D. D., Cruz, M. G., & Morr, M. C. (2000). Pattern violations and perceptions of deception. *Communication Reports, 13,* 1–10.

Heritage, J. (1984). *Garfinkel and ethnomethodology.* Oxford: Basil Blackwell.

Heritage, J. (1985). Recent developments in conversation analysis. *Sociolinguistics, 15* (1), 1–18.

Herman, A., & Sloop, J. M. (1998). The politics of authenticity in postmodern rock culture: The case of Negativland and *The Letter 'U' and the Numeral '2'. Critical Studies in Mass Communication, 15,* 1–20.

Hess, J. A. (2000). Maintaining nonvoluntary relationships with disliked partners: An investigation into the use of distancing behaviors. *Human Communication Research, 26,* 458–488.

Hickson, M., III, Stacks, D. W., & Bodon, J. (1999). The status of research productivity in communication: 1915–1995. *Communication Monographs, 66,* 178–197.

Hill, F. (1972). Conventional wisdom—traditional form—the President's message of November 3, 1969. In S. K. Foss, *Rhetorical criticism: Exploration and practice* (pp. 93–108). Prospect Heights, IL: Waveland Press.

Hiltz, S. R., Johnson, K., & Turoff, M. (1986). Experiments in group decision making: Communication processes and outcomes in face-to-face versus computerized conferences. *Human Communication Research, 13,* 225–252.

Hinkle, L. (1999). Nonverbal immediacy communication behaviors and liking in marital relationships. *Communication Research Reports, 16,* 81–90.

Hirokawa, R. Y. (1980). A comparative analysis of communication patterns within effective and ineffective decision-making groups. *Communication Monographs, 47,* 312–321.

Hochmuth Nichols, M. (1955). *A history and criticism of American public address, Vol. 3,* London: Longmans-Green.

Hoffman, E. W., & Heald, G. R. (2000). Tobacco and alcohol advertisements in popular African-American and general audience magazines. *Communication Research Reports, 17,* 415–425.

Hollingshead, A. B. (1996). Information suppression and status persistence in group decision-making: The effects of communication media. *Human Communication Research, 23,* 193–219.

Holmes, S. (2001). *Empirical rule.* [Online]. Available: www.stat.stanford.edu/~susan/courses.html.

Honeycutt, L. (2001). Comparing e-mail and synchronous conferencing in online peer response. *Written Communication, 18,* 26–60.

hooks, b. (1989). *Talking back: Thinking feminist, thinking black.* Boston: South End Press.

hooks, b. (1990). *Yearning: Race, gender, and cultural politics.* Boston: South End Press.

hooks, b. (1992). *Black looks: Race and representation.* Boston: South End Press.

hooks, b. (1994). *Outlaw culture: Resisting representations.* New York: Routledge.

hooks, b. (2000). *Where we stand: Class matters.* New York: Routledge.

Hoppe, M. J. (2000). The relative costs and benefits of telephone interviews versus self-administered diaries for daily data collection. *Evaluation Review, 24,* 102–117.

Hopper, R. (1992). *Telephone conversation.* Bloomington: Indiana University Press.

Hsu, C. F. (2002). The influence of self-construals, family and teacher communication patterns on communication apprehension among college students in Taiwan. *Communication Reports, 15,* 125–132.

Hubbard, R. C. (1985). Relationship styles in popular romance novels, 1950 to 1983. *Communication Quarterly, 33,* 113–125.

Hummert, M. L., Shaner, J., Garstka, T. A., & Henry, C. (1998). Communication with older adults: The influence of age stereotypes, context, and communicator age. *Human Communication Research, 25,* 124–151.

Hutchby, I., & Wooffitt, R. (1998). *Conversation analysis: Principles, practices, and applications.* Cambridge: Polity Press.

Hymes, D. (1962). Models of the interaction of language and social life. In J. J. Gumperz & D. Hymes (Eds.), *Directions in sociolinguistics* (pp. 35–71). New York: Holt, Rinehart, & Winston.

Hymes, D. (1974). Ways of speaking. *Foundations in sociolinguistics: An ethnographic approach.* Philadelphia: University of Pennsylvania Press.

Infante, D. A. (1987). Enhancing the prediction of response to a communication situation from communication traits. *Communication Quarterly, 35,* 308–316.

Infante, D. (1989). Response to high argumentativeness: Message and sex differences. *Southern Communication Journal, 54,* 159–170.

Infante, D., & Wigley, C. J., III (1986). Verbal aggressiveness: An interpersonal model and measure. *Communication Monographs, 53,* 61–69.

Jackson, B. G. (2000). A fantasy theme analysis of Peter Senge's learning organization. *Journal of Applied Behavioral Science, 36,* 193–210.

Jackson, S. (1986). Building a case for claims about discourse structure. In C. H. Tardy (Ed.), *Contemporary issues in language and discourse processes.* Hillsdale, NJ: Lawrence Erlbaum.

Jackson, S., Jacobs, S., Burrell, N., & Allen, M. (1986). Characterizing ordinary argument: Substantive and methodological issues. *Journal of American Forensic Association, 23,* 42–57.

Jacobs, S. (1990). On the especially nice fit between qualitative analysis and the known properties of conversation. *Communication Monographs, 57,* 243–249.

Jaksa, J. A., & Pritchard, M. S. (1988). *Communication ethics: Methods of analysis.* Belmont, CA: Wadsworth.

Jamieson, K. H. (1973). Generic constraints and the rhetorical situation. *Philosophy and Rhetoric, 6,* 162–170.

Jamieson, K. H., & Campbell, K. K. (1982). Rhetorical hybrids: Fusion of generic elements. *Quarterly Journal of Speech, 68,* 146–157.

Janesick, V. J. (1998). The dance of qualitative research design: Metaphor, methodalatry, and meaning (pp. 35–55). In N. K. Denzin & Y. S. Lincoln (Eds.), *Strategies of qualitative inquiry,* Thousand Oaks, CA: Sage.

Jarmon, L. (1996). Performance as a resource in the practice of conversation analysis. *Text and Performance Quarterly, 16,* 336–355.

Jenkins, M. (1999). What to do if you find out you have breast cancer. *Magazine, 17,* 197–201.

Jenkins, M. (2000). *A credit to her country.* A staged play based on oral history interviews, produced by the author, and performed in San Francisco and San Diego, CA, and in Phoenix, AZ.

Johanson, J.-E. (2000). Intraorganizational influence: Theoretical clarification and empirical assessment of intraorganizational social influence. *Management Communication Quarterly, 13,* 393–426.

Johnson, A. J., Smith, S. W., Mitchell, M. M., Orrego, V. O., & Yun, K. A. (1999). Expert advice on daytime talk television: A beneficial source of information for the general public? *Communication Research Reports, 16,* 91–101.

Johnson, D., & Sellnow, T. (1995). Deliberative rhetoric as a step in organizational crisis management: Exxon as a case study. *Communication Reports, 8,* 54–61.

Johnstone, C. L. (1995). Reagan, rhetoric, and the public philosophy: Ethics and politics in the 1984 campaign. *Southern Communication Journal, 60,* 93–108.

Jones, D. (1992). Postmodern perspectives on organisational communication. *Australian Journal of Communication, 19,* 30–37.

Jones, S. G. (Ed.). (1998a). *Cybersociety 2.0: Revisiting computer-mediated communication and community.* Thousand Oaks, CA: Sage.

Jones, S. (1998b). Understanding micropolis and compunity. *The Electronic Journal of Communication, 8* (3 & 4), 1–8.

Jorgensen, D. L. (1989). *Participant observation: A methodology for human studies.* Newbury Park, CA: Sage.

Kaid, L. L., & Holtz-Bacha, C. (2000). Gender reactions to TV political broadcasts: A multicountry comparison. *Harvard International Journal of Press/Politics, 5,* 17–30.

Kassing, J. W., & Avtgis, T. A. (2001). Dissension in the organization as it relates to control expectancies. *Communication Research Reports, 18,* 118–127.

Kassing, J. W., & Infante, D. A. (1999). Aggressive communication in the coach-athlete relationship. *Communication Research Reports, 16,* 110–120.

Katriel, T. (1995). From "context" to "contexts" in intercultural communication research. In R. Wiseman (Ed.), *Intercultural communication theory* (pp. 271–284). Thousand Oaks, CA: Sage.

Katzer, J., Cook, K. H., & Crouch, W. W. (1982). *Evaluating information: A guide for users of social science research* (2nd ed.). New York: Random House.

Katzer, J., Cook, K. H., & Crouch, W. W. (1998). *Evaluating information: A guide for users of social science research* (4th ed.). Boston: McGraw-Hill.

Kendig, D. (1997). Transforming gender scripts: Life after *You just don't understand. Text and Performance Studies, 17,* 197–216.

Kennedy, G. (1963). *The art of persuasion in Greece.* Princeton, NJ: Princeton University Press.

Kenny, R. W. (2000). The rhetoric of Kevorkian's battle. *Quarterly Journal of Speech, 86,* 386–401.

Kerlinger, F. N. (1973). *Foundations of behavioral research* (2nd ed.). New York: Holt, Rinehart, & Winston.

Kerlinger, F. N. (1986). *Foundations of behavioral research* (3rd ed.). New York: Holt Rinehart, & Winston.

Keshishian, F. (1997). Political bias and nonpolitical news: A content analysis of an Armenian and Iranian earthquake in the *New York Times* and the *Washington Post*. *Critical Studies in Mass Communication, 14,* 323–343.

Kessler, R. A. (1995). *Beyond smile sheets: Evaluating a presentation skills training program for industry.* Unpublished master's thesis. San Francisco State University, San Francisco, CA.

Kim, M. S. (1999). Cross-cultural perspectives on motivations of verbal communication: Review, critique, and a theoretical framework. *Communication Yearbook, 22,* 51–89.

Kim, Y. Y., Lujan, P., & Dixon, L. D. (1998). "I can walk both ways": Identity integration of American Indians in Oklahoma. *Human Communication Research, 25,* 252–274.

Kirkman, B. L., & Shapiro, D. L. (2000). Understanding why team members won't share. *Small Group Research, 31,* 175–210.

Kline, S. L., and Clinton, B. L. (1998). Developments in children's persuasive message practices. *Communication Education. 47,* 120–136.

Kolko, B., & Reid, E. (1998). Dissolution and fragmentation: Problems in on-line communities. In S. G. Jones (Ed.), *Cybersociety 2.0: Revisiting computer-mediated communication and community,* pp. 212–229. Thousand Oaks, CA: Sage.

Kraidy, M. M. (1999). The global, the local, and the hybrid: A native ethnography of globalization. *Critical Studies in Mass Communication, 16,* 456–476.

Kraidy, M. M. (2002). Hybridity in cultural globalization. *Communication Theory, 12,* 316–339.

Kramer, M. W., & Pier, P. M. (1999). Students' perceptions of effective and ineffective communication by college teachers. *Southern Communication Journal, 65,* 16–33.

Kremar, M., & Valkenburg, P. M. (1999). A scale to assess children's interpretations of justified and unjustified violence and its relationship to television viewing. *Communication Research, 26,* 608–634.

Krippendorf, K. (1980). *Content analysis: An introduction to its methodology.* Beverly Hills, CA: Sage.

Krueger, R. A. (1994). *Focus groups: A practical guide for applied research.* Newbury Park, CA: Sage.

Kruml, S. M., & Geddes, D. (2000). Exploring the dimensions of emotional labor. *Management Communication Quarterly, 14,* 8–50.

Kuypers, J. A. (2000). From science, moral-poetics: Dr. James Dobson's response to the fetal tissue research initiative. *Quarterly Journal of Speech, 86,* 146–167.

Lakoff, G., & Johnson, M. (1980). *Metaphors we live by.* Chicago: University of Chicago Press.

Lannamann, J. W. (1991). Interpersonal communication research as ideological practice. *Communication Theory, 3,* 179–203.

LaRose, R., & Whitten, P. (2000). Re-thinking instructional immediacy for Web courses: A social cognitive exploration. *Communication Education, 49,* 320–338.

Larson, M. S. (2001). Interactions, activities, and gender in children's television commercials: A content analysis. *Journal of Broadcasting and Electronic Media, 45,* 41–56.

Lasswell, H. D. (1927). *Propaganda techniques in the World War.* New York: Knopf.

Lawrence, S. G. (1999). The preoccupation with problems of understanding in communication research. *Communication Theory, 9,* 265–286.

Lears, T. J. (1985). The concept of cultural hegemony: Problems and possibilities. *American Historical Review, 90,* 567–593.

Lechte, J. (1994). *Fifty key contemporary thinkers: From structuralism to post-modernity.* London: Routledge.

LeCompte, M. D., & Goetz, J. P. (1982). Problems of reliability and validity in ethnographic research. *Review of Educational Research, 52,* 31–60.

Lee, R. (1995). Humility and the political servant: Jimmy Carter's post-presidential rhetoric of virtue and power. *Southern Communication Journal, 60,* 120–130.

Lee, W. S. (1998a). In the names of Chinese women. *Quarterly Journal of Speech, 84,* 283–302.

Lee, W. S. (1998b). Patriotic breeders or colonized converts: A postcolonial feminist approach to antifootbinding discourse in China. *International and intercultural annual, 21,* 11–33.

Leff, M. (1999). The habitation of rhetoric. In J. L. Lucaites, C. M. Condit, & S. Caudill, (Eds.). *Contemporary rhetorical theory: A reader* (pp. 52–64). New York: Guilford.

Leidner, R. (1991). Serving hamburgers and selling insurance: Gender, work, and identity in interactive service jobs. *Gender & Society, 5,* 154–177.

Lemke, J. L. (1999). Discourse and organizational dynamics: Website communication and institutional change. *Discourse and Society, 10* (1), 21–47.

Le Poire, B. A., Shepard, C., & Duggan, A. (1999). Nonverbal involvement, expressiveness, and pleasantness as predicted by parental and partner attachment style. *Communication Monographs, 66,* 293–311.

Le Poire, B. A., & Yoshimura, S. M. (1999). The effects of expectancies and actual communication on nonverbal adaptation and communication outcomes: A test of interaction adaptation theory. *Communication Monographs, 66,* 1–30.

Lessl, T. M. (1999). The Galileo legend as scientific folklore. *Quarterly Journal of Speech, 85,* 268–284.

Lewis, C. (1997). Hegemony in the ideal: Wedding photography, consumerism, and patriarchy. *Women's Studies in Communication, 20,* 167–187.

Lichter, S. R., Lichter, L. S., & Amundson, D. (1997). Does Hollywood hate business or money? *Journal of Communication, 47,* 68–84.

Lieberg, M. (1995). Teenagers and public space. *Communication Research, 22,* 720–745.

Lin, C. A. (1997). Beefcake versus cheesecake in the 1990s: Sexist portrayals of both genders in television commercials. *The Howard Journal of Communications, 8,* 237–249.

Lincoln, J. R. (1990, Dec.). Review of *Social structures: A network approach,* by Wellman, B., & Berkowitz, S. D., Eds. In *Administrative Science Quarterly,* pp. 746–748.

Lincoln, Y. S., & Guba, E. G. (1985). *Naturalistic inquiry.* Beverly Hills, CA: Sage.

Lindlof, T. R. (1995). *Qualitative communication research methods.* Thousand Oaks, CA: Sage.

Lindlof, T. R., & Schatzer, M. J. (1998). Media ethnography in virtual space: Strategies, limits, and possibilities. *Journal of Broadcasting & Electronic Media, 42* (2), 170–193.

Lindsay, S. A. (1999). Waco and Andover: An application of Kenneth Burke's concept of psychotic entelechy. *Quarterly Journal of Speech, 85,* 268–284.

Lindsley, S. L. (1999). A layered model of problematic intercultural communication in U.S. owned maquiladoras in Mexico. *Communication Monographs, 66,* 145–167.

Littlejohn, S. (1996). *Theories of human communication* (5th ed.) Belmont, CA: Wadsworth Thompson Publishing.

Littlejohn, S. (2000). *Theories of human communication* (6th ed.). Belmont, CA: Wadsworth Thompson Publishing.

Littlejohn, S. (2002). *Theories of human communication* (7th ed.). Belmont, CA: Wadsworth Thompson Publishing.

Lofland, J., & Lofland, L. H. (1984). *Analyzing social settings: A guide to qualitative observation and analysis* (2nd ed.). Belmont, CA: Wadsworth Publishing Company.

Lombard, M., & Reich, R. D. (2000). Presence and television: The role of screen size. *Human Communication Research, 26,* 75–99.

Lombard, M., Snyder-Duch, J., & Bracken, C. C. (2002). Content analysis in mass communication: Assessment and reporting of intercoder reliability. *Human Communication Research, 28* (4, October), 587–604.

Lucaites, J. L., Condit, C. M., & Caudill, S. (Eds.). (1999). *Contemporary rhetorical theory: A reader.* New York: Guilford.

Lucchetti, A. E. (1999). Deception in disclosing one's sexual history: Safe-sex avoidance or ignorance? *Communication Quarterly, 47,* 300–314.

Lyotard, F. (1984). *The Postmodern condition: A report on knowledge* (G. Bennington & B. Massumi, Trans.). Minneapolis: University of Minnesota Press.

Mabrito, M. (1995). The e-mail discussion group: An opportunity for discourse analysis. *Business Communication Quarterly, 58* (2), 10–12.

Malinowski, B. (1922). *Argonauts of the western Pacific.* London: Routledge.

Mandelbaum, J. (1987). Couples sharing stories. *Communication Quarterly, 35,* 144–170.

Manusov, V., & Trees, A. R. (2002). "Are you kidding me?": The role of nonverbal cues in the verbal accounting process. *Journal of Communication, 52,* 640–656.

Markham, A. (1996). Designing discourse: A critical analysis of strategic ambiguity and workplace control. *Management Communication Quarterly, 9,* 389–421.

Marshall, J. (1993). Viewing organizational communication from a feminist perspective: A critique and some offerings. In S. Deetz (Ed.), *Communication Yearbook, 16* (pp. 122–143). Newbury Park, CA: Sage.

Martin, J. (1990). Deconstructing organizational taboos: The suppression of gender conflict in organizations. *Organization Science, 11,* 339–359.

Martin, J. N., & Flores, L.A. (1998). Colloquy: Challenges in contemporary culture and communication research. *Human Communication Research, 25,* 293–299.

Martin, J. N., Hammer, M. R., & Bradford, L. (1994). The influence of cultural and situational context on Hispanic and non-Hispanic communication competence behaviors. *Communication Quarterly, 42,* 160–179.

Matabane, P., & Merritt, B. (1996). African-Americans on television: 25 years after Kerner. *The Howard Journal of Communications, 7,* 329–337.

Mathison, S. (1988). Why triangulate? *Educational Researcher, 17* (2), 13–17.

Mattson, M., & Brann, M. (2002). Managed care and the paradox of patient confidentiality: A case study analysis from a communication boundary management perspective. *Communication Studies, 53* (4), 337–358.

May, R. A., & Pattillo-McCoy, M. (2000). Do you see what I see? Examining a collaborative ethnography. *Qualitative Inquiry, 6,* 65–87.

McCain, G., & Segal, E. M. (1988). *The game of science* (5th ed.). Pacific Grove, CA: Brooks/Cole Publishing Co.

McClure, K. R. (2000). Frederick Douglass' use of comparison in his Fourth of July oration: A textual criticism. *Western Journal of Communication, 64,* 425–444.

McComas, K., & Shanahan, J. (1999). Telling stories about global climate change: Measuring the impact of narratives on issue cycles. *Communication Research, 26,* 30–57.

McCroskey, J. (1982). *An introduction to rhetorical communication* (4th ed.). Englewood Cliffs, NJ: Prentice Hall.

McCroskey, J. C., & Young, T. J. (1981). Ethos and credibility: The construct and its measurement after three decades. *Central States Speech Journal, 32,* 24–34.

McDermott, R. P., Gospodinoff, K., & Aron, J. (1978). Criteria for an ethnographically adequate description of concerted activities and their contexts. *Semiotica, 24,* 245–275.

McDevitt, M., & Chaffee, S. (2000). Closing gaps in political communication and knowledge. *Communication Research, 27,* 259–293.

McGee, B. R. (1998). Witnessing and *ethos:* The evangelical conversion of David Duke. *Western Journal of Communication, 62,* 217–244.

McKee, K. B., & Pardun, C. J. (1996). Mixed messages: The relationship between sexual and religious imagery in rock, country, and Christian videos. *Communication Reports, 9,* 163–172.

McLaughlin, L. (1991). Discourses of prostitution /discourses of sexuality. *Critical Studies in Mass Communication, 8,* 249–272.

McLaughlin, M. L. (1984). *Conversation: How talk is organized.* Beverly Hills, CA: Sage.

McLeod, J. M., Scheufele, D. A., Moy, P., Horowitz, E. M., Holbert, E. M., Zhang, W., Zubric, S., & Zubric, J. (1999). Understanding deliberation: The effects of discussion networks on participation in a public forum. *Communication Research, 26,* 743–774.

McMillan, J. J., & Cheney, G. (1996). The student as consumer: The implications and limitations of a metaphor. *Communication Education, 45,* 1–15.

McNeil, L. M. (1986). Contradictions of control: School structure and school knowledge. London: Routledge & Kegan.

McNeill, K. (2001). *Statistical concepts.* [On-line]. Available: www.wizard.ucr.edu/~kmcneill/stats.html.

McPhail, M. L. (1998). From complicity to coherence: Rereading the rhetoric of Afrocentricity. *Western Journal of Communication, 62,* 114–140.

Mertens, D. M. (1998). *Research methods in education and psychology: Integrating diversity with quantitative & qualitative approaches.* Thousand Oaks, CA: Sage.

Merton, R. K. (1968). *Social theory and social structure.* New York: Free Press.

Merton, T. (1962). Personal letter to Czeslaw Milosz, as cited in *San Francisco Examiner* column by S. Salter (date unknown), titled "It's not faith—it's work."

Messman, S. J., & Mikesell, R. L. (2000). Competition and interpersonal conflict in dating relationships. *Communication Reports, 13,* 21–34.

Messner, B. A. (1996). "Sizing up" codependency recovery. *Western Journal of Communication, 60,* 1–24.

Meyer, J. C. (1997). Humor in member narratives: Uniting and dividing at work. *Western Journal of Communication, 61,* 188–209.

Meyers, R. A., & Brashers, D. E. (1998). Argument in group decision making: Explicating a process model and investigating the argument-outcome link. *Communication Monographs, 65,* 261–281.

Mies, M. (1991). Women's research or feminist research? The debate surrounding feminist science and methodology. In M. M. Fonow & J. A. Cook (Eds.), *Beyond methodology: Feminist scholarship as lived research* (pp. 60–84). Bloomington: Indiana University Press.

Mikesell, R. L., & Messman, S. J. (1994). Competition in romantic relationships: A preliminary investigation. Paper presented at the Central States Communication Association annual convention, Oklahoma City, OK.

Miles, M. B., & Huberman, A. M. (1994). *Qualitative data analysis: An expanded sourcebook* (2nd ed.). Thousand Oaks, CA: Sage.

Miller, C. R. (1998). Genre as social action. In T. B. Farrell (Ed.), *Landmark essays on contemporary rhetoric* (pp. 123–141). Mahwah, NJ: Lawrence Erlbaum.

Miller, D. L., Creswell, J. W., & Olander, L. S. (1998). Writing and retelling multiple ethnographic tales of a soup kitchen for the homeless. *Qualitative Inquiry, 4,* 469–491.

Miller, G. R. (1970}. Research setting: Laboratory studies. In P. Emmert & W. Brooks (Eds.), *Methods of research in communication,* pp. 77–104. Boston: Houghton Mifflin.

Miller, J. M. (2000). Language use, identity, and social interaction: Migrant students in Australia. *Research on Language and Social Interaction, 33* (1), 69–100.

Miller, K. (2002). The experience of emotion in the workplace: Professing in the midst of tragedy. *Management Communication Quarterly, 15,* 571–600.

Miller, M. (1995). An intergenerational case study of suicidal tradition and mother-daughter communication. *Journal of Applied Communication Research, 23,* 247–270.

Miller, M. L. (1999). Public argument and legislative debate in the rhetorical construction of public policy: The case of Florida midwifery legislation. *Quarterly Journal of Speech, 85,* 361–379.

Mitchell, C. J. (1983). Case and situation analysis. *Sociological Review, 31,* 187–211.

Mitchell, G. R. (2000). Placebo defense: Operation desert mirage? The rhetoric of Patriot missile accuracy in the 1991 Persian Gulf War. *Quarterly Journal of Speech, 86,* 121–145.

Monahan, J. L., & Lannutti, P. J. (2000). Alcohol as social lubricant: Alcohol myopia theory, social self-esteem, and social interaction. *Human Communication Research, 26,* 175–202.

Monge, P. (1987). The network level of analysis. In C. Berger & S. Chaffee (Eds.), *Handbook of communication science* (pp. 239–270). Beverly Hills, CA: Sage.

Mongeau, P. A., Hale, J. L., & Alles, M. (1994). An experimental investigation of accounts and attributions following sexual infidelity. *Communication Monographs, 61,* 326–344.

Montgomery, B. M., & Norton, R. W. (1981). Sex differences and similarities in communicator style. *Communication Monographs, 48,* 121–132.

Moraga, C., & Anzaldua, G. (Eds.). (1983). *This bridge called my back: Writings by radical women of color.* New York: Kitchen Table.

Morgan, D. L. (1988). *Focus groups as qualitative research.* Newbury Park, CA: Sage.

Morse, J. M. (1998). Designing funded qualitative research. In N. Denzin & Y. Lincoln (Eds.), *Strategies of qualitative inquiry* (pp. 56–85). Thousand Oaks, CA: Sage.

Morton, T. A., & Duck, J. M. (2000). Social identity and media dependency in the gay community: The prediction of safe sex attitudes. *Communication Research, 27,* 438–460.

Mumby, D. K. (1988). *Communication and power in organizations: Discourse, ideology, and domination.* Norwood, NJ: Ablex.

Mumby, D. K. (1993). Critical organizational communication studies: The next 10 years. *Communication Monographs, 60,* 18–25.

Mumby, D. K. (1997a). Modernism, postmodernism, and communication studies: A rereading of an ongoing debate. *Communication Theory, 7,* 1–28.

Mumby, D. K. (1997b). The problem of hegemony: Rereading Gramsci for organizational communication studies. *Western Journal of Communication, 61,* 343–375.

Mumby, D. K., & Putnam, L. L. (1992). The politics of emotion: A feminist reading of bounded rationality. *Academy of Management Review, 17,* 465–486.

Mumby, D., & Stohl, C. (1991). Power and discourse in organizational studies: Absence and the dialectic of control. *Discourse & Society, 2,* 313–332.

Murillo, E. G., Jr. (1996, Nov.). *Pedagogy of a Latin-American festival: A mojado ethnography.* Paper presented at the Annual Meeting of the American Educational Studies Association in Montreal, Quebec, Canada.

Murphy, J. M. (1997). Inventing authority: Bill Clinton, Martin Luther King, Jr., and the orchestration of rhetorical traditions. *Quarterly Journal of Speech, 83,* 71–89.

Myers, S. A. (2002). Perceived aggressive instructor communication and student state motivation, learning, and satisfaction. *Communication Reports, 15,* 113–121.

Nakayama, T. K. (1998). Les voix de l'autre. *Western Journal of Communication, 61,* 235–242.

Nakayama, T. K., & Krizek, R. L. (1995). Whiteness: A strategic rhetoric. *Quarterly Journal of Speech, 81,* 291–309.

Nathanson, A. I. (1999). Identifying and explaining the relationship between parental mediation and children's aggression. *Communication Research, 26,* 124–144.

Nathanson, A. I. (2001). Parents versus peers: Exploring the significance of peer mediation of antisocial television. *Communication Research, 28,* 251–274.

Neruda, P. (1972). *New poems: 1968–1970.* B. Belitt (Ed.). New York: Grove Press.

Neuliep, J. W., Chaudoir, M., & McCroskey, J. C. (2001). A cross-cultural comparison of ethnocentrism among Japanese and United States college students. *Communication Research Reports, 18,* 137–146.

Neuman, W. L. (1994). *Social research methods.* Boston: Allyn & Bacon.

Newman, I., & Benz, C. R. (1998). *Qualitative-quantitative research methodology: Exploring the interactive continuum.* Carbondale, IL: SIU Press.

Neyer, F. J. (1997). Free recall or recognition in collecting egocentered networks: The role of survey techniques. *Journal of Social and Personal Relationships, 14* (3), 305–316.

Nieves, E. (2000, Nov. 5). Mission district fights case of dot-com fever. *NY Times,* New York, p. 1.27.

Niquette, M., & Buxton, W. J. (1997). Meet me at the fair: Sociability and reflexivity in nineteenth-century world expositions. *Canadian Journal of Communication, 22,* 81–113.

Noelle Ignacis, E. (2000). Ain't I a Filipino woman?: An analysis of authorship/authority through the construction of 'Filipina' on the Net. *Sociological Quarterly, 41,* 551–572.

Ochs, E. (1979). Transcription as theory. In E. Ochs & B. B. Schieffelin (Eds.), *Developmental pragmatics* (pp. 251–268). New York: Academic Press.

O'Keefe, D. (1980). Ethnomethodology. *Journal for the Theory of Social Behavior, 9,* 187–219.

Oliver, M. (1992). Changing the social relations of research production? *Disability, Handicap, & Society, 7,* 101–114.

Ono, K. A. (1998). A letter/essay I've been longing to write in my personal/academic voice. *Western Journal of Communication, 61,* 114–125.

Osborn, M. (1967). Archetypal metaphor in rhetoric: The light-dark family. *Quarterly Journal of Speech, 53,* 115–126.

Ott, B. L., & Aoki, E. (2001). Popular imagination and identity politics: Reading the future in *Star Trek: The Next Generation. Western Journal of Communication, 65,* 392–415.

Papa, M. J., Auwal, M. A., & Singhal, A. (1995). Dialectic of control and emancipation in organizing for social change: A multitheoretic study of the Grameen Bank in Bangladesh. *Communication Theory, 5,* 189–223.

Papa, M. J., Auwal, M. A., & Singhal, A. (1997). Organizing for social change within concertive control systems: Member identification, empowerment, and the masking of discipline. *Communication Monographs, 64,* 219–249.

Park, H. W. (1998). A Gramscian approach to interpreting international communication. *Journal of Communication, 48* (4), 79–99.

Parker, M. (1992). Post-modern organizations or postmodern organizational theory? *Organization Studies, 13,* 1–17.

Parks, M. R. (1997). Ideology in interpersonal communication: Beyond the couches, talk shows, and bunkers. *Communication Yearbook, 18,* 480–497.

Parks, M. R., & Aldeman, M. B. (1983). Communication networks and the development of romantic relationships. *Human Communication Research, 10,* 55–79.

Parks, M. R., & Floyd, K. (1996). Making friends in cyberspace. *Journal of Communication, 46,* 80–97.

Parks, M. R., & Roberts, L. D. (1998). "Making MOOsic": The development of personal relationships on line and a comparison to their off-line counterparts. *Journal of Social and Personal Relationships, 15,* 517–537.

Patterson, B. R., & Gojdycz, T. K. (2000). The relationship between computer-mediated communication and communication related anxieties. *Communication Research Reports, 17,* 278–287.

Patterson, B. R., Neupauer, N. C., Burant, P. A., Koehn, S. C., & Reed, A. T. (1996). A preliminary examination of conversation analytic techniques: Rates of inter-transcriber reliability. *Western Journal of Communication, 60,* 76–91.

Patton, M. Q. (1990). *Qualitative evaluation and research methods* (2nd ed.). Newbury Park, CA: Sage.

Pauley, G. E. (1998). Rhetoric and timeliness: An analysis of Lyndon B. Johnson's voting rights address. *Western Journal of Communication, 62,* 26–54.

Pauley, J. L, II (1998). Reshaping public persona and the prophetic *ethos:* Louis Farrakhan at the Million Man March. *Western Journal of Communication, 62,* 512–537.

Pearce, W. B. (1998). On putting social justice in the discipline of communication and putting enriched concepts of communication in social justice research and practice. *Journal of Applied Communication Research, 26,* 272–278.

Pedhazur, E. J. (1982). *Multiple regression in behavioral research: Explanation and prediction* (2nd ed.). New York: Holt, Rinehart, & Winston.

Peirce, C. S. (1992). *Reasoning and the logic of things: The Cambridge Conference lectures of 1898.* K. L. Ketner (Ed.). Cambridge: Harvard University Press.

Pelias, R. (in press). Remembering Viet Nam. *A methodology of the heart: Life and higher education.* Walnut Creek, CA: AltaMira.

Perry, P. (2001). White means never having to say you're ethnic: White youth and the construction of "cultureless" identities. *Journal of Contemporary Ethnography, 30,* 56–92.

Perse, E. M., & Ferguson, D. A. (2000). The benefits and costs of web surfing. *Communication Quarterly, 48,* 343–359.

Peshkin, A. (1988). In search of subjectivity—one's own. *Educational Researcher, 17,* 17–22.

Philipsen, G. (1975). Speaking "like a man" in Teamsterville: Cultural patterns of role enactment in an urban neighborhood. *Quarterly Journal of Speech, 61,* 13–22.

Philipsen, G. (1976). Places for speaking in Teamsterville. *Quarterly Journal of Speech, 62,* 15–25.

Philipsen, G. (1977). Linearity of research design in ethnographic studies of speaking. *Communication Quarterly, 25,* 42–50.

Philipsen, G. (1982). The qualitative case study as a strategy in communication inquiry. *The Communicator, 12,* 4–17.

Philipsen, G. (1989). An ethnographic approach to communication studies. In B. Dervin, L. Grossberg, B. J. O'Keefe, & E. Wartella (Eds.), *Rethinking communication 2: Paradigm exemplars* (pp. 258–267). Newbury Park, CA: Sage.

Philipsen, G. (1992). *Speaking culturally: Explorations in social communication.* Albany: State University of New York Press.

Philipsen, G. (1997). A theory of speech codes. In G. Philipsen & T. Albrecht (Eds.), *Developing communication theories* (pp. 119–156). Albany: State University of New York Press.

Phillips, K. R. (1999). The rhetoric of controversy. *Western Journal of Communication, 63,* 488–511.

Pittman, J., & Gallois, C. (1997). Language strategies in the attribution of blame for HIV and AIDS. *Communication Monographs, 64,* 201–218.

Pomerantz, A. (1978). Compliment responses: Notes on the co-operation of multiple constraints (pp. 79–112). In J. Schenkein (Ed.), *Studies in the organization of conversational interaction.* New York: Academic Press.

Pomerantz, A. (1990). Chautauqua: On the validity and generalizability of conversational analysis methods. Conversation analytic claims. *Communication Monographs, 57,* 231–235.

Popper, K. (1962). On the sources of knowledge and ignorance. *Encounter, 19,* 42–57.

Potter, J., & Wetherall, M. (1987). *Discourse and social psychology.* Newbury Park, CA: Sage.

Pragg, L., Wiseman, R. L., Cody, M. J., & Wendt, P. F. (1999). Interrogative strategies and information exchange in computer-mediated communication. *Communication Quarterly, 47* (1), 46–66.

Pyrczak, F., & Bruce, R. R. (1992). *Writing empirical research reports: A basic guide for students of behavioral and social sciences.* Los Angeles: Pyrczak Publishing.

Ragsdale, J. D. (1996). Gender, satisfaction level, and the use of relational maintenance strategies in marriage. *Communication Monographs, 63,* 354–369.

Ramazanoglu, C. (1992). On feminist methodology: Male reason versus female empowerment. *Sociology, 26,* 207–212.

Ramsey, S. (1999). A benchmark study of elaboration and sourcing in science stories for eight American newspapers. *Journalism & Mass Communication Quarterly, 76,* 87–98.

Ray, E. B. (1993). When the links become chains: Considering dysfunctions of supportive communication in the workplace. *Communication Monographs, 60,* 106–111.

Reed, L. (2000). Domesticating the personal computer: The mainstreaming of a new technology and the cultural management of a widespread technophobia, *Critical Studies in Media Communication, 17,* 159–185.

Richmond, V. P., & McCroskey, J. C. (2000). The impact of supervisor and subordinate immediacy on relational and organizational outcomes. *Communication Monographs, 67,* 85–96.

Ritter, K. W. (1980). American political rhetoric and the jeremiad tradition: Presidential nomination acceptance speeches, 1960–1976. *Central States Speech Journal, 31,* 153–171.

Roach, K. D., & Olaniran, B. A. (2001). Intercultural willingness to communicate and communication anxiety in international teaching assistants. *Communication Research Reports, 18,* 26–35.

Robinson, J. D. (1998). Getting down to business: Talk, gaze, and body orientation during openings of doctor-patient consultations. *Human Communication Research, 25,* 97–123.

Robinson, J. D., & Stivers, T. (2001). Achieving activity transition in physician-patient encounters: From history-taking to physical examination. *Human Communication Research, 27,* 253–298.

Rogers, E. M. (1994). *A history of communication study: A biographical approach.* New York: The Free Press.

Romaine, S. (1982). What is a speech community? In *Sociolinguistic variation in speech communities* (pp. 13–24). London: Edward Arnold.

Ropers-Huilman, B. (1996). Still waters run deep: Meanings of silence in feminist classrooms. *Feminist Teacher, 10* (1), 3–7.

Rossler, P. (2001). Between online heaven and cyberhell: The framing of "the Internet" by traditional media coverage in Germany. *New Media & Society, 3,* 49–66.

Rothman, B. K. (1986). Reflections: On hard work. *Qualitative Sociology, 9,* 48–53.

Rowland, R. C. (1987). Narrative: Mode of discourse or paradigm? *Communication Monographs, 54,* 264–275.

Roy, A., & Harwood, J. (1997). Underrepresented, positively portrayed: Older adults in television commercials. *Journal of Applied Communication Research, 25,* 39–56.

Ruben, B. D. (1993). What patients remember: A content analysis of critical incidents in health care. *Health Communication, 5,* 99–112.

Rubin, R. B., Rubin, A. M., & Jordan, F. F. (1997). Effects of instruction on communication apprehension and communication competence. *Communication Education, 46,* 104–114.

Rubin, R. B., Rubin, A. M., & Piele, L. J. (2000). *Communication research: Strategies and sources* (5th ed.). Belmont, CA: Wadsworth.

Rueckert, W. H. (1982). *Kenneth Burke and the drama of human relations* (2nd ed.). Berkeley: University of California Press.

Ruud, G. (1995). The symbolic construction of organizational identities and community in a regional symphony. *Communication Studies, 46,* 201–222.

Rybacki, K., & Rybacki, D. (1991). *Communication criticism: Approaches and genres.* Belmont, CA: Wadsworth.

Sachweh, S. (1998). Granny darling's nappies: Secondary babytalk in German nursing homes for the aged. *Journal of Applied Communication Research, 26,* 52–65.

Sacks, H. (1972). An initial investigation of the usability of conversational data for doing sociology. In D. Sudnow (Ed.), *Studies in social interaction.* New York: Free Press.

Sacks, H. (1984). Notes on methodology. In J. Atkinson & J. Heritage (Eds.), *Structures of social action: Studies in conversation analysis.* Cambridge: Cambridge University Press.

Sacks, H., Schegloff, E., & Jefferson, G. (1974). A simplest systematic for the organization of turn taking for conversation. *Language, 50,* 696–735.

Said, E. (1984). Permission to narrate. *Journal of Palestine Studies, 13,* 27–48.

Scanlon, J. (1993). Challenging the imbalances of power in feminist oral history: Developing a give-and-take methodology. *Women's Studies International Forum, 16,* 639–645.

Scharrer, E. (2001). From wise to foolish: The portrayal of the sitcom father, 1950s–1990s. *Journal of Broadcasting and Electronic Media, 45,* 23–40.

Scheibel, D. (1994). Graffiti and "film school" culture: Displaying alienation. *Communication Monographs, 61,* 1–18.

Scheibel, D. (1996). Appropriating bodies: Organ(izing) ideology and cultural practice in medical school. *Journal of Applied Communication Research, 24,* 310–331.

Scheibel, D. (1999). "If your roommate dies, you get a 4.0": Reclaiming rumor with Burke and organizational culture. *Western Journal of Communication, 63,* 169–192.

Schely-Newman, E. (1997). Finding one's place: Locale narratives in an Israeli Moshav. *Quarterly Journal of Speech, 83,* 401–415.

Schenck-Hamlin, W. J., Procter, D. E., & Rumsey, D. J. (2000). The influence of negative advertising frames on political cynicism and politician accountability. *Human Communication Research, 26,* 53–74.

Schenkein, J. (1978). Sketch of an analytic mentality for the study of conversational interaction. *Studies in the organization of conversational interaction.* New York: Academic.

Schiffrin, D. (1997). Theory and method in discourse analysis: What context for what unit? *Language & Communication, 17* (2), 75–92.

Schlegoff, E. A. (1968). Preliminaries to preliminaries: "Can I ask you a question?" *Sociological Inquiry, 50,* 104–152.

Schlegoff, E. A., & Sacks, H. (1973). Opening up closings. *Semiotica, 8,* 289–327.

Schönfeldt-Aultman, S. M., & Yep, G. A. (2002). (Re)building a nation: South Africa's Heritage Day as a site of renaming, reimaging, and remembering. In L. K. Fuller (Ed.), *National Days/National Ways.* Westport, CO: Greenwood Press.

Schutz, A. (1967). *The phenomenology of the social world* (G. Walsh & F. Lehnert, Trans.). Evanston, IL: Northwestern University Press.

Schwartz, H. S. (1987). [Review of the book *The reflective practitioner: How professionals think in action*]. *Administrative Science Quarterly, 32,* 614–617.

Schwartzman, H. B. (1993). *Ethnography in organizations.* Thousand Oaks, CA: Sage (Qualitative Research Methods Series #27).

Scott, C. R., & Fontenot, J. C. (1999). Multiple identifications during team meetings: A comparison of conventional and computer-supported interactions. *Communication Reports, 12* (2), 91–100.

Scott, J. B. (2001). Putting women and newborns to the HIV test: A case study of public policy *topos. Southern Communication Journal, 66,* 101–119.

Scotton, C. M. (1985). What the heck, sir: Style shifting and lexical colouring as features of powerful language (pp. 103–119). In R. L. Street & J. N. Cappella (Eds.), *Sequence and pattern in conversational behavior.* Baltimore, MD: E. Arnold.

Seale, C. (1999). Quality in qualitative research. *Qualitative Inquiry, 5,* 465–478.

Searle, J. (1991). Communication at work: An ethnography of checkout operators. *Open Letter, 2* (1), 28–39.

Sequeira, D. L. (1993). Personal address as negotiated meaning in an American church community. *Research on Language and Social Interaction, 26,* 259–285.

Sheared, V. (1994). Giving voice: An inclusive model of instruction—a womanist perspective. *New Directions for Continuing and Adult Education, 61,* 27–37.

Shimanoff, S. B. (1980). *Communication rules.* Beverly Hills, CA: Sage.

Shimanoff, S. B. (1985). Rules governing the verbal expression of emotions between married couples. *Western Journal of Speech Communication, 49,* 147–165.

Shome, R. (1998). Caught in the term "post-colonial": Why the "post-colonial" still matters. *Critical Studies in Mass Communication, 15,* 203–212.

Shugart, H. A. (1997). Counterhegemonic acts: Appropriation as a feminist rhetorical strategy. *Quarterly Journal of Speech, 83,* 210–229.

Shugart, H. A. (1999). Postmodern irony as a subversive rhetorical strategy. *Western Journal of Communication, 63,* 433–455.

Siebold, D. R., Kudsi, S., & Rude, M. (1993). Does communication training make a difference? Evidence for the effectiveness of a presentation skills training program. *Journal of Applied Communication, 21,* 111–131.

Sigman, S. J. (1985). Some common mistakes students make when learning discourse analysis. *Communication Education, 34,* 119–127.

Sigman, S. J., Sullivan, S. J., & Wendell, M. (1988). Conversation: Data acquisition and analysis. In C. H. Tardy (Ed.), *A handbook for the study of human communication: Methods and instruments for observing, measuring, and assessing communication processes.* Norwood, NJ: Ablex.

Signorelli, N. (2000). Sex on prime-time in the 90's. *Communication Research Reports, 17,* 70–78.

Sillars, A. L. (1980). Attribution and communication in roommate conflicts. *Communication Monographs, 47,* 180–200.

Silverman, D. (1993). *Interpreting qualitative data: Methods for analyzing talk, text and interaction.* London: Sage.

Slemon, J. (1995). "The scramble for post-colonialism." In B. Ashcraft, G. Griffiths, & H. Tiffin (Eds.), *The post-colonial studies reader.* London: Routledge.

Sloop, J. M. (2000). Disciplining the transgendered: Brandon Teena, public representation, and normativity. *Western Journal of Communication, 64,* 165–189.

Sloop, J. M., & Ono, K. A. (1997). Out-law discourse: The critical politics of material judgment. *Philosophy and Rhetoric, 30,* 50–69.

Smart, G. (1998). Mapping conceptual worlds: Using interpretive ethnography to explore knowledge-making in a professional community. *Journal of Business Communication, 35,* 111–127.

Smith, M. J. (1988). *Contemporary communication research methods.* Belmont, CA: Wadsworth.

Snow, D. A. (1980). The disengagement process: A neglected problem in participant-observation research. *Qualitative Sociology, 3,* 100–122.

Snyder, L. (2000). Invitation to transcendence: The *Book of Revelation. Quarterly Journal of Speech, 86,* 402–416.

Sparks, G. G., Pellechia, M., & Irvine, C. (1999). The repressive coping style and fright reactions to mass media. *Communication Research, 26,* 176–193.

Speer, S. A., & Potter, J. (2000). The management of heterosexist talk: Conversational repairs and prejudiced claims. *Discourse & Society, 11,* 543–572.

Spitzberg, B., & Cupach, W. (1984). *Interpersonal communication competence.* Beverly Hills, CA: Sage.

Spitzberg, B., & Hecht, M. (1984). A component model of relational competence. *Human Communication Research, 10,* 575–599.

Spradley, J. P. (1980). *Participant observation.* New York: Holt, Rinehart and Winston.

Sprague, J. (1992). Critical perspectives on teacher empowerment. *Communication Education, 41,* 181–203.

Stablein, R. (1996). Data in organization studies. In S. R. Clegg, C. Hardy, & W. R. Nord (Eds.), *Handbook of organization studies.* London: Sage.

Stage, F. K., & Russell, R. V. (1992). Using method triangulation in college student research. *Journal of College Student Development, 33,* 485–491.

Stake, R. E. (1998). Case studies. In N. Denzin & Y. Lincoln (Eds.), *Strategies of qualitative inquiry* (pp. 86–109). Thousand Oaks, CA: Sage.

Stamp, G. H. (1999). A qualitatively constructed interpersonal communication model: A grounded theory analysis. *Human Communication Research, 25,* 531–547.

Staton, A., Johnson, G., & Jorgensen-Earp, C. (1995). Communication in the socialization of new university freshmen. *Communication Education, 44,* 334–352.

Staton, A. Q., & Peeples, J. A. (2000). Educational reform discourse: President George Bush on "America 2000." *Communication Education, 49,* 303–319.

Steinberg, P. E., & McDowell, S. D. (2003). Mutiny on the bandwidth: The semiotics of statehood in the internet domain name registries of Pitcairn Island and Niue. *New Media & Society, 5* (1), 47–67.

Stephen, T. (1999). Computer-assisted concept analysis of HCR's first 25 years. *Human Communication Research, 25,* 498–513.

Stephenson, M. T., Palmgreen, P., Hoyle, R. H., Donohew, L., Lorch, E. P., & Colon, S. E. (1999). Short-term effects of an anti-marijuana media campaign targeting high sensation seeking adolescents. *Journal of Applied Communication Research, 27,* 175–195.

Stewart, A. (1998). *The ethnographer's method.* Thousand Oaks, CA: Sage (Qualitative Research Methods Series #46).

Stewart, C. M, Shields, S. F., & Sen, N. (1998). Diversity in on-line discussions: A study of cultural and gender differences in listservs. *Electronic Journal of Communication, 8 (3/4)*, File Stewart V8N398, 1–15.

Stiles, W. B. (1980). Comparison of dimensions derived from rating versus coding of dialogue. *Journal of Personality and Social Psychology, 38,* 359–374.

Stoda, M. (2000). Jeremiad at Harvard: Solzhenitsyn and "The world split apart." *Western Journal of Communication, 64,* 28–53.

Stokoe, E. H., & Smithson, J. (2001). Making gender relevant: Conversational analysis and gender categories in interaction. *Discourse & Society, 12,* 217–244.

Stoller, E. P. (1993). Gender and the organization of lay health care: A socialist-feminist perspective. *Journal of Aging Studies, 7 (2),* 151–170.

Strauss, A., & Corbin, J. (1998). Grounded theory methodology: An overview. In N. K. Denzin & Y. Lincoln (Eds.), *Strategies of qualitative inquiry* (pp. 158–83). Newbury Park, CA: Sage.

Stringer Cawyer, C. S., & Smith-Dupré, A. (1995). Communicating social support: Identifying supportive episodes in an HIV/AIDS support group. *Communication Quarterly, 43,* 243–258.

Stroud, S. R. (2001). Technology and mythic narrative: *The Matrix* as technological hero-quest. *Western Journal of Communication, 65,* 416– 441.

Stutts, N. B., & Barker, R. T. (1999). The use of Narrative Paradigm Theory in assessing audience value conflict in image advertising. *Management Communication Quarterly, 13,* 209–245.

Sunwolf & Seibold, D. R. (1998). Jurors' intuitive rules for deliberation: A structurational approach to communication in jury decision making. *Communication Monographs, 65,* 282–307.

Sutter, D. L., & Martin, M. M. (1998). Verbal aggression during disengagement of dating relationships. *Communication Research Reports, 15,* 318–326.

Swanson, D. L. (1993). Fragmentation, the field, and the future. *Journal of Communication, 43 (4),* 163–192.

Tamborini, R., Mastro, D. E., Chory-Assad, R. M., & Huang, R. H. (2000). The color of crime and the court: A content analysis of minority representation on television. *Journal & Mass Communication Quarterly, 77,* 639–651.

Tanno, D. V., & Jandt, F. E. (1994). Redefining the "other" in multicultural research. *The Howard Journal of Communications, 5,* 36–45.

Tardy, R. W., & Hale, C. L. (1998). Getting "plugged in": A network analysis of health-information seeking among "stay-at-home Moms." *Communication Monographs, 65,* 336–357.

Tavener, J. (2000). Media, morality, and madness: The case against sleaze TV. *Critical Studies in Mass Communication, 17,* 63–85.

Taylor, C. R., & Bang, H. (1997). Portrayals of Latinos in magazine advertising. *Journalism and Mass Communication Quarterly, 74,* 285–303.

Taylor, S. J., & Bogdan, R.C. (1998). *Introduction to qualitative research methods: A guidebook and resource* (3rd ed.). New York: Wiley.

ten Have, P. (1999). *Doing conversation analysis: A practical guide.* London: Sage.

Tesch, R. (1990). *Qualitative research: Analysis types and software tools.* New York: Falmer.

Tesch, R. (1991). Computers and qualitative data II [Special issues, Parts 1 & 2]. *Qualitative Sociology, 14 (3 & 4).*

Thimm, C., Rademacher, U., & Kruse, L. (1998). Age stereotypes and patronizing messages: Features of age-adapted speech in technical instructions to the elderly. *Journal of Applied Communication Research, 26,* 66–82.

Thomas, J. (1993). *Doing critical ethnography.* Newbury Park, CA: Sage.

Thomas, S. (1994). Artifactual study in the analysis of culture: A defense of content analysis in a postmodern age. *Communication Research, 21,* 683–697.

Thonssen, L., & Baird, A. C. (1948). *Speech criticism.* New York: Ronald.

Toulmin, S., Rieke, R., & Janik, A. (1984). *An introduction to reasoning* (2nd ed.). New York: Macmillan Publishing.

Townsley, N. C., & Geist, P. (2000). The discursive enactment of hegemony: Sexual harassment and academic organizing. *Western Journal of Communication, 64,* 190–217.

Tracy, K. (1995). Action-implicative discourse analysis. *Journal of Language & Social Psychology, 14,* 195–216.

Tracy, K., & Tracy, S. J. (1998). Rudeness at 911: Reconceptualizing face and face attack. *Human Communication Research, 25,* 225–251.

Trees, A. R., & Manusov, V. (1998). Managing face concerns in criticism: Integrating nonverbal behaviors as a dimension of politeness in female friendship dyads. *Human Communication Research, 24,* 564–583.

Tretheway, A. (1997). Resistance, identity, and empowerment: A postmodern feminist analysis of clients in a human service organization. *Communication Monographs, 64,* 281–301.

Trost, M. R., Langan, E. J., & Kellar-Guenther, Y. (1999). Not everyone listens when you "just say no": Drug resistance in relational context. *Journal of Applied Communication Research, 27,* 120–138.

Trujillo, N. (1991). Hegemonic masculinity on the mound: Media representations of Nolan Ryan and American sports culture. *Critical Studies in Mass Communication, 8,* 290–308.

Trujillo, N. (1992). Interpreting (the work and the talk of) baseball: Perspectives on ballpark culture. *Western Journal of Communication, 56,* 350–371.

Trujillo, N. (1993). Interpreting November 22: A critical ethnography of an assassination site. *Quarterly Journal of Speech, 79,* 447–466.

Trujillo, N. (1999). Teaching ethnography in the twenty-first century using collaborative learning. *Journal of Contemporary Ethnography, 28,* 705–719.

University of Chicago Press. (1993). *The Chicago manual of style* (14th ed.). Chicago: University of Chicago Press.

Valdes, G., & Pino, C. (1981). Muy a tus ordenes: Compliment responses among Mexican-American bilinguals. *Language and Society, 10,* 53–72.

Valkenburg, P. M., Cantor, J., & Peeters, A. L. (2000). Fright reactions to television: A child survey. *Communication Research, 27,* 82–99.

Valkenburg, P. M., & Janssen, S. C. (1999). What do children value in entertainment programs? A cross-cultural investigation. *Journal of Communication, 49,* 3–21.

Valkenburg, P. M., & Semetko, H. A. (1999). The effects of news frames on readers' thoughts and recall. *Communication Research, 26,* 550–570.

Vande Berg, L. R.. (1997). Editor's introduction: Special series on "voices." *Western Journal of Communication, 61,* 87–88.

Van der Molen, J. H. W., & van der Voort, T. H. A. (2000). Children's and adults' recall of television and print news in children's and adult news formats. *Communication Research, 27,* 132–160.

Van Maanen, J. (1988). *Tales of the field: On writing ethnography.* Chicago: University of Chicago Press.

Van Oosting, J. (1996). Acoustic writers and electronic readers: Literature through the back door. *Communication Education, 45,* 108–111.

Varallo, S. M., Ray, E. B., & Ellis, B. H. (1998). Speaking of incest: The research interview as social justice. *Journal of Applied Communication Research, 26,* 254–271.

Wagoner, R., & Waldron, V. R. (1999). How supervisors convey routine bad news: Facework at UPS. *Southern Communication Journal, 64,* 193–210.

Waldeck, J. H., Kearney, P., & Plax, T. G. (2001). Teacher e-mail message strategies and students' willingness to communicate online. *Journal of Applied Communication Research, 29,* 54–70.

Waldron, V. (1990). Constrained rationality: Situational influences on information acquisition plans and tactics. *Communication Monographs, 57,* 184–201.

Walther, J. B., Slovacek, C. L., & Tidwell, L. C. (2001). Is a picture worth a thousand words? Photographic images in long-term and short-term computer-mediated communication. *Communication Research, 28,* 105–135.

Ware, B. L., & Linkugel, W. A. (1973). They spoke in defense of themselves: On the generic criticism of apologia. *Quarterly Journal of Speech, 59,* 273–283.

Warnick, B. (1987). The narrative paradigm: Another story. *Quarterly Journal of Speech, 73,* 172–182.

Watkins, S. C. (2001). A nation of millions: Hip hop culture and the legacy of black nationalism. *Communication Review, 4,* 373–398.

Watson, G., & Goulet, J. (1998). What can ethnomethodology say about power? *Qualitative Inquiry, 4,* 96–113.

Watt, J. H., & van den Berg, S. A. (1995). *Research methods for communication science.* Boston: Allyn & Bacon.

Watts, E. K., & Orbe, M. P. (2002). The spectacular consumption of the "True" African American culture: "Whassup" with the Budweiser Guys? *Critical Studies in Mass Communication, 19,* 1–20.

Weaver, J. B., III (1991). Are "slasher" horror films sexually violent? A content analysis. *Journal of Broadcasting and Electronic Media, 35,* 385–392.

Weaver Lariscy, R. A., & Tinkham, S. F. (1999). The sleeper effect and negative political advertising. *Journal of Advertising, 28,* 13–31.

Weber, K., Martin, M. M, & Patterson, B. R. (2001). Teacher behavior, student interest and affective learning: Putting theory into practice. *Journal of Applied Communication Research, 29,* 71–90.

Weick, K. (1989). [Review of the book *Tales of the field: On writing ethnography*]. *Administrative Science Quarterly, 34,* 307–311.

Weitzel, A. (1994). King's "I Have a Dream" speech: A case study of incorporating orality in rhetorical criticism. *Communication Reports, 7,* 50–57.

Weitzel, A., & Geist, P. (1998). Parliamentary procedure in a community group: Communication and vigilant decision making. *Communication Monographs, 65,* 244–260.

West, C. (1982). Why can't a woman be more like a man? *Work and Occupations, 9,* 5–29.

West, C., & Zimmerman, D. (1983). Small insults: A study of interruptions in cross-sex conversations between unacquainted persons. In B. Thorne, C. Kramerae, & N. Henley (Eds.), *Language, gender, and society* (pp. 102–117). Rowley, MA: Newbury House.

Whalen, M., & Zimmerman, D. (1987). Sequential and institutional contexts in calls for help. *Social Psychology Quarterly, 50,* 172–185.

White, W. J. (1999). Academic topographies: A network analysis of disciplinarity among communication faculty. *Human Communication Research, 25,* 604–617.

Wichelns, H. A. (1925). The literary criticism of oratory. In A. M. Drummond (Ed.), *Rhetoric and public speaking in honor of James A. Winans* (pp. 181–216). New York: Century.

Wiemann, J. M. (1981). Effects of laboratory videotaping procedures on selected conversational behaviors. *Human Communication Research, 7,* 302–311.

Wilson, S. R., Aleman, C. G., & Leatham, G. B. (1998). Identity implications of influence goals: A revised analysis of face-threatening acts and application to seeking compliance with same-sex friends. *Human Communication Research, 25,* 64–96.

Wimmer, R. D., & Dominick, J. R. (1991). Content analysis (pp. 156–179), *Mass media research: An introduction* (3rd ed.). Belmont, CA: Wadsworth.

Windt, T. O., Jr. (1972). The diatribe: Last resort for protest. *Quarterly Journal of Speech, 58,* 1–14.

Witmer, D. F. (1997). Communication and recovery: Structuration as an ontological approach to organizational culture. *Communication Monographs, 64,* 324–349.

Wittig, M. (1990). The straight mind. In R. Ferguson, M. Gever, T. T. Minh-Ha, & C. West (Eds.), *Out there: Marginalization and contemporary culture* (pp. 51–58). Cambridge, MA: MIT Press.

Wong, J. (2000). The token "yeah" in nonnative speaker English conversation. *Research on Language & Social Interaction, 33,* 39–67.

Wood, J. T. (1997). *Communication theories in action: An introduction.* Belmont, CA: Wadsworth.

Wood, J. T., & Inman, C. C. (1993). In a different mode: Masculine styles of communicating closeness. *Journal of Applied Communication Research, 21,* 279–295.

Wright, K. B., & O'Hair, D. (1999). Seeking and resisting compliance: Selection and evaluation of tactics in a simulated college student drinking context. *Communication Research Reports, 16,* 266–275.

Yep, G. (1997). My three cultures: Navigating the multicultural identity landscape. *Magazine, 15* (2), 43–55.

Yep, G. A. (2000). Encounters with the "other": Personal notes for a reconceptualization of intercultural communication competence. *CATESOL Journal, 12,* 117–144.

Yep, G. A., Lovaas, K. E., & Ho, P. C. (2001). Communication in "Asian American" families with queer members: A relational dialectics perspective. In M. Bernstein & R. Reimann (Eds.), *Queer families, queer politics: Challenging culture and the state* (pp. 152–172). New York: Columbia University Press.

Yep, G. A., Lovaas, K. E., & Pagonis, A. V. (2002). The case of "riding bareback": Sexual practices and the paradoxes of identity in the era of AIDS. *Journal of Homosexuality, 42,* 1–13.

Zimmerman, D. (1988). On conversation: The conversation analytic perspective. In J. Andersen (Ed.), *Communication yearbook, 11* (pp. 406–432). Newbury Park, CA: Sage.

Zoch, L. M., & Turk, J. V. (1998). Women making news: Gender as a variable in source selection and use. *Journalism & Mass Communication Quarterly, 75,* 762–775.

INDEX

(2) 26 Action Research
(2) 25 Associative Claim
(3) 54 Anonymity
(3) 38 Archive
(3) 40 Bias
(1) 2– Claim
(2) 25 Casual Claim
(3) 49 Cohort Studies
(3) 42 Convience Sampling
(1) 12-13 Constructivism
(2) 25 Dep & Indep Variable
(3) 37, 38, 39 Data Collection
(2) 25 Evaluative Claim
(2) 26 Explanatory Claim
(2) 22 Hypothesis
(3) 39 Field Setting

(3) 44 Interactive data collection
(1) 3 Laws
(3) 39 Lab settings
(3) 49 Longitudinal research design
(1) 10 Modernism
(3) 44 Maximum variation sampling
(3) 41 Multistage cluster sampling
(1) 80B Naturalism
(2) 25 Predictive Claim
(1) 4-5 Paradigm
(1) 12 Phenomenology
(3) 43 Quota Sampling
(2) 28 Reportist claim
(3) 40 Random selection and ...
(3) 37 Self Report
(3) 40 Sampling Frames

(3) 50 Triangulation
(3) 38 Text
(3) 49 Trends Study
Unobstructive data collection procedure
(3) 47 Variables
(1) Warrant 2-3

Knowing By Discovery 5
  " Authority 4
  " Method of Sci 7-8
  " Tenacity 3-4
  " Priori 4

Generalizations → Grouping or Categorizing objects together
    by their similarities → p 6-7